Dictionary of
Marketing

fourth edition

BLOOMSBURY

First published by *Peter Collin Publishing*
This fourth edition published 2011

Third edition published 2003
Second edition published 1996
First edition published 1989

Bloomsbury Publishing Plc
50 Bedford Square
London WC1B 3DP

A CIP record for this book is available from the British Library

ISBN: 9781 4081 5208 9

The publishers use paper produced with elemental chlorine
free pulp, harvested from managed sustainable forests.

Text typeset by RefineCatch Ltd, Bungay, Suffolk
Printed in Croatia by Zrinski

Preface

This dictionary provides the user with a comprehensive vocabulary of terms used in marketing. It covers such aspects of the subject as market research, advertising, promotional aids and selling techniques.

The main words are explained in simple English, and, where appropriate, examples are given to show how the words are used in context. Quotations are also given from various magazines and journals, which give an idea of how the terms are used in real life.

The Supplement, which starts on page 303, gives some further information which may be of use to the user, including VALS Lifestyle Segmentation, SWOT Analysis, Social Classes in the UK and Technical Information for a Periodical.

Business terminology changes rapidly, and this edition includes a variety of new terms and expressions which have come into use since the first edition was published, including the many new terms that have come into marketing with the growth of e-commerce and the Internet. We have also included new examples and quotations from recent magazines.

Also included is a pronunciation guide for the main entry words.

Pronunciation

The following symbols have been used to show the pronunciation of the main words in the dictionary.

Stress has been indicated by a main stress mark (') and a secondary stress mark (,). Note that these are only guides as the stress of the word changes according to its position in the sentence.

	Vowels		*Consonants*
æ	back	b	buck
ɑː	harm	d	dead
ɒ	stop	ð	other
aɪ	type	dʒ	jump
aʊ	how	f	fare
aɪə	hire	g	gold
aʊə	hour	h	head
ɔː	course	j	yellow
ɔɪ	annoy	k	cab
e	head	l	leave
eə	fair	m	mix
eɪ	make	n	nil
eʊ	go	s	save
ɜː	word	ʃ	shop
iː	keep	t	take
i	happy	tʃ	change
ə	about	θ	theft
ɪ	fit	v	value
ɪə	near	w	work
u	annual	x	loch
uː	pool	ʒ	measure
ʊ	book	z	zone
ʊə	tour		
ʌ	shut		

A

AB /ˌeɪ ˈbiː/ *noun* the highest socio-economic group, consisting of professionals with a high disposable income

ABC method /ˌeɪ biː ˈsiː ˌmeθəd/ *noun* a sales method, where the customer's attention is attracted, the salesperson then shows the benefits of the product to the customer, and finally closes the deal. Full form **attention, benefit, close**

ABCs *abbreviation* Audit Bureau of Circulations

AB deadline /ˌeɪ biː ˈdedlaɪn/ *noun* same as **advance booking deadline**

above-the-fold /əˌbʌv ðə ˈfəʊld/ *noun* the part of a webpage which is seen first without having to scroll, and so is preferred for advertising

above-the-line /əˌbʌv ðə ˈlaɪn/ *adjective, adverb* **1.** used to describe entries in a company's profit and loss accounts that appear above the line which separates entries showing the origin of the funds that have contributed to the profit or loss from those that relate to its distribution. Exceptional and extraordinary items appear above the line. ○ *Exceptional items are noted above the line in company accounts.* ⇨ **below-the-line 2.** relating to revenue items in a government budget

above-the-line advertising /əˌbʌv ðə laɪn ˈædvətaɪzɪŋ/ *noun* advertising for which commission is paid to the advertising agency, e.g. an advertisement in a magazine or a stand at a trade fair. Compare **below-the-line advertising** (NOTE: as opposed to direct marketing)

absenteeism /ˌæbs(ə)nˈtiːɪz(ə)m/ *noun* the practice of staying away from work for no good reason ○ *Low produc-tivity is largely due to the high level of absenteeism.* ○ *Absenteeism is high in the week before Christmas.*

'…but the reforms still hadn't fundamentally changed conditions on the shop floor: absenteeism was as high as 20% on some days' [*Business Week*]

absolute /ˈæbsəluːt/ *adjective* complete or total

absolute advantage /ˌæbsəluːt ədˈvɑːntɪdʒ/ *noun* an advantage enjoyed by an area of the world which can produce a product more cheaply than other areas ○ *For climatic reasons, tropical countries have an absolute advantage in that type of production.*

absolute cost /ˌæbsəluːt ˈkɒst/ *noun* the actual cost of placing an advertisement in a magazine or other advertising medium

absolute monopoly /ˌæbsəluːt məˈnɒpəli/ *noun* a situation where only one producer produces or only one supplier supplies something ○ *The company has an absolute monopoly of imports of French wine.* ○ *The supplier's absolute monopoly of the product meant that customers had to accept her terms.*

absorb /əbˈzɔːb/ *verb* to take in a small item so that it forms part of a larger one □ **overheads have absorbed all our profits** all our profits have gone in paying overhead expenses □ **to absorb a loss by a subsidiary** to include a subsidiary company's loss in the group accounts □ **a business which has been absorbed by a competitor** a small business which has been made part of a larger one

absorption /əbˈzɔːpʃən/ *noun* the process of making a smaller business part of a larger one, so that the smaller company, in effect, no longer exists

absorption costing /əbˈzɔːpʃən ˌkɒstɪŋ/ *noun* a form of costing for a product that includes both the direct costs of production and the indirect overhead costs as well

A/B split /ˌeɪ biː ˈsplɪt/ *noun* a two-way direct mail marketing test which compares a control sample to a variety of single-variable test samples in order to improve response rates

accelerated depreciation /əkˌseləreɪtɪd dɪpriːʃɪˈeɪʃ(ə)n/ *noun* a system of depreciation which reduces the value of assets at a high rate in the early years to encourage companies, as a result of tax advantages, to invest in new equipment

acceleration factor /əkˌseləˈreɪʃ(ə)n ˌfæktə/ *noun* the idea that increased efficiency in communication and transport links speeds up the exchange of information, which has an immediate impact on the media

accelerator /əkˈseləreɪtə/ *noun* the theory that a change in demand for consumer goods will result in a greater change in demand for the capital goods used in their production

accept /əkˈsept/ *verb* **1.** to take something which is being offered □ **to accept delivery of a shipment** to take goods into the warehouse officially when they are delivered **2.** to say 'yes' or to agree to something ○ *She accepted the offer of a job in Australia.* ○ *He accepted $2,000 instead of one week's notice.* **3.** to agree formally to receive something or to be responsible for something

acceptable /əkˈseptəb(ə)l/ *adjective* easily accepted ○ *Both parties found the offer acceptable.* ○ *The terms of the contract of employment are not acceptable to the candidate.*

acceptance /əkˈseptəns/ *noun* □ **acceptance of an offer** the act of agreeing to an offer □ **to give an offer a conditional acceptance** to accept an offer provided that specific things happen or that specific terms apply □ **we have their letter of acceptance** we have received a letter from them accepting the offer

acceptance against documents /əkˌseptəns əgenst ˈdɒkjʊmənts/ *noun* a transaction where the seller takes charge of the shipping documents for a consignment of goods when a buyer accepts a bill of exchange ○ *Acceptance against documents protects the seller when sending goods which are not yet paid for.*

acceptance sampling /əkˈseptəns ˌsɑːmplɪŋ/ *noun* the process of testing a small sample of a batch to see if the whole batch is good enough to be accepted

accepted bill /əkˌseptɪd ˈbɪl/ *noun* a bill of exchange which has been signed, and therefore accepted by the buyer

acceptor /əkˈseptə/ *noun* a person who accepts a bill of exchange by signing it, thus making a commitment to pay it by a specified date

access /ˈækses/ *noun* □ **to have access to something** a way of obtaining or reaching something ○ *She has access to large amounts of venture capital.* ■ *verb* to call up data which is stored in a computer ○ *She accessed the address file on the computer.* ◇ **access to the market 1.** the legal right to sell in a particular market **2.** the ability to reach a market by promotion and distribution

accessibility /əkˌsesɪˈbɪlɪti/ *noun* the ability of a market to be reached by promotion and distribution ○ *There is much demand in the market, but, because of the great distances involved, accessibility is a problem.* ○ *We must analyse the geographical aspects in assessing the market's accessibility.*

access panel /ˈækses ˌpæn(ə)l/ *noun* a group of people that allows their television watching habits to be monitored for research purposes. Also called **panel**

access time /ˈækses taɪm/ *noun* the time taken by a computer to find data stored in it

accommodation bill /əˌkɒməˈdeɪʃ(ə)n ˌbɪl/ *noun* a bill of exchange where the person signing (the 'drawee') is helping another company (the 'drawer') to raise a loan

accordion fold /əˈkɔːdiən fəʊld/ *noun* a method of folding a printed sheet in parallel folds, with one fold in one direction, and the next in the other, so that it will unfold sideways. Also called **concertina fold, fanfold**

accordion insert /əˈkɔːdiən ˌɪnsɜːt/ *noun* an insert in a magazine which is folded in the accordion method

account /əˈkaʊnt/ *noun* **1.** a record of financial transactions over a period of time, such as money paid, received, borrowed or owed ○ *Please send me an itemised account.* **2.** *(in a shop)* an arrangement in which a customer acquires goods and pays for them at a later date, usually the end of the month ○ *to have an account with Harrods* ○ *Charge it to my account.* □ **to open an account** *(of a customer)* to ask a shop to supply goods which you will pay for at a later date □ **to open an account, to close an account** *(of a shop)* to start or to stop supplying a customer on credit □ **to settle an account** to pay all the money owed on an account □ **to stop an account** to stop supplying a customer until payment has been made for goods supplied **3.** □ **on account** as part of a total bill □ **to pay money on account** to pay to settle part of a bill □ **advance on account** money paid as a part payment **4.** a customer who does a large amount of business with a firm and has an account with it ○ *Smith Brothers is one of our largest accounts.* ○ *Our sales people call on their best accounts twice a month.* **5.** □ **to keep the accounts** to write each sum of money in the account book ○ *The bookkeeper's job is to keep the accounts.* **6.** □ **overdrawn account** an account where you have taken out more money than you have put in, i.e. the bank is effectively lending you money □ **to open an account** to start an account by putting money in ○ *She opened an account with Santander.* □ **to close an account** to take all money out of a bank account and stop the account ○ *We closed our account with Lloyds.* **7.** a period during which shares are traded for credit, and at the end of which the shares bought must be paid for (NOTE: On the London Stock Exchange, there are twenty-four accounts during the year, each running usually for ten working days.) **8.** a notice □ **to take account of inflation, to take inflation into account** to assume that there will be a specific percentage of inflation when

making calculations **9.** an arrangement which a company has with an advertising agency, where the agency deals with all promotion for the company ○ *The company has moved its $3m account to another agency.* ○ *The small agency lost the account when the company decided it needed a different marketing approach.* ○ *Three agencies were asked to make presentations, as the company had decided to switch its account.* ■ *verb* □ **to account for** to explain and record a money transaction ○ *to account for a loss* ○ *The reps have to account for all their expenses to the sales manager.*

accountancy /əˈkaʊntənsi/ *noun* the work of an accountant ○ *They are studying accountancy* or *They are accountancy students.*

accountant /əˈkaʊntənt/ *noun* **1.** a person who keeps a company's accounts or deals with an individual person's tax affairs ○ *The chief accountant of a manufacturing group.* **2.** a person who advises a company on its finances ○ *I send all my income tax queries to my accountant.* **3.** a person who examines accounts

account book /əˈkaʊnt bʊk/ *noun* a book with printed columns which is used to record sales and purchases

account director /əˈkaʊnt daɪˌrektə/ *noun* a person who works in an advertising agency and who oversees various account managers who are each responsible for specific clients

account executive /əˈkaʊnt ɪgˌzekjʊtɪv/ *noun* **1.** an employee who looks after customers or who is the link between customers and the company **2.** an employee of an organisation such as a bank, public relations firm or advertising agency who is responsible for looking after particular clients and handling their business with the organisation

account handler /əˈkaʊnt ˌhændlə/, **account manager** /əˈkaʊnt ˌmænɪdʒə/ *noun* a person who works in an advertising agency, and who is responsible for a particular client

'…we have moved the account because we thought it would be better suited in a smaller agency' [*Marketing Week*]

accounting /əˈkaʊntɪŋ/ *noun* the work of recording money paid, received, borrowed, or owed ○ *accounting methods* ○ *accounting procedures* ○ *an accounting machine*

'...applicants will be professionally qualified and have a degree in Commerce or Accounting' [*Australian Financial Review*]

accounts department /ə'kaʊnts dɪˌpɑːtmənt/ *noun* a department in a company which deals with money paid, received, borrowed, or owed

accounts manager /ə'kaʊnts ˌmænɪdʒə/ *noun* the manager of an accounts department

accounts payable /əˌkaʊnts 'peɪəb(ə)l/ *plural noun* money owed by a company. Abbreviation **AP**

accredited agent /əˌkredɪtɪd 'eɪdʒənt/ *noun* an agent who is appointed by a company to act on its behalf

accurate /'ækjʊrət/ *adjective* correct ○ *The sales department made an accurate forecast of sales.* ○ *The designers produced an accurate copy of the plan.*

accurate description /ˌækjʊrət dɪ'skrɪpʃən/ *noun* an honest and true description of a product or service in an advertisement or catalogue ○ *As the advertisement was clearly not an accurate description of the product, the company had to pay a fine.* ○ *It is not an accurate description of the product to state that it gives out more light than the sun.*

accurately /'ækjʊrətli/ *adverb* correctly ○ *The second quarter's drop in sales was accurately forecast by the computer.*

acknowledge /ək'nɒlɪdʒ/ *verb* to tell a sender that a letter, package, or shipment has arrived ○ *He has still not acknowledged my letter of the 24th.* ○ *We acknowledge receipt of your letter of June 14th.*

acknowledgement /ək'nɒlɪdʒmənt/ *noun* the act of acknowledging ○ *She sent an acknowledgement of receipt.* ○ *The company sent a letter of acknowledgement after I sent in my job application.*

ACORN /'eɪkɔːn/ *noun* a classification of residential areas into categories, based on the type of people who live in them, the type of houses, etc., much used in consumer research ○ *ACORN will help us plan where to concentrate our sales visits.* Full form **a classification of residential neighbourhoods**

acquire /ə'kwaɪə/ *verb* to buy ○ *to acquire a company* ○ *We have acquired a new office building in the centre of town.*

acquirer /ə'kwaɪərə/ *noun* a person or company which buys something

acquisition /ˌækwɪ'zɪʃ(ə)n/ *noun* **1.** something bought ○ *The chocolate factory is our latest acquisition.* **2.** the act of getting or buying something □ **data acquisition, acquisition of data** obtaining and classifying data **3.** the action of acquiring new customers, as opposed to retention, which is keeping the loyalty of existing customers

acquisition cost /ˌækwɪ'zɪʃ(ə)n kɒst/ *noun* the cost to a company of winning new customers through advertising

acquisition rate /ˌækwɪ'zɪʃ(ə)n reɪt/ *noun* a figure that indicates how much new business is being won by a company's marketing activities

Acrobat /'ækrəʊbæt/ a trademark for a file format developed by Adobe Systems, which describes a graphics, text and indexing system that allows the same screen image or page layout file to be displayed on different hardware

acronym /'ækrənɪm/ *noun* a word which is made up from the initials of other words ○ *The name of the company was especially designed to provide a catchy acronym.* ○ *BASIC is an acronym for Beginner's All-purpose Symbolic Instruction Code.*

across-the-board /əˌkrɒs ðə 'bɔːd/ *adjective* (*of an advertisement*) running for five consecutive days from Monday to Friday

action shot /'ækʃən ʃɒt/ *noun* a scene with movement either in a film or on TV

activity sampling /æk'tɪvɪti ˌsɑːmplɪŋ/ *noun* an observation of tasks and their performances, carried out at random intervals ○ *Activity sampling was carried out to see how fast the machinists worked.*

ad /æd/ *noun* same as **advertisement** (*informal*) ○ *We put an ad in the paper.* ○ *She answered an ad in the paper.* ○ *He found his job through an ad in the paper.*

Ad-A-Card /ˈæd ə kɑːd/ *noun US* a type of perforated card bound into a magazine which a reader can tear off and return to the advertiser

adapt /əˈdæpt/ *verb* to change something a little to fit in with changing circumstances ○ *This product must be adapted in line with recent technological developments.* ○ *The device has been adapted for use on board aircraft.*

adaptable /əˈdæptəb(ə)l/ *adjective* able to change or be changed

adaptation /ˌædæpˈteɪʃ(ə)n/ *noun* **1.** a change which has been, or can be, made to something ○ *With a few minor adaptations, the machine will cut square holes as well as round ones.* **2.** the process of changing something, or of being changed, to fit new conditions ○ *adaptation to new surroundings*

adaptive control model /əˌdæptɪv kənˈtrəʊl ˌmɒd(ə)l/ *noun US* a model for planning advertising expenditure in line with changes in consumer responses to advertising

ad banner /ˈæd ˌbænə/ *noun* same as **banner**

ad click /ˈæd klɪk/ *noun* same as **click-through**

ad click rate /ˈæd klɪk ˌreɪt/ *noun* same as **click-through rate**

added value /ˌædɪd ˈvæljuː/ *noun* an amount added to the value of a product or service, equal to the difference between its cost and the amount received when it is sold. Wages, taxes, etc. are deducted from the added value to give the profit. ⇨ **VAT** ■ *noun, adjective* any extra promotion that a publication can offer its advertisers, such as press events, supplements or special sections

add-on sales /ˈæd ɒn ˌseɪlz/ *plural noun* the sale of items which complement items being bought, e.g., washing powder sold with a dishwasher

address label /əˈdres ˌleɪb(ə)l/ *noun* a label with an address on it

address list /əˈdres lɪst/ *noun* a list of names and addresses of people and companies

ad hoc /ˌæd ˈhɒk/ *adjective* for this particular purpose ○ *They run ad hoc surveys to test customer reaction when products are launched.* ○ *Shipping by airfreight was an ad hoc arrangement initially.*

ad hoc research /ˌæd hɒk rɪˈsɜːtʃ/ *noun* research carried out for a particular client or in a particular market

ad impression /ˈæd ɪmˌpreʃ(ə)n/ *noun* same as **ad view**

adjacency /əˈdʒeɪs(ə)nsi/ *noun* a commercial which is run between two TV programmes

adjust /əˈdʒʌst/ *verb* to change something to fit new conditions ○ *Prices are adjusted for inflation.*

'…inflation-adjusted GNP moved up at a 1.3% annual rate' [*Fortune*]

'Saudi Arabia will no longer adjust its production to match short-term supply with demand' [*Economist*]

'…on a seasonally-adjusted basis, output of trucks, electric power, steel and paper decreased' [*Business Week*]

adman /ˈædmæn/ *noun* a man who works in advertising (*informal*) ○ *The admen are using balloons as promotional material.*

administer /ədˈmɪnɪstə/ *verb* to organise, manage or direct the whole of an organisation or part of one ○ *She administers a large pension fund.*

administered channel /ədˌmɪnɪstəd ˈtʃæn(ə)l/ *noun* a distribution channel in which there is cooperation between businesses

administered price /ədˈmɪnɪstəd praɪs/ *noun US* a price fixed by a manufacturer which cannot be varied by a retailer (NOTE: The UK term is **resale price maintenance**.)

administration /ədˌmɪnɪˈstreɪʃ(ə)n/ *noun* the running of a company in receivership by an administrator appointed by the courts

administration costs /ədˌmɪnɪˈstreɪʃ(ə)n ˌkɒsts/, **administration expenses** /ədˌmɪnɪˈstreɪʃ(ə)n ɪkˌspensɪz/ *plural noun* the costs of management, not including production, marketing or distribution costs

administrative /ədˈmɪnɪstrətɪv/ *adjective* referring to administration

○ *administrative details* ○ *administrative expenses*

administrator /ədˈmɪnɪstreɪtə/ *noun* **1.** a person who directs the work of other employees in a business ○ *After several years as a college teacher, she hopes to become an administrator.* **2.** a person appointed by a court to manage the affairs of someone who dies without leaving a will

Adobe /əˈdəʊbi/ a trade name for a leading producer of graphics and desktop publishing software

Adobe Acrobat /əˌdəʊbi ˈækrəbæt/ a trade name for a piece of software that converts documents and formatted pages into a file format that can be viewed on almost any computer platform or using a web browser on the Internet

Adobe Illustrator /əˌdəʊbi ˈɪləstreɪtə/ a trade name for a vector image and editing software, or a drawing program

Adobe InDesign /əˌdəʊbi ˈɪndɪzaɪn/ a trade name for a design and page layout software

Adobe Pagemaker /əˌdəʊbi ˈpeɪdʒmeɪkə/ a trade name for a design and page layout software, an older form of Adobe InDesign

Adobe Photoshop /əˌdəʊbi ˈfəʊtəʊʃɒp/ a trade name for an image creation, editing and format translation software

Adobe Type Manager /əˌdəʊbi taɪp ˈmænɪdʒə/ a trade name for a group of software technology programs used for describing scalable fonts. It is most commonly used to provide fonts that can be scaled to almost any point size, and printed on almost any printer. Abbreviation **ATM**

adopt /əˈdɒpt/ *verb* to agree to something or to accept something

adopter /əˈdɒptə/ *noun* a customer who adopts a particular product

adoption /əˈdɒpʃən/ *noun* the decision to buy or use a particular product ○ *More promotion was needed to speed up adoption of the product.* ○ *Widespread adoption of its new shampoo range has made the company the market leader.*

adoption curve /əˈdɒpʃən kɜːv/ *noun* a line on a graph showing how many consumers adopt or buy a new product at various time periods after the launch date ○ *The adoption curve shows that most people who buy the product do so at a fairly late stage.*

Adshel /ˈædʃel/ *noun* a trademark for a poster site for advertisements in a bus shelter

adspeak /ˈædspiːk/ *noun* jargon used in the advertising trade

adspend /ˈædspend/ *noun* the amount of money spent on advertising

ad transfer /ˈæd ˌtrænsfɜː/ *noun* same as **click-through**

ad valorem duty /ˌæd vəˈlɔːrəm ˌdjuːti/ *noun* the duty calculated on the sales value of the goods

advance /ədˈvɑːns/ *noun* **1.** money paid as a loan or as a part of a payment to be made later ○ *She asked if she could have a cash advance.* ○ *We paid her an advance on account.* ○ *Can I have an advance of $100 against next month's salary?* **2.** an increase **3.** □ **in advance** early, before something happens ○ *freight payable in advance* ○ *prices fixed in advance* ■ *adjective* early, or taking place before something else happens ○ *advance payment* ○ *Advance holiday bookings are up on last year.* ○ *You must give seven days' advance notice of withdrawals from the account.* ■ *verb* **1.** to pay an amount of money to someone as a loan or as a part of a payment to be made later ○ *The bank advanced him $100,000 against the security of his house.* **2.** to increase ○ *Prices generally advanced on the stock market.* **3.** to make something happen earlier ○ *The date of the shipping has been advanced to May 10th.* ○ *The meeting with the German distributors has been advanced from 11.00 to 9.30.*

advance blurb /ədˌvɑːns ˈblɜːb/ *noun* a quote or review which is prepared before a book or film is released and is used to publicise it

advance booking deadline /ədˌvɑːns ˌbʊkɪŋ ˈdedlaɪn/ *noun* the date by which an advertiser must book a particular media slot in order to guarantee the best rates and quality. Also called **AB deadline**

advance freight /ədˈvɑːns freɪt/ *noun* freight which is payable in advance

advance man /əd'vɑːns mæn/
noun US a person who publicises a performance and sells tickets for it before the performers arrive

advert /'ædvɜːt/ *noun* same as **advertisement** (*informal*) ○ *to put an advert in the paper* ○ *to answer an advert in the paper* ○ *classified adverts* ○ *display adverts*

advertise /'ædvətaɪz/ *verb* to arrange and pay for publicity designed to help sell products or services or to find new employees ○ *to advertise a vacancy* ○ *to advertise for a secretary* ○ *to advertise a new product*

advertisement /əd'vɜːtɪsmənt/ *noun* **1.** a notice which shows that something is for sale, that a service is offered, that someone wants something, or that a job is vacant **2.** a short film on television or a short announcement on the radio which tries to persuade people to use a product or service **3.** the public promotion of a product or service, in forms such as posters, short television or radio broadcasts and announcements in the press. Abbreviation **ad**

advertisement manager /əd'vɜːtɪsmənt ˌmænɪdʒə/ *noun* the manager in charge of the advertisement section of a newspaper

advertisement panel /əd'vɜːtɪsmənt ˌpæn(ə)l/ *noun* a specially designed large advertising space in a newspaper

advertiser /'ædvətaɪzə/ *noun* a person or company that advertises ○ *The catalogue gives a list of advertisers.*

advertising /'ædvətaɪzɪŋ/ *noun* the business of announcing that something is for sale or of trying to persuade customers to buy a product or service ○ *She works in advertising She has a job in advertising.* ○ *Their new advertising campaign is being launched next week.* ○ *The company has asked an advertising agent to prepare a presentation.* □ **to take advertising space in a paper** to book space for an advertisement in a newspaper

advertising agency /'ædvətaɪzɪŋ ˌeɪdʒənsi/ *noun* a company which plans, designs and manages advertising for other companies

advertising appeal /'ædvətaɪzɪŋ əˌpiːl/ *noun* the appeal of an advertisement to the intended audience

advertising appropriation /'ædvətaɪzɪŋ əˌprəuprieɪʃ(ə)n/ *noun* money set aside by an organisation for its advertising ○ *The marketing director and the chief accountant have yet to fix the advertising appropriation.* ○ *We cannot afford as large an advertising appropriation as last year.*

advertising brief /'ædvətaɪzɪŋ briːf/ *noun* basic objectives and instructions concerning an advertising campaign, given by an advertiser to an advertising agency ○ *The brief stressed the importance of the market segment to be targeted.* ○ *The advertising brief was not detailed enough and did not show what sort of product image the advertiser wanted to create.*

advertising budget /'ædvətaɪzɪŋ ˌbʌdʒɪt/ *noun* money planned for spending on advertising ○ *Our advertising budget has been increased.*

advertising campaign /'ædvətaɪzɪŋ kæmˌpeɪn/ *noun* a co-ordinated publicity or advertising drive to sell a product

advertising control /'ædvətaɪzɪŋ kənˌtrəʊl/ *noun* legislative and other measures to prevent abuses in advertising ○ *If voluntary advertising control doesn't work, then the government will step in with legislation.*

advertising department /'ædvətaɪzɪŋ dɪˌpɑːtmənt/ *noun* the department in a company that deals with the company's advertising

advertising expenditure /'ædvətaɪzɪŋ ɪkˌspendɪtʃə/ *noun* the amount a company spends on its advertising

advertising hoarding /'ædvətaɪzɪŋ ˌhɔːdɪŋ/ *noun* a billboard or wooden surface onto which advertising posters are stuck ○ *Advertising hoardings have been taken down since the city council banned posters.* ○ *Giant hoardings were placed in fields on either side of the road.*

advertising jingle /'ædvətaɪzɪŋ ˌdʒɪŋg(ə)l/ *noun* a short and easily remembered tune or song to advertise a product on television, etc.

advertising manager /ˈædvətaɪzɪŋ ˌmænɪdʒə/ *noun* the manager in charge of advertising a company's products

advertising medium /ˈædvətaɪzɪŋ ˌmiːdiəm/ *noun* a type of advertisement, e.g. a TV commercial ○ *The product was advertised through the medium of the trade press.* (NOTE: The plural for this meaning is **media**.)

advertising message /ˈædvətaɪzɪŋ ˌmesɪdʒ/ *noun* whatever a company is trying to communicate in an advertisement ○ *Bad copywriting made the advertising message unclear.* ○ *The advertising message was aimed at the wrong target audience and therefore got little response.* ○ *The poster does not use words to get its advertising message across.*

advertising rates /ˈædvətaɪzɪŋ reɪts/ *plural noun* the amount of money charged for advertising space in a newspaper or advertising time on TV

advertising space /ˈædvətaɪzɪŋ speɪs/ *noun* a space in a newspaper set aside for advertisements

advertising specialities /ˌædvətaɪzɪŋ ˌspeʃiˈælɪtiz/ *plural noun* special items given away as part of an advertising campaign, e.g. T-shirts, mugs, umbrellas, etc.

Advertising Standards Authority /ˌædvətaɪzɪŋ ˈstændədz ɔːˌθɒrɪti/ *noun* the independent body which oversees the system of self-regulation in the British advertising industry. Abbreviation **ASA**

advertising time /ˈædvətaɪzɪŋ taɪm/ *noun* the time on television or radio set aside for advertising ○ *Advertising time is cheapest in the afternoon.* ○ *They spent a month selling advertising time over the telephone.* ○ *How much advertising time does this programme allow for?*

advertising value equivalent /ˌædvətaɪzɪŋ ˌvæljuː ɪˈkwɪvələnt/ *noun* a measure used in the public relations industry to establish the benefit to a client from media coverage of a PR campaign. Advertising value equivalents commonly measure the size of the coverage gained and its placement, and calculate what the equivalent amount of space, if paid for as advertising, would cost.

advertising weight /ˈædvətaɪzɪŋ weɪt/ *noun* the amount of advertising given to a brand

advertorial /ˌædvɜːˈtɔːriəl/ *noun* text in a magazine which is not written by the editorial staff but by an advertiser

advice /ədˈvaɪs/ *noun* a notification telling someone what has happened ◇ **as per advice** according to what is written on the advice note

advice note /ədˈvaɪs nəʊt/ *noun* the written notice to a customer giving details of goods ordered and shipped but not yet delivered. Also called **letter of advice**

advice of dispatch /ədˌvaɪs əv dɪˈspætʃ/ *noun* communication from seller to buyer stating that goods have been sent, specifying time and place of arrival ○ *We have paid for the goods but as yet have received no advice of dispatch.* ○ *The advice of dispatch informed the buyer that the goods would arrive at Southampton on the morning of the 10th.*

ad view /ˈæd vjuː/ *noun* the number of times an advertisement is downloaded from a webpage and assumed to have been seen by a potential customer

advise /ədˈvaɪz/ *verb* to tell someone what has happened ○ *We have been advised that the shipment will arrive next week.*

advocacy advertising /ˈædvəkəsi ˌædvətaɪzɪŋ/ *noun* advertising by a business that expresses a particular point of view on some issue ○ *Because of its prestige as a producer, the company's advocacy advertising had great influence.* ○ *The food company's advocacy advertising condemned unhealthy additives in canned produce.* ○ *Advocacy advertising has changed the public's attitude to smoking.*

aerial advertising /ˌeəriəl ˈædvətaɪzɪŋ/ *noun* advertising displayed in the air from balloons or planes or in smoke designs ○ *Aerial advertising proved to be an effective gimmick.* ○ *Aerial advertising was used to attract the attention of people on the beach.*

affiliate /əˈfɪlieɪt/ *noun* a local TV station which is part of a national network

affiliated /əˈfɪlieɪtɪd/ *adjective* connected with or owned by another company ○ *Smiths Ltd is one of our affiliated companies.*

affiliate directory /əˌfɪliət daɪˈrektəri/ *noun* a directory that lists websites belonging to affiliate programmes (NOTE: Affiliate directories provide information both to companies that want to subscribe to a programme and to those who want to set up their own affiliate programmes.)

affiliate marketing /əˈfɪliət ˌmaːkɪtɪŋ/ *noun* marketing that uses affiliate programmes

affiliate partner /əˈfɪliət ˌpaːtnə/ *noun* a company which puts advertising onto its website for other companies, who pay for this service

affiliate programme /əˈfɪliət ˌprəʊgræm/ *noun* a form of advertising on the web, in which a business persuades other businesses to put banners and buttons advertising its products or services on their websites and pays them a commission on any purchases made by their customers. Also called **associate programme**

affinity card /əˈfɪnɪti kaːd/ *noun* a credit card where a percentage of each purchase made is given by the credit card company to a stated charity

affinity marketing /əˈfɪnɪti ˌmaːkɪtɪŋ/ *noun* marketing targeted at individuals sharing common interests that predispose them towards a product, e.g. a car accessories manufacturer targeting motoring magazine readers. Also, a campaign jointly sponsored by a number of disparate organisations that are non-competitive but have a particular interest in common.

affluence /ˈæfluəns/ *noun* wealth and a high standard of living

'For many older Koreans, who 20 years ago worked more than 60 hours a week to barely scrape by, such affluence is unimaginable' [*Business Week*]

affluent /ˈæfluənt/ *adjective* rich ○ *Our more affluent clients prefer the luxury model.* □ **the affluent** rich people □ **the mass affluent** people with more than £50,000 in liquid assets

affluent society /ˌæfluənt səˈsaɪəti/ *noun* a type of society where most people are rich

affluenza /ˌæfluˈenzə/ *noun* **1.** a term used by critics of capitalism and consumerism to describe the unfulfilled feeling that results from an effort to 'keep up with the Joneses' ○ *There is an affluenza epidemic throughout the world.* **2.** an unsustainable addiction to economic growth

affordable method /əˈfɔːdəb(ə)l ˌmeθəd/ *noun* a method of budgeting how much can be spent on marketing and promotion, which is based on what you can afford, rather than what you want to achieve ○ *Affordable method appeals to accountants, but won't help us achieve a high enough market share for the product.*

after-date /ˈaːftə deɪt/ *noun* a reference on a bill of exchange to the length of time allowed for payment after a specific date ○ *The after-date allowed the buyer three months in which to pay.*

after-sales service /ˌaːftə seɪlz ˈsɜːvɪs/ *noun* a service of a machine carried out by the seller for some time after the machine has been bought

after-sight /ˈaːftə saɪt/ *noun* a type of bill of exchange which is due to be paid on a specific day after acceptance

agate /ˈægət/ *noun US* a measurement of advertising space in a newspaper, equal to one-fourteenth of an inch

age group /ˈeɪdʒ gruːp/, **age bracket** *noun* a category including all people whose ages fall between two established points ○ *What age groups is this product meant to appeal to?* ○ *Research shows an increase in smoking among the 18–20 age group.*

agency /ˈeɪdʒənsi/ *noun* **1.** an office or job of representing another company in an area ○ *They signed an agency agreement.* **2.** an office or business which arranges things for other companies

agency commission /ˈeɪdʒənsi kəˌmɪʃ(ə)n/ *noun* the commission charged by an advertising agency

agency mark-up /ˌeɪdʒənsi ˈmaːk ʌp/ *noun* an amount added by an advertising agency to purchases, which forms part of the agency's commission

agency roster /ˈeɪdʒənsi ˌrɒstə/ *noun* a group of different advertising agencies all working for a large company

agent /ˈeɪdʒənt/ *noun* **1.** a person who represents a company or another person in an area ○ *to be the agent for BMW cars* ○ *to be the agent for IBM* **2.** a person in charge of an agency ○ *an advertising agent* ○ *The estate agent sent me a list of properties for sale.* ○ *Our trip was organised through our local travel agent.*

agent's commission /ˌeɪdʒənts kəˈmɪʃ(ə)n/ *noun* money, often a percentage of sales, paid to an agent

age profile /ˈeɪdʒ ˌprəʊfaɪl/ *noun* the audience a particular media product is targeted at, defined by age group, such as teenagers or over-60s

aggregate /ˈæɡrɪɡət/ *adjective* total, with everything added together ○ *aggregate output*

aggregate demand /ˌæɡrɪɡət dɪˈmɑːnd/ *noun* the total demand for goods and services from all sectors of the economy including individuals, companies and the government ○ *Economists are studying the recent fall in aggregate demand.* ○ *As incomes have risen, so has aggregate demand.*

aggregate supply /ˌæɡrɪɡət səˈplaɪ/ *noun* all goods and services on the market ○ *Is aggregate supply meeting aggregate demand?*

aggregator /ˈæɡrɪɡeɪtə/ *noun* a website which collects news from other websites, allowing rapid syndication of information

AGM *abbreviation* Annual General Meeting

agree /əˈɡriː/ *verb* **1.** to decide and approve something together with another person or other people ○ *The figures were agreed between the two parties.* ○ *We have agreed the budgets for next year.* ○ *The terms of the contract are still to be agreed.* **2.** □ **to agree on something** to come to a decision that is acceptable to everyone about something ○ *We all agreed on the need for action.* **3.** □ **to agree to something** to say that you accept something that is suggested ○ *After some discussion he agreed to our plan.* □ **to agree to do something** to say that you will do something ○ *She agreed to be chairman.* ○ *Will the finance director agree to resign?*

agree with /əˈɡriː wɪð/ *phrasal verb* **1.** to say that your opinions are the same as someone else's ○ *I agree with*

the chairman that the figures are lower than normal. **2.** to be the same as ○ *The auditors' figures do not agree with those of the accounts department.*

agreed /əˈɡriːd/ *adjective* having been accepted by everyone ○ *We pay an agreed amount each month.* ○ *The agreed terms of employment are laid down in the contract.*

agreed price /əˌɡriːd ˈpraɪs/ *noun* a price which has been accepted by both the buyer and seller

agreement /əˈɡriːmənt/ *noun* a spoken or written contract between people or groups which explains how they will act ○ *a written agreement* ○ *an unwritten* or *verbal agreement* ○ *to draw up* to *draft an agreement* ○ *to break an agreement* ○ *to sign an agreement* ○ *to reach an agreement* or *to come to an agreement on something* ○ *a collective wage agreement*

'...after three days of tough negotiations the company has reached agreement with its 1,200 unionized workers' [*Toronto Star*]

agreement of sale /əˌɡriːmənt əv ˈseɪl/ *noun* a written contract that sets out in detail the terms agreed between the buyer and the seller when a property is sold

AICPA *abbreviation* American Institute of Certified Public Accountants

aid /eɪd/ *noun* something which helps ■ *verb* to help

AIDA *noun* a model showing stages in the effects of advertising on consumers, i.e. you attract their Attention, keep their Interest, arouse a Desire, and provoke Action to purchase. Full form **attention, interest, desire, action**

aided recall /ˌeɪdɪd ˈriːkɔːl/ *noun* a test to see how well someone remembers an advertisement by giving the respondent some help such as a picture which he or she might associate with it ○ *Even aided recall brought no reaction from the respondent.* ○ *Aided recall has shown that we must make our advertising more striking.* (NOTE: also called **prompted recall**)

aid-to-trade /ˌeɪd tə ˈtreɪd/ *noun* a service which supports trade, e.g. banking and advertising ○ *The recession has affected aids-to-trade and the industries* *they support and supply.* ○ *At that time, advertising was the fastest expanding aid-to-trade.*

aim /eɪm/ *noun* something which you try to do ○ *One of our aims is to increase the quality of our products.* □ **the company has achieved all its aims** the company has done all the things it had hoped to do ■ *verb* to try to do something ○ *Each member of the sales team must aim to double their previous year's sales.* ○ *We aim to be No. 1 in the market within two years.*

air /eə/ *noun* a method of travelling or sending goods using aircraft ○ *to send a letter a shipment by air*

air carrier /ˈeə ˌkæriə/ *noun* a company which sends cargo or passengers by air

air forwarding /ˈeə ˌfɔːwədɪŋ/ *noun* the process of arranging for goods to be shipped by air

air freight /ˈeə freɪt/ *noun* the transportation of goods in aircraft, or goods sent by air ○ *to send a shipment by air freight* ○ *Air freight tariffs are rising.*

airfreight /ˈeəfreɪt/ *verb* to send goods by air ○ *to airfreight a consignment to Mexico* ○ *We airfreighted the shipment because our agent ran out of stock.*

airline /ˈeəlaɪn/ *noun* a company which carries passengers or cargo by air

airmail /ˈeəmeɪl/ *noun* a postal service which sends letters or parcels by air ○ *to send a package by airmail* ○ *Airmail charges have risen by 15%.* ■ *verb* to send letters or parcels by air ○ *We airmailed the document to New York.*

airmail envelope /ˈeəmeɪl ˌenvələʊp/ *noun* a very light envelope for sending airmail letters

airmail transfer /ˈeəmeɪl ˌtrænsfɜː/ *noun* an act of sending money from one bank to another by airmail

airtight /ˈeətaɪt/ *adjective* which does not allow air to get in ○ *The goods are packed in airtight containers.*

air time /ˈeə taɪm/, **airtime** *noun* the time set aside for advertising on television or radio ○ *How much air time do we need for this commercial?* ○ *We should look for air time on the new radio*

station. ○ *All the air time in the world won't sell this product.*

AIUAPR *noun* a buying decision model which represents awareness, interest, understanding, attitudes, purchase, and repeat purchase

à la carte /ˌæ læ ˈkɑːt/ *noun* a system whereby advertisers use the services of a whole range of businesses rather than relying on one agency over a long period

all-in price /ˌɔːl ɪn ˈpraɪs/ *noun* a price which covers all items in a purchase such as goods, delivery, tax or insurance

all-in rate /ˌɔːl ɪn ˈreɪt/ *noun* a price which covers all the costs connected with a purchase, such as delivery, tax and insurance, as well as the cost of the goods themselves

allowable expenses /əˌlaʊəb(ə)l ɪkˈspensɪz/ *plural noun* business expenses which can be claimed against tax

allowance /əˈlaʊəns/ *noun* money removed in the form of a discount ○ *an allowance for depreciation* ○ *an allowance for exchange loss*

'…the compensation plan includes base, incentive and car allowance totalling $50,000+' [*Globe and Mail (Toronto)*]

alpha activity /ˈælfə ækˌtɪvɪti/ *noun* the measurement of a person's brain activity as a way of measuring their reaction to an advertisement

alternate media /ɔːlˌtɜːnət ˈmiːdiə/ *noun* forms of advertising which are not direct mailing, e.g. TV commercials, magazine inserts, etc.

alternative close /ɔːlˈtɜːnətɪv kləʊz/ *noun* an act of ending a sales negotiation by asking the customer to choose something such as a method of payment

ambient advertising /ˌæmbiənt ˈædvətaɪzɪŋ/ *noun* advertising such as posters on the side of a bus or in a public toilet, to which people are exposed during their everyday activities

ambient media /ˌæmbiənt ˈmiːdiə/ *noun* advertising media outdoors, e.g. posters, advertisements on the sides of buses, etc.

ambush marketing /ˈæmbʊʃ ˌmɑːkɪtɪŋ/ *noun* the linking of a promotion campaign to an event such as a sporting contest which is sponsored by another manufacturer without paying a fee

American Institute of Certified Public Accountants /ə,merɪkən ,ɪnstɪtjuːt əv ,sɜːtɪfaɪd ,pʌblɪk ə'kaʊntənts/ *noun* the national association for certified public accountants in the US. Abbreviation **AICPA**

analyse /'ænəlaɪz/, **analyze** *verb* to examine someone or something in detail ○ *to analyse a statement of account* ○ *to analyse the market potential*

analysis /ə'næləsɪs/ *noun* a detailed examination and report ○ *a job analysis* ○ *market analysis* ○ *Her job is to produce a regular sales analysis.* (NOTE: The plural is **analyses**.)

analyst /'ænəlɪst/ *noun* a person who analyses ○ *a market analyst* ○ *a systems analyst*

ancillary-to-trade /æn,sɪləri tə 'treɪd/ *noun* a service which supports trade, e.g. banking and advertising ○ *The recession has affected ancillaries-to-trade and the industries they support and supply.* ○ *Advertising was the fastest expanding ancillary-to-trade at that time.*

animatic /,ænɪ'mætɪk/ *noun* a rough outline version of a television commercial shown to the advertiser for approval ○ *The animatic was sent back to the agency with several criticisms.* ○ *The animatic impressed the advertiser because it put the message over stylishly.* ○ *If the animatic is approved, the creative team will begin work on the final product.*

animation /,ænɪ'meɪʃ(ə)n/ *noun* a cartoon film, a film made from drawings

annual /'ænjuəl/ *adjective* for one year ○ *an annual statement of income* ○ *They have six weeks' annual leave.* ○ *The company has an annual growth of 5%.*

'...real wages have risen at an annual rate of only 1% in the last two years' [*Sunday Times*]

'...the remuneration package will include an attractive salary, profit sharing and a company car together with four weeks' annual holiday' [*Times*]

annual accounts /,ænjuəl ə'kaʊnts/ *plural noun* the accounts prepared at the end of a financial year

○ *The annual accounts have been sent to the shareholders.*

annual depreciation /,ænjuəl dɪ,priːʃi'eɪʃ(ə)n/ *noun* a reduction in the book value of an asset at a particular rate per year. ⇨ **straight line depreciation**

Annual General Meeting /,ænjuəl ,dʒen(ə)rəl 'miːtɪŋ/ *noun* an annual meeting of all shareholders of a company, when the company's financial situation is presented by and discussed with the directors, when the accounts for the past year are approved and when dividends are declared and audited. Abbreviation **AGM** (NOTE: The US term is **annual meeting** or **annual stockholders' meeting**.)

annual income /,ænjuəl 'ɪnkʌm/ *noun* money received during a calendar year

annual meeting /,ænjuəl 'miːtɪŋ/ *noun US* same as **Annual General Meeting**

Annual Percentage Rate /,ænjuəl pə'sentɪdʒ ,reɪt/ *noun* a rate of interest (such as on a hire-purchase agreement) shown on an annual compound basis, and including fees and charges. Abbreviation **APR**

annual report /,ænjuəl rɪ'pɔːt/ *noun* a report of a company's financial situation at the end of a year, sent to all the shareholders

anonymous product /ə,nɒnɪməs 'prɒdʌkt/ *noun* a product with no apparent brand name, used in advertisements to highlight the product being promoted ○ *Brand X is the anonymous product which never gets your washing completely white.* ○ *No one watching the commercial would believe the anonymous product was as bad is it seemed.* ○ *What happens if the respondent chooses the anonymous product instead of ours?*

Ansoff matrix /'ænsɒf ,meɪtrɪks/ *noun* a category management tool which relates market position to market strategy

anti- /ænti/ *prefix* against

anti-dumping /,ænti 'dʌmpɪŋ/ *adjective* intended to stop surplus goods being sold in foreign markets at a price that is lower than their marginal cost

'…just days before the Department of Commerce decides on anti-dumping duties for Chinese wooden bedroom furniture' [*Forbes*]

anti-inflationary measure /ˌænti ɪnˈfleɪʃ(ə)n(ə)ri ˌmeʒə/ *noun* a measure taken to reduce inflation

anti-site /ˈænti saɪt/ *noun* same as **hate site**

anti-trust /ˌænti ˈtrʌst/ *adjective* attacking monopolies and encouraging competition ○ *anti-trust measures*

antitrust law /ˈæntitrʌst lɔː/ *noun* US a law that promotes or maintains market competition by regulating anti-competitive behaviour

any other business /ˌeni ˌʌðə ˈbɪznɪs/ *noun* an item at the end of an agenda, where any matter can be raised. Abbreviation **AOB**

AOB *abbreviation* any other business

appeal /əˈpiːl/ *noun* the fact of being attractive

appendix /əˈpendɪks/ *noun* additional pages at the back of a book

apperception /ˌæpəˈsepʃ(ə)n/ *noun* → **thematic apperception test**

application form /ˌæplɪˈkeɪʃ(ə)n ˌfɔːm/ *noun* a form to be filled in when applying for a new issue of shares or for a job

appraisal /əˈpreɪz(ə)l/ *noun* a calculation of the value of someone or something

'…we are now reaching a stage in industry and commerce where appraisals are becoming part of the management culture. Most managers now take it for granted that they will appraise and be appraised' [*Personnel Management*]

appraisee /əpreɪˈziː/ *noun* an employee who is being appraised by his or her manager in an appraisal interview

appraiser /əˈpreɪzə/ *noun* a person who conducts an appraisal interview

appro /ˈæprəʊ/ *noun* same as **approval** (*informal*) □ **to buy something on appro** to buy something which you will only pay for if it is satisfactory

approach /əˈprəʊtʃ/ *noun* an act of getting in touch with someone with a proposal ○ *The company made an approach to the supermarket chain.* ○ *The board turned down all approaches*

on the subject of mergers. ○ *We have had an approach from a Japanese company to buy our car division.* ○ *She has had an approach from a firm of headhunters.* ■ *verb* to get in touch with someone with a proposal ○ *He approached the bank with a request for a loan.* ○ *The company was approached by an American publisher with the suggestion of a merger.* ○ *We have been approached several times but have turned down all offers.* ○ *She was approached by a headhunter with the offer of a job.*

appropriate /əˈprəʊpriət/ *adjective* suitable ○ *I leave it to you to take appropriate action.*

appropriation /əˌprəʊpriˈeɪʃ(ə)n/ *noun* the act of putting money aside for a special purpose ○ *appropriation of funds to the reserve*

appropriation account /əˌprəʊpriˈeɪʃ(ə)n əˌkaʊnt/ *noun* the part of a profit and loss account which shows how the profit has been dealt with, e.g., how much has been given to the shareholders as dividends and how much is being put into the reserves

approval /əˈpruːv(ə)l/ *noun* **1.** the act of saying or thinking that something is good ○ *to submit a budget for approval* **2.** □ **on approval** in order to be able to use something for a period of time and check that it is satisfactory before paying for it ○ *to buy a photocopier on approval*

approve /əˈpruːv/ *verb* **1.** □ **to approve of something** to think something is good ○ *The chairman approves of the new company letter heading.* ○ *The sales staff do not approve of interference from the accounts division.* **2.** to agree to something officially ○ *to approve the terms of a contract* ○ *The proposal was approved by the board.*

APR *abbreviation* Annual Percentage Rate

area /ˈeəriə/ *noun* **1.** a subject ○ *a problem area* or *an area for concern* **2.** a part of a country, a division for commercial purposes ○ *Her sales area is the North West.* ○ *He finds it difficult to cover all his area in a week.* **3.** a part of a room, factory, restaurant, etc. ○ *a no-smoking area*

area code /ˈeəriə kəʊd/ *noun* a special telephone number which is given to a particular area ○ *The area code for central London is 0207.*

area manager /ˌeəriə ˈmænɪdʒə/ *noun* a manager who is responsible for a company's work in a specific part of the country

argument /ˈɑːgjʊmənt/ *noun* a reason for supporting or rejecting something ○ *The document gives the management's arguments in favour of flexible working hours.*

arithmetic mean /ˌærɪθmetɪk ˈmiːn/ *noun* a simple average calculated by dividing the sum of two or more items by the number of items

armchair research /ˌɑːmtʃeə rɪˈsɜːtʃ/ *noun* looking for information that has already been compiled and published in reference books such as directories ○ *Most of our armchair research can be done in libraries.* ○ *If we cannot find all the data through armchair research, we shall have to do a market survey of our own.* (NOTE: also called **desk research**)

arrears /əˈrɪəz/ *plural noun* **1.** money which is owed, but which has not been paid at the right time ○ *a salary with arrears effective from 1st January* ○ *We are pressing the company to pay arrears of interest.* ○ *You must not allow the mortgage payments to fall into arrears.* **2.** □ **in arrears** owing money which should have been paid earlier ○ *The payments are six months in arrears.* ○ *He is six weeks in arrears with his rent.*

art director /ˈɑːt daɪˌrektə/ *noun* a coordinator of creative work in advertising ○ *The art director briefed the copywriter and illustrator on the main points of the campaign.* ○ *After three years as an agency photographer, he was made art director.*

article /ˈɑːtɪk(ə)l/ *noun* **1.** a product or thing for sale ○ *to launch a new article on the market* ○ *a black market in luxury articles* **2.** a section of a legal agreement such as a contract or treaty ○ *See article 8 of the contract.*

article numbering system /ˌɑːtɪk(ə)l ˈnʌmbərɪŋ ˌsɪstəm/ *noun* a universal system of identifying articles for sale, used especially in Europe and Japan, using a series of digits which can be expressed as bar codes

artificial obsolescence /ˌɑːtɪfɪʃ(ə)l ˌɒbsəˈles(ə)ns/ *noun* the practice of deliberately making old models seem out of date by bringing out new ones with changes and additional features which will attract the customer ○ *Artificial obsolescence is making our products seem cheap and disposable.* ○ *Artificial obsolescence means that no product can be fashionable for very long.*

artwork /ˈɑːtwɜːk/ *noun* an original work to be used for an advertisement, e.g. drawings, layouts, photographs

ASA *abbreviation* Advertising Standards Authority

asking price /ˈɑːskɪŋ ˌpraɪs/ *noun* a price which the seller is hoping will be paid for the item being sold ○ *the asking price is $24,000*

assay mark /ˈæseɪ mɑːk/ *noun* a mark put on gold, silver or platinum items to show that the metal is of the correct quality

assembly /əˈsembli/ *noun* **1.** the process of putting an item together from various parts ○ *There are no assembly instructions to show you how to put the computer together.* ○ *We can't put the machine together because the instructions for assembly are in Japanese.* **2.** an official meeting

assembly line /əˈsembli laɪn/ *noun* a production system where a product such as a car moves slowly through the factory with new sections added to it as it goes along ○ *She works on an assembly line* or *She is an assembly line worker.*

assessment /əˈsesmənt/ *noun* a calculation of value ○ *a property assessment* ○ *a tax assessment* ○ *They made a complete assessment of each employee's contribution to the organisation.*

asset /ˈæset/ *noun* something which belongs to a company or person, and which has a value ○ *He has an excess of assets over liabilities.* ○ *Her assets are only $640 as against liabilities of $24,000.*

asset stripping /ˈæset ˌstrɪpɪŋ/ *noun* the practice of buying a company at a lower price than its asset value, and then selling its assets

asset value /ˈæset ˌvæljuː/ *noun* the value of a company calculated by adding together all its assets

associate programme /əˈsəʊsiət ˌprəʊɡræm/ *noun* same as **affiliate programme**

assortment /əˈsɔːtmənt/ *noun* a combination of goods sold together ○ *The box contains an assortment of chocolates with different centres.*

assumptive close /əˈsʌmptɪv ˌkləʊz/ *noun* an act of ending the sales negotiation by assuming that the customer has agreed to buy, and then asking further details of payments, delivery, etc.

asterisk law /ˈæstərɪsk lɔː/ *noun* a law which prevents telemarketing agencies from trying to sell to people who have indicated that they do not want to be approached by telephone salesmen by putting an asterisk against their names in the phone book

ATM /ˌeɪ tiː ˈem/ *abbreviation* automated teller machine

'Swiss banks are issuing new cards which will allow cash withdrawals from ATMs in Belgium, Denmark, Spain, France, the Netherlands, Portugal and Germany' [*Banking Technology*]

'…the major supermarket operator is planning a new type of bank that would earn 90% of its revenue from fees on automated teller machine transactions. With the bank setting up ATMs at 7,000 group outlets nationwide, it would have a branch network at least 20 times larger than any of the major banks' [*Nikkei Weekly*]

atmosphere /ˈætməsfɪə/ *noun* **1.** the general feeling in a shop or shopping area **2.** the effect that the medium itself through which an advertisement is presented has on the audience

atmospherics /ˌætməsˈferɪks/ *noun* **1.** a way of encouraging customer interest by using the senses such as smell and sound **2.** creating an overall image of a company through the design of its premises and products

atomistic competition /ˌætəmɪstɪk ˌkɒmpəˈtɪʃ(ə)n/ *noun* same as **perfect competition**

ATR /ˌeɪ tiː ˈɑː/ *noun* a model showing stages in the effects of advertising on the consumer, where the customer becomes aware of the product, buys it once to try it, and then buys it again when he finds it is satisfactory. Full form **awareness, trial, repeat**

atrium /ˈeɪtriəm/ *noun* a very large open space in a building, usually with a glass roof, fountains, and plants, which acts as a central meeting point, linking shopping and office areas and restaurants

attention /əˈtenʃən/ *noun* careful thought or consideration

attitude /ˈætɪtjuːd/ *noun* the way in which a person behaves or thinks □ **a person's attitude towards an advertisement** a person's reaction to an advertisement

attitude measurement /ˈætɪtjuːd ˌmeʒəmənt/, **attitude testing** /ˈætɪtjuːd ˌtestɪŋ/ *noun* the act of ascertaining the way in which a person views something by assigning scores to various factors ○ *Attitude measurement has given us a good idea of how consumers view our product.* ○ *Will attitude testing lead to the redesigning of these heaters?*

attitude research /ˈætɪtjuːd rɪˈsɜːtʃ/, **attitude survey** /ˈætɪtjuːd ˌsɜːveɪ/ *noun* research that is intended to reveal what people think and feel about an organisation, its products or services, and its activities (NOTE: Attitude research can be used to discover the opinions either of consumers and the general public or of an organisation's own employees.)

attitude scale /ˈætɪtjuːd skeɪl/ *noun* a device which measures or tests attitudes by analysing a subject's responses

attrition /əˈtrɪʃ(ə)n/ *noun* a decrease in the loyalty of consumers to a product, due to factors such as boredom or desire for a change ○ *We must adapt our products if we are to avoid attrition.* ○ *Attrition showed the company that brand loyalty could not be taken for granted.*

auction /ˈɔːkʃən/ *noun* a method of selling goods where people who want to buy compete with each other by saying how much they will offer for something, and the item is sold to the person who makes the highest offer ○ *Their furniture will be sold in the auction rooms next week.* ○ *They announced a sale by auction of the fire-damaged stock.* ○ *The equipment was sold by auction at auction.* □ **to put an item up for**

auction to offer an item for sale at an auction ■ *verb* to sell something at an auction ○ *The factory was closed and the machinery was auctioned off.*

auctioneer /ˌɔːkʃəˈnɪə/ *noun* the person who conducts an auction

auction house /ˈɔːkʃən haʊs/ *noun* a company which specialises in holding auction sales, especially of items such as antiques or paintings

auction mart /ˈɔːkʃən mɑːt/ *noun* US auction rooms

audience /ˈɔːdiəns/ *noun* **1.** the number of people who watch a TV programme or listen to a radio programme **2.** the number of people who are exposed to an advertisement

audience accumulation /ˌɔːdiəns əkjuːmjʊˈleɪʃ(ə)n/ *noun* the building up of an audience by repeating advertisements over a period of time

audience appreciation /ˌɔːdiəns əˌpriːʃiˈeɪʃ(ə)n/ *noun* a measure of how an audience responded to a media product, used as a factor in ratings research alongside the bare statistics of how many people were watching

Audience Appreciation Index /ˌɔːdiəns əˌpriːʃiˈeɪʃ(ə)n ˌɪndeks/ *noun* a study of audience opinions on programmes they have watched. Abbreviation **AI**

audience composition /ˌɔːdiəns kɒmpəˈzɪʃ(ə)n/ *noun* the way an audience is made up, i.e. the age range, sex, lifestyles, etc.

audience differentiation /ˌɔːdiəns ˌdɪfərenʃiˈeɪʃ(ə)n/ the process of splitting an audience into groups according to age, social status and considering the needs of each group

audience measurement /ˈɔːdiəns ˌmeʒəmənt/ research into how many people are receiving a particular media product and what they are like, their social status etc.

audience research /ˌɔːdiəns rɪˈsɜːtʃ/ *noun* research into the attitudes of an audience to an advertising campaign

audimeter /ˈɔːdɪmiːtə/ *noun* an electronic device attached to a TV set,

which records details of a viewer's viewing habits

audiovisual /ˌɔːdiəʊ ˈvɪʒuəl/ *noun* media that can be seen and heard, e.g. a TV commercial ○ *The exhibition was devoted to the latest in audiovisual equipment.*

audit /ˈɔːdɪt/ *noun* **1.** the examination of the books and accounts of a company ○ *to carry out the annual audit* **2.** a detailed examination of something in order to assess it ○ *A thorough job audit was needed for job evaluation.* ○ *A manpower audit showed up a desperate lack of talent.*

Audit Bureau of Circulations /ˌɔːdɪt ˌbjʊərəʊ əv ˌsɜːkjʊˈleɪʃ(ə)nz/ *noun* an organisation which verifies and publishes the circulation of magazines and newspapers. Abbreviation **ABCs**

audited circulation /ˌɔːdɪtəd ˌsɜːkjʊˈleɪʃ(ə)n/ *noun* circulation figures for newspapers or magazines that have been independently verified

augmented product /ɔːgˌmentɪd ˈprɒdʌkt/ *noun* a product with added benefits such as warranties or installation service etc.

aural signature /ˌɔːrəl ˈsɪgnɪtʃə/ *noun* musical sounds used as a signature to identify a product or service

automated teller machine /ˌɔːtəmeɪtɪd ˈtelə məˌʃiːn/ *noun* US same as **cash dispenser**

automatic /ˌɔːtəˈmætɪk/ *adjective* working or taking place without any person making it happen ○ *There is an automatic increase in salaries on 1st January.*

automatic merchandising /ˌɔːtəmætɪk ˈmɜːtʃəndaɪzɪŋ/, **automatic selling** /ˌɔːtəmætɪk ˈselɪŋ/ **automatic vending** /ˌɔːtəmætɪk ˈvendɪŋ/ *noun* selling through a machine ○ *Automatic selling is popular because of the low labour costs involved.*

automatic vending machine /ˌɔːtəmætɪk ˈvendɪŋ məˌʃiːn/ *noun* a machine which provides drinks, cigarettes etc., when a coin is put in

automation /ˌɔːtəˈmeɪʃ(ə)n/ *noun* the use of machines to do work with very little supervision by people

availability /ə,veɪlə'bɪlɪti/ *noun*
1. the fact of being easy to obtain
□ **offer subject to availability** the offer
is valid only if the goods are available
2. the time and number of advertising
slots which are available to be used

avatar /'ævətɑː/ *noun* an animated
or graphic character, cartoon or picture used to represent an individual in a
game, chat room or website ○ *Her avatar was often seen playing online computer games.*

average /'æv(ə)rɪdʒ/ *noun* **1.** a
number calculated by adding several figures together and dividing by the number of figures added ○ *the average for
the last three months* ○ *sales average* or
average of sales **2.** □ **on average, on an
average** in general ○ *On average, $15
worth of goods are stolen every day.*
■ *adjective* **1.** equal to the average of a
set of figures ○ *the average increase in
salaries* ○ *The average cost per unit is too
high.* ○ *The average sales per representative are rising.* **2.** not very good ○ *The
company's performance has been only
average.* ○ *He's only an average worker.*

'…a share with an average rating might yield
5% and have a PER of about 10' [*Investors
Chronicle*]

'…the average price per kilogram for this
season to the end of April has been 300 cents'
[*Australian Financial Review*]

average out /,æv(ə)rɪdʒ 'aʊt/
phrasal verb to come to a figure as an
average ○ *It averages out at 10% per
annum.* ○ *Sales increases have aver-
aged out at 15%.*

average cost pricing /,æv(ə)rɪdʒ
'kɒst ,praɪsɪŋ/ *noun* pricing based on
the average cost of producing one unit
of a product

average due date /,æv(ə)rɪdʒ
'djuː ,deɪt/ *noun* the average date
when several different payments fall due

average frequency /,æv(ə)rɪdʒ
'friːkwənsi/ *noun* the average number
of times a consumer will see a particular
advertisement ○ *We will have to buy a
lot of advertising time to attain a high
average frequency.* ○ *What average frequency do we need to get this advertisement across to the target audience?*

average quarter-hour figure
/,æv(ə)rɪdʒ ,kwɔːtər 'aʊə ,fɪɡə/
adjective the average number of people
watching a TV programme during a
15-minute period

awareness /ə'weənəs/ *noun* the
state of being conscious of an advertisement's message or of a brand's existence
and qualities ○ *The survey after the
campaign showed advertising awareness had remained low.* ⇨ **ATR, maximal awareness**

B

B2B /ˌbiː tə ˈbiː/ *adjective* referring to products or services that are aimed at other businesses rather than at consumers (NOTE: The word is most commonly used of business-to-business dealings conducted over the Internet.)

'…rather than opening markets to greater competition, B2B exchanges could become powerful monopolistic tools' [*Economist*]

B2B auction /ˌbiː tə biː ˈɔːkʃən/ *noun* a web marketplace where supplier companies bid against one another to offer the lowest price for a particular product or service, while the buyer company waits until the sellers have reduced the price to one that it can afford (NOTE: Businesses have to register to take part in B2B auctions by providing their credit-card information and shipping preferences, and also have to agree to the site's code of conduct.)

B2B commerce /ˌbiː tə biː ˈkɒmɜːs/ *noun* business done by companies with other companies, rather than with individual consumers

B2B exchange /ˌbiː tə biː ɪksˈtʃeɪndʒ/ *noun* same as **exchange**

B2B web exchange /ˌbiː tə biː ˈweb ɪksˌtʃeɪndʒ/ *noun* same as **exchange**

B2B website /ˌbiː tə biː ˈwebsaɪt/ *noun* a website that is designed to help businesses trade with each other on the Internet

B2C /ˌbiː tə ˈsiː/ *adjective* referring to products or services that are aimed at consumers rather than at other businesses (NOTE: The word is most commonly used of business-to-consumer dealings conducted over the Internet.)

'While B2C companies were the target of choice last May, this spring they ranked fourth: The

leaders were B2B outfits, e-marketplaces, and online service companies' [*Business Week*]

B2C website /ˌbiː tə siː ˈwebsaɪt/ *noun* an online shop that sells products to consumers via its website

baby boomer /ˈbeɪbi ˌbuːmə/ *noun* a person born during the period from 1945 to 1965, when the population of the UK and US increased rapidly

back /bæk/ *noun* the opposite side to the front ○ *Write your address on the back of the envelope.* ○ *Please endorse the cheque on the back.* ■ *adjective* referring to the past ○ *a back payment* ■ *verb* **1.** to help someone, especially financially ○ *The bank is backing us to the tune of $10,000.* ○ *She is looking for someone to back her project.* **2.** □ **to back a bill** to sign a bill promising to pay it if the person it is addressed to is not able to do so

'…the businesses we back range from start-up ventures to established companies in need of further capital for expansion' [*Times*]

backbone /ˈbækbəʊn/ *noun* a high-speed communications link for Internet communications across an organisation or country or between countries

back cover /ˌbæk ˈkʌvə/ *noun* the back of a magazine cover, which can be used for advertising

backdate /bækˈdeɪt/ *verb* **1.** to put an earlier date on a document such as a cheque or an invoice ○ *Backdate your invoice to 1st April.* **2.** to make something effective from an earlier date than the current date ○ *The pay increase is backdated to 1st January.*

backdoor selling /ˌbækdɔː ˈselɪŋ/ *noun* the practice of bypassing an organisation's bureaucracy and selling direct to the chief decision-maker in it ○ *If we* *did not resort to backdoor selling the right department might never hear of us.* ○ *The chairman was asked out for a meal by the sales director of the other company to try a little backdoor selling.*

backer /'bækə/ *noun* **1.** a person or company that backs someone ○ *One of the company's backers has withdrawn.* **2.** □ **the backer of a bill** the person who backs a bill **3.** a piece of publicity material placed at the back of a display or stand

background /'bækgraʊnd/ *noun* past work or experience ○ *My background is in the steel industry.* ○ *The company is looking for someone with a background in the electronics industry.* ○ *She has a publishing background.* ○ *What is his background?* ○ *Do you know anything about his background?*

background music /'bækgraʊnd ˌmjuːzɪk/ *noun* music played over the tannoy in a shop, supermarket, atrium etc., as a means of pleasing or calming potential customers

backing /'bækɪŋ/ *noun* support, especially financial support ○ *She has the backing of an Australian bank.* ○ *The company will succeed only if it has sufficient backing.*

'…the company has received the backing of a number of oil companies who are willing to pay for the results of the survey' [*Lloyd's List*]

backload /'bækləʊd/ *verb* to make sure that most of the costs of a promotional campaign come in the later stages, so that they can be regulated according to the response received. The campaign can then be cut back if the response rate is inadequate. This is opposed to front-loading, where most of the costs are incurred in the early stages. Compare **frontload**

backlog /'bæklɒg/ *noun* an amount of work, or of items such as orders or letters, which should have been dealt with earlier but is still waiting to be done ○ *The warehouse is trying to cope with a backlog of orders.* ○ *We're finding it hard to cope with the backlog of paperwork.*

back of book /ˌbæk əv 'bʊk/ *noun* the last pages of a magazine containing advertisements

back-of-the-house services /ˌbæk əv ðə haʊs 'sɜːvɪsɪz/ *plural noun* services which are in the back part of a shop

back orders /'bæk ˌɔːdəz/ *plural noun* orders received and not yet fulfilled, usually because the item is out of stock ○ *It took the factory six weeks to clear all the accumulated back orders.*

back pay /'bæk peɪ/ *noun* a salary which has not been paid ○ *I am owed £500 in back pay.*

back payment /'bæk ˌpeɪmənt/ *noun* the act of paying money which is owed

backup /'bækʌp/ *adjective* supporting or helping ○ *We offer a free backup service to customers.* ○ *After a series of sales tours by representatives, the sales director sends backup letters to all the contacts.*

backup ad /'bækʌp æd/ *noun* an advertisement designed to accompany editorial material in a publication

backup copy /'bækʌp ˌkɒpi/ *noun* a copy of a computer file to be kept in case the original file is damaged

back wages /ˌbæk 'weɪdʒɪz/ *plural noun* same as **back pay**

backward integration /ˌbækwəd ˌɪntɪ'greɪʃ(ə)n/ *noun* a process of expansion in which a business that deals with the later stages in the production and sale of a product acquires a business that deals with an earlier stage in the same process, usually a supplier ○ *Buying up rubber plantations is part of the tyre company's backward integration policy.* ○ *Backward integration will ensure cheap supplies but forward integration would bring us nearer to the market.* Also called **vertical integration**. Opposite **forward integration**

bad bargain /ˌbæd 'bɑːgɪn/ *noun* an item which is not worth the price asked

bad debt /ˌbæd 'det/ *noun* a debt which will not be paid, usually because the debtor has gone out of business, and which has to be written off in the accounts ○ *The company has written off $30,000 in bad debts.*

bait /beɪt/ *noun* an article which is sold at a loss to attract customers ○ *This is an attractive enough product to use as* *bait.* ○ *The shop's best bargains were displayed in the window as bait.*

bait ad /'beɪt æd/ *noun* an advertisement for low-priced goods, used to attract customers into a shop

bait and switch /ˌbeɪt ənd 'swɪtʃ/ *noun* a sales technique where the salesperson offers what looks like an attractive bargain and then says at the last minute that it is not available and replaces it with something inferior

balance of payments /ˌbæləns əv 'peɪmənts/ *noun* a comparison between total receipts and payments arising from a country's international trade in goods, services and financial transactions. Abbreviation **BOP**

balance sheet /'bæləns ʃiːt/ *noun* a statement of the financial position of a company at a particular time, such as the end of the financial year or the end of a quarter, showing the company's assets and liabilities ○ *Our accountant has prepared the balance sheet for the first half-year.* ○ *The company balance sheet for the last financial year shows a worse position than for the previous year.*

COMMENT: The balance sheet shows the state of a company's finances at a certain date. The profit and loss account shows the movements which have taken place since the end of the previous accounting period. A balance sheet must balance, with the basic equation that assets (i.e. what the company owns, including money owed to the company) must equal liabilities (i.e. what the company owes to its creditors) plus capital (i.e. what it owes to its shareholders). A balance sheet can be drawn up either in the horizontal form, with (in the UK) liabilities and capital on the left-hand side of the page (in the US, it is the reverse) or in the vertical form, with assets at the top of the page, followed by liabilities, and capital at the bottom. Most are usually drawn up in the vertical format, as opposed to the more old-fashioned horizontal style.

balanced scorecard /ˌbælənst 'skɔːkaːd/ *noun* a system of measurement and assessment that uses a variety of indicators, particularly customer relations, internal efficiency, financial performance and innovation, to find out how well an organisation is doing in its attempts to achieve its main objectives

balloon loan /bə'luːn ləʊn/ *noun* a loan where the last repayment is larger than the others

balloon payment /bə'luːn ˌpeɪmənt/ *noun* the last payment, usually much larger than the others, that is made when repaying a balloon loan

ballot /'bælət/ *noun* a vote where voters decide on an issue by marking a piece of paper

banded offer /ˌbændɪd 'ɒfə/ *noun* a type of sales promotion involving the offer of an additional item along with the main one ○ *The banded offer consisted of a full-sized bottle of shampoo along with a small bottle of hair conditioner.*

banded pack /ˌbændɪd 'pæk/ *noun* a pack which includes two items attached to form a pack, or with an additional different item bound along with the main one ○ *These banded packs have been specially designed for our sales promotion drive.*

bandwidth /'bændwɪdθ/ *noun* a measurement of the capacity of a fibre-optic cable to carry information to and from the Internet (NOTE: The higher the bandwidth, the faster information passes through the cable.)

bangtail /'bæŋteɪl/ *noun US* a type of folded mailer, with a pocket for an information card or reply coupon and a flap that tucks in

bankable paper /ˌbæŋkəb(ə)l 'peɪpə/ *noun* a document which a bank will accept as security for a loan

bank account /'bæŋk əˌkaʊnt/ *noun* an account which a customer has with a bank, where the customer can deposit and withdraw money ○ *to open a bank account* ○ *to close a bank account* ○ *How much money do you have in your bank account?* ○ *If you let the balance in your bank account fall below $1,000, you have to pay bank charges.*

bank bill /'bæŋk bɪl/ *noun* **1.** same as **banker's bill 2.** *US* same as **banknote**

bank card /'bæŋk kaːd/ *noun* a credit card or debit card issued to a customer by a bank for use instead of cash when buying goods or services (NOTE: There are internationally recognised rules that govern the authorisation of the use of bank cards and the clearing and settlement of transactions in which they are used.)

bank charge /ˈbæŋk tʃɑːdʒ/ *noun* same as **service charge**

bank credit /ˈbæŋk ˌkredɪt/ *noun* loans or overdrafts from a bank to a customer

bank draft /ˈbæŋk drɑːft/ *noun* an order by one bank telling another bank, usually in another country, to pay money to someone

banker's bill /ˈbæŋkəz bɪl/ *noun* an order by one bank telling another bank, usually in another country, to pay money to someone. Also called **bank bill**

bank manager /ˈbæŋk ˌmænɪdʒə/ *noun* the person in charge of a branch of a bank ○ *They asked their bank manager for a loan.*

banknote /ˈbæŋk nəʊt/ *noun* a piece of printed paper money ○ *a counterfeit £20 banknote* (NOTE: The US term is **bill**.)

bank transfer /ˈbæŋk ˌtrænsfɜː/ *noun* an act of moving money from a bank account to another account

banner /ˈbænə/ *noun* **1.** material stretched between two walls or buildings, carrying an advertising message ○ *There were banners across the street advertising the charity run.* **2.** an online interactive advertisement that appears on a webpage, usually at the top or bottom, and contains a link to the website of the business whose products or services are being advertised (NOTE: Banner ads often use graphics, images and sound as well as text.)

banner advertising /ˈbænə ˌædvətaɪzɪŋ/ *noun* website advertising which runs across the top of a webpage, similar to newspaper headlines

banner exchange /ˈbænə ɪks-ˌtʃeɪndʒ/ *noun* an agreement between two or more businesses, in which each allows the others' advertising banners to be displayed on its website

banner headline /ˌbænə ˈhedlaɪn/ *noun* a headline set in very large black type, running across a page

bar chart /ˈbɑː tʃɑːt/ *noun* a chart where values or quantities are shown as columns of different heights set on a base line, the different lengths expressing the quantity of the item or unit. Also called **bar graph** or **histogram**

bar code /ˈbɑː kəʊd/ *noun* a system of lines printed on a product which, when read by a computer, give a reference number or price

bar coding /ˈbɑː ˌkəʊdɪŋ/ *noun* the process of attaching an identifying label, written in machine-readable code and able to be read by a scanner, to a product or container (NOTE: Bar codes are useful for stock control and order picking and can be used to trace a product through every stage of a transaction from packaging to customer delivery.)

bargain /ˈbɑːgɪn/ *noun* **1.** an agreement on the price of something ○ *to strike a bargain* or *to make a bargain* □ **to drive a hard bargain** to be a difficult person to negotiate with **2.** something which is cheaper than usual ○ *That car is a (real) bargain at $500.* ■ *verb* to try to reach agreement about something, especially a price, usually with each person or group involved putting forward suggestions or offers which are discussed until a compromise is arrived at ○ *You will have to bargain with the dealer if you want a discount.* ○ *They spent two hours bargaining over the price.* (NOTE: You bargain **with** someone **over** or **about** or **for** something.)

bargain basement /ˌbɑːgɪn ˈbeɪsmənt/ *noun* a basement floor in a shop where goods are sold cheaply □ **I'm selling this at a bargain basement price** I'm selling this very cheaply

bargain hunter /ˈbɑːgɪn ˌhʌntə/ *noun* a person who looks for cheap deals

bargaining /ˈbɑːgɪnɪŋ/ *noun* the act of trying to reach agreement about something, e.g. a price or a wage increase for workers

bargaining position /ˈbɑːgɪnɪŋ pəˌzɪʃ(ə)n/ *noun* the offers or demands made by one group during negotiations

bargaining power /ˈbɑːgɪnɪŋ ˌpaʊə/ *noun* the strength of one person or group when discussing prices or wage settlements

bargain offer /ˌbɑːgɪn ˈɒfə/ *noun* the sale of a particular type of goods at a cheap price ○ *This week's bargain offer – 30% off all carpet prices.*

bargain price /ˌbɑːgɪn ˈpraɪs/ *noun* a cheap price ○ *These carpets are for sale at a bargain price.*

bargain sale /ˌbɑːgɪn 'seɪl/ *noun* the sale of all goods in a store at cheap prices

bar graph /'bɑː grɑːf/ *noun* same as **bar chart**

barrier /'bæriə/ *noun* anything which makes it difficult for someone to do something, especially to send goods from one place to another □ **to impose trade barriers on certain goods** to restrict the import of some goods by charging high duty ○ *They considered imposing trade barriers on some food products.* □ **to lift trade barriers from imports** to remove restrictions on imports ○ *The government has lifted trade barriers on foreign cars.*

'…a senior European Community official has denounced Japanese trade barriers, saying they cost European producers $3 billion a year' [*Times*]

'…to create a single market out of the EC member states, physical, technical and tax barriers to free movement of trade between member states had to be removed. Imposing VAT on importation of goods from other member states was seen as one such tax barrier' [*Accountancy*]

barrier to entry /ˌbæriə tʊ 'entri/ *noun* a factor that makes it impossible or unprofitable for a company to try to start selling its products in a particular market (NOTE: Barriers to entry may be created, for example, when companies already in a market have patents that prevent their goods from being copied, when the cost of the advertising needed to gain a market share is too high, or when an existing product commands very strong brand loyalty.)

barrier to exit /ˌbæriə tʊ 'egzɪt/ *noun* a factor that makes it impossible or unprofitable for a company to leave a market where it is currently doing business (NOTE: Barriers to exit may be created, for example, when a company has invested in specialist equipment that is only suited to manufacturing one product, when the costs of retraining its workforce would be very high, or when withdrawing one product would have a bad effect on the sales of other products in the range.)

barter /'bɑːtə/ *noun* **1.** a system in which goods are exchanged for other goods and not sold for money **2.** a system in which advertising space or time is exchanged for goods from the advertiser ■ *verb* to exchange goods for other goods and not for money ○ *They agreed a deal to barter tractors for barrels of wine.*

'…under the barter agreements, Nigeria will export 175,000 barrels a day of crude oil in exchange for trucks, food, planes and chemicals' [*Wall Street Journal*]

bartering /'bɑːtərɪŋ/ *noun* the act of exchanging goods for other goods and not for money

base /beɪs/ *noun* **1.** the lowest or first position ○ *Turnover increased by 200%, but started from a low base.* **2.** a place where a company has its main office or factory, or a place where a business person's office is located ○ *The company has its base in London and branches in all the European countries.* ○ *She has an office in Madrid which she uses as a base while travelling in Southern Europe.* ■ *verb* to set up a company or a person in a place ○ *The European manager is based in our London office.* ○ *Our overseas branch is based in the Bahamas.*

'…the base lending rate, or prime rate, is the rate at which banks lend to their top corporate borrowers' [*Wall Street Journal*]

'…other investments include a large stake in the Chicago-based insurance company' [*Lloyd's List*]

base line /'beɪs laɪn/ *noun* the part of promotional material that contains basic information about the organisation such as its name and address

basement /'beɪsmənt/ *noun* a section of a shop which is underground

base year /'beɪs jɪə/ *noun* the first year of an index, against which changes occurring in later years are measured

basic /'beɪsɪk/ *adjective* **1.** normal **2.** most important **3.** simple, or from which everything starts ○ *She has a basic knowledge of the market.* ○ *To work at the cash desk, you need a basic qualification in maths.*

basic commodities /ˌbeɪsɪk kə'mɒdɪtiz/ *plural noun* ordinary farm produce, produced in large quantities, e.g. corn, rice or sugar

basic discount /ˌbeɪsɪk 'dɪskaʊnt/ *noun* a normal discount without extra percentages ○ *Our basic discount is 20%,* *but we offer 5% extra for rapid settlement.*

basic industry /ˌbeɪsɪk ˈɪndəstri/ *noun* the most important industry of a country, e.g. coal, steel or agriculture

basic necessities /ˌbeɪsɪk nəˈsesɪtiz/ *plural noun* the very least that people need to live, e.g. food and clothing ○ *Being unemployed makes it difficult to afford even the basic necessities.*

basic price /ˌbeɪsɪk ˈpraɪs/, **basic rate** /ˌbeɪsɪk ˈreɪt/ *noun* the price of a product or service that does not include any extras ○ *This is a rather high basic price.* ○ *Please make clear whether $1,000 is the basic rate or whether it is inclusive of spare parts.*

basic product /ˌbeɪsɪk ˈprɒdʌkt/ *noun* the main product made from a raw material

basics /ˈbeɪsɪks/ *plural noun* simple and important facts or principles ○ *She has studied the basics of foreign exchange dealing.* □ **to get back to basics** to consider the main facts or principles again

basis /ˈbeɪsɪs/ *noun* **1.** a point or number from which calculations are made ○ *We forecast the turnover on the basis of a 6% price increase.* (NOTE: The plural is **bases**.) **2.** the general terms of agreement or general principles on which something is decided or done ○ *This document should form the basis for an agreement.* ○ *We have three people working on a freelance basis.* (NOTE: The plural is **bases**.) □ **on a short-term or long-term basis** for a short or long period ○ *He has been appointed on a short-term basis.*

basket of currencies /ˌbɑːskɪt əv ˈkʌrənsiz/ *noun* same as **currency basket**

batch /bætʃ/ *noun* a group of items which are made at one time ○ *This batch of shoes has the serial number 25–02.* ■ *verb* to put items together in groups ○ *to batch invoices* or *cheques*

batch number /ˈbætʃ ˌnʌmbə/ *noun* a number attached to a batch ○ *When making a complaint always quote the batch number on the packet.*

batch production /ˈbætʃ prəˌdʌkʃən/ *noun* production in batches

battle /ˈbæt(ə)l/ *noun* a fight □ **battle of the brands** competition in the market between existing product brands ○ *This battle of the brands will lead to dramatic price-cutting.*

Bayesian decision theory /ˌbeɪziən dɪˈsɪʒ(ə)n ˌθɪəri/ *noun* a method for helping decision-making, often applied to new product development. The decision-maker is aware of alternatives, can work out the probable advantages or disadvantages of the alternatives, and makes up his or her mind according to the value of the best alternative.

BDI *abbreviation* brand development index

bear hug /ˈbeə hʌg/ *noun* an offer made by one company to buy the shares of another for a much higher per-share price than what that company is worth, usually made when there is doubt that the target company's management will be willing to sell ○ *The bear hug often comes before a full hostile bid.*

beginning inventory /bɪˈgɪnɪŋ ˌɪnvənt(ə)ri/ *noun US* same as **opening stock**

behavioural segmentation /bɪˌheɪvjərəl ˌsegmənˈteɪʃ(ə)n/, **behaviouristic segmentation** *noun* the segmentation or division of the market according to customers' buying habits and usage of a product ○ *Behavioural segmentation will mean there are several distinct target audiences for our product.*

behavioural targeting /bɪˌheɪvjərəl ˈtɑːgətɪŋ/ *noun* a technique used to improve the effectiveness of online campaigns by targeting individuals' web-browsing behaviour and then displaying advertisements to those individuals that match their interests

behind schedule /bɪˌhaɪnd ˈʃedʒuːl/ *noun* late ○ *The agency is way behind schedule with the promotional material.*

believer /bɪˈliːvə/ *noun* in the VALS lifestyle classification, someone with conventional values and strong principles who buy traditional, well-known products

bells and whistles /ˌbelz ənd ˈwɪs(ə)lz/ *plural noun* every possible feature that has been included in an advertising campaign

below-the-fold /bɪˌləʊ ðə ˈfəʊld/ *adjective* relating to the parts of a webpage that can be seen only by scrolling down the page and that are therefore less commercially valuable for marketing purposes

below-the-line /bɪˌləʊ ðə ˈlaɪn/ *adjective, adverb* used to describe entries in a company's profit and loss account that show how the profit is distributed, or where the funds to finance the loss originate. ⇨ **above-the-line 1**

'…the move represents a considerable promotion for the executive who ran the innovative below-the-line initiative. The club allows the company to target its customers by name through direct marketing, a significant advance on previous above-the-line campaigns' [*Marketing Week*]

below-the-line advertising /bɪˌləʊ ðə laɪn ˈædvətaɪzɪŋ/ *noun* advertising which is not paid for and for which no commission is paid to the advertising agency, e.g. work by staff who are manning an exhibition. Compare **above-the-line advertising**

below-the-line expenditure /bɪˌləʊ ðə laɪn ɪkˈspendɪtʃə/ *noun* **1.** payments which do not arise from a company's usual activities, e.g. redundancy payments **2.** extraordinary items which are shown in the profit and loss account below net profit after taxation, as opposed to exceptional items which are included in the figure for profit before taxation

benchmark /ˈbentʃmaːk/ *noun* **1.** a standard used to measure performance (NOTE: a benchmark was originally a set of computer programs that was used to measure how well a particular computer performed in comparison with similar models.) **2.** a point in an index which is important, and can be used to compare with other figures

benchmarking /ˈbentʃmaːkɪŋ/ *noun* the testing of an audience's response using a benchmark

benchmark measure /ˈbentʃmaːk ˌmeʒə/ *noun* the measure of a target audience's response at the beginning of an advertising campaign which are then

compared to responses at the end of the campaign to test its efficiency

benefit /ˈbenɪfɪt/ *noun* **1.** something of value given to an employee in addition to their salary **2.** the way in which a product or service will improve the quality of life of the purchaser, as opposed to 'features' which highlight the particular important aspects of the product or service itself

benefit-cost analysis /ˌbenɪfɪt ˈkɒst əˌnælɪsɪs/ *noun* same as **cost-benefit analysis**

benefit segmentation /ˌbenɪfɪt ˌsegmənˈteɪʃ(ə)n/ *noun* the division of a market into segments according to the types of benefit obtained by the customer from a product such as ease of availability, light weight

berth /bɜːθ/ *noun* the place in a harbour where a ship can tie up ■ *verb* to tie up at a berth ○ *The ship will berth at Rotterdam on Wednesday.*

berth cargo /ˈbɜːθ ˌkaːgəʊ/ *noun* cargo carried at especially low rates ○ *If we do not send the goods as berth cargo we will have to charge the buyer more.*

bespoke /bɪˈspəʊk/ *adjective* made to order or made to fit the requirements of the customer

bespoke tailoring /bɪˌspəʊk ˈteɪlərɪŋ/ *noun* the making of clothing for customers, to fit their individual measurements or requirements

best-before date /ˌbest bɪˈfɔː deɪt/ *noun* the date stamped on the label of a food product, which is the last date on which the product is guaranteed to be of good quality. ⇨ **sell-by date, use-by date**

best-in-class /ˌbest ɪn ˈklaːs/ *adjective* more effective and efficient, especially in acquiring and processing materials and in delivering products or services to customers, than any other organisation in the same market or industrial sector

best practice /ˌbest ˈpræktɪs/ *noun* the most effective and efficient way to do something or to achieve a particular aim (NOTE: In business, best practice is often determined by benchmarking, that is by comparing the method one organisation uses to carry out a task with the methods used by other similar organisations and determining which method is most efficient and effective.)

'For the past 25 years, managers have been taught that the best practice for valuing assets…is to use a discounted-cash-flow (DCF) methodology' [*Harvard Business Review*]

best-selling /ˌbest 'selɪŋ/ *adjective* selling better than any other ○ *These smartphones are our best-selling line.*

best value /ˌbest 'væljuː/ *noun* a system adopted by the UK government to ensure that local authorities provide services to the public in the most efficient and cost-effective way possible (NOTE: Best value, which came into force with the Local Government Act 1999, replaced the previous system of compulsory competitive tendering (CCT). It requires local authorities to review all their services over a five-year period, to set standards of performance, and to consult with local taxpayers and service users.)

Better Business Bureau /ˌbetə 'bɪznɪs ˌbjʊərəʊ/ *US* an organisation of local businesses whose purpose is to establish a good relationship between businesses and consumers by promoting ethical business practices

bias /'baɪəs/ *noun* the practice of favouring of one group or person rather than another ○ *A postal survey will do away with bias.* ○ *The trainee interviewers were taught how to control bias and its effects.*

bid /bɪd/ *noun* **1.** an offer to buy something at a specific price. ⇨ **takeover bid** □ **to make a bid for something** to offer to buy something ○ *We made a bid for the house.* ○ *The company made a bid for its rival.* □ **to make a cash bid** to offer to pay cash for something □ **to put in or enter a bid for something** to offer to buy something, usually in writing **2.** an offer to sell something or do a piece of work at a specific price ○ *She made the lowest bid for the job.* ■ *verb* to offer to buy (NOTE: **bidding – bid – has bid**)□ **to bid for something** *(at an auction)* to offer to buy something □ **he bid £1,000 for the jewels** he offered to pay £1,000 for the jewels

bidder /'bɪdə/ *noun* a person who makes a bid, usually at an auction ○ *Several bidders made offers for the house.* □ **the property was sold to the highest bidder** to the person who had made the highest bid or who offered the most money □ **the tender will go to the lowest bidder** to the person who offers the best terms or the lowest price for services

bidding /'bɪdɪŋ/ *noun* the act of making offers to buy, usually at an auction □ **the bidding started at £1,000** the first and lowest bid was £1,000 □ **the bidding stopped at £250,000** the last bid, i.e. the successful bid, was for £250,000 □ **the auctioneer started the bidding at £100** the auctioneer suggested that the first bid should be £100

big box store /ˌbɪɡ bɒks 'stɔː/ *noun* a large retail superstore that sells a very wide range of merchandise from groceries to refrigerators or televisions

big business /ˌbɪɡ 'bɪznɪs/ *noun* very large commercial firms

big idea /ˌbɪɡ aɪ'dɪə/ *noun* the main new idea behind an advertising campaign, the aim of which is to attract potential customers

Big Mac Index /ˌbɪɡ 'mæk ˌɪndeks/ *noun* an informal way of measuring the purchasing power parity between two currencies and tests the extent to which market exchange rates result in goods costing the same in different countries ○ *The Big Mac Index aims to make exchange-rate theory more digestible.*

big picture /ˌbɪɡ 'pɪktʃə/ *noun* a broad view of a subject that takes into account all the factors that are relevant to it and considers the future consequences of action taken now (*informal*)

big-ticket /ˌbɪɡ 'tɪkɪt/ *adjective* costing a lot of money

big ticket item /ˌbɪɡ 'tɪkɪt ˌaɪtəm/ *noun* a large expensive item, e.g. a car, washing machine, etc.

bilateral /baɪ'læt(ə)rəl/ *adjective* between two parties or countries ○ *The minister signed a bilateral trade agreement.*

bilateralism /baɪ'læt(ə)rəlɪz(ə)m/ *noun* a system whereby a country balances its trade with another ○ *With luck, bilateralism will put an end to the trade war.*

bill /bɪl/ *noun* **1.** a written list of charges to be paid ○ *The bill is made out to Smith Ltd* ○ *The sales assistant wrote out the bill.* ○ *Does the bill include VAT?* ○ *The builder sent in his bill.* ○ *She left the country without paying her bills.* **2.** a written paper promising to pay money **3.** *US* same as **banknote** ○ *a $5 bill* **4.** a draft of a new law which will be discussed in Parliament **5.** a small poster □ **'stick no bills'** the unauthorised putting up of posters is prohibited ■ *verb* to present a bill to someone so that it can be paid ○ *The plumbers billed us for the repairs.*

billboard /'bɪlbɔːd/ *noun* **1.** a poster site of double crown size (30 × 20 inches) **2.** *US* same as **hoarding 3.** a short announcement which identifies an advertiser at the beginning, end, or in the breaks of a broadcast

billing /'bɪlɪŋ/ *noun* the work of writing invoices or bills

bill of entry /ˌbɪl əv 'entri/ *noun* the written details of goods that have to go through customs

bill of exchange /ˌbɪl əv ɪks'tʃeɪndʒ/ *noun* a document, signed by the person authorising it, which tells another person or a financial institution to pay money unconditionally to a named person on a specific date (NOTE: Bills of exchange are usually used for payments in foreign currency.) □ **to accept a bill** to sign a bill of exchange to show that you promise to pay it □ **to discount a bill** to buy or sell a bill of exchange at a lower price than that written on it in order to cash it later □ **to retire a bill** to pay a bill of exchange when it is due

bill of lading /ˌbɪl əv 'leɪdɪŋ/ *noun* a document listing goods that have been shipped, sent by the transporter to the seller and entered in the seller's accounts as money owed but not yet paid, and therefore as an asset

bill of sale /ˌbɪl əv 'seɪl/ *noun* a document which the seller gives to the buyer to show that the sale has taken place

bill poster /'bɪl ˌpəʊstə/ *noun* a person who sticks up small posters. ⇨ **fly poster**

bills payable /ˌbɪlz 'peɪəb(ə)l/ *plural noun* bills, especially bills of exchange, which a company will have to pay to its creditors. Abbreviation **B/P**

bills receivable /ˌbɪlz rɪ'siːvəb(ə)l/ *plural noun* bills, especially bills of exchange, which are due to be paid by a company's debtors. Abbreviation **B/R**

bin /bɪn/ *noun* a separate section of shelves in a warehouse

Bingo card /'bɪŋgəʊ kɑːd/ *noun* a printed card bound into a magazine, with a squared grid of numbers and letters which a reader can mark. The numbers refer to products advertised in the magazine, and the card is returned post free to the publisher, who passes the card to the advertiser for further response.

bipolar scale /ˌbaɪpəʊlə 'skeɪl/ *noun* a scale used in questionnaires which contains two extreme points between which an interviewee can choose an answer

birth rate /'bɜːθ reɪt/ *noun* the number of children born per 1,000 of the population

BIS *abbreviation* Department for Business, Innovation and Skills

BlackBerry® /'blækbəri/ a trade name for a portable handheld device that combines functions such as email, web browsing, text messaging, scheduling and a mobile phone ○ *She kept up to date with her emails on her BlackBerry.*

black economy /ˌblæk ɪ'kɒnəmi/ *noun* goods and services which are paid for in cash, and therefore not declared for tax. Also called **hidden economy, parallel economy, shadow economy**

black list /'blæk lɪst/ *noun* a list of goods, people, or companies which have been identified as not appropriate to do business with

blacklist /'blæklɪst/ *verb* to put goods, people, or a company on a black list ○ *Their firm was blacklisted by the government.*

black market /ˌblæk 'mɑːkɪt/ *noun* the buying and selling of goods or currency in a way which is not allowed by law ○ *There is a flourishing black market in spare parts for cars.* □ **to pay black market prices** to pay high prices to get items which are not easily available

black-market economy /ˌblæk ˌmɑːkɪt ɪˈkɒnəmi/ *noun* an economy, or part of an economy, that functions by illegally trading goods that are normally subject to official controls

black space /ˌblæk ˈspeɪs/ *noun* the business opportunities that a company has formally targeted and organised itself to capture. ⇨ **white space**

blank cheque /ˌblæŋk ˈtʃek/ *noun* a cheque with the amount of money and the payee left blank, but signed by the drawer

blanket agreement /ˌblæŋkɪt əˈgriːmənt/ *noun* an agreement which covers many different items

blanket branding /ˌblæŋkɪt ˈbrændɪŋ/ *noun* giving a whole group or line of products the same brand name ○ *Blanket branding will make the brand a household name.*

blanket coverage /ˌblæŋkɪt ˈkʌv(ə)rɪdʒ/ *noun* advertising to the general public with no particular target audience in mind ○ *We will go for blanket coverage first and then see what kind of people buy the product.*

blanket insurance (cover) /ˌblæŋkɪt ɪnˈʃʊərəns ˌkʌvə/ *noun* insurance which covers various items such as a house and its contents

blanket refusal /ˌblæŋkɪt rɪˈfjuːz(ə)l/ *noun* a refusal to accept many different items

bleed /bliːd/ *noun* an illustration or text which runs right to the edge of the printed page ■ *verb* to allow advertising space to run to the edge of a printed page

blind offer /ˌblaɪnd ˈɒfə/ *noun* a premium offer which is hidden away in an advertisement so as to find out how many readers read the advertisement

blindside /ˈblaɪndsaɪd/ *verb* to attack a competitor unexpectedly and in a way which it is difficult to respond to

blind testing /ˌblaɪnd ˈtestɪŋ/ *noun* the practice of testing a product on consumers without telling them what brand it is

blister pack /ˈblɪstə pæk/ *noun* a type of packing where the item for sale is covered with a stiff plastic cover sealed to a card backing. Also called **bubble pack**

blitz /blɪts/ *noun* a marketing campaign which starts at full pressure, as opposed to a gradual build-up

blog /blɒg/ *noun* same as **web log** (*informal*)

blogger /ˈblɒgə/ *noun* a person who creates or runs a web log

blogging /ˈblɒgɪŋ/ *noun* the act of creating or maintaining a web log

blogosphere /ˈblɒgəˌsfɪə/ *noun* the parts of the World Wide Web where bloggers communicate with each other

blogware /ˈblɒgweə/ *noun* computer software that is designed to help people create web logs

blow-in /ˈbləʊ ɪn/ *noun US* a postcard-size advertising card inserted in a magazine

blue-hair /ˌbluː ˈheə/ *adjective US* referring to elderly women

blue-sky thinking /ˌbluː ˌskaɪ ˈθɪŋkɪŋ/ *noun* extremely idealistic and often unconventional ideas

'Researchers are also doing blue-sky thinking about technologies that might step to the fore once magnetic recording has reached its limit' [*Business Week*]

Bluetooth /ˈbluːtuːθ/ *trademark* a type of technology allowing for communication between mobile phones, computers, and the Internet

blur /blɜː/ *noun* a period in which a great many important changes take place in an organisation very quickly

blurb /blɜːb/ *noun* a brief description of a book, printed in a publisher's catalogue or on the cover of the book itself

body copy /ˈbɒdi ˌkɒpi/ *noun* the main part of the text of an advertisement ○ *The body copy is OK, though the company's address doesn't need to be included.* ○ *The body copy on the poster is too long for passers-by to read it all.*

body language /ˈbɒdi ˌlæŋgwɪdʒ/ *noun* gestures, expressions, and movements which show what somebody's response is to a situation ○ *Trainee salespeople learn how to interpret a customer's body language.* ○ *The interviewer of prospective marketing managers observed the body language of the candidates very carefully.* ○ *The candidate claimed to be very confident about* *taking the job, but her body language was saying the opposite.*

bogof /ˈbɒgɒf/ *noun* the practice of giving free gifts to customers, e.g. one free item for each one bought. Full form **buy one get one free**

boilerplate /ˈbɔɪləpleɪt/ *noun* a basic standard version of a contract that can be used again and again

bonded warehouse /ˌbɒndɪd ˈweəhaʊs/ *noun* a warehouse where goods are stored until excise duty has been paid

bonus /ˈbəʊnəs/ *noun* an extra payment in addition to a normal payment

bonus offer /ˈbəʊnəs ˌɒfə/ *noun* a special offer, especially one to launch a new product, which includes a bonus or free gift

bonus pack /ˈbəʊnəs pæk/ *noun* a pack with extra contents or extra items for which no extra charge is made ○ *We are offering bonus packs in order to attract new customers to the product.*

bonus size /ˈbəʊnəs saɪz/ *noun* an extra large size of pack sold at the usual price as a form of sales promotion ○ *Bonus size packs are 20% larger, but are sold at the normal price.*

bonus spot /ˈbəʊnəs spɒt/ *noun* a free television or radio spot offered to an advertiser as part of an advertising package

book /bʊk/ *noun* **1.** a set of sheets of paper attached together □ **a company's books** the financial records of a company **2.** a statement of a dealer's exposure to the market, i.e. the amount which he or she is due to pay or has borrowed

book club /ˈbʊk klʌb/ *noun* a group of people who pay a small subscription and buy books regularly by mail order

booking /ˈbʊkɪŋ/ *noun* an arrangement by which something such as a room or seat is kept for someone's use at a specific time ○ *Hotel bookings have fallen since the end of the tourist season.*

booking clerk /ˈbʊkɪŋ klɑːk/ *noun* a person who sells tickets in a booking office

booking office /ˈbʊkɪŋ ˌɒfɪs/ *noun* an office where you can book seats at a theatre or tickets for the railway

bookmark /ˈbʊkmɑːk/ *verb* to make a special mental note of somebody or something so that you remember them in the future ■ *noun* a software tool in a web browser that enables users to select and store webpages that they want to look at often and to access them quickly and conveniently

book sales /ˈbʊk seɪlz/ *plural noun* sales as recorded in the sales book

book token /ˈbʊk ˌtəʊkən/ *noun* a voucher bought in a shop which is given as a present and which must be exchanged for books

book value /ˈbʊk ˌvæljuː/ *noun* the value of an asset as recorded in the company's balance sheet

boom /buːm/ *noun* a time when sales, production or business activity are increasing ○ *a period of economic boom* ○ *the boom of the 1990s* □ **the boom years** years when there is an economic boom ■ *verb* to expand or to become prosperous ○ *business is booming* ○ *sales are booming*

'…starting in 1981, a full-blown real estate boom took off in Texas' [*Business*]

boom industry /ˈbuːm ˌɪndəstri/ *noun* an industry which is expanding rapidly

booming /ˈbuːmɪŋ/ *adjective* expanding or becoming prosperous ○ *a booming industry company* ○ *Technology is a booming sector of the economy.*

boom share /ˈbuːm ʃeə/ *noun* a share in a company which is expanding

BOP *abbreviation* balance of payments

borderless world /ˌbɔːdələs ˈwɜːld/ *noun* the global economy in the age of the Internet, which is thought to have removed all the previous barriers to international trade

borderline case /ˌbɔːdəlaɪn ˈkeɪs/ *noun* a worker who may or may not be recommended for a particular type of treatment, such as for promotion or dismissal

Boston Box /ˌbɒstən ˈbɒks/ *noun* a system used to indicate a company's potential by analysing the relationship between its market share and its growth rate (NOTE: The Boston Box was devised by the Boston Consulting Group in the

1970s to help companies decide which businesses they should invest in and which they should withdraw from. In this system businesses with a high market share and high growth rate are called *stars*, businesses with a low market share and low growth rate are called *dogs*, businesses with a high market share and a low growth rate are called *cash cows* and businesses with a low market share and a high growth rate are called *question marks*.)

Boston matrix /ˌbɒstən ˈmeɪtrɪks/ *noun* a type of product portfolio analysis, in which products are identified as stars, question marks, cash cows, or dogs. Full form **Boston Consulting Group Share/Growth Matrix**

bottle hanger /ˈbɒt(ə)l ˌhæŋə/ *noun* an advertisement in the form of a card which hangs round the neck of a bottle

bottleneck /ˈbɒt(ə)lnek/ *noun* a situation which occurs when one section of an operation cannot cope with the amount of work it has to do, which slows down the later stages of the operation and business activity in general ○ *a bottleneck in the supply system* ○ *There are serious bottlenecks in the production line.*

bottom /ˈbɒtəm/ *noun* the lowest part or point □ **the bottom has fallen out of the market** sales have fallen below what previously seemed to be the lowest point □ **rock-bottom price** the lowest price of all ■ *verb* to reach the lowest point

bottom line /ˌbɒtəm ˈlaɪn/ *noun* **1.** the last line on a balance sheet indicating profit or loss **2.** the final decision on a matter ○ *The bottom line was that the work had to completed within budget.*

bottom price /ˈbɒtəm praɪs/ *noun* the lowest price

bounce back /ˌbaʊns ˈbæk/ *verb* (of emails) to be returned to the sender because the address is incorrect or the user is not known at the mail server

bounce-back coupon /ˌbaʊns ˈbæk ˌkuːpɒn/ *noun* a coupon offer made to existing customers in order to persuade them to continue purchasing the brand

bounce rate /ˈbaʊns ˌreɪt/ *noun* the percentage of visitors to a website

that enter the site but leave it immediately and do not continue to view other pages on the site

box /bɒks/ *noun* a cardboard, wooden, or plastic container ○ *The goods were sent in thin cardboard boxes.* ○ *The watches are prepacked in plastic display boxes.* □ **paperclips come in boxes of two hundred** paperclips are packed two hundred to a box

boxed /bɒkst/ *adjective* put or sold in a box

box store /ˈbɒks stɔː/ *noun* a supermarket like a warehouse, with not much service or promotion, where goods are sold from their original packing cases ○ *The school bought stationery in large quantities from the box store.* ○ *With low overheads, box stores can offer cut-rate prices.*

boycott /ˈbɔɪkɒt/ *noun* a refusal to buy or to deal in certain products ○ *The union organised a boycott against of imported cars.* ■ *verb* to refuse to buy or deal in a product ○ *We are boycotting all imports from that country.* □ **the management has boycotted the meeting** the management has refused to attend the meeting

B/P *abbreviation* bills payable

B/R *abbreviation* bills receivable

BRAD *abbreviation* British Rate and Data

brainstorming /ˈbreɪnˌstɔːmɪŋ/ *noun* an intensive discussion by a small group of people as a method of producing new ideas or solving problems

brainstorming session /ˈbreɪnˌstɔːmɪŋ ˌseʃ(ə)n/ *noun* a meeting to thrash out problems, where everyone puts forward different ideas

branch /brɑːntʃ/ *noun* the local office of a bank or large business, or a local shop which is part of a large chain

branch out /ˌbrɑːntʃ ˈaʊt/ *phrasal verb* to start a new but usually related type of business ○ *From car retailing, the company branched out into car leasing.*

branch manager /ˌbrɑːntʃ ˈmænɪdʒə/ *noun* a person in charge of a branch of a company

'...a leading manufacturer of business, industrial and commercial products requires a branch manager to head up its mid-western Canada operations based in Winnipeg' [*Globe and Mail (Toronto)*]

brand /brænd/ *noun* a make of product, which can be recognised by a name or by a design ○ *the top-selling brands of toothpaste* ○ *The company is launching a new brand of soap.*

'...the multiple brought the price down to £2.49 in some stores. We had not agreed to this deal and they sold out very rapidly. When they reordered we would not give it to them. This kind of activity is bad for the brand and we cannot afford it' [*The Grocer*]

'...you have to look much further down the sales league to find a brand which has not been around for what seems like ages' [*Marketing*]

'...major companies are supporting their best existing brands with increased investment' [*Marketing Week*]

brand awareness /ˈbrænd əˌweənəs/ *noun* consciousness by the public of a brand's existence and qualities ○ *How can you talk about brand awareness when most people don't even know what the product is supposed to do?* ○ *Our sales staff must work harder to increase brand awareness in this area.*

brand building /ˈbrænd ˌbɪldɪŋ/, **brand development** /ˈbrænd dɪˌveləpmənt/ *noun* the expansion of the total awareness and sales of a brand in a given market

brand champion /ˈbrænd ˌtʃæmpiən/ *noun* an executive who is passionate about a brand and promotes it vigorously worldwide

brand development index /ˌbrænd dɪˈveləpmənt ɪnˌdeks/ *noun* an index that compares the percentage of a brand's total sales in a given market to the percentage of the total population in the market. Abbreviation **BDI**

branded goods /ˌbrændɪd ˈgʊdz/ *plural noun* goods sold under brand names

brand equity /ˈbrænd ˌekwɪti/ *noun* the extra value brought to a product by being a brand, both value as seen by the customer as well as financial value to the company

brand extension strategy /ˌbrænd ɪkˈstenʃən ˌstrætədʒi/ *noun* the applying of an existing brand name to a new product

brand image /ˌbrænd ˈɪmɪdʒ/ *noun* an opinion of a product which people associate in their minds with the brand name. Brand image is developed and protected carefully by companies to make sure that their product or service is adopted by its target customers.

branding /ˈbrændɪŋ/ *noun* the act of giving brand names to products or services. Branding is an important part of a marketing strategy as it helps organisations reach their key customers.

'...marketing and branding are becoming more important in the hotel and restaurant business. There is increasing competition in hotels and reviews of brand image are commonplace' [*Marketing Week*]

brand leader /ˌbrænd ˈliːdə/ *noun* the brand with the largest market share

brand life cycle /ˌbrænd ˈlaɪf ˌsaɪk(ə)l/ *noun* stages in the life of a brand in terms of sales and profitability, from its launch to its decline

brand loyalty /ˌbrænd ˈlɔɪəlti/ *noun* the feeling of trust and satisfaction that makes a customer always buy the same brand of product

brand management /ˌbrænd ˈmænɪdʒmənt/ *noun* directing the making and selling of a brand as an independent item

brand manager /ˌbrænd ˈmænɪdʒə/ *noun* the manager or executive responsible for the marketing of a particular brand ○ *The brand manager and the production manager met to discuss changes to be made to the company's leading brand of soap.*

brand name /ˈbrænd neɪm/ *noun* a name of a particular make of product

brand positioning /ˌbrænd pəˈzɪʃ(ə)nɪŋ/ *noun* the practice of placing a brand in a particular position in the market, so that it is recognisable to the public ○ *Intensive television advertising is a key part of our brand positioning strategy.* (NOTE: also called **product positioning**)

brand recognition /ˌbrænd ˌrekəɡˈnɪʃ(ə)n/ *noun* the ability of the consumer to recognise a brand on sight

brand switching /ˈbrænd ˌswɪtʃɪŋ/ *noun* the practice of changing from buying one brand to another, showing little brand loyalty ○ *We can't rely on steady sales with such a lot of brand switching going on.* ○ *Brand switching makes shopping more fun for consumers.*

brand value /ˈbrænd ˌvæljuː/ *noun* the value of a brand name

brand wagon /ˈbrænd ˌwægən/ *noun* the tendency for marketers to see branding as the only way to promote a product

brandwidth /ˈbrændwɪdθ/ *noun* the amount of customer recognition which a brand enjoys

brand X /ˌbrænd ˈeks/ *noun* the anonymous brand used in TV commercials to compare with the named brand being advertised

breach /briːtʃ/ *noun* a failure to carry out the terms of an agreement

breach of contract /ˌbriːtʃ əv ˈkɒntrækt/ *noun* the failure to do something which has been agreed in a contract

bread-and-butter line /ˌbred ən ˈbʌtə laɪn/ *noun* a range of items which are found in all stores of one category, and which provide a solid basis of continuing sales

break /breɪk/ *noun* a pause between periods of work ○ *She keyboarded for two hours without a break.* ■ *verb* □ to **break bulk** to split into small quantities for retail sale after having bought a large quantity □ **to break even** to balance costs and receipts, but not make a profit ○ *Last year the company only just broke even.* ○ *We broke even in our first two months of trading.* (NOTE: [all verb senses] **breaking – broke – has broken**)

break up /ˌbreɪk ˈʌp/ *phrasal verb* to split something large into small sections ○ *The company was broken up and separate divisions sold off.*

break-even analysis /ˌbreɪkˈiːv(ə)n əˌnæləsɪs/ *noun* **1.** the analysis of fixed and variable costs and sales that determines at what level of production the break-even point will be reached ○ *The break-even analysis showed that the company will only break even if it sells at least 1,000 bicycles a month.*

2. a method of showing the point at which a company's income from sales will be equal to its production costs so that it neither makes a profit nor makes a loss (NOTE: Break-even analysis is usually shown in the form of a chart and can be used to help companies make decisions, set prices for their products, and work out the effects of changes in production or sales volume on their costs and profits.)

break-even point /ˈbreɪkˌiːv(ə)n ˌpɔɪnt/ *noun* the point or level of financial activity at which expenditure equals income, or the value of an investment equals its cost so that the result is neither a profit nor a loss. Abbreviation **BEP**

breaking bulk /ˌbreɪkɪŋ ˈbʌlk/ *noun* the practice of buying in bulk and then selling in small quantities to many customers

break-up value /ˈbreɪk ʌp ˌvæljuː/ *noun* **1.** the value of the material of a fixed asset ○ *What would the break-up value of our old machinery be?* ○ *Scrap merchants were asked to estimate the tractors' break-up value.* **2.** the value of various parts of a company taken separately

bricks-and-mortar /ˌbrɪks ən ˈmɔːtə/ *adjective* conducting business in the traditional way in buildings such as shops and warehouses and not being involved in e-commerce. Compare **clicks-and-mortar**

bridge /brɪdʒ/ *verb* to print an advertisement across the centre of a double-page spread in a magazine

brief /briːf/ *verb* to explain something to someone in detail ○ *The salespeople were briefed on the new product.* ○ *The managing director briefed the board on the progress of the negotiations.*

briefing /ˈbriːfɪŋ/ *noun* an act of telling someone details ○ *All sales staff have to attend a sales briefing on the new product.*

British Rate and Data /ˌbrɪtɪʃ ˌreɪt ən ˈdeɪtə/ *noun* a regular publication which lists British newspapers and magazines, giving all relevant information about their circulation, rates, frequency and other advertising services offered ○ *You should consult BRAD to find the* *most suitable newspaper to carry our advertising.* Abbreviation **BRAD** (NOTE: The comparable American publication is **Standard Rate and Data Service**.)

broadband /'brɔːdbænd/ *noun* a data transmission system that allows large amounts of data to be transferred very quickly

broadband communications /ˌbrɔːdbænd kəˌmjuːnɪ'keɪʃ(ə)nz/ *plural noun* the number of different communications channels which are available using broadband cable

broadcast /'brɔːdkaːst/ *noun* a radio or TV programme ■ *verb* to send out on radio or TV

broadcasting media /'brɔːdkaːstɪŋ ˌmiːdiə/ *plural noun* media such as radio or TV

broadsheet /'brɔːdʃiːt/ *noun* a large size of newspaper page (as opposed to tabloid). Compare **tabloid**

broadside /'brɔːdsaɪd/ *noun US* a large format publicity leaflet

brochure /'brəʊʃə/ *noun* a publicity booklet ○ *We sent off for a brochure about holidays in Greece or about postal services.*

brochure site /'brəʊʃə saɪt/ *noun* a website that gives details of a company's products and contact information

brochureware /'brəʊʃəweə/ *noun* a website that provides information about products and services in the same way as a printed brochure (NOTE: The word is often used negatively to refer to electronic advertising for planned but nonexistent products.)

broken lot /ˌbrəʊkən 'lɒt/ *noun* an incomplete set of goods for sale ○ *We'll give you a discount since it is a broken lot, with two items missing.*

broker /'brəʊkə/ *noun* **1.** a dealer who acts as a middleman between a buyer and a seller **2.** □ **(stock)broker** a person or firm that buys and sells shares or bonds on behalf of clients

brown goods /'braʊn gʊdz/ *plural noun* electrical equipment for home entertainment, e.g. television sets, hi-fi equipment. Compare **white goods**

browser /'braʊzə/ *noun* a piece of software that enables computer users to

have access to the Internet and World Wide Web

bubble card /'bʌb(ə)l kaːd/, **bubble pack** /'bʌb(ə)l pæk/ *noun* a type of packaging, where the item for sale is covered by a stiff plastic sheet sealed to a card backing

bubble pack /'bʌb(ə)l pæk/ *noun* same as **blister pack**

bubble wrap /'bʌb(ə)l ræp/ *noun* a sheet of clear plastic with bubbles of air in it, used as a protective wrapping material

bucket shop /'bʌkɪt ʃɒp/ *noun* **1.** a firm that sells cheap airline or other travel tickets (*informal*) **2.** a firm of brokers or dealers that sells shares that may be worthless

'...at last something is being done about the thousands of bucket shops across the nation that sell investment scams by phone' [*Forbes Magazine*]

budget /'bʌdʒɪt/ *noun* **1.** a plan of expected spending and income for a period of time ○ *We have agreed on the budgets for next year.* **2.** □ **the Budget** the annual plan of taxes and government spending. In the US the Office of Management and Budget prepares the budget based on requests for funds by the various agencies. The President then submits the budget to Congress, which passes legislation to appropriate and authorise the funds. In the UK the budget is proposed by a finance minister and drawn up by the Chancellor of the Exchequer. ○ *The minister put forward a budget aimed at boosting the economy.* □ **to balance the budget** to plan income and expenditure so that they balance ○ *The president is planning for a balanced budget.* ■ *adjective* cheap □ **budget prices** low prices ■ *verb* to plan probable income and expenditure ○ *We are budgeting for $10,000 of sales next year.*

'...he budgeted for further growth of 150,000 jobs (or 2.5%) in the current financial year' [*Sydney Morning Herald*]

'...the Federal government's budget targets for employment and growth are within reach according to the latest figures' [*Australian Financial Review*]

budget account /'bʌdʒɪt əˌkaʊnt/ *noun* a bank account where you plan income and expenditure to allow for periods when expenditure is high, by paying a set amount each month

budgetary /ˈbʌdʒɪt(ə)ri/ *adjective* referring to a budget

budgetary control /ˌbʌdʒɪt(ə)ri kənˈtrəʊl/ *noun* controlled spending according to a planned budget

budgetary policy /ˌbʌdʒɪt(ə)ri ˈpɒlɪsi/ *noun* the policy of planning income and expenditure

budgetary requirements /ˌbʌdʒɪt(ə)ri rɪˈkwaɪəməntz/ *plural noun* the rate of spending or income required to meet the budget forecasts

budget department /ˈbʌdʒɪt dɪˌpɑːtmənt/ *noun* a department in a large store which sells cheaper goods

budgeting /ˈbʌdʒɪtɪŋ/ *noun* the preparation of budgets to help plan expenditure and income

budget surplus /ˌbʌdʒɪt ˈsɜːpləs/ *noun* a situation where there is revenue than was planned for in the budget

budget variance /ˈbʌdʒɪt ˌveəriəns/ *noun* the difference between the cost as estimated for a budget and the actual cost

build-up approach /ˈbɪld ʌp əˌprəʊtʃ/ *noun* a method of calculating the budget for promotion by determining the tasks that have to be carried out and estimating the costs of performing them

built-in /ˌbɪlt ˈɪn/ *adjective* forming part of the system or of a machine ○ *The PC has a built-in modem.* ○ *The accounting system has a series of built-in checks.*

built-in obsolescence /ˈbɪlt ɪn ɒbsəˌles(ə)ns/ *noun* a method of ensuring continuing sales of a product by making it in such a way that it will soon become obsolete

bulk /bʌlk/ *noun* a large quantity of goods □ **in bulk** in large quantities ○ *to buy rice in bulk*

bulk breaking /ˈbʌlk ˌbreɪkɪŋ/ *noun* same as **breaking bulk**

bulk buying /ˌbʌlk ˈbaɪɪŋ/ *noun* the act of buying large quantities of goods at low prices

bulk carrier /ˌbʌlk ˈkæriə/ *noun* a ship which carries large quantities of loose goods such as corn or coal

bulk discount /ˌbʌlk ˈdɪskaʊnt/ *noun* a discount given to a purchaser who buys in bulk

bulk rate /ˈbʌlk reɪt/ *noun* a cheap rate offered to advertisers who take large amounts of advertising space

bulk shipment /ˌbʌlk ˈʃɪpmənt/ *noun* a shipment of large quantities of goods

bulky /ˈbʌlki/ *adjective* large and awkward ○ *The Post Office does not accept bulky packages.*

bulldog /ˈbʊldɒg/ *noun* the first edition of a daily newspaper

bulletin /ˈbʊlɪtɪn/ *noun* a short note, newsletter, or report, issued regularly ○ *Bulletins were regularly sent to the sales force.* ○ *The bulletin contained sales figures for the month.*

bulletin board /ˈbʊlɪtɪn bɔːd/ *noun* **1.** *US* same as **noticeboard** **2.** a website that allows members of an interest group to exchange emails, chat online, and access software

bumper sticker /ˈbʌmpə ˌstɪkə/ *noun* an advertising sticker put onto the bumper of a car

bundle /ˈbʌnd(ə)l/ *verb* to market a package that contains various products or services at a special price

bundling /ˈbʌndlɪŋ/ *noun* putting several items together to form a package deal, especially offering software as part of the purchase of computer hardware

buppies /ˈbʌpiz/ *plural noun* young professional people with relatively high incomes (NOTE: Short for **Black Upwardly-Mobile Professionals**)

burst /bɜːst/ *noun* a large number of advertisements for a product placed over a short period ○ *Shall we go for a burst or for a more prolonged campaign?*

business /ˈbɪznɪs/ *noun* **1.** work in buying, selling, or doing other things to make a profit ○ *We do a lot of business with Japan.* ○ *Business is expanding.* ○ *Business is slow.* ○ *Repairing cars is 90% of our business.* ○ *We did more business in the week before Christmas than we usually do in a month.* ○ *Strikes* *are very bad for business.* ○ *What's your line of business?* □ **to be in business** to run a commercial firm □ **on business** doing commercial work ○ *She had to go abroad on business.* ○ *The chairman is in Holland on business.* **2.** a commercial company ○ *He owns a small car repair business.* ○ *She runs a business from her home.* ○ *I set up in business as an insurance broker.* **3.** the affairs discussed ○ *The main business of the meeting was finished by 3 p.m.*

business address /ˈbɪznɪs əˌdres/ *noun* the details of number, street, and city or town where a company is located

business agent /ˈbɪznɪs ˌeɪdʒənt/ *noun US* the chief local official of a trade union

business call /ˈbɪznɪs kɔːl/ *noun* a visit to talk to someone about business

business card /ˈbɪznɪs kɑːd/ *noun* a card showing a businessperson's name and the name and address of the company he or she works for

business case /ˈbɪznɪs keɪs/ *noun* a statement that explains why a particular course of action would be advantageous or profitable to an organisation (NOTE: A business case depends on the preparation and presentation of a viable business plan and is intended to weed out ideas that may seem promising but have no real long-term value to an organisation.)

business centre /ˈbɪznɪs ˌsentə/ *noun* the part of a town where the main banks, shops and offices are located

business class /ˈbɪznɪs klɑːs/ *noun* a type of airline travel which is less expensive than first class and more comfortable than economy class

business community /ˈbɪznɪs kəˌmjuːnɪti/ *noun* the business people living and working in the area

business computer /ˈbɪznɪs kəmˌpjuːtə/ *noun* a powerful small computer that runs software written to manage a business

business correspondence /ˈbɪznɪs kɒrɪˌspɒndəns/ *noun* letters concerned with a business

business correspondent /ˈbɪznɪs kɒrɪˌspɒndənt/ *noun* a journalist who writes articles on business news for newspapers

business cycle /ˈbɪznɪs ˌsaɪk(ə)l/ *noun* the period during which trade expands, slows down and then expands again. Also called **trade cycle**

business efficiency exhibition /ˌbɪznɪs ɪˈfɪʃ(ə)nsi eksɪˌbɪʃ(ə)n/ *noun* an exhibition which shows products such as computers and word-processors which help businesses to be efficient

business environment /ˌbɪznɪs ɪnˈvaɪrənmənt/ *noun* the elements or factors outside a business organisation which directly affect it, such as the supply of raw materials and product demand ○ *The unreliability of supplies is one of the worst features of our business environment.*

business equipment /ˈbɪznɪs ɪˌkwɪpmənt/ *noun* the machines used in an office

business expenses /ˈbɪznɪs ɪkˌspensɪz/ *plural noun* money spent on running a business, not on stock or assets

business game /ˈbɪznɪs geɪm/ *noun* a game, often run on a computer, in which individuals or teams compete to do business in an imaginary market ○ *Students on management courses are often asked to take part in business games to improve their decision-making skills.*

business gift /ˈbɪznɪs gɪft/ *noun* a present received by a customer, either attached to a product bought or given to him by the retailer or producer on proof of purchase of a minimum quantity of goods

business hours /ˈbɪznɪs ˌaʊəz/ *plural noun* the time when a business is open, usually 9.00 a.m. to 5.30 p.m.

business intelligence /ˈbɪznɪs ɪnˌtelɪdʒ(ə)ns/ *noun* information that may be useful to a business when it is planning its strategy

'…a system that enables its employees to use cell phones to access the consulting firm's business information database' [*Information Week*]

business letter /ˈbɪznɪs ˌletə/ *noun* a letter which deals with business matters

business mailing list /ˌbɪznɪs ˈmeɪlɪŋ lɪst/ *noun* a list of names and addresses of businesses

businessman /ˈbɪznɪsmæn/ *noun* a man engaged in business

business park /ˈbɪznɪs pɑːk/ *noun* a group of small factories or warehouses, especially near a town ○ *He has rented a unit in the local business park.*

business plan /ˈbɪznɪs plæn/ *noun* a document drawn up to show how a business is planned to work, with cash flow forecasts, sales forecasts, etc., often used when trying to raise a loan, or when setting up a new business

business portfolio analysis /ˌbɪznɪs pɔːtˈfəʊliəʊ əˌnæləsɪs/ *noun* a method of categorising a firm's products according to their relative competitive position and business growth rate in order to lay the foundations for sound strategic planning

business publication /ˈbɪznɪs ˌpʌblɪkeɪʃ(ə)n/ *noun* a magazine or newspaper which is only concerned with business matters, e.g. trade journals

business-to-business /ˌbɪznɪs tə ˈbɪznɪs/ *adjective* full form of **B2B**

business-to-business advertising /ˌbɪznɪstəˈbɪznɪsˌædvətaɪzɪŋ/ *noun* advertising aimed at businesses, not at households or private purchasers

business-to-consumer /ˌbɪznɪs tə kənˈsjuːmə/ *adjective* full form of **B2C**

business transaction /ˈbɪznɪs trænˌzækʃən/ *noun* an act of buying or selling

business unit /ˈbɪznɪs juːnɪt/ *noun* a unit within an organisation that operates as a separate department, division, or stand-alone business and is usually treated as a separate profit centre

businesswoman /ˈbɪznɪsmæn/ *noun* a woman engaged in business

busy season /ˈbɪzi ˌsiːz(ə)n/ *noun* the period when a company is busy

buy /baɪ/ *verb* to get something by paying money ○ *to buy wholesale and sell retail* ○ *to buy for cash* ○ *She bought 10,000 shares.* ○ *The company has been bought by its leading supplier.* (NOTE: **buying – bought**) □ **buy one get one free** giving free gifts to customers such as one free item for each one bought. Abbreviation **bogof**

buy back /ˌbaɪ ˈbæk/ *phrasal verb* to buy something which you sold earlier ○ *She sold the shop last year and is now trying to buy it back.*

buy forward /ˌbaɪ ˈfɔːwəd/ *phrasal verb* to buy foreign currency before you need it, in order to be sure of the exchange rate

buy in /ˌbaɪ ˈɪn/ *phrasal verb (of a seller at an auction)* to buy the thing which you are trying to sell because no one will pay the price you want

buy-back agreement /ˈbaɪ bæk əˌgriːmənt/ *noun* an agreement that a producer will buy back goods from a distributor on a specific date if the distributor has not been able to sell them

buy classes /ˈbaɪ ˌklɑːsɪz/ *plural noun* categories of buying based on how much the purchasing decisions of an organisation have changed from the time of the previous purchase

buyer /ˈbaɪə/ *noun* **1.** a person who buys □ **there were no buyers** no one wanted to buy **2.** a person who buys stock on behalf of a trading organisation for resale or for use in production **3.** in B2B selling, a person who has made a commitment to buy, but has not finalised the deal

buyer expectation /ˌbaɪə ˌeks-pekˈteɪʃ(ə)n/ *noun* same as **customer expectation**

buyer's guide /ˈbaɪəz gaɪd/ *noun* a book or pamphlet which gives advice to purchasers on the prices, availability, and reliability of products or services

buyer's market /ˈbaɪəz ˌmɑːkɪt/ *noun* a market where products are sold cheaply because there are few people who want to buy them. Opposite **seller's market**

buyer's risk /ˌbaɪəz ˈrɪsk/ *noun* the risk taken by a buyer when accepting goods or services without a guarantee

buyer's surplus /ˌbaɪəz ˈsɜːpləs/ *noun* an extra margin generated when an item is bought at a higher discount than usual ○ *When the brand manager realised how great the buyer's surplus was, she decided to lower the price of the product.*

buy grid /ˈbaɪ ɡrɪd/ *noun* a method used for objective assessment of competing products, especially when purchasing industrial supplies

buying /ˈbaɪɪŋ/ *noun* the act of getting something for money

buying agent /ˈbaɪɪŋ ˌeɪdʒənt/ *noun* a person who buys for a business or another person, and earns a commission ○ *Our buying agent is presently looking for materials in Portugal.* ○ *The buying agent knows a whole network of suppliers round the country.*

buying department /ˈbaɪɪŋ dɪˌpɑːtmənt/ *noun* the department in a company which buys raw materials or goods for use in the company (NOTE: The US term is **purchasing department**.)

buying habits /ˈbaɪɪŋ ˌhæbɪtz/ *plural noun* the general way in which some people select and buy goods

buying power /ˈbaɪɪŋ ˌpaʊə/ *noun* an assessment of an individual's or organisation's disposable income regarded as conferring the power to make purchases

○ *The buying power of the dollar has fallen over the last five years.*

buying service /ˈbaɪɪŋ ˌsɜːvɪs/ *noun* an agency which buys advertising space or time for its clients

buyout /ˈbaɪaʊt/ *noun* the purchase of a controlling interest in a company

'…we also invest in companies whose growth and profitability could be improved by a management buyout' [*Times*]

'…in a normal leveraged buyout, the acquirer raises money by borrowing against the assets or cash flow of the target company' [*Fortune*]

buy phases /ˈbaɪ ˌfeɪzɪz/ *plural noun* phases in the buying of industrial products. The main phases are the recognition of a want, the identification of a product, comparison with other competing products on the market, evaluation of possible courses of action, and final decision-making.

buzz marketing /ˈbʌz ˌmɑːkɪtɪŋ/ *noun* buzz marketing uses 'word-of-mouth' advertising: potential customers pass round information about a product through email, social networking, websites and face-to-face contact

by-line /ˈbaɪ laɪn/ *noun* the journalist's name which appears before a newspaper report

C

C2C commerce /ˌsiː tə siː ˈkɒmɜːs/ noun same as **consumer-to-consumer commerce**

CA abbreviation Consumers Association

cable television /ˌkeɪb(ə)l ˌtelɪˈvɪ-ʒ(ə)n/, **cable TV** /ˌkeɪb(ə)l ˌtiːˈviː/ noun a television service which a viewer receives via a cable from a particular station and pays for on subscription

caging /ˈkeɪdʒɪŋ/ noun the handling of cash and cheques in a direct-mail operation

call /kɔːl/ noun a visit ○ *The salespeople make six calls a day.* ■ verb □ **to call on someone** to visit someone ○ *Our salespeople call on their best accounts twice a month.*

call in /ˌkɔːl ˈɪn/ phrasal verb **1.** to visit ○ *Their sales representative called in twice last week.* **2.** to telephone to make contact ○ *We ask the reps to call in every Friday to report the week's sales.*

call bird /ˈkɔːl bɜːd/ noun a low-priced product advertised to attract customers to the point-of-sale where they can then be sold more profitable goods ○ *We need a call bird to attract more customers.*

call centre /ˈkɔːl ˌsentə/ noun a department or business that operates a large number of telephones and specialises in making calls to sell products or in receiving calls from customers to provide information or after-sales services (NOTE: A call centre often acts as the central point of contact between an organisation and its customers.)

call cycle /ˈkɔːl ˌsaɪk(ə)l/ noun the time between a salesperson's visits to the same customer ○ *Because we now have*

more customers to deal with, call cycles are getting longer.

call frequency /ˈkɔːl ˌfriːkwənsi/ noun the number of times a salesperson visits a specific customer during a period of time

calling line identification /ˈkɔːlɪŋ laɪn aɪdentɪfɪˌkeɪʃ(ə)n/ noun ➡ **computer telephony integration**

call letters /ˈkɔːl ˌletəz/ plural noun US a series of letters used to identify a radio station

call rate /ˈkɔːl reɪt/ noun the number of calls per day or per week which a salesperson makes on customers

call report /ˈkɔːl rɪˌpɔːt/ noun a report made by a salesperson after a visit to a customer ○ *In his call report, the sales rep explained why he was experiencing sales resistance.* ○ *The call reports have to be handed in each week to the sales manager.*

call to action /ˌkɔːl tʊ ˈækʃən/ noun a prompt which encourages a potential Internet purchaser to do something such as click to see a range of colours

camp /kæmp/ verb □ **to camp on the line** to have to wait on hold for a long time until someone answers your telephone call

campaign /kæmˈpeɪn/ noun a series of co-ordinated activities to reach an objective

cancellation clause /ˌkænsəˈleɪʃ(ə)n klɔːz/ noun a clause in a contract which states the terms on which the contract may be cancelled

cancellation date /ˌkænsəˈleɪʃ(ə)n deɪt/ noun the final date by which an advertisement must be cancelled if the advertiser does not wish to proceed

canned presentation /ˌkænd prez(ə)nˈteɪʃ(ə)n/ *noun* a standard sales presentation which some salespeople use all the time ○ *When trainee sales reps are not sure how to approach customers they fall back on canned presentations.* ○ *The sales manager feels that the artificiality of canned presentations makes them ineffective.*

cannibalisation, cannibalization /ˌkænɪbəlaɪˈzeɪʃ(ə)n/, **cannibalism** /ˈkænɪbəlɪz(ə)m/, *noun* a situation where a company launches a new product which sells well at the expense of another established product ○ *Though the new product sold well, the resultant cannibalisation damaged the company's overall profits for the year.* ○ *Cannibalism became a real problem because the new product made the existing line seem obsolete.*

canvass /ˈkænvəs/ *verb* to visit people to ask them to buy goods, to vote, or to say what they think ○ *He's canvassing for customers for his hairdresser's shop.* ○ *We've canvassed the staff about raising the prices in the staff restaurant.*

canvasser /ˈkænvəsə/ *noun* a person who canvasses

canvassing /ˈkænvəsɪŋ/ *noun* the practice of asking people to buy, to vote, or to say what they think ○ *door-to-door canvassing* ○ *canvassing techniques*

capital /ˈkæpɪt(ə)l/ *noun* **1.** the money, property, and assets used in a business ○ *a company with $10,000 capital or with a capital of $10,000* □ **capital structure of a company** the way in which a company's capital is made up from various sources **2.** money owned by individuals or companies, which they use for investment □ **movements of capital** changes of investments from one country to another □ **flight of capital** the rapid movement of capital out of one country because of lack of confidence in that country's economic future

capital account /ˈkæpɪt(ə)l əˌkaʊnt/ *noun* an account that states the value of funds and assets invested in a business by the owners or shareholders

capital allowances /ˌkæpɪt(ə)l əˈlaʊənsɪz/ *plural noun* the allowances based on the value of fixed assets which may be deducted from a company's profits and so reduce its tax liability

COMMENT: Under current UK law, depreciation is not allowable for tax on profits, whereas capital allowances, based on the value of fixed assets owned by the company, are tax-allowable.

capital assets /ˌkæpɪt(ə)l ˈæsets/ *plural noun* the property, machines, and other assets which a company owns and uses but which it does not buy and sell as part of its regular trade. Also called **fixed assets**

capital city /ˌkæpɪt(ə)l ˈsɪti/ *noun* the main city in a country, where the government is located

capital gain /ˌkæpɪt(ə)l ˈɡeɪn/ *noun* an amount of money made by selling a fixed asset. Opposite **capital loss**

capital gains tax /ˌkæpɪt(ə)l ˈɡeɪnz tæks/ *noun* a tax on the difference between the gross acquisition cost and the net proceeds when an asset is sold. In the UK, this tax also applies when assets are given or exchanged, although each individual has an annual capital gains tax allowance that exempts gains within that tax year below a stated level. In addition, certain assets may be exempt, e.g., a person's principal private residence and transfers of assets between spouses. Abbreviation **CGT**

capital goods /ˈkæpɪt(ə)l ɡʊdz/ *plural noun* machinery, buildings, and raw materials which are used to make other goods

capital-intensive industry /ˌkæpɪt(ə)l ɪnˈtensɪv ˌɪndəstri/ *noun* an industry which needs a large amount of capital investment in plant to make it work

capitalise /ˈkæpɪt(ə)laɪz/, **capitalize** *verb* to supply money to a working company

'…at its last traded price the bank was capitalized at around $1.05 billion with 60% in the hands of the family' [*South China Morning Post*]

capitalise on /ˈkæpɪt(ə)laɪz ɒn/ *phrasal verb* to make a profit from ○ *We* *are seeking to capitalise on our market position.*

capitalism /ˈkæpɪt(ə)lɪz(ə)m/ *noun* the economic system in which each person has the right to invest money, to work in business and to buy and sell, with no restrictions from the state

capitalist /ˈkæpɪt(ə)lɪst/ *adjective* working according to the principles of capitalism ○ *the capitalist system* ○ *the capitalist countries world* ■ *noun* a person who invests capital in business enterprises

capitalist economy /ˌkæpɪt(ə)lɪst ɪˈkɒnəmi/ *noun* an economy in which each person has the right to invest money, to work in business and to buy and sell, with no restrictions from the state

capital levy /ˌkæpɪt(ə)l ˈlevi/ *noun* a tax on the value of a person's property and possessions

capital loss /ˌkæpɪt(ə)l ˈlɒs/ *noun* a loss made by selling assets. Opposite **capital gain**

capital transfer tax /ˌkæpɪt(ə)l ˈtrænsfɜː ˌtæks/ *noun* in the UK, a tax on the transfer of assets that was replaced in 1986 by inheritance tax

captain /ˈkæptɪn/ *noun* same as **channel captain**

caption /ˈkæpʃən/ *noun* a short description at the bottom of an illustration or photograph ○ *Having no caption at the bottom of the illustration created more reader interest in the product.* ○ *It took the copywriter days to think of a suitable caption for the photograph.*

captive audience /ˌkæptɪv ˈɔːdiəns/ *noun* the people who cannot avoid being exposed to an advertisement ○ *Advertisers like to have their posters in underground stations where there is a large captive audience.*

captive market /ˌkæptɪv ˈmaːkɪt/ *noun* a market where one supplier has a monopoly and the buyer has no choice over the product which he or she must purchase

capture /ˈkæptʃə/ *verb* to take or get control of something □ **to capture 10% of the market** to sell hard, and so take a

10% market share □ **to capture 20% of a company's shares** to buy shares in a company rapidly and so own 20% of it

car boot sale /ˌkaː ˈbuːt ˌseɪl/ *noun* a type of jumble sale, organised in a large car park or sports field, where people sell unwanted items from the back of their cars

car card /ˈkaː kaːd/ *noun* an advertisement display card which is placed in a vehicle such as a bus, taxi, or train

card /kaːd/ *noun* a small piece of cardboard or plastic, usually with information printed on it ○ *He showed his staff card to get a discount in the store.*

card deck /ˈkaːd dek/ *noun* a series of small cards, advertising different products or services, which are mailed as a pack in a plastic envelope to prospective customers

cardholder /ˈkaːdˌhəʊldə/ *noun* an individual or company that has an account with a credit card company and whose name usually appears on the card

card-issuing bank /ˈkaːd ɪsjuɪŋ ˌbæŋk/ *noun* same as **issuer**

card-not-present merchant account /ˌkaːd nɒt prez(ə)nt ˈmɜː-tʃənt əˌkaʊnt/ *noun* an account that enables businesses operating on the web to receive payments by credit card without the buyer or card being physically present when the transaction is made

card rate /ˈkaːd reɪt/ *noun* an advertising charge which is based on the charges listed in a rate card, i.e. without any discounts. ⇨ **escalator card, showcard**

careline /ˈkeəlaɪn/ *noun* a telephone number which links people to services which can help them, such as social services departments, hospitals, or a similar service offered by shops to their customers

cargo /ˈkaːgəʊ/ *noun* a load of goods which are sent in a ship or plane, etc. □ **the ship was taking on cargo** the ship was being loaded with goods □ **to load cargo** to put cargo on a ship

cargo liner /ˈkaːgəʊ ˌlaɪnə/ *noun* a cargo ship with a regular schedule ○ *If the cargo liner's schedule doesn't* *suit us, we'll have to charter a ship.* ○ *The cargo liner makes regular trips between Southampton and Lisbon.*

cargo ship /ˈkɑːɡəʊ ʃɪp/ *noun* a ship which carries cargo, not passengers

car mart /ˈkɑː mɑːt/ *noun US* a secondhand car salesroom

carnet /ˈkɑːneɪ/ *noun* an international document which allows dutiable goods to cross several European countries by road without paying duty until the goods reach their final destination

carriage /ˈkærɪdʒ/ *noun* **1.** the transporting of goods from one place to another ○ *to pay for carriage* **2.** the cost of transport of goods ○ *to allow 10% for carriage* ○ *Carriage is 15% of the total cost.* □ **carriage free** a deal where the customer does not pay for the shipping □ **carriage paid** a deal where the seller has paid for the shipping □ **carriage prepaid** a note showing that the transport costs have been paid in advance

carrier /ˈkæriə/ *noun* **1.** a company that transports goods ○ *We only use reputable carriers.* **2.** a vehicle or ship that transports goods

carrier bag /ˈkæriə bæɡ/ *noun* a disposable shopping bag made of plastic or paper

carrier's risk /ˌkæriəz ˈrɪsk/ *noun* the responsibility of a carrier to pay for damage or loss of goods being shipped

carry /ˈkæri/ *verb* **1.** to take from one place to another ○ *a tanker carrying oil from the Gulf* ○ *The truck was carrying goods to the supermarket.* **2.** to keep in stock ○ *to carry a line of goods* ○ *We do not carry pens.* (NOTE: [all senses] **carries – carrying – carried**)

carry over /ˌkæri ˈəʊvə/ *phrasal verb* **1.** □ **to carry over a balance** to take a balance from the end of one page or period to the beginning of the next **2.** □ **to carry over stock** to hold stock from the end of one stocktaking period to the beginning of the next

carrying /ˈkæriɪŋ/ *noun* transporting from one place to another ○ *carrying charges* ○ *carrying cost*

carry-over effect /ˌkæri ˈəʊvər ɪˌfekt/ *noun* the effect of something after it has happened ○ *The carry-over*

effect of the currency devaluation was a good few years of lucrative exporting. ○ *The political unrest in our key export markets had disastrous carry-over effects on our international marketing.*

cart /kɑːt/ *noun* a receptacle for carrying goods; typically goods bought online ○ *He added his purchases to the shopping cart.*

cartage /ˈkɑːtɪdʒ/ *noun* the activity of carrying goods by road

cartel /kɑːˈtel/ *noun* a group of companies which try to fix the price or to regulate the supply of a product so that they can make more profit

carter /ˈkɑːtə/ *noun* a person who transports goods by road

carton /ˈkɑːt(ə)n/ *noun* a box made of cardboard ○ *a carton of milk*

case /keɪs/ *noun* **1.** a cardboard or wooden box for packing and carrying goods □ **six cases of wine** six boxes, each containing twelve bottles **2.** a typical example of something ○ *The company has had several cases of petty theft in the post room.* **3.** reasons for doing something ○ *The negotiators put forward the union's case for a pay rise.*

case study /ˈkeɪs ˌstʌdi/ *noun* a true or invented business situation used in business training to practise decision-making ○ *The marketing case study consisted of a long history of the company, the present situation, and a choice of strategic plans.* ○ *The case study was about territory-planning in a city in which there were a number of accounts of varying importance.*

cash /kæʃ/ *noun* **1.** money in the form of coins or notes **2.** the using of money in coins or notes □ **to pay cash down** to pay in cash immediately ■ *verb* □ **to cash a cheque** to exchange a cheque for cash

cash out *phrasal verb US* same as **cash up**

cash up /ˌkæʃ ˈʌp/ *phrasal verb* to add up the cash in a shop at the end of the day

cashable /ˈkæʃəb(ə)l/ *adjective* able to be cashed ○ *A crossed cheque is not cashable at any bank.*

cash account /ˈkæʃ əˌkaʊnt/ noun an account which records the money which is received and spent

cash advance /ˌkæʃ ədˈvɑːns/ noun a loan in cash against a future payment

cash against documents /ˌkæʃ əgenst ˈdɒkjʊmənts/ noun a system whereby a buyer receives documents for the goods on payment of a bill of exchange

cash and carry /ˌkæʃ ən ˈkæri/ noun a large store selling goods at low prices, where the customer pays cash and takes the goods away immediately ○ *We get our supplies every morning from the cash and carry.*

'...the small independent retailer who stocks up using cash and carries could be hit hard by the loss of footfall associated with any increase in smuggled goods' [*The Grocer*]

cashback /ˈkæʃbæk/ noun a discount system where a purchaser receives a cash discount on the completion of the purchase

'... he mentioned BellSouth's DSL offer of $75 a month, plus a one-month cash-back rebate' [*Business Week*]

cash balance /ˈkæʃ ˌbæləns/ noun a balance that represents cash alone, as distinct from a balance that includes money owed but as yet unpaid

cash book /ˈkæʃ bʊk/ noun a book in which all cash payments and receipts are recorded. In a double-entry bookkeeping system, the balance at the end of a given period is included in the trial balance and then transferred to the balance sheet itself.

cash budget /ˈkæʃ ˌbʌdʒɪt/ noun a plan of cash income and expenditure. Also called **cash-flow budget**

cash card /ˈkæʃ kɑːd/ noun a plastic card used to obtain money from a cash dispenser

cash cow /ˈkæʃ kaʊ/ noun a product or subsidiary company that consistently generates good profits but does not provide growth

cash deal /ˌkæʃ ˈdiːl/ noun a sale done for cash

cash desk /ˈkæʃ desk/ noun the place in a store where you pay for the goods bought

cash discount /ˌkæʃ ˈdɪskaʊnt/ noun a discount given for payment in cash. Also called **discount for cash**

cash dispenser /ˈkæʃ dɪˌspensə/ noun a machine which gives out money when a special card is inserted and instructions given

cash float /ˈkæʃ fləʊt/ noun cash put into the cash box at the beginning of the day or week to allow change to be given to customers

cash flow /ˈkæʃ fləʊ/ noun cash which comes into a company from sales (cash inflow) or the money which goes out in purchases or overhead expenditure (cash outflow) □ **the company is suffering from cash flow problems** cash income is not coming in fast enough to pay the expenditure going out

cash-flow budget /ˈkæʃ fləʊ ˌbʌdʒɪt/ noun same as **cash budget**

cash-flow forecast /ˈkæʃ fləʊ ˌfɔːkɑːst/ noun a forecast of when cash will be received or paid out

cash-flow statement /ˈkæʃ fləʊ ˌsteɪtmənt/ noun a record of a company's cash inflows and cash outflows over a specific period of time, typically a year

cashier /kæˈʃɪə/ noun **1.** a person who takes money from customers in a shop or who deals with the money that has been paid in **2.** a person who deals with customers in a bank and takes or gives cash at the counter

cash in hand /ˌkæʃ ɪn ˈhænd/ noun money and notes, kept to pay small amounts but not deposited in the bank

cash items /ˈkæʃ ˌaɪtəmz/ plural noun goods sold for cash

cash offer /ˈkæʃ ˌɒfə/ noun an offer to pay in cash, especially an offer to pay cash when buying shares in a takeover bid

cash payment /ˈkæʃ ˌpeɪmənt/ noun payment in cash

cash purchase /ˈkæʃ ˌpɜːtʃɪs/ noun a purchase made for cash

cash sale /ˈkæʃ seɪl/ noun a transaction paid for in cash

cash terms /ˈkæʃ tɜːmz/ plural noun lower terms which apply if the customer pays cash

cash transaction /ˈkæʃ træn͵zæk-ʃən/ *noun* a transaction paid for in cash, as distinct from a transaction paid for by means of a transfer of a financial instrument

cash voucher /ˈkæʃ ͵vaʊtʃə/ *noun* a piece of paper which can be exchanged for cash ○ *With every $20 of purchases, the customer gets a cash voucher to the value of $2.*

catalogue /ˈkæt(ə)lɒg/ *noun* a publication which lists items for sale, usually showing their prices ○ *an office equipment catalogue* ○ *They sent us a catalogue of their new range of products.* ■ *verb* to put an item into a catalogue (NOTE: [all senses] The usual US spelling is **catalog**.)

catalogue house /ˈkæt(ə)lɒg haʊs/ *noun* a company which mainly or solely sells by catalogue

catalogue price /ˈkæt(ə)lɒg praɪs/ *noun* a price as marked in a catalogue or list

catalogue store /ˈkæt(ə)lɒg stɔː/, **catalogue showroom** /ˈkæt(ə)lɒg ʃəʊruːm/ *noun* a shop where customers can examine a catalogue and choose goods from it

catchment area /ˈkætʃmənt ͵eəriə/ *noun* the area around a shop or shopping centre, where the customers live

catchpenny /ˈkætʃpeni/ *noun* an article which has only superficial appeal, but which attracts buyers ○ *A closer look at the doll showed it to be just a shoddily made catchpenny.*

category extension /ˈkætɪg(ə)ri ɪk͵stenʃən/ *noun* the applying of an existing brand name to a new product category

category management /ˈkætɪg(ə)ri ͵mænɪdʒmənt/ *noun* a system where managers have responsibility for the marketing of a particular category or line of products

cater /ˈkeɪtər/ *verb*

cater for /ˈkeɪtə fɔː/ *phrasal verb* to deal with or provide for ○ *The store caters mainly for overseas customers.*

cause related marketing /ˈkɔːz rɪ͵leɪtɪd ͵maːkɪtɪŋ/ *noun* a partnership between a company or brand and a charity or 'cause' by which the 'cause' benefits financially from the sale of specific products ○ *The alcohol awareness campaign launched by the wine distributor shows a commitment to cause related marketing.*

caveat emptor /͵kæviæt ˈemptɔː/ *phrase* a Latin phrase meaning 'let the buyer beware', which indicates that the buyer is responsible for checking that what he or she buys is in good order

'…the idea that buyers at a car boot sale should have any rights at all is laughable. Even those who do not understand Latin know that caveat emptor is the rule' [*Times*]

CCTV /͵siː siː tiː ˈviː/ *abbreviation* closed circuit television

ceiling /ˈsiːlɪŋ/ *noun* the highest point that something can reach, e.g. the highest rate of a pay increase ○ *to fix a ceiling for a budget* ○ *There is a ceiling of $100,000 on deposits.* ○ *Output reached its ceiling in June and has since fallen back.*

census /ˈsensəs/ *noun* an official count of a country's population, including such data as the age, sex, and occupation of individuals ○ *The market research department made a careful study of the census in different areas of the country to see where demand would be highest.* ⇨ **distribution census**

central /ˈsentrəl/ *adjective* organised from one main point

centralise /ˈsentrəlaɪz/ *verb* to organise from a central point ○ *All purchasing has been centralised in our main office.* ○ *The company has become very centralised, and far more staff work at headquarters.*

centralised distribution /͵sentrəlaɪzd ͵dɪstrɪˈbjuːʃ(ə)n/ *noun* a system of distribution of goods to retail stores in a chain, from a central or local warehouse, so avoiding direct distribution from the manufacturer, and making stock control easier

centralised organisational structure /͵sentrəlaɪzd ɔːgənaɪ͵zeɪʃ(ə)n(ə)l ˈstrʌktʃə/ *noun* a method of organising international advertising and promotion where all decisions are made in a company's central office ○ *The group benefits from a highly centralised organisational structure.*

centralised system /ˌsentrəlaɪzd ˈsɪstəm/ *noun* a system where advertising and other marketing activities are run from one central marketing department

central office /ˌsentrəl ˈɒfɪs/ *noun* the main office which controls all smaller offices

Central Office of Information /ˌsentrəl ˌɒfɪs əv ɪnfəˈmeɪʃ(ə)n/ a British government organisation which provides a publicity service and advice on international trade for British companies wishing to export. Abbreviation **COI**

central purchasing /ˌsentrəl ˈpɜːtʃɪsɪŋ/ *noun* purchasing organised by a central office for all branches of a company

centre spread /ˌsentə ˈspred/ *noun* two facing pages in the centre of a newspaper or magazine used by an advertiser for one advertisement ○ *The whole centre spread for three days cost the advertiser $150,000.* ○ *The centre spread was taken up with a large advertisement for a new model of car.*

certificate of approval /səˌtɪfɪkət əv əˈpruːv(ə)l/ *noun* a document showing that an item has been approved officially

certificate of origin /səˌtɪfɪkət əv ˈɒrɪdʒɪn/ *noun* a document showing where imported goods come from or were made

certified mail /rɪˌkɔːdɪd dɪˈlɪv(ə)ri/ *noun US* same as **recorded delivery**

certified public accountant /ˌsɜː tɪfaɪd ˌpʌblɪk əˈkaʊntənt/ *noun US* same as **chartered accountant**

CGT *abbreviation* capital gains tax

chain /tʃeɪn/ *noun* a series of stores or other businesses belonging to the same company ○ *a chain of hotels* or *a hotel chain* ○ *the chairman of a large do-it-yourself chain* ○ *He runs a chain of shoe shops.* ○ *She bought several garden centres and gradually built up a chain.*

'...the giant US group is better known for its chain of cinemas and hotels rather than its involvement in shipping' [*Lloyd's List*]

chairman and managing director /ˌtʃeəmən ən ˌmænɪdʒɪŋ daɪˈrektə/ *noun* a managing director who is also chairman of the board of directors

challenger /ˈtʃælɪndʒə/ *noun* a company which challenges other companies which are already established in the marketplace

channel /ˈtʃæn(ə)l/ *noun* a means by which information or goods pass from one place to another □ **to go through the official channels** to deal with government officials, especially when making a request □ **channels of influence** the ways in which a company can influence consumers to buy their products, i.e. personal influence channels such as salesmen, or non-personal channels such as press advertising ○ *Owing to lack of capital there were not many channels of influence open to the company.* ○ *It was decided that personal selling was the most effective channel of influence for such a specialised product.*

channel captain /ˈtʃæn(ə)l ˌkæptɪn/ *noun* a business which controls or has the most influence in a distribution channel ○ *The production company became a channel captain by acquiring a number of important retail outlets.* ○ *Only businesses with enough financial resources to acquire other companies can become channel captains.*

channel communications /ˈtʃæn(ə)l kəmjuːnɪˌkeɪʃ(ə)nz/ *plural noun* communications to a marketing channel such as the company's sales force or to selected retailers

channel management /ˈtʃæn(ə)l ˌmænɪdʒmənt/ *noun* the managing of a marketing channel and the business partners which form part of it

channel marketing strategy /ˈtʃæn(ə)l ˌmɑːkɪtɪŋ ˌstrætədʒi/ *noun* a strategic approach to winning new customers by identifying the sales channels and processes that will yield the most new business

channel members /'tʃæn(ə)l ˌmembəz/ *plural noun* the various companies which form a distribution channel

channel of distribution /ˌtʃæn(ə)l əv ˌdɪstrɪ'bjuːʃ(ə)n/ *noun* same as **distribution channel**

channel power /'tʃæn(ə)l paʊə/ *noun* the influence which one company in a trading channel has over the other companies in the channel

channel strip /'tʃæn(ə)l strɪp/ *noun* the front edge of a shelf on which details of the products displayed can be put such as price, weight, code numbers

channel support /'tʃæn(ə)l səˌpɔːt/ *noun* support given to a marketing channel, that is to the people or companies that help to sell the product

character /'kærɪktə/ *noun* a letter, number, or sign used in typesetting, e.g. a letter of the alphabet, a number, or a punctuation mark

charge /tʃɑːdʒ/ *noun* **1.** money which must be paid, or the price of a service ○ *to make no charge for delivery* ○ *to make a small charge for rental* ○ *There is no charge for this service* or *No charge is made for this service.* □ **charges forward** charges which will be paid by the customer **2.** a debit on an account ○ *It appears as a charge on the accounts.* ■ *verb* **1.** to ask someone to pay for services later □ **to charge the packing to the customer, to charge the customer with the packing** the customer has to pay for packing **2.** to ask for money to be paid ○ *to charge $5 for delivery* ○ *How much does he charge?*

chargeable /'tʃɑːdʒəb(ə)l/ *adjective* able to be charged ○ *repairs chargeable to the occupier*

charge account /'tʃɑːdʒ əˌkaʊnt/ *noun US* same as **credit account** (NOTE: The customer will make regular monthly payments into the account and is allowed credit of a multiple of those payments.)

charges forward /ˌtʃɑːdʒɪz 'fɔːwəd/ *plural noun* charges which will be paid by the customer

charity /'tʃærɪti/ *noun* an organisation which offers free help or services to those in need ○ *Because the organisation is a charity it does not have to pay taxes.* ○ *The charity owes its success to clever marketing strategies in its fund-raising.*

charity shop /'tʃærɪti ʃɒp/ *noun* a shop organised by a charity, usually paying low rent and manned by volunteer staff, selling second-hand or specially bought products

chart /tʃɑːt/ *noun* a diagram displaying information as a series of lines, blocks, etc.

charter /'tʃɑːtə/ *noun* the action or business of hiring transport for a special purpose □ **boat on charter to Mr Smith** a boat which Mr Smith has hired for a voyage ■ *verb* to hire for a special purpose ○ *to charter a plane* or *a bus*

chartered /'tʃɑːtəd/ *adjective* □ **a chartered ship or bus or plane** a ship, bus or plane which has been hired for a special purpose

chartered accountant /ˌtʃɑːtəd ə'kaʊntənt/ *noun* an accountant who has passed the necessary professional examinations and is a member of the Institute of Chartered Accountants. Abbreviation **CA**

charterer /'tʃɑːtərə/ *noun* a person who hires a ship etc. for a special purpose

chartering /'tʃɑːtərɪŋ/ *noun* the act of hiring for a special purpose

charter party /'tʃɑːtə ˌpɑːti/ *noun* a contract between the owner and the charterer of a ship

chat group /'tʃæt gruːp/ *noun* a group of people who share a common interest and exchange messages about it online

chat room /'tʃæt ruːm/ *noun* a website where computer users can exchange messages in real time

cheap money /ˌtʃiːp 'mʌni/ *noun* money which can be borrowed at a low rate of interest

check /tʃek/ *noun* **1.** *US (in a restaurant)* a bill **2.** same as **cheque**

checkbook /'tʃekbʊk/ *noun US* same as **cheque book**

check card /'tʃek kɑːd/ *noun US* same as **cheque card**

checklist /'tʃeklɪst/ *noun* a list of points which have to be checked before something can be regarded as finished, or as part of a procedure for evaluating something

checkout /'tʃekaʊt/ *noun* the place where goods are paid for in a shop or supermarket ○ *We have opened two more checkouts to cope with the Saturday rush.*

checkout staff /'tʃekaʊt stɑːf/ *noun* the people who work at checkouts

check sample /'tʃek ˌsɑːmp(ə)l/ *noun* a sample to be used to see if a consignment is acceptable

cheque /tʃek/ *noun* a note to a bank asking them to pay money from your account to the account of the person whose name is written on the note ○ *a cheque for £10 a £10 cheque.*) (NOTE: The US spelling is **check**.) □ **cheque to the bearer** a cheque with no name written on it, so that the person who holds it can cash it □ **to endorse a cheque** to sign a cheque on the back to show that you accept it □ **to pay a cheque into your account** to deposit a cheque □ **the bank referred the cheque to the drawer** the bank returned the cheque to the person who wrote it because there was not enough money in the account to pay it □ **to sign a cheque** to sign on the front of a cheque to show that you authorise the bank to pay the money from your account □ **to stop a cheque** to ask a bank not to pay a cheque which has been signed and sent

cheque account /'tʃek əˌkaʊnt/ *noun* same as **current account**

cheque book /'tʃek bʊk/ *noun* a booklet with new blank cheques (NOTE: The usual US term is **checkbook**.)

cheque card /'tʃek kɑːd/, **cheque guarantee card** /ˌtʃek ˌgærən'tiː kɑːd/ *noun* a plastic card from a bank which guarantees payment of a cheque up to some amount, even if the user has no money in his account

cherry-picking /'tʃeri ˌpɪkɪŋ/ *noun* **1.** going from shop to shop or from supplier to supplier, looking for special bargains ○ *Cherry-picking has become so widespread that prices may be forced down.* **2.** the practice of choosing only the best or most valuable items from among a group

'Though it doesn't cherry-pick the best applicants – students are selected randomly by zip codes – its student body tends to be better off than those at the toughest schools' [Forbes]

chip and pin /ˌtʃɪp ən 'pɪn/ *noun* a government-backed initiative in the UK where credit/debit cards contain an embedded microchip and are authenticated automatically using the customer's PIN. ⇨ **PIN**

churn /tʃɜːn/ *verb* **1.** to persuade an investor to change the shares in his or her portfolio frequently because the broker is paid every time the investor buys a new share **2.** to be in a situation where many employees stay for only a short time and then leave and have to be replaced **3.** to buy many different products or services one after the other without showing loyalty to any of them (NOTE: Churning often happens when companies have competitive marketing strategies and continually undercut their rivals' prices. This encourages customers to switch brands constantly in order to take advantage of cheaper or more attractive offers.)

churn rate /'tʃɜːn reɪt/ *noun* a measurement of how often new customers try a product or service and then stop using it

'The customer churn rate…also increased, from 2.2% in the year ago quarter to 3.4% this quarter' [*Information Week*]

CIF /ˌsiː aɪ 'ef/, **c.i.f.** *abbreviation* cost, insurance, and freight

cinema advertising /'sɪnɪmə ˌædvətaɪzɪŋ/ *noun* advertising by short films or still messages on cinema screens

circular /'sɜːkjʊlə/ *adjective* sent to many people ■ *noun* a leaflet or letter sent to many people ○ *They sent out a circular offering a 10% discount.*

circularise /'sɜːkjʊləraɪz/, **circularize** *verb* to send a circular to ○ *The committee has agreed to circularise the members of the society.* ○ *They circularised all their customers with a new list of prices.*

circular letter /ˌsɜːkjʊlə 'letə/ *noun* a letter sent to many people

circular letter of credit /ˌsɜːkjʊlə ˌletər əv ˈkredɪt/ *noun* a letter of credit sent to all branches of the bank which issues it

circulate /ˈsɜːkjʊleɪt/ *verb* 1. □ **to circulate freely** *(of money)* to move about without restriction by the government 2. to send information to ○ *They circulated a new list of prices to all their customers.* ○ *They circulated information about job vacancies to all colleges in the area.*

circulation /ˌsɜːkjʊˈleɪʃ(ə)n/ *noun* the number of readers of a newspaper or magazine. It is audited and is not the same as 'readership'.

circulation battle /ˌsɜːkjʊˈleɪʃ(ə)n ˌbæt(ə)l/ *noun* a competition between two papers to try to sell more copies in the same market

city /ˈsɪti/ *noun* a large town ○ *The largest cities in Europe are linked by hourly flights.*

city centre /ˌsɪti ˈsentə/ *noun* the centre of a large town, usually where the main shops and offices are situated

CKD *abbreviation* Completely Knocked Down products

claim form /ˈkleɪm fɔːm/ *noun* a form which has to be filled in when making an insurance claim

class /klɑːs/ *noun* a category or group into which things are classified

classification /ˌklæsɪfɪˈkeɪʃ(ə)n/ *noun* arrangement into classes or categories according to specific characteristics ○ *the classification of employees by ages or skills* ○ *Jobs in this organisation fall into several classifications.*

classified advertisements /ˌklæsɪfaɪd ədˈvɜːtɪsmənts/, **classified ads** /ˈklæsɪfaɪd ædz/ *plural noun* advertisements listed in a newspaper under special headings such as 'property for sale' or 'jobs wanted' ○ *Look in the small ads to see if anyone has a laptop for sale.*

classified catalogue /ˌklæsɪfaɪd ˈkæt(ə)lɒg/ *noun* a catalogue which groups articles into categories ○ *The classified catalogue is divided into two sections, electrical and non-electrical products.* ○ *The department store pub-lishes a classified catalogue with a section for each department.* ○ *There is no entry for garden furniture in the classified catalogue.*

classified directory /ˌklæsɪfaɪd daɪˈrekt(ə)ri/ *noun* a list of businesses grouped under various headings such as computer shops or newsagents

classified display advertising /ˌklæsɪfaɪd dɪsˈpleɪ ˌædvətaɪzɪŋ/ *noun* advertising that, although it is classified, may also have individual features such as its own box border or the company logo

classify /ˈklæsɪfaɪ/ *verb* to put into classes or categories according to specific characteristics (NOTE: **classifies – classifying – classified**)

clause /klɔːz/ *noun* a section of a contract ○ *There are ten clauses in the contract of employment.* ○ *There is a clause in this contract concerning the employer's right to dismiss an employee.*

claused bill of lading /ˌklɔːzd bɪl əv ˈleɪdɪŋ/ *noun* a bill of lading stating that goods did not arrive on board in good condition

clean /kliːn/ *adjective* straightforward or with no complications

clean acceptance /ˌkliːn əkˈseptəns/ *noun* an unconditional acceptance of a bill of lading ○ *A clean acceptance ensures a quick and uncomplicated transaction.*

clean bill of lading /ˌkliːn bɪl əv ˈleɪdɪŋ/ *noun* a bill of lading with no note to say the shipment is faulty or damaged

clear /klɪə/ *verb* 1. to sell something cheaply in order to get rid of stock ○ *'Demonstration models to clear'* 2. to obtain a slot for broadcasting an advertisement

clearance /ˈklɪərəns/ *noun* 1. □ **to effect customs clearance** to clear goods through customs 2. □ **clearance of a cheque** the passing of a cheque through the banking system, transferring money from one account to another ○ *You should allow six days for cheque clearance.*

clearance sale /ˈklɪərəns seɪl/ *noun* a sale of items at low prices to get rid of stock

clear profit /ˌklɪə ˈprɒfɪt/ *noun* a profit after all expenses have been paid ○ *We made $6,000 clear profit on the deal.*

clerical error /ˌklerɪk(ə)l ˈerə/ *noun* a mistake made by someone doing office work

click /klɪk/ *verb* to press a key or button on a keyboard or mouse

clickable corporation /ˌklɪkəbl ˌkɔːpəˈreɪʃ(ə)n/ *noun* a company that operates on the Internet

click rate /ˈklɪk reɪt/ *noun* same as **click-through rate**

clicks and bricks /ˌklɪks ən ˈbrɪks/ *noun* a way of doing business that combines e-commerce and traditional shops

clicks-and-mortar /ˌklɪks ən ˈmɔːtə/ *adjective* conducting business both through e-commerce and also in the traditional way in buildings such as stores and warehouses. Compare **bricks-and-mortar**

'...there may be a silver lining for 'clicks-and-mortar' stores that have both an online and a high street presence. Many of these are accepting returns of goods purchased online at their traditional stores. This is a service that may make them more popular as consumers become more experienced online shoppers' [*Financial Times*]

clicks-and-mortar business /ˌklɪks ən ˈmɔːtə ˌbɪznɪs/ *noun* a business that uses both e-commerce and buildings such as shops to market its products

clickstream /ˈklɪkstriːm/ *noun* a record of how a user navigates around a website, sometimes used in marketing research

clickstream data /ˈklɪkstriːm ˌdeɪtə/ *noun* a record of a user's activity on the Internet, including every website the user visits, how long the user was on a page or site, any newsgroups that the user participates in, and the email addresses of mail that the user sends and receives

click-through /ˈklɪk θruː/ *noun* an act of clicking on a banner or other on-screen advertising that takes the user through to the advertiser's website (NOTE: The number of times users click on an advertisement can be counted, and the total number of click-throughs is a way of measuring how successful the advertisement has been.)

click-through rate /ˈklɪk θruː ˌreɪt/ *noun* a method of charging an advertiser for the display of a banner advertisement on a website. Each time a visitor clicks on a displayed advertisement which links to the advertiser's main site, the advertiser is charged a fee. A click-through rate of just a few percent is common and most advertisers have to pay per thousand impressions of their banner ad, sometimes written CTM (click-through per thousand). (NOTE: The click-through rate is expressed as a percentage of *ad views* and is used to measure how successful an advertisement has been.)

client /ˈklaɪənt/ *noun* a person with whom business is done or who pays for a service ○ *One of our major clients has defaulted on her payments.*

client base /ˈklaɪənt beɪs/ *noun* same as **client list**

clientele /ˌkliːɒnˈtel/ *noun* all the clients of a business or all the customers of a shop

client list /ˈklaɪənt lɪst/ *noun* a list of clients of an advertising agency

clip /klɪp/ *noun* a short extract from a film

clipping /ˈklɪpɪŋ/ *noun US* same as **cutting**

clipping service /ˈklɪpɪŋ ˌsɜːvɪs/ *noun* the service of cutting out references to a client in newspapers or magazines and sending them to him

close /kləʊz/ *noun* the end of a sales negotiation ■ *verb* **1.** to bring something to an end □ **to close a sale** to end a sales negotiation and persuade a buyer to make a purchase **2.** *(business, shop)* to stop doing business for the day ○ *The office closes at 5.30.* ○ *We close early on Saturdays.* **3.** □ **to close a market** to restrict a market to one agent or distributor, and refuse to allow others to deal in the area **4.** to stop something being open

close down /ˌkləʊz ˈdaʊn/ *phrasal verb* **1.** to shut a shop, factory, or service for a long period or for ever ○ *The company is closing down its London office.* ○ *The accident closed down the station* *for a period.* **2.** *(of a shop, factory, or service)* to stop doing business or operating

'...the best thing would be to have a few more plants close down and bring supply more in line with current demand' [*Fortune*]

closed /kləʊzd/ *adjective* **1.** not open for business, or not doing business ○ *The office is closed on Mondays.* ○ *These warehouses are usually closed to the public.* **2.** restricted

closed market /ˌkləʊzd 'mɑːkɪt/ *noun* a market where a supplier deals only with one agent or distributor and does not supply any others direct ○ *They signed a closed-market agreement with an Egyptian company.*

closing /'kləʊzɪŋ/ *adjective* **1.** final or coming at the end **2.** at the end of an accounting period ○ *At the end of the quarter the bookkeeper has to calculate the closing balance.* ■ *noun* □ **the closing of an account** the act of stopping supply to a customer on credit

closing bid /'kləʊzɪŋ bɪd/ *noun* the last bid at an auction, the bid which is successful

closing date /'kləʊzɪŋ deɪt/ *noun* the last date ○ *The closing date for tenders to be received is May 1st.*

closing-down sale /ˌkləʊzɪŋ 'daʊn ˌseɪl/ *noun* the sale of goods when a shop is closing for ever

closing price /'kləʊzɪŋ praɪs/ *noun* the price of a share at the end of a day's trading

closing sentence /ˌkləʊzɪŋ 'sentəns/ *noun* the last sentence in a marketing email which pushes the customer to take action

closing stock /ˌkləʊzɪŋ 'stɒk/ *noun* a business's remaining stock at the end of an accounting period. It includes finished products, raw materials, or work in progress and is deducted from the period's costs in the balance sheets. ○ *At the end of the month the closing stock was 10% higher than at the end of the previous month.*

closing technique /'kləʊzɪŋ tek-ˌniːk/ *noun* a special technique of persuasion used by salespeople to close sales ○ *The training manager demon-*

strated some presentation and closing techniques. ○ *Most of our sales force develop their own selling methods, including closing techniques.*

closing time /'kləʊzɪŋ taɪm/ *noun* the time when a shop or office stops work

closure /'kləʊʒə/ *noun* the act of closing

cluster /'klʌstə/ *noun* a group of things or people taken together

cluster analysis /'klʌstər əˌnælə-sɪs/ *noun* a method whereby samples are classified into groups according to characteristics

cluster sampling /'klʌstə ˌsɑːm-plɪŋ/ *noun* sampling on the basis of well-defined groups ○ *Cluster sampling was used in the survey since there were several very distinct groups in the population under study.*

clutter /'klʌtə/ *noun* a mass of advertising units shown together, so that any single advertisement or commercial tends to get lost

CMS *abbreviation* content management system

co-browsing /ˌkəʊ 'braʊzɪŋ/ *noun* the synchronisation of two or more browsers so that their users can see the same web pages at the same time. Also called **page pushing**

code /kəʊd/ *noun* a system of signs, numbers, or letters which mean something

code of practice /ˌkəʊdəv'præktɪs/ *noun* the formally established ways in which members of a profession agree to work ○ *Advertisers have agreed to abide by the code of practice set out by the advertising council.*

coefficient of correlation /ˌkəʊɪ-ˌfɪʃ(ə)nt əv kɒrəˈleɪʃ(ə)n/ *noun* a measurement of correlation or relationship between two sets of data on a continuum from −1 to +1

cognitive dissonance /ˌkɒgnətɪv 'dɪsənəns/ *noun* the feeling of dissatisfaction experienced by a person who cannot reconcile apparently contradictory information, as when making buying decisions or comparing purchases with the claims made for them in advertising

cognitive processing /ˌkɒgnɪtɪv ˈprəʊsesɪŋ/ *noun* the way in which a person changes external information into patterns of thought and how these are used to form judgements or choices

COI *abbreviation* Central Office of Information

cold /kəʊld/ *adjective* without being prepared

'…the board is considering the introduction of a set of common provisions on unsolicited calls to investors. The board is aiming to permit the cold calling of customer agreements for the provision of services relating to listed securities. Cold calling would be allowed when the investor is not a private investor' [*Accountancy*]

cold call /ˌkəʊld ˈkɔːl/ *noun* a telephone call or sales visit where the salesperson has no appointment and the client is not an established customer

cold list /ˈkəʊld lɪst/ *noun* a list of names and addresses of people who have not been approached before by a seller

cold start /ˌkəʊld ˈstɑːt/ *noun* the act of beginning a new business or opening a new shop with no previous turnover to base it on

collateral /kəˈlæt(ə)rəl/ *adjective* used to provide a guarantee for a loan ▪ *noun* a security, such as negotiable instruments, shares or goods, used to provide a guarantee for a loan

'…examiners have come to inspect the collateral that thrifts may use in borrowing from the Fed' [*Wall Street Journal*]

collateral services /kəˌlæt(ə)rəl ˈsɜːvɪsɪz/ *plural noun* agencies which provide specialised services such as package design, production of advertising material, or marketing research

colleague /ˈkɒliːg/ *noun* a person who works in the same organisation as another

collect /kəˈlekt/ *verb* **1.** to get money which is owed to you by making the person who owes it pay □ **to collect a debt** to go and make someone pay a debt **2.** to take things away from a place ○ *We have to collect the stock from the warehouse.* □ **letters are collected twice a day** mail workers take letters from the letter box to the post office for dispatch ▪ *adverb, adjective* used to describe a

phone call which the person receiving the call agrees to pay for

collectables /kəˈlektɪb(ə)lz/ *plural noun* items which people collect, e.g. stamps, playing cards, or matchboxes

collecting agency /kəˈlektɪŋ ˌeɪdʒənsi/ *noun* an agency which collects money owed to other companies for a commission

collocation hosting /ˌkɒləˌkeɪʃ(ə)n ˈhəʊstɪŋ/ *noun* a (**hosting option**) in which a business places its own servers with a hosting company and controls everything that happens on its website. The hosting company simply provides an agreed speed of access to the Internet and an agreed amount of (**data transfer**), and ensures that the business's server is up and running.

colour supplement /ˈkʌlə ˌsʌplɪmənt/ *noun* a magazine which accompanies a newspaper, usually with the weekend issue, printed in colour on art paper, and containing a lot of advertising ○ *The colour supplements were mostly devoted to holiday advertising.* ○ *The clothing company bought advertising space on three pages of the colour supplement.*

colour swatch /ˈkʌlə swɒtʃ/ *noun* a small sample of colour which the finished product must look like

colour theory /ˈkʌlə ˌθɪəri/ *noun* knowledge about colours and their psychological effect on prospective customers

column /ˈkɒləm/ *noun* a section of printed words in a newspaper or magazine

combination commercial /ˌkɒmbɪˈneɪʃ(ə)n kəˌmɜːʃ(ə)l/ *noun* a television advertisement which combines still pictures with action shots

combination rate /ˌkɒmbɪˈneɪʃ(ə)n ˌreɪt/ *noun* a special rate or discount for advertising in two or more magazines

comeback /ˈkʌmbæk/ *noun* a means of getting compensation for a complaint or claim ○ *If you throw away the till receipt you will have no comeback if the goods turn out to be faulty.*

comfortable belongers /ˌkʌmf-(ə)təb(ə)l bɪˈlɒŋəz/ *plural noun* a large group of consumers who are conservative in outlook and happy with their existence

commando selling /kəˈmɑːndəʊ ˌselɪŋ/ *noun* hard intensive selling ○ *Commando selling campaigns were started in all the new markets where the company's products were virtually unknown.* ○ *Commando selling is needed to obtain a reasonable market share in a market dominated by a powerful competitor.*

commerce /ˈkɒmɜːs/ *noun* the buying and selling of goods and services

commerce service provider /ˌkɒmɜːs ˈsɜːvɪs prəˌvaɪdə/ *noun* an organisation that provides a service that helps companies with some aspect of e-commerce, e.g., by acting as an Internet payment gateway

commercial /kəˈmɜːʃ(ə)l/ *adjective* **1.** referring to business **2.** profitable □ **not a commercial proposition** not likely to make a profit ■ *noun* an advertisement on television

'…commercial radio has never had it so good – more stations, more listeners, and soaring advertising revenue' [*Marketing Week*]

commercial agent /kəˌmɜːʃ(ə)l ˈeɪdʒənt/ *noun* a person or business selling a company's products or services for a commission ○ *The commercial agent earned a 30% commission on sales he made.* ○ *As a commercial agent, she represents several companies.*

commercial artist /kəˌmɜːʃ(ə)l ˈɑːtɪst/ *noun* an artist who designs advertisements, posters, etc. for payment

commercial break /kəˌmɜːʃ(ə)l ˈbreɪk/ *noun* the time set aside for commercials on television ○ *The advertiser wished to specify exactly when in the commercial break the advertisements were to appear.* ○ *The advertising manager placed one advertisement in each commercial break of the day on the radio channel.*

commercial counsellor /kəˌmɜːʃ(ə)l ˈkaʊns(ə)lə/ *noun* a person who advises on commercial matters in an embassy ○ *The commercial counsellor gave us sound advice on marketing in the country he represented.*

commercialisation /kəˌmɜːʃ(ə)laɪˈzeɪʃ(ə)n/, **commercialization** *noun* the act of making something into a business run for profit ○ *the commercialisation of museums*

commercialise /kəˈmɜːʃəlaɪz/, **commercialize** *verb* to make something into a business ○ *The holiday town has become unpleasantly commercialised.*

commercial law /kəˌmɜːʃ(ə)l ˈlɔː/ *noun* the laws regarding the conduct of businesses

commercial load /kəˌmɜːʃ(ə)l ˈləʊd/ *noun* the amount of goods or number of passengers which a bus, train, or plane has to carry to make a profit

commercially /kəˈmɜːʃ(ə)li/ *adverb* **1.** for the purpose of making a profit □ **not commercially viable** not likely to make a profit **2.** in the operation of a business

commercial port /kəˌmɜːʃ(ə)l ˈpɔːt/ *noun* a port which has only goods traffic and no passengers

commercial protection /kəˌmɜːʃ(ə)l prəˈtekʃən/ *noun* the guarantee that rival products will not be advertised directly before or after a particular advertisement

commercial radio /kəˌmɜːʃ(ə)l ˈreɪdiəʊ/, **commercial TV** /kəˌmɜːʃ(ə)l tiːˈviː/ *noun* a radio or TV station which broadcasts advertisements, which help to pay for its programming costs

commercial services /kəˌmɜːʃ(ə)l ˈsɜːvɪsɪz/ *plural noun* services which support trade, e.g. banking and advertising ○ *The recession has affected commercial services and the industries they support and supply.*

commercial time /kəˈmɜːʃ(ə)l taɪm/ *noun* the time that a television or radio station devotes to advertising ○ *The TV station is extending its commercial time in order to increase revenue.*

commercial traveller /kəˌmɜːʃ(ə)l ˈtræv(ə)lə/ *noun* a salesperson who travels round an area visiting customers on behalf of his or her company (NOTE: The modern term for a commercial traveller is **sales representative**.)

commercial value /kəˌmɜːʃ(ə)l ˈvæljuː/ *noun* the value that a thing would have if it were offered for sale □ **'sample only – of no commercial value'** these goods are intended only as a sample and would not be worth anything if sold

commission /kəˈmɪʃ(ə)n/ *noun* money paid to a salesperson or agent, usually a percentage of the sales made ○ *She gets 10% commission on everything she sells.*□ **he charges 10% commission** he asks for 10% of sales as his payment

commission agent /kəˈmɪʃ(ə)n ˌeɪdʒənt/ *noun* an agent who is paid a percentage of sales

commission rebating /kəˈmɪʃ(ə)n ˌriːbeɪtɪŋ/ *noun* an advertising agency's discounting of invoices for media costs sent to clients, in effect taking them out of its own commission or profit margin

commission rep /kəˈmɪʃ(ə)n rep/ *noun* a representative who is not paid a salary but receives a commission on sales

commitment /kəˈmɪtmənt/ *noun* **1.** something which you have agreed to do ○ *The company has a commitment to provide a cheap service.* **2.** money which you have agreed to spend

commodity /kəˈmɒdɪti/ *noun* something sold in very large quantities, especially a raw material such as a metal or a food such as wheat

commodity exchange /kəˈmɒdɪti ɪksˌtʃeɪndʒ/ *noun* a place where commodities are bought and sold

commodity futures /kəˌmɒdɪti ˈfjuːtʃəz/ *plural noun* commodities traded for delivery at a later date ○ *Silver rose 5% on the commodity futures market yesterday.*

commodity trader /kəˈmɒdɪti ˌtreɪdə/ *noun* a person whose business is buying and selling commodities

common /ˈkɒmən/ *adjective* **1.** happening frequently ○ *Unrealistic salary expectations in younger staff was a common problem they had to deal with.* **2.** belonging to several different people or to everyone

common carrier /ˌkɒmən ˈkæriə/ *noun* a firm which carries goods or passengers, and which anyone can use

Common Market /ˌkɒmən ˈmaːkɪt/ *noun* an association of nations who join together in order to remove or reduce the barriers to trade between them

common ownership /ˌkɒmən ˈəʊnəʃɪp/ *noun* a situation where a business is owned by the employees who work in it

common pricing /ˌkɒmən ˈpraɪsɪŋ/ *noun* the illegal fixing of prices by several businesses so that they all charge the same price

communication /kəˌmjuːnɪˈkeɪʃ(ə)n/ *noun* the passing on of views or information ○ *A house journal was started to improve communication between management and staff.* ○ *Customers complained about the lack of communication about the unexpected delay.* □ **to enter into communication with someone** to start discussing something with someone, usually in writing ○ *We have entered into communication with the relevant government department.*

communication objectives /kəˌmjuːnɪˈkeɪʃ(ə)n əbˌdʒektɪvz/ *plural noun* objectives that a company tries to achieve through its advertising, e.g. creating awareness, knowledge, images, attitudes, preferences, or purchase intentions

communications /kəˌmjuːnɪˈkeɪʃ(ə)nz/ *plural noun* **1.** the fact of being able to contact people or to pass messages ○ *After the flood all communications with the outside world were broken.* **2.** systems or technologies used for sending and receiving messages, e.g. postal and telephone networks **3.** messages sent from one individual or organisation to another

communications channel /kəˌmjuːnɪˈkeɪʃ(ə)nz ˌtʃæn(ə)l/ *noun* a means of passing messages from one individual or organisation to another (NOTE: Communications channels include the spoken, written, and printed word, and media such as radio and television, telephones, video-conferencing and electronic mail.)

communication skills /kə,mjuː-nɪˈkeɪʃ(ə)n skɪlz/ *plural noun* the ability to pass information to others easily and intelligibly

communications management /kə,mjuːnɪˈkeɪʃ(ə)nz ˌmænɪdʒ-mənt/ *noun* the managing of communications, so that advertising messages are sent efficiently to people who need to receive them

communications strategy /kə,m-juːnɪˈkeɪʃ(ə)nz ˌstrætədʒi/ *noun* planning the best way of communicating with potential customers

communication task /kə,mjuː-nɪˈkeɪʃ(ə)n tɑːsk/ *noun* things that can be attributed to advertising, e.g. awareness, comprehension, conviction, and action, following the DAGMAR approach to setting advertising goals and objectives

communisuasion /kə,mjuːnɪ-ˈsweɪʒ(ə)n/ *noun US* communication that is intended to persuade ○ *The sales reps are being trained in the subtleties of communisuasion.*

community /kəˈmjuːnɪti/ *noun* a group of people living or working in the same place

community initiative /kə,mjuːnɪti ɪˈnɪʃətɪv/ *noun* a particular scheme set up by a business organisation with the aim of making a positive contribution to the life of the community by helping local people take practical action to solve their problems

community involvement /kə-,mjuːnɪti ɪnˈvɒlvmənt/ *noun* the contribution that business organisations make to the life of their local community in the form of community initiatives (NOTE: Community involvement developed as a result of the growing emphasis on the social responsibility of business in the 1960s and 1970s and often involves companies not only giving money to finance local projects but also sending trained staff to help set them up.)

Community legislation /kə,mjuː-nɪti ledʒɪˈsleɪʃ(ə)n/ *noun* directives issued by the EU commission

Community ministers /kə,mjuː-nɪti ˈmɪnɪstəz/ *plural noun* the ministers of member states of the EU

company /ˈkʌmp(ə)ni/ *noun* a business organisation, a group of people organised to buy, sell, or provide a service, usually for profit

company report /ˌkʌmp(ə)ni rɪˈpɔːt/ *noun* a document that sets out in detail what a company has done and how well it has performed (NOTE: Companies are legally required to write *annual reports* and financial reports and to submit them to the authorities in the country where they are registered, but they may also produce other reports on specific subjects, for example, on the environmental or social impact of a project they are undertaking.)

comparative /kəmˈpærətɪv/ *adjective* which can be compared with something else

comparative advertising /kəm-ˌpærətɪv ˈædvətaɪzɪŋ/ *noun* advertising which compares a company's product with competing brands to its own advantage ○ *Disparaging remarks in comparative advertising were strongly discouraged in the industry.* ○ *The company uses comparative advertising to highlight the advantages of its products.*

comparative analysis /kəm-ˌpærətɪv əˈnæləsɪs/ *noun* an analysis of different media and vehicle options by an advertiser ○ *A tight advertising budget made a thorough comparative analysis essential.* ○ *Comparative analysis is difficult when the various media offer such different advantages.*

comparative pricing /kəm,pærə-tɪv ˈpraɪsɪŋ/ *noun* the indication of a price by comparing it with another, e.g. '15% reduction'

comparison /kəmˈpærɪs(ə)n/ *noun* the act of comparing one thing with another ○ *Sales are down in comparison with last year.*

comparison-shop /kəmˈpærɪs(ə)n ʃɒp/ *verb* to compare prices and features of items for sale in different shops to find the best deal

compete /kəmˈpiːt/ *verb* □ **to compete with someone or with a company** to try to do better than another person or another company ○ *We have to compete with cheap imports from the Far East.* ○ *They were competing unsuccessfully with local companies on their home territory.* □ **the two companies are competing for a market share** *or* **for a contract** each company is trying to win a larger part of the market, trying to win the contract

competence framework /ˈkɒmpɪt(ə)ns ˌfreɪmwɜːk/ *noun* the set of duties or tasks performed as part of a job with the standards which should be achieved in these duties

competing /kəmˈpiːtɪŋ/ *adjective* which competes □ **competing firms** firms which compete with each other □ **competing products** products from different companies which have the same use and are sold in the same markets at similar prices

competition /ˌkɒmpəˈtɪʃ(ə)n/ *noun* **1.** a situation where companies or individuals are trying to do better than others, e.g. trying to win a larger share of the market, or to produce a better or cheaper product or to control the use of resources □ **keen competition** strong competition ○ *We are facing keen competition from European manufacturers.* **2.** □ **the competition** companies which are trying to compete with your product (*singular, but can take a plural verb in this sense*) ○ *We have lowered our prices to beat the competition.* ○ *The competition have brought out a new range of products.* **3.** a sales promotion which enables consumers who can show that they have bought a minimum number of purchases to compete in a game ○ *The company uses competitions to sell off an excess supply of tinned food.* ○ *Competitions involve prizes ranging from washing-machines to overseas holidays.* ○ *Competitions and free gifts make up a large part of the company's sales promotions.*

'…profit margins in the industries most exposed to foreign competition are worse than usual' [*Sunday Times*]

'…competition is steadily increasing and could affect profit margins as the company tries to retain its market share' [*Citizen (Ottawa)*]

competition law /ˌkɒmpəˈtɪʃ(ə)n ˌlɔː/ *noun* a law that promotes or maintains market competition by regulating anti-competitive behaviour

competition-oriented pricing /ˌkɒmpəˌtɪʃ(ə)n ˌɔːrientɪd ˈpraɪsɪŋ/ *noun* the act of putting low prices on goods so as to compete with other competing products

competitive /kəmˈpetɪtɪv/ *adjective* **1.** involving competition **2.** intended to compete with others, usually by being cheaper or better □ **competitive price** a low price aimed to compete with a rival product □ **competitive product** a product made or priced to compete with existing products

'…the company blamed fiercely competitive market conditions in Europe for a £14m operating loss last year' [*Financial Times*]

competitive advantage /kəmˌpetɪtɪv ədˈvɑːntɪdʒ/ *noun* same as **competitive edge**

'A four-year, ten-nation study of the patterns of competitive success in leading countries concludes that companies achieve competitive advantage through acts of innovation' [*Harvard Business Review*]

competitive analysis /kəmˌpetɪtɪv əˈnæləsɪs/ *noun* analysis for marketing purposes that can include industry, customer, and competitor analysis and aims to discover how competitive an organisation, project, or product is, especially by evaluating the capabilities of key competitors

competitive check /kəmˌpetɪtɪv ˈtʃek/ *noun* analysing rival advertising levels and patterns, often conducted on the basis of data supplied by monitoring organisations

competitive demand /kəmˌpetɪtɪv dɪˈmaːnd/ *noun* demand for products that are competing for sales

competitive edge /kəmˌpetɪtɪv ˈedʒ/ *noun* a factor that gives a special advantage to a nation, company, group, or individual when it is competing with others ○ *Any competitive edge we have in this market is due to our good after-sales service.* ○ *Why does this product have the competitive edge over its rivals?* Also called **competitive advantage**

competitive forces /kəmˌpetɪtɪv ˈfɔːsɪz/ *plural noun* economic and business factors that force an organisation to become more competitive if wants to survive and succeed

competitive intelligence /kəm-ˌpetɪtɪv ɪnˈtelɪdʒəns/ *noun* information, especially information concerning the plans, activities, and products of its competitors, that an organisation gathers and analyses in order to make itself more competitive (NOTE: Competitive intelligence may sometimes be gained through *industrial espionage*.)

competitively /kəmˈpetɪtɪvli/ *adverb* □ **competitively priced** sold at a low price which competes with the price of similar products from other companies

competitiveness /kəmˈpetɪtɪvnəs/ *noun* the fact of being competitive

'…farmers are increasingly worried by the growing lack of competitiveness for their products on world markets' [*Australian Financial Review*]

competitiveness index /kəmˈpetɪtɪvnəs ˌɪndeks/ *noun* a list that uses economic and other data to rank countries in order according to the competitiveness of their industries and products

competitive parity /kəmˌpetɪtɪv ˈpærɪti/ *noun* a method of budgeting marketing or promotional expenses according to the amounts being spent by competitors

competitive pricing /kəmˌpetɪtɪv ˈpraɪsɪŋ/ *noun* the practice of putting low prices on goods so as to compete with other products

competitive products /kəm-ˌpetɪtɪv ˈprɒdʌkts/ *plural noun* products made to compete with existing products

competitive separation /kəm-ˌpetɪtɪv ˌsepəˈreɪʃ(ə)n/ *noun* a guarantee that rival products will not be advertised directly before or after a particular advertisement ○ *If our advertising campaign is to be really effective, we must insist on competitive separation.*

competitive tender /kəmˌpetɪtɪv ˈtendə/ *noun* a form of tender where different organisations are asked to tender for a contract, especially for government or local government work

competitor /kəmˈpetɪtə/ *noun* a person or company that is competing

with another ○ *Two German firms are our main competitors.*

'…sterling labour costs continue to rise between 3% and 5% a year faster than in most of our competitor countries' [*Sunday Times*]

competitor analysis /kəmˌpetɪtə əˈnæləsɪs/ *noun* the process of analysing information about competitors and their products in order to build up a picture of where their strengths and weaknesses lie

competitor profiling /kəmˌpetɪtə ˈprəʊfaɪlɪŋ/ *noun* same as **competitor analysis**

complaint /kəmˈpleɪnt/ *noun* a statement that you feel something is wrong ○ *complaints from the workforce about conditions in the factory* ○ *She sent her letter of complaint to the managing director.*

complaints department /kəmˈpleɪnts dɪˌpɑːtmənt/ *noun* a department in a company or store to which customers can send or bring complaints about its products or service

complaints management /kəmˈpleɪnts ˌmænɪdʒmənt/ *noun* the management of complaints from customers

complementary /ˌkɒmplɪˈment(ə)ri/ *adjective* which adds to or completes something else

complementary demand /ˌkɒmplɪment(ə)ri dɪˈmɑːnd/ *noun* demand for two or more products that are needed together ○ *The demand for cars and petrol was an example of complementary demand.*

complementary goods /ˌkɒmplɪment(ə)ri ˈɡʊdz/, **complementary products** /ˌkɒmplɪment(ə)ri ˈprɒdʌkts/ *plural noun* a product for which demand is dependent on the demand for another product

complementary supply /ˌkɒmplɪment(ə)ri səˈplaɪ/ *noun* the supply of two or more products from the same production process

complementor /ˈkɒmplɪmentə/ *noun* a company that makes something that your product needs in order to function successfully. For example, software companies are complementors to computer companies. (NOTE: Software companies, for example, are complementors to computer companies.)

Completely Knocked Down products /kəm,pliːt(ə)li nɒkt daʊn ˈprɒdʌktz/ *plural noun* products which are sold in pieces, which the purchaser has to assemble, and are therefore sold at reasonably low prices ○ *Many low-income buyers buy CKD products.* ○ *CKD products are popular with DIY enthusiasts.* Abbreviation **CKD products**

compliance documentation /kəmˈplaɪəns dɒkjʊmenˈteɪʃ(ə)n/ *noun* documents that a company has to publish when it issues shares in order to comply with the regulations governing share issues

compliance officer /kəmˈplaɪəns ,ɒfɪsə/ *noun* an employee of a financial organisation whose job is to make sure that the organisation complies with the regulations governing its business

complimentary /,kɒmplɪˈment-(ə)ri/ *adjective* free

complimentary ticket /,kɒmplɪment(ə)ri ˈtɪkɪt/ *noun* a free ticket, given as a present

compliments slip /ˈkɒmplɪmənts slɪp/ *noun* a piece of paper with the name of the company printed on it, sent with documents or gifts etc. instead of a letter

component /kəmˈpəʊnənt/ *noun* a piece of machinery or a part which will be put into a final product ○ *The assembly line stopped because the supply of a vital component was delayed.*

components factory /kəmˈpəʊnənts ,fækt(ə)ri/ *noun* a factory which makes parts that are used in other factories to make finished products

composite demand /ˈkɒmpəzɪt dɪ,mɑːnd/ *noun* the total demand for a product that has many uses ○ *Composite demand for the construction equipment came from construction companies and DIY enthusiasts.*

computer error /kəm,pjuːtər ˈerə/ *noun* a mistake made by a computer

computer file /kəmˈpjuːtə faɪl/ *noun* a section of information on a computer, e.g. the payroll, list of addresses, or list of customer accounts

computer hardware /kəm,pjuːtə ˈhɑːdweə/ *noun* machines used in data processing, including the computers and printers, but not the programs

computerise /kəmˈpjuːtəraɪz/, **computerize** *verb* to change something from a manual system to one using computers ○ *We have computerised all our records.* ○ *Stock control is now completely computerised.*

computer magazine /kəmˈpjuːtə mægə,ziːn/ *noun* a magazine with articles on computers and programs

computer manager /kəmˈpjuːtə ,mænɪdʒə/ *noun* a person in charge of a computer department

computer network /kəmˈpjuːtə ,netwɜːk/ *noun* a computer system where several PCs are linked so that they all draw on the same database

computer-readable /kəm,pjuːtə ˈriːdəb(ə)l/ *adjective* able to be read and understood by a computer ○ *computer-readable codes*

computer run /kəmˈpjuːtə rʌn/ *noun* a period of work done by a computer

computer services /kəm,pjuːtə ˈsɜːvɪsɪz/ *plural noun* work using a computer, done by a computer bureau

computer system /kəmˈpjuːtə ,sɪstəm/ *noun* a set of programs, commands, etc., which run a computer

computer telephony integration /kəm,pjuːtə tə,lefəni ,ɪntɪˈgreɪʃ(ə)n/ *noun* a technology that links computers and telephones and enables computers to dial telephone numbers and send and receive messages (NOTE: One product of computer telephony integration is *calling line identification*, which identifies the telephone number a customer is calling from, searches the customer database to identify the caller, and displays his or her account on a computer screen.)

computer time /kəmˈpjuːtə taɪm/ *noun* the time when a computer is being used, paid for at an hourly rate

computer worm /kəmˈpjuːtə wɜːm/ *noun* a type of computer virus that does damage by making as many copies of itself as it can as quickly in order to clog up communication channels on the Internet

'New features in a free Windows upgrade will give your PC a lot of much-needed protection from viruses, worms, and other nuisances' [*Fortune*]

computing /kəm'pju:tɪŋ/ *noun* the operating of computers

computing speed /kəm'pju:tɪŋ spi:d/ *noun* the speed at which a computer calculates

concentrated marketing /ˌkɒnsən treɪtɪd 'mɑ:kətɪŋ/, **concentrated segmentation** /ˌkɒnsəntreɪtɪd ˌsegmən'teɪʃ(ə)n/ *noun* niche marketing, the promotion of a product aimed at one particular area of the market ○ *When it became obvious that the general public was interested in our product, we switched from concentrated marketing to a much broader approach.* ▷ **differentiated marketing strategy, undifferentiated product**

concentration /ˌkɒnsən'treɪ-ʃ(ə)n/ *noun* the degree to which a small number of businesses control a large section of the market ○ *Too much concentration created resentment among small businesses trying to enter the market.* ○ *Concentration has meant too little competition and therefore higher prices to the consumer.*

concept /'kɒnsept/ *noun* an idea

concept board /'kɒnsept bɔ:d/ *noun* a visual and/or verbal aid for presenting an idea for a product, service or advertisement ○ *The advertising team used a concept board to show their ideas to the client.*

concept testing /'kɒnsept ˌtestɪŋ/ *noun* the evaluation of a new product idea, usually by consulting representatives from all the main departments in a company, and/or by interviewing a sample of consumers ○ *The new product idea did not survive concept testing because it didn't answer an existing demand.* ○ *After thorough concept testing the idea of a disposable pen was rejected as the company's production capacity was too limited.*

concertina fold /ˌkɒnsə'ti:nə fəʊld/ *noun* same as **accordion fold**

concession /kən'seʃ(ə)n/ *noun* **1.** the right to use someone else's property for business purposes **2.** the right to be the only seller of a product in a place ○ *She runs a jewellery concession in a department store.* **3.** the act of allowing something to be done, which is not normally done ○ *The union obtained some important concessions from management during negotiations.*

concessionaire /kənˌseʃə'neə/ *noun* a person or business that has the right to be the only seller of a product in a place

concession close /kən'seʃ(ə)n kləʊz/ *noun* the act of offering a concession to a potential buyer in order to close a sale ○ *The trainee sales reps were told to resort to concession closes only when meeting with strong sales resistance.* ○ *A full morning's bargaining finally ended with a concession close.*

condition /kən'dɪʃ(ə)n/ *noun* something which has to be carried out as part of a contract or which has to be agreed before a contract becomes valid □ **on condition that** provided that ○ *They were granted the lease on condition that they paid the legal costs.*

conditional /kən'dɪʃ(ə)n(ə)l/ *adjective* provided that specific conditions are taken into account □ **to give a conditional acceptance** to accept, provided that specific things happen or that specific terms apply □ **the offer is conditional on the board's acceptance** the offer is only valid provided the board accepts

conditional offer /kənˌdɪʃ(ə)nəl 'ɒfə/ *noun* an offer to buy provided that specific terms apply

conditions of sale /kənˌdɪʃ(ə)nz əv 'seɪl/ *plural noun* special features that apply to a particular sale, e.g. discounts or credit terms

conference /'kɒnf(ə)rəns/ *noun* a meeting of people to discuss problems ○ *Many useful tips can be picked up at a sales conference.* ○ *The conference of HR managers included talks on pay-*

ment and recruitment policies. □ **to be in conference** to be in a meeting

conference call /ˈkɒnf(ə)rəns kɔːl/ *noun* a telephone call that connects three or more lines so that people in different places can talk to one another (NOTE: Conference calls reduce the cost of meetings by making it unnecessary for the participants to spend time and money on getting together in one place.)

confidence /ˈkɒnfɪd(ə)ns/ *noun* the state of feeling sure or being certain ○ *The sales teams do not have much confidence in their manager.* ○ *The board has total confidence in the managing director.*

confidence level /ˈkɒnfɪd(ə)ns ˌlev(ə)l/ *noun* a measurement, shown as a percentage, of how reliable or accurate the results of a survey can be expected to be

confidentiality agreement /ˌkɒnfɪdenʃiˈælɪti əˌɡriːmənt/ *noun* an agreement in which an organisation that has important information about the plans and activities of another organisation promises not to pass that information on to outsiders (NOTE: Confidentiality agreements are often used when someone is planning to buy a company and is given access to confidential information and in partnerships and benchmarking programmes.)

confirm /kənˈfɜːm/ *verb* to say again that something agreed before is correct ○ *to confirm a hotel reservation* or *a ticket an agreement a booking* □ **to confirm someone in a job** to say that someone is now permanently in the job

confirmation /ˌkɒnfəˈmeɪʃən/ *noun* **1.** the act of making certain □ **confirmation of a booking** the act of checking that a booking is certain **2.** a document which confirms something ○ *She received confirmation from the bank that the deeds had been deposited.*

confirmed credit /kənˌfɜːmd ˈkredɪt/ *noun* credit that is official and binding

confirming house /kənˈfɜːmɪŋ haʊs/ *noun* an organisation that confirms a buyer's order with a supplier

and makes transport arrangements ○ *A reputable confirming house acted for the buyers of the machinery.* ○ *We will need a confirming house to arrange for a new supply of office furniture to be delivered to our shop by December.*

conflict of interest /ˌkɒnflɪkt əv ˈɪntrəst/ *noun* a situation where a person or firm may profit personally from decisions taken in an official capacity

conglomerate /kənˈɡlɒmərət/ *noun* a group of subsidiary companies linked together and forming a group, each making very different types of products

conjoint analysis /kənˌdʒɔɪnt əˈnæləsɪs/ *noun* a research method aimed at discovering the best combination of features for a product or service, e.g. price and size

connectivity /ˌkɒnekˈtɪvɪti/ *noun* the ability of an electronic product to connect with other similar products, or the extent to which individuals, companies and countries can connect with one another electronically

consign /kənˈsaɪn/ *verb* □ **to consign goods to someone** to send goods to someone for them to use or to sell for you

consignation /ˌkɒnsaɪˈneɪʃ(ə)n/ *noun* the act of consigning

consignee /ˌkɒnsaɪˈniː/ *noun* a person who receives goods from someone for their own use or to sell for the sender

consignment /kənˈsaɪnmənt/ *noun* the sending of goods to someone who will sell them for you □ **goods on consignment** goods kept for another company to be sold on their behalf for a commission

'…some of the most prominent stores are gradually moving away from the traditional consignment system, under which manufacturers agree to repurchase any unsold goods, and in return dictate prices and sales strategies and even dispatch staff to sell the products' [*Nikkei Weekly*]

consignment note /kənˈsaɪnmənt nəʊt/ *noun* a note saying that goods have been sent

consignor /kənˈsaɪnə/ *noun* a person who consigns goods to someone

consolidate /kənˈsɒlɪdeɪt/ *verb* **1.** to include the accounts of several subsidiary companies as well as the holding company in a single set of accounts **2.** to group goods together for shipping

consolidated profit and loss account /kən,sɒlɪdeɪtɪd ,prɒfɪt ən 'lɒs ə,kaʊnt/ *noun* profit and loss accounts of the holding company and its subsidiary companies, grouped together into a single profit and loss account (NOTE: The US term is **profit and loss statement** or **income statement**.)

consolidated shipment /kən,- sɒlɪdeɪtɪd 'ʃɪpmənt/ *noun* a single shipment of goods from different companies grouped together

consolidation /kən,sɒlɪ'deɪʃ(ə)n/ *noun* the grouping together of goods for shipping

consolidator /kən'sɒlɪdeɪtə/ *noun* a firm which groups together orders from different companies into one shipment

consortium /kən'sɔːtiəm/ *noun* a group of companies which work together ○ *A consortium of Canadian companies A Canadian consortium has tendered for the job.* (NOTE: The plural is **consortia**.)

'…the consortium was one of only four bidders for the £2 billion contract to run the lines, seen as potentially the most difficult contract because of the need for huge investment' [*Times*]

conspicuous consumption /kən,spɪkjuəs kən'sʌmpʃən/ *noun* the consumption of goods for show or to get approval, rather than because they are useful

consult /kən'sʌlt/ *verb* to ask an expert for advice ○ *We consulted our accountant about our tax.*

consultancy /kən'sʌltənsi/ *noun* the act of giving specialist advice ○ *a consultancy firm* ○ *She offers a consultancy service.*

consultant /kən'sʌltənt/ *noun* a specialist who gives advice ○ *an engineering consultant* ○ *a management consultant* ○ *a tax consultant*

consulting /kən'sʌltɪŋ/ *adjective* giving specialist advice ○ *a consulting engineer*

consumable goods /kən,sjuː- məb(ə)l 'ɡʊdz/ *plural noun* goods which are bought by members of the public and not by companies. Also called **consumer goods, consumables**

consumables /kən'sjuːməb(ə)lz/ *plural noun* same as **consumable goods**

consumer /kən'sjuːmə/ *noun* a person or company that buys and uses goods and services ○ *Gas consumers are protesting at the increase in prices.* ○ *The factory is a heavy consumer of water.*

'…forecasting consumer response is one problem which will never be finally solved' [*Marketing Week*]

'…consumer tastes in the UK are becoming much more varied' [*Marketing*]

'…the marketing director's brief will be to develop the holiday villages as a consumer brand, aimed at the upper end of the tourist market' [*Marketing Week*]

consumer advertising /kən'sjuː- mə ,ædvətaɪzɪŋ/ *noun* advertising direct to individual consumers, as opposed to businesses

consumer cooperative /kən,sjuː- mə kəʊ'ɒp(ə)rətɪv/ *noun* a retailing business owned by consumers who share in its profits

consumer council /kən,sjuːmə 'kaʊns(ə)l/ *noun* a group representing the interests of consumers

consumer credit /kən,sjuːmə 'kredɪt/ *noun* credit given by shops, banks and other financial institutions to consumers so that they can buy goods (NOTE: Lenders have to be licensed under the **Consumer Credit Act, 1974**.)

Consumer Credit Act, 1974 /kən,sjuːmə 'kredɪt ækt/ *noun* an Act of Parliament which licenses lenders, and requires them to state clearly the full terms of loans which they make, including the APR

consumer culture /kən'sjuːmə ,kʌltʃə/ *noun* a view of society as dominated by consumerism

consumer durables /kən,sjuːmə 'djʊərəb(ə)lz/ *plural noun* items which are bought and used by the public, e.g. washing machines, refrigerators or cookers

consumer goods /kən,sjuːmə 'ɡʊdz/ *plural noun* same as **consumable goods**

consumerism /kən'sjuːmərɪz- (ə)m/ *noun* the activities concerned with protecting the rights and interests of consumers

consumer list /kən'sjuːmə lɪst/ *noun* a list of individuals who can be mailed with details of a product or service, e.g. from the electoral register

consumer magazine /kən'sjuːmə mægə,ziːn/ *noun* a magazine published for consumers, giving details of product tests, special legal problems regarding services offered, etc.

consumer mailing list /kən,sjuːmə 'meɪlɪŋ lɪst/ *noun* same as **consumer list**

consumer market /kən'sjuːmə ,maːkɪt/ *noun* the customers who buy consumer goods ○ *There is a growing consumer market for construction materials owing to the increased popularity of DIY.* ○ *Both consumer markets and industrial markets have been affected by the recession.*

consumer panel /kən'sjuːmə ,pæn(ə)l/ *noun* a group of consumers who report on products they have used so that the manufacturers can improve them or use what the panel says about them in advertising

Consumer Price Index /kən,sjuːmə 'praɪs ,ɪndeks/ *noun* a US index showing how prices of consumer goods have risen over a period of time, used as a way of measuring inflation and the cost of living. Abbreviation **CPI** (NOTE: The UK term is **retail prices index**.)

'...analysis of the consumer price index for the first half of the year shows that the rate of inflation went down by about 12.9%' [*Business Times (Lagos)*]

consumer profile /kən,sjuːmə 'prəʊfaɪl/ *noun* a description of the relevant details of the average customer for a product or service

Consumer Protection Act, 1987 /kən,sjuːmə prə'tekʃən ,ækt/ *noun* an Act of Parliament which bans the use of misleading information given to potential purchasers to encourage them to buy

consumer research /kən,sjuːmə rɪ'sɜːtʃ/ *noun* research into why consumers buy goods and what goods they may want to buy

consumer resistance /kən,sjuːmə rɪ'zɪstəns/ *noun* a lack of interest by consumers in buying a new product ○ *The new product met no consumer resistance even though the price was high.*

Consumers Association /kən'sjuːməz əsəʊsi,eɪʃ(ə)n/ *noun* an independent organisation which protects consumers and represents their interests, and reports on the quality of products and services in its regular magazine. Abbreviation **CA**

consumer society /kən,sjuːmə sə'saɪəti/ *noun* a type of society where consumers are encouraged to buy goods

consumer sovereignty /kən,sjuːmə 'sɒvrɪnti/ *noun* the power of consumers to influence trends in production and marketing

consumer spending /kən,sjuːmə 'spendɪŋ/ *noun* spending by private households on goods and services

'...companies selling in the UK market are worried about reduced consumer spending as a consequence of higher interest rates and inflation' [*Business*]

consumer's surplus /kən,sjuːməz 'sɜːpləs/ *noun* the difference between what a consumer is willing to pay for something and what he or she actually does pay for it ○ *When the brand manager realised how big the consumer's surplus was she decided to raise the price of the product.*

consumer survey /kən,sjuːmə 'sɜːveɪ/ *noun* a survey of existing and potential demand for a product

consumer-to-consumer commerce /kən,sjuːmə tə kən'sjuːmə ,kɒmɜːs/ *noun* business, especially e-business, done by one individual with another and not involving any business organisation

consumption /kən'sʌmpʃ(ə)n/ *noun* the act of buying or using goods or services ○ *a car with low petrol consumption* ○ *The factory has a heavy consumption of coal.*

contain /kən'teɪn/ *verb* to hold something inside ○ *a barrel contains 250 litres* ○ *Each crate contains two computers and their peripherals.* ○ *We have* *lost a file containing important documents.*

container /kən'teɪnə/ *noun* **1.** a box, bottle, can, etc. which can hold goods ○ *The gas is shipped in strong metal containers.* ○ *The container burst during shipping.* **2.** a very large metal case of a standard size for loading and transporting goods on trucks, trains, and ships ○ *to ship goods in containers* □ **a container-load of spare parts** a shipment of spare parts sent in a container

containerisation /kən,teɪnəraɪ'zeɪʃ(ə)n/, **containerization** *noun* the act of shipping goods in containers

containerise /kən'teɪnəraɪz/, **containerize** *verb* to put or ship goods in containers

content /'kɒntent/ *noun* the text, illustrations, and graphics of a piece of publicity

content management /'kɒntent ,mænɪdʒmənt/ *noun* the management of the textual and graphical material contained on a website (NOTE: Owners of large sites with thousands of pages often invest in a content management application system to help with the creation and organisation of the content of these sites.)

content management system /,kɒntent 'mænɪdʒmənt ,sɪstəm/ *noun* software that allows a user to manage the textual and graphical material contained on a website. Abbreviation **CMS**

contest /'kɒntest/ *noun* a type of promotion where prizes are given to people who give the right answers to a series of questions

contested takeover /kən,testɪd 'teɪkəʊvə/ *noun* a takeover bid where the board of the target company does not recommend it to the shareholders and tries to fight it. Also called **hostile bid**

context /'kɒntekst/ *noun* additional information about a product that is considered to be helpful to customers and is shown on a website. For example, reviews by other customers displayed on the site for a particular book.

contingency plan /kən'tɪndʒənsi plæn/ *noun* a plan which will be put into action if something unexpected happens

contingent liability /kən,tɪndʒənt ,laɪə'bɪlɪti/ *noun* a liability which may or may not occur, but for which provision is made in a company's accounts, as opposed to 'provisions', where money is set aside for an anticipated expenditure

continuity /,kɒntɪ'njuːɪti/ *noun* the act of maintaining a continuous stable level of advertising activity ○ *Continuity must be the watchword of this promotional campaign to keep the product firmly in the minds of the target audience.* ○ *Should we aim for a sudden short blast of advertising or should continuity be the essence of our strategy?*

continuity programme /,kɒntɪ'njuːɪti ,prəʊɡræm/ *noun* a marketing programme which offers a series of products which are sent to customers at regular intervals

continuous /kən'tɪnjʊəs/ *adjective* with no end or with no breaks ○ *a continuous production line*

continuous process production /kən,tɪnjʊəs 'prəʊses prə,dʌkʃən/ *noun* automated production of many identical products

continuous research /kən,tɪnjʊəs rɪ's3ːtʃ/ *noun* regular ongoing market research ○ *Continuous research will tell us if sales are dropping off.*

contra /'kɒntrə/ *verb* □ **to contra an entry** to enter a similar amount in the opposite side of an account

contra account /'kɒntrə ə,kaʊnt/ *noun* an account which offsets another account, e.g. where a company's supplier is not only a creditor in that company's books but also a debtor because it has purchased goods on credit

contraband /'kɒntrəbænd/ *noun* goods brought into a country illegally, without paying customs duty

contract *noun*/'kɒntrækt/ **1.** a legal agreement between two parties ○ *to draw up a contract* ○ *to draft a contract* ○ *to sign a contract* □ **the contract is binding on both parties** both parties signing the contract must do what is agreed □ **under contract** bound by the terms of a contract ○ *The firm is under contract to deliver the goods by November.* □ **to void**

a **contract** to make a contract invalid **2.** □ **by private contract** by private legal agreement **3.** an agreement for the supply of a service or goods ○ *to enter into a contract to supply spare parts* ○ *to sign a contract for $10,000 worth of spare parts* □ **to put work out to contract** or to decide that work should be done by another company on a contract, rather than by employing members of staff to do it □ **to award a contract to a company** *or* **to place a contract with a company** to decide that a company shall have the contract to do work for you □ **to tender for a contract** to put forward an estimate of cost for work under contract ■ *verb*/ kən'trækt/ to agree to do some work on the basis of a legally binding contract ○ *to contract to supply spare parts to contract for the supply of spare parts* □ **the supply of spare parts was contracted out to Smith Ltd** Smith Ltd was given the contract for supplying spare parts □ **to contract out of an agreement** to withdraw from an agreement with the written permission of the other party

contract carrier /'kɒntrækt ˌkæriə/ *noun* a carrier or transportation company which has special contracts with businesses ○ *a contract carrier which ships coffee beans from Brazil to coffee wholesalers in Britain*

contract hire /'kɒntrækt haɪə/ *noun* a system that allows organisations to hire equipment that they need to use for a long period, e.g. cars or office machines, from other organisations instead of buying it, on condition that they sign a contract for the hire with owners (NOTE: Contract hire agreements often include arrangements for maintenance and replacement.)

contracting company /kənˌtræktɪŋ 'kʌmp(ə)ni/ *noun* an independent broadcasting company that sells advertising time ○ *With two new contracting companies being set up this year, advertisers will have more choice.*

contracting party /kənˌtræktɪŋ 'pɑːti/ *noun* a person or company that signs a contract

contract manufacturing /ˌkɒntrækt mænjʊ'fæktʃərɪŋ/ *noun* an agreement which allows an overseas manufacturer to manufacture or assem-

ble your products in that country for sale there ○ *Under a contract manufacturing agreement a local company is making our cars in France.*

contract note /'kɒntrækt nəʊt/ *noun* a note showing that shares have been bought or sold but not yet paid for, also including the commission

contractor /kən'træktə/ *noun* a person or company that does work according to a written agreement

contractual /kən'træktʃuəl/ *adjective* according to a contract ○ *contractual conditions* □ **to fulfil your contractual obligations** to do what you have agreed to do in a contract

contractual liability /kənˌtrækt-ʃuəl ˌlaɪə'bɪlɪti/ *noun* a legal responsibility for something as stated in a contract

contractually /kən'træktjuəli/ *adverb* according to a contract ○ *The company is contractually bound to pay our expenses.*

contractual obligation /kənˌtrækt-tʃuəl ˌɒblɪ'geɪʃ(ə)n/ *noun* something that a person is legally forced to do through having signed a contract to do □ **to fulfil your contractual obligations** to do what you have agreed to do in a contract □ **he is under no contractual obligation to buy** he has signed no agreement to buy

contract work /'kɒntrækt wɜːk/ *noun* work done according to a written agreement

contra deal /'kɒntrə ˌdiːl/ *noun* a deal between two businesses to exchange goods and services

contra entry /'kɒntrə ˌentri/ *noun* an entry made in the opposite side of an account to make an earlier entry worthless, i.e. a debit against a credit

contribute /kən'trɪbjuːt/ *verb* to give money or add to money ○ *We agreed to contribute 10% of the profits.* ○ *They had contributed to the pension fund for 10 years.*

contributed content website /kənˌtrɪbjuːtd ˌkɒntent 'websaɪt/ *noun* a website that allows visitors to add their contributions to its content, e.g., to write reviews of books that are advertised on the site

contribution /ˌkɒntrɪˈbjuːʃ(ə)n/ noun something that is contributed

contribution analysis /ˌkɒntrɪ-ˈbjuːʃ(ə)n əˌnæləsɪs/ noun an analysis of how much each of a company's products contributes to fixed costs, based on its profit margin and sales ○ *Contribution analysis helps to streamline production and marketing.* ○ *Thorough contribution analysis led to six products being dropped from the product range.*

contribution margin /ˌkɒntrɪ-ˈbjuːʃ(ə)n ˌmɑːdʒɪn/ noun a way of showing how much individual products or services contribute to net profit

'The provider of rehabilitation services cited the negative impact of Part B therapy caps on estimated Contract Therapy contribution margins' [*Business Week*]

contribution of capital /ˌkɒntrɪ-ˌbjuːʃ(ə)n əv ˈkæpɪt(ə)l/ noun money paid to a company as additional capital

contribution pricing /ˌkɒntrɪ-ˈbjuːʃ(ə)n ˌpraɪsɪŋ/ noun a pricing method based on maximising the contribution of each product to fixed costs

contributor /kənˈtrɪbjʊtə/ noun a person who gives money □ **contributor of capital** person who contributes capital

control /kənˈtrəʊl/ noun **1.** the power or ability to direct something ○ *The company is under the control of three shareholders.* □ **to lose control of a business** to find that you have less than 50% of the shares in a company, and so are no longer able to direct it ○ *The family lost control of its business.* **2.** the act of restricting or checking something or making sure that something is kept in check □ **under control** kept in check ○ *Expenses are kept under tight control.* ○ *The company is trying to bring its overheads back under control.* □ **out of control** not kept in check ○ *Costs have got out of control.* ■ verb **1.** □ **to control a business** to direct a business ○ *The business is controlled by a company based in Luxembourg.* ○ *The company is controlled by the majority shareholder.* **2.** to make sure that something is kept in check or is not allowed to develop ○ *The government is fighting to control inflation* or *to control the rise in*

the cost of living. (NOTE: **controlling – controlled**)

control group /kənˈtrəʊl gruːp/ noun a small group which is used to check a sample group

controllable /kənˈtrəʊləb(ə)l/ adjective which can be controlled

controllable variables /kənˌtrəʊ-ləb(ə)l ˈveəriəb(ə)lz/ plural noun factors that can be controlled, e.g. a company's marketing mix ○ *Because there were so few controllable variables the outcome of the marketing plan was very uncertain.*

controlled /kənˈtrəʊld/ adjective ruled or kept in check

controlled circulation /kənˌtrəʊld ˌsɜːkjʊˈleɪʃ(ə)n/ noun the distribution of a publication to a specialist readership who are members of a particular organisation or profession (often with controlled circulation, where the magazine is distributed free to key executives, and is paid for by the advertisers) ○ *The professional institute publishes a quarterly magazine with a controlled circulation.* ○ *The newspaper has a controlled circulation and is suitable for advertisements for highly specialised products.*

controlled circulation magazine /kənˌtrəʊld ˌsɜːkjʊleɪʃ(ə)n ˌmægə-ˈziːn/ noun a magazine which is sent free to a limited number of readers, and is paid for by the advertising it contains

controlled economy /kənˌtrəʊld ɪˈkɒnəmi/ noun an economy where most business activity is directed by orders from the government

control question /kənˈtrəʊl ˌkwestʃən/ noun a question in a questionnaire designed to check that answers are consistent ○ *A control question was included to check that respondents were not lying about their age.* ○ *If control questions show that answers are not honest, the interview is ended.*

control systems /kənˈtrəʊl ˌsɪs-təmz/ plural noun the systems used to check that a computer system is working correctly

convenience /kənˈviːniəns/ noun □ **at your earliest convenience** as soon as you find it possible

convenience food /kən'viːniəns fuːd/ *noun* food which is prepared by the shop before it is sold, so that it needs only heating to be made ready to eat

convenience goods /kən'viːniəns gʊdz/ *plural noun* ordinary everyday products that people have to buy but which command little or no brand loyalty ○ *Price competition is very fierce in the convenience goods market.*

convenience store /kən'viːniəns stɔː/ *noun* a small store selling food or household goods, open until late at night, or even 24 hours per day

'…the nation's largest convenience store chain has expanded the range of bills it takes payments for to include gas and telephone services' [*Nikkei Weekly*]

convenient /kən'viːniənt/ *adjective* suitable or handy ○ *A bank draft is a convenient way of sending money abroad.* ○ *Is 9.30 a convenient time for the meeting?*

conversion /kən'vɜːʃ(ə)n/ *noun* the action of converting a prospective customer into an actual purchaser

conversion rate /kən'vɜːʃ(ə)n reɪt/ *noun* the proportion of contacts, by mailing, advertising, or email marketing, who actually end up purchasing the product or service

convertible currency /kən,vɜː-təb(ə)l 'kʌrənsi/ *noun* a currency which can easily be exchanged for another

cooling-off laws /,kuːlɪŋ 'ɒf lɔːz/ *plural noun* US state laws allowing cancellation of an order within a specific period after signing an agreement ○ *Cooling-off laws are making buyers less hesitant about placing large orders.*

cooling-off period /,kuːlɪŋ 'ɒf ,pɪəriəd/ *noun* 1. (*during an industrial dispute*) a period when negotiations have to be carried on and no action can be taken by either side 2. a period during which someone who is about to enter into an agreement may reflect on all aspects of the arrangement and change his or her mind if necessary ○ *New York has a three day cooling-off period for telephone sales.*

co-op /'kəʊ ɒp/ *noun* same as **cooperative** noun1

co-operate /,kəʊ 'ɒpəreɪt/ *verb* to work together ○ *The regional governments are cooperating in the fight against piracy.* ○ *The two firms have cooperated on the computer project.*

co-operation /kəʊ ,ɒpə'reɪʃ(ə)n/ *noun* the act of working together ○ *The project was completed ahead of schedule with the cooperation of the workforce.*

co-operative /kəʊ 'ɒp(ə)rətɪv/ *adjective* willing to work together ○ *The workforce has not been cooperative over the management's productivity plan.* ■ *noun* 1. a business run by a group of employees who are also the owners and who share the profits ○ *The product is marketed by an agricultural cooperative.* ○ *They set up a workers' cooperative to run the factory.* 2. a business which organises cooperative mailing or advertising for different companies

co-operative advertising /kəʊ-,ɒp(ə)rətɪv 'ædvətaɪzɪŋ/ *noun* 1. the sharing by two companies, often a producer and a distributor, of advertising costs ○ *A cooperative advertising agreement means that two companies can enjoy quantity discounts offered by the media.* 2. mailing advertising material from different companies in the same mailing pack

co-operative marketing /kəʊ,ɒp-(ə)rətɪv 'maːkɪtɪŋ/ *noun* an arrangement whereby various producers cooperate in the marketing of their products or services ○ *Cooperative marketing proved an economic method of selling for companies with few financial resources.*

co-operative movement /kəʊ'ɒp-(ə)rətɪv ,muːvmənt/ *noun* a movement that encourages the setting-up of cooperative businesses that are jointly owned by their members who share the profits and benefits they gain from trading amongst themselves (NOTE: The movement was founded in Rochdale, Lancashire, in 1844 by 28 weavers and, in Britain, has launched not only a chain of shops, but also manufacturing and wholesale businesses as well as insurance and financial services.)

co-opetition /kəʊ,ɒpə'tɪʃ(ə)n/ *noun* cooperation between competing companies

copier /ˈkɒpiə/ *noun* a machine which makes copies of documents

copy /ˈkɒpi/ *verb* to make a second document which is like the first ○ *He copied the company report and took it home.* (NOTE: **copies – copying – copied**)

copy brief /ˈkɒpi briːf/ *noun* the instructions from an advertiser to a copywriter explaining the objectives of an advertising campaign ○ *The copy brief made it clear that the advertisements were to be aimed at young people.* ○ *The advertisers blamed the agency for not paying enough attention to the copy brief.*

copy clearance /ˈkɒpi ˌklɪərəns/ *noun* the passing of an advertiser's copy as neither misleading nor offensive ○ *It is doubtful the advertisement will get copy clearance since it directly disparages the competition.* ○ *The advertisement has received copy clearance because all its claims can be substantiated.* ○ *You will not get copy clearance for this ad because the caption is sure to offend a lot of women readers.*

copy date /ˈkɒpi deɪt/ *noun* the date by which an advertisement must be delivered to the media concerned ○ *The creative teams are working flat out because the copy date is only one week away.* ○ *Let's work on the advertisements with the earliest copy dates.*

copy fitting /ˈkɒpi ˌfɪtɪŋ/ *noun* the arrangement of advertising text so it fits the space allowed for it

copy platform /ˈkɒpi ˌplætfɔːm/ *noun* the main theme of an advertisement's copy ○ *There is no point in discussing details until we decide on a copy platform.*

copyright /ˈkɒpiraɪt/ *noun* **1.** an author's legal right to publish his or her own work and not to have it copied, lasting seventy years after the author's death **2.** a legal right which protects the creative work of writers and artists and prevents others from copying or using it without authorisation, and which also applies to such things as company logos and brand names ■ *adjective* covered by the laws of copyright ○ *It is illegal to photocopy a copyright work.*

copy testing /ˈkɒpi ˌtestɪŋ/ *noun* the act of testing the effectiveness of an advertisement's copy ○ *Copy testing led to the copywriter having to rethink the wording of the message.* ○ *Copy testing will tell us whether or not the advertisements are offensive to the public in general.*

copywriter /ˈkɒpiraɪtə/ *noun* a person who writes advertisements

copywriting /ˈkɒpiˌraɪtɪŋ/ *noun* the writing of copy for advertisements

core /kɔː/ *noun* the central or main part

core activity /ˈkɔːr ækˌtɪvɪti/ *noun* the central activity of a company, which is its basic product or service

core business /ˈkɔː ˌbɪznɪs/ *noun* the most important work that an organisation does, that it is most expert at, that makes it different from other organisations, that contributes most to its success and, usually, that it was originally set up to do (NOTE: The concept of core business became prominent in the 1980s when attempts at diversification by large companies proved less successful than expected.)

core capability /ˌkɔː ˌkeɪpəˈbɪlɪti/ *noun* same as **core competence**

core competence /ˌkɔː ˈkɒmpɪt(ə)ns/ *noun* a skill or an area of expertise possessed by an organisation that makes it particularly good at doing some things and makes an important contribution to its success by giving it competitive advantage over other organisations

core product /ˌkɔː ˈprɒdʌkt/ *noun* **1.** the main product which a company makes or sells **2.** a basic product, without added benefits such as credit terms, installation service, etc.

core values /ˌkɔː ˈvæljuːz/ *plural noun* the main commercial and moral principles that influence the way an organisation is run and the way it conducts its business, and that are supposed to be shared by everyone in the organisation from senior management to ordinary employees (NOTE: Core values are often reflected in an organisation's *mission statement.*)

corner /ˈkɔːnə/ *verb* □ **to corner the market** to own most or all of the supply of a commodity and so control the price

○ *The syndicate tried to corner the market in silver.*

corporate /ˈkɔːp(ə)rət/ *adjective* referring to corporations or companies, or to a particular company as a whole

'…the prime rate is the rate at which banks lend to their top corporate borrowers' [*Wall Street Journal*]

'…if corporate forecasts are met, sales will exceed $50 million next year' [*Citizen (Ottawa)*]

corporate advertising /ˌkɔːp(ə)rət ˈædvətaɪzɪŋ/ *noun* the advertising of an organisation rather than a product ○ *Our corporate advertising is designed to present us as a caring organisation.* ○ *No amount of corporate advertising will ever persuade the consumer that the company stands for quality.*

corporate brand /ˌkɔːp(ə)rət ˈbrænd/ *noun* the overall image that a company presents to the outside world, or the image of it that exists in the minds of its customers, its employees, and the public, and that encapsulates what it does and what it stands for

'A corporate brand, which is based on the characteristics of the firm as well as its products, can play a critical role in a company's brand portfolio' [*Harvard Business Review*]

corporate communication /ˌkɔːp(ə)rət kəmjuːnɪˈkeɪʃ(ə)n/ *noun* the activities undertaken by an organisation to pass on information both to its own employees and to its existing and prospective customers and the general public

corporate culture /ˌkɔːp(ə)rət ˈkʌltʃə/ *noun* the often unspoken beliefs and values that determine the way an organisation does things, the atmosphere that exists within it, and the way people who work for it behave (NOTE: The culture of an organisation is often summed up as 'the way we do things around here'.)

'Executives may have no idea how differently minority colleagues can view the corporate culture that treats whites so well' [*Fortune*]

corporate discount /ˌkɔːp(ə)rət ˈdɪskaʊnt/ *noun* a reduction in advertising charges calculated on the basis of the total advertising revenue from all the brands of a company

corporate hospitality /ˌkɔːp(ə)rət hɒspɪˈtælɪti/ *noun* entertainment provided by an organisation, originally intended to help salespeople build relationships with customers, but now increasingly used as an incentive for staff and in team-building and training exercises for employees

corporate identity /ˌkɔːp(ə)rət aɪˈdentɪti/ *noun* the way in which a corporation is distinguished from others

corporate image /ˌkɔːp(ə)rət ˈɪmɪdʒ/ *noun* an idea which a company would like the public to have of it

corporate name /ˌkɔːp(ə)rətˈneɪm/ *noun* the name of a large corporation

corporate plan /ˌkɔːp(ə)rətˈplæn/ *noun* a plan for the future work of a whole company

corporate planning /ˌkɔːp(ə)rət ˈplænɪŋ/ *noun* the process of planning the future work of a whole company

corporate portal /ˌkɔːp(ə)rətˈpɔː-t(ə)l/ *noun* a main website that allows access to all the information and software applications held by an organisation and provides links to information from outside it (NOTE: A corporate portal is a development of *intranet* technology and, ideally, should allow users to access groupware, email, and desktop applications, and to customise the way information is presented and the way it is used.)

corporate profits /ˌkɔːp(ə)rət ˈprɒfɪts/ *plural noun* the profits of a corporation

'…corporate profits for the first quarter showed a 4% drop from last year' [*Financial Times*]

corporate strategy /ˌkɔːp(ə)rət ˈstrætədʒi/ *noun* the plans for future action by a corporation

corporate vision /ˌkɔːp(ə)rət ˈvɪʒ(ə)n/ *noun* the overall aim or purpose of an organisation that all its business activities are designed to help it achieve (NOTE: An organisation's corporate vision is usually summed up in its **vision statement**.)

corporation /ˌkɔːpəˈreɪʃ(ə)n/ *noun* **1.** a large company **2.** US a company which is incorporated in the US

corporation income tax /ˌkɔː-pəreɪʃ(ə)n ˈɪnkʌm tæks/ *noun* a tax on profits made by incorporated companies

corporation tax /ˌkɔːpəˈreɪʃ(ə)n tæks/ *noun* a tax on profits and capital gains made by companies, calculated before dividends are paid. Abbreviation **CT**

correlation /ˌkɒrəˈleɪʃ(ə)n/ *noun* the degree to which there is a relationship between two sets of data ○ *Is there any correlation between people's incomes and the amount they spend on clothing?* ⇨ **coefficient of correlation, multiple, correlation**

cosmetic /kɒzˈmetɪk/ *adjective* referring to the appearance of people or things ○ *We've made some cosmetic changes to our product line.* ○ *Packaging has both practical as well as cosmetic importance.*

cost /kɒst/ *noun* the amount of money paid to acquire, produce or maintain something, e.g. the money paid for materials, labour and overheads in the manufacture of a product produced and sold by a business ○ *What is the cost of a first class ticket to New York?* ○ *Production costs are falling each year.* ○ *We cannot afford the cost of two cars.* □ **to cover costs** to produce enough money in sales to pay for the costs of production ○ *The sales revenue barely covers the advertising costs.* □ **to sell at cost** to sell at a price which is the same as the cost of manufacture or the wholesale cost ■ *verb* **1.** to have as its price ○ *How much does the machine cost?* ○ *This cloth costs $10 a metre.* (NOTE: **costing – cost**) **2.** to cause money to be spent or lost (NOTE: **costing – cost**) **3.** to determine the cost of something (NOTE: **costing – cost**) □ **to cost a product** to calculate how much money will be needed to make a product, and so work out its selling price

cost, insurance, and freight /ˌkɒst ɪnˌʃʊərəns ən ˈfreɪt/ *noun* the estimate of a price, which includes the cost of the goods, the insurance, and the transport charges. Abbreviation **CIF, c.i.f.**

cost accountant /ˈkɒst əˌkaʊntənt/ *noun* an accountant who gives managers information about their business costs

cost accounting /ˈkɒst əˌkaʊntɪŋ/ *noun* the process of preparing special accounts of manufacturing and sales costs

cost analysis /ˈkɒst əˌnæləsɪs/ *noun* the process of calculating in advance what a new product will cost

cost-benefit analysis /ˌkɒst ˈbenɪfɪt əˌnæləsɪs/ *noun* the process of comparing the costs and benefits of various possible ways of using available resources. Also called **benefit-cost analysis**

cost centre /ˈkɒst ˌsentə/ *noun* **1.** a person or group whose costs can be itemised and to which costs can be allocated in accounts **2.** a unit, a process or an individual that provides a service needed by another part of an organisation and whose cost is therefore accepted as an overhead of the business

cost-cutting /ˈkɒst ˌkʌtɪŋ/ *noun* the process of reducing costs ○ *As a result of cost-cutting, we have had to make three staff redundant.*

cost driver /ˈkɒst ˌdraɪvə/ *noun* a factor that determines how much it costs to carry out a particular task or project, e.g. the amount of resources needed for it, or the activities involved in completing it

cost-effective /ˌkɒstɪ ˈfektɪv/ *adjective* giving good value when compared with the original cost ○ *We find advertising in the Sunday newspapers very cost-effective.*

cost-effectiveness /ˌkɒstɪˈfektɪvnəs/, **cost efficiency** /ˌkɒst ɪˈfɪʃənsi/ *noun* the quality of being cost-effective ○ *Can we calculate the cost-effectiveness of air freight against shipping by sea?*

cost factor /ˈkɒst ˌfæktə/ *noun* any activity or item of material, equipment or personnel that incurs a cost

costing /ˈkɒstɪŋ/ *noun* a calculation of the manufacturing costs, and so the selling price, of a product ○ *The costings give us a retail price of $2.95.* ○ *We cannot do the costing until we have details of all the production expenditure.*

costly /ˈkɒstli/ *adjective* costing a lot of money, or costing too much money ○ *Defending the court case was a costly process.* ○ *The mistakes were time-consuming and costly.*

cost of entry /ˌkɒst əv ˈentri/ *noun* the cost of going into a market for the first time

cost of goods sold /ˌkɒst əv ˌgʊdz ˈsəʊld/ *noun* same as **cost of sales**

cost-of-living increase /ˌkɒst əv ˈlɪvɪŋ ˌɪnkriːs/ *noun* an increase in salary to allow it to keep up with the increased cost of living

cost-of-living index /ˌkɒst əv ˈlɪvɪŋ ˌɪndeks/ *noun* a way of measuring the cost of living which is shown as a percentage increase on the figure for the previous year. It is similar to the consumer price index, but includes other items such as the interest on mortgages.

cost of sales /ˌkɒst əv ˈseɪlz/ *noun* all the costs of a product sold, including manufacturing costs and the staff costs of the production department, before general overheads are calculated. Also called **cost of goods sold**

cost per acquisition /kɒst pə ˌækwɪˈzɪʃ(ə)n/ *noun* the average cost for each acquisition of a new customer in response to an advertisement. Abbreviation **CPA**

cost per click-through /ˌkɒst pə ˈklɪk θruː/ *noun* a method of pricing online advertising, based on the principle that the seller gets paid whenever a visitor clicks on an advertisement

cost per customer /ˌkɒst pə ˈkʌstəmə/ *noun* a measure of cost-effectiveness based on the cost per sale generated

cost per inquiry /ˌkɒst pər ɪnˈkwaɪəri/ *noun* the average cost for each inquiry in response to an advertisement

cost per order /ˌkɒst pə ˈɔːdə/ *noun* a measure used to determine the number of orders generated compared to the cost of running the advertisement. Abbreviation **CPO**

cost per sale /ˌkɒst pə ˈseɪl/ *noun* a method of pricing based on the number of sales transactions generated by a company's advertisement. Abbreviation **CPS**

cost per thousand /ˌkɒst pə ˈθaʊz(ə)nd/, **cost per mille** /ˌkɒst pə ˈmɪl/ *noun* the cost of an advertisement, calculated as the cost for every thousand people reached or the cost of a thousand impressions for a website ○ *This newspaper has the highest cost per thousand but a very high proportion of its readers fall within our target audience.* Abbreviation **CPT**, **CPM**

cost plus /ˌkɒst ˈplʌs/ *noun* a system of calculating a price, by taking the cost of production of goods or services and adding a percentage to cover the supplier's overheads and margin ○ *We are charging for the work on a cost plus basis.*

cost-plus pricing /ˌkɒst ˈplʌs ˌpraɪsɪŋ/ *noun* a pricing method that involves basing the price on the production costs and adding a percentage for margin

cost price /ˈkɒst praɪs/ *noun* a selling price that is the same as the price paid by the seller, which results in no profit being made

costs /kɒsts/ *plural noun* the expenses involved in a court case ○ *The judge awarded costs to the defendant.* ○ *Costs of the case will be borne by the prosecution.*

cottage industry /ˌkɒtɪdʒˈɪndəstri/ *noun* the production of goods or some other type of work, carried out by people working in their own homes

counter /ˈkaʊntə/ *noun* a long flat surface in a shop for displaying and selling goods □ **goods sold over the counter** retail sales of goods in shops ○ *Some drugs are sold over the counter, but others need to be prescribed by a doctor.* □ **under the counter** illegally

counter- /kaʊntə/ *prefix* against

counteradvertising /ˌkaʊntərˈædvətaɪzɪŋ/ *noun* advertising aimed as a reply to a competitor's advertisements

counter-argument /ˈkaʊntərˌɑːgjʊmənt/ *noun* a response that is opposed to the position advocated in an advertising message

counterbid /ˈkaʊntəbɪd/ *noun* a higher bid in reply to a previous bid ○ *When I bid $20 she put in a counterbid of $25.*

counter-jumper /ˈkaʊntəˌdʒʌmpə/ *noun* a person who sells goods over the counter (*informal*) ○ *He was a counter-jumper for many years before he became a manager.* ○ *Five years as a counter-jumper gave her plenty of experience of customer relations.*

countermand /ˌkaʊntəˈmɑːnd/ *verb* to say that an order must not be carried out ○ *to countermand an order*

counter-offer /ˈkaʊntər ˌɒfə/ *noun* a higher or lower offer made in reply to another offer ○ *Smith Ltd made an offer of $1m for the property, and Blacks replied with a counter-offer of $1.4m.*

'…the company set about paring costs and improving the design of its product. It came up with a price cut of 14%, but its counter-offer – for an order that was to have provided 8% of its workload next year – was too late and too expensive' [*Wall Street Journal*]

counterpack /ˈkaʊntəpæk/ *noun* a box for the display of goods for sale, placed on the counter or on another flat surface in a shop

counter-programming /ˈkaʊntə ˌprəʊɡræmɪŋ/ *noun* the presenting of TV programmes that are designed to appeal to the audience of competing programmes run during at the same time

countersign /ˈkaʊntəsaɪn/ *verb* to sign a document which has already been signed by someone else ○ *All our cheques have to be countersigned by the finance director.* ○ *The sales director countersigns all my orders.*

counter staff /ˈkaʊntə stɑːf/ *noun* sales staff who serve behind counters

country of origin /ˌkʌntri əv ˈɒrɪdʒɪn/ *noun* a country where a product is manufactured or where a food product comes from ○ *All produce must be labelled to show the country of origin.*

coupon /ˈkuːpɒn/ *noun* **1.** a piece of paper used in place of money **2.** a piece of paper which replaces an order form

coupon ad /ˈkuːpɒn æd/ *noun* an advertisement with a form attached, which you cut out and return to the advertiser with your name and address for further information

couponed /ˈkuːpɒnd/ *adjective* with a coupon attached ○ *The agency is using couponed direct response advertising.*

couponing /ˈkuːpɒnɪŋ/ *noun* a selling method using coupons delivered to homes, giving special discounts on some items

'…it employs selective mailings and package inserts such as the couponed offers sent out with credit card statements' [*PR Week*]

course /kɔːs/ *noun* a series of lessons or a programme of instruction ○ *She has finished her marketing course.* ○ *The company has paid for her to attend a course for trainee sales managers.* ○ *Management trainees all took a six-month course in business studies.* ○ *The training officer was constantly on the lookout for new courses in management studies.* ○ *The company sent her on a management course.*

courtesy /ˈkɜːtəsi/ *adjective* supplied free of charge ○ *A courtesy sample is sent with the sales literature.*

courtesy car /ˈkɜːtəsi kɑː/ *noun* the use of a car offered free to a customer

cover /ˈkʌvə/ *noun* **1.** the proportion of a target audience reached by advertising **2.** one of the outside pages of a publication. The four cover pages are front cover, inside front cover, inside back cover, and back cover. ○ *We could never afford to advertise on the cover of this magazine.*

coverage /ˈkʌv(ə)rɪdʒ/ *noun* the proportion of a target market that is reached by an advertisement ○ *The advertisement itself was effective but it had very poor coverage.* ○ *We must consider both the cost of the advertisement and its coverage before committing ourselves any further.*

'…from a PR point of view it is easier to get press coverage when you are selling an industry and not a brand' [*PR Week*]

cover charge /ˈkʌvə tʃɑːdʒ/ *noun* (*in restaurants*) a charge for a place at the table in addition to the charge for food

covered market /ˌkʌvəd ˈmɑːkɪt/ *noun* a market which is held in a special building

covering letter /ˌkʌvərɪŋ ˈletə/, **covering note** /ˌkʌvərɪŋ ˈnəʊt/ *noun* a letter sent with documents to say why they are being sent ○ *She sent a covering letter with her curriculum vitae, explaining why she wanted the job.* ○ *The job advertisement asked for a CV and a covering letter.*

cover note /ˈkʌvə nəʊt/ *noun* a letter from an insurance company giving details of an insurance policy and confirming that the policy exists

cover page /ˈkʌvə peɪdʒ/ *noun* the front or back cover of a publication

cover price /ˈkʌvə praɪs/ *noun* the price of a newspaper or magazine which is printed on the cover and paid by the final purchaser

CPA *abbreviation* cost per acquisition

CPM *abbreviation* cost per mille

CPO *abbreviation* cost per order

CPS *abbreviation* cost per sale

CPT *abbreviation* cost per thousand

crash-test /ˈkræʃ test/ *verb* to establish the safety and reliability of something by testing it in different ways

creaming /ˈkriːmɪŋ/ *noun* the act of fixing a high price for a product in order to achieve high short-term profits

create /kriˈeɪt/ *verb* to make something new ○ *By acquiring small unprofitable companies he soon created a large manufacturing group.* ○ *The government scheme aims at creating new jobs for young people.*

'…he insisted that the tax advantages he directed towards small businesses will help create jobs and reduce the unemployment rate' [*Toronto Star*]

creative /kriˈeɪtɪv/ *adjective* relating to the conceptual or artistic side of advertising ○ *There are three copywriters and four illustrators in the agency's creative department.* ○ *He has had good experience working on both the creative and the administrative sides of advertising.* ■ *noun* someone who works in the conceptual or artistic side of a business

'…agencies are being called on to produce great creative work and at the same time deliver value for money' [*Marketing Week*]

creative director /kriˌeɪtɪv daɪ-ˈrektə/ *noun* an employee of an advertising agency who is in overall charge of finding the right words and images to promote the product during an advertising campaign

creative selling /kriˌeɪtɪv ˈselɪŋ/ *noun* a sales technique where the main emphasis is on generating new business

creative shop /kriˌeɪtɪv ˈʃɒp/, **creative boutique** /kriˌeɪtɪv buːˈtiːk/ *noun* a highly specialised business offering creative customer advertising services ○ *A group of copywriters and designers have left the agency to set up their own creative shop.* ○ *The creative shop made short advertising films and designed some press ads for us.*

creative strategy /kriˈeɪtɪv ˌstræ-tədʒi/ *noun* a strategy to determine what message an advertisement will communicate

creativity /ˌkriːeɪˈtɪvɪti/, **creative thinking** /kriˌeɪtɪv ˈθɪŋkɪŋ/ *noun* the ability to generate new ideas, especially by taking a fresh and imaginative approach to old problems or existing procedures (NOTE: Creativity is considered important not just in the development of new products and services, but also in organisational *decision-making* and *problem-solving*, and many organisations try to encourage it through their corporate culture and by using techniques such as *brainstorming* and *lateral thinking*.)

credere /ˈkreɪdəri/ *noun* ➡ del credere agent

credibility /ˌkredɪˈbɪlɪti/ *noun* the state of being trusted

credibility gap /ˌkredɪˈbɪlɪti gæp/ *noun* a discrepancy between claims for a product made by the manufacturer and acceptance of these claims by the target audience ○ *The credibility gap that we face is partly due to our product's bad performance record.* ⇨ **source credibility**

credit /ˈkredɪt/ *noun* **1.** a period of time allowed before a customer has to pay a debt incurred for goods or services ○ *to give someone six months' credit* ○ *to sell on good credit terms* □ **to open a line of credit** *or* **a credit line** to make credit available to someone □ **on credit** without paying immediately ○ *to live on credit* ○ *We buy everything on sixty days' credit.* ○ *The company exists on credit from its suppliers.* **2.** an amount entered in accounts to show a decrease in assets or expenses or an increase in liabilities, revenue or capital. In accounts, credits are entered in the right-hand column. ○ *to enter $100 to someone's credit* ○ *to pay in $100 to the credit of Mr Smith* Compare **debit** □ **account in credit** an account where the credits are higher than the debits **3.** money set against a client's account because an advertisement was not run at the correct time

credit account /ˈkredɪt əˌkaʊnt/ *noun* an account which a customer has with a shop which allows him or her to buy goods and pay for them later

credit agency /ˈkredɪt ˌeɪdʒənsi/ *noun* a company which reports on the creditworthiness of customers to show whether they should be allowed credit. Also called **credit bureau**

credit bank /ˈkredɪt bæŋk/ *noun* a bank which lends money

credit bureau /ˈkredɪt ˌbjʊərəʊ/ *noun US* same as **credit agency**

credit card /ˈkredɪt kɑːd/ *noun* a plastic card which allows someone to borrow money and to buy goods up to a certain limit without paying for them immediately, but only after a period of grace of about 25–30 days

credit card sale /ˈkredɪt kɑːd ˌseɪl/ *noun* the act of selling where the buyer uses a credit card to pay

credit column /ˈkredɪt ˌkɒləm/ *noun* the right-hand column in accounts showing money received

credit control /ˈkredɪt kənˌtrəʊl/ *noun* a check that customers pay on time and do not owe more than their credit limit

credit crunch /ˈkredɪt krʌntʃ/, **credit crisis** /ˈkredɪt ˌkraɪsɪs/ *noun* a reduction in the general availability of loans or credit or a tightening on conditions required to obtain a loan from the banks ○ *Small businesses have been worst hit by the credit crunch.* ○ *We've had to tighten our belts because of the credit crunch.* Also called **credit squeeze**

credit crunch lunch /ˈkredɪt krʌntʃ ˌlʌntʃ/ *noun* a special offer by restaurants for discounted meals to attract more customers during the credit crunch of 2008–9

credit entry /ˈkredɪt ˌentri/ *noun* an entry on the credit side of an account

credit facilities /ˈkredɪt fəˌsɪlɪtiz/ *plural noun* an arrangement with a bank or supplier to have credit so as to buy goods

credit freeze /ˈkredɪt friːz/ *noun* a period when lending by banks is restricted by the government

credit history /ˈkredɪt ˌhɪst(ə)ri/ *noun* a record of how a potential borrower has repaid his or her previous debts

'...failed to consider numerous factors, such as an applicant's credit history and ability to repay based on income' [*Economist*]

credit limit /ˈkredɪt ˌlɪmɪt/ *noun* the largest amount of money which a customer can borrow □ **he has exceeded his credit limit** he has borrowed more money than he is allowed to

credit memorandum /ˈkredɪt ˌmemərændəm/, **credit memo** /ˈkredɪt ˌmeməʊ/ *noun US* a note showing that money is owed to a customer ○ *When the buyer paid too much money for the goods he was immediately sent a credit memorandum.* ○ *I hope we receive a credit memo from the suppliers for the money they owe us.*

credit note /ˈkredɪt nəʊt/ *noun* a note showing that money is owed to a customer ○ *The company sent the wrong order and so had to issue a credit note.* Abbreviation **C/N**

creditor /ˈkredɪtə/ *noun* a person or company that is owed money, i.e. a company's creditors are its liabilities

creditors' meeting /ˈkredɪtəz ˌmiːtɪŋ/ *noun* a meeting of all the people to whom an insolvent company owes money, to decide how to obtain the money owed

credit rating agency /ˈkredɪt reɪtɪŋ ˌeɪdʒənsi/ *noun US* a company used by businesses and banks to assess the creditworthiness of people

credit-reference agency /ˈkredɪt ˌrefər(ə)ns ˌeɪdʒənsi/ *noun* same as **credit agency**

credits /ˈkredɪts/ *plural noun* a list of the names of people who have worked on a film, TV programme, etc.

credit sale /'kredɪt seɪl/ *noun* a sale where the purchaser will pay for the goods bought at a later date

credit scoring /'kredɪt ˌskɔːrɪŋ/ *noun* a calculation made when assessing the creditworthiness of someone or something

credit side /'kredɪt saɪd/ *noun* the right-hand column of accounts showing money received

credit squeeze /'kredɪt skwiːz/ *noun* same as **credit crunch**

credit system /'kredɪt ˌsɪstəm/ *noun* the system that governs the way that loans are made to people and organisations, especially the regulations that relate to loans and to organisations that provide loans

credit union /'kredɪt ˌjuːnjən/ *noun* a group of people who pay in regular deposits or subscriptions which earn interest and are used to make loans to other members of the group

creditworthiness /'kredɪtˌwɜːðinəs/ *noun* the extent to which an individual or organisation is creditworthy

creditworthy /'kredɪtwɜːði/ *adjective* judged as likely to be able to repay money borrowed, either, in the case of an individual, by a credit reference agency, or, in the case of an organisation, by a credit rating agency ○ *We will do some checks on her to see if she is creditworthy.*

criminal record /ˌkrɪmɪn(ə)l 'rekɔːd/ *noun* same as **police record**

crisis /'kraɪsɪs/ *noun* a serious situation where decisions have to be taken rapidly

crisis management /'kraɪsɪs ˌmænɪdʒmənt/ *noun* management of a business or a country's economy during a period of crisis

critical mass /ˌkrɪtɪk(ə)l 'mæs/ *noun* the point at which an organisation or a project is generating enough income or has gained a large enough market share to be able to survive on its own or to be worth investing more money or resources in

critical path analysis /ˌkrɪtɪk(ə)l 'pɑːθ əˌnæləsɪs/ *noun* **1.** an analysis of the way a project is organised in terms of the minimum time it will take to complete, calculating which parts can be delayed without holding up the rest of the project **2.** same as **critical-path method**

critical-path method /ˌkrɪtɪk(ə)l 'pɑːθ ˌmeθəd/ *noun* a technique used in project management to identify the activities within a project that are critical to its success, usually by showing on a diagram or flow chart the order in which activities must be carried out so that the project can be completed in the shortest time and at the least cost

'…need initial project designs to be more complex or need to generate Critical Path Method charts or PERT reports' [*Information Week*]

CRM *abbreviation* customer relations management *or* customer relationship management

cross /krɒs/ *verb* **1.** to go across ○ *The Concorde only took three hours to cross the Atlantic.* ○ *To get to the bank, you turn left and cross the street at the post office.* **2.** □ **to cross a cheque** to write two lines across a cheque to show that it has to be paid into a bank

crossed cheque /ˌkrɒst 'tʃek/ *noun* a cheque with two lines across it showing that it can only be deposited at a bank and not exchanged for cash

cross elasticity of demand /ˌkrɒs ɪlæˌstɪsɪti əv dɪ'mɑːnd/ *noun* changes in demand for an item depending on the selling price of a competing product

cross-media advertising /ˌkrɒs ˌmiːdiə 'ædvətaɪzɪŋ/ *noun* advertising the same product or service in several different types of media which are offered by a single-company media provider

cross-over /'krɒs ˌəʊvə/ *noun* a media product which was made for one genre, but gains popularity in another

cross-promotion /ˌkrɒs prə'məʊ-ʃ(ə)n/ *noun* a process in which two or more advertisers of a product or service associate themselves with each other to increase their profile, reach more people etc.

cross-selling /ˌkrɒs 'selɪŋ/ *noun* **1.** the act of selling two products which go with each other, by placing them side by side in a store **2.** the selling of a new product which goes with another product a customer has already bought

cross-tracks /ˈkrɒs træks/ *noun* a poster site next to a railway track

cryptography /ˌkrɪpˈtɒɡrəfi/ *noun* the use of codes and ciphers, especially as a way of restricting access to part or all of a website, so that only a user with a key can read the information

CTM /ˌsiː tiː ˈem/ *noun* click through per thousand. ⇨ **click-through rate**

CTR /kənˈtrəʊl/ *abbreviation* click-through rate

cume /kjuːm/ *noun* same as **cumulative audience** (*informal*)

cumulative /ˈkjuːmjʊlətɪv/ *adjective* added to regularly over a period of time

cumulative audience /ˌkjuːmjʊlətɪv ˈɔːdiəns/ *noun* the number of people reached by an advertisement at least once over a period of time

cumulative interest /ˌkjuːmjʊlətɪv ˈɪntrəst/ *noun* the total amount of interest that has been charged on a loan up to a given point

cumulative quantity discount /ˌkjuːmjʊlətɪv ˌkwɒntəti ˈdɪskaʊnt/ *noun* a discount based on a quantity bought or the value of purchases over a period of time ○ *We have purchased only from these suppliers over the last few months in order to enjoy a cumulative quantity discount.*

cumulative reach /ˌkjuːmjʊlətɪv ˈriːtʃ/ *noun* same as **cumulative audience**

curbside conference /ˌkɜːbsaɪd ˈkɒnf(ə)rəns/ *noun US* US spelling of **kerbside conference**

currency /ˈkʌrənsi/ *noun* money in coins and notes which is used in a particular country

'…today's wide daily variations in exchange rates show the instability of a system based on a single currency, namely the dollar' [*Economist*]

'…the level of currency in circulation increased to N4.9 billion in the month of August' [*Business Times (Lagos)*]

currency backing /ˈkʌrənsi ˌbækɪŋ/ *noun* gold or government

securities which maintain the strength of a currency

currency basket /ˈkʌrənsi ˌbɑːskɪt/ *noun* a group of currencies, each of which is weighted, calculated together as a single unit against which another currency can be measured

currency note /ˈkʌrənsi nəʊt/ *noun* a bank note

current /ˈkʌrənt/ *adjective* referring to the present time ○ *the current round of wage negotiations*

'…crude oil output plunged during the past month and is likely to remain at its current level for the near future' [*Wall Street Journal*]

current account /ˈkʌrənt əˌkaʊnt/ *noun* **1.** an account in an bank from which the customer can withdraw money when he or she wants. Current accounts do not always pay interest. ○ *to pay money into a current account* Also called **cheque account** (NOTE: The US term is **checking account**.) **2.** an account of the balance of payments of a country relating to the sale or purchase of raw materials, goods and invisibles

current assets /ˌkʌrənt ˈæsets/ *plural noun* the assets used by a company in its ordinary work, e.g. materials, finished goods, cash and monies due, and which are held for a short time only

current cost accounting /ˌkʌrənt ˈkɒst əˌkaʊntɪŋ/ *noun* a method of accounting in which assets are valued at the amount it would cost to replace them, rather than at the original cost. Abbreviation **CCA**. Also called **replacement cost accounting**

current liabilities /ˌkʌrənt ˌlaɪəˈbɪlɪtiz/ *plural noun* the debts which a company has to pay within the next accounting period. In a company's annual accounts, these would be debts which must be paid within the year and are usually payments for goods or services received.

current price /ˌkʌrənt ˈpraɪs/ *noun* today's price

current rate of exchange /ˌkʌrənt reɪt əv ɪksˈtʃeɪndʒ/ *noun* today's rate of exchange

current yield /ˌkʌrənt ˈjiːld/ *noun* a dividend calculated as a percentage of the current price of a share on the stock market

curriculum vitae /kə,rɪkjʊləm 'viːtaɪ/ *noun* a summary of a person's work experience and qualifications sent to a prospective employer by someone applying for a job ○ *Candidates should send a letter of application with a curriculum vitae to the HR manager.* ○ *The curriculum vitae listed all the candidate's previous jobs and her reasons for leaving them.* Abbreviation **CV** (NOTE: The plural is **curriculums** or **curricula vitae**. The US term is **résumé**.)

curve /kɜːv/ *noun* a line which is not straight, e.g. a line on a graph ○ *The graph shows an upward curve.*

custom /'kʌstəm/ *noun* **1.** the use of a shop by regular shoppers □ **to lose someone's custom** to do something which makes a regular customer go to another shop **2.** a thing which is usually done ○ *It is the custom of the book trade to allow unlimited returns for credit.* □ **the customs of the trade** the general way of working in a trade

custom-built /'kʌstəm bɪlt/ *adjective* made specially for one customer ○ *He drives a custom-built Rolls Royce.*

customer /'kʌstəmə/ *noun* a person or company that buys goods ○ *The shop was full of customers.* ○ *Can you serve this customer first please?* ○ *She's a regular customer of ours.* (NOTE: The customer may not be the consumer or end user of the product.)

'…unless advertising and promotion is done in the context of an overall customer orientation, it cannot seriously be thought of as marketing' [*Quarterly Review of Marketing*]

customer appeal /'kʌstəmərə,piːl/ *noun* what attracts customers to a product

customer capital /,kʌstəmə 'kæpɪt(ə)l/ *noun* an organisation's relationships with its customers considered as a business asset

customer care /,kʌstəmə 'keə/ *noun* the activity of looking after customers, so that they do not become dissatisfied

customer-centric model /,kʌstəmə 'sentrɪk ,mɒd(ə)l/ *noun* a business

model that is based on an assessment of what the customer needs

customer complaint /,kʌstəmə kəm'pleɪnt/ *noun* same as **complaint**

customer expectation /,kʌstəmər ekspek'teɪʃ(ə)n/ *noun* the ideas and feelings that a customer has about a product or service, based on what he or she needs from it and expects it to do (NOTE: Customer expectation can be created by previous experience, advertising, what other people say about it, awareness of competitors' products, and ***brand image***. If customer expectations are met, then customer satisfaction results.)

customer flow /'kʌstəmə fləʊ/ *noun* the number of customers in a store and the pattern of their movements around the store

customer focus /,kʌstəmə'fəʊkəs/ *noun* the aiming of all marketing operations towards the customer

customer lifetime value /,kʌstəmə 'laɪftaɪm ,væljuː/ *noun* the value of exactly how much each customer is worth in monetary terms over their lifetime, and therefore how much a marketing department should spend to acquire each customer. Abbreviation **LTV**

customer loyalty /,kʌstəmə 'lɔɪəlti/ *noun* the feeling of customers who always shop at the same shop

'…a difficult market to get into, China nevertheless offers a high degree of customer loyalty once successfully entered' [*Economist*]

customer profile /,kʌstəmə 'prəʊfaɪl/ *noun* a description of an average customer for a product or service ○ *The customer profile shows our average buyer to be male, aged 25–30, and employed in the service industries.*

customer profitability /,kʌstəmə ,prɒfɪtə'bɪlɪti/ *noun* the amount of profit generated by each individual customer. Usually a small percentage of customers generate the most profit.

customer relations /,kʌstəmə rɪ'leɪʃ(ə)nz/ *plural noun* relations between a company and its customers

customer relationship management /,kʌstəmə rɪ'leɪʃ(ə)nʃɪp ,mænɪdʒmənt/ *noun* the management of relations between a company and its customers, keeping them informed of new products or services and dealing sympathetically with their complaints or inquiries. Abbreviation **CRM**

customer retention /ˌkʌstəmə rɪ-ˈtenʃən/ *noun* same as **retention**

customer satisfaction /ˌkʌstəmə ˌsætɪsˈfækʃən/ *noun* the act of making customers pleased with what they have bought

customer segmentation /ˌkʌstə-mə ˌsegmənˈteɪʃ(ə)n/ *noun* the act of dividing a customer base into groups of individuals that have similar characteristics e.g. age, gender, interests, and spending habits and then targeting these groups with more effective campaigns

customer service /ˌkʌstəmə ˈsɜːvɪs/ *noun* a service given to customers once they have made their decision to buy, including delivery, after-sales service, installation, training, etc.

customer service department /ˌkʌstəmə ˈsɜːvɪs dɪˌpɑːtmənt/ *noun* a department which deals with customers and their complaints and orders

customisation /ˌkʌstəmaɪˈzeɪ-ʃ(ə)n/, **customization** *noun* the process of making changes to products or services that enable them to satisfy the particular needs of individual customers

customise /ˈkʌstəmaɪz/, **customize** *verb* to change something to fit the special needs of a customer ○ *We use customised computer terminals.*

customised service /ˌkʌstəmaɪzd ˈsɜːvɪs/ *noun* a service that is specifically designed to satisfy the particular needs of an individual customer

custom publisher /ˈkʌstəm ˌpʌblɪʃə/ *noun* a company which creates a magazine for a company to use as publicity

customs /ˈkʌstəmz/ *plural noun* the government department which organises the collection of taxes on imports, or an office of this department at a port or airport ○ *He was stopped by customs.* ○ *Her car was searched by customs.*
□ **to go through customs** to pass through the area of a port or airport where customs officials examine goods

□ **to take something through customs** to carry something illegal through a customs area without declaring it □ **the crates had to go through a customs examination** the crates had to be examined by customs officials

customs broker /ˈkʌstəmz ˌbrəukə/ *noun* a person or company that takes goods through customs for a shipping company

customs clearance /ˈkʌstəmz ˌklɪərəns/ *noun* **1.** the act of passing goods through customs so that they can enter or leave the country **2.** a document given by customs to a shipper to show that customs duty has been paid and the goods can be shipped ○ *to wait for customs clearance*

customs declaration /ˈkʌstəmz dekləˌreɪʃ(ə)n/ *noun* a statement showing goods being imported on which duty will have to be paid ○ *to fill in a customs declaration form*

customs entry point /ˈkʌstəmz ˈentri pɔɪnt/ *noun* a place at a border between two countries where goods are declared to customs

customs invoice /ˈkʌstəmz ˌɪnvɔɪs/ *noun* a customs form containing a list of goods with their values in both the exporter's and importer's countries

customs seal /ˈkʌstəmz siːl/ *noun* a seal attached by a customs officer to a box, to show that the contents have not passed through customs

customs tariff /ˈkʌstəmz ˌtærɪf/ *noun* a list of taxes to be paid on imported goods

customs warehouse /ˈkʌstəmz ˌweəhaʊs/ *noun* a government-run warehouse where goods are stored until duty is paid ○ *The goods will remain in the customs warehouse until the buyer claims them.*

cut-off /ˈkʌt ɒf/ *noun* the time after which a spot cannot be broadcast, usually late at night

cut-price /ˌkʌt ˈpraɪs/ *adjective* cheaper than usual

cut-price store /ˌkʌt praɪs ˈstɔː/ *noun* a store selling cut-price goods

cut-throat competition /ˌkʌt θrəʊt ˌkɒmpəˈtɪʃ(ə)n/ *noun* sharp competition which cuts prices and offers high discounts

cutting /'kʌtɪŋ/ *noun* a piece cut out of a publication which refers to an item of particular interest

cutting-edge /ˌkʌtɪŋ 'edʒ/ *adjective* using or involving the latest and most advanced techniques and technologies

CV /ˌsiː 'viː/ *abbreviation* curriculum vitae ○ *Please apply in writing, enclosing a current CV.*

cybercrime /'saɪbəkraɪm/ *noun* a crime committed using the Internet ○ ... *the treaty...names four types of cybercrime: confidentiality offenses, notably breaking into computers; fraud and forgery; content violations, such as child pornography and racism; and copyright offenses*

cyber mall /'saɪbə mɑːl/ *noun* a website that provides information and links for a number of online businesses

cybermarketing /'saɪbəˌmɑːkɪtɪŋ/ *noun* marketing that uses any kind of Internet-based promotion, e.g. targeted emails, bulletin boards, websites, or sites from which the customer can download files

cybershopping /'saɪbəʃɒpɪŋ/ *noun* the activity of making purchases using the Internet

cycle /'saɪk(ə)l/ *noun* a set of events which happen in a regularly repeated sequence

cycle models /'saɪk(ə)l ˌmɒd(ə)lz/ *plural noun* models which are used to explain cyclical change ○ *Cycle models were used in the case study to show recent developments in retailing.*

cyclical /'sɪklɪk(ə)l/ *adjective* happening in cycles

cyclical factors /ˌsɪklɪk(ə)l 'fæktəz/ *plural noun* the way in which a trade cycle affects businesses

D

DAGMAR /'dægmɑː/ *noun* a model showing stages in the effect of advertising on a consumer, e.g. awareness, comprehension, conviction, and action. Full form **defining advertising goals for measured advertising results**

DAR *abbreviation* day after recall test

data /'deɪtə/ *noun* information available on computer, e.g. letters or figures ○ *All important data on employees was fed into the computer.* ○ *To calculate the weekly wages, you need data on hours worked and rates of pay.* (NOTE: takes a singular or plural verb) □ **data bank, bank of data** a store of information in a computer

data acquisition /'deɪtə ˌækwɪˈzɪʃ(ə)n/ *noun* the act of gathering information about a subject

database /'deɪtəbeɪs/ *noun* a set of data stored in an organised way in a computer system ○ *We can extract the lists of potential customers from our database.*

database cleaning /'deɪtəbeɪs ˌkliːnɪŋ/, **database cleansing** /'deɪtəbeɪs ˌklenzɪŋ/ *noun* checking the details of a database to make sure they are correct

database management system /ˌdeɪtəbeɪs 'mænɪdʒmənt ˌsɪstəm/ *noun* a computer program that is specially designed to organise and process the information contained in a database

database marketing /'deɪtəbeɪs ˌmɑːkɪtɪŋ/ *noun* using a database to market a product or service by building up a relationship with customers

database modelling /'deɪtəbeɪs ˌmɒdəlɪŋ/ *noun* using the information from a database to create a website or to forecast trends in a market

database publishing /'deɪtəbeɪs ˌpʌblɪʃɪŋ/ *noun* the publishing of information selected from a database, either online where the user pays for it on a per-page inspection basis or as a CD-ROM

data capture /'deɪtə ˌkæptʃə/, **data entry** /ˌdeɪtə 'entri/ *noun* the act of putting information onto a computer by keyboarding or by scanning

data cleansing /'deɪtə ˌklenzɪŋ/, **data cleaning** /'deɪtə ˌkliːnɪŋ/ *noun* checking data to make sure it is correct

data mining /'deɪtə ˌmaɪnɪŋ/ *noun* the use of advanced software to search online databases and identify statistical patterns or relationships in the data that may be commercially useful

'…it used decision-science-based analytical tools and database marketing. This deep data mining has succeeded because Harrah's has simultaneously maintained its focus on satisfying its customers' [*Harvard Business Review*]

data protection /'deɪtə prəˌtekʃən/ *noun* making sure that computerised information about people is not misused

data sheet /'deɪtə ʃiːt/ *noun* a leaflet with data *or* information about a product

data warehouse /'deɪtə ˌweəhaʊs/ *noun* a large collection data that is collected over a period of time from different sources and stored on a computer in a standard format so that is easy to retrieve. It can be used, e.g. to support managerial decision-making. (NOTE: Organisations often use data warehouses for marketing purposes, for example, in order to store and analyse customer information.)

date coding /'deɪt ˌkəʊdɪŋ/ *noun* the act of showing the date by which a product should be consumed

dated /ˈdeɪtɪd/ *adjective* out-of-date ○ *The unions have criticised management for its dated ideas.*

date-in-charge /ˌdeɪt ɪn ˈtʃɑːdʒ/ *noun* the date from which a poster site is charged ○ *We will have three weeks of exposure from the date-in-charge.*

day /deɪ/ *noun* one of the days of the week

day after recall test /ˌdeɪ ˌɑːftə ˈriːkɔːl ˌtest/ *noun* an advertising research test to see how much someone can remember of an advertisement, the day after it appeared or was broadcast. Abbreviation **DAR**

day in the sun /ˌdeɪ ɪn ðə ˈsʌn/ *noun* the period of time during which a product is in demand and sells well in the marketplace (*informal*)

daypart /ˈdeɪpɑːt/ *noun* a section of a day, used for measuring audience ratings on TV

day work /ˈdeɪ wɜːk/ *noun* work done during a day

DBS *abbreviation* direct broadcast by satellite

dead /ded/ *adjective* not working □ **the line went dead** the telephone line suddenly stopped working

dead account /ˌded əˈkaʊnt/ *noun* an account which is no longer used

dead freight /ˌded ˈfreɪt/ *noun* payment by a charterer for unfilled space in a ship or plane ○ *Too much dead freight is making it impossible for the company to continue to charter ships.*

deadline /ˈdedlaɪn/ *noun* the date by which something has to be done □ **to meet a deadline** to finish something in time □ **to miss a deadline** to finish something later than it was planned ○ *We've missed our October 1st deadline.*

dead loss /ˌded ˈlɒs/ *noun* a total loss ○ *The car was written off as a dead loss.*

dead season /ˈded ˌsiːz(ə)n/ *noun* the time of year when there are few tourists about

deadweight /ˈdedweɪt/ *noun* heavy goods, e.g. coal, iron, or sand

deadweight cargo /ˌdedweɪt ˈkɑːgəʊ/ *noun* a heavy cargo which is charged by weight, not by volume

deal /diːl/ *noun* a business agreement, affair or contract ○ *The sales director set up a deal with a Russian bank.* ○ *The deal will be signed tomorrow.* ○ *They did a deal with an American airline.* □ **to call off a deal** to stop an agreement ○ *When the chairman heard about the deal he called it off.* ■ *verb* **1.** □ **to deal with** to organise something ○ *Leave it to the filing clerk – he'll deal with it.* □ **to deal with an order** to work to supply an order **2.** to buy and sell (NOTE: **dealing – dealt**) □ **to deal with someone** to do business with someone □ **to deal in leather** *or* **options** to buy and sell leather or options □ **he deals on the stock exchange** his work involves buying and selling shares on the stock exchange for clients

Deal and Kennedy /ˌdiːl ən ˈkenədi/ *noun* the Deal and Kennedy model of corporate cultures defines four types of organisation based on how quickly feedback and rewards are received and the levels of risk taken. The four types are: tough-guy macho, work hard/play hard, process, and bet-the-company.

dealer /ˈdiːlə/ *noun* a person who buys and sells ○ *a used-car dealer*

dealer aids /ˈdiːlər eɪdz/ *plural noun* types of advertising material used by shops to stimulate sales

dealer's brand /ˈdiːləz brænd/ *noun* a brand owned by a distributor rather by a producer ○ *I bought the dealer's brand of soap since the store is well known for its high quality goods.*

dealership /ˈdiːləʃɪp/ *noun* **1.** the authority to sell some products or services **2.** a business run by an authorised dealer

dealer tie-in /ˌdiːlə ˈtaɪ ˌɪn/ *noun* advertising which includes the names of local dealers that stock the product being advertised

deal in /ˈdiːl ɪn/ *noun* sales promotion to the trade

deal out /ˈdiːl aʊt/ *noun* sales promotion to consumers

dear money /ˈdɪə ˌmʌni/ *noun* money which has to be borrowed at a high interest rate, and so restricts expenditure by companies. Also called **tight money**

deaveraging /diːˈæv(ə)rɪdʒɪŋ/ *noun* the act of treating customers in different ways according to the amount they buy, by rewarding the best and penalising the worst

debit /ˈdebɪt/ *noun* an amount entered in accounts which shows an increase in assets or expenses or a decrease in liabilities, revenue or capital. In accounts, debits are entered in the left-hand column. Compare **credit** ■ *verb* □ **to debit an account** to charge an account with a cost ○ *His account was debited with the sum of £25.*

debitable /ˈdebɪtəb(ə)l/ *adjective* able to be debited

debit card /ˈdebɪt kaːd/ *noun* a plastic card, similar to a credit card, but which debits the holder's account immediately through an EPOS system

debit column /ˈdebɪt ˌkɒləm/ *noun* the left-hand column in accounts showing the money paid or owed to others

debit entry /ˈdebɪt ˌentri/ *noun* an entry on the debit side of an account

debit note /ˈdebɪt nəʊt/ *noun* a note showing that a customer owes money ○ *We undercharged Mr Smith and had to send him a debit note for the extra amount.*

debits and credits /ˌdebɪts ən ˈkredɪts/ *plural noun* money which a company owes and money it receives, or figures which are entered in the accounts to record increases or decreases in assets, expenses, liabilities, revenue or capital

debt /det/ *noun* money owed for goods or services ○ *The company stopped trading with debts of over £1 million.* □ **to be in debt** to owe money □ **he is in debt to the tune of £250,000** he owes £250,000 □ **to get into debt** to start to borrow more money than you can pay back □ **the company is out of debt** the company does not owe money any more □ **to pay back a debt** to pay all the money owed □ **to pay off a debt** to finish paying money owed □ **to service a debt** to pay interest on a debt ○ *The company is having problems in servicing its debts.* □ **debts due** money owed which is due for repayment

debt collection /ˈdet kəˌlekʃən/ *noun* the act of collecting money which is owed

debt collector /ˈdet kəˌlektə/ *noun* a person who collects debts

debtor /ˈdetə/ *noun* a person who owes money

debtor side /ˈdetə saɪd/ *noun* the debit side of an account

decentralise /diːˈsentrəlaɪz/, **decentralize** *verb* to move power or authority or action from a central point to local areas

decentralised system /diːˌsentrəlaɪzd ˈsɪstəm/ *noun* a system where responsibility for marketing, advertising, and promotion lies with a product manager rather than a centralised department

deception /dɪˈsepʃən/ *noun* telling a lie in order to mislead a customer

decide /dɪˈsaɪd/ *verb* to make up your mind to do something ○ *to decide on a course of action* ○ *to decide to appoint a new managing director*

decider /dɪˈsaɪdə/ *noun* a person who makes decisions, especially the person who makes the decision to buy

deciding factor /dɪˌsaɪdɪŋ ˈfæktə/ *noun* the most important factor which influences a decision ○ *A deciding factor in marketing our range of sports goods in the country was the rising standard of living there.*

decision /dɪˈsɪʒ(ə)n/ *noun* a choice made after thinking about what to do ○ *It took the committee some time to come to a decision* or *to reach a decision.*

decision-maker /dɪˈsɪʒ(ə)n ˌmeɪkə/ *noun* a person who takes decisions

decision-making /dɪˈsɪʒ(ə)n ˌmeɪkɪŋ/ *noun* the act of coming to a decision

decision-making unit /dɪˈsɪʒ(ə)n ˌmeɪkɪŋ juːnɪt/ *noun* a group of people who decide on the purchase of a product. For the purchase of a new piece of equipment, they would be the manager, the financial controller, and the operator who will use the equipment. Abbreviation **DMU**

decision theory /dɪˈsɪʒ(ə)n ˌθɪəri/ *noun* the mathematical methods for weighing the various factors in making decisions ○ *In practice it is difficult to apply decision theory to our planning.* ○ *Students study decision theory to help them suggest strategies in case-studies.*

decision tree /dɪˈsɪʒ(ə)n triː/ *noun* a model for decision-making, showing the possible outcomes of different decisions ○ *This business plan incorporates a decision tree.*

deck /dek/ *noun* a flat floor in a ship

deck cargo /ˈdek ˌkɑːɡəʊ/ *noun* the cargo carried on the open top deck of a ship

decline /dɪˈklaɪn/ *noun* **1.** a gradual fall ○ *the decline in the value of the dollar* ○ *a decline in buying power* ○ *The last year has seen a decline in real wages.* **2.** the final stage in the life cycle of a product when the sales and profitability are falling off and the product is no longer worth investing in ■ *verb* to fall slowly or decrease ○ *Shares declined in a weak market.* ○ *New job applications have declined over the last year.* ○ *The economy declined during the last government.*

'Saudi oil production has declined by three quarters to around 2.5m barrels a day' [*Economist*]

'…this gives an average monthly decline of 2.15% during the period' [*Business Times (Lagos)*]

'…share prices disclosed a weak tendency right from the onset of business and declined further, showing losses over a broad front' [*The Hindu*]

decode /diːˈkəʊd/ *verb* to translate and interpret a coded message

deduplication /diːˌdjuːplɪˈkeɪʃ(ə)n/ *noun* removing duplicate entries from a database

deep-rooted demand /ˌdiːp ˌruːtɪd dɪˈmɑːnd/ *noun* brand loyalty which survives even if the product no longer offers value for money ○ *There is deep-rooted demand for this product which is a household name.*

de facto standard /ˌdeɪ ˌfæktəʊ ˈstændəd/ *noun* a standard that is set by a product or service that is very successful in a particular market

defensive spending /dɪˌfensɪv ˈspendɪŋ/ *noun* a budget strategy that promotes areas where sales are currently strong rather than potential areas where sales could be made

defer /dɪˈfɜː/ *verb* to put back to a later date, to postpone ○ *We will have to defer payment until January.* ○ *The decision has been deferred until the next meeting.* (NOTE: **deferring – deferred**)

deferment /dɪˈfɜːmənt/ *noun* the act of leaving until a later date ○ *deferment of payment* ○ *deferment of a decision*

deferred /dɪˈfɜːd/ *adjective* put back to a later date

deferred creditor /dɪˌfɜːdˈkredɪtə/ *noun* a person who is owed money by a bankrupt but who is paid only after all other creditors

deferred payment /dɪˌfɜːd ˈpeɪmənt/ *noun* **1.** money paid later than the agreed date **2.** payment for goods by instalments over a long period

deferred rebate /dɪˌfɜːd ˈriːbeɪt/ *noun* a discount given to a customer who buys up to a specified quantity over a specified period

deferred shares /dɪˌfɜːd ˈʃeəz/, **deferred stock** /dɪˌfɜːd ˈstɒk/ *noun* shares that receive a dividend only after all other dividends have been paid

deficit /ˈdefɪsɪt/ *noun* the amount by which spending is higher than income □ **the accounts show a deficit** the accounts show a loss □ **to make good a deficit** to put money into an account to balance it

deficit financing /ˈdefɪsɪt ˌfaɪnænsɪŋ/ *noun* a type of financial planning by a government in which it borrows money to cover the difference between its tax income and its expenditure

deflate /diːˈfleɪt/ *verb* □ **to deflate the economy** to reduce activity in the economy by cutting the supply of money

deflation /diːˈfleɪʃ(ə)n/ *noun* a general reduction in economic activity as a result of a reduced supply of money and credit, leading to lower prices ○ *The oil crisis resulted in worldwide deflation.* Opposite **inflation**

'…the reluctance of people to spend is one of the main reasons behind 26 consecutive months of price deflation, a key economic ill that has led to price wars, depressed the profit margins of state enterprises and hit incomes among the rural population' [*Financial Times*]

deflationary /diːˈfleɪʃ(ə)n(ə)ri/ *adjective* causing deflation ○ *The government has introduced some deflationary measures in the budget.*

delay /dɪˈleɪ/ *noun* the time when someone or something is later than planned ○ *There was a delay of thirty minutes before the AGM started* or *the AGM started after a thirty-minute delay.* ○ *We are sorry for the delay in supplying your order in replying to your letter.* ■ *verb* to make someone or something late ○ *The company has delayed payment of all invoices.* ○ *She was delayed because her taxi was involved in an accident.*

delayed response /dɪˌleɪd rɪˈspɒns/ *noun* a slower than expected response by consumers to a company's promotion ○ *If there is a delayed response we will only reap the benefits next year.* ○ *A delayed response is not usual in such a new product.*

del credere agent /ˌdel ˈkreɪdəri ˌeɪdʒənt/ *noun* an agent who receives a high commission because he or she guarantees payment by customers

delegation /ˌdelɪˈɡeɪʃ(ə)n/ *noun* **1.** a group of delegates ○ *A Chinese trade delegation is visiting the UK* ○ *The management met a union delegation.* **2.** an act of passing authority or responsibility to someone else

delete /dɪˈliːt/ *verb* to remove a product from a company's product range ○ *We have decided to delete three old products as the new ones are coming on stream.*

deletion /dɪˈliːʃ(ə)n/ *noun* the act of removing an old product from the market ○ *The product has lost market share and is a candidate for deletion.*

delight factor /dɪˈlaɪt ˌfæktə/ *noun* the customer's pleasure at making a purchase

deliver /dɪˈlɪvə/ *verb* to transport goods to a customer □ **goods delivered free** or **free delivered goods** goods transported to the customer's address at a price which includes transport costs □ **goods delivered on board** goods transported free to the ship or plane but not to the customer's warehouse

delivered price /dɪˈlɪvəd praɪs/ *noun* a price which includes packing and transport

delivery /dɪˈlɪv(ə)ri/ *noun* **1.** the transporting of goods to a customer ○ *allow 28 days for delivery* ○ *parcels awaiting delivery* ○ *free delivery delivery free* ○ *a delivery date* ○ *Delivery is not allowed for* or *is not included.* ○ *We have a pallet of parcels awaiting delivery.* □ **to take delivery of goods** to accept goods when they are delivered ○ *We took delivery of the stock into our warehouse on the 25th.* **2.** a consignment of goods being delivered ○ *We take in three deliveries a day.* ○ *There were four items missing in the last delivery.*

delivery note /dɪˈlɪv(ə)ri nəʊt/ *noun* a list of goods being delivered, given to the customer with the goods

delivery of goods /dɪˌlɪv(ə)ri əv ˈɡʊdz/ *noun* the transport of goods to a customer's address

delivery order /dɪˈlɪv(ə)ri ˌɔːdə/ *noun* the instructions given by the customer to the person holding her goods, to tell her where and when to deliver them

delivery receipt /dɪˈlɪv(ə)ri rɪˌsiːt/ *noun* a delivery note when it has been signed by the person receiving the goods

delivery service /dɪˈlɪv(ə)ri ˌsɜːvɪs/ *noun* a transport service organised by a supplier or a shop to take goods to customers

delivery time /dɪˈlɪv(ə)ri taɪm/ *noun* the number of days before something will be delivered

delphi method /ˈdelfaɪ ˌmeθəd/ *noun* a method of forming strategies by soliciting individual estimates on the time-scale of projected developments and then inviting further estimates on the basis of all those already made until a consensus is reached

demand /dɪˈmɑːnd/ *noun* an act of asking for payment □ **payable on demand** which must be paid when payment is asked for ■ *verb* **1.** the need that customers have for a product or their eagerness to buy it ○ *There was an active demand for oil shares on the stock market.* ○ *The factory had to cut* *production when demand slackened.* ○ *The office cleaning company cannot keep up with the demand for its services.* □ **there is not much demand for this item** not many people want to buy it □ **this book is in great demand** *or* **there is a great demand for this book** many people want to buy it □ **to meet** *or* **fill a demand** to supply what is needed ○ *The factory had to increase production to meet the extra demand.* **2.** to ask for something and expect to get it ○ *She demanded a refund.* ○ *The suppliers are demanding immediate payment of their outstanding invoices.* ○ *The shop stewards demanded an urgent meeting with the managing director.*

'…spot prices are now relatively stable in the run-up to the winter's peak demand' [*Economist*]

'…the demand for the company's products remained strong throughout the first six months of the year with production and sales showing significant increases' [*Business Times (Lagos)*]

'…growth in demand is still coming from the private rather than the public sector' [*Lloyd's List*]

demand bill /dɪˈmaːnd bɪl/ *noun* a bill of exchange which must be paid when payment is asked for

demand deposit /dɪˈmaːnd dɪˌpɒzɪt/ *noun US* money in a deposit account which can be taken out when you want it by writing a cheque

demand forecasting /dɪˈmaːnd ˌfɔːkaːstɪŋ/ *noun* estimating what demand would exist at various prices, used as a method of calculating prices

demand-led inflation /dɪˌmaːnd led ɪnˈfleɪʃ(ə)n/, **demand-pull inflation** /dɪˌmaːnd pʊl ɪnˈfleɪʃ(ə)n/ *noun* inflation caused by rising demand which cannot be met

demand price /dɪˈmaːnd praɪs/ *noun* the price at which a quantity of goods will be bought

demand schedule /dɪˈmaːnd ˌʃedʒuːl/ *noun* a table showing demand for a product or service at different prices

demand theory /dɪˈmaːnd ˌθɪəri/ *noun* a branch of economics concerned with consumer buying habits and factors which determine demand

demarketing /diːˈmaːkɪtɪŋ/ *noun* the act of attempting to reduce the demand for a product ○ *Demarketing was the keynote in the industry when rationing was introduced.*

demassifying /ˌdiːˈmæsɪfaɪɪŋ/ *noun* the process of changing a mass medium into one that is customised to fit the needs of individual consumers

demographic /ˌdemə'græfɪk/ *adjective* referring to demography or demographics ○ *A full demographic study of the country must be done before we decide how to export there.*

demographic edition /ˌdemə'græfɪk ɪˌdɪʃ(ə)n/ *noun* a special edition of a magazine targeted at a specific demographic group

demographics /ˌdemə'græfɪks/ *plural noun* the details of the population of a country, in particular its size, density, distribution, and the birth, death, and marriage rates, which affect marketing (NOTE: takes a singular verb)

demographic segmentation /ˌdemə,græfɪk ˌsegmen'teɪʃ(ə)n/ *noun* the act of dividing a market up into segments according to the age, sex, income levels, etc. of the potential customers

demography /dɪˈmɒɡrəfi/ *noun* the study of populations and population statistics such as size, density, distribution, and birth, death, and marriage rates

demonstrate /ˈdemənstreɪt/ *verb* to show how something works ○ *He was demonstrating a new tractor when he was killed.* ○ *The managers saw the new stock-control system being demonstrated.*

demonstration /ˌdemən'streɪʃ(ə)n/ *noun* an act of showing or explaining how something works ○ *We went to a demonstration of new laser equipment.*

demonstration effect /ˌdemən'streɪʃ(ə)n ɪˌfekt/ *noun* the theory stating that people buy products to impress or keep up with their neighbours ○ *The promotion of luxury goods is intended to exploit the demonstration effect.*

demonstration model /ˌdemən'streɪʃ(ə)n ˌmɒd(ə)l/ *noun* a piece of equipment used in demonstrations and later sold off cheaply

demonstrator /ˈdemənstreɪtə/ *noun* **1.** a person who demonstrates pieces of equipment **2.** same as **demonstration model**

demurrage /dɪˈmʌrɪdʒ/ *noun* money paid to a customer when a shipment is delayed at a port or by customs

department /dɪˈpɑːtmənt/ *noun* **1.** a specialised section of a large organisation ○ *Trainee managers work for a while in each department to get an idea of the organisation as a whole.* **2.** a section of a large store selling one type of product ○ *You will find beds in the furniture department.*

departmental manager /ˌdiː-pɑːtment(ə)l ˈmænɪdʒə/ *noun* the manager of a department

departmental system /ˌdiːpɑːt-ˈment(ə)l ˌsɪstəm/ *noun* a way of organising an advertising agency into departments such as creative, media, administration, etc.

Department for Business, Innovation and Skills /dɪˌpɑːtmənt fə ˌbɪznəs ˌɪnəveɪʃ(ə)n ən ˈskɪlz/ *noun* a British government department which deals with areas such as commerce, international trade and the stock exchange. Abbreviation **BIS**

Department for Work and Pensions /dɪˌpɑːtmənt fə ˌwɜːk ən ˈpenʃənz/ *noun* a British government department responsible for services to people of working age, pensioners and families. Abbreviation **DWP**

depend /dɪˈpend/ *verb* **1.** □ **to depend on** to need someone or something to exist ○ *The company depends on efficient service from its suppliers.* ○ *We depend on government grants to pay the salary bill.* **2.** to happen because of something ○ *The success of the launch will depend on the publicity campaign.* □ **depending on** which varies according to something

dependent /dɪˈpendənt/ *adjective* supported financially by someone else ○ *Employees may be granted leave to care for dependent relatives.*

dependent variable /dɪˌpendənt ˈveəriəb(ə)l/ *noun* a variable or factor

which changes as a result of a change in another (the 'independent variable') ○ *We are trying to understand the effects of several independent variables on one dependent variable, in this case, sales.*

deposit /dɪˈpɒzɪt/ *noun* money given in advance so that the thing which you want to buy will not be sold to someone else ○ *to pay a deposit on a watch* ○ *to leave £10 as a deposit*

depot /ˈdepəʊ/ *noun* a central warehouse or storage area for goods, or a place for keeping vehicles used for transport ○ *a goods depot* ○ *an oil storage depot* ○ *a freight depot* ○ *a bus depot*

depreciate /dɪˈpriːʃieɪt/ *verb* **1.** to make an allowance in accounts for the loss of value of an asset over time ○ *We depreciate our company cars over three years.* **2.** to lose value ○ *a share that has depreciated by 10% over the year* ○ *The pound has depreciated by 5% against the dollar.*

COMMENT: Various methods of depreciating assets are used, such as the 'straight line method', where the asset is depreciated at a constant percentage of its cost each year and the 'reducing balance method', where the asset is depreciated at a constant percentage which is applied to the cost of the asset after each of the previous years' depreciation has been deducted.

depreciation /dɪˌpriːʃiˈeɪʃ(ə)n/ *noun* **1.** a reduction in value of an asset **2.** a loss of value ○ *a share that has shown a depreciation of 10% over the year* ○ *the depreciation of the pound against the dollar*

depreciation rate /dɪˌpriːʃiˈeɪʃ(ə)n reɪt/ *noun* the rate at which an asset is depreciated each year in the company accounts

depress /dɪˈpres/ *verb* to reduce something ○ *Reducing the money supply has the effect of depressing demand for consumer goods.*

depressed area /dɪˌprest ˈeəriə/ *noun* a part of a country suffering from depression

depressed market /dɪˌprest ˈmɑːkɪt/ *noun* a market where there are more goods than customers

depression /dɪˈpreʃ(ə)n/ *noun* a period of economic crisis with high unemployment and loss of trade ○ *The* *country entered a period of economic depression.*

depth /depθ/ *noun* the variety in a product line

depth interview /'depθ ˌɪntəvjuː/ *noun* an interview with no preset questions and following no fixed pattern, but which can last a long time and allows the respondent time to express personal views and tastes ○ *Depth interviews elicited some very original points of view.*

deregulation /diːˌregjʊ'leɪʃ(ə)n/ *noun* the reduction of government control over an industry ○ *the deregulation of the airlines*

'...after the slump in receipts last year that followed liner shipping deregulation in the US, carriers are probably still losing money on their transatlantic services. But with a possible contraction in capacity and healthy trade growth, this year has begun in a much more promising fashion than last' [*Lloyd's List*]

derived demand /dɪˌraɪvd dɪ'maːnd/ *noun* a demand for a product because it is needed to produce another product which is in demand

describe /dɪ'skraɪb/ *verb* to say what someone or something is like ○ *The leaflet describes the services the company can offer.* ○ *The managing director described the difficulties the company was having with cash flow.*

description /dɪ'skrɪpʃən/ *noun* a detailed account of what something is like □ **false description of contents** the act of wrongly stating the contents of a packet to trick customers into buying it

design /dɪ'zaɪn/ *noun* **1.** the planning or drawing of a product before it is built or manufactured **2.** the planning of the visual aspect of an advertisement ■ *verb* to plan or to draw something before it is built or manufactured ○ *He designed a new car factory.* ○ *She designs garden furniture.*

designate /'dezɪgneɪt/ *verb* to identify something or someone in a particular way

designated market area /ˌdezɪgneɪtɪd 'maːkɪt ˌeəriə/ *noun* geographical areas used in measuring the size of an audience. Abbreviation **DMA**

design audit /dɪ'zaɪn ˌɔːdɪt/ *noun* the checking and evaluating of design,

especially in advertising materials or on a website

design consultancy /dɪ'zaɪn kənˌsʌltənsi/ *noun* a firm which gives specialist advice on design

design department /dɪ'zaɪn dɪˌpaːtmənt/ *noun* the department in a large company which designs the company's products or its advertising

designer /dɪ'zaɪnə/ *noun* a person who designs ○ *She is the designer of the new packaging.* ■ *adjective* expensive and fashionable ○ *designer jeans*

designer product /dɪˌzaɪnə 'prɒdʌkt/ *noun* a fashionable product created by a well-known designer ○ *Recent wealth in the cities has increased the demand for designer products.* ○ *Jeans and sportswear are only some of our designer products.*

design factor /dɪ'zaɪn ˌfæktə/ *noun* the ratio of sampling error of a complex sample or sample design to that of a completely random sample

design for manufacturability /dɪˌzaɪn fə ˌmænjʊfæktʃərə'bɪlɪti/ *noun* the process of adapting the design of a product so that it fits as well as possible into the manufacturing system of an organisation, thus reducing the problems of bringing the product to market (NOTE: The manufacturing issues that need to be taken into account in design for manufacturability include selecting appropriate materials, making the product easy to assemble, and minimising the number of machine set-ups required.)

design protection /dɪ'zaɪn prəˌtekʃən/ *noun* making sure that a design is not copied by an unauthorised user

design studio /dɪ'zaɪn ˌstjuːdiəʊ/ *noun* an independent firm which specialises in creating designs

desire /dɪ'zaɪə/ *noun* the wish to do something

desire to purchase /dɪˌzaɪə tə 'pɜːtʃɪs/ *noun* the feeling of a customer that he or she needs to purchase a product. ⇨ **AIDA**

desk /desk/ *noun* a writing table in an office, usually with drawers for stationery ○ *a desk diary* ○ *a desk drawer* ○ *a desk lamp*

desk research /'desk rɪˌsɜːtʃ/ *noun* the process of looking for information which is in printed sources such as directories

desk researcher /'desk rɪˌsɜːtʃə/ *noun* a person who carries out desk research

devaluation /ˌdiːvæljuˈeɪʃ(ə)n/ *noun* a reduction in the value of a currency against other currencies ○ *the devaluation of the rand*

devalue /diːˈvæljuː/ *verb* to reduce the value of a currency against other currencies ○ *The pound has been devalued by 7%.*

develop /dɪˈveləp/ *verb* **1.** to plan and produce ○ *to develop a new product* **2.** to plan and build an area ○ *to develop an industrial estate*

developed country /dɪˌveləpt ˈkʌntri/ *noun* a country which has an advanced manufacturing system

'…developed countries would gain $135 billion a year and developing countries, such as the former centrally planned economies of Eastern Europe, would gain $85 billion a year. The study also notes that the poorest countries would lose an annual $7 billion' [*Times*]

developing country /dɪˌveləpɪŋ ˈkʌntri/, **developing nation** /dɪˌveləpɪŋ ˈneɪʃ(ə)n/ *noun* a country which is not fully industrialised

development /dɪˈveləpmənt/ *noun* the work of planning the production of a new product and constructing the first prototypes ○ *We spend a great deal on research and development.*

development cycle /dɪˈveləpmənt ˌsaɪk(ə)l/ *noun* the various stages which are involved in the development of a product from the initial concept to its manufacture and marketing

deviation /ˌdiːviˈeɪʃ(ə)n/ *noun* a change of route or strategy ○ *Advertising in the tabloids will mean a deviation from our normal marketing strategy.*

diadic test /daɪˌædɪk ˈtest/ *noun* a product test in which respondents compare two products

diagram /'daɪəgræm/ *noun* a drawing which presents information visually ○ *a diagram showing sales locations* ○ *a diagram of the company's organisational structure* ○ *The first diagram shows how our decision-making processes work.*

diagrammatic /ˌdaɪəgrəˈmætɪk/ *adjective* □ **in diagrammatic form** in the form of a diagram

diagrammatically /ˌdaɪəgrəˈmætɪkli/ *adverb* using a diagram ○ *The chart shows the sales pattern diagrammatically.*

dial /'daɪəl/ *verb* to call a telephone number on a telephone ○ *to dial a number* ○ *to dial the operator* (NOTE: **dialling – dialled**. The US spelling is **dialing – dialed**.)

dial-and-smile /ˌdaɪəl ən ˈsmaɪl/ *verb* to try to appear pleasant when cold-calling potential customers

diarise /'daɪəraɪz/, **diarize** *verb* to enter a date you have to remember in a diary

diary /'daɪəri/ *noun* a book in which you can write notes or appointments for each day of the week ○ *She checked her engagements in her desk diary.*

diary method /'daɪəri ˌmeθəd/ *noun* a market research method whereby respondents keep a regular written account of advertising noticed or purchases made or products used

diary panel /'daɪəri ˌpæn(ə)l/ *noun* a group of people who are asked to keep notes of their purchases on a daily basis

dichotomous question /daɪˌkɒtəməs ˈkwestʃən/ *noun* a question in a questionnaire that can only be answered by 'yes' or 'no'

differential /ˌdɪfəˈrenʃəl/ *adjective* showing a difference ■ *noun* □ **to erode wage differentials** to reduce differences in salary gradually

differential advantage /ˌdɪfərenʃəl ədˈvɑːntɪdʒ/ *noun* an advantage that one product has over rival products in the market ○ *We are confident that our toothpaste has a differential advantage.*

differential pricing /ˌdɪfərenʃəl ˈpraɪsɪŋ/ *noun* the act of giving different products in a range of different prices so as to distinguish them from each other

differential tariffs /ˌdɪfərenʃəl ˈtærɪfs/ *plural noun* different tariffs for different classes of goods as, e.g., when imports from some countries are taxed more heavily than similar imports from other countries

differentiated marketing strategy /ˌdɪfəˌrenʃieɪtɪd ˈmɑːkɪtɪŋ ˌstrætɪdʒi/ *noun* a method of marketing where the product is modified to suit each potential market. ⇨ **concentrated marketingun, differentiated product**

differentiation /ˌdɪfərenʃiˈeɪʃ(ə)n/ *noun* the act of ensuring that a product has some unique features that distinguish it from competing products ○ *We are adding some extra features to our watches in the interest of product differentiation.* ○ *The aim of differentiation should be to catch the customer's eye.*

diffusion /dɪˈfjuːʒ(ə)n/ *noun* the process by which a product is gradually adopted by consumers

diffusion curve /dɪˈfjuːʒ(ə)n kɜːv/ *noun* the geographical representation of how many consumers adopt a product at different times. ⇨ **exponential diffusion**

digerati /ˌdɪdʒəˈrɑːti/ *plural noun* people who claim to have a sophisticated understanding of Internet or computer technology (*slang*)

digital /ˈdɪdʒɪt(ə)l/ *adjective* converted into a form that can be processed by computers and accurately reproduced

digital cash /ˌdɪdʒɪt(ə)l ˈkæʃ/ *noun* a form of digital money that can be used like physical cash to make online purchases and is anonymous because there is no way of obtaining information about the buyer when it is used

digital colour proof /ˌdɪdʒɪt(ə)l ˌkʌlə ˈpruːf/ *noun* a colour proof taken from digital files prior to film output at high or low resolution

digital economy /ˌdɪdʒɪt(ə)l ɪˈkɒnəmi/ *noun* an economy that is based on electronic commerce, e.g., trade on the Internet

digital goods /ˌdɪdʒɪt(ə)l ˈɡʊdz/ *plural noun* goods that are sold and delivered electronically, usually over the Internet

digital marketing /ˌdɪdʒɪt(ə)l ˈmɑːkɪtɪŋ/ *noun* the use of digital technology e.g. the Internet, email, mobile phones, interactive TV, and wireless media to promote brands and develop and distribute products and services

digital money /ˌdɪdʒɪt(ə)l ˈmʌni/ *noun* a series of numbers that has a value equivalent to a sum of money in a physical currency

digital nervous system /ˌdɪdʒɪt(ə)l ˈnɜːvəs ˌsɪstəm/ *noun* a digital information system that gathers, manages, and distributes knowledge in a way that allows an organisation to respond quickly and effectively to events in the outside world

digital TV /ˌdɪdʒɪt(ə)l tiːˈviː/ *noun* TV where the picture has been changed into a form which a computer can process

digital wallet /ˌdɪdʒɪt(ə)l ˈwɒlɪt/ *noun* a piece of personalised software on the hard drive of a user's computer that contains, in coded form, such items as credit card information, digital cash, a digital identity certificate, and standardised shipping information, and can be used when paying for a transaction electronically. Also called **e-purse, electronic purse**

digitisable /ˈdɪdʒɪtɪzəb(ə)l/ *adjective* able to be converted into digital form for distribution via the Internet or other networks

Dinkies /ˈdɪŋkiz/ *plural noun* couples who are both wage-earners and have no children (NOTE: short for **Double Income No Kids**)

direct /daɪˈrekt/ *verb* to manage or organise something ○ *He directs our South-East Asian operations.* ○ *She was directing the development unit until last year.* ■ *adjective* straight or without interference ■ *adverb* with no third party involved ○ *We pay income tax direct to the government.*

direct-action advertising /daɪˌrekt ˌækʃən ˈædvətaɪzɪŋ/ *noun* advertising which aims to get a quick response ○ *We'll need some direct-action advertising if we're not to fall behind our competitors this spring.* ○ *Directaction advertising will only help us in the short term.*

direct-action marketing /daɪˌrekt ˌækʃən ˈmɑːkɪtɪŋ/ *noun* same as **direct response advertising**

direct broadcast by satellite /daɪˌrekt ˌbrɔːdkɑːst baɪ ˈsætəlaɪt/ *noun* TV and radio signals broadcast over a wide area from an earth station via a satellite, received with a dish aerial. Abbreviation **DBS**

direct channel /daɪˌrekt ˈtʃæn(ə)l/ *noun* a marketing channel where a producer and consumer deal directly with one another

direct close /daɪˌrekt ˈkləʊz/ *noun* the act of ending a sale by asking the customer if they want to buy

direct demand /daɪˌrekt dɪˈmɑːnd/ *noun* demand for a product or service for its own sake, and not for what can be derived from it

direct export /daɪˌrekt ˈekspɔːt/ *noun* selling a product direct to the overseas customer without going through a middleman ○ *Direct export is the only way to keep down the retail price.* ○ *Our overseas marketing consists mainly of direct export to German department stores.*

direct headline /daɪˌrekt ˈhedlaɪn/ *noun* an eye-catching headline that presents its message directly to its target audience

direction /daɪˈrekʃən/ *noun* **1.** the process of organising or managing ○ *He took over the direction of a multinational group.* **2.** □ **directions for use** instructions showing how to use something

directional /daɪˈrekʃən(ə)l/ *adjective* pointing in a specific direction

directional medium /daɪˌrekʃən(ə)l ˈmiːdiəm/ *noun* an advertising medium that tells potential customers where to find products or services, e.g. a directory

directive interview /daɪˈrektɪv ˈɪntəvjuː/ *noun* an interview using preset questions and following a fixed pattern

direct labour /daɪˌrekt ˈleɪbə/ *noun* the cost of the workers employed which can be allocated to a product, not including materials or overheads

directly /daɪˈrektli/ *adverb* with no third party involved ○ *We deal directly with the manufacturer, without using a wholesaler.*

direct mail /daɪˌrekt ˈmeɪl/ *noun* the practice of selling a product by sending publicity material to possible buyers through the post ○ *These calculators are only sold by direct mail.* ○ *The company runs a successful direct-mail operation.*

'…all of those who had used direct marketing techniques had used direct mail, 79% had used some kind of telephone technique and 63% had tried off-the-page selling' [*Precision marketing*]

direct-mail advertising /daɪˌrekt ˈmeɪl ˌædvətaɪzɪŋ/ *noun* advertising by sending leaflets to people through the post

direct mailing /daɪˌrekt ˈmeɪlɪŋ/ *noun* the sending of publicity material by post to possible buyers

direct mail preference scheme /daɪˌrekt meɪl ˈpref(ə)rəns skiːm/ *noun* a scheme where an addressee can have his or her name removed from a mailing list

direct marketing /daɪˌrekt ˈmɑːkɪtɪŋ/ *noun* same as **direct response advertising**

'…after five years of explosive growth, fuelled by the boom in financial services, the direct marketing world is becoming a lot more competitive' [*Marketing Workshop*]

'…direct marketing is all about targeting the audience, individualising the message and getting a response' [*PR Week*]

direct-marketing media /daɪˌrekt ˈmɑːkɪtɪŋ ˌmiːdiə/ *plural noun* media that are used for direct marketing, e.g. direct mail, telemarketing, and TV

director /daɪˈrektə/ *noun* **1.** a senior employee appointed by the shareholders to help run a company, who is usually in charge of one or other of its main functions, e.g. sales or human relations, and usually, but not always, a member of the board of directors **2.** the person who is in charge of a project, an official institute, or other organisation ○ *the director of the government research institute* ○ *She was appointed director of the trade association.*

'…the research director will manage and direct a team of business analysts reporting on the latest developments in retail distribution throughout the UK' [*Times*]

directorate /daɪˈrekt(ə)rət/ *noun* a group of directors

directorship /daɪˈrektəʃɪp/ *noun* the post of director ○ *She was offered a directorship with Smith Ltd.*

directors' report /daɪˈrektəz rɪˌpɔːt/ *noun* the annual report from the board of directors to the shareholders

directory /daɪˈrekt(ə)ri/ *noun* a reference book containing information on companies and their products

direct response /daɪˌrekt rɪˈspɒns/ a form of advertising designed to solicit a direct response from the consumer which is specific and quantifiable

direct response advertising /daɪˌrekt rɪˈspɒns ˌædvətaɪzɪŋ/ *noun* advertising in such a way as to get customers to send in inquiries or orders directly by mail

direct response agency /daɪˌrekt rɪˈspɒns ˌeɪdʒənsi/ *noun* a company which provides direct marketing services to its clients such as database management, direct mail, and response collecting

direct response marketing /daɪˌrekt rɪˈspɒns ˌmɑːkɪtɪŋ/ *noun* same as **direct response advertising**

direct selling /daɪˌrekt ˈselɪŋ/ *noun* the work of selling a product direct to the customer without going through a shop

direct services /daɪˌrekt ˈsɜːvɪsɪz/ *plural noun* personal services to the public, e.g. catering, dentistry, or hairdressing ○ *There is little manufacturing industry in the area, and direct services account for most of the wealth.*

dirty /ˈdɜːti/ *adjective* not clean

dirty bill of lading /ˌdɜːti bɪl əv ˈleɪdɪŋ/ *noun* a bill of lading stating that the goods did not arrive on board in good condition. Also called **foul bill of lading**

disclosure of information /dɪsˌkləʊʒər əv ˌɪnfəˈmeɪʃ(ə)n/ *noun* the passing on of information that was intended to be kept secret or private to someone else

discount *noun*/ˈdɪskaʊnt/ **1.** the percentage by which the seller reduces the full price for the buyer ○ *to give a discount on bulk purchases* □ **to sell goods at a discount** *or* **at a discount price**

to sell goods below the normal price □ **10% discount for cash, 10% cash discount** you pay 10% less if you pay in cash **2.** the amount by which something is sold for less than its value ■ *verb*/dɪsˈkaʊnt/ **1.** □ **to discount bills of exchange** to buy or sell bills of exchange for less than the value written on them in order to cash them later **2.** to react to something which may happen in the future, such as a possible takeover bid or currency devaluation □ **shares are discounting a rise in the dollar** shares have risen in advance of a rise in the dollar price

discountable /ˈdɪskaʊntəb(ə)l/ *adjective* possible to discount ○ *These bills are not discountable.*

discounted value /ˌdɪskaʊntɪd ˈvæljuː/ *noun* the difference between the face value of a share and its lower market price

discounter /ˈdɪskaʊntə/ *noun* a person or company that discounts bills or invoices, or sells goods at a discount

discount for cash /ˌdɪskaʊnt fə ˈkæʃ/ *noun* same as **cash discount**

discount house /ˈdɪskaʊnt haʊs/ *noun* **1.** a financial company which specialises in discounting bills **2.** a shop which specialises in selling cheap goods bought at a high discount

discount price /ˈdɪskaʊnt praɪs/ *noun* the full price less a discount

discount rate /ˈdɪskaʊnt reɪt/ *noun* the rate charged by a central bank on any loans it makes to other banks

discount store /ˈdɪskaʊnt stɔː/ *noun* a shop which specialises in cheap goods bought at a high discount

discount table /ˈdɪskaʊnt ˌteɪb(ə)l/ *noun* same as **table of discounts**

discrepancy /dɪˈskrepənsi/ *noun* a lack of agreement between figures in invoices or accounts

discretion /dɪˈskreʃ(ə)n/ *noun* the ability to decide what should be done □ **I leave it to your discretion** I leave it for you to decide what to do □ **at the discretion of someone** according to what someone decides ○ *Membership is at the discretion of the committee.*

discretionary /dɪ'skreʃ(ə)n(ə)ri/ *adjective* possible if someone wants □ **the governor's discretionary powers** powers which the governor could use if he or she thought it necessary

discretionary income /dɪˌskreʃ(ə)n(ə)ri 'ɪnkʌm/ *noun* income left after fixed payments have been made and whose spending is therefore subject to advertising influence ○ *Discretionary incomes generally increase in a recession.*

discrimination test /dɪˌskrɪmɪ-'neɪʃ(ə)n test/ *noun* a product test designed to show how one product differs from another ○ *The discrimination test showed our product to be superior to that of our closest competitor.*

discussion board /dɪ'skʌʃ(ə)n bɔːd/, **discussion group** /dɪ'skʌʃ-(ə)n gruːp/ *noun* a group of people who discuss something by sending emails to the group and where each member can respond and see the responses of other members

discussion list /dɪ'skʌʃ(ə)n lɪst/ *noun* a list of addresses of members of a discussion board

diseconomies of scale /dɪs-ɪˌkɒnəmiz əv 'skeɪl/ *plural noun* a situation where increased production leads to a higher production cost per unit or average production cost

disequilibrium /ˌdɪsiːkwɪ'lɪbriəm/ *noun* an imbalance in the economy when supply does not equal demand

dishoarding /dɪs'hɔːdɪŋ/ *noun* putting goods back onto the market when they have been hoarded or stored for some time

dishonour /dɪs'ɒnə/ *verb* □ **to dishonour a bill** not to pay a bill (NOTE: The US spelling is **dishonor**.)

dishonoured cheque /dɪsˌɒnəd 'tʃek/ *noun* a cheque which the bank will not pay because there is not enough money in the account to pay it

disintegration /dɪsˌɪntɪ'greɪʃ(ə)n/ *noun* the decision to stop producing some goods or supplies and to buy them in instead ○ *Disintegration has meant we now have to buy all of our plastic parts.* ○ *Part of the company's disintegration policy involved selling off the factories.*

disintermediation /dɪsˌɪntəmiːdi-'eɪʃ(ə)n/ *noun* the removal of any intermediaries from a process so that, e.g., manufacturers sell direct to consumers instead of selling their products through wholesalers and retailers

dismiss /dɪs'mɪs/ *verb* to refuse to accept ○ *The court dismissed the claim.*

disparage /dɪ'spærɪdʒ/ *verb* to criticise

disparaging copy /dɪˌspærɪdʒɪŋ 'kɒpi/ *noun* advertising copy which is critical of another company's products ○ *Their disparaging copy has given them a bad name in the industry.* Also called **knocking copy**

dispatch /dɪ'spætʃ/ *noun* **1.** the sending of goods to a customer ○ *Production difficulties held up dispatch for several weeks.* **2.** goods which have been sent ○ *The weekly dispatch went off yesterday.* ■ *verb* to send goods to customers ○ *The goods were dispatched last Friday.*

dispatch department /dɪ'spætʃ dɪˌpɑːtmənt/ *noun* the department which deals with the packing and sending of goods to customers

dispatcher /dɪ'spætʃə/ *noun* a person who sends goods to customers

dispatch note /dɪ'spætʃ nəʊt/ *noun* a note saying that goods have been sent

dispatch rider /dɪ'spætʃ ˌraɪdə/ *noun* a motorcyclist who delivers messages or parcels in a town

dispenser /dɪ'spensə/ *noun* a machine which automatically provides something such as an object, a drink, or an item of food, often when money is put in ○ *an automatic dispenser* ○ *a towel dispenser*

dispersion /dɪ'spɜːʃ(ə)n/ *noun* the attempt by a distributor to distribute a product to a market

display /dɪ'spleɪ/ *noun* the showing of goods for sale ○ *an attractive display of kitchen equipment* ○ *The shop has several car models on display.* ■ *verb* to show ○ *The company was displaying three new car models at the show.*

display advertisement /dɪˈspleɪ ədˌvɜːtɪsmənt/, **display ad** /dɪˈspleɪ æd/ *noun* an advertisement which is well designed or printed in bold type to attract attention

display advertising /dɪˈspleɪ ˌædvətaɪzɪŋ/ *noun* advertising that has individual features such as photographs, its own box border, or the company logo in addition to text

display material /dɪˈspleɪ məˌtɪəriəl/ *noun* material used to attract attention to goods which are for sale, e.g. posters and photographs

display outer /dɪˈspleɪ ˌaʊtə/ *noun* a container for protecting goods in transit which can also be used as an attractive display container for the goods in a shop

display panel /dɪˈspleɪ ˌpæn(ə)l/ *noun* a flat area for displaying goods in a shop window

disposable /dɪˈspəʊzəb(ə)l/ *adjective* which can be used and then thrown away ○ *The machine serves soup in disposable paper cups.*

disposable income /dɪˌspəʊzəb(ə)l ˈɪnkʌm/, **disposable personal income** /dɪˌspəʊzəb(ə)l ˌpɜːs(ə)nəl ˈɪnkʌm/ *noun* the income left after tax and national insurance have been deducted

disposal /dɪˈspəʊz(ə)l/ *noun* a sale ○ *a disposal of securities* ○ *The company has started a systematic disposal of its property portfolio.* □ **lease** *or* **business for disposal** a lease or business for sale

dispose /dɪˈspəʊz/ *verb* □ **to dispose of** to get rid of or to sell, especially cheaply ○ *He is planning to dispose of excess stock* ○ *He is planning to dispose of his business in the new year.*

disrewarding /ˌdɪsrɪˈwɔːdɪŋ/ *noun* the penalising of bad customers to allow the company to give special terms to the best customers

dissonance/attribution model /ˌdɪsənəns ˌætrɪˈbjuːʃ(ə)n ˌmɒd(ə)l/ *noun* a response model which follows the opposite sequence from normal:

consumers first act in a specific way, then develop feelings as a result of their behaviour, and then look for information that supports their attitude and behaviour

dissonance reduction /ˈdɪsənəns rɪˌdʌkʃən/ *noun* a reduction in worries experienced by the purchaser after a product has been purchased, by increasing their awareness of the positive features of the product and reducing their fears about its negative features. ⇨ **cognitive dissonance**

distance freight /ˈdɪstəns freɪt/ *noun* freight charges based on the distance over which the goods are transported

distinctive competence /dɪˌstɪŋktɪv ˈkɒmpɪt(ə)ns/ *noun* an advantage that one company or producer has over competitors in the market ○ *Our distinctive competence is a highly professional sales force.* ○ *The company could not survive with high costs and no distinctive competence.*

distress merchandise /dɪˈstres ˌmɜːtʃəndaɪs/ *noun* US goods sold cheaply to pay a company's debts

distress sale /dɪˈstres seɪl/ *noun* a sale of goods at low prices to pay a company's debts

distress selling /dɪˈstres ˌselɪŋ/ *noun* the sale of goods cheaply in order to pay off debts ○ *Difficult circumstances forced the producers to resort to distress selling.*

distribute /dɪˈstrɪbjuːt/ *verb* **1.** to share out dividends ○ *Profits were distributed among the shareholders.* **2.** to send out goods from a manufacturer's warehouse to retail shops ○ *Smith Ltd distributes for several smaller companies.* ○ *All orders are distributed from our warehouse near Oxford.*

distribution /ˌdɪstrɪˈbjuːʃ(ə)n/ *noun* **1.** the act of sending goods from the manufacturer to the wholesaler and then to retailers ○ *Stock is held in a distribution centre which deals with all order processing.* ○ *Distribution costs have risen sharply over the last 18 months.* ○ *She has several years' experience as distribution manager.* **2.** the act of sharing something among several people

'British distribution companies are poised to capture a major share of the European market' [*Management News*]

distribution census /ˌdɪstrɪˈbjuː-ʃ(ə)n ˌsensəs/ *noun* official statistics regarding the number of distributors and their businesses ○ *Using the distribution census, we drew up a list of wholesalers who were worth approaching.*

distribution centre /ˌdɪstrɪˈbjuː-ʃ(ə)n ˌsentə/ *noun* a place where goods are collected and stored temporarily but whose main function is to send them on to wholesalers, retailers, or consumers

distribution channel /ˌdɪstrɪˈbjuː-ʃ(ə)n ˌtʃæn(ə)l/ *noun* the route by which a product or service reaches a customer after it leaves the producer or supplier (NOTE: A distribution channel usually consists of a chain of intermediaries, for example **wholesalers** and **retailers**, that is designed to move goods from the point of production to the point of consumption in the most efficient way.)

'...there is evidence that distribution channels are supply driven' [*Quarterly Review of Marketing*]

distribution management /ˌdɪs-trɪˈbjuːʃ(ə)n ˌmænɪdʒmənt/ *noun* the management of the efficient transfer of goods from the place where they are manufactured to the place where they are sold or used (NOTE: Distribution management involves such activities as **warehousing, materials handling**, packaging, and **stock control**, order processing, and transport.)

distribution network /ˌdɪstrɪ-ˈbjuːʃ(ə)n ˌnetwɜːk/ *noun* a series of points or small warehouses from which goods are sent all over a country

distribution resource planning /dɪstrɪˌbjuːʃ(ə)n rɪˈsɔːs ˌplænɪŋ/ *noun* planning, especially using a computerised system, that is intended to ensure the most efficient use of the resources used in distributing goods (NOTE: Effective distribution resource planning integrates distribution with manufacturing and synchronises supply and demand by identifying requirements for finished goods and by producing schedules for the movement

of goods along the distribution chain so that they reach the customer as soon as possible.)

distributive /dɪˈstrɪbjʊtɪv/ *adjective* referring to distribution

distributive trades /dɪˈstrɪbjʊtɪv ˌtreɪdz/ *plural noun* all businesses involved in the distribution of goods

distributor /dɪˈstrɪbjʊtə/ *noun* a company which sells goods for another company which makes them □ **a network of distributors** a number of distributors spread all over a country

distributor's brand /dɪˈstrɪbjʊtəz ˌbrænd/ *noun* goods specially packed for a store with the store's name printed on them ○ *I bought the distributor's brand of soap because it was the cheapest.*

distributorship /dɪˈstrɪbjʊtəʃɪp/ *noun* the position of being a distributor for a company

distributor support /dɪˌstrɪbjʊtə səˈpɔːt/ *noun* the action of a supplier of a product or service in providing help to distributors, by offering training, promotional material, etc.

divergent marketing /daɪˌvɜːd-ʒənt ˈmaːkɪtɪŋ/ *noun* a separate marketing treatment for each of a company's products ○ *Divergent marketing is giving way to a more co-ordinated and integrated marketing effort.*

diversification /daɪˌvɜːsɪfɪˈkeɪ-ʃ(ə)n/ *noun* the process in which a company begins to engage in a new and different type of business

diversify /daɪˈvɜːsɪfaɪ/ *verb* **1.** to add new types of business to existing ones ○ *The company is planning to diversify into new products.* **2.** to invest in different types of shares or savings so as to spread the risk of loss

divert /daɪˈvɜːt/ *verb* **1.** to send to another place or in another direction **2.** to buy stock in a special offer and then sell it on to customers living outside the special-offer area

divestment /daɪˈvestmənt/ *noun* the dropping or sale of a whole product line, to allow the company to concentrate on other products

division /dɪˈvɪʒ(ə)n/ *noun* **1.** the main section of a large company

○ *the marketing division* ○ *the production division* ○ *the retail division* ○ *the hotel division of the leisure group* **2.** a company which is part of a large group ○ *Smith's is now a division of the Brown group of companies.* **3.** the act of separating a whole into parts ○ *the division of responsibility between managers*

divisional /dɪ'vɪʒ(ə)n(ə)l/ *adjective* relating to a division ○ *a divisional director* ○ *the divisional headquarters*

DM *abbreviation* direct marketing

DMA /ˌdiː em 'eɪ/ *abbreviation* designated market area

DMU *abbreviation* decision-making unit

document /'dɒkjʊmənt/ *noun* a paper, especially an official paper, with written information on it ○ *He left a file of documents in the taxi.* ○ *She asked to see the documents relating to the case.*

documentary /ˌdɒkjʊ'ment(ə)ri/ *adjective* in the form of documents ○ *documentary evidence* ■ *noun* a film concerning actual facts or real events

documentation /ˌdɒkjʊmen'teɪʃ(ə)n/ ■ *noun* all the documents referring to something ○ *Please send me the complete documentation concerning the sale.*

document of title /ˌdɒkjʊmənt əv 'taɪt(ə)l/ *noun* a document allowing the holder to handle goods as if they own them

documents against acceptance /ˌdɒkjʊmənts əˌgenst ək'septəns/ *noun* an arrangement whereby buyers receive documents for the goods on their acceptance of a bill of exchange

documents against cash /ˌdɒkjʊmənts əˌgenst 'kæʃ/, **documents against presentation** /ˌdɒkjʊmənts əˌgenst prez(ə)n'teɪʃ(ə)n/ *noun* an arrangement whereby a buyer receives documents for the goods on payment of a bill of exchange

dog /dɒg/ *noun* a product that has a low market share and a low growth rate, and so is likely to be dropped from the company's product line

dog-eat-dog /ˌdɒg iːt 'dɒg/ *noun* marketing activity where everyone fights for their own product and attacks competitors mercilessly (*informal*)

do-it-yourself /ˌduː ɪt jə'self/ *adjective* done by an ordinary person, not by a skilled worker. Abbreviation **DIY**

do-it-yourself magazine /ˌduː ɪt jə'self ˌmægəziːn/ *noun* a magazine with articles on work which the average person can do to repair or paint his or her house

domestic /də'mestɪk/ *adjective* **1.** referring to the home market or the market of the country where the business is situated ○ *Domestic sales have increased over the last six months.* **2.** for use in the home ○ *Glue which is intended for both domestic and industrial use.*

domestic appliances /dəˌmestɪk ə'plaɪənsɪz/ *plural noun* electrical machines which are used in the home, e.g. washing machines

domestic consumption /dəˌmestɪk kən'sʌmpʃən/ *noun* use in the home country ○ *Domestic consumption of oil has fallen sharply.*

domestic market /dəˌmestɪk 'mɑːkɪt/ *noun* the market in the country where a company is based ○ *They produce goods for the domestic market.*

domestic production /dəˌmestɪk prə'dʌkʃən/ *noun* the production of goods for use in the home country

door drop /'dɔː drɒp/ *noun* a delivery of promotional literature by hand to all the houses in an area

door-to-door /ˌdɔː tə 'dɔː/ *adjective* going from one house to the next, asking the occupiers to buy something or to vote for someone ○ *door-to-door canvassing* ○ *We have 200 door-to-door salesmen.* ○ *Door-to-door selling is banned in this part of the village.*

door-to-door salesman /ˌdɔː tə dɔː 'seɪlzmən/ *noun* a man who goes from one house to the next, asking people to buy something

door-to-door service /ˌdɔː tə dɔː 'sɜːvɪs/ *noun* a transportation service that takes goods directly to the buyer's address

dormant /'dɔːmənt/ *adjective* no longer active or no longer operating

dormant account /ˌdɔːmənt ə'kaʊnt/ *noun* a bank account which is no longer used

dot.com /ˌdɒt ˈkɒm/, **dot-com** /ˌdɒt ˈkɒm/ *noun* a business that markets its products through the Internet, rather than by using traditional marketing channels

double /ˈdʌb(ə)l/ *adjective* twice as large or two times the size ○ *Their turnover is double ours.* □ **to be on double time** to earn twice the usual wages for working on Sundays or other holidays □ **in double figures** with two figures, from 10 to 99 ○ *Inflation is in double figures.* ○ *We have had double-figure inflation for some years.* ■ *verb* to become twice as big, or make something twice as big ○ *We have doubled our profits this year* or *our profits have doubled this year.* ○ *The company's borrowings have doubled.*

double column /ˌdʌb(ə)l ˈkɒləm/ *noun* two columns spanned by an advertisement

double crown /ˌdʌb(ə)l ˈkraʊn/ *noun* a basic poster size, 30 inches deep by 20 inches wide

double-decker /ˌdʌb(ə)l ˈdekə/ *noun* two advertising panels, one on top of the other

double-digit /ˌdʌb(ə)l ˈdɪdʒɪt/ *adjective* more than 10 and less than 100 ○ *double-digit inflation*

double opt-in /ˌdʌb(ə)l ˈɒpt ˌɪn/ *noun* a method by which users who want to receive information or services from a website can register themselves as subscribers

double-page spread /ˌdʌb(ə)l peɪdʒ ˈspred/ *noun* two facing pages in a magazine or newspaper, used by an advertiser

double-pricing /ˌdʌb(ə)l ˈpraɪsɪŋ/ *noun* the practice of showing two prices on a product, to make buyers think there has been a price reduction

double-spotting /ˌdʌb(ə)l ˈspɒtɪŋ/ *noun* running an advertising spot twice

down /daʊn/ *adverb, preposition* in a lower position or to a lower position ○ *The inflation rate is gradually coming down.* ○ *Shares are slightly down on the day.* ○ *The price of petrol has gone down.* □ **to pay money down** to pay a deposit ○ *They paid £50 down and the rest in monthly instalments.*

down tools *phrasal verb* to stop working ○ *The entire workforce downed tools in protest.*

downmarket /ˌdaʊnˈmɑːkɪt/ *adverb, adjective* cheaper or appealing to a less wealthy section of the population ○ *The company has adopted a downmarket image.*

downside /ˈdaʊnsaɪd/ *noun* □ **the sales force have been asked to give downside forecasts** they have been asked for pessimistic forecasts

downside factor /ˈdaʊnsaɪd ˌfæktə/, **downside potential** /ˌdaʊnsaɪd pəˈtenʃ(ə)l/ *noun* the possibility of making a loss in an investment

down time /ˈdaʊn taɪm/ *noun* time when a worker cannot work because machines have broken down or because components are not available

downturn /ˈdaʊntɜːn/ *noun* a downward trend in sales or profits ○ *a downturn in the market price* ○ *The last quarter saw a downturn in the economy.*

draft /drɑːft/ *noun* an order for money to be paid by a bank ○ *We asked for payment by banker's draft.* □ **to make a draft on a bank** to ask a bank to pay money for you

draw /drɔː/ *verb* **1.** to take money away ○ *to draw money out of an account* □ **to draw a salary** to have a salary paid by the company ○ *The chairman does not draw a salary.* **2.** to write a cheque ○ *She paid the invoice with a cheque drawn on an Egyptian bank.* (NOTE: **drawing – drew – has drawn**)

drawback /ˈdrɔːbæk/ *noun* **1.** something which is not convenient or which is likely to cause problems ○ *One of the main drawbacks of the scheme is that it will take six years to complete.* **2.** a rebate on customs duty for imported goods when these are then used in producing exports

drawee /drɔːˈiː/ *noun* the person or bank asked to make a payment by a drawer

drawer /ˈdrɔːə/ *noun* the person who writes a cheque or a bill asking a drawee to pay money to a payee □ **the bank returned the cheque to drawer** the bank would not pay the cheque because the person who wrote it did not have enough money in the account to pay it

drawing account /ˈdrɔːɪŋəˌkaʊnt/
noun a current account, or any account from which the customer may take money when he or she wants

dress code /ˈdres kəʊd/ *noun* a policy on which type of clothes are considered suitable for a specific activity, especially the clothes worn at work ○ *The dress code is suit and tie for men or smart casual clothes on Fridays.* ○ *The company has a strict dress code for members of staff who meet the public.*

drilling down /ˌdrɪlɪŋ ˈdaʊn/ *noun* the act of sorting data into hierarchies, each of which is more detailed than the previous one

drip /ˈdrɪp kæmˌpeɪn/, **drip campaign** /ˈdrɪp kæmˌpeɪn/, **drip method** /ˈdrɪp ˌmeθəd/ *noun* the placing of advertisements for a product at fairly long intervals, making a long-drawn-out advertising campaign

drive /draɪv/ *noun* an energetic way of doing things □ **she has a lot of drive** she is very energetic in business

driver /ˈdraɪvə/ *noun* something or someone that provides an impetus for something to happen

drive time /ˈdraɪv taɪm/ *noun* the time when people are most likely to be listening to the radio in their cars, hence a good time for broadcasting commercials

driving licence /ˈdraɪvɪŋ ˌlaɪs-(ə)ns/ *noun* the official document which shows that someone is legally allowed to drive a car, truck, or other vehicle ○ *Applicants for the job should hold a valid driving licence.* (NOTE: The US term is **driver's license.**)

drop /drɒp/ *noun* a fall ○ *a drop in sales* ○ *Sales show a drop of 10%.* ○ *The drop in prices resulted in no significant increase in sales.* ■ *verb* **1.** to fall ○ *Sales have dropped by 10% or have dropped 10%.* ○ *The pound dropped three points against the dollar.* **2.** not to keep in a product range ○ *We have dropped these items from the catalogue because they've been losing sales steadily for some time.* (NOTE: **dropping – dropped**)

'...while unemployment dropped by 1.6% in the rural areas, it rose by 1.9% in urban areas during the period under review' [*Business Times (Lagos)*]

'...corporate profits for the first quarter showed a 4% drop from last year's final three months' [*Financial Times*]

'...since last summer American interest rates have dropped by between three and four percentage points' [*Sunday Times*]

drop ship *phrasal verb* to deliver a large order direct to a customer

drop shipment /ˈdrɒp ˈʃɪpmənt/ *noun* the delivery of a large order from the manufacturer direct to a customer's shop or warehouse without going through an agent or wholesaler

dud /dʌd/ *noun, adjective* referring to a coin or banknote that is false or not good, or something that does not do what it is supposed to do (*informal*) ○ *The £50 note was a dud.*

dud cheque /ˌdʌd ˈtʃek/ *noun* a cheque which cannot be cashed because the person writing it does not have enough money in the account to pay it

due /djuː/ *adjective* **1.** owed ○ *a sum due from a debtor* □ **to fall or become due** to be ready for payment □ **bill due on May 1st** a bill which has to be paid on May 1st □ **balance due to us** the amount owed to us which should be paid **2.** expected to arrive **3.** correct and appropriate in the situation □ **in due form** written in the correct legal form ○ *a receipt in due form* ○ *a contract drawn up in due form* □ **after due consideration of the problem** after thinking seriously about the problem □ **due to** caused by ○ *The company pays the wages of staff who are absent due to illness.*

'...many expect the US economic indicators for April, due out this Thursday, to show faster economic growth' [*Australian Financial Review*]

dues /djuːz/ *plural noun* orders taken but not supplied until new stock arrives □ **to release dues** to send off orders which had been piling up while a product was out of stock ○ *We have recorded thousands of dues for that item and our supplier cannot supply it.*

dummy /ˈdʌmi/ *noun* an imitation product to test the reaction of potential customers to its design

dummy pack /ˈdʌmi pæk/ *noun* an empty pack for display in a shop

dump /dʌmp/ *verb* □ **to dump goods on a market** to get rid of large quantities of excess goods cheaply in an overseas market

'…a serious threat lies in the 400,000 tonnes of subsidized beef in European cold stores. If dumped, this meat will have disastrous effects in Pacific Basin markets' [*Australian Financial Review*]

dump bin /'dʌmp bɪn/ *noun* a display container like a large box which is filled with goods for sale

dump display /'dʌmp dɪˌspleɪ/ *noun* goods on special display in a container for purchasers to select themselves in a shop ○ *We will use dump displays with price reductions clearly marked.* ○ *There are several dump displays near the counters in the supermarket.*

dumping /'dʌmpɪŋ/ *noun* the act of getting rid of excess goods cheaply in an overseas market ○ *The government has passed anti-dumping legislation.* ○ *Dumping of goods on the European market is banned.* □ **panic dumping of sterling** a rush to sell sterling at any price because of possible devaluation

duopoly /djuˈɒpəli/ *noun* the existence of only two producers or suppliers in a market ○ *The duopoly meant that the two businesses collaborated to keep prices at very high levels.* ○ *When they took over their only competitor in the market, the duopoly became a monopoly.* Compare **monopoly**

duplication /ˌdjuːplɪˈkeɪʃ(ə)n/ *noun* running an advertisement twice to the same audience

durable /'djʊərəb(ə)l/ *adjective* □ **durable effects** effects which will be felt for a long time ○ *These demographic changes will have durable effects on the economy.*

durable goods /'djʊərəb(ə)l ɡʊdz/ *plural noun* goods which will be used for a long time, e.g. washing machines or refrigerators

duration /djʊˈreɪʃ(ə)n/ *noun* the amount of time that an advertising poster is visible to the average passer-by

dustbin check /'dʌstbɪn tʃek/ *noun* a consumer audit for which a panel of householders keep the empty containers of products bought so that these can be regularly checked for product type, size, and brand

Dutch auction /ˌdʌtʃ 'ɔːkʃən/ *noun* an auction in which the auctioneer offers an item for sale at a high price and then gradually reduces the price until someone makes a bid

dutiable goods /ˌdjuːtiəb(ə)l 'ɡʊdz/ *plural noun* goods on which a customs duty has to be paid

duty /'djuːti/ *noun* a tax that has to be paid ○ *Traders are asking the government to take the duty off alcohol* or *to put a duty on cigarettes.* □ **goods which are liable to duty** goods on which customs or excise tax has to be paid

'Canadian and European negotiators agreed to a deal under which Canada could lower its import duties on $150 million worth of European goods' [*Globe and Mail (Toronto)*]

'…the Department of Customs and Excise collected a total of N79m under the new advance duty payment scheme' [*Business Times (Lagos)*]

duty-free /ˌdjuːti 'friː/ *adjective, adverb* sold with no duty to be paid ○ *She bought duty-free perfume at the airport.* ○ *He bought the watch duty-free.*

duty-free shop /ˌdjuːti 'friː ʃɒp/ *noun* a shop at an airport or on a ship where goods can be bought without paying duty

duty-paid goods /ˌdjuːti 'peɪd ɡʊdz/ *plural noun* goods where the duty has been paid

DWP *abbreviation* Department for Work and Pensions

dyadic communication /daɪˌædɪk kəˌmjuːnɪˈkeɪʃ(ə)n/ *noun* direct conversation between two people such as a salesperson and a customer

Dynamic HTML /daɪˌnæmɪk ˌeɪtʃ tiː em 'el/ *noun* a tool for creating limited animated graphics on a website that can be viewed by most browsers. Its major advantage is that it does not require a plug-in to be viewed by users. Abbreviation **DHTML**

dynamic obsolescence /daɪˌnæmɪk ˌɒbsəˈles(ə)ns/ *noun* the redesigning of a company's product in order to make previous models and other products on the market obsolete

dynamic pricing /daɪˌnæmɪk 'praɪsɪŋ/ *noun* pricing that changes when the demand for something increases or decreases

E

e-alliance /ˈiː əˌlaɪəns/ *noun* a partnership between organisations that do business over the web. Studies show that the most successful e-alliances have been those that link traditional off-line businesses with businesses that specialise in operating online entities.

ear /ɪə/ *noun* a space at the top left or right corner of the front page of a newspaper, set aside for advertising

early /ˈɜːlɪ/ *adjective, adverb* before the usual time ○ *The mail arrived early.* □ **at an early date** very soon

early adopter /ˌɜːli əˈdɒptə/ *noun* an individual or organisation that is one of the first to make use of a new technology

'...early adopters of electronic-product-code RFID systems will wait for a return on investment longer than perhaps they'd anticipated' [*Information Week*]

early majority /ˌɜːli məˈdʒɒrɪti/ *noun* a category of buyers of a product who buy it later than the early adopters

earned rate /ˌɜːnd ˈreɪt/ *noun* the actual rate for a printed advertising space after taking discounts into account

earnest /ˈɜːnɪst/ *noun* money paid as an initial payment by a buyer to a seller, to show commitment to the contract of sale

earning potential /ˈɜːnɪŋ pəˌten-ʃəl/ *noun* **1.** the amount of money a person should be able to earn in his or her professional capacity **2.** the amount of dividend which a share is capable of earning

easy terms /ˌiːzi ˈtɜːmz/ *plural noun* financial terms which are not difficult to accept ○ *The shop is let on very easy terms.*

e-business /ˈiː ˌbɪznɪs/ *noun* **1.** business activities, e.g. buying and selling, servicing customers, and communicating with business partners, that are carried out electronically, especially on the Internet. Also called **electronic commerce 2.** a company that does its business using the Internet

'...the enormous potential of e-business is that it can automate the link between suppliers and customers' [*Investors Chronicle*]

ECGD *abbreviation* Export Credit Guarantee Department

ecoconsumer /ˈiːkəʊkənˌsjuːmə/ *noun* a customer who will buy goods that have been produced in a way that does not harm the environment

ecolabel /ˈiːkəʊleɪb(ə)l/ *noun* a label used to mark products that are produced and can be used and disposed of in a way that does not harm the environment

e-commerce /ˌiː ˈkɒmɜːs/ *noun* the exchange of goods, information, products, or services via an electronic medium such as the Internet. Also called **electronic commerce** (NOTE: Although e-commerce was originally limited to buying and selling, it has now evolved and includes such things as customer service, marketing, and advertising.)

'...the problem is that if e-commerce takes just a 3% slice of the market that would be enough to reduce margins to ribbons' [*Investors Chronicle*]

'...the new economy requires new company structures. He believes that other blue-chip organizations are going to find that new set-ups would be needed to attract and retain the best talent for e-commerce' [*Times*]

e-commerce mall /ˈiː kɒmɜːs mɔːl/ *noun* same as **cyber mall**

e-company /ˈiː ˌkʌmp(ə)ni/ *noun* a company that does all its business using the Internet

econometrics /ɪˌkɒnəˈmetrɪks/ *noun* the study of the statistics of economics, using computers to analyse these statistics and make forecasts using mathematical models

economic /ˌiːkəˈnɒmɪk/ *adjective* **1.** providing enough money to make a profit ○ *The flat is let at an economic rent.* ○ *It is hardly economic for the company to run its own warehouse.* **2.** referring to the financial state of a country ○ *economic planning* ○ *economic trends* ○ *Economic planners are expecting a consumer-led boom.* ○ *The government's economic policy is in ruins after the devaluation.* ○ *The economic situation is getting worse.* ○ *The country's economic system needs more regulation.*

'...each of the major issues on the agenda at this week's meeting is important to the government's success in overall economic management' [*Australian Financial Review*]

economical /ˌiːkəˈnɒmɪk(ə)l/ *adjective* saving money or materials or being less expensive ○ *This car is very economical.* □ **economical car** a car which does not use much petrol □ **an economical use of resources** the fact of using resources as carefully as possible

economic development /ˌiːkənɒmɪk dɪˈveləpmənt/ *noun* improvements in the living standards and wealth of the citizens of a country ○ *The government has offered tax incentives to speed up the economic development of the region.* ○ *Economic development has been relatively slow in the north, compared with the rest of the country.*

economic growth /ˌiːkənɒmɪk ˈɡrəʊθ/ *noun* the rate at which a country's national income grows

economic indicator /ˌiːkənɒmɪk ˈɪndɪkeɪtəz/ *noun* various statistics, e.g. for the unemployment rate or overseas trade, which show how the economy is going to perform in the short or long term

economic infrastructure /ˌiːkənɒmɪk ˈɪnfrəstrʌktʃə/ *noun* the road and rail systems of a country

economic model /ˌiːkənɒmɪk ˈmɒd(ə)l/ *noun* a computerised plan of a country's economic system, used for forecasting economic trends

economic order quantity /ˌiːkənɒmɪk ˈɔːdə ˌkwɒntɪti/ *noun* the quantity of stocks which a company should hold, calculated on the basis of the costs of warehousing, of lower unit costs because of higher quantities purchased, the rate at which stocks are used, and the time it takes for suppliers to deliver new orders. Abbreviation **EOQ**

economic planning /ˌiːkənɒmɪk ˈplænɪŋ/ *noun* plans made by a government for the future financial state of a country

economics /ˌiːkəˈnɒmɪks/ *noun* the study of the production, distribution, selling and use of goods and services ■ *plural noun* the study of financial structures to show how a product or service is costed and what returns it produces ○ *I do not understand the economics of the coal industry.* (NOTE: [all senses] takes a singular verb)

economic stagnation /ˌiːkənɒmɪk stæɡˈneɪʃ(ə)n/ *noun* a lack of expansion in the economy

economic trend /ˌiːkənɒmɪk ˈtrend/ *noun* the way in which a country's economy is moving

economies of scale /ɪˌkɒnəmiz əv ˈskeɪl/ *plural noun* the cost advantages of a company producing a product in larger quantities so that each unit costs less to make. Compare **diseconomies of scale**

economist /ɪˈkɒnəmɪst/ *noun* a person who specialises in the study of economics ○ *Government economists are forecasting a growth rate of 3% next year.* ○ *An agricultural economist studies the economics of the agriculture industry.*

economy /ɪˈkɒnəmi/ *noun* **1.** an action which is intended to stop money or materials from being wasted, or the quality of being careful not to waste money or materials □ **to introduce economies *or* economy measures into the system** to start using methods to save money or materials **2.** the financial state of a country, or the way in which a country makes and uses its money ○ *The country's economy is in ruins.*

economy drive /ɪˈkɒnəmi draɪv/ *noun* a vigorous effort to save money or materials

economy measure /ɪˈkɒnəmi ˌmeʒə/ *noun* an action to save money or materials

economy size /ɪˈkɒnəmi saɪz/ *noun* a large size or large packet which is cheaper than usual

EDI /ˌiː diː ˈaɪ/ *abbreviation* electronic data interchange

editing /ˈedɪtɪŋ/ *noun* **1.** the process of checking the results of a survey to confirm that data has been collected correctly **2.** the process of modifying or correcting a text or film ○ *This sales literature needs editing to make it less long-winded.*

edition /ɪˈdɪʃ(ə)n/ *noun* an issue of a publication such as a newspaper, trade magazine, or book ○ *We are too late to advertise in this month's edition.* ○ *There will be too many competing advertisements in that edition.*

editorial /ˌedɪˈtɔːriəl/ *adjective* referring to editors or to editing ■ *noun* the main article in a newspaper, written by the editor

editorial advertisement /ˌedɪtɔːriəl ədˈvɜːtɪsmənt/ *noun* an advertisement in the form of text material in a magazine

editorial board /ˌedɪˈtɔːriəl ˌbɔːd/ *noun* a group of editors on a newspaper or other publication

editorial environment /ˌedɪtɔːriəl ɪnˈvaɪrənmənt/ *noun* the general editorial tone and philosophy of a medium

editorial matter /ˌedɪˈtɔːriəl ˌmætə/ *noun* the text of a magazine which is written by journalists, and not part of an advertisement

editorial publicity /edɪˌtɔːriəl pʌbˈlɪsɪti/ *noun* free publicity which is given to a product by a newspaper or magazine in an editorial or article, rather than in an advertisement which must be paid for

EDMA *abbreviation* European Direct Marketing Association

EDP /ˌiː diː ˈpiː/ *abbreviation* electronic data processing

educational advertising /ˌedjʊˈkeɪʃ(ə)nəl ˌædvətaɪzɪŋ/ *noun* advertising that informs consumers about a product, particularly important when the product has only recently been introduced ○ *Educational advertising has made the public aware that our product is just as safe as more traditional devices on the market.*

e-economy /ˈiː ɪˌkɒnəmi/ *noun* an economy in which the use of the Internet and information technology plays a major role

effect /ɪˈfekt/ *noun* **1.** a result ○ *The effect of the pay increase was to raise productivity levels.* **2.** an operation □ **terms of a contract which take effect** *or* **come into effect from 1st January** terms which start to operate on 1st January □ **prices are increased 10% with effect from 1st January** new prices will apply from 1st January □ **to remain in effect** to continue to be applied **3.** meaning □ **a clause to the effect that** a clause which means that □ **we have made provision to this effect** we have put into the contract terms which will make this work ■ *verb* to carry out □ **to effect a payment** to make a payment □ **to effect customs clearance** to clear something through customs □ **to effect a settlement between two parties** to bring two parties together and make them agree to a settlement

effective /ɪˈfektɪv/ *adjective* **1.** actual, as opposed to theoretical **2.** □ **a clause effective as from 1st January** a clause which starts to be applied on 1st January **3.** producing results ○ *Advertising in the Sunday papers is the most effective way of selling.* ○ *She is an effective marketing manager.* ➪ **cost-effective**

effective cover /ɪˌfektɪv ˈkʌvə/ *noun* a situation where consumers in the target audience will have seen the advertisement at least four times on average

effective date /ɪˈfektɪv deɪt/ *noun* the date on which a rule or contract starts to be applied, or on which a transaction takes place

effective demand /ɪˌfektɪv dɪˈmɑːnd/ *noun* demand for a product made by individuals and institutions with sufficient wealth pay for it

effectiveness /ɪˈfektɪvnəs/ *noun* the quality of working successfully or producing results ○ *I doubt the effectiveness of television advertising.* ➪ **cost-effectiveness**

effective reach /ɪˌfektɪv ˈriːtʃ/ *noun* the actual number of people who will see an advertisement once

effective sample size /ɪˌfektɪv ˈsɑːmpəl ˌsaɪz/ *noun* the size of a sample after all irrelevant factors have been removed

effectual /ɪˈfektʃuəl/ *adjective* which produces a correct result

efficient consumer response /ɪˌfɪʃ(ə)nt kənˌsjuːmə rɪˈspɒns/ *noun* having the right product in the right place at the right price with the right promotions

EFTPOS /ˈeftpɒz/ *abbreviation* electronic funds transfer at point of sale

EFQM *abbreviation* European Foundation for Quality Management

EFQM Excellence Model *noun* the EFQM Excellence Model is a framework for organisational management systems, promoted by the European Foundation for Quality Management (EFQM) and designed for helping organisations in their drive towards being more competitive

eighty/twenty law /ˌeɪti ˈtwenti ruːl/, **80/20 law** *noun* the rule that a small percentage of customers may account for a large percentage of sales. ➪ **Pareto's Law**

elastic /ɪˈlæstɪk/ *adjective* able to expand or contract easily because of small changes in price

elastic demand /ɪˌlæstɪk dɪˈmɑːnd/ *noun* demand which experiences a comparatively large percentage change in response to a change in price

elasticity /ˌɪlæˈstɪsɪti/ *noun* the ability to change easily in response to a change in circumstances ☐ **elasticity of supply and demand** changes in supply and demand of an item depending on its market price

elastic supply /ɪˌlæstɪk səˈplaɪ/ *noun* supply which experiences a comparatively large percentage change in response to a change in price

elect /ɪˈlekt/ *verb* to choose to do something ○ *He elected to take early retirement.*

electronic /ˌelekˈtrɒnɪk/ *adjective* referring to computers and electronics

electronic cash /ˌelektrɒnɪk ˈkæʃ/ *noun* same as **digital cash**

electronic catalogue /ˌelektrɒnɪk ˈkæt(ə)lɒg/ *noun* a catalogue of the goods that a supplier has for sale, which can be viewed in an electronic format, e.g. on a website

electronic commerce /ˌelektrɒnɪk ˈkɒmɜːs/ *noun* same as **e-commerce**

electronic data capture /ˌelektrɒnɪk ˈdeɪtə ˌkæptʃə/ *noun* the use of data-processing equipment to collect data, especially the use of electronic point-of-sale equipment to collect, validate, and submit data when credit or debit cards are used in transactions

electronic data interchange /ˌelektrɒnɪk ˈdeɪtə ˌɪntətʃeɪndʒ/ *noun* a standard format used when business documents such as invoices and purchase orders are exchanged over electronic networks such as the Internet. Abbreviation **EDI**

electronic data processing /ˌelektrɒnɪk ˈdeɪtə ˌprəʊsesɪŋ/ *noun* the process of selecting and examining data stored in a computer to produce information. Abbreviation **EDP**

electronic funds transfer at point of sale /ˌelektrɒnɪk ˌfʌndz ˌtrænsfɜː ət ˌpɔɪnt əv ˈseɪl/ *noun* the payment for goods or services by a bank customer using a card that is swiped through an electronic reader on the till, thereby transferring the cash from the customer's account to the retailer's or service provider's account. Abbreviation **EFTPOS**

electronic mail /ˌelektrɒnɪk ˈmeɪl/ *noun* same as **email noun 1**

electronic media /ˌelektrɒnɪk ˈmiːdiə/ *plural noun* electronic-based media, e.g. television and radio ○ *Advertising in the electronic media would certainly increase sales, but we can only afford to advertise in the press.*

electronic payment system /ˌelektrɒnɪk ˈpeɪmənt ˌsɪstəm/ *noun* a means of making payments over an electronic network such as the Internet

electronic point of sale /ˌelektrɒnɪk ˌpɔɪnt əv ˈseɪl/ *noun* a system where sales are charged automatically to a customer's credit card and stock is controlled by the shop's computer. Abbreviation **epos**

electronic purse /ˌelektrɒnɪk ˈpɜːs/ *noun* same as **digital wallet**

electronic shopping /ˌelektrɒnɪk ˈʃɒpɪŋ/ *noun* shopping for goods or services which takes place over an electronic network such as the Internet

eliminate /ɪˈlɪmɪneɪt/ *verb* to remove ○ *to eliminate defects in the system* ○ *Using a computer should eliminate all possibility of error.* ○ *We have decided to eliminate this series of old products from our range.* ○ *Most of the candidates were eliminated after the first batch of tests.*

elimination /ɪˌlɪmɪˈneɪʃ(ə)n/ *noun* the act of removing something

email /ˈiːmeɪl/, **email** /ˈiː meɪl/ *noun* **1.** a system of sending messages from one computer terminal to another, using a modem and telephone lines ○ *You can contact me by phone or email if you want.* **2.** a message sent electronically ○ *I had six emails from him today.* ■ *verb* to send a message from one computer to another, using a modem and telephone lines ○ *She emailed her order to the warehouse.* ○ *I emailed him about the meeting.*

email campaign /ˈiː meɪl kæmˌpeɪn/ *noun* a series of emails which deliver marketing messages to individuals

email mailing list /ˌiːmeɪl ˈmeɪlɪŋ ˌlɪst/ *noun* a marketing technique that involves contacting a group of people from anywhere in the world and inviting them to discuss a particular topic and share information and experience by email (NOTE: An email mailing list is run by a *moderator* who compiles a list of email addresses for possible members, mails them with the theme for discussion, collects their contributions, and publishes them by email so that other members of the group can respond to them.)

e-marketing /ˈiː ˌmɑːkɪtɪŋ/ *noun* marketing using the Internet, concentrating on methods such as web page design, advertising, newsgroup targeting, sales emails etc

e-marketplace /ˌiː ˈmɑːkɪtpleɪs/ *noun* a network of connections that brings business-to-business buyers and sellers together on the Internet and enables them to trade more efficiently online

embargo /ɪmˈbɑːgəʊ/ *noun* **1.** a government order which stops a type of trade □ **to impose** *or* **put an embargo on trade with a country** to say that trade with a country must not take place ○ *The government has put an embargo on the export of computer equipment.* □ **to lift an embargo** to allow trade to start again ○ *The government has lifted the embargo on the export of computers.* □ **to be under an embargo** to be forbidden **2.** a period of time during which specific information in a press release must not be published (NOTE: The plural is **embargoes**.) ■ *verb* **1.** to stop trade, or to not allow something to be traded ○ *The government has embargoed trade with countries that are in breach of international agreements.* **2.** not to allow publication of information for a period of time ○ *The news of the merger has been embargoed until next Wednesday.*

e-money /ˈiː ˌmʌni/ *noun* same as **digital money**

emotional appeal /ɪˌməʊʃ(ə)n(ə)l əˈpiːl/ *noun* an attempt by advertising to persuade through an emotional rather than a rational message ○ *The charity used the emotional appeal of starving children to raise funds.* ○ *Emotional appeal was an obvious feature in all the political parties' campaign films.*

empirical data /ɪmˌpɪrɪk(ə)lˈdeɪtə/ *noun* data or information which comes from actual observation or which can be proved ○ *We have no empirical data concerning our competitors' sales last year.*

employer's association /ɪmˌplɔɪəz əˌsəʊsiˈeɪʃ(ə)n/ *noun* same as **employers' organisation**

employers' liability insurance /ɪmˌplɔɪəz ˌlaɪəˈbɪlɪti ɪnˌʃʊərəns/ *noun* insurance to cover accidents which may happen at work, and for which the company may be responsible

employers' organisation /ɪmˈplɔɪəz ˌɔːgənaɪzeɪʃ(ə)n/, **employers' association** /ɪmˈplɔɪəz əsəʊsiˌeɪʃ(ə)n/ *noun* a group of employers with similar interests

employment agency /ɪm'plɔɪ-mənt ˌeɪdʒənsi/, **employment bureau** /ɪm'plɔɪmənt ˌbjʊərəʊ/ *noun* an office or company that finds jobs for people

emporium /ɪm'pɔːriəm/ *noun* a large shop (NOTE: The plural is **emporia**.)

empty nesters /ˌempti 'nestəz/ *plural noun* couples whose children have grown up and left the home

emulator /'emjʊleɪtə/ *noun* someone who is trying to become an achiever

enc, encl *abbreviation* enclosure

enclose /ɪn'kləʊz/ *verb* to put something inside an envelope with a letter ○ *to enclose an invoice with a letter* ○ *I am enclosing a copy of the contract.* ○ *Please find the cheque enclosed herewith.* ○ *Please enclose a recent photograph with your CV.*

enclosure /ɪn'kləʊʒə/ *noun* a document enclosed with a letter or package ○ *The enclosure turned out to be a free sample of perfume.* ○ *Sales material on other products was sent out as an enclosure.*

encode /ɪn'kəʊd/ *verb* to write something in a code so that it cannot be read or used by other people

end /end/ *noun* the final point or last part ○ *at the end of the contract period*

end consumer /end kən'sjuːmə/ *noun* a person who uses a product ○ *The survey was designed to assess the attitudes of end consumers to the product.*

end of season sale /ˌend əv 'siːz(ə)n seɪl/ *noun* a sale of goods at a lower price when the season in which they would be used is over, such as summer clothes sold cheaply in the autumn

endorse /ɪn'dɔːs/ *verb* to say that a product is good □ **to endorse a bill** *or* **a cheque** to sign a bill or cheque on the back to show that you accept it

endorsee /ˌendɔː'siː/ *noun* a person whose name is written on a bill or cheque as having the right to cash it

endorsement /ɪn'dɔːsmənt/ *noun* **1.** the act of endorsing **2.** a signature on a document which endorses it

endorsement advertising /ɪn'dɔːsmənt ˌædvətaɪzɪŋ/ *noun* same as **product endorsement**

endorser /ɪn'dɔːsə/ *noun* a person who endorses a bill or cheque which is then paid to him or her

end user /ˌend 'juːzə/ *noun* a person who actually uses a product

enhancement /ɪn'hɑːnsmənt/ *noun* increase or improvement in quality of service, value for money, etc.

ent /ent/ *noun* a test of number sequences for large quantities of data

enterprise /'entəpraɪz/ *noun* **1.** a system of carrying on a business **2.** a business

enterprise portal /ˌentəpraɪz 'pɔːt(ə)l/ *noun* a website that contains a wide variety of information and services useful to the employees of a particular organisation for their work (NOTE: The essential difference between an enterprise portal and an intranet is that an enterprise portal also provides external content that may be useful, e.g. specialist news feeds and access to industry research reports.)

enterprise zone /'entəpraɪz zəʊn/ *noun* an area of the country where businesses are encouraged to develop by offering special conditions such as easy planning permission for buildings or a reduction in the business rate

entrant /'entrənt/ *noun* a company which goes into a market for the first time

entrepot port /'ɒntrəpəʊ pɔːt/ *noun* a town with a large international commercial port dealing in re-exports

entrepot trade /'ɒntrəpəʊ treɪd/ *noun* the exporting of imported goods

entrepreneur /ˌɒntrəprə'nɜː/ *noun* a person who is willing to take commercial risks by starting or financing commercial enterprises

entrepreneurial /ˌɒntrəprə'nɜːriəl/ *adjective* taking commercial risks ○ *an entrepreneurial decision*

entry barrier /'entri ˌbæriə/ *noun* same as **barrier to entry**

envelope stuffer /'envələʊp ˌstʌfə/ *noun* advertising material which is mailed in an envelope

environment /ɪn'vaɪrənmənt/ *noun* the area in which an organisation works

environmental analysis /ɪnˌvaɪrənmənt(ə)l əˈnæləsɪs/ *noun* the analysis of factors outside an organisation such as demography or politics, in order to make strategic planning more effective ○ *Our environmental analysis must cover all the countries we sell in.* ○ *Environmental analysis made clear that some markets were too unstable to enter.*

environmental management /ɪnˌvaɪrənmənt(ə)l ˈmænɪdʒmənt/ *noun* a planned approach to minimising an organisation's impact on the environment

EOQ *abbreviation* economic order quantity

epos /ˈiːpɒs/, **EPOS EPoS** *abbreviation* electronic point of sale

e-purse /ˈiː pɜːs/ *noun* same as **digital wallet**

equilibrium /ˌiːkwɪˈlɪbriəm/ *noun* the state of balance in the economy where supply equals demand or a country's balance of payments is neither in deficit nor in excess

equity capital /ˈekwɪti ˌkæpɪt(ə)l/ *noun* the nominal value of the shares owned by the ordinary shareholders of a company (NOTE: Preference shares are not equity capital. If the company were wound up, none of the equity capital would be distributed to preference shareholders.)

e-retailer /ˈiː ˌriːteɪlə/ *noun* a business that uses an electronic network such as the Internet to sell its goods or services

erode /ɪˈrəʊd/ *verb* to wear away gradually □ **to erode wage differentials** to reduce gradually differences in salary between different grades

error /ˈerə/ *noun* a mistake ○ *He made an error in calculating the total.* ○ *Someone must have made a keyboarding error.*

error rate /ˈerə reɪt/ *noun* the number of mistakes per thousand entries or per page

escalate /ˈeskəleɪt/ *verb* to increase steadily

escalation /ˌeskəˈleɪʃ(ə)n/ *noun* a steady increase ○ *an escalation of wage demands* ○ *The union has threatened an escalation in strike action.* □ **escalation of prices** a steady increase in prices

escalation clause /ˌeskəˈleɪʃ(ə)n klɔːz/ *noun* same as **escalator clause**

escalator /ˈeskəleɪtə/ *noun* a moving staircase

escalator card /ˈeskəleɪtə kɑːd/ *noun* an advertisement on either side of an escalator in underground stations ○ *The media buyer compared the cost of posters and escalator cards.*

escalator clause /ˈeskəleɪtə klɔːz/ *noun* a clause in a contract allowing for regular price increases because of increased costs, or regular wage increases because of the increased cost of living

escrow /ˈeskrəʊ/ *noun US* an agreement between two parties that something should be held by a third party until conditions are fulfilled □ **in escrow** held in safe keeping by a third party □ **document held in escrow** a document given to a third party to keep and to pass on to someone when money has been paid

escrow account /ˈeskrəʊə ˌkaʊnt/ *noun US* an account where money is held in escrow until a contract is signed or until goods are delivered

essential /ɪˈsenʃəl/ *adjective* very important ○ *It is essential that an agreement be reached before the end of the month.* ○ *The factory is lacking essential spare parts.*

essential goods /ɪˌsenʃəl ˈɡʊdz/, **essential products** /ɪˌsenʃəl ˈprɒdʌktz/ *plural noun* basic goods or products necessary for everyday life

estate duty /ɪˈsteɪt ˌdjuːti/ *noun* a tax paid on the property left by a dead person (NOTE: now called **inheritance tax**)

estimate *noun* /ˈestɪmət/ **1.** a calculation of the probable cost, size or time of something ○ *Can you give me an estimate of how much time was spent on the job?* □ **these figures are only an estimate** these are not the final accurate figures **2.** a calculation by a contractor or seller of a service of how much something is likely to cost, given to a client in advance of an order ○ *You should ask for an estimate before committing yourselves.* ○ *Before we can give the grant we must have an estimate of the total costs involved.* ○ *Unfortunately the final bill was quite* *different from the estimate.* □ **to put in an estimate** to give someone a written calculation of the probable costs of carrying out a job ○ *Three firms put in estimates for the job.* ■ *verb*/'estɪmeɪt/ **1.** to calculate the probable cost, size, or time of something ○ *to estimate that it will cost £1m* ○ *We estimate current sales at only 60% of last year.* **2.** □ **to estimate for a job** to state in writing the future costs of carrying out a piece of work so that a client can make an order ○ *Three firms estimated for the refitting of the offices.*

estimated /'estɪmeɪtɪd/ *adjective* calculated approximately ○ *estimated sales* ○ *Costs were slightly more than the estimated figure.*

estimation /ˌestɪ'meɪʃ(ə)n/ *noun* an approximate calculation

estimator /'estɪmeɪtə/ *noun* a person whose job is to calculate estimates for carrying out work

e-tailer /'iː ˌteɪlə/ *noun* same as **e-retailer**

e-tailing /'iː ˌteɪlɪŋ/ *noun* **1.** the selling of goods and services using an electronic network such as the Internet **2.** same as **e-commerce**

ethics /'eθɪks/ *noun* the moral aspects of decision-making ○ *Whether or not we use such aggressive sales tactics is a matter of ethics.* (NOTE: takes a singular verb)

ethnic /'eθnɪk/ *adjective* relating to people who share the same race, culture, and traditions

ethnic media /ˌeθnɪk 'miːdiə/ *plural noun* magazines or TV stations which appeal to ethnic audiences

ethnic monitoring /ˌeθnɪk 'mɒnɪt(ə)rɪŋ/ *noun* the recording of the racial origins of employees or customers in order to ensure that all parts of the population are represented

ethnocentric stage /ˌeθnəʊsentrɪk 'steɪdʒ/ *noun US* an early stage in a company's marketing when goods are sent overseas with no concessions to local needs or tastes

e-ticket /'iː ˌtɪkɪt/ *noun* a booking, especially for air travel, made on the Internet for which no paper ticket is issued to the customer

EU /'iː'juː/ *abbr* European Union ○ *EU ministers met today in Brussels.* ○ *The US is increasing its trade with the EU.*

European Community /ˌjʊərəpiːən kə'mjuːnɪti/ *noun* formerly, the name of the European Union. Abbreviation **EC**

European Direct Marketing Association /ˌjʊərəpiːən daɪˌrekt 'mɑːkɪtɪŋ əˌsəʊsieɪʃ(ə)n/ *noun* an organisation based in Switzerland which monitors new techniques in direct marketing and represents the interests of its members. Abbreviation **EDMA**

European Union /ˌjʊərəpiːən 'juːnjən/ *noun* a group of European countries linked together by the Treaty of Rome. Abbreviation **EU**

evaluate /ɪ'væljueɪt/ *verb* to examine something to see how good it is

evaluation /ɪˌvælju'eɪʃ(ə)n/ *noun* the examination of a product to see how good it is

evaluative /ɪ'væljuətɪv/ *adjective* referring to the calculation of value

evaluative criteria /ɪˌvæljuətɪv kraɪ'tɪəriə/ *plural noun* the criteria used to compare different products or services

event /ɪ'vent/ *noun* a thing which happens, e.g. a trade exhibition, an end of season sale

event marketing /ɪ'vent ˌmɑːkɪtɪŋ/ *noun* promotional activity to advertise an event

event sponsorship /ɪ'vent ˌspɒnsəʃɪp/ *noun* a promotional deal by which a company sponsors a particular event such as a concert, sporting event, or other activity, on a regular basis

evoke /ɪ'vəʊk/ *verb* to call up an image

evoked set /ɪˌvəʊkt 'set/ *noun* the various brands which are identified by a consumer as possible purchases and which he or she considers during the alternative evaluation process

ex /eks/ *prefix* out of or from □ **price ex warehouse** a price for a product which is to be collected from the manufacturer's or agent's warehouse and so does not include delivery □ **price ex works** or **ex factory** a price not including transport from the maker's factory ■ *adverb* without

ex- /eks/ *prefix* former ○ *an ex-director of the company*

excess /'ekses//ɪk'ses/ *noun, adjective* an amount which is more than what is allowed ○ *an excess of expenditure over revenue*

excess capacity /ˌekses kə'pæsɪti/ *noun* spare capacity which is not being used

excess demand /ˌekses dɪ-'mɑːnd/ *noun* more demand at the present price than sellers can satisfy ○ *Much more machinery and labour must be acquired to meet excess demand.*

excess profit /ˌekses 'prɒfɪt/ *noun* a level of profit that is higher than a level regarded as normal

excess supply /ˌekses sə'plaɪ/ *noun* more supply at the present price than buyers want to buy

exchange /ɪks'tʃeɪndʒ/ *noun* **1.** the act of giving one thing for another □ **exchange of contracts** the point in the sale of property when the buyer and the seller both sign the contract of sale which then becomes binding **2.** a market for shares, commodities, futures, etc. ■ *verb* **1.** □ **to exchange something (for something else)** to give one thing in place of something else ○ *He exchanged his motorcycle for a car.* ○ *Goods can be exchanged only on production of the sales receipt.* **2.** □ **to exchange contracts** to sign a contract when buying a property, carried out by both buyer and seller at the same time **3.** to change money of one country for money of another ○ *to exchange euros for pounds*

'…under the barter agreements, Nigeria will export crude oil in exchange for trucks, food, planes and chemicals' [*Wall Street Journal*]

exchangeable /ɪks'tʃeɪndʒəb(ə)l/ *adjective* possible to exchange

exchange control /ɪks'tʃeɪndʒ kən,trəʊl/ *noun* the control by a government of the way in which its currency may be exchanged for foreign currencies

exchange controls /ɪks'tʃeɪndʒ kən,trəʊlz/ *plural noun* government

restrictions on changing the local currency into foreign currency ○ *The government had to impose exchange controls to stop the rush to buy dollars.* ○ *They say the government is going to lift exchange controls.*

exchange dealer /ɪks'tʃeɪndʒ ˌdiːlə/ *noun* a person who buys and sells foreign currency

exchange dealings /ɪks'tʃeɪndʒ ˌdiːlɪŋz/ *plural noun* the buying and selling of foreign currency

exchange economy /ɪks'tʃeɪndʒ ɪˌkɒnəmi/ *noun* an economy based on the exchange of goods and services

exchange premium /ɪks'tʃeɪndʒ ˌpriːmiəm/ *noun* an extra cost above the usual rate for buying a foreign currency

exchanger /ɪks'tʃeɪndʒə/ *noun* a person who buys and sells foreign currency

exchange rate /ɪks'tʃeɪndʒ reɪt/ *noun* a figure that expresses how much a unit of one country's currency is worth in terms of the currency of another country

exchange transaction /ɪks'tʃeɪndʒ trænˌzækʃən/ *noun* a purchase or sale of foreign currency

excise duty /'eksaɪz ˌdjuːti/ *noun* a tax on goods such as alcohol and petrol which are produced in a given country

exclusion clause /ɪk'skluːʒ(ə)n klɔːz/ *noun* a clause in an insurance policy or warranty which says which items or events are not covered

exclusive /ɪk'skluːsɪv/ *adjective* **1.** limited to one person or group □ **to have exclusive right to market a product** to be the only person who has the right to market a product **2.** □ **exclusive of** not including ○ *The invoice is exclusive of VAT.* ■ *noun* the exclusive rights to a news story or the story itself

exclusive agreement /ɪkˌskluːsɪv ə'griːmənt/ *noun* an agreement where a person is made sole agent for a product in a market

exclusivity /ˌekskluː'sɪvɪti/ *noun* the exclusive right to market a product

ex dividend /ˌeks 'dɪvɪdend/, **ex div** /ˌeks 'dɪv/ *adjective* used to describe a share that does not have the right to receive the next dividend ○ *The shares went ex dividend yesterday.* Abbreviation **xd**

exempt /ɪgˈzempt/ *adjective* not forced to do something, especially not forced to obey a particular law or rule, or not forced to pay something ○ *Anyone over 65 is exempt from charges.* □ **exempt from tax** not required to pay tax ○ *As a non-profit-making organisation we are exempt from tax.*

'Companies with sales under $500,000 a year will be exempt from the minimum-wage requirements' [*Nation's Business*]

exempt rating /ɪgˈzempt ˌreɪtɪŋ/ *noun* the legal right of a business not to add VAT to the prices of some products or services

exempt supplies /ɪgˌzempt səˈplaɪz/ *plural noun* products or services on which the supplier does not have to charge VAT, e.g., the purchase of, or rent on, property and financial services

ex gratia /ˌeks ˈɡreɪʃə/ *adjective* as an act of favour, without obligation

ex gratia payment /eks ˌɡreɪʃə ˈpeɪmənt/ *noun* a payment made as a gift, with no other obligations

exhibit /ɪgˈzɪbɪt/ *noun* **1.** a thing which is shown ○ *The buyers admired the exhibits on our stand.* **2.** a single section of an exhibition ○ *the British Trade Exhibit at the International Computer Fair* ■ *verb* □ **to exhibit at the Motor Show** to display new models of cars at the Motor Show

exhibition /ˌeksɪˈbɪʃ(ə)n/ *noun* an occasion for the display of goods so that buyers can look at them and decide what to buy ○ *The government has sponsored an exhibition of good design.* ○ *We have a stand at the Ideal Home Exhibition.* ○ *The agricultural exhibition grounds were crowded with visitors.*

exhibition stand /ˌeksɪˈbɪʃ(ə)n stænd/ *noun* a separate section of an exhibition where a company exhibits its products or services

exhibitor /ɪgˈzɪbɪtə/ *noun* a person or company that shows products at an exhibition

exorbitant /ɪgˈzɔːbɪtənt/ *adjective* unreasonably high in price ○ *$10,000 a minute; that's exorbitant and totally unjustified.* ○ *Their fees may seem exorbitant, but their costs are very high.*

expand /ɪkˈspænd/ *verb* to get bigger, or make something bigger ○ *an expanding economy* ○ *The company is expanding fast.* ○ *We have had to expand our sales force.*

expansion /ɪkˈspænʃən/ *noun* an increase in size ○ *The expansion of the domestic market.* ○ *The company had difficulty in financing its current expansion programme.*

'...inflation-adjusted GNP moved up at a 1.3% annual rate, its worst performance since the economic expansion began' [*Fortune*]

'...the businesses we back range from start-up ventures to established businesses in need of further capital for expansion' [*Times*]

'...the group is undergoing a period of rapid expansion and this has created an exciting opportunity for a qualified accountant' [*Financial Times*]

expect /ɪkˈspekt/ *verb* to hope that something is going to happen ○ *We are expecting him to arrive at 10:45.* ○ *They are expecting a cheque from their agent next week.* ○ *The house was sold for more than the expected price.*

'...he observed that he expected exports to grow faster than imports in the coming year' [*Sydney Morning Herald*]

'American business as a whole has seen profits well above the levels normally expected at this stage of the cycle' [*Sunday Times*]

expectation /ˌekspekˈteɪʃ(ə)n/ *noun* **1.** what someone believes will happen, especially concerning their future prosperity **2.** what someone believes about an item or service to be purchased, which is one of the reasons for making the purchase

expected price /ɪkˈspektɪd praɪs/ *noun* the price of a product which consumers consider corresponds to its true value

expense /ɪkˈspens/ *noun* money spent ○ *It is not worth the expense.* ○ *The expense is too much for my bank balance.* ○ *The likely profits do not justify the expense of setting up the project.* ○ *It was well worth the expense to get really high-quality equipment.*

expense account /ɪk'spens ə,kaʊnt/ *noun* an allowance of money which a business pays for an employee to spend on travelling and entertaining clients in connection with that business

expenses /ɪk'spensɪz/ *plural noun* money paid to cover the costs incurred by someone when doing something ○ *The salary offered is £10,000 plus expenses.* □ **all expenses paid** with all costs paid by the company ○ *The company sent him to San Francisco all expenses paid.* □ **to cut down on expenses** to reduce spending

expensive /ɪk'spensɪv/ *adjective* which costs a lot of money ○ *First-class air travel is becoming more and more expensive.*

experience /ɪk'spɪəriəns/ *noun* knowledge or skill that comes from having had to deal with many different situations ○ *She has a lot of experience of dealing with German companies.* ○ *I gained most of my experience abroad.* ○ *Considerable experience is required for this job.* ○ *The applicant was pleasant, but did not have any relevant experience.*

experience curve /ɪk'spɪəriəns kɜːv/ *noun* a graph showing the relationship between the cumulative amount of products produced and the production cost per unit ○ *The experience curve shows how increasing efficiency has brought down our costs.*

experience effect /ɪk'spɪəriəns ɪ,fekt/ *noun* the role of experience in improving business efficiency ○ *The experience effect is evident in the rise in our profits as our workforce becomes more skilled.*

experiencer /ɪk'spɪəriənsə/ *noun* in the VALS lifestyle classification system, a young person who likes new and unusual things and spends a lot of money on hobbies and socialising

experiential /ek,spɪəri'enʃəl/ *noun* a lifestyle segment according to VALS, people who are attracted to others

experiential advertising /ek,spɪərienʃəl 'ædvətaɪzɪŋ/ *noun* advertising which conveys to the customer the real sensation of using the product

experimental method /ɪk,sperɪ'ment(ə)l ,meθəd/ *noun* the use of controlled experiments to discover the influence of various variables in marketing such as types of promotion and sales training

expert /'eksp3ːt/ *noun* a person who knows a lot about something ○ *an expert in the field of electronics* ○ *The company asked a financial expert for advice.* □ **expert's report** a report written by an expert

expertise /,ekspə'tiːz/ *noun* specialist knowledge or skill in a particular field ○ *We hired Mr Smith because of his financial expertise* or *because of his expertise in finance.* ○ *With years of experience in the industry, we have plenty of expertise to draw on.* ○ *Lack of marketing expertise led to low sales figures.*

expert system /'eksp3ːt ,sɪstəm/ *noun* a computer program that is designed to imitate the way a human expert in a particular field thinks and makes decisions (NOTE: Expert systems, which are an application of **artificial intelligence**, are used for a wide variety of tasks including medical diagnostics and financial decision-making and can be used by non-experts to solve well-defined problems when human experts are unavailable.)

exploit /ɪk'splɔɪt/ *verb* to use something to make a profit ○ *The company is exploiting its contacts in the Ministry of Trade.* ○ *We hope to exploit the oil resources in the China Sea.*

exponential diffusion /ekspə,-nenʃ(ə)l dɪ'fjuːʒ(ə)n/, **exponential growth** /ekspə,nenʃ(ə)l 'grəʊθ/ *noun* a typical growth pattern of new products that involves a slow start, followed by acceleration and finally a slowing down

exponential smoothing /ekspə,-nenʃ(ə)l 'smuːðɪŋ/ *noun* a technique for working out averages while allowing for recent changes in values by moving forward the period under consideration at regular intervals

export *noun*/'ekspɔːt/ the practice or business of sending goods to foreign countries to be sold ○ *50% of the* *company's profits come from the export trade the export market.* ⇨ **exports**

■ *verb*/ɪk'spɔːt/ to send goods to foreign countries for sale ○ *50% of our production is exported.* ○ *The company imports raw materials and exports the finished products.*

'...in the past, export documentation was a major stumbling block for some companies' [*Marketing & Sales Management*]

'Europe's gross exports of white goods climbed to 2.4 billion, about a quarter of total production' [*Economist*]

'...the New Zealand producers are now aiming to export more fresh meat as opposed to frozen which has formed the majority of its UK imports in the past' [*Marketing*]

export agent /'ekspɔːt ˌeɪdʒənt/ *noun* a person who sells overseas on behalf of a company and earns a commission ○ *An export agent is developing our business in West Africa.* ○ *She is working in London as an export agent for a French company.*

exportation /ˌekspɔː'teɪʃ(ə)n/ *noun* the act of sending goods to foreign countries for sale

export bounty /'ekspɔːt ˌbaʊnti/ *noun* a government payment to businesses to encourage specific types of export

Export Credit Guarantee Department /ˌekspɔːt ˌkredɪt ˌgærən'tiː dɪˌpaːtmənt/ *noun* a British government department which insures sellers of exports sold on credit against the possibility of non-payment by the purchasers. Abbreviation **ECGD**

export department /'ekspɔːt dɪˌpaːtmənt/ *noun* the section of a company which deals in sales to foreign countries

export duty /'ekspɔːt ˌdjuːti/ *noun* a tax paid on goods sent out of a country for sale

exporter /ɪk'spɔːtə/ *noun* a person, company, or country that sells goods in foreign countries ○ *a major furniture exporter* ○ *Canada is an important exporter of oil an important oil exporter.*

export house /'ekspɔːt haʊs/ *noun* a company which specialises in the export of goods manufactured by other companies

exporting /ek'spɔːtɪŋ/ *adjective* sending goods out of a country □ **oil-exporting countries** countries which produce oil and sell it to other countries

export licence /'ekspɔːt ˌlaɪs(ə)ns/ *noun* a government permit allowing something to be exported ○ *The government has refused an export licence for computer parts.*

export manager /'ekspɔːt ˌmænɪdʒə/ *noun* the person in charge of an export department in a company ○ *The export manager planned to set up a sales force in Southern Europe.* ○ *Sales managers from all export markets report to our export manager.*

exports /'ekspɔːts/ *plural noun* goods sent to a foreign country to be sold ○ *Exports to Africa have increased by 25%.* ⇨ **export** (NOTE: Usually used in the plural, but the singular form is used before a noun.)

exposition /ˌekspə'zɪʃ(ə)n/ *noun* US same as **exhibition**

exposure /ɪk'spəʊʒə/ *noun* publicity given to an organisation or product ○ *Our company has achieved more exposure since we decided to advertise nationally.*

'...it attributed the poor result to the bank's high exposure to residential mortgages, which showed a significant slowdown in the past few months' [*South China Morning Post*]

express /ɪk'spres/ *adjective* rapid or very fast ○ *an express letter* ■ *verb* to send something very fast ○ *We expressed the order to the customer's warehouse.*

expressage /ɪk'spresɪdʒ/ *noun* US a very fast transport service

express delivery /ɪkˌspres dɪ'lɪv(ə)ri/ *noun* a very fast delivery

extend /ɪk'stend/ *verb* **1.** to offer something ○ *to extend credit to a customer* **2.** to make something longer ○ *Her contract of employment was extended for two years.* ○ *We have extended the deadline for making the appointment by two weeks.*

extended credit /ɪkˌstendɪd 'kredɪt/ *noun* credit allowing the borrower a very long time to pay ○ *We sell to Australia on extended credit.*

extended guarantee /ɪkˌstendɪd gærən'tiː/ *noun* a guarantee, offered by a dealer on consumer durables such as dishwashers, which goes beyond the time specified in the manufacturer's guarantee

extension /ɪkˈstenʃən/ *noun* an additional period of time allowed for something, e.g. the repayment of a debt □ **to get an extension of credit** to get more time to pay back □ **extension of a contract** the continuing of a contract for a further period

extension strategy /ɪkˈstenʃən ˌstrætədʒi/ *noun* a marketing strategy aimed at extending the life of a product either by making small changes in it, finding new uses for it, or finding new markets ○ *An extension strategy is needed to ensure demand for another few years.* ○ *The extension strategy consisted in providing a greater choice of colours and upholstery for the range of cars.*

extensive /ɪkˈstensɪv/ *adjective* very large or covering a wide area ○ *an extensive network of sales outlets*

extensive marketing /ɪkˌstensɪv ˈmɑːkɪtɪŋ/ *noun* the practice of using a wide network of distributors and a great variety of promotional activities to gain as large a section of the market as possible ○ *Only a company with vast resources could embark on this type of extensive marketing.*

extensive problem-solving /ɪkˌstensɪv ˈprɒbləm ˌsɒlvɪŋ/ *noun* detailed research and decision-making by a buyer who needs to examine carefully all options open to him or her

external /ɪkˈstɜːn(ə)l/ *adjective* **1.** outside a country. Opposite **internal** **2.** outside a company

external account /ɪkˌstɜːn(ə)l əˈkaʊnt/ *noun* an account in a British bank belonging to someone who is living in another country

external analysis /ɪkˌstɜːn(ə)l əˈnæləsɪs/ *noun* the analysis of an organisation's customers, market segments, competitors, and marketing environment

external audience /ɪkˌstɜːn(ə)l ˈɔːdiəns/ *noun* people, such as the general public, who do not belong to an organisation

external audit /ɪkˌstɜːn(ə)l ˈɔːdɪt/ *noun* an evaluation of the effectiveness

of a company's public relations carried out by an outside agency

external communication /ɪkˌstɜːn(ə)l kəˌmjuːnɪˈkeɪʃ(ə)n/ *noun* the exchange of information and messages between an organisation and other organisations, groups, or individuals that are not part of it (NOTE: External communication includes the fields of *public relations*, media relations, advertising, and marketing management.)

external desk research /ɪkˌstɜːn(ə)l ˈdesk rɪˌsɜːtʃ/ *noun* research based on material outside the company's own records, e.g. in libraries or government departments

external search /ɪkˌstɜːn(ə)l ˈsɜːtʃ/ *noun* a method of finding information from external sources such as advertising, or from the web using a search engine

external search engine /ɪkˌstɜːn(ə)l ˈsɜːtʃ ˌendʒɪn/ *noun* a search engine that allows the user to search millions of Internet pages rapidly

external trade /ɪkˌstɜːn(ə)l ˈtreɪd/ *noun* trade with foreign countries. Opposite **internal trade**

extra /ˈekstrə/ *adjective* which is added or which is more than usual ○ *to charge 10% extra for postage* ○ *There is no extra charge for heating.* ○ *Service is extra.* ○ *We get £25 extra pay for working on Sunday.*

extranet /ˈekstrənet/ *noun* a closed network of websites and email systems that is accessible to the people who belong to an organisation and to some others who do not, and that allows the outsiders access to the organisation's internal applications or information – usually subject to some kind of signed agreement (NOTE: Like *intranets*, extranets provide all the benefits of Internet technology (browsers, web servers, HTML, etc.) with the added benefit of security, since the network cannot be used by the general public.)

extraordinary item /ɪkˈstrɔːd(ə)n(ə)ri ˌaɪtəm/ *noun* a large item of income or expenditure entered into accounts that is unusual in nature and also occurs very infrequently

extrapolation /ɪkˌstræpəˈleɪʃ(ə)n/ *noun* a forecasting technique which involves projecting past trends into the future ○ *We are using extrapolation to forecast demand for a new product based on the demand for a similar product over the last five years.*

extras /ˈekstrəz/ *plural noun* items which are not included in a price ○ *Packing and postage are extras.*

eyeballing /ˈaɪbɔːlɪŋ/ *noun* simply looking at statistical data to make a quick and informal assessment of the results (*informal*)

eyeballs /ˈaɪbɔːlz/ *plural noun* a measure of the number of visits made to a website (*slang*)

eye candy /ˈaɪ ˌkændi/ *noun* visually attractive material (*slang*)

eye-movement test /ˈaɪ ˌmuːvmənt ˌtest/, **eye tracking** /ˈaɪ ˌtrækɪŋ/ *noun* an advertising research test which involves recording the movement of a person's eyes as they look at an advertisement to see which parts are of special interest ○ *The eye-movement test will tell us what to highlight in future advertisements.*

e-zine /ˈiː ziːn/ *noun* a publication on a particular topic that is distributed regularly in electronic form, mainly via the Web but also by email

F

face-lift /feɪs lɪft/ *noun* an improvement to the design of products and packaging or of an organisation's image ○ *These products need a face-lift if they are going to retain their appeal.*

face out /ˈfeɪs aʊt/ *adverb* used to refer to the displaying of books on bookshop shelves, showing the front cover

face time /ˈfeɪs taɪm/ *noun* time spent communicating with other people face-to-face as opposed to time spent communicating with them electronically (*informal*)

face-to-face selling /ˌfeɪs tə feɪs ˈselɪŋ/ *noun* person-to-person or direct selling, involving a meeting between seller and buyer ○ *Six months of face-to-face selling will give trainees direct experience of the market.* ○ *We need confident outgoing people to do our face-to-face selling.*

face value /ˌfeɪs ˈvæljuː/ *noun* the value written on a coin, banknote or share certificate

'…travellers cheques cost 1% of their face value – some banks charge more for small amounts' [*Sunday Times*]

Facebook /ˈfeɪsˌbʊk/ a trade name for a social networking website where users can create and customise their own profiles with photos, videos and personal information. People can browse other people's profiles and write messages on their *wall*.

facia /ˈfeɪʃə/ *noun* another spelling of **fascia**

facilities /fəˈsɪlɪtiz/ *plural noun* services, equipment or buildings which make it possible to do something ○ *Our storage facilities are the best in the region.* ○ *Transport facilities in the area are not satisfactory.* ○ *There are no facilities for disabled visitors.*

facility /fəˈsɪlɪti/ *noun* **1.** the total amount of credit which a lender will allow a borrower **2.** *US* a single large building ○ *We have opened our new warehouse facility.*

facing /ˈfeɪsɪŋ/ *adjective* opposite

facing matter /ˈfeɪsɪŋ ˌmætə/, **facing text matter** /ˌfeɪsɪŋ ˈtekst ˌmætə/ *noun* an advertisement on a page opposite to one containing editorial matter

facing page /ˈfeɪsɪŋ peɪdʒ/ *noun* the page opposite

facsimile /fækˈsɪmɪli/ *noun* an exact copy of a text or illustration

fact /fækt/ *noun* a piece of information ○ *The chairman asked to see all the facts on the income tax claim.* ○ *The sales director can give you the facts and figures about the African operation.*

fact book /ˈfækt bʊk/ *noun* data put together about a product on the market that can be used for reference by the producers or by an advertising agency

fact-finding mission /ˈfækt faɪndɪŋ ˌmɪʃ(ə)n/ *noun* a visit by a person or group of people, usually to another country, to obtain information about a specific issue ○ *The minister went on a fact-finding tour of the region.*

factor /ˈfæktə/ *noun* **1.** something which is important, or which is taken into account when making a decision ○ *The drop in sales is an important factor in the company's lower profits.* ○ *Motivation was an important factor in drawing up the new pay scheme.* **2.** a person who sells for a business or another person and earns a commission ■ *verb* to buy debts from a company at a discount

'…factors 'buy' invoices from a company, which then gets an immediate cash advance representing most of their value. The balance is paid when the debt is met. The client company is charged a fee as well as interest on the cash advanced' [*Times*]

factorage /'fæktərɪdʒ/ *noun* a commission earned by a factor ○ *What percentage is the factorage?*

factor analysis /'fæktə ə,næləsɪs/ *noun* a process of identifying key factors that influence the results in an attitude research programme

factoring /'fæktərɪŋ/ *noun* the business of buying debts from a firm at a discount and then enforcing the payment of the debt

factoring agent /'fæktərɪŋ ,eɪdʒənt/ *noun* a person who sells for a business or another person and earns a commission

factoring charges /'fæktərɪŋ,tʃɑːdʒɪz/ *plural noun* the cost of selling debts to a factor for a commission

factory /'fækt(ə)ri/ *noun* a building where products are manufactured ○ *a car factory* ○ *a shoe factory* ○ *The company is proposing to close three of its factories with the loss of 200 jobs.*

factory gate price /,fækt(ə)ri 'geɪt praɪs/ *noun* the actual cost of manufacturing goods before any mark-up is added to give profit (NOTE: The factory gate price includes direct costs such as labour, *raw materials* and energy, and indirect costs such as interest on loans, plant maintenance or rent.)

factory outlet /'fækt(ə)ri ,aʊt(ə)let/ *noun* a shop where merchandise is sold direct to the public from the factory, usually at wholesale prices

factory unit /'fækt(ə)ri juːnɪt/ *noun* a single building on an industrial estate

fact sheet /'fækt ʃiːt/ *noun* a sheet of paper giving information about a product or service which can be used for publicity purposes

fad /fæd/ *noun* a short-lived fashion or craze

failure /'feɪljə/ *noun* the fact of not doing something which you promised to do

failure fee /'feɪljə fiː/ *noun* a fee charged by a distributor to the manufacturer of a product whose sales are less than those agreed in advance

fair /feə/ *noun* same as **trade fair** ○ *The employment fair runs from 1st to 6th April.* ■ *adjective* reasonable, with equal treatment

fair deal /,feə 'diːl/ *noun* an arrangement where both parties are treated equally ○ *The employees feel they did not get a fair deal from the management.*

fairly /'feəli/ *adverb* reasonably or equally ○ *The union representatives put the employees' side of the case fairly and without argument.*

fair price /,feə 'praɪs/ *noun* a good price for both buyer and seller

fair trade /,feə 'treɪd/ *noun* an international business system where countries agree not to charge import duties on some items imported from their trading partners

fall /fɔːl/ *noun* a sudden reduction or loss of value ○ *a fall in the exchange rate* ○ *a fall in the price of gold* ○ *a fall on the stock exchange* ○ *Profits showed a 10% fall.* ■ *verb* **1.** to be reduced suddenly to a lower price or value ○ *Shares fell on the market today.* ○ *Gold shares fell 10%* or *fell 45 cents on the stock exchange.* ○ *The price of gold fell for the second day running.* ○ *The pound fell against the euro.* (NOTE: **falling – fell – has fallen**) **2.** to happen or to take place ○ *The public holiday falls on a Tuesday.* (NOTE: **falling – fell – has fallen**) □ **payments which fall due** payments which are now due to be made

'…market analysts described the falls in the second half of last week as a technical correction to the market' [*Australian Financial Review*]

'…for the first time since mortgage rates began falling in March a financial institution has raised charges on homeowner loans' [*Globe and Mail (Toronto)*]

'…interest rates were still falling as late as June, and underlying inflation remains below the government's target of 2.5%' [*Financial Times*]

fall away *phrasal verb* to become less ○ *Hotel bookings have fallen away since the tourist season ended.*

fall back *phrasal verb* to become lower or cheaper after rising in price ○ *Shares fell back in light trading.*

fall back on *phrasal verb* to have to use something kept for emergencies ○ *to fall back on cash reserves* ○ *The management fell back on the usual old excuses.*

fall behind *phrasal verb* to be late in doing something ○ *They fell behind with their mortgage repayments.*

fall off *phrasal verb* to become lower, cheaper, or less ○ *Sales have fallen off since the tourist season ended.*

fall out *phrasal verb* □ **the bottom has fallen out of the market** sales have fallen below what previously seemed to be their lowest point

fall through /ˌfɔːl ˈθruː/ *phrasal verb* not to happen or not to take place ○ *The plan fell through at the last moment.*

fall-back price /ˈfɔːl bæk ˌpraɪs/ *noun* the lowest price which a seller will accept ○ *The buyer tries to guess the seller's fall-back price.* ○ *The fall-back price must not be any lower or there won't be any profit in the deal.*

falling /ˈfɔːlɪŋ/ *adjective* becoming smaller or dropping in price

'…falling profitability means falling share prices' [*Investors Chronicle*]

falling market /ˌfɔːlɪŋ ˈmɑːkɪt/ *noun* a market where prices are coming down

falling pound /ˌfɔːlɪŋ ˈpaʊnd/ *noun* the pound when it is losing its value against other currencies

false /fɔːls/ *adjective* not true or not correct ○ *to make a false claim for a product* ○ *to make a false entry in the balance sheet*

false claim /ˌfɔːls ˈkleɪm/ *noun* an untrue or exaggerated claim made in the advertising of a product ○ *A voluntary control body was set up to discourage false claims in the advertising business.*

false weight /ˌfɔːls ˈweɪt/ *noun* a weight as measured on shop scales which is wrong and so cheats customers

falsification /ˌfɔːlsɪfɪˈkeɪʃ(ə)n/ *noun* the act of making false entries in accounts

falsify /ˈfɔːlsɪfaɪ/ *verb* to change something to make it wrong ○ *They were accused of falsifying the accounts.*

family /ˈfæm(ə)li/ *noun* a group of products which are linked by a brand name or by their packaging

family branding /ˌfæm(ə)li ˈbrænd-ɪŋ/ *noun* the practice of selling a variety of different products under the same brand name

family life cycle /ˌfæm(ə)li ˈlaɪf ˌsaɪk(ə)l/ *noun* the stages through which consumers pass in their lives, as they have families, e.g. 'young singles', 'young marrieds', 'young couples with small children', 'couples with adolescent children still at home' and 'retired couples', which correspond to different types of buying behaviour

family packaging /ˌfæm(ə)li ˈpækɪdʒɪŋ/ *noun* the practice of selling a whole range of products in similar packaging ○ *We hope that family packaging will make for a clear company image.*

fancy goods /ˈfænsi ɡʊdz/ *plural noun* small attractive items

fanfold /ˈfænfəʊld/ *noun* same as **accordion fold**

fascia /ˈfeɪʃə/, **facia** /ˈfeɪʃə/ *noun* **1.** a board over a shop on which the name of the shop is written **2.** a board above an exhibition stand on which the name of the company represented is written

fast /fɑːst/ *adjective, adverb* quick or quickly ○ *The train is the fastest way of getting to our supplier's factory.* ○ *Toys sell fast in the pre-Christmas period.*

fast food /ˈfɑːst fʊd/ *noun* food that can be cooked and sold quickly to customers, often using franchises, e.g. hamburgers and pizzas

fastmarketing /ˈfɑːstˌmɑːkɪtɪŋ/ *noun* the concept of concentrating all promotions into a short space of time, so that customers cannot avoid being affected

'…fastmarketing tactics mark a radical departure from more traditional marketing. Instead of dotting commercials over a four or five week campaign, fastmarketers try to squeeze them into just a few days' [*Times*]

fast-moving consumer goods /ˌfɑːst ˌmuːvɪŋ kənˈsjuːmə ˌɡʊdz/ *plural noun* essential low-price goods which get repeat orders ○ *He couldn't work in FMCGs because his only experience was in industrial selling.* Abbreviation **FMCGs**

fast-selling item /ˌfɑːst ˌselɪŋ ˈaɪtəm/ *noun* an item which sells quickly

favourable /ˈfeɪv(ə)rəb(ə)l/ *adjective* giving an advantage (NOTE: The US spelling is **favorable**.) □ **on favourable terms** on especially good terms ○ *The shop is let on very favourable terms.*

favourable balance of trade /ˌfeɪv(ə)rəb(ə)l ˌbæləns əv 'treɪd/, **favourable trade balance** /ˌfeɪv-(ə)rəb(ə)l 'treɪd ˌbæləns/ *noun* a situation where a country's exports are larger than its imports

fax /fæks/ *noun* **1.** a system for sending the exact copy of a document via telephone lines ○ *Can you confirm the booking by fax?* **2.** a document sent by this method ○ *We received a fax of the order this morning.* ■ *verb* to send a message by fax ○ *The details of the offer were faxed to the brokers this morning.* ○ *I've faxed the documents to our New York office.*

faxback /'fæksbæk/ *noun* a system of responding by fax, e.g. by downloading pages from a website direct to a fax machine, or where customers dial a fax number and get a fax back on their fax machine

FCC *abbreviation* Federal Communications Commission

fear /fɪə/ *noun* the feeling of being afraid

fear appeal /'fɪə əˌpiːl/ *noun* an advertising message that makes the reader anxious about something, especially about not doing something

feasibility report /ˌfiːzə'bɪlɪti rɪˌpɔːt/ *noun* a document which says if it is worth undertaking something

feasibility study /ˌfiːzə'bɪlɪti ˌstʌdi/ *noun* the careful investigation of a project to see whether it is worth undertaking ○ *We will carry out a feasibility study to decide whether it is worth setting up an agency in the USA.*

feasibility test /ˌfiːzə'bɪlɪti test/ *noun* a test to see if something is possible

feature /'fiːtʃə/ *noun* an article in a newspaper or magazine that deals with one subject in depth ○ *There is a feature in the next issue describing the history of our company.*

features /'fiːtʃəz/ *plural noun* the particular important aspects of a product or service which are advertised as an attraction to the purchaser, as opposed to 'benefits' which show how the product or service will improve the quality of life of the purchaser

Federal Communications Commission /ˌfed(ə)rəl kəˌmjuːnɪ'keɪ-ʃ(ə)nz kəˌmɪʃən/ *noun* a regulatory body in the US whose job is to monitor all non-government communications and broadcasts. Abbreviation **FCC**

Federal Trade Commission /ˌfed(ə)rəl 'treɪd kəˌmɪʃ(ə)n/ *noun* a federal agency established to keep business competition free and fair

feed /fiːd/ *verb* to give information or tips to another salesperson regarding promising customers or areas for sales ○ *I can feed you some interesting sales leads.* (NOTE: **feeding – fed**)

feedback /'fiːdbæk/ *noun* information, especially about the result of an activity which allows adjustments to be made to the way it is done in future ○ *We are getting positive feedback about our after-sales service.* ○ *It would be useful to have some feedback from people who had a test drive but didn't buy the car.* ○ *Are we getting any feedback on customer reaction to our new product?*

…the service is particularly useful when we are working in a crisis management area and we need fast feedback from consumers [*PR Week*]

field /fiːld/ *noun* **1.** an area of study or interest □ **first in the field** being the first company to bring out a product or to start a service ○ *Smith Ltd has a great advantage in being first in the field with a reliable electric car.* **2.** □ **in the field** outside the office, among the customers ○ *We have sixteen reps in the field.*

field of experience /ˌfiːld əv ɪk'spɪərəns/ *noun* the general experience that a sender and receiver of a message use in considering the message

field research /'fiːld rɪˌsɜːtʃ/ *noun* the process of looking for information that is not yet published and must be obtained in surveys ○ *They had to do a lot of fieldwork before they found the right market for the product.* ○ *Field research is carried out to gauge potential demand.*

field sales force /ˌfiːld 'seɪlz ˌfɔːs/ *noun* salespeople working outside the company's offices, in the field ○ *After working for a year in the field sales force, she became field sales man-*

ager. ○ *The field sales force operates in three main areas.*

field sales manager /fiːld 'seɪlz ˌmænɪdʒə/ *noun* the manager in charge of a group of salespeople

field trial /'fiːld traɪəlz/, **field test** /'fiːld test/ *noun* a test of a new product or of something such as an advertisement on real customers

field work /'fiːld wɜːk/ *noun* same as **field research** ○ *They had to do a lot of field work to find the right market for the product.*

fill /fɪl/ *verb* □ **to fill a gap** to provide a product or service which is needed, but which no one has provided before ○ *The new range of small cars fills a gap in the market.*

filler /'fɪlə/ *noun* something which fills a space ○ a filler ad

filter /'fɪltə/ *noun* a process of analysis applied to incoming information in order to identify any material that could be of interest to an organisation

filter question /'fɪltə ˌkwestʃən/ *noun* a question in a questionnaire designed to separate respondents who are worth questioning further from those who are not

finance /'faɪnæns/ *noun* **1.** money used by a company, provided by the shareholders or by loans ○ *Where will they get the necessary finance for the project?* (NOTE: The US term is **financing**) **2.** the business of managing money ■ *verb* to provide money to pay for something ○ *They plan to finance the operation with short-term loans.*

'…an official said that the company began to experience a sharp increase in demand for longer-term mortgages at a time when the flow of money used to finance these loans diminished' [*Globe and Mail*]

Finance Act /'faɪnæns ækt/ *noun* an annual Act of Parliament which gives the government the power to obtain money from taxes as proposed in the Budget

finance department /'faɪnæns dɪˌpɑːtmənt/, **finance committee** /'faɪnæns kəˈmɪti/ *noun* the department or committee which manages the money used in an organisation

finance market /'faɪnæns ˌmɑːkɪt/ *noun* a place where large sums of money can be lent or borrowed

finances /'faɪnænsɪz/ *plural noun* money or cash which is available ○ *the bad state of the company's finances*

financial /faɪˈnænʃəl/ *adjective* relating to money

financial accounting /faɪˌnæn-ʃ(ə)l əˈkaʊntɪŋ/, **financial accountancy** /faɪˌnænʃ(ə)l əˈkaʊntənsi/ *noun* the form of accounting in which financial reports are produced to provide investors or other external parties with information on a company's financial status. Compare **management accounting**

financial advertising /faɪˌnænʃ(ə)l 'ædvətaɪzɪŋ/ *noun* advertising by companies in the field of financial investment

financial audit /faɪˌnænʃəl 'ɔːdɪt/ *noun* an examination of the books and accounts of an advertising agency

financial correspondent /faɪˌn-ænʃəl ˌkɒrɪsˈpɒndənt/ *noun* a journalist who writes articles on money matters for a newspaper

financial institution /faɪˌnænʃəl ˌɪnstɪˈtjuːʃ(ə)n/ *noun* a bank, investment trust or insurance company whose work involves lending or investing large sums of money

financially /fɪˈnænʃəli/ *adverb* regarding money □ **a company which is financially sound** a company which is profitable and has strong assets

financial position /faɪˌnænʃəl pəˈzɪʃ(ə)n/ *noun* the state of a person's or company's bank balance in terms of assets and debts

financial resources /faɪˌnænʃəl rɪˈzɔːsɪz/ *plural noun* the supply of money for something ○ *a company with strong financial resources*

financial risk /faɪˌnænʃəl 'rɪsk/ *noun* the possibility of losing money ○ *The company is taking a considerable financial risk in manufacturing 25 million units without doing any market research.* ○ *There is always some financial risk in selling on credit.*

financial statement /faɪˌnænʃəl ˈsteɪtmənt/ *noun* a document which shows the financial situation of a company ○ *The accounts department has prepared a financial statement for the shareholders.*

Financial Times Index /faɪˌnænʃəl ˈtaɪmz ɪnˌdeks/ *noun* an index which shows percentage rises or falls in share prices on the London Stock Exchange based on a small group of major companies

financier /faɪˈnænsiə/ *noun* a person who lends large amounts of money to companies or who buys shares in companies as an investment

financing /ˈfaɪnænsɪŋ/ *noun* the act of providing money for a project ○ *The financing of the project was done by two international banks.*

find time /ˈfaɪnd taɪm/ *noun* the time taken by a customer to find what he or she wants in a store

fine /faɪn/ *adverb* very thin or very small □ **we are cutting our margins very fine** we are reducing our margins to the smallest possible amount

finished goods /ˌfɪnɪʃt ˈɡʊdz/ *plural noun* manufactured goods which are ready to be sold

fire-fight /ˈfaɪə faɪt/ *verb* to fight bad publicity for a client ○ *The agency has done fire-fighting work for the egg producers.*

fire sale /ˈfaɪə seɪl/ *noun* **1.** a sale of fire-damaged goods **2.** a sale of anything at a very low price

firm /fɜːm/ *noun* a company, business or partnership ○ *a manufacturing firm* ○ *an important publishing firm* ○ *She is a partner in a law firm.* ■ *adjective* **1.** unchangeable ○ *to make a firm offer for something* ○ *to place a firm order for two aircraft* **2.** not dropping in price and possibly going to rise ○ *Sterling was firmer on the foreign exchange markets.* ○ *Shares remained firm.* ■ *verb* to remain at a price and seem likely to rise ○ *The shares firmed at £1.50.*

'…some profit-taking was noted, but underlying sentiment remained firm' [*Financial Times*]

firm up *phrasal verb* to agree on the final details of something ○ *We expect to firm up the deal at the next trade fair.*

firm price /ˌfɜːm ˈpraɪs/ *noun* a price which will not change ○ *They are quoting a firm price of $1.23 a unit.*

first choice /ˌfɜːst ˈtʃɔɪs/ *noun* a prospective customer who chooses the first option available, as opposed to a 'tyrekicker' who wants to examine every option before coming to a decision

firsthand /ˌfɜːst ˈhænd/ *adjective* **1.** coming directly from the original source **2.** new or unused ○ *I actually bought the TV firsthand, but at a second-hand price.*

firsthand information /ˌfɜːsthænd ˌɪnfəˈmeɪʃ(ə)n/ *noun* information from an original source ○ *We had a firsthand account of what happened at the sales meeting from one of the salesreps who was there.*

first-line management /ˌfɜːst laɪn ˈmænɪdʒmənt/ *noun* the managers who have immediate contact with the workforce

first mover /ˌfɜːst ˈmuːvə/ *noun* a person or company that is the first to launch a product in a market

first mover advantage /fɜːst ˈmuːvə ədˌvɑːntɪdʒ/ *noun* the advantage a company gets in being the first to enter a market

first-run syndication /ˌfɜːst rʌn sɪndɪˈkeɪʃ(ə)n/ *noun* material produced specifically for the syndication market

fishy-back freight /ˈfɪʃi bæk ˌfreɪt/ *noun* US the transportation of trucks or freight-train cars on ferries or barges (NOTE: compare **piggy-back freight**)

fix /fɪks/ *verb* **1.** to arrange or to agree ○ *to fix a budget* ○ *to fix a meeting for 3 p.m.* ○ *The date has still to be fixed.* ○ *The price of gold was fixed at $300.* ○ *The mortgage rate has been fixed at 5%.* **2.** to mend ○ *The technicians are coming to fix the phone system.* ○ *Can you fix the photocopier?*

'…coupons are fixed by reference to interest rates at the time a gilt is first issued' [*Investors Chronicle*]

fixed /fɪkst/ *adjective* unable to be changed or removed

'…you must offer shippers and importers fixed rates over a reasonable period of time' [*Lloyd's List*]

fixed assets /ˌfɪkst ˈæsets/ *plural noun* property or machinery which a company owns and uses, but which the company does not buy or sell as part of its regular trade, including the company's investments in shares of other companies

fixed break /ˌfɪkst ˈbreɪk/ *noun* the placing of a television or radio advertisement in a specific commercial break on a specific day, at the advertiser's insistence

fixed costs /ˌfɪkst ˈkɒsts/ *plural noun* business costs which do not change with the quantity of the product made

fixed expenses /ˌfɪkst ɪkˈspensɪz/ *plural noun* expenses which do not vary with different levels of production, e.g. rent, staff salaries and insurance

fixed-fee arrangement /ˌfɪkst ˈfiːəˌreɪndʒmənt/ *noun* a way of agreeing the fees for an agency before the agency starts work on a project

fixed position /ˌfɪkst pəˈzɪʃ(ə)n/ *noun* the placing of an advertisement in a specific location in a publication, or running a commercial at a fixed time of day, at the advertiser's insistence

fixed-price agreement /ˌfɪkst ˈpraɪs əˌgriːmənt/ *noun* an agreement where a company provides a service or a product at a price which stays the same for the whole period of the agreement

fixed rate /ˌfɪkst ˈreɪt/ *noun* a rate, e.g. an exchange rate, which does not change

fixed scale of charges /ˌfɪkst skeɪl əv ˈtʃɑːdʒɪz/ *noun* a set of charges that do not vary according to individual circumstances but are applied consistently in all cases of a particular kind

fixed spot /ˌfɪkst ˈspɒt/ *noun* the placing of a TV or radio commercial in a specific position, at the advertiser's insistence

fixing /ˈfɪksɪŋ/ *noun* **1.** arranging ○ *the fixing of charges* ○ *the fixing of a mortgage rate* **2.** a regular meeting to set a price

flagship /ˈflæɡʃɪp/ *noun* the key product in a range, on which the reputation of the producer most depends

flagship store /ˈflæɡʃɪp stɔː/, **flagship hotel** /ˈflæɡʃɪp həʊˌtel/ *noun* the main store or hotel in a chain

flash pack /ˈflæʃ pæk/ *noun* a pack or package which shows a price reduction very clearly in order to attract customers ○ *Flash packs are displayed at eye-level on the supermarket shelves to attract the attention of passing customers.*

flat rate /ˌflæt ˈreɪt/ *noun* a charge which always stays the same ○ *a flat-rate increase of 10%* ○ *We pay a flat rate for electricity each quarter.* ○ *He is paid a flat rate of £2 per thousand.*

Flexible Work Regulations /ˌfleksɪb(ə)l ˈwɜːk reɡjʊˌleɪʃ(ə)nz/ *plural noun* (*in the UK*) the legal right for a parent with a child under the age of 6, or with a disabled child under the age of 18, to ask that their working hours should be arranged to help them with their responsibilities

flier /ˈflaɪə/ *noun* a promotional leaflet

flight /flaɪt/ *verb* to arrange a scheduling pattern for something

flighting by number /ˌflaɪtɪŋ baɪ ˈnʌmbə/ *noun* scheduling things in a series of groups, with the same number in each group

floating population /ˌfləʊtɪŋ pɒpjʊˈleɪʃ(ə)n/ *noun* people who move from place to place

flog /flɒɡ/ *verb* to publicise something very aggressively

flood /flʌd/ *noun* a large quantity ○ *We received a flood of orders.* ○ *Floods of tourists filled the hotels.* ■ *verb* to fill with a large quantity of something ○ *The market was flooded with cheap imitations.* ○ *The sales department is flooded with orders* or *with complaints.*

floor /flɔː/ *noun* all the rooms on one level in a building ○ *Her office is on the 26th floor.* (NOTE: In the UK, the floor at street level is the **ground floor**, but in the US it is the **first floor**. Each floor in the USA is one number higher than the same floor in Britain.)

floor manager /ˈflɔː ˌmænɪdʒə/ *noun* US a person in charge of the sales staff in a department store

floor space /ˈflɔː speɪs/ *noun* an area of floor in an office or warehouse ○ *We have 3,500 square metres of floor space to let.*

floor stand /'flɔː stænd/ *noun* a display stand which stands on the floor, as opposed to one which stands on a table or counter

floorwalker /'flɔːwɔːkə/ *noun* an employee of a department store who advises customers, and supervises the shop assistants in a department

flop /flɒp/ *noun* a failure, or something which has not been successful ○ *The new model was a flop.* ■ *verb* to fail or not be a success ○ *The launch of the new shampoo flopped badly.* (NOTE: **flopping – flopped**)

flow chart /'fləʊ tʃɑːt/, **flow diagram** /'fləʊ ˌdaɪəgræm/ *noun* a chart which shows the arrangement of work processes in a series

fluff /flʌf/ *verb* □ **fluff it and fly it** give a product an attractive appearance and then sell it (*informal*)

fluidity /fluˈɪdɪti/ *noun* ease of movement or change

fluidity of labour /fluˌɪdɪti əv 'leɪbə/ *noun* the extent to which employees move from one place to another to work or from one occupation to another

fly poster /'flaɪ ˌpəʊstə/ *noun* a poster which is pasted to a site without permission and without being paid for

fly-posting /'flaɪ ˌpəʊstɪŋ/ *noun* the practice of sticking posters up illegally, without permission of the site owner and without making any payment

FMCGs *abbreviation* fast-moving consumer goods

focus group /'fəʊkəs gruːp/ *noun* a group of people who are brought together to discuss informally a market-research question

fold-out /'fəʊld aʊt/ *noun* a folded page in a publication, which opens out to show a much larger advertisement

follow /'fɒləʊ/ *verb* **1.** to come behind or to come afterwards ○ *The samples will follow by surface mail.* ○ *We will pay £10,000 now, with the balance to follow in six months' time.* **2.** to subscribe to another user's profile page on *Twitter*

follow up *phrasal verb* to examine something further ○ *I'll follow up your idea of targeting our address list with a*

special mailing. □ **to follow up an initiative** to take action once someone else has decided to do something

follower /'fɒləʊə/ *noun* **1.** a company which follows others into a market **2.** someone who subscribes to another user's profile page on Twitter ○ *The company's profile has attracted more than a thousand followers since it was created.*

following reading matter /ˌfɒləʊɪŋ 'riːdɪŋ ˌmætə/ *noun* a good position for an advertisement, which follows an interesting article in a newspaper or magazine

font /fɒnt/ *noun* a set of characters all of the same size and face

foot /fʊt/ *verb* □ **to foot the bill** to pay the costs

footer /'fʊtə/ *noun* a section at the bottom of a webpage, which usually contains any essential links and information on how to contact the organisation that owns the page and on its copyright and privacy policy

footfall /'fʊtfɔːl/ *noun* the number of customers who come into and walk round a shop

'…the small independent retailer who stocks up using cash and carries could be hit hard by the loss of footfall associated with any increase in smuggled goods' [*The Grocer*]

force /fɔːs/ *noun* **1.** strength □ **to be in force** to be operating or working ○ *The rules have been in force since 1986.* □ **to come into force** to start to operate or work ○ *The new regulations will come into force on 1st January.* **2.** a group of people ■ *verb* to make someone do something ○ *Competition has forced the company to lower its prices.* ○ *After the takeover several of the managers were forced to take early retirement.*

force down *phrasal verb* to make something such as prices become lower □ **to force prices down** to make prices come down ○ *Competition has forced prices down.*

force up *phrasal verb* to make something become higher □ **to force prices up** to make prices go up ○ *The war forced up the price of oil.*

forced consumption /ˌfɔːst kən'sʌmpʃən/ *noun* the attempt to impose a rate or type of consumption on consumers

forced sale /ˌfɔːst 'seɪl/ *noun* a sale which takes place because a court orders it or because it is the only way to avoid a financial crisis

force majeure /ˌfɔːs mæ'ʒɜː/ *noun* something that happens which is out of the control of the parties who have signed a contract, e.g. a strike, war, or storm

forecast /'fɔːkɑːst/ *noun* a description or calculation of what will probably happen in the future ○ *The chairman did not believe the sales director's forecast of higher turnover.* ■ *verb* to calculate or to say what will probably happen in the future ○ *She is forecasting sales of £2m.* ○ *Economists have forecast a fall in the exchange rate.* (NOTE: **forecasting – forecast**)

forecasting /'fɔːkɑːstɪŋ/ *noun* the process of calculating what will probably happen in the future ○ *Manpower planning will depend on forecasting the future levels of production.*

foreign /'fɒrɪn/ *adjective* not belonging to your own country ○ *Foreign cars have flooded our market.* ○ *We are increasing our trade with foreign countries.*

'…a sharp setback in foreign trade accounted for most of the winter slowdown' [*Fortune*]

'…the dollar recovered a little lost ground on the foreign exchanges yesterday' [*Financial Times*]

foreign currency /ˌfɒrɪn 'kʌrənsi/ *noun* money of another country

foreign currency account /ˌfɒrɪn 'kʌrənsi əˌkaʊnt/ *noun* a bank account in the currency of another country, e.g. a dollar account in a UK bank

foreign currency reserves /ˌfɒrɪn 'kʌrənsi rɪˌzɜːvz/ *plural noun* a country's reserves held in currencies of other countries. Also called **foreign exchange reserves, international reserves**

'…the treasury says it needs the cash to rebuild its foreign reserves which have fallen from $19 billion when the government took office to $7 billion in August' [*Economist*]

foreign exchange market /ˌfɒrɪn ɪks'tʃeɪndʒ ˌmɑːkɪt/ *noun* **1.** a market where people buy and sell foreign currencies ○ *She trades on the foreign exchange market.* **2.** dealings in foreign currencies ○ *Foreign exchange markets were very active after the dollar devalued.*

foreign exchange reserves /ˌfɒrɪn ɪks'tʃeɪndʒ rɪˌzɜːvz/ *plural noun* foreign money held by a government to support its own currency and pay its debts

foreign exchange transfer /ˌfɒrɪn ɪks'tʃeɪndʒ ˌtrænsfɜː/ *noun* the sending of money from one country to another

foreign goods /ˌfɒrɪn 'gʊdz/ *plural noun* goods manufactured in other countries

foreign investments /ˌfɒrɪn ɪn'vestmənts/ *plural noun* money invested in other countries

forfeit /'fɔːfɪt/ *noun* the fact of having something taken away as a punishment □ **the goods were declared forfeit** the court said that the goods had to be taken away from the person who was holding them ■ *verb* to have something taken away as a punishment □ **to forfeit a deposit** to lose a deposit which was left for an item because you have decided not to buy that item

forfeit clause /'fɔːfɪt klɔːz/ *noun* a clause in a contract which says that goods or a deposit will be taken away if the contract is not obeyed

forfeiture /'fɔːfɪtʃə/ *noun* the act of forfeiting a property

form /fɔːm/ *noun* **1.** □ **form of words** words correctly laid out for a legal document □ **receipt in due form** a correctly written receipt **2.** an official printed paper with blank spaces which have to be filled in with information ○ *You have to fill in form A20.* ○ *Each passenger was given a customs declaration form.* ○ *The reps carry pads of order forms.*

forma /'fɔːmə/ *noun* ➡ **pro forma**

format /'fɔːmæt/ *noun* **1.** the general page design or size of a publication **2.** the general style of an email or electronic marketing piece

form utility /'fɔːm juːˌtɪlɪti/ *noun* a use for a product created by the introduction of the product

forty-eight sheet /ˌfɔːti 'eɪt ʃiːt/ *noun* a large poster-sized sheet of paper

forum /'fɔːrəm/ *noun* an online area where Internet users can read, post, and respond to messages

forward /'fɔːwəd/ *adjective* in advance or to be paid at a later date ■ *adverb* **1.** □ **to date a cheque forward** to put a later date than the present one on a cheque **2.** □ **to sell forward** to sell foreign currency, commodities, etc., for delivery at a later date **3.** □ **balance brought forward, carried forward** balance which is entered in an account at the end of a period and is then taken to be the starting point of the next period ■ *verb* □ **to forward something to someone** to send something to someone ○ *to forward a consignment to Nigeria* □ **'please forward', 'to be forwarded'** words written on an envelope, asking the person receiving it to send it on to the person whose name is written on it

forward contract /'fɔːwəd ˌkɒntrækt/ *noun* a one-off agreement to buy currency, shares or commodities for delivery at a later date at a specific price

forwarding /'fɔːwədɪŋ/ *noun* the act of arranging shipping and customs documents

forwarding address /'fɔːwədɪŋ əˌdres/ *noun* the address to which a person's mail can be sent on

forwarding agent /'fɔːwədɪŋ ˌeɪdʒənt/ *noun* a person or company which arranges shipping and customs documents

forward integration /ˌfɔːwəd ˌɪntəˈɡreɪʃ(ə)n/ *noun* a process of expansion in which a company becomes its own distributor or takes over a company in the same line of business as itself ○ *Forward integration will give the company greater control over its selling.* ○ *Forward integration has brought the company closer to its consumers and has made it aware of their buying habits.* Compare **backward integration**

forward market /ˌfɔːwəd 'mɑːkɪt/ *noun* a market for purchasing foreign currency, oil or commodities for delivery at a later date

forward price /'fɔːwəd praɪs/ *noun* a price of goods which are to be delivered in the future

forward sales /'fɔːwəd seɪlz/ *plural noun* sales of shares, commodities or foreign exchange for delivery at a later date

foul bill of lading /ˌfaʊl bɪl əv 'leɪdɪŋ/ *noun* a bill of lading which says that the goods were in bad condition when received by the shipper

four-colour process /ˌfɔː kʌlə 'prəʊses/ *noun* a printing process where the three primary colours and black are used to create a wide range of shades

four Cs /fɔː 'siz/ *plural noun* a simple way of referring to the four important points regarding customers: value to the Customer, Cost, Convenience for the customer, and Communication between seller and buyer

four Os /ˌfɔːr 'əʊz/ *plural noun* a simple way of summarising the essentials of a marketing operation, which are Objects, Objectives, Organisation, and Operations

four-plus cover /fɔː 'plʌs ˌkʌvə/ *noun* a situation where consumers in the target audience will have seen an advertisement at least four times on average

four Ps /ˌfɔː 'piːz/ *plural noun* a simple way of summarising the essentials of the marketing mix, which are Product, Price, Promotion, and Place

fraction /'frækʃən/ *noun* a part of a whole

fragment /fræɡ'ment/ *verb* to split into sections

'…the consumer market is fragmenting, which means that brand advertising to the whole market is no longer enough' [*Financial Times*]

fragmentation /ˌfræɡmənˈteɪʃ(ə)n/ *noun* the use of a variety of media for a publicity campaign

fragmented market /fræɡˌmentɪd 'mɑːkɪt/ *noun* a market which is split into many small segments, which are more difficult to sell into

frame /freɪm/ *noun* same as **sampling frame**

franchise /'fræntʃaɪz/ *noun* a licence to trade using a brand name and paying a royalty for it ○ *He's bought a printing franchise* or *a pizza franchise.* ■ *verb* to sell licences for people to trade using a brand name and paying a royalty ○ *His sandwich bar was so successful that he decided to franchise it.*

'...many new types of franchised businesses will join the ranks of the giant chains of fast-food restaurants, hotels and motels and rental car agencies' [*Franchising Opportunities*]

'...a quarter of a million Britons are seeking to become their own bosses by purchasing franchises' [*Marketing Week*]

'...feelings are already running high over the question of how to allocate the next TV franchises' [*Marketing*]

franchise agreement /'fræntʃaɪz ə‚griːmənt/, **franchise contract** /'fræntʃaɪz ‚kɒntrækt/ *noun* a legal contract to trade using a brand name and paying a royalty for it

franchise-building promotion /'fræntʃaɪz ‚bɪldɪŋ prə‚məʊʃ(ə)n/ *noun* a sales promotion aimed at building up long-term repeat sales and customer loyalty

franchise chain /'fræntʃaɪz tʃeɪn/ *noun* a series of retail stores or fast-food outlets which are operated as franchises from the main operator

franchisee /‚fræntʃaɪ'ziː/ *noun* a person who runs a franchise

franchiser /'fræntʃaɪzə/ *noun* a person who licenses a franchise

franchising /'fræntʃaɪzɪŋ/ *noun* the act of selling a licence to trade as a franchise ○ *She runs her sandwich chain as a franchising operation.*

franchisor /'fræntʃaɪzə/ *noun* another spelling of **franchiser**

franco /'fræŋkəʊ/ *adverb* free

fraudulent misrepresentation /‚frɔːdjʊlənt mɪs‚reprɪzen'teɪʃ(ə)n/ *noun* the act of making a false statement with the intention of tricking a customer

free /friː/ *adjective, adverb* **1.** not costing any money ○ *I have been given a free ticket to the exhibition.* ○ *The price includes free delivery.* ○ *All goods in the store are delivered free.* ○ *A catalogue will be sent free on request.* □ **free alongside ship** referring to a price that includes all costs up to delivery of goods next to the ship on the quay □ **free docks** referring to a price that includes all costs up to delivery of goods to the

docks □ **free of charge** with no payment to be made □ **free on quay** referring to a price that includes all costs up to delivery of goods next to the ship on the quay □ **free overboard** *or* **free overside** referring to a price that includes up to arrival of the ship at a port **2.** with no restrictions □ **free of tax** with no tax having to be paid ○ *Interest is paid free of tax.* □ **free of duty** with no duty to be paid ○ *to import wine free of duty* **3.** not busy or not occupied ○ *Are there any free tables in the restaurant?* ○ *I shall be free in a few minutes.* ○ *The chairman always keeps Friday afternoon free for a game of bridge.* ■ *verb* to make something available or easy ○ *The government's decision has freed millions of pounds for investment.*

'American business as a whole is increasingly free from heavy dependence on manufacturing' [*Sunday Times*]

free advertisement /friː əd'vɜː-tɪsmənt/ *noun* an advertisement shown without any charge to the advertiser ○ *The newspaper agreed to place a free advertisement for the charity on the back page.*

freebie /'friːbi/ *noun* a product or service supplied free of charge, especially a gift to an agent or journalist (*informal*)

free collective bargaining /‚friː kə‚lektɪv 'baːgɪnɪŋ/ *noun* negotiations between management and trade unions about wage increases and working conditions

free competition /‚friː ‚kɒmpə-'tɪʃ(ə)n/ *noun* the fact of being free to compete without government interference

free currency /‚friː 'kʌrənsi/ *noun* a currency which is allowed by the government to be bought and sold without restriction

free delivery area /friː dɪ'lɪv(ə)-ri ‚eəriə/ *noun* an area within which a seller will deliver purchases free ○ *The total price will be low as the goods are being delivered in a free delivery area.*

free enterprise /‚friː 'entəpraɪz/ *noun* a system of business free from government interference

free gift /‚friː 'gɪft/ *noun* a present given by a shop to a customer who buys a specific amount of goods ○ *There is a free gift worth £25 to any customer buying a washing machine.*

free market /ˌfriː ˈmɑːkɪt/ *noun* a market in which there is no government control of supply and demand, and the rights of individuals and organisations to physical and intellectual property are upheld

free market economy /ˌfriː ˌmɑːkɪt ɪˈkɒnəmi/ *noun* an economic system where the government does not interfere in business activity in any way

free on board /ˌfriː ɒn ˈbɔːd/ *adjective* **1.** including in the price all the seller's costs until the goods are on the ship for transportation. Abbreviation **f.o.b. 2.** including in the price all the seller's costs until the goods are delivered to a place

free paper /ˌfriː ˈpeɪpə/ *noun* a newspaper which is given away free, and which relies on its advertising for its income

freephone /ˈfriːfəʊn/, **freefone** *noun* a system where you can telephone to reply to an advertisement, to place an order, or to ask for information and the seller pays for the call

free port /ˈfriː pɔːt/ *noun* a port where there are no customs duties to be paid

freepost /ˈfriːpəʊst/ *noun* a system where someone can write to an advertiser to place an order or to ask for information to be sent, without paying for a stamp. The company paying for the postage on receipt of the envelope.

free sample /ˌfriː ˈsɑːmpəl/ *noun* a sample given free to advertise a product

freesheet /ˈfriːʃiːt/ *noun* same as **free paper**

free-standing insert /ˌfriː stændɪŋ ˈɪnsɜːt/ *noun* advertising material on one or more pages which is inserted into a newspaper. Abbreviation **FSI**

free trade /ˌfriː ˈtreɪd/ *noun* a system where goods can go from one country to another without any restrictions

free trader /ˌfriː ˈtreɪdə/ *noun* a person who is in favour of free trade

free trade zone /ˌfriː ˈtreɪd ˌzəʊn/ *noun* an area where there are no customs duties

free trial /ˌfriː ˈtraɪəl/ *noun* an opportunity to test a machine or product with no payment involved

freeware /ˈfriːweə/ *noun* free software programs

freeze /friːz/ *verb* to keep something such as money or costs at their present level and not allow them to rise ○ *to freeze wages and prices* ○ *to freeze credits* ○ *to freeze company dividends* ○ *We have frozen expenditure at last year's level.* (NOTE: **freezing – froze – frozen**)

freeze out *phrasal verb* □ **to freeze out the competition** to trade successfully and cheaply and so prevent competitors from operating

freight /freɪt/ *noun* **1.** the cost of transporting goods by air, sea, or land ○ *At an auction, the buyer pays the freight.* **2.** goods which are transported □ **to take on freight** to load goods onto a ship, train, or truck ■ *verb* □ **to freight goods** to send goods ○ *We freight goods to all parts of the country.*

freightage /ˈfreɪtɪdʒ/ *noun* the cost of transporting goods

freight collect /ˈfreɪt kəˌlekt/ *noun* US an arrangement whereby the customer pays for transporting the goods

freight costs /ˈfreɪt kɒsts/ *plural noun* money paid to transport goods

freight depot /ˈfreɪt ˌdepəʊ/ *noun* a central point where goods are collected before being shipped

freight elevator /ˈfreɪt ˌeləveɪtə/ *noun* a strong lift for carrying goods up and down inside a building

freighter /ˈfreɪtə/ *noun* **1.** an aircraft or ship which carries goods **2.** a person or company that organises the transport of goods

freight forward /ˌfreɪt ˈfɔːwəd/ *noun* a deal where the customer pays for transporting the goods

freight forwarder /ˈfreɪt ˌfɔːwədə/ *noun* a person or company that arranges shipping and customs documents for several shipments from different companies, putting them together to form one large shipment

'...the airline will allow freight forwarder customers to track and trace consignments on the airline's website' [*Lloyd's List*]

freight plane /'freɪt pleɪn/ *noun* an aircraft which carries goods, not passengers

frequency /'friːkwənsi/ *noun* **1.** the number of times something happens **2.** the number of times an advertisement appears in a specific period ○ *The plan is to have larger advertisements but less frequency.* **3.** the number of times a person sees an advertisement during a campaign ○ *We feel that a frequency of two showings per night is enough for the first week of the campaign.*

frequency analysis /'friːkwənsi əˌnæləsɪs/ *noun* analysis of frequency distribution statistics

frequency discount /'friːkwənsi ˌdɪskaʊnt/ *noun* reduced rates offered for frequent use of a advertising medium

frequency distribution /'friːkwənsi dɪstrɪˌbjuːʃ(ə)n/ *noun* statistics, usually in the form of a graph, showing how often a sample group responded in a certain way to a questionnaire

frequent /'friːkwənt/ *adjective* which comes, goes or takes place often ○ *There is a frequent ferry service to France.* ○ *We send frequent faxes to New York.* ○ *How frequent are the planes to Birmingham?*

frequently /'friːkwəntli/ *adverb* often ○ *The photocopier is frequently out of use.* ○ *We email our New York office very frequently – at least four times a day.*

friction-free market /ˌfrɪkʃən friː 'maːkɪt/ *noun* a market in which there are few differences between competing products, so that the customer has an exceptionally free choice

'…economists predict that a new era of nearly friction-free markets will arrive. Companies that don't move quickly to the new technology risk being left behind.' [*Business Week*]

fringe account /'frɪndʒ əˌkaʊnt/ *noun* accounts or customers that are not very profitable for the supplier ○ *The salespeople are not giving priority to these fringe accounts.* ○ *It is hoped that some of these fringe accounts will soon start buying in larger quantities.*

fringe benefit /'frɪndʒ ˌbenɪfɪt/ *noun* an extra item given by a company to employees in addition to a salary, e.g. company cars or private health insurance ○ *The fringe benefits make up for the poor pay.* ○ *Use of the company recreation facilities is one of the fringe benefits of the job.*

fringe time /'frɪndʒ taɪm/ *noun* TV time around prime time where there is usually more availability

front /frʌnt/ *noun* a part of something which faces away from the back ○ *The front of the office building is on the High Street.* ○ *Our ad appeared on the front page of the newspaper.* ○ *There is a photograph of the managing director on the front page of the company report.*

frontage /'frʌntɪdʒ/ *noun* the width of a shop which faces onto the street

front cover /ˌfrʌnt 'kʌvə/ *noun* the front outside page of a publication, as opposed to the back cover

front end /'frʌnt end/ *noun* the part of an organisation that meets and deals with customers face-to-face

front-line management /ˌfrʌnt laɪn 'mænɪdʒmənt/ *noun* managers who have immediate contact with the employees

frontload /'frʌntləʊd/ *verb* to plan a publicity campaign where most costs are incurred in the early stages. Compare **backload**

front man /'frʌnt mæn/ *noun* a person who seems honest but is hiding an illegal trade

front of book /ˌfrʌnt əv 'bʊk/ *noun* the first few pages of a magazine

FSI *abbreviation* free-standing insert

fudge /fʌdʒ/ *noun* a mistake made in an advertisement

fulfil /fʊl'fɪl/ *verb* to complete something in a satisfactory way ○ *The clause regarding payments has not been fulfilled.* (NOTE: **fulfilling- fulfilled**. The US spelling is **fulfill**.) □ **to fulfil an order** to supply the items which have been ordered ○ *We are so understaffed that we cannot fulfil any more orders before Christmas.*

fulfilment /fʊl'fɪlmənt/ *noun* the act of carrying something out in a satisfactory way (NOTE: The US spelling is **fulfillment**.)

fulfilment house /fʊl'fɪlmənt haʊs/ *noun* a company which supplies orders on behalf of a mail-order company

full /fʊl/ *adjective* **1.** complete, including everything □ **we are working at full capacity** we are doing as much work as possible **2.** □ **in full** completely ○ *a full refund a refund paid in full* ○ *Give your full name and address your name and address in full.* ○ *He accepted all our conditions in full.*

'…a tax-free lump sum can be taken partly in lieu of a full pension' [*Investors Chronicle*]

full cost pricing /ˌfʊl kɒst 'praɪsɪŋ/ *noun* a pricing method based on assessing the full production cost of each product unit and adding a profit margin

full costs /ˌfʊl 'kɒsts/ *plural noun* all the costs of manufacturing a product, including both fixed and variable costs

full cover /ˌfʊl 'kʌvə/ *noun* insurance cover against a wide range of risks

full employment /ˌfʊl ɪm'plɔɪ mənt/ *noun* a situation where all the people who can work have jobs

full-function wholesaler /ˌfʊl fʌŋkʃ(ə)n 'həʊlseɪlə/ *noun* a distributor performing all the normal functions of a wholesaler such as storage and transport ○ *There is room for only one full-function wholesaler dealing with this product in the Southampton area.*

full-line forcing /ˌfʊl laɪn 'fɔːsɪŋ/ *noun* a situation where a supplier pressures a customer to buy from that supplier only ○ *If the supplier succeeds in full-line forcing, he will probably raise prices.*

full nester /ˌfʊl 'nestə/ *noun* an older customer who has their own home and who is interested in a good quality of life, eats in restaurants, buys new gadgets, and is not influenced by advertising. ➾ **empty nesters**

full page /'fʊl peɪdʒ/ *noun* a size of advertisement taking up one complete page

full price /ˌfʊl 'praɪs/ *noun* a price with no discount ○ *She bought a full-price ticket.*

full rate /ˌfʊl 'reɪt/ *noun* the standard charge for a service, with no special discounts applied

full-scale /'fʊl skeɪl/ *adjective* complete or very thorough ○ *The MD ordered a full-scale review of credit terms.*

'…the administration launched a full-scale investigation into maintenance procedures' [*Fortune*]

full-service advertising agency /ˌfʊl ˌsɜːvɪs 'ædvətaɪzɪŋ ˌeɪdʒənsi/, **full-service agency** /fʊl ˌsɜːvɪs 'eɪdʒənsi/ *noun* an advertising agency offering a full range of services such as sales promotion, design of house style, advice on public relations and market research, and creating stands for exhibitions ○ *We have so little marketing expertise, we'll need a full-service advertising agency.*

full-time /'fʊl taɪm/ *adjective, adverb* working all the usual working time, i.e. about eight hours a day, five days a week ○ *She's in full-time work She works full-time She's in full-time employment.* ○ *He is one of our full-time staff.*

full-timer /ˌfʊl 'taɪmə/ *noun* a person who works full-time

fully connected world /ˌfʊli kəˌnektɪd 'wɜːld/ *noun* a world where most people and organisations are linked by the Internet or similar networks

function /'fʌŋkʃən/ *noun* a duty or job ■ *verb* to work ○ *The advertising campaign is functioning smoothly.* ○ *The new management structure does not seem to be functioning very well.*

functional /'fʌŋkʃən(ə)l/ *adjective* which can function properly

functional consequences /ˌfʌŋkʃən(ə)l 'kɒnsɪkwensɪz/ *plural noun* the tangible effects of a product or service which a customer experiences directly

functional discount /ˌfʌŋkʃən(ə)l 'dɪskaʊnt/ *noun* a discount offered on goods sold to distributors

functional product differentiation /ˌfʌŋkʃən(ə)l 'prɒdʌkt dɪfərenʃiˌeɪʃ(ə)n/ *noun* the process of ensuring that a product has some functional features that distinguish it from competing ones

functional title /'fʌŋkʃən(ə)l ˌtaɪt(ə)l/ *noun* a job title, the description of a person's job which is used as part of his or her address, e.g. 'marketing manager' or 'head buyer'

fund /fʌnd/ *noun* money set aside for a special purpose

funded debt /ˌfʌndɪd 'det/ *noun* the part of the British National Debt which pays interest, but with no date for repayment of the principal

future /'fjuːtʃə/ *adjective* referring to time to come or to something which has not yet happened ■ *noun* the time which has not yet happened ○ *Try to be more careful in future.* ○ *In future all reports must be sent to Australia by air.*

future delivery /ˌfjuːtʃə dɪ'lɪv(ə)ri/ *noun* delivery at a later date

futurology /ˌfjuːtʃə'rɒlədʒi/ *noun* the prediction and study of future trends

G

gable end /ˈɡeɪb(ə)l end/ *noun* the end of a building which is used as a poster site

gain /ɡeɪn/ *noun* **1.** an increase, or the act of becoming larger □ **gain in experience** the act of getting more experience □ **gain in profitability** the act of becoming more profitable **2.** an increase in profit, price, or value ○ *Oil shares showed gains on the stock exchange.* ○ *Property shares put on gains of 10%–15%.* ■ *verb* **1.** to get or to obtain ○ *She gained some useful experience working in a bank.* □ **to gain control of a business** to buy more than 50% of the shares so that you can direct the business **2.** to rise in value ○ *The dollar gained six points on the foreign exchange markets.*

galleria /ˌɡæləˈriːə/ *noun* a large shopping complex with many different stores under one roof, usually built round a large open space, with fountains, plants, etc.

galley /ˈɡæli/, **galley proof** /ˈɡæli pruːf/ *noun* the first proof of typesetting, before the text is made up into pages

galloping inflation /ˌɡæləpɪŋ ɪnˈfleɪʃ(ə)n/ *noun* very rapid inflation which is almost impossible to reduce

game /ɡeɪm/ *noun* a form of promotional material where people have a chance of winning a prize

game theory /ˈɡeɪm ˌθɪəri/ *noun* a mathematical method of analysis used in operational research to predict the outcomes of games of strategy and conflicts of interest. It is used to assess the likely strategies that people will adopt in situations governed by a particular set of rules and to identify the best approach to a particular problem or conflict.

gap /ɡæp/ *noun* an empty space □ **gap in the market** an opportunity to make a product or provide a service which is needed but which no one has sold before ○ *to look for to find a gap in the market* ○ *This laptop has filled a real gap in the market.*

'…these savings are still not great enough to overcome the price gap between American products and those of other nations' [*Duns Business Month*]

gap analysis /ˈɡæp əˌnæləsɪs/ *noun* analysis of a market to try to find a particular area that is not at present being satisfied ○ *Gap analysis showed that there was a whole area of the market we were not exploiting.* ○ *The computer performed a gap analysis and came up with suggestions for a medium-priced machine suitable for the small business market.*

gatefold /ˈɡeɪtfəʊld/ *noun* a double-page spread in which both pages are folded over, and which open out like a gate to give a spread of almost four pages

gatekeeper /ˈɡeɪtˌkiːpə/ *noun* a person who controls the flow of information within an organisation and so has a great influence on its policy

GDP *abbreviation* gross domestic product

general cargo /ˌdʒen(ə)rəl ˈkɑːɡəʊ/ *noun* a cargo made up of various types of goods ○ *The ship left the port with a general cargo bound for various destinations.*

general preplanning input /ˌdʒen(ə)rəl priːˈplænɪŋ ˌɪnpʊt/ *noun* market research which can be used to prepare the initial stages of an advertising campaign

general store /ˌdʒen(ə)rəl ˈstɔː/ *noun* a small shop which sells a wide range of goods

general trading /ˌdʒen(ə)rəl ˈtreɪdɪŋ/ noun dealing in all types of goods

general wholesaler /ˌdʒen(ə)rəl ˈhəʊlseɪlə/ noun a wholesaler selling a variety of goods

generation /ˌdʒenəˈreɪʃ(ə)n/ noun a stage in the development of a product. Each new generation is a new version of the product with certain technical improvements on the preceding version.

Generation X /ˌdʒenəreɪʃ(ə)n ˈeks/ noun the generation of people who were born between 1963 and 1976 and began their working lives from the 1980s onwards (NOTE: The people who belong to Generation X are said to have challenged traditional corporate expectations by not being solely motivated by money. Instead they want to establish a balance between their professional and personal lives, being in favour of flexible working practices and valuing opportunities for learning and self-advancement.)

generic /dʒəˈnerɪk/ adjective which is shared by a group, and does not refer to one individual ■ noun **1.** a product sold without a brand name ○ *Generics are cheap since they have no name to advertise.* **2.** a brand name which is now given to a product rather than to a particular brand, e.g. hoover, kleenex, or thermos

generic product /dʒə,nerɪk ˈprɒdʌkt/ noun same as **generic** noun 1 ○ *Next to the brightly packaged branded goods the generic products on display were easily overlooked.*

generic term /dʒə,nerɪk ˈtɜːm/, **generic name** /dʒə,nerɪk ˈneɪm/ noun same as **generic** noun 2

gentleman's agreement /ˈdʒent(ə)lmənz ə,griːmənt/ noun a verbal agreement between two parties who trust each other

geocentric stage /ˌdʒiːəʊsentrɪk ˈsteɪdʒ/ noun US an advanced stage in a company's international marketing when there is great co-ordination of overseas marketing activities

geodemographics /ˌdʒiːəʊ,deməˈgræfɪks/ noun a method of analysis combining geographic and demographic variables such as *ACORN* ○ *The company used geodemographics to help ensure its* luxury goods advertising targeted at the right audience.

geographical /ˌdʒiːəˈgræfɪk(ə)l/ adjective referring to an area

geographical concentration /dʒiːə,græfɪk(ə)l,kɒnsənˈtreɪʃ(ə)n/ noun the degree to which consumers in a market are concentrated or dispersed in a country or area ○ *The number of sales personnel needed will depend on the geographical concentration of the market.*

geographical information system /,dʒiːəgræfɪk(ə)l ,ɪnfəˈmeɪʃ(ə)n ,sɪstəm/ noun a type of database which is sorted on geographical data, such as a census, or one which provides maps on-screen. Abbreviation **GIS**

geographical segmentation /dʒiːə,græfɪk(ə)l ,segmənˈteɪʃ(ə)n/ noun the division of a market according to areas or regions

geographical weighting /dʒiːə,græfɪk(ə)l ˈweɪtɪŋ/ noun a statistical process which gives more importance to some geographic areas than others in the process of reaching a final figure or result

geotargeting /,dʒiːəʊˈtaːgɪtɪŋ/ noun a method of analysing what a visitor to a website is viewing or doing and deducing his or her location, then displaying custom content or advertisements accordingly

gestation period /dʒeˈsteɪʃ(ə)n ,pɪəriəd/ noun the period of time between the initial inquiry about a product and the placing of an order ○ *The long gestation period is due to inefficient decision-making procedures in the buying company.*

GHI abbreviation guaranteed homes impressions

ghosting /ˈgəʊstɪŋ/ noun the practice of showing a little of the product itself by removing a small part of the packaging

GHR abbreviation guaranteed homes ratings

giant retailer /,dʒaɪənt ˈriːteɪlə/ noun a very large retailing group, e.g. a department store or chain store

GIF /gɪf/ noun a common file format for web graphics and banners. Full form **graphic interchange format**

GIF89 /ˌgɪf eɪti ˈnaɪn/ *noun* a commonly used version of GIF

gift coupon /ˈgɪft ˌkuːpɒn/, **gift token** /ˈgɪft ˌtəʊkən/**gift voucher** /ˈgɪft ˌvaʊtʃə/ *noun* a card that can be used to buy specified goods up to the value printed on it, often issued by chain stores. The person receiving the voucher is able to redeem it in any store in the chain. ○ *We gave her a gift token for her birthday.*

gift-wrap /ˈgɪft ræp/ *verb* to wrap a present in attractive paper ○ *Do you want this book gift-wrapped?* (NOTE: **gift-wrapping – gift-wrapped**)

gimmick /ˈgɪmɪk/ *noun* a clever idea or trick ○ *a publicity gimmick*

give /gɪv/ *verb*

give away *phrasal verb* to give something as a free present ○ *We are giving away a pocket calculator with each purchase.*

giveaway /ˈgɪvəweɪ/ *adjective* □ **to sell at giveaway prices** to sell at very cheap prices ■ *noun* something which is given as a free gift when another item is bought

giveaway paper /ˈgɪvəweɪ ˌpeɪpə/ *noun* a newspaper which is given away free, and which relies for its income on its advertising

GLAM /glæm/ *noun* a demographic term which describes middle-aged people who have considerable disposable income and leisure time. Full form **greying, leisured, affluent, and middle-aged**

global /ˈgləʊb(ə)l/ *adjective* referring to the whole world ○ *We offer a 24-hour global delivery service.*

global advertising /ˌgləʊb(ə)l ˈædvətaɪzɪŋ/ *noun* using the same advertising message to advertise the same product internationally

global brand /ˌgləʊb(ə)l ˈbrænd/ *noun* a famous brand name which is recognised and sold all over the world

globalisation /ˌgləʊbəlaɪˈzeɪʃ(ə)n/, **globalization** *noun* the process of making something international or worldwide, especially the process of expanding business interests, operations, and strategies to countries all over the world (NOTE: Globalisation is due to technological developments that make global communications possible, political developments such as the fall of communism, and developments in transport that make travelling faster and more frequent. It can benefit companies by opening up new markets, giving access to new raw materials and investment opportunities, and enabling them to take advantage of lower operating costs in other countries.)

global marketing /ˌgləʊb(ə)l ˈmaːkɪtɪŋ/ *noun* using a common marketing plan to sell the same product or services everywhere in the world

global product /ˌgləʊb(ə)l ˈprɒdʌkt/ *noun* a product with a famous brand name which is recognised and sold all over the world

global retailer /ˌgləʊb(ə)l ˈriːteɪlə/ *noun* a company which sells its products all over the world

glocalisation /ˌgləʊkəlaɪˈzeɪʃ(ə)n/ *noun* the process of adapting globalised products or services to fit the needs of different local markets and communities around the world (NOTE: The word is a combination of globalisation and localisation.)

glue /gluː/ *noun* something such as information that unifies organisations, supply chains, and other commercial groups

glut /glʌt/ *noun* □ **a glut of produce** too much produce, which is then difficult to sell ○ *a coffee glut* or *a glut of coffee* □ **a glut of money** a situation where there is too much money available to borrowers ■ *verb* to fill the market with something which is then difficult to sell ○ *The market is glutted with cheap cameras.* (NOTE: **glutting – glutted**)

GM *abbreviation* gross margin

GNP *abbreviation* gross national product

goal /gəʊl/ *noun* something which you try to achieve ○ *Our goal is to break even within twelve months.* ○ *The company achieved all its goals.*

going rate /ˌgəʊɪŋ ˈreɪt/ *noun* the usual or current rate of payment ○ *We pay the going rate for consultants.* ○ *The going rate is £10 per hour.*

gondola /ˈgɒndələ/ *noun* a free-standing display in a supermarket which shoppers can walk round

gone aways /ˈgɒn əˌweɪz/ *plural noun* people who have moved away from the address they have in a mailing list

good industrial relations /gʊd ɪnˌdʌstrɪəl rɪˈleɪʃ(ə)nz/ *plural noun* a situation where management and employees understand each others' problems and work together for the good of the company

goods /gʊdz/ *plural noun* **1.** □ **goods and chattels** movable personal possessions □ **goods in progress** the value of goods being manufactured which are not complete at the end of an accounting period ○ *Our current assets are made up of stock, goods in progress, and cash.* □ **goods sold loose** goods sold by weight, not prepacked in bags **2.** items which can be moved and are for sale

'…profit margins are lower in the industries most exposed to foreign competition – machinery, transportation equipment and electrical goods' [*Sunday Times*]

'…the minister wants people buying goods ranging from washing machines to houses to demand facts on energy costs' [*Times*]

goods depot /ˈgʊdz ˌdepəʊ/ *noun* a central warehouse where goods can be stored until they are moved

goodwill /gʊdˈwɪl/ *noun* good feeling towards someone ○ *To show goodwill, the management increased the terms of the offer.*

GOTS *abbreviation* gross opportunity to see

government contractor /ˌgʌv(ə)nmənt kənˈtræktə/ *noun* a company which supplies the government with goods by contract

government-controlled /ˈgʌv(ə)nmənt kənˌtrəʊld/ *adjective* under the direct control of the government ○ *Advertisements cannot be placed in the government-controlled newspapers.*

government economic indicators /ˌgʌv(ə)nmənt ˌiːkənɒmɪk ˈɪndɪkeɪtəz/ *plural noun* statistics which show how the country's economy is going to perform in the short or long term

government organisation /ˌgʌv(ə)nmənt ˌɔːgənaɪˈzeɪʃ(ə)n/ *noun* an official body run by the government

government sector /ˌgʌv(ə)nmənt ˈsektə/ *noun* same as **public sector**

grade /greɪd/ *noun* a level or rank ○ *to reach the top grade in the civil service* ■ *verb* **1.** to sort something into different levels of quality ○ *to grade coal* **2.** to make something rise in steps according to quantity □ **graded advertising rates** rates which become cheaper as you take more advertising space

graded hotel /ˌgreɪdɪd həʊˈtel/ *noun* a good-quality hotel

graded tax /ˌgreɪdɪd ˈtæks/ *noun US* **1.** a tax in which the rate rises as income increases **2.** a tax on property in which vacant land is taxed at a higher rate than structures, in order to encourage development

grade level /ˈgreɪd ˌlev(ə)l/ *noun* the classification of a product's quality written on a label attached to the product ○ *Many consumers do not properly understand the grade levels.*

grand /grænd/ *adjective* important □ **grand plan** *or* **grand strategy** a major plan ○ *They explained their grand plan for redeveloping the factory site.* ■ *noun* one thousand pounds or dollars (*informal*) ○ *They offered him fifty grand for the information.*

grand total /ˌgrænd ˈtəʊt(ə)l/ *noun* the final total made by adding several subtotals

grapevine /ˈgreɪpvaɪn/ *noun* an informal and unofficial communications network within an organisation that passes on information by word of mouth (NOTE: A grapevine may distort information or spread gossip and rumour, but it can also back up the official communications network, provide feedback, and strengthen social relationships within the organisation.)

graph /grɑːf/ *noun* a diagram which shows the relationship between two sets of quantities or values, each of which is represented on an axis ○ *A graph was used to show salary increases in relation to increases in output.* ○ *According to the graph, as average salaries have risen so has absenteeism.* ○ *We need to set out the results of the questionnaire in a graph.*

graphics /ˈgræfɪks/ *plural noun* designs and illustrations in printed work, especially designs which are created by computers ○ *In this series of* *advertisements the graphics do not do justice to the copy.*

gratis /'grætɪs/ *adverb* free or not costing anything ○ *We got into the exhibition gratis.*

green investment /ˌgriːn ɪn'vestmənt/ *noun* an investment that focuses on companies or projects that are committed to environmentally conscious business practices

green issues /'griːn ɪsjuːz/ *plural noun* same as **environmental management**

green marketing /'griːn ˌmaːkɪtɪŋ/ *noun* marketing products and services on the basis of their environmental acceptability

grey market /'greɪ ˌmaːkɪt/ *noun* **1.** the unofficial legal buying and selling of scarce, highly priced goods ○ *If the government puts a ceiling on prices for these products the grey market will become a black market.* **2.** a market formed of people over 60 years of age. ⇨ **silver market**

grid /grɪd/ *noun* a graph with lines crossing at right angles and items written in the boxes, used for comparison

gross /grəʊs/ *adverb* with no deductions ○ *My salary is paid gross.* ■ *verb* to make as a gross profit or earn as gross income ○ *The group grossed £25m in 2010.*

gross audience /ˌgrəʊs 'ɔːdiəns/ *noun* the total number of people who have seen an advertisement, multiplied by the number of times it has been run

gross circulation /grəʊs ˌsɜː-kjʊ'leɪʃ(ə)n/ *noun* the total sales of a publication before adjusting for error or discounting unsold copies

gross cover /ˌgrəʊs 'kʌvə/ *noun* the number of times a television or radio spot has been seen based on television ratings

gross domestic product /ˌgrəʊs də,mestɪk 'prɒdʌkt/ *noun* the annual value of goods sold and services paid for inside a country. Abbreviation **GDP**

gross earnings /ˌgrəʊs 'ɜːnɪŋz/ *plural noun* total earnings before tax and other deductions

gross impressions /grəʊs ɪm'preʃ(ə)nz/ *plural noun* the total

number of people who have seen an advertisement, multiplied by the number of times it has been run. ⇨ **guaranteed homes impressions**

gross margin /ˌgrəʊs 'maːdʒɪn/ *noun* the percentage difference between the received price and the unit manufacturing cost or purchase price of goods for resale. Abbreviation **GM**

gross national product /ˌgrəʊs ˌnæʃ(ə)nəl 'prɒdʌkt/ *noun* the annual value of goods and services in a country including income from other countries. Abbreviation **GNP**

gross opportunity to see /ˌgrəʊs ˌɒpətjuːnɪti tə 'siː/ *noun* the number of opportunities that an average member of the target audience will have to see the advertisements in an advertising campaign. Abbreviation **GOTS**

gross profit /ˌgrəʊs 'prɒfɪt/ *noun* a profit calculated as sales income less the cost of the goods sold, i.e. without deducting any other expenses

gross rating point /ˌgrəʊs 'reɪtɪŋ ˌpɔɪnt/ *noun US* a way of calculating the effectiveness of outdoor advertising, where each point represents one per cent of the population in a specific market. Abbreviation **GRP**

gross reach /grəʊs 'riːtʃ/ *noun* the total number of opportunities for people to see a company's advertisements in a campaign, i.e. the total number of publications sold multiplied by the number of advertisements appearing in each one

gross receipts /ˌgrəʊs rɪ'siːts/ *plural noun* the total amount of money received before expenses are deducted

gross sales /ˌgrəʊs 'seɪlz/ *plural noun* money received from sales before deductions for goods returned, special discounts, etc. ○ *Gross sales are impressive since many buyers seem to be ordering more than they will eventually need.*

gross weight /ˌgrəʊs 'weɪt/ *noun* the weight of both the container and its contents

ground transportation /'graʊnd trænspɔːˌteɪʃ(ə)n/ *noun* the means of transport available to take passengers from an airport to the town, e.g. buses, taxis, or trains

group /gruːp/ noun **1.** several things or people together ○ *A group of managers has sent a memo to the chairman complaining about noise in the office.* ○ *The respondents were interviewed in groups of three or four, and then singly.* **2.** several companies linked together in the same organisation ○ *the group chairman* or *the chairman of the group* ○ *group turnover* or *turnover for the group* ○ *the Granada Group* ■ *verb* □ **to group together** to put several items together ○ *Sales from six different agencies are grouped together under the heading 'European sales'.*

group discussion /gruːp dɪ'skʌʃ(ə)n/ noun a survey method in which a focus group is brought together to discuss informally a market-research question ○ *The group discussion was taken over by one or two strong personalities.* ○ *A sample of young people took part in a group discussion on the new shampoo.*

group interview /gruːp 'ɪntəvjuː/ noun an interview with a group of respondents such as a family in order to discover the views of the group as a whole ○ *There were group interviews with all the classes in the school in order to gauge reactions to the new educational programme.*

group results /ˌgruːp rɪ'zʌlts/ plural noun the end-of-year financial statements and accounts of a group of companies

group system /'gruːp ˌsɪstəm/ noun a system of organising an advertising agency in groups, each group having specialists in creative, media, marketing services, and other areas, and each group dealing with particular accounts

groupware /'gruːpweə/ noun software that enables a group of people who are based in different locations to work together and share information (NOTE: Groupware usually provides communal diaries, address books, work planners, bulletin boards, and newsletters in electronic format on a closed network.)

grow /grəʊ/ verb to cause something such as a business to develop or expand

'…the thrift had grown from $4.7 million in assets to $1.5 billion' [*Barrons*]

growth /grəʊθ/ noun **1.** the fact of becoming larger or increasing □ **the company is aiming for growth** the company is aiming to expand rapidly **2.** the second stage in a product life cycle, following the launch, when demand for the product increases rapidly

'…a general price freeze succeeded in slowing the growth in consumer prices' [*Financial Times*]

'…growth in demand is still coming from the private rather than the public sector' [*Lloyd's List*]

'…population growth in the south-west is again reflected by the level of rental values' [*Lloyd's List*]

growth area /'grəʊθ ˌeəriə/ noun an area where sales are increasing rapidly

growth index /'grəʊθ ˌɪndeks/ noun an index showing the growth in a company's revenues, earnings, dividends or other figures

growth industry /'grəʊθ ˌɪndəstri/ noun an industry that is expanding or has the potential to expand faster than other industries

growth market /'grəʊθ ˌmaːkɪt/ noun a market where sales are increasing rapidly ○ *We plan to build a factory in the Far East, which is a growth market for our products.*

growth rate /'grəʊθ reɪt/ noun the speed at which something grows

growth share matrix /'grəʊθ ʃeə ˌmeɪtrɪks/ noun a model for a marketing strategy with various categories of product based on present performance and growth rate ○ *The growth share matrix helped to decide what products needed extra marketing efforts.*

growth vector matrix /'grəʊθ ˌvektə ˌmeɪtrɪks/ noun a model for a marketing strategy with various choices and combinations of strategy based on product and market development

GRP *abbreviation* gross rating point

guarantee /ˌgærən'tiː/ noun **1.** a legal document in which the producer agrees to compensate the buyer if the product is faulty or becomes faulty before a specific date after purchase ○ *a certificate of guarantee* or *a guarantee certificate* ○ *The guarantee lasts for two years.* ○ *It is sold with a* *twelve-month guarantee.* □ **the car is still under guarantee** the car is still covered by the maker's guarantee **2.** a promise that someone will pay another person's debts □ **to go guarantee for someone** to act as security for someone's debts **3.** something given as a security ○ *to leave share certificates as a guarantee* ■ *verb* **1.** to give a promise that something will happen □ **to guarantee a debt** to promise to pay another person's debts if he or she should fail to □ **to guarantee an associate company** to promise that an associate company will pay its debts □ **to guarantee a bill of exchange** to promise that the bill will be paid **2.** □ **the product is guaranteed for twelve months** the manufacturer says that the product will work well for twelve months, and will mend it free of charge if it breaks down

guaranteed circulation /ˌgærən-tiːd ˌsɜːkjʊˈleɪʃ(ə)n/ *noun* the audited circulation of a magazine which is used as a basis for calculating advertising rates

guaranteed homes impressions /ˌgærəntiːd ˈhəʊmz ɪmˌpreʃ(ə)nz/, **guaranteed homes ratings** /ˌgæ-rəntiːd ˈhəʊmz ˌreɪtɪŋz/ *plural noun* an advertising package offered by television companies which guarantees the advertisers that their advertising will reach a specified number of people, but leaves it to the TV company to choose the number and timing of the spots. Abbreviation **GHI, GHR**

guaranteed prices /ˌgærəntiːd ˈpraɪsɪz/ *plural noun* minimum prices guaranteed to an industry by the government, with the payment of a subsidy to make up for market prices that fall below this level ○ *Guaranteed prices help bring some security to a notoriously unstable industry.*

guaranteed wage /ˌgærəntiːd ˈweɪdʒ/ *noun* a wage which a company promises will not fall below a specific figure

guarantor /ˌgærənˈtɔː/ *noun* a person who promises to pay another person's debts if he or she should fail to ○ *She stood guarantor for her brother.*

guard book /ˈgɑːd bʊk/ *noun* a hardcover album which allows pages to be inserted into it, e.g. for showing samples or advertising material

guerrilla marketing /gəˈrɪlə ˌmɑːkɪtɪŋ/ *noun* a form of unconventional flexible marketing, adapted to the products or services sold, or to the type of customer targeted

guesstimate /ˈgestɪmət/ *noun* a rough calculation (*informal*)

gutter /ˈgʌtə/ *noun* the area where the two pages meet in a book or magazine. It can be left blank as a centre margin, or can be printed across to form a double-page spread.

H

habit /'hæbɪt/ *noun* the practice of doing something regularly ○ *Most consumers continue to buy the same brands from force of habit.*

habit buying /'hæbɪt ˌbaɪɪŋ/ *noun* the practice of buying a particular product again and again out of habit, without making any conscious decision to buy

haggle /'hæg(ə)l/ *verb* to discuss prices and terms and try to reduce them ○ *to haggle about* or *over the details of a contract* ○ *After two days' haggling the contract was signed.*

half-price sale /ˌhɑːf praɪs 'seɪl/ *noun* a sale of items at half the usual price

hallmark /'hɔːlmɑːk/ *noun* a mark put on gold or silver items to show that the metal is of the correct quality ■ *verb* to put a hallmark on a piece of gold or silver ○ *a hallmarked spoon*

hallmark of excellence /ˌhɔːlmɑːk əv 'eksələns/ *noun* the reputation that a brand name has for high quality

hall test /'hɔːl test/ *noun* a market-research test where respondents are asked to go into a public building or central place to answer questions or to test new products ○ *The hall test was conducted in the town's main school.*

halo effect /'heɪləʊ ɪˌfekt/ *noun* a series of positive impressions of a product which consumers retain and which can be revealed by a respondent when questioned in a survey

hand /hænd/ *noun* □ **in hand** kept in reserve ○ *we have £10,000 in hand* □ **balance in hand** or **cash in hand** cash held to pay small debts and running costs □ **work in hand** work which is in progress but not finished

handbill /'hændbɪl/ *noun* a sheet of printed paper handed out to members of the public as an advertisement

handbook /'hændbʊk/ *noun* a book which gives instructions on how to use something ○ *The handbook does not say how you open the photocopier.*

handed-overs /'hændɪd ˌəʊvəz/ *plural noun* sales leads which have been passed on to the client to pursue

handle /'hænd(ə)l/ *verb* **1.** to deal with something or to organise something ○ *The accounts department handles all the cash.* ○ *We can handle orders for up to 15,000 units.* ○ *They handle all our overseas orders.* **2.** to sell or to trade in a type of product ○ *We do not handle foreign cars.* ○ *They will not handle goods produced by other firms.*

handling /'hændlɪŋ/ *noun* the process of receiving, storing and sending off goods

'…shipping companies continue to bear the extra financial burden of cargo handling operations at the ports' [*Business Times (Lagos)*]

handling charge /'hændlɪŋ tʃɑːdʒ/ *noun* money to be paid for packing, invoicing and dealing with goods which are being shipped

handout /'hændaʊt/ *noun* a free gift, especially of money ○ *The company exists on handouts from the government.*

hard bounce /ˌhɑːd 'baʊns/ *noun* an email message that is returned to the sender because the recipient's address is invalid, either because the domain name does not exist or because the recipient is unknown

hard cash /ˌhɑːd 'kæʃ/ *noun* money in notes and coins, as opposed to cheques or credit cards

hard currency /ˌhɑːd ˈkʌrənsi/ *noun* the currency of a country which has a strong economy, and which can be changed into other currencies easily ○ *to pay for imports in hard currency* ○ *to sell raw materials to earn hard currency* Also called **scarce currency**. Opposite **soft currency**

hardening /ˈhɑːd(ə)nɪŋ/ *adjective* (*of a market*) slowly moving upwards □ **a hardening of prices** prices which are becoming settled at a higher level

hardness /ˈhɑːdnəs/ *noun* □ **hardness of the market** the state of the market when it is strong and not likely to fall

hard sell /ˌhɑːd ˈsel/ *noun* □ **to give a product the hard sell** to make great efforts to persuade people to buy a product □ **he tried to give me the hard sell** he put a lot of effort into trying to make me buy

hard selling /ˌhɑːd ˈselɪŋ/ *noun* the act of selling by using great efforts ○ *A lot of hard selling went into that deal.*

hardware /ˈhɑːdweə/ *noun* machines used in data processing, including the computers and printers, but not the programs

harvesting /ˈhɑːvɪstɪŋ/ *noun* the practice of cutting marketing investment on a particular product prior to withdrawing it from the market

hate site /ˈheɪt saɪt/ *noun* a website devoted to attacking a particular company or organisation. A hate site often imitates the target organisation's own site and is usually set up by a customer who has a complaint against the organisation that he or she has been unable to express on the organisation's own site. Also called **anti-site**

haulage /ˈhɔːlɪdʒ/ *noun* the cost of transporting goods by road ○ *Haulage is increasing by 5% per annum.*

haulage contractor /ˈhɔːlɪdʒ kənˌtræktə/ *noun* a company which transports goods by contract

hawk /hɔːk/ *verb* to sell goods from door to door or in the street □ **to hawk something round** to take a product, an idea, or a project to various companies to see if one will accept it ○ *He hawked his idea for a plastic car body round all the major car constructors.*

hawker /ˈhɔːkə/ *noun* a person who sells goods from door to door or in the street

head buyer /ˌhed ˈbaɪə/ *noun* the most important buyer in a store

headhunt /ˈhedhʌnt/ *verb* to look for managers and offer them jobs in other companies □ **she was headhunted** she was approached by a headhunter and offered a new job

headhunter /ˈhedhʌntə/ *noun* a person or company whose job is to find suitable top managers to fill jobs in companies

headline /ˈhedlaɪn/ *noun* the heading of an article or advertisement, which is set in much larger type than the rest

head-on position /ˈhed ɒn pəˌzɪʃ(ə)n/ *noun* a poster site directly facing traffic ○ *Let's try to obtain a head-on position in the central part of town.*

heads of agreement /ˌhedz əv əˈɡriːmənt/ *plural noun* the most important parts of a commercial agreement

heavy /ˈhevi/ *adjective* large or in large quantities ○ *a programme of heavy investment overseas* ○ *He suffered heavy losses on the stock exchange.* ○ *The government imposed a heavy tax on luxury goods.* □ **heavy costs** *or* **heavy expenditure** large sums of money that have to be spent

'…heavy selling sent many blue chips tumbling in Tokyo yesterday' [*Financial Times*]

heavy half /ˌhevi ˈhɑːf/ *noun* a situation where a small number of customers make up more than half of the total demand for a product

heavy industry /ˌhevi ˈɪndəstri/ *noun* an industry which deals in heavy raw materials such as coal or makes large products such as ships or engines

heavy user /ˌhevi ˈjuːzə/ *noun* a consumer who buys more of a product than average ○ *Heavy users will be particularly affected by the price rise.*

heavy viewer /ˌhevi ˈvjuːə/ *noun* a person who watches a lot of television, and is part of the target audience for commercials ○ *Heavy viewers gave us the most interesting comments on our advertising.*

helicopter view /ˈhelɪkɒptə vjuː/ *noun* a general or broad view of a problem as a whole, which does not go into details (*slang*)

helpline /ˈhelplaɪn/ *noun* a telephone number which links people to services that can give them specialist advice, or a similar service offered by shops to their customers. Also called **careline**

heterogeneous /ˌhetərəʊˈdʒiːniəs/ *adjective* varied

heterogeneous shopping goods /ˌhetərəʊdʒiːniəs ˈʃɒpɪŋ ˌɡʊdz/ *plural noun* goods which vary in quality and style from brand to brand and which consumers spend time in choosing. Compare **homogeneous shopping goods**

heuristics /hjʊəˈrɪstɪks/ *noun* simple decision rules used by ordinary customers when choosing what to buy, e.g. buying whatever is cheapest

hidden economy /ˌhɪd(ə)n ɪˈkɒnəmi/ *noun* same as **black economy**

hierarchy /ˈhaɪəraːki/ *noun* a series of items ranged in order of importance □ **hierarchy of needs** the theory that needs of individuals are arranged in an order based on their importance, such as safety, social needs, esteem, etc.

hierarchy of effects /ˌhaɪəraːki əv ɪˈfekts/ *noun* a model showing the stages in the effect of advertising on a consumer such as awareness, knowledge, liking, preference, conviction, and purchase

high /haɪ/ *adjective* **1.** tall ○ *The shelves are 30 cm high.* ○ *The door is not high enough to let us get the machines into the building.* ○ *They are planning a 30-storey-high office block.* **2.** large, not low ○ *High overhead costs increase the unit price.* ○ *High prices put customers off.* ○ *They are budgeting for a high level of expenditure.* ○ *High interest rates are crippling small businesses.* □ **high sales** a large amount of revenue produced by sales □ **high taxation** taxation which imposes large taxes on incomes or profits □ **highest tax bracket** the group which pays the most tax □ **high volume (of sales)** a large number of items sold **3.** □ **the highest bidder** the person who

offers the most money at an auction ○ *The tender will be awarded to the highest bidder.* ○ *The property was sold to the highest bidder.* ■ *adverb* □ **prices are running high** prices are above their usual level ■ *noun* a point where prices or sales are very large ○ *Prices have dropped by 10 per cent since the high of 2nd January.* □ **sales volume has reached an all-time high** the sales volume has reached the highest point it has ever been at

'American interest rates remain exceptionally high in relation to likely inflation rates' [*Sunday Times*]

'…faster economic growth would tend to push US interest rates, and therefore the dollar, higher' [*Australian Financial Review*]

'…in a leveraged buyout the acquirer raises money by selling high-yielding debentures to private investors' [*Fortune*]

high concept /ˌhaɪ ˈkɒnsept/ *noun* an important and persuasive idea expressed clearly and in few words

high-end /ˈhaɪ end/ *adjective* more expensive, more advanced, or more powerful than the other items in a range of things, e.g. computers

high finance /ˌhaɪ ˈfaɪnæns/ *noun* the lending, investing and borrowing of very large sums of money organised by financiers

high-grade /ˈhaɪ ɡreɪd/ *adjective* of very good quality ○ *high-grade petrol* □ **high-grade trade delegation** a delegation made up of very important people

'…the accepted wisdom built upon for well over 100 years that government and high-grade corporate bonds were almost riskless' [*Forbes Magazine*]

high-involvement product /ˌhaɪ ɪnˈvɒlvmənt ˌprɒdʌkt/ *noun* a high-priced or high-tech product that is carefully considered by a consumer before being bought

high pressure /ˌhaɪ ˈpreʃə/ *noun* a strong insistence that somebody should do something □ **working under high pressure** working very hard, with a manager telling you what to do and to do it quickly, or with customers asking for supplies urgently

high-pressure salesman /ˌhaɪ ˌpreʃə ˈseɪlzmən/, **high-pressure**

saleswoman *noun* a salesman or saleswoman who forces a customer to buy something he or she does not really want

high-pressure sales technique /ˌhaɪ ˌpreʃə 'seɪlz tekˌniːk/ *noun* an attempt to force a customer to buy something he or she does not really want

high-quality /ˌhaɪ 'kwɒlɪti/ *adjective* of very good quality ○ *high-quality goods* ○ *a high-quality product*

high season /ˌhaɪ 'siːz(ə)n/ *noun* the period when there are the most travellers and tourists

high street /'haɪ striːt/ *noun* **1.** the main shopping street in a British town ○ *the high street shops* ○ *a high street bookshop* **2.** a main street considered as an important retail area

High Street banks /ˌhaɪ striːt 'bæŋks/ *plural noun* the main British banks which accept deposits from individual customers

hire purchase /ˌhaɪə 'pɜːtʃɪs/ *noun* a system of buying something by paying a sum regularly each month ○ *to buy a refrigerator on hire purchase* (NOTE: The US term is **installment credit**, **installment plan** or **installment sale**.)

hire-purchase company /ˌhaɪə 'pɜːtʃɪs ˌkʌmp(ə)ni/ *noun* a company which provides money for hire purchase

histogram /'hɪstəɡræm/ *noun* same as **bar chart**

historic /hɪ'stɒrɪk/, **historical** /hɪ'stɒrɪk(ə)l/ *adjective* dating back over a period of time

'…the Federal Reserve Board has eased interest rates in the past year, but they are still at historically high levels' [*Sunday Times*]

'…the historic p/e for the FTSE all-share index is 28.3 and the dividend yield is barely 2%. Both indicators suggest that the stock markets are very highly priced' [*Times*]

historical cost /hɪˌstɒrɪk(ə)l 'kɒst/, **historic cost** /hɪˌstɒrɪk 'kɒst/ *noun* the actual cost of purchasing something which was bought some time ago

historical figures /hɪˌstɒrɪk(ə)l 'fɪɡəz/ *plural noun* figures that were correct at the time of purchase or payment, as distinct from, e.g. a current saleable value or market value

historical trend /hɪˌstɒrɪk(ə)l 'trend/ *noun* a trend detected in the past on the basis of historical data ○ *Historical trends may help us to predict how the economy will develop in the future.* ○ *It is difficult to detect any clear historical trends in consumer reaction to our past product launches.*

hit /hɪt/ *noun* **1.** a response to a request sent from an Internet browser (NOTE: When a browser conducts a search, the number of hits it gets is the number of websites, files, or images it finds that fit the criteria set for the search.) **2.** a successful match or search of a database

hit rate /'hɪt reɪt/ *noun* the rate at which a target is reached such as the number of mail shots needed before a customer makes an order for a product advertised on them, or the number of customers who reply to a mail shot compared to the total number of customers mailed

hive /haɪv/ *verb* **hive off** *phrasal verb* to split off part of a large company to form a smaller subsidiary ○ *The new managing director hived off the retail sections of the company.*

hoard /hɔːd/ *verb* **1.** to buy and store goods in case of need **2.** to keep cash instead of investing it

hoarder /'hɔːdə/ *noun* a person who buys and stores goods in case of need

hoarding /'hɔːdɪŋ/ *noun* **1.** □ **hoarding of supplies** the buying of large quantities of goods to keep in case of need **2.** a large wooden board for posters (NOTE: The US term is **billboard**.)

'…as a result of hoarding, rice has become scarce with prices shooting up' [*Business Times (Lagos)*]

home audit /həʊm 'ɔːdɪt/ *noun* a survey method whereby a panel of householders keeps records of purchases so that these can be regularly checked for quantity and brand ○ *The home audit showed that although wholesalers were buying the product in large quantities, consumers were not.* ○ *The home audit suggested that there is little brand loyalty for this type of product.*

home country /ˌhəʊm 'kʌntri/ *noun* a country where a company is based

homegrown /ˈhəʊmɡrəʊn/ *adjective* which has been developed in a local area or in a country where the company is based ○ *a homegrown computer industry* ○ *India's homegrown car industry*

home industry /həʊm ˈɪndəstri/ *noun* productive work carried out by people at home ○ *In third world countries there are still many home industries.* ○ *Home industries are disappearing as mass production takes over.*

home market /ˌhəʊm ˈmɑːkɪt/ *noun* the market in the country where the selling company is based ○ *Sales in the home market rose by 22%.*

homepage /ˈhəʊmpeɪdʒ/ *noun* the first page that is displayed when you visit a site on the Internet

home-produced product /ˌhəʊm prəˌdjuːst ˈprɒdʌkt/ *noun* a product manufactured in the country where the company is based

home shopping /ˌhəʊm ˈʃɒpɪŋ/ *noun* buying items direct from the customer's house, using a computer linked to the telephone which is linked to the store's ordering department

home trade /ˌhəʊm ˈtreɪd/ *noun* trade in the country where a company is based

homeward /ˈhəʊmwəd/ *adjective* going towards the home country ○ *The ship is carrying homeward freight.* ○ *The liner left Buenos Aires on her homeward journey.*

homewards /ˈhəʊmwədz/ *adverb* towards the home country ○ *cargo homewards*

homogeneous /ˌhəʊməʊˈdʒiːniəs/ *adjective* uniform or unvaried

homogeneous shopping goods /ˌhəʊməʊdʒiːniəs ˈʃɒpɪŋ ɡʊdz/ *plural noun* goods which vary little in style and quality from brand to brand and which consumers spend little time choosing. Compare **heterogeneous shopping goods**

homogenisation /həˌmɒdʒənaɪˈzeɪʃ(ə)n/ *noun* the tendency for different products, markets and cultures to lose their characteristic differences and become the same (NOTE: Globalisation is often blamed for homogenisation.)

horizontal /ˌhɒrɪˈzɒnt(ə)l/ *adjective* at the same level or with the same status ○ *Her new job is a horizontal move into a different branch of the business.*

horizontal communication /ˌhɒrɪzɒnt(ə)l kəˌmjuːnɪˈkeɪʃ(ə)n/ *noun* communication between employees at the same level

horizontal co-operative advertising /ˌhɒrɪzɒnt(ə)l kəʊˌɒp(ə)rətɪv ˈædvətaɪzɪŋ/ *noun* cooperative advertising where the advertising is sponsored by a group of retailers

horizontal industrial market /ˌhɒrɪzɒnt(ə)l ɪnˌdʌstriəl ˈmɑːkɪt/ *noun* a market in which a product is used by many industries

horizontal integration /ˌhɒrɪzɒnt(ə)l ˌɪntɪˈɡreɪʃ(ə)n/ *noun* the process of joining similar companies or taking over a company in the same line of business as yourself

horizontal marketing system /ˌhɒrɪzɒnt(ə)l ˈmɑːkɪtɪŋ ˌsɪstəm/ *noun* cooperation between or merger of two or more companies whose assets are complementary and who therefore all gain from coming together

horizontal publication /ˌhɒrɪzɒnt(ə)l ˌpʌblɪˈkeɪʃ(ə)n/ *noun* a publication which is aimed at people in similar levels of occupation in different industries

horizontal rotation /ˌhɒrɪzɒnt(ə)l rəʊˈteɪʃ(ə)n/ *noun* distributing broadcast spots on different days of the week at the same time of day

horizon scanning /həˈraɪz(ə)n ˌskænɪŋ/ *noun* the exploration of future developments, opportunities and threats. Horizon scanning may explore existing issues and trends, as well as identifying new or potential issues.

horse trading /ˈhɔːs ˌtreɪdɪŋ/ *noun* hard bargaining which ends with someone giving something in return for a concession from the other side

hostess party selling /ˌhəʊstes ˈpɑːti ˌselɪŋ/ *noun* a method of selling certain items such as household goods directly by the manufacturer's agent at a party to which potential customers are invited

hostile bid /ˌhɒstaɪl ˈbɪd/ *noun* same as **contested takeover**

hosting /ˈhəʊstɪŋ/ *noun* the business of putting websites onto the Internet so that people can visit them. ➪ **hosting option**

hosting option /ˌhəʊstɪŋ ˈɒpʃən/ *noun* any of the different kinds of hosting that a business may use when putting a website on the Internet and that are usually provided by specialist hosting companies. ➪ **collocation hosting, managed hosting, non-virtual hosting, virtual hosting**

host service /ˈhəʊst ˌsɜːvɪs/, **hosting service provider** /ˈhəʊstɪŋ ˌsɜːvɪs prəˌvaɪdə/ *noun* a company that provides connections to the Internet and storage space on its computers, which can store the files for a user's website

hot button /ˈhɒt ˌbʌt(ə)n/ *noun* the immediate interest a customer has in a product or service offered for sale

hotelling /həʊˈtelɪŋ/ *noun* the practice of using a desk or workspace in an office belonging to someone who is not your employer. Hotelling is normally carried out by consultants or sales people, who spend more time with their customers than at their base.

hotline /ˈhɒtlaɪn/ *noun* a special telephone ordering service set up for a special period ○ *a Christmas hotline*

hot money /ˌhɒt ˈmʌni/ *noun* money which is moved from country to country to get the best returns

house /haʊs/ *noun* **1.** the building in which someone lives **2.** a company ○ *the largest London finance house* ○ *a publishing house*

house advertisment /ˈhaʊs æd/, **house ad** *noun* an advertisement in a publication which is placed by the publication itself, e.g. one offering a readers' advice service or selling back numbers of the publication

house agency /ˈhaʊs ˌeɪdʒənsi/ *noun* an advertising agency owned and used by a large company, and which other companies may also use

house agent /ˈhaʊz ˌeɪdʒənt/ *noun* an estate agent who deals in buying or selling houses or flats

house brand /ˈhaʊs brænd/ *noun* a brand owned by a retailer rather than by the producer

household /ˈhaʊshəʊld/ *noun* a unit formed of all the people living together in a single house or flat, whether it is a single person living alone, a married couple, or a large family

'…the extent of single women households has implications for marketing' [*Precision Marketing*]

household goods /ˌhaʊshəʊld ˈɡʊdz/ *plural noun* items which are used in the home

household name /ˌhaʊshəʊld neɪm/ *noun* a brand name which is recognised by a large number of consumers

households using television /ˌhaʊshəʊldz ˌjuːzɪŋ ˌtelɪˈvɪʒ(ə)n/ *noun* the percentage of homes watching television during a specific time period and within a specific area. Abbreviation **HUT**

house journal /ˈhaʊs ˌdʒɜːn(ə)l/, **house magazine** /ˈhaʊs mægəˌziːn/ *noun* a magazine produced for the employees or shareholders in a company to give them news about the company

house property /ˈhaʊs ˌprɒpəti/ *noun* private houses or flats, not shops, offices, or factories

house style /ˌhaʊs ˈstaɪl/ *noun* a company's own design which is used in all its products, including packaging and stationery

house-to-house /ˌhaʊs tə ˈhaʊs/ *adjective* going from one house to the next, asking people to buy something or to vote for someone ○ *house-to-house canvassing* ○ *He trained as a house-to-house salesman.* ○ *House-to-house selling is banned in this area.*

housing market /ˈhaʊzɪŋ ˌmɑːkɪt/ *noun* the sale of houses. Also called **property market**

HR *abbreviation* human resources

HTML /ˌeɪtʃ tiː em ˈel/ *noun* the standard computer code used to build and develop webpages. Full form **Hyper Text Markup Language**

human resources /ˌhjuːmən rɪˈsɔːsɪz/ *plural noun* the employees which an organisation has available ○ *Our human resources must be looked after and developed if we are to raise productivity successfully.* Abbreviation **HR.** Also called **personnel**

'...effective use and management of human resources hold the key to future business development and success' [*Management Today*]

human resources department /ˌhjuːmən rɪˈzɔːsɪz dɪˌpɑːtmənt/ *noun* the section of the company which deals with its staff

human resources officer /ˌhjuːmən rɪˈzɔːsɪz ˌɒfɪsə/ *noun* a person who deals with the staff in a company, especially interviewing candidates for new posts

hunch marketing /ˈhʌntʃ ˌmɑːkɪtɪŋ/ *noun* the process of making marketing decisions following a hunch, rather than relying on market research

HUT *abbreviation* households using television

hype /haɪp/ *noun* excessive claims made in advertising ○ *all the hype surrounding the launch of the new soap* ○ *Many consumers were actually put off by all the media hype surrounding the launch of the new magazine.* ■ *verb* to make excessive claims in advertising

hyperlink /ˈhaɪpəlɪŋk/ *noun* **1.** an image or a piece of text that a user clicks on in order to move directly from one webpagew to another (NOTE: Hyperlinks can be added to webpages by using simple HTML commands; they can also be used in email messages, for example, to include the address of a company's website.) **2.** a series of commands attached to a button or word on one webpage that link it to another page, so that if a user clicks on the button or word, the hyperlink will move the user to another position or display another page

hypermarket /ˈhaɪpəmɑːkɪt/ *noun* a very large supermarket, usually outside a large town, with car-parking facilities

hypertext /ˈhaɪpətekst/ *noun* a system of organising information in which certain words in a document link to other documents and display the text when the word is selected

hypertext link /ˈhaɪpətekst lɪŋk/ *noun* same as **hyperlink**

Hyper Text Markup Language /ˌhaɪpətekst ˈmɑːkʌp ˌlæŋgwɪdʒ/ *noun* full form of **HTML**

hypoing /ˈhaɪpəʊɪŋ/ *noun* using special promotions to increase the audience of a TV station during the sweep periods and so affect the ratings

hypothesis /haɪˈpɒθəsɪs/ *noun* an assumption or theory which must be tested to be confirmed or proved correct ○ *Let us assume, as a working hypothesis, that we can win a 5% market share within two years of the launch.* ○ *Surveys proved that our original hypothesis about likely consumer behaviour was by and large correct.* (NOTE: plural is **hypotheses**)

I

iceberg principle /ˈaɪsbɜːɡ ˌprɪn-sɪp(ə)l/ *noun* the principle that strong needs and desires lie deep in the human personality and that advertising must work at this level if it is to be effective

ident /ˈaɪdent/ *noun* a short TV image which identifies a channel

image /ˈɪmɪdʒ/ *noun* the general idea that the public has of a product, brand, or company ○ *They are spending a lot of advertising money to improve the company's image.* ○ *The company has adopted a downmarket image.* □ **to promote the corporate image** to publicise a company so that its reputation is improved

'…charities are also ready to buy air time to promote their corporate image' [*Marketing Week*]

image advertising /ˈɪmɪdʒ ˌædvə-taɪzɪŋ/ *noun* advertising with the aim of making a brand or company name easily remembered

image-maker /ˈɪmɪdʒ ˌmeɪkə/ *noun* someone who is employed to create a favourable public image for an organisation, product, or public figure

image manipulation /ˈɪmɪdʒ mə,nɪpjʊleɪʃ(ə)n/ *noun* alteration of digital images using special computer software

image setter /ˈɪmɪdʒ ˌsetə/ *noun* a typesetting device that can process a PostScript page and produce a high-resolution output

image transfer /ˈɪmɪdʒ ˌtrænsfɜː/ *noun* the technique of transferring images from one medium to another, e.g. from a photograph to a CD ROM

IMF *abbreviation* International Monetary Fund

imitate /ˈɪmɪteɪt/ *verb* to do what someone else does ○ *They imitate all our sales gimmicks.*

imitation /ˌɪmɪˈteɪʃ(ə)n/ *noun* something which is a copy of an original □ **beware of imitations** be careful not to buy low-quality goods which are made to look like other more expensive items

immediate /ɪˈmiːdiət/ *adjective* happening at once ○ *We wrote an immediate letter of complaint.* ○ *Your order will receive immediate attention.*

immediate environment /ɪˌmiː-diət ɪnˈvaɪrənmənt/ *noun* elements or factors outside a business organisation which directly affect its work, such as the supply of raw materials and demand for its products ○ *The unreliability of our suppliers is one of the worst features of our immediate environment.*

impact /ˈɪmpækt/ *noun* a shock or strong effect ○ *the impact of new technology on the cotton trade* ○ *The new design has made little impact on the buying public.*

impactaplan /ɪmˈpæktəplæn/ *noun* an extensive poster advertising campaign

impact scheduling /ˈɪmpækt ˌʃedjuːlɪŋ/ *noun* the practice of running advertisements for the same product close together so as to make a strong impression on the target audience ○ *Impact scheduling can achieve rapid brand awareness.*

imperfect /ɪmˈpɜːfɪkt/ *adjective* having defects ○ *They are holding a sale of imperfect items.* ○ *Check the batch for imperfect products.*

imperfect competition /ɪmˌpɜːfɪkt ˌkɒmpəˈtɪʃ(ə)n/ *noun* the degree of competition in a market which is somewhere between a monopoly at one extreme and perfect competition at the other. Also called **monopolistic competition**

imperfection /ˌɪmpəˈfekʃən/ *noun* a defect in something ○ *to check a batch for imperfections*

implied close /ɪmˌplaɪd ˈkləʊz/ *noun* an act of ending a sale by assuming that the customer will make the purchase

import /ɪmˈpɔːt/ *verb* to bring goods from abroad into a country for sale ○ *The company imports television sets from Japan.* ○ *This car was imported from France.*

importation /ˌɪmpɔːˈteɪʃ(ə)n/ *noun* the act of importing ○ *The importation of arms is forbidden.* ○ *The importation of livestock is subject to very strict controls.*

import ban /ˈɪmpɔːt bæn/ *noun* a government order forbidding imports of a particular kind or from a particular country ○ *The government has imposed an import ban on arms.*

import duty /ˈɪmpɔːt ˌdjuːti/ *noun* a tax on goods imported into a country

importer /ɪmˈpɔːtə/ *noun* a person or company that imports goods ○ *a cigar importer* ○ *The company is a big importer of foreign cars.*

import-export /ˌɪmpɔːt ˈekspɔːt/ *adjective, noun* referring to business which deals with both bringing foreign goods into a country and sending locally made goods abroad ○ *Rotterdam is an important centre for the import-export trade.* ○ *She works in import-export.*

importing /ɪmˈpɔːtɪŋ/ *adjective* bringing goods into a country ○ *oil-importing countries* ○ *an importing company* ■ *noun* the act of bringing foreign goods into a country for sale ○ *The importing of arms into the country is illegal.*

import levy /ˈɪmpɔːt ˌlevi/ *noun* a tax on imports, especially in the EU a tax on imports of farm produce from outside the EU

import licence /ˈɪmpɔːt ˌlaɪs-(ə)ns/, **import permit** *noun* an official document which allows goods to be imported

import quota /ˈɪmpɔːt ˌkwəʊtə/ *noun* a fixed quantity of a particular type of goods which the government allows to be imported ○ *The government has imposed a import quota on cars.*

import restrictions /ˈɪmpɔːt rɪˌstrɪkʃ(ə)nz/ *plural noun* actions taken by a government to reduce the level of imports by imposing quotas, duties, etc.

imports /ˈɪmpɔːts/ *plural noun* goods brought into a country from abroad for sale ○ *Imports from Poland have risen to $1m a year.* (NOTE: Usually used in the plural, but the singular is used before a noun.)

import surcharge /ˈɪmpɔːt ˌsɜː-tʃɑːdʒ/ *noun* the extra duty charged on imported goods, to try to stop them from being imported and to encourage local manufacture

impression /ɪmˈpreʃ(ə)n/ *noun* **1.** one person's single exposure to an advertisement ○ *One impression can be enough to induce a consumer to buy.* ○ *Too many impressions can put consumers off.* **2.** the number of times an ad banner is displayed

impression cover /ɪmˈpreʃ(ə)n ˌkʌvə/ *noun* the amount of advertising necessary to ensure the required number of impressions

impulse /ˈɪmpʌls/ *noun* a sudden decision □ **to do something on impulse** to do something because you have just thought of it, not because it was planned

impulse buyer /ˈɪmpʌls ˌbaɪə/ *noun* a person who buys something on impulse, not because he or she intended to buy it

impulse buying /ˈɪmpʌls ˌbaɪɪŋ/ *noun* the practice of buying items which you have just seen, not because you had planned to buy them

impulse purchase /ˈɪmpʌls ˌpɜː-tʃɪs/ *noun* something bought as soon as it is seen

incentive /ɪnˈsentɪv/ *noun* something which encourages a customer to buy, or employees to work better

'…some further profit-taking was seen yesterday as investors continued to lack fresh incentives to renew buying activity' [*Financial Times*]

'...a well-designed plan can help companies retain talented employees and offer enticing performance incentives – all at an affordable cost' [*Fortune*]

'...the right incentives can work when used strategically' [*Management Today*]

'...an additional incentive is that the Japanese are prepared to give rewards where they are due' [*Management Today*]

incentive-based system /ɪn'sen-tɪv beɪst ˌsɪstəm/ *noun* a payment system by which an advertising agency's commission depends on how well it performs

incentive marketing /ɪn'sentɪv ˌmɑːkɪtɪŋ/ *noun* any additional incentives to buy apart from advertising, e.g. free gifts ○ *We will have to use incentive marketing to break down sales resistance.*

incentive scheme /ɪn'sentɪv skiːm/ *noun* a plan to encourage better work by paying higher commission or bonuses ○ *Incentive schemes are boosting production.*

inch rate /'ɪnʃ reɪt/ *noun* an advertising rate for periodicals, calculated on a normal column width, one inch in depth

inclusive charge /ɪnˌkluːsɪv 'tʃɑːdʒ/, **inclusive sum** /ɪnˌkluːsɪv 'sʌm/ *noun* a charge which includes all items or costs

income /'ɪnkʌm/ *noun* money which a person receives as salary or dividends □ **lower income bracket** *or* **upper income bracket** the groups of people who earn low or high salaries considered for tax purposes

'...there is no risk-free way of taking regular income from your money much higher than the rate of inflation' [*Guardian*]

income distribution /'ɪnkʌm dɪsˌtrɪˌbjuːʃ(ə)n/ *noun* the way in which the national income is distributed among the various classes and occupations in a country

income effect /'ɪnkʌm ɪˌfekt/ *noun* the effect that a change in a person's income has on his or her spending

incomes policy /'ɪnkʌmz ˌpɒlɪsi/ *noun* the government's ideas on how incomes should be controlled

incoming /'ɪnkʌmɪŋ/ *adjective* referring to someone who has recently been elected or appointed ○ *the incoming chairman*

indemnity /ɪn'demnɪti/ *noun* a guarantee of payment after a loss ○ *She had to pay an indemnity of £100.*

indent *noun*/'ɪndent/ **1.** an order placed by an importer for goods from overseas ○ *They put in an indent for a new stock of soap.* **2.** a line of typing which starts several spaces from the left-hand margin ■ *verb*/ɪn'dent/ **1.** □ **to indent for something** to put in an order for something ○ *The department has indented for a new computer.* **2.** to start a line of typing several spaces from the left-hand margin ○ *Indent the first line three spaces.*

independent /ˌɪndɪ'pendənt/ *adjective* not under the control or authority of anyone else

independent company /ˌɪndɪ-pendənt 'kʌmp(ə)ni/ *noun* a company which is not controlled by another company

independents /ˌɪndɪ'pendənts/ *plural noun* shops or companies which are owned by private individuals or families

'...many independents took advantage of the bank holiday period when the big multiples were closed' [*The Grocer*]

independent television /ˌɪndɪ-pendənt 'telɪvɪʒ(ə)n/ *noun* British commercial television

Independent Television Commission /ˌɪndɪpendənt 'telɪvɪ-ʒ(ə)n kəˌmɪʃ(ə)n/ *noun* the British statutory body which operated transmitting stations and oversaw commercial television and radio until 2003 when licensing and regulating duties were transferred to DFCOM. Abbreviation **ITC**

independent trader /ˌɪndɪpen-dənt 'treɪdə/, **independent shop** /ˌɪndɪpendənt 'ʃɒp/ *noun* a shop which is owned by an individual proprietor, not by a chain

independent variable /ˌɪndɪ-pendənt 'veərɪəb(ə)l/ *noun* a factor whose value, when it changes, influences one or more other variables called 'dependent variables' ○ *In this model personal income is the independent variable and expenditure the dependent variable.*

index /ˈɪndeks/ *noun* a regular statistical report which shows rises and falls in prices, values, or levels (NOTE: The plural is **indexes** or **indices**.)

'…the index of industrial production sank 0.2% for the latest month after rising 0.3% in March' [*Financial Times*]

'…an analysis of the consumer price index for the first half of the year shows that the rate of inflation went down by 12.9%' [*Business Times (Lagos)*]

indexation /ˌɪndekˈseɪʃ(ə)n/ *noun* the linking of something to an index

indexation of wage increases /ˌɪndekseɪʃ(ə)n əv ˈweɪdʒ ˌɪnkriːsɪz/ *noun* the linking of wage increases to the percentage rise in the cost of living

indexing /ˈɪndeksɪŋ/ *noun* a method of showing changes in a value over time by starting with a simple base point such as 100, which then serves as a reference point for future years ○ *Indexing is used to show the rise in the cost of living over a ten-year period.*

index-linked /ˈɪndeks ˌlɪŋkt/ *adjective* rising automatically by the percentage increase in the cost of living ○ *index-linked government bonds* ○ *Inflation did not affect her as she has an index-linked pension.*

'…two-year index-linked savings certificates now pay 3% a year tax free, in addition to index-linking' [*Financial Times*]

indicate /ˈɪndɪkeɪt/ *verb* to show something ○ *The latest figures indicate a fall in the inflation rate.* ○ *Our sales for last year indicate a move from the home market to exports.*

indicator /ˈɪndɪkeɪtə/ *noun* a factor of a situation that gives an indication of a general trend

'…it reduces this month's growth in the key M3 indicator from about 19% to 12%' [*Sunday Times*]

'…we may expect the US leading economic indicators for April to show faster economic growth' [*Australian Financial Review*]

'…other indicators, such as high real interest rates, suggest that monetary conditions are extremely tight' [*Economist*]

indicia /ɪnˈdɪsɪə/ *noun US* a stamp printed on an envelope to show that postage has been paid by the sender

indifference curve /ɪnˈdɪf(ə)rəns kɜːv/ *noun* a line on a graph that joins various points, each point representing a combination of two commodities, each combination giving the customer equal satisfaction

indigenous /ɪnˈdɪdʒɪnəs/ *adjective* belonging to a particular country or area ○ *Cocoa is not indigenous to the area, but has been grown there for some years.*

indirect /ˌɪndaɪˈrekt/ *adjective* not direct

indirect channel /ˌɪndaɪrekt ˈtʃæn(ə)l/ *noun* a marketing channel where intermediaries such as wholesalers and retailers are used to sell a product, as opposed to using a direct sales force

indirect exporting /ˌɪndaɪrekt ˈekspɔːtɪŋ/ *noun* selling products to a customer overseas through a middleman in your own country ○ *There is no need for indirect exporting as we can sell directly to the major department stores in Spain.* ○ *Indirect exporting saved the company from having to worry about export documentation and transportation.*

indirect headline /ˌɪndaɪrekt ˈhedlaɪn/ *noun* a headline which does not directly try to sell a product or service but rather tries to attract the customer's attention or plays on his or her emotions

indirect labour costs /ˌɪndaɪrekt ˈleɪbə ˌkɒsts/ *plural noun* the cost of paying employees not directly involved in making a product, such as cleaners or administrative staff. Such costs cannot be allocated to a cost centre.

individual /ˌɪndɪˈvɪdʒuəl/ *noun* one single person ○ *a savings plan tailored to the requirements of the private individual* ■ *adjective* single or belonging to one person ○ *a pension plan designed to meet each person's individual requirements* ○ *We sell individual portions of ice cream.*

individual demand /ˌɪndɪvɪdʒuəl dɪˈmaːnd/ *noun* demand from one single consumer

industrial /ɪnˈdʌstrɪəl/ *adjective* referring to manufacturing work □ **to take industrial action** to go on strike or go-slow

'…indications of renewed weakness in the US economy were contained in figures on industrial production for April' [*Financial Times*]

industrial advertising /ɪnˌdʌstriəl ˈædvətaɪzɪŋ/ *noun* advertising to businesses, not to private individuals

industrial capacity /ɪnˌdʌstriəl kəˈpæsɪti/ *noun* the amount of work which can be done in a factory or several factories

industrial centre /ɪnˈdʌstriəl ˌsentə/ *noun* a large town with many industries

industrial consumer /ɪnˌdʌstriəl kənˈsjuːmə/ *noun* a business which buys industrial goods

industrial design /ɪnˌdʌstriəl dɪˈzaɪn/ *noun* the design of products made by machines such as cars and refrigerators

industrial development /ɪnˌdʌstriəl dɪˈveləpmənt/ *noun* the planning and building of new industries in special areas

industrial espionage /ɪnˌdʌstriəl ˈespiənɑːʒ/ *noun* the practice of trying to find out the secrets of a competitor's work or products, usually by illegal means

industrial expansion /ɪnˌdʌstriəl ɪkˈspænʃən/ *noun* the growth of industries in a country or a region

industrial goods /ɪnˌdʌstriəl ˈɡʊdz/, **industrial products** /ɪnˌdʌstriəl ˈprɒdʌkts/ *plural noun* **1.** goods or products bought by producers to be used in production processes ○ *Our industrial products are advertised in the specialised press.* ○ *He is an engineer by profession and sells industrial goods to factories.* **2.** goods produced for use by industry, which include processed or raw materials and goods such as machinery and equipment that are used to produce other goods

industrial injury /ɪnˌdʌstriəl ˈɪndʒəriz/ *noun* an injury to an employee that occurs in the workplace

industrialisation /ɪnˌdʌstriəlaɪˈzeɪʃ(ə)n/, **industrialization** *noun* the process of change by which an economy becomes based on industrial production rather than on agriculture

industrialise /ɪnˈdʌstriəˌlaɪz/, **industrialize** *verb* to set up industries in a country which had none before

'…central bank and finance ministry officials of the industrialized countries will continue work on the report' [*Wall Street Journal*]

industrialised society /ɪnˌdʌstriəlaɪzd səˈsaɪəti/ *noun* a country which has many industries

industrialist /ɪnˈdʌstriəlɪst/ *noun* an owner or director of a factory

industrial market /ɪnˈdʌstriəl ˌmɑːkɪt/ *noun* customers who buy goods to be used in production

industrial marketing /ɪnˌdʌstriəl ˈmɑːkɪtɪŋ/ *noun* the marketing of industrial products ○ *After doing a course in industrial marketing, I got a job selling machinery to aircraft manufacturers.*

industrial market research /ɪnˌdʌstriəl mɑːkɪt rɪˈsɜːtʃ/ *noun* market research into selling to businesses as opposed to private individuals

industrial practices /ɪnˌdʌstriəl ˈpræktɪsɪz/ *plural noun* ways of managing or working in business, industry or trade (NOTE: also called **trade practices**)

industrial services marketing /ɪnˌdʌstriəl ˈsɜːvɪsɪz ˌmɑːkɪtɪŋ/ *noun* the marketing to business customers of such services as debt collection, office cleaning, etc.

industrial user /ɪnˌdʌstriəl ˈjuːzə/ *noun* a customer who buys industrial products to use in production

industry /ˈɪndəstri/ *noun* **1.** all factories, companies, or processes involved in the manufacturing of products ○ *All sectors of industry have shown rises in output.* **2.** a group of companies making the same type of product or offering the same type of service ○ *the aircraft industry* ○ *the food-processing industry* ○ *the petroleum industry* ○ *the advertising industry*

'…with the present overcapacity in the airline industry, discounting of tickets is widespread' [*Business Traveller*]

inelastic demand /ɪnɪˌlæstɪk dɪˈmɑːnd/ *noun* demand which experiences a comparatively small percentage change in response to a percentage change in price ○ *Where a product is a household necessity, you almost always find an inelastic demand.*

inelastic supply /ɪnɪˌlæstɪk sə-ˈplaɪ/ *noun* supply which experiences a comparatively small percentage change in response to a percentage change in price

inertia selling /ɪˈnɜːʃə ˌselɪŋ/ *noun* a method of selling items by sending them when they have not been ordered and assuming that if the items are not returned, the person who has received them is willing to buy them

inferior /ɪnˈfɪəriə/ *adjective* not as good as others ○ *products of inferior quality*

inferior product /ɪnˌfɪəriə ˈprɒdʌkt/ *noun* a product which consumers buy less of as their incomes rise ○ *Margarine was clearly an inferior product before it came to be considered healthier than butter.* ○ *As the recession hit, sales of inferior products soared.*

inflation /ɪnˈfleɪʃ(ə)n/ *noun* a greater increase in the supply of money or credit than in the production of goods and services, resulting in higher prices and a fall in the purchasing power of money ○ *to take measures to reduce inflation* ○ *High interest rates tend to increase inflation.* □ **we have 3% inflation or inflation is running at 3%** prices are 3% higher than at the same time last year

inflationary /ɪnˈfleɪʃ(ə)n(ə)ri/ *adjective* tending to increase inflation ○ *inflationary trends in the economy* □ **the economy is in an inflationary spiral** the economy is in a situation where price rises encourage higher wage demands which in turn make prices rise

'…inflationary expectations fell somewhat this month, but remained a long way above the actual inflation rate, according to figures released yesterday. The annual rate of inflation measured by the consumer price index has been below 2% for over 18 months' [*Australian Financial Review*]

inflight advertising /ˌɪnflaɪt ˈædvətaɪzɪŋ/ *noun* advertising on TV screens inside a plane

inflight audience /ˌɪnflaɪt ˈɔː-diəns/ *noun* travellers, especially business executives, seen as a market for advertisers

influencer /ˈɪnfluənsə/ *noun* an expert in the decision-making unit who advises on technical aspects of the product or service under consideration

infoholic /ˌɪnfəʊˈhɒlɪk/ *noun* a person who is obsessed with obtaining information, especially on the Internet (*slang*)

infomediary /ˈɪnfəʊˌmiːdiəri/ *noun* a business or website that collects information about customers for use by other companies (NOTE: The plural is **infomediaries**.)

'BioInformatics' position as an infomediary is facilitating the firm's expansion into markets adjacent to its current niche.' [Forbes]

infomercial /ˌɪnfəʊˈmɜːʃ(ə)l/ *noun* a TV commercial that is longer than the normal 30 seconds, and contains information about the product or service being sold

inform /ɪnˈfɔːm/ *verb* to tell someone officially ○ *I regret to inform you that your tender was not acceptable.* ○ *We are pleased to inform you that you have been selected for interview.* ○ *We have been informed by the Department that new regulations are coming into force.*

informant /ɪnˈfɔːmənt/ *noun* a person who answers questions in a survey ○ *So far only two informants have said that they never buy the product.*

information /ˌɪnfəˈmeɪʃ(ə)n/ *noun* details which explain something ○ *Please send me information on* or *about holidays in the US* ○ *to disclose a piece of information* ○ *to answer a request for information* ○ *Have you any information on* or *about deposit accounts?* ○ *I enclose this leaflet for your information.* ○ *For further information, please write to Department 27.* □ **disclosure of confidential information** the act of telling someone information which should be secret

informational appeal /ɪnfəˌmeɪʃ(ə)n(ə)l əˈpiːl/ *noun* same as **rational appeal**

information and communications technologies /ˌɪnfəmeɪʃ(ə)n ən kəˌmjuːnɪˈkeɪʃ(ə)nz tekˌnɒlədʒiz/ *plural noun* computer and telecommunications technologies considered together (NOTE: It is the coming together of information and communications technology that has made possible such things as the *Internet, videoconferencing, groupware, intranets*, and third-generation mobile phones.)

information architecture /ˌɪnfə-ˈmeɪʃ(ə)n ˌɑːkɪtektʃə/ *noun* the methods used in designing the navigation, search and content layout for a website

information blizzard /ˌɪnfəˈmeɪʃ(ə)n ˌblɪzəd/ *noun* the overload of information that the media exposes people to, which is difficult to take in and make sense of

information management /ˌɪnfə-ˈmeɪʃ(ə)n ˌmænɪdʒmənt/ *noun* the task of controlling information and the flow of information within an organisation, which involves acquiring, recording, organising, storing, distributing, and retrieving it (NOTE: Good information management has been described as getting the right information to the right person in the right format at the right time.)

information officer /ˌɪnfəˈmeɪʃ(ə)n ˌɒfɪsə/ *noun* **1.** a person whose job is to give information about a company, an organisation or a government department to the public **2.** a person whose job is to give information to other departments in the same organisation

information processing model /ˌɪnfəmeɪʃ(ə)n ˈprəʊsesɪŋ ˌmɒd-(ə)l/ *noun* a way of evaluating the effect of advertising by seeing the receiver of the message as someone who processes information and deals with problems

information retrieval /ˌɪnfəˈmeɪʃ(ə)n rɪˌtriːv(ə)l/ *noun* the finding of stored data in a computer

infotainment /ˌɪnfəʊˈteɪnmənt/ *noun* entertainment that is informative, especially television programmes that deal with serious issues or current affairs in an entertaining way

ingredient /ɪnˈɡriːdiənt/ *noun* material or a substance which goes to make something

ingredient sponsored cooperative advertising /ɪnˌɡriːdiənt ˌspɒnsəd kəʊˌɒp(ə)rətɪv ˈædvətaɪzɪŋ/ *noun* advertising sponsored by the producers of raw materials which aims

to encourage the production of products that use these raw materials

inherent drama /ɪnˌhɪərənt ˈdrɑːmə/ *noun* advertising that emphasises the benefits of purchasing a product or service and the vital interest which the user has in the product such as the speed of a car, the nutrition value of cereals, etc.

inherent vice /ɪnˌhɪərənt ˈvaɪs/ *noun* the tendency of some goods to spoil during transportation ○ *Inherent vice discouraged us from importing tropical fruit.*

in-home selling /ˌɪn həʊm ˈselɪŋ/, **in-home retailing** /ˌɪn həʊm ˈriːtaɪlɪŋ/ *noun* selling to a customer in his or her home, either by direct contact or by telephone ○ *In-home selling is the national strategy for our products.* ○ *In-home selling is useful when housewives are the target market.*

in-house /ˌɪn ˈhaʊs/ *adverb, adjective* done by someone employed by a company on their premises, not by an outside contractor ○ *the in-house staff* ○ *We do all our data processing in-house.*

in-house agency /ˌɪn haʊs ˈeɪdʒənsi/ *noun* an advertising agency which is owned and operated by a company and is responsible for the company's advertising programme

in-house newsletter /ˌɪn haʊs ˈnjuːzletə/ *noun* same as **newsletter**

initial /ɪˈnɪʃ(ə)l/ *adjective* first or starting ○ *The initial response to the TV advertising has been very good.*

'…the founding group has subscribed NKr 14.5m of the initial NKr 30m share capital' [*Financial Times*]

'…career prospects are excellent for someone with potential, and initial salary is negotiable around $45,000 per annum' [*Australian Financial Review*]

initial capital /ɪˌnɪʃ(ə)l ˈkæpɪt-(ə)l/ *noun* capital which is used to start a business

initial sales /ɪˌnɪʃ(ə)l ˈseɪlz/ *plural noun* the first sales of a new product

ink-jet printing /ˈɪŋk dʒet ˌprɪntɪŋ/, **ink-jet imaging** /ˈɪŋk dʒet ˌɪmɪdʒɪŋ/ *noun* a printing process where text is reproduced by projecting dots of electronically charged ink onto the paper

inland port /ˌɪnlənd 'pɔːt/ *noun* a port on a river or canal

innovate /'ɪnəʊveɪt/ *verb* to bring in new ideas or new methods

innovation /ˌɪnə'veɪʃ(ə)n/ *noun* the development of new products or new ways of selling

'…if innovation equates with daring, then 'who dares wins' will be a marketing commandment' [*Marketing Workshop*]

innovation–adoption model /ɪn-ə,veɪʃ(ə)n ə'dɒpʃ(ə)n ,mɒd(ə)l/ *noun* a model that shows the stages in the adoption process for a new product by a consumer, which are: awareness, interest, evaluation, trial, and adoption

innovative /'ɪnəveɪtɪv/ *adjective* referring to a person or thing which is new and makes changes

'…small innovative companies in IT have been hampered for lack of funds' [*Sunday Times*]

innovator /'ɪnəveɪtə/ *noun* 1. a person or company that brings in new ideas and methods 2. a person who buys a new product first

in-pack /'ɪn pæk/ *noun* something placed inside the packaging with the product ○ *In-pack promotion may include information on other products in the same line.*

input tax /'ɪnpʊt tæks/ *noun* VAT which is paid by a company on goods or services bought

inquiry /ɪn'kwaɪəri/ *noun* a request for information about a product

inquiry test /ɪŋ'kwaɪəri test/ *noun* a measuring of the effectiveness of advertising based on responses following the advertisement such as requests for information, phone calls, or the number of coupons redeemed

insert *noun*/'ɪnsɜːt/ a form or leaflet which is put inside something, usually a magazine or newspaper □ **an insert in a magazine mailing, a magazine insert** an advertising sheet put into a magazine when it is mailed ■ *verb*/ɪn'sɜːt/ to put something in ○ *to insert a clause into a contract* ○ *to insert a publicity piece into a magazine mailing*

insertion /ɪn'sɜːʃ(ə)n/ *noun* the act of putting an advertisement into a magazine or newspaper

insertion rate /ɪn'sɜːʃ(ə)n reɪt/ *noun* the rate charged for a single insertion of an advertisement

inset /'ɪnset/ *noun* same as **insert**

inside back cover /ˌɪnsaɪd bæk 'kʌvə/ the page on the inside of the back cover used for advertising ○ *We have advertised on the inside back cover of every issue this year.* ○ *The survey is trying to establish how much notice readers take of the inside back cover.*

inside front cover /ˌɪnsaɪd ˌfrʌnt 'kʌvə/ *noun* the page on the inside of the front cover of a magazine, used for advertisements

instability /ˌɪnstə'bɪlɪti/ *noun* the state of being unstable or moving up and down □ **a period of instability in the money markets** a period when currencies fluctuate rapidly

install /ɪn'stɔːl/ *verb* 1. to put a machine into an office or into a factory ○ *We are planning to install the new machinery over the weekend.* ○ *They must install a new data processing system because the old one cannot cope with the mass of work involved.* 2. to set up a piece of machinery or equipment, e.g. a new computer system, so that it can be used 3. to configure a new computer program to the existing system requirements

installation /ˌɪnstə'leɪʃ(ə)n/ *noun* 1. the act of putting new machines into an office or a factory ○ *to supervise the installation of new equipment* 2. machines, equipment and buildings ○ *Harbour installations were picketed by striking dockers.* ○ *The fire seriously damaged the oil installations.* 3. the act of setting up a piece of equipment

installment plan /ɪn'stɔːlmənt plæn/, **installment sales** /ɪn'stɔːlmənt seɪlz/ **installment buying** /ɪn,stɔːlmənt 'baɪɪŋ/ **installment credit** /ɪn,stɔːlmənt 'kredɪt/ *noun* US same as **hire purchase** ○ *to buy a car on the installment plan*

instalment /ɪn'stɔːlmənt/ *noun* a part of a payment which is paid regularly until the total amount is paid ○ *The first instalment is payable on signature of the agreement.* (NOTE: The US spelling is

installment.) □ **the final instalment is now due** the last of a series of payments should be paid now □ **to pay £25 down and monthly instalments of £20** to pay a first payment of £25 and the rest in payments of £20 each month □ **to miss an instalment** not to pay an instalment at the right time

institution /ˌɪnstɪˈtjuːʃ(ə)n/ *noun* an organisation or society set up for a particular purpose. ⇨ **financial institution**

institutional /ˌɪnstɪˈtjuːʃ(ə)n(ə)l/ *adjective* relating to an institution, especially a financial institution

'...during the 1970s commercial property was regarded by big institutional investors as an alternative to equities' [*Investors Chronicle*]

institutional advertising /ˌɪnstɪ-ˈtjuːʃ(ə)n(ə)l ˌædvətaɪzɪŋ/ *noun* advertising an organisation rather than a product

institutional investor /ˌɪnstɪtjuː-ʃ(ə)n(ə)l ɪnˈvestə/ *noun* a financial institution which invests money in securities

in-store /ˈɪn stɔː/ *adjective* inside a store

'...dissatisfied with traditional media advertising, manufacturers in the USA are shifting their money into in-store promotion. The reason why marketers in the US put more effort into in-store marketing is the greater penetration of EPOS' [*Marketing Week*]

in-store demonstration /ˌɪn stɔː ˌdemənˈstreɪʃ(ə)n/ *noun* a demonstration of a product such as a piece of kitchen equipment inside a store

in-store media /ˌɪn stɔː ˈmiːdiə/ *noun* promotional material used inside a store, e.g. POS material, display banners, and advertisements on trolleys

in-store promotion /ˌɪn stɔː prəˈməʊʃ(ə)n/ *noun* a promotion of a product inside a shop, e.g. by demonstrations or special gift counters

instrument /ˈɪnstrʊmənt/ *noun* a legal document

instrumental conditioning /ˌɪn-strʊment(ə)l kənˈdɪʃ(ə)nɪŋ/ *noun* same as **operant conditioning**

insurance rates /ɪnˈʃʊərəns reɪts/ *plural noun* the amount of premium which has to be paid per £1000 of insurance

intangible assets /ɪnˌtændʒɪb(ə)l ˈæsets/, **intangible fixed assets** /ɪnˌtændʒɪb(ə)l fɪkst ˈæsets/ **intangibles** /ɪnˈtændʒɪb(ə)lz/ *plural noun* assets that have a value but which cannot be seen, e.g. goodwill or a trademark

integrate /ˈɪntɪɡreɪt/ *verb* to link things together to form one whole group

integrated information response model /ˌɪntɪɡreɪtɪd ˌɪnfəmeɪʃ(ə)n rɪˈspɒns ˌmɒd(ə)l/ *noun* a model showing the response process to an advertising message which suggests that advertising leads to a low acceptance rate of information, but that after trials of the product the acceptance rate increases and this in turn leads to brand loyalty

integrated lifestyle segment /ˌɪntɪɡreɪtɪd ˈlaɪfstaɪl ˌsegmənt/ *noun* according to VALS, the group of people in society who are satisfied with their way of life

integrated marketing /ˌɪntɪɡreɪtɪd ˈmaːkɪtɪŋ/ *noun* co-ordination of all of a company's marketing activities in establishing marketing strategies such as packaging, media promotion, POS material, or after-sales service ○ *The separation of departments makes integrated marketing difficult to achieve.*

integrated marketing communications concept /ˌɪntɪɡreɪtɪd ˌmaːkɪtɪŋ kəˌmjuːnɪˈkeɪʃ(ə)nz ˌkɒnsept/ *noun US* the concept or principle that a company should link all its promotions, either of its own image or of the products and services it sells, in a consistent way on several different levels

integrated marketing communications objectives /ˌɪntɪɡreɪtɪd ˌmaːkɪtɪŋ kəˌmjuːnɪˈkeɪʃ(ə)nz əbˈdʒektɪvz/ *plural noun* the listed objectives of an integrated marketing communications programme such as communication tasks, anticipated sales, and increased market share

integrated processes /ˌɪntɪ-ɡreɪtɪd ˈprəʊsesɪz/ *plural noun* the processes by which knowledge of products, and beliefs about their excellence, combine to help the purchaser evaluate alternative products

integration /ˌɪntɪˈɡreɪʃ(ə)n/ *noun* the act of bringing several businesses together under a central control

intellectual property /ˌɪntɪlekt-ʃʊəl ˈprɒpəti/ *noun* ideas, designs, and inventions, including copyrights, patents, and trademarks, that were created by and legally belong to an individual or an organisation (NOTE: Intellectual property is protected by law in most countries, and the World Intellectual Property Organization is responsible for harmonising the law in different countries and promoting the protection of intellectual property rights.)

intensive distribution /ɪnˌtensɪv ˌdɪstrɪˈbjuːʃ(ə)n/ *noun* the use by a producer of as wide a network of distributors as possible to sell products ○ *Without intensive distribution we cannot hope to achieve these ambitious sales targets.* ○ *Intensive distribution makes us rely on too many retailers and wholesalers.*

intention to buy /ɪnˌtenʃ(ə)n tə ˈbaɪ/ *noun* a statement by a respondent that he or she intends to buy a product or service, which may or may not be true

interactive /ˌɪntərˈæktɪv/ *adjective* allowing the customer and seller to influence the presentation of information or the development of strategies

'Last year Hongkong Telecom launched the first commercial interactive television (ITV) service in the world, offering video and music on demand, along with high-speed Internet access, to 70% of the city's homes' [Economist]

interactive marketing /ˌɪntəræk-tɪv ˈmaːkɪtɪŋ/ *noun* marketing strategies which are developed as a result of decisions taken by both salespeople and customers

interactive media /ˌɪntəræktɪv ˈmiːdiə/ *plural noun* media that allow the customer to interact with the source of the message, receiving information and replying to questions, etc.

interactive voice response /ˌɪntəræktɪv ˈvɔɪs rɪˌspɒns/ *noun* a telephone or Internet system which is activated by the voice of the caller and responds to the caller's queries. Abbreviation **IVR**

intercompany comparison /ˌɪntəkʌmpəni kəmˈpærɪs(ə)n/, **interfirm comparison** /ˌɪntəfɜːm kəmˈpærɪs(ə)n/ *noun* a comparison of different companies to see how much they spend on promotion, what their return on investment is, etc.

interconnect /ˌɪntəkəˈnekt/ *noun* two or more cable systems joined together for advertising purposes so as to give a wider geographical spread

interest /ˈɪntrəst/ *noun* **1.** special attention ○ *The buyers showed a lot of interest in our new product range.* **2.** payment made by a borrower for the use of money, calculated as a percentage of the capital borrowed ■ *verb* to attract someone's attention ○ *She tried to interest several companies in her new invention.* ○ *The company is trying to interest a wide range of customers in its products.*

interest charges /ˈɪntrəst ˌtʃaː-dʒɪz/ *plural noun* money paid as interest on a loan

interest rate /ˈɪntrəst reɪt/ *noun* a figure which shows the percentage of the capital sum borrowed or deposited which is to be paid as interest. Also called **rate of interest**

interface /ˈɪntəfeɪs/ *noun* a point where two groups of people come into contact

intermedia comparison /ˌɪntə-miːdiə kəmˈpærɪs(ə)n/ *noun* a comparison of different media to decide how suitable they are for advertising ○ *We will carry out intermedia comparisons before deciding on our promotional strategy.* Compare **intramedia comparison**

intermediate goods /ˌɪntəmiːdiət ˈɡʊdz/ *plural noun* goods bought for use in the production of other goods

internal /ɪnˈtɜːn(ə)l/ *adjective* **1.** inside a company □ **we decided to make an internal appointment** we decided to appoint an existing member of staff to the post, and not bring someone in from outside the company **2.** inside a country or a region

internal analysis /ɪnˌtɜːn(ə)l əˈnæləsɪs/ *noun* detailed examination and reports on the product or service offered and the company itself

internal communication /ɪnˌtɜː-n(ə)l kəˌmjuːnɪˈkeɪʃ(ə)n/ *noun* communication between employees or departments of the same organisation (NOTE: Internal communication can take various forms such as *team briefings, interviewing,* employee or *works councils, meetings, memos,* an *intranet, newsletters, suggestion schemes,* the *grapevine,* and reports.)

internal desk research /ɪnˌtɜː-n(ə)l ˈdesk rɪˌsɜːtʃ/ *noun* research based on information in a company's own records such as customer accounts and sales reports

internalisation /ɪnˌtɜːnəlaɪˈzeɪ-ʃ(ə)n/, **internalization** *noun* a process by which individuals identify information which is relevant to them personally and so acquire values and norms which allow them to make decisions

internally /ɪnˈtɜːn(ə)li/ *adverb* inside a company ○ *The job was advertised internally.*

internal marketing /ɪnˌtɜːn(ə)l ˈmɑːkɪtɪŋ/ *noun* marketing conducted inside a large organisation, where independent departments sell goods or services to each other

Internal Revenue Service /ɪn-ˌtɜːn(ə)l ˈrevənjuː ˌsɜːvɪs/ *noun* in the US, the branch of the federal government charged with collecting the majority of federal taxes. Abbreviation **IRS**

internal search /ɪnˌtɜːn(ə)l ˈsɜːtʃ/ *noun* the process by which a consumer acquires information from past experience or something he or she has remembered

internal telephone /ɪnˌtɜːn(ə)l ˈtelɪfəʊn/ *noun* a telephone which is linked to other telephones in an office

internal trade /ɪnˌtɜːn(ə)l ˈtreɪd/ *noun* trade between various parts of a country. Opposite **external trade**

international /ˌɪntəˈnæʃ(ə)nəl/ *adjective* working between countries

international marketing /ˌɪntən-æʃ(ə)nəl ˈmɑːkɪtɪŋ/ *noun* the marketing of a company's products abroad ○ *Our international marketing so far consists of exporting to three countries.* ○ *The next stage in the company's inter-national marketing was the setting up of factories overseas.*

international media /ˌɪntənæʃ(ə)nəl ˈmiːdiə/ *plural noun* advertising media that cover several countries and can be used to reach audiences in them

International Monetary Fund /ˌɪntənæʃ(ə)nəl ˈmʌnɪt(ə)ri ˌfʌnd/ *noun* a type of bank which is part of the United Nations and helps member states in financial difficulties, gives financial advice to members and encourages world trade. Abbreviation **IMF**

international monetary system /ˌɪntənæʃ(ə)nəlˈmʌnɪt(ə)riˌsɪstəm/ *noun* methods of controlling and exchanging currencies between countries

international postal reply coupon /ˌɪntənæʃ(ə)nəl ˌpəʊst(ə)l rɪˈplaɪ kuːˌpɒn/ *noun* a coupon which can be used in another country to pay the postage of replying to a letter ○ *She enclosed an international reply coupon with her letter.*

international reserves /ˌɪn-tənæʃ(ə)nəl rɪˈzɜːvz/ *plural noun* same as **foreign currency reserves**

international trade /ˌɪntənæʃ(ə)-nəl ˈtreɪd/ *noun* trade between different countries

Internet /ˈɪntənet/ *noun* the global, public network of computers and telephone links that houses websites, allows email to be sent, and is accessed with the aid of a modem ○ *Much of our business is done on the Internet.* ○ *Internet sales form an important part of our turnover.* ○ *He searched the Internet for information on cheap tickets to the USA.*

'…they predict a tenfold increase in sales via internet or TV between 1999 and 2004' [*Investors Chronicle*]

'…in two significant decisions, the Securities and Exchange Board of India today allowed trading of shares through the Internet and set a deadline for companies to conform to norms for good corporate governance' [*The Hindu*]

Internet commerce /ˈɪntənet ˌkɒmɜːs/ *noun* the part of e-commerce that consists of commercial business transactions conducted over the Internet

Internet marketing /ˈɪntənet ˌmɑːkɪtɪŋ/ *noun* the marketing of products or services over the Internet

Internet merchant /ˈɪntənet ˌmɜːtʃənt/ *noun* a businessman or businesswoman who sells a product or service over the Internet

Internet payment system /ˌɪntənet ˈpeɪmənt ˌsɪstəm/ *noun* any mechanism that enables funds to be transferred from a customer to seller or from one business to another via the Internet

Internet security /ˌɪntənet sɪˈkjʊərɪti/ *noun* the means used to protect websites and other electronic files against attacks by hackers and viruses and to ensure that business can be safely conducted over the Internet

interpolation /ɪnˌtɜːpəˈleɪʃ(ə)n/ *noun* a method of estimating a value between two established values

interstate commerce /ˌɪntəsteɪt ˈkɒmɜːs/ *noun US* commerce between different states which is therefore subject to federal government control

interstitial /ˌɪntəˈstɪʃ(ə)l/ *noun* a page of advertising which is inserted into a website

interview /ˈɪntəvjuː/ *noun* a meeting in order to talk to a person who is applying for a job to find out whether they are suitable for it ○ *We called six people for interview.* ○ *I have an interview next week* or *I am going for an interview next week.* ■ *verb* to talk to a person applying for a job to see if they are suitable ○ *We interviewed ten candidates, but found no one suitable.*

interviewee /ˌɪntəvjuːˈiː/ *noun* the person who is being interviewed ○ *The interviewer did everything to put the interviewee at ease.* ○ *The interviewees were all nervous as they waited to be called into the interview room.*

interviewer /ˈɪntəvjuːə/ *noun* the person who is conducting an interview

intramedia comparison/ˌɪntrəmiːdiə kəmˈpærɪs(ə)n/ *noun* a comparison of different advertising options within the same medium ○ *After extensive intramedia comparison we now know all the possibilities of TV advertising.* Compare **intermedia comparison**

intranet /ˈɪntrənet/ *noun* a network of computers and telephone links that uses Internet technology but is accessible only to the employees of a particular organisation

intransient /ɪnˌtrænziənt ˈædvətaɪzɪŋ/ *adjective* referring to an advertisement which the target audience can keep and look at again, e.g. in a newspaper or magazine, as opposed to a transient advertisement on TV or radio

intrinsic value /ɪnˌtrɪnsɪk ˈvæljuː/ *noun* the material value of something ○ *These objects have sentimental value, but no intrinsic value at all.* ○ *The intrinsic value of jewellery makes it a good investment.*

introduce /ˌɪntrəˈdjuːs/ *verb* to make someone get to know somebody or something □ **to introduce a client** to bring in a new client and make them known to someone □ **to introduce a new product on the market** to produce a new product and launch it on the market

introductory offer /ˌɪntrədʌkt(ə)ri ˈɒfə/ *noun* a special price offered on a new product to attract customers

inventory /ˈɪnvənt(ə)ri/ *noun* **1.** *especially US* all the stock or goods in a warehouse or shop ○ *to carry a high inventory* ○ *to aim to reduce inventory* Also called **stock 2.** a list of the contents of a building such as a house for sale or an office for rent ○ *to draw up an inventory of fixtures and fittings* □ **to agree the inventory** to agree that the inventory is correct **3.** advertising time or space which is not used and is available ■ *verb* to make a list of stock or contents

inventory control /ˈɪnvənt(ə)ri kənˌtrəʊl/ *noun US* same as **stock control**

investment /ɪnˈvestmənt/ *noun* the placing of money so that it will produce interest and increase in value ○ *They called for more government investment in new industries.* ○ *She was advised to make investments in oil companies.*

'…investment trusts, like unit trusts, consist of portfolios of shares and therefore provide a spread of investments' [*Investors Chronicle*]

'…investment companies took the view that prices had reached rock bottom and could only go up' [*Lloyd's List*]

investment advertising /ɪnˈvestmənt ˌædvətaɪzɪŋ/ *noun* large expenditure on advertising to achieve long-term objectives

investment spending /ɪn'vest-mənt ˌspendɪŋ/ *noun* spending more than normal on advertising with the expectation of increased sales and profits

investor relations research /ɪn-ˌvestə rɪ'leɪʃ(ə)nz rɪˌsɜːtʃ/ *noun* research that allows a company to see how financial institutions such as merchant banks view the company

invisible /ɪn'vɪzɪb(ə)l/ *adjective* not recorded or reflected in economic statistics

invisible assets /ɪnˌvɪzɪb(ə)l 'æsets/ *plural noun US* same as **intangible assets**

invisible exports /ɪnˌvɪzɪb(ə)l 'ekspɔːts/ *plural noun* services, e.g. banking, insurance and tourism, that are provided to customers overseas and paid for in foreign currency. Opposite **visible exports**

invisible imports /ɪnˌvɪzɪb(ə)l 'ɪmpɔːts/ *plural noun* services that overseas companies provide to domestic customers who pay for them in local currency. Opposite **visible imports**

invisibles /ɪn'vɪzɪb(ə)lz/ *plural noun* invisible imports and exports

invitation to tender /ˌɪnvɪteɪʃ(ə)n tə 'tendə/ *noun* a formal request, sent to a small number of suppliers, asking them to submit a detailed proposal for completing a particular piece of work

invoice /'ɪnvɔɪs/ *noun* a note asking for payment for goods or services supplied ○ *your invoice dated November 10th* ○ *to make out an invoice for £250* ○ *to settle* or *to pay an invoice* ○ *They sent in their invoice six weeks late.* □ **the total is payable within thirty days of invoice** the total sum has to be paid within thirty days of the date on the invoice ■ *verb* to send an invoice to someone ○ *to invoice a customer* □ **we invoiced you on November 10th** we sent you the invoice on November 10th

invoice clerk /'ɪnvɔɪs klɑːk/ *noun* an office employee who deals with invoices

invoice number /'ɪnvɔɪs ˌnʌmbə/ *noun* the reference number printed on an invoice or order

invoice price /'ɪnvɔɪs praɪs/ *noun* the price as given on an invoice, including any discount and VAT

invoicing /'ɪnvɔɪsɪŋ/ *noun* the work of sending invoices ○ *All our invoicing is done by computer.* □ **invoicing in triplicate** the preparation of three copies of invoices

invoicing department /'ɪnvɔɪsɪŋ dɪˌpɑːtmənt/ *noun* the department in a company which deals with preparing and sending in voices

inward /'ɪnwəd/ *adjective* towards the home country

inward bill /ˌɪnwəd 'bɪl/ *noun* a bill of lading for goods arriving in a country

inward mission /ˌɪnwəd 'mɪʃ-(ə)n/ *noun* a visit to your home country by a group of foreign businesspeople

IP address /ˌaɪ 'piː əˌdres/ *noun* a unique 32-bit number that defines the precise location of a computer connected to a network or the Internet

irrevocable /ɪ'revəkəb(ə)l/ *adjective* unchangeable

irrevocable acceptance /ɪˌre-vəkəb(ə)l ək'septəns/ *noun* an acceptance which cannot be withdrawn

island display /'aɪlənd dɪsˌpleɪ/ *noun* same as **island site**

island position /'aɪlənd pəˌzɪ-ʃ(ə)n/ *noun* advertising space separated from other advertising space in a newspaper or magazine ○ *An island position is expensive but will attract great attention.*

island site /'aɪlənd saɪt/, **island display** /'aɪlənd dɪsˌpleɪ/ *noun* an exhibition stand separated from others ○ *There are only two island sites at the exhibition and we have one of them.* ○ *An island site means that visitors can approach the stand from several directions.*

issue /'ɪʃuː/ *noun* the number of a newspaper or magazine ○ *We have an ad in the January issue of the magazine.* ■ *verb* to put out or to give out ○ *to issue a letter of credit* ○ *to issue shares in a* *new company* ○ *to issue a writ against someone* ○ *The government issued a report on London's traffic.*

'...the company said that its recent issue of 10.5% convertible preference shares at A$8.50 a share has been oversubscribed' [*Financial Times*]

issue life /ˈɪʃuː laɪf/ *noun* the time between one issue of a publication and another ○ *The reason the magazine's advertising rates are so expensive is because it has an issue life of three months.*

issuer /ˈɪʃuə/ *noun* a financial institution that issues credit and debit cards and maintains the systems for billing and payment

ITC *abbreviation* Independent Television Commission

item /ˈaɪtəm/ *noun* **1.** something for sale □ **we are holding orders for out-of-stock items** we are holding orders for goods which are not in stock ○ *Please find enclosed an order for the following items from your catalogue.* **2.** a piece of information ○ *items on a balance sheet* □ **item of expenditure** goods or services which have been paid for and appear in the accounts **3.** a point on a list □ **we will now take item four on the agenda** we will now discuss the fourth point on the agenda

itemise /ˈaɪtəmaɪz/, **itemize** *verb* to make a detailed list of things ○ *Itemising the sales figures will take about two days.*

itemised account /ˌaɪtəmaɪzd əˈkaʊnt/ *noun* a detailed record of money paid or owed

itemised invoice /ˌaɪtəmaɪzd ˈɪnvɔɪs/ *noun* an invoice which lists each item separately

itinerary /aɪˈtɪnərəri/ *noun* a list of places to be visited on one journey ○ *a sales rep's itinerary*

IVR *abbreviation* interactive voice response

J

jargon /'dʒɑːgən/ *noun* a special sort of language used by a trade or profession or particular group of people

'The very term "open-source software" sounds like the kind of computer jargon most managers would prefer to leave to their IT experts' [*Harvard Business Review*]

JIT *abbreviation* just-in-time

job /dʒɒb/ *noun* an order being worked on ○ *We are working on six jobs at the moment.* ○ *The shipyard has a big job starting in August.*

jobber /'dʒɒbə/ *noun US* a wholesaler

jobbing /'dʒɒbɪŋ/ *noun* the practice of doing small pieces of work

jobbing font /'dʒɒbɪŋ fɒnt/ *noun* a display font used for advertisements and posters

jobbing printer /'dʒɒbɪŋ ˌprɪntə/ *noun* a person who does small printing jobs

jobbing production /'dʒɒbɪŋ prə-ˌdʌkʃən/ *noun* the production of several different articles, each to individual requirements

job classification /'dʒɒb klæsɪfɪ-ˌkeɪʃ(ə)n/ *noun* the process of describing jobs listed in various groups

job description /'dʒɒb dɪˌs-krɪpʃən/ *noun* a description of what a job consists of and what skills are needed for it ○ *The letter enclosed an application form and a job description.*

job lot /ˌdʒɒb 'lɒt/ *noun* a group of miscellaneous items sold together ○ *They sold the household furniture as a job lot.*

job opening /'dʒɒb ˌəʊp(ə)nɪŋ/ *noun* a job which is empty and needs filling ○ *We have job openings for office staff.*

job opportunities /'dʒɒb ɒpəˌ-tjuːnɪtiz/ *plural noun* new jobs which are available ○ *The increase in export orders has created hundreds of job opportunities.*

job satisfaction /'dʒɒb sætɪs-ˌfækʃən/ *noun* an employee's feeling that he or she is happy at work and pleased with the work he or she does

job specification /'dʒɒb ˌspe-sɪfɪkeɪʃ(ə)n/ *noun* a very detailed description of what is involved in a job

joined-up /'dʒɔɪnd ʌp/ *adjective* involving two or more individuals or organisations who share information and co-ordinate their activities in order to achieve their aims more effectively

joint account /'dʒɔɪnt əˌkaʊnt/ *noun* a bank or building society account shared by two people ○ *Many married couples have joint accounts so that they can pay for household expenses.*

Joint Photographics Experts Group *noun* full form of **JPEG**

journal /'dʒɜːn(ə)l/ *noun* **1.** a book with the account of sales and purchases made each day **2.** a magazine

journalist /'dʒɜːn(ə)lɪst/ *noun* 1. a person who writes for a newspaper

journey /'dʒɜːni/ *noun* a long trip, especially a trip made by a salesperson ○ *She planned her journey so that she could visit all her accounts in two days.*

journey mapping /'dʒɜːni ˌmæpɪŋ/ *noun* a method of calculating how many people pass a poster site ○ *Journey mapping allows us to pinpoint the ten key sites we will be renting for the next three months.*

journey order /'dʒɜːni ˌɔːdə/ *noun* an order given by a shopkeeper to a salesperson when they call

journey planning /'dʒɜːni ˌplæn-ɪŋ/ *noun* the act of planning what calls a salesperson will make and how they will be reached most efficiently, giving priority to the more profitable accounts ○ *The sales manager will stress how good journey planning will save precious time.* ○ *Inefficient journey planning means miles of unnecessary travelling for the sales force every day.*

JPEG /'dʒeɪpeg/ *noun* a file format used to compress and store photographic images for transfer over the Internet

judgement /'dʒʌdʒmənt/, **judgment** *noun* an assessment or evaluation of the quality of someone or something

judgement forecasting /'dʒʌd-ʒmənt ˌfɔːkɑːstɪŋ/ *noun* forecasting based on judgement rather than on any scientific techniques ○ *We need more precise information so that we can extrapolate rather than use judgement forecasting.* ○ *Market research departments find judgement forecasting too subjective and unreliable.*

judgement sampling /'dʒʌdʒ-mənt ˌsɑːmplɪŋ/ *noun* the choosing of a sample for a survey based on judgement of what criteria would be especially significant rather than applying any scientific techniques ○ *Judgement sampling can produce an insufficiently representative sample.*

jumbo /'dʒʌmbəʊ/ *adjective* very large ○ *jumbo-sized pack*

junior staff /ˌdʒuːniə 'stɑːf/ *noun* people in less important positions in a company

junk mail /'dʒʌŋk meɪl/ *noun* **1.** unsolicited advertising material sent through the post and usually thrown away immediately by the people who receive it **2.** unsolicited advertising material sent by email

jury of executive opinion /ˌdʒʊəri əv ɪgˌzekjʊtɪv ə'pɪnjən/ *noun* a panel of executives used to contribute to forecasting

just-in-time /ˌdʒʌst ɪn 'taɪm/ *noun* a system in which goods are made or purchased just before they are needed, so as to avoid carrying high levels of stock. Abbreviation **JIT**

K

KAM *abbreviation* key account management

keen /kiːn/ *adjective* **1.** eager or active □ **keen competition** strong competition ○ *We are facing some keen competition from European manufacturers.* □ **keen demand** wide demand ○ *There is a keen demand for home computers.* **2.** □ **keen prices** prices which are kept low so as to be competitive ○ *Our prices are the keenest on the market.*

kerb appeal /ˈkɜːb əˌpiːl/ *noun* an estate agency term to describe the attractive appearance of a property for sale as seen from the roadside, creating a favourable first impression on a potential buyer ○ *Their house looks impressive from the street. It definitely has kerb appeal.*

kerbside conference /ˌkɜːbsaɪd ˈkɒnf(ə)rəns/ *noun* a discussion of selling techniques between a trainee salesperson and the person training them after making a sales call ○ *In the kerbside conference, the sales trainer described a number of different approaches that might have been made to a particular customer.*

key /kiː/ *adjective* important ○ *a key factor* ○ *key industries* ○ *key personnel* ○ *a key member of our management team* ○ *She has a key post in the organisation.* ○ *We don't want to lose any key staff in the reorganisation.*

'…he gave up the finance job in September to devote more time to his global responsibilities as chairman and to work more closely with key clients' [*Times*]

key account /ˈkiː əˌkaʊnt/ *noun* an important account or client, e.g. of an advertising agency

key account management /ˈkiː əˌkaʊnt ˌmænɪdʒmənt/ *noun* the management of the small number of key accounts which represent the bulk of a company's business. Abbreviation **KAM**

keyboard /ˈkiːbɔːd/ *noun* the part of a computer or other device with keys which are pressed to make letters or figures ■ *verb* to press the keys on a keyboard to type something ○ *She is keyboarding our address list.*

keyboarder /ˈkiːbɔːdə/ *noun* a person who types information into a computer

keyboarding /ˈkiːbɔːdɪŋ/ *noun* the act of typing on a keyboard ○ *Keyboarding costs have risen sharply.*

key code /ˈkiː kəʊd/ *noun* a letter and number code printed on mailshots so that the respondents can be identified

keyed advertisement /ˌkiːd ədˈvɜːtɪsmənt/ *noun* an advertisement which asks people to write to a specially coded address which will indicate where they saw it, thus helping the advertisers to evaluate the effectiveness of advertising in that particular newspaper or magazine

key number /ˈkiː ˌnʌmbə/ *noun* the number used in a keyed advertisement

keypad /ˈkiːpæd/ *noun* a set of keys on a computer

key prospects /ˌkiː ˈprɒspekts/ *plural noun* potential customers ○ *In this sales campaign we will be concentrating on key prospects.* ○ *This is bad journey planning since it does not allow sufficient time to visit all the key prospects.*

keyword /ˈkiːwɜːd/ *noun* a word used by a search engine to help it locate a particular type of website (NOTE: Companies need to think very carefully about the keywords they place in their webpages in order to attract relevant search-engine traffic.)

keyword density /ˈkiːwɜːd ˌdensɪti/ *noun* the number of times a keyword or phrase appears on a webpage compared to the total number of words on the page, expressed as a percentage, which is especially important in search engine optimisation

keyword search /ˌkiːwɜːd ˈsɜːtʃ/ *noun* **1.** a search for documents containing one or more words that are specified by a search-engine user **2.** a search of a website to find documents or articles, etc. that contain one or more words specified by the user

kickback /ˈkɪkbæk/ *noun* an illegal commission paid to someone, especially a government official, who helps in a business deal

Kimball tag /ˈkɪmb(ə)l tæg/ *noun* a paper tag attached to an item for sale, which is removed when the item has been sold and is kept by the store so that it can be used for stock control

king-size /ˈkɪŋ saɪz/ *adjective* **1.** referring to an extra large container of a product, usually comparatively economical to buy **2.** referring to a very large size of poster

kiosk /ˈkiːɒsk/ *noun* a small wooden shelter, for selling goods out of doors ○ *She had a newspaper kiosk near the station for 20 years.*

KISS /kɪs/ *noun* the need to make sure your advertising is clear and concise so as to improve its chances of getting a response. Full form **keep it simple, stupid**

Kitemark /ˈkaɪtmɑːk/ *trademark* a mark on goods to show that they meet official standards

knock /nɒk/ *verb* □ **to knock the competition** to hit competing firms hard by vigorous selling

'…for some years butter advertising tended to knock other fats such as margarine' [*Marketing Week*]

knock down *phrasal verb* □ **to knock something down to a bidder** to sell something to somebody at an auction ○ *The furniture was knocked down to him for £100.*

knock off *phrasal verb* to reduce a price by a particular amount ○ *She knocked £10 off the price for cash.*

knockdown /ˈnɒkdaʊn/ *noun* □ **knockdown goods** goods sold in parts, which must be assembled by the buyer

knockdown price /ˌnɒkdaʊn ˈpraɪs/ *noun* a very low price ○ *He sold me the car at a knockdown price.*

knocking copy /ˈnɒkɪŋ ˌkɒpi/ *noun* advertising material which criticises competing products

know-how /ˈnəʊ haʊ/ *noun* knowledge or skill in a particular field ○ *to acquire computer know-how*

knowledge capital /ˈnɒlɪdʒ ˌkæpɪt(ə)l/ *noun* knowledge, especially specialist knowledge, that a company and its employees possess and that can be put to profitable use

knowledge management /ˈnɒlɪdʒ ˌmænɪdʒmənt/ *noun* **1.** the task of co-ordinating the specialist knowledge possessed by employees so that it can be exploited to create benefits and competitive advantage for the organisation **2.** same as **information management**

L

label /'leɪb(ə)l/ *noun* a piece of paper or card attached to something to show its price or an address or instructions for use ■ *verb* to attach a label to something (NOTE: **labelling – labelled**. The US spelling is **labeling – labeled**.)

labelling /'leɪb(ə)lɪŋ/ *noun* the act of putting a label on something

labelling department /'leɪb(ə)lɪŋ dɪ,pɑːtmənt/ *noun* a section of a factory where labels are attached to the product

laboratory test /lə'bɒrət(ə)ri test/ *noun* a test carried out under controlled conditions, e.g. of the reactions of consumers to advertising

labour-intensive industry /,leɪbər ɪn,tensɪv 'ɪndəstri/ *noun* an industry which needs large numbers of employees and where labour costs are high in relation to turnover

labour market /'leɪbə ,mɑːkɪt/ *noun* the number of people who are available for work ○ *25,000 school-leavers have just come on to the labour market.*

ladder /'lædə/ *noun* a series of different levels through which an employee may progress

ladder of loyalty /,lædə əv 'lɔɪəlti/ *noun* a marketing communications tool that aims to move a consumer along a path from a prospect ('not yet purchased') to advocate ('brand insistence') through customer ('trialist') and client ('repeat purchases') by using integrated marketing communications techniques. As a consumer travels up the ladder they become increasingly loyal to the brand. Also called **brand ladder**

lading /'leɪdɪŋ/ *noun* the work of putting goods on a ship

laggards /'lægədz/ *plural noun* a category of buyers of a product who are the last to buy it or use it

laissez-faire economy /,leseɪ 'feər ɪ,kɒnəmi/ *noun* an economy where the government does not interfere because it believes it is right to let the economy run itself

land /lænd/ *verb* to put goods or passengers on to land after a voyage by sea or by air ○ *The ship landed some goods at Mombasa.* ○ *The plane stopped for thirty minutes at the local airport to land passengers and mail.*

landed costs /,lændɪd 'kɒsts/ *plural noun* the costs of goods which have been delivered to a port, unloaded, and passed through customs

landing charges /'lændɪŋ ,tʃɑːdʒɪz/ *plural noun* payments for putting goods on land and paying customs duties

landing order /'lændɪŋ ,ɔːdə/ *noun* a permit which allows goods to be unloaded into a bonded warehouse without paying customs duty

landing page /'lændɪŋ peɪdʒ/ *noun* the page on a website where the user arrives, in particular the page you arrive on when directed by a hyperlink

landscape /'lændskeɪp/ *noun* an illustration, page, or book whose width is greater than its height. Compare **portrait**

laser printer /'leɪzə ,prɪntə/ *noun* a computer printer which uses a laser source to print high-quality dot matrix characters on paper

laser printing /'leɪzə ,prɪntɪŋ/ *noun* printing using a laser printer

late /leɪt/ *adjective* **1.** after the time stated or agreed ○ *We apologise for the* *late arrival of the plane from Amsterdam.* □ **there is a penalty for late delivery** if delivery is later than the agreed date, the supplier has to pay a fine **2.** at the end of a period of time □ **latest date for signature of the contract** the last acceptable date for signing the contract ■ *adverb* after the time stated or agreed ○ *The shipment was landed late.* ○ *The plane was two hours late.*

late majority /ˌleɪt məˈdʒɒrɪti/ *noun* a category of buyers of a product who buy it later than the early majority but before the laggards

latent /ˈleɪt(ə)nt/ *adjective* present but not yet developed □ **latent market** a potential market which has not so far been touched

latent demand /ˌleɪt(ə)nt dɪˈmaːnd/ *noun* a situation where there is demand for a product but potential customers are unable to pay for it ○ *We will have to wait for the economy to improve in countries where there is latent demand.* ○ *Situation analysis has shown that there is only latent demand.*

lateral /ˈlæt(ə)rəl/ *adjective* at the same level or with the same status ○ *Her transfer to Marketing was something of a lateral move.*

lateral diversification /ˌlæt(ə)rəl daɪˌvɜːsɪfɪˈkeɪʃ(ə)n/ *noun* the act of diversifying into quite a different type of business

lateral integration /ˌlæt(ə)rəl ɪntəˈɡreɪʃ(ə)n/ *noun* the act of joining similar companies or taking over a company in the same line of business as yourself ○ *Lateral integration will allow a pooling of resources.* ○ *Lateral integration in the form of a merger will improve the efficiency of both businesses involved.*

lateral thinking /ˌlæt(ə)rəl ˈθɪŋkɪŋ/ *noun* an imaginative approach to problem-solving which involves changing established patterns of thinking to help make a breakthrough ○ *Lateral thinking resulted in finding a completely new use for an existing product.* ○ *Brainstorming sessions encourage lateral thinking and originality.*

latest /ˈleɪtɪst/ *adjective* most recent ○ *He always drives the latest model of*

car. ○ *Here are the latest sales figures.*

launch /lɔːntʃ/ *verb* to put a new product on the market, usually spending money on advertising it ○ *They launched their new car model at the motor show.* ○ *The company is spending thousands of pounds on launching a new brand of soap.* ■ *noun* the act of putting a new product on the market ○ *The launch of the new model has been put back three months.* ○ *The management has decided on a September launch date.* ○ *The company is geared up for the launch of its first tablet computer.*

launch date /ˈlɔːntʃ deɪt/ *noun* the date when a new product is officially shown to the public for the first time

launch party /ˈlɔːntʃɪŋ ˌpaːti/ *noun* a party held to advertise the launching of a new product

launching /ˈlɔːntʃɪŋ/ *noun* the act of putting a new product on the market

launching costs /ˈlɔːntʃɪŋ kɒsts/ *plural noun* the costs of publicity for a new product

law /lɔː/ *noun* a rule governing some aspect of human activity made and enforced by the state

law of diminishing returns /ˌlɔː əv dɪˌmɪnɪʃɪŋ rɪˈtɜːnz/ *noun* a general rule that as more factors of production such as land, labour, and capital are added to the existing factors, so the amount they produce is proportionately smaller

law of inertia of large numbers /ˌlɔː əv ɪˌnɜːʃər əv ˌlaːdʒ ˈnʌmbəz/ *noun* a general rule that larger samples are more likely to be representative of the population than small ones

law of statistical regularity /ˌlɔː əv stəˌtɪstɪk(ə)l reɡjʊˈlærɪti/ *noun* a general rule that a group of people or objects taken from a larger group of people or objects will tend to resemble the larger group

law of supply and demand /ˌlɔː əv səˌplaɪ ən dɪˈmaːnd/ *noun* a general rule that the amount of a product which is available is related to the needs of potential customers

layout /ˈleɪaʊt/ *noun* **1.** the arrangement of the inside space of a building or its contents ○ *They have altered the layout of the offices.* **2.** the arrangement of words and pictures on a printed page, in an advertisement, on an email advertising message, etc., including the headline, illustrations, text, and trademarks ○ *I like the illustration and the copy but not the layout.* ○ *The layout needs to be changed so that other features are highlighted.*

lead /liːd/ *verb* to be the main person in a group ○ *She will lead the trade mission to Nigeria.* ○ *The tour of American factories will be led by a Commerce Department official.* (NOTE: **leading – led**) ■ *noun* **1.** information which may lead to a sale ○ *It has been difficult starting selling in this territory with no leads to follow up.* ○ *I was given some useful leads by the sales rep who used to cover this territory.* **2.** a prospective purchaser who is the main decision-maker when buying a product or service

leader /'liːdə/ *noun* **1.** a person who manages or directs others ○ *the leader of the construction workers' union* or *the construction workers' leader* ○ *She is the leader of the trade mission to Nigeria.* **2.** a product which sells best

leader pricing /'liːdə ˌpraɪsɪŋ/ *noun* the practice of cutting prices on some goods in the hope that they attract customers to the shop where more profitable sales can be made

lead generation /'liːd dʒenəˌreɪʃ(ə)n/ *noun* the process of finding prospective purchasers

leading question /ˌliːdɪŋ 'kweʃtʃən/ *noun* a question in a questionnaire which, by its phrasing, suggests a certain answer ○ *Interviewers were trained to avoid bias and leading questions.* ○ *The leading question pressurised the respondent into answering untruthfully.*

lead partner /'liːd ˌpɑːtnə/ *noun* the organisation that takes the leading role in a business alliance

lead sourcing /'liːd ˌsɔːsɪŋ/ *noun* searching through online databases to find the addresses of potential customers

leaflet /'liːflət/ *noun* a sheet of paper giving information, used to advertise something ○ *to mail leaflets advertising a new hairdressing salon* ○ *They are handing out leaflets describing the financial services they offer.* ○ *We made a leaflet mailing to 20,000 addresses.*

leakage /'liːkɪdʒ/ *noun* an amount of goods lost in storage, e.g. by going bad or by being stolen or by leaking from the container

learning curve /'lɜːnɪŋ kɜːv/ *noun* a process of learning something that starts slowly and then becomes faster

learning organisation /'lɜːnɪŋ ɔːgənaɪˌzeɪʃ(ə)n/ *noun* an organisation whose employees are willing and eager to share information with each other, to learn from each other, and to work as a team to achieve their goals

lease /liːs/ *noun* a written contract for letting or renting a building, a piece of land or a piece of equipment for a period against payment of a fee ○ *to rent office space on a twenty-year lease* □ **the lease expires next year** or **the lease runs out next year** the lease comes to an end next year

leave leaflet /'liːv ˌliːflət/ *noun* a promotional leaflet left by a salesperson with a prospective customer

ledger /'ledʒə/ *noun* a book in which accounts are written

legal /'liːg(ə)l/ *adjective* **1.** according to the law or allowed by the law **2.** referring to the law □ **to take legal action** to sue someone or to take someone to court □ **to take legal advice** to ask a lawyer to advise about a legal problem

legal adviser /ˌliːg(ə)l əd'vaɪzə/ *noun* a person who advises clients about the law

legal currency /ˌliːg(ə)l 'kʌrənsi/ *noun* money which is legally used in a country

legalisation /ˌliːgəlaɪ'zeɪʃ(ə)n/, **legalization** *noun* the act of making something legal ○ *the campaign for the legalisation of cannabis*

legalise /'liːgəlaɪz/, **legalize** *verb* to make something legal

legality /lɪ'ɡælɪti/ *noun* the fact of being allowed by law ○ *There is doubt about the legality of the company's action in dismissing him.*

legally /ˈliːgəli/ *adverb* according to the law □ **the contract is legally binding** according to the law, the contract has to be obeyed □ **the directors are legally responsible** the law says that the directors are responsible

legend /ˈledʒənd/ *noun* a short note printed underneath an illustration to explain it

legislation /ˌledʒɪˈsleɪʃ(ə)n/ *noun* laws

legs /legz/ *plural noun* the ability of an advertising campaign, a film, a book, or other usually short-lived product to interest people for a much longer time than normal (*informal*)

leisure market /ˈleʒə ˌmɑːkɪt/ *noun* people who have plenty of leisure time and are willing to buy products or services to occupy their time

lemon /ˈlemən/ *noun* **1.** a product, especially a car, that is defective in some way **2.** an investment that is performing poorly

lending limit /ˈlendɪŋ ˌlɪmɪt/ *noun* a restriction on the amount of money a bank can lend

letter /ˈletə/ *noun* a piece of writing sent from one person or company to another to ask for or to give information

COMMENT: First names are commonly used between business people in the US and UK; they are less often used in other European countries (France and Germany), for example, where business letters tend to be more formal.

letterhead /ˈletəhed/ *noun* the name and address of a company printed at the top of a piece of notepaper

letter of acknowledgement /ˌletər əv əkˈnɒlɪdʒmənt/ *noun* a letter which says that something has been received

letter of advice /ˌletər əv ədˈvaɪs/ *noun* same as **advice note** ○ *The letter of advice stated that the goods would be at Southampton on the morning of the 6th.* ○ *The letter of advice reminded the customer of the agreed payment terms.*

letter of agreement /ˌletər əv əˈgriːmənt/ *noun* a document that sets out what has been agreed between two people or organisations and acts as a simple form of contract

letter of complaint /ˌletər əv kəmˈpleɪnt/ *noun* a letter in which someone complains

letter of credit /ˌletər əv ˈkredɪt/ *noun* a document issued by a bank on behalf of a customer authorising payment to a supplier when the conditions specified in the document are met. Abbreviation **L/C**

letter of indemnity /ˌletər əv ɪnˈdemnɪti/ *noun* a letter promising payment as compensation for a loss

letter of inquiry /ˌletər əv ɪnˈkwaɪəri/ *noun* a letter from a prospective buyer to a supplier inquiring about products and their prices ○ *The letter of inquiry requested us to send our catalogues and price lists.* ○ *We received a letter of inquiry concerning possible trade discounts.*

lettershop /ˈletəʃɒp/ *noun* a company that puts together the various elements of a direct mailing shot, and sorts the envelopes by addresses

letters of administration /ˌletəz əv ədˌmɪnɪˈstreɪʃ(ə)n/ *plural noun* a letter given by a court to allow someone to deal with the estate of a person who has died

letters patent /ˌletəz ˈpeɪtənt/ *plural noun* the official term for a patent

level /ˈlev(ə)l/ *noun* the position of something compared to others ○ *low levels of productivity* or *low productivity levels* ○ *to raise the level of employee benefits* ○ *to lower the level of borrowings*

'…figures from the Fed on industrial production for April show a decline to levels last seen in June 1984' [*Sunday Times*]

'…applications for mortgages are running at a high level' [*Times*]

'…employers having got their staff back up to a reasonable level are waiting until the scope for overtime working is exhausted before hiring' [*Sydney Morning Herald*]

level playing field /ˌlev(ə)l ˈpleɪɪŋ fiːld/ *noun* a situation in which the same rules apply for all competitors and none of them has any special advantage over the others

levy /ˈlevi/ *noun* money which is demanded and collected by the government □ **levies on luxury items** taxes on luxury items

liabilities /ˌlaɪəˈbɪlɪtiz/ *plural noun* the debts of a business, including dividends owed to shareholders ○ *The balance sheet shows the company's assets and liabilities.* □ **he was not able to meet his liabilities** he could not pay his debts □ **to discharge your liabilities in full** to pay everything which you owe

liability /ˌlaɪəˈbɪlɪti/ *noun* **1.** a legal responsibility for damage, loss or harm □ **to accept liability for something** to agree that you are responsible for something □ **to refuse liability for something** to refuse to agree that you are responsible for something **2.** responsibility for a payment such as the repayment of a loan

liable /ˈlaɪəb(ə)l/ *adjective* □ **liable for** legally responsible for ○ *The customer is liable for breakages.* ○ *The chairman was personally liable for the company's debts.*

licence /ˈlaɪs(ə)ns/ *noun* an official document which allows someone to do something (NOTE: The US spelling is **license**.) □ **goods manufactured under licence** goods made with the permission of the owner of the copyright or patent

licence agreement /ˈlaɪs(ə)ns əˌgriːmənt/ *noun* a legal document which comes with a software product and defines how you can use the software and how many people are allowed to use it

license /ˈlaɪs(ə)ns/ *noun* US spelling of **licence** ■ *verb* to give someone official permission to do something for a fee, e.g. when a company allows another company to manufacture its products abroad ○ *licensed to sell beers, wines and spirits* ○ *to license a company to manufacture spare parts* ○ *She is licensed to run an employment agency.*

licensee /ˌlaɪs(ə)nˈsiː/ *noun* a person who has a licence, especially a licence to sell alcohol or to manufacture something

licensing /ˈlaɪs(ə)nsɪŋ/ *adjective* referring to licences ○ *a licensing agreement* ○ *licensing laws*

licensing agreement /ˈlaɪs(ə)nsɪŋ əˌgriːmənt/ *noun* an agreement where a person or company is granted a licence to manufacture something or to use something, but not an outright sale

licensing hours /ˈlaɪs(ə)nsɪŋ ˌaʊəz/ *plural noun* the hours of the day when alcohol can be sold

licensing laws /ˈlaɪs(ə)nsɪŋ ˌlɔːz/ *plural noun* the laws which control when and where alcohol can be sold

licensor /ˈlaɪsensə/ *noun* a person who licenses someone

lien /ˈliːən/ *noun* the legal right to hold someone's goods and keep them until a debt has been paid

life /laɪf/ *noun* the period of time for which something or someone exists

life cycle /ˈlaɪf ˌsaɪk(ə)l/ *noun* a concept used for charting the different stages in the life of people, animals, or products

life expectancy /ˈlaɪf ɪkˌspektənsi/ *noun* the number of years a person is likely to live

lifestyle /ˈlaɪfstaɪl/ *noun* the way of living of a particular section of society ○ *These upmarket products appeal to people with an extravagant lifestyle.* ○ *The magazine ran a series of articles on the lifestyles of some successful businessmen.*

lifestyle segmentation /ˈlaɪfstaɪl segmenˌteɪʃ(ə)n/ *noun* the dividing of a market into segments according to the way in which customers live. ⇨ **VALS**

lifetime /ˈlaɪftaɪm/ *noun* the time when you are alive

lifetime customer value /ˌlaɪftaɪm ˈkʌstəmə ˌvæljuː/, **lifetime value** /ˈlaɪftaɪm ˌvæljuː/ *noun* the value of a customer to a firm during the customer's lifetime, which can be charted using technology and market research

light /laɪt/ *adjective* not heavy, not very busy or active

light industry /ˌlaɪt ˈɪndəstri/ *noun* an industry making small products such as clothes, books, or calculators

light pen /ˈlaɪt pen/ *noun* a type of electronic pen that directs a beam of light which, when passed over a bar code, can read it and send information back to a computer

light viewer /ˌlaɪt ˈvjuːə/ *noun* a person who watches little television ○ *If too many of the target audience are light viewers, the impact of the commercials will be wasted.*

limit /ˈlɪmɪt/ *noun* the point at which something ends or the point where you can go no further □ **to set limits to imports**, **to impose import limits** to allow only a specific amount of imports ■ *verb* **1.** to stop something from going beyond a specific point, to restrict the number or amount of something □ **the banks have limited their credit** the banks have allowed their customers only a specific amount of credit □ **each agent is limited to twenty-five units** each agent is allowed only twenty-five units to sell **2.** to restrict the number or amount of something

'…the biggest surprise of 1999 was the rebound in the price of oil. In the early months of the year commentators were talking about a fall to $5 a barrel but for the first time in two decades, the oil exporting countries got their act together, limited production and succeeded in pushing prices up' [*Financial Times*]

limitation /ˌlɪmɪˈteɪʃ(ə)n/ *noun* the act of allowing only a specific quantity of something ○ *The contract imposes limitations on the number of cars which can be imported.* □ **limitation of liability** the fact of making someone liable for only a part of the damage or loss

limited /ˈlɪmɪtɪd/ *adjective* restricted

limited company /ˌlɪmɪtɪd ˈkʌmp(ə)ni/ *noun* a company in which each shareholder is responsible for the company's debts only to the amount that he or she has invested in the company. Limited companies must be formed by at least two directors. Abbreviation **Ltd**. Also called **limited liability company**

limited function wholesaler /ˌlɪmɪtɪd ˈfʌŋkʃən ˌhəʊlseɪlə/ *noun* a distributor performing only some of the functions of a wholesaler ○ *As a limited function wholesaler the dealer did not provide a delivery service to retailers.*

limited liability /ˌlɪmɪtɪd ˌlaɪə-ˈbɪlɪti/ *noun* a situation where someone's liability for debt is limited by law

limited liability company /ˌlɪmɪtɪd ˌlaɪəbɪlɪti ˈkʌmp(ə)ni/ *noun* same as **limited company**

limited market /ˌlɪmɪtɪd ˈmɑːkɪt/ *noun* a market which can take only a specific quantity of goods

limiting /ˈlɪmɪtɪŋ/ *adjective* not allowing something to go beyond a point, restricting ○ *a limiting clause in a contract* ○ *The short holiday season is a limiting factor on the hotel trade.*

line /laɪn/ *noun* **1.** a long mark printed or written on paper ○ *paper with thin blue lines* ○ *I prefer notepaper without any lines.* ○ *She drew a thick line before the column of figures.* **2.** a row of letters or figures on a page **3.** a series of things, one after another **4.** same as **product line 5.** a short letter

'…cash paid for overstocked lines, factory seconds, slow sellers, etc.' [*Australian Financial Review*]

lineage /ˈlɪniɪdʒ/ *noun* a method of measuring a classified advertisement by counting the lines, used for charging purposes

linear /ˈlɪniə/ *adjective* calculated by length

linear measurement /ˌlɪniəˈmeʒə-mənt/, **linear footage** /ˌlɪniə ˈfʊ-tɪdʒ/ *noun* a measurement of how long something is such as the length of shelving available for a display

line block /ˈlaɪn blɒk/ *noun* a printing block for line drawings

line chart /ˈlaɪn tʃɑːt/ *noun* a chart or graph using lines to indicate values

line divestment /ˈlaɪn daɪˌvest-mənt/ *noun* the dropping or selling of an entire product line so as to concentrate on other products

line drawing /ˈlaɪn ˌdrɔːɪŋ/, **line illustration** /ˈlaɪn ɪləˌstreɪʃ(ə)n/ *noun* a drawing or illustration consisting only of lines and no tones. Shades are shown by lines drawn close together.

line extension /ˈlaɪn ɪkˌstenʃən/ *noun* the adding of another product to a product line

line filling /ˈlaɪn ˌfɪlɪŋ/ *noun* the filling of gaps in a product line

line management /ˈlaɪn ˌmænɪdʒ-mənt/ *noun* the organisation of a company where each manager is responsible for doing what their superior tells them to do. Also called **line organisation**

line of credit /ˌlaɪn əv ˈkredɪt/ *noun* **1.** the amount of money made available to a customer by a bank as an overdraft □ **to open a line of credit** *or* **a credit line** to make credit available to someone **2.** the borrowing limit on a credit card

line rate /ˈlaɪn reɪt/ *noun* the rate charged for advertising space, based on the line space used in a newspaper or magazine

line simplification /ˈlaɪn sɪmplɪ-fɪˌkeɪʃ(ə)n/ *noun* the removal of some products from a product line to make the whole line more easily manageable

link /lɪŋk/ *noun* same as **hyperlink**

LinkedIn /ˌlɪŋkdˈɪn/ a trade name for a business-oriented social networking site aimed at professionals looking to make new business contacts or to keep in touch with clients

linking /ˈlɪŋkɪŋ/ *noun* the process of connecting two or more websites or documents by inserting links that enable users to move from one to the other

liquid assets /ˌlɪkwɪd ˈæsets/ *plural noun* cash, or investments which can be quickly converted into cash

liquor licence /ˈlɪkə ˌlaɪs(ə)ns/ *noun* a government document allowing someone to sell alcohol

liquor store /ˈɒf ˌlaɪs(ə)ns/ *noun US* same as **off-licence**

list /lɪst/ *noun* **1.** several items written one after the other ○ *They have an attractive list of products* or *product list.* ○ *I can't find that item on our stock list.* ○ *Please add this item to the list.* ○ *She crossed the item off her list.* **2.** a catalogue ■ *verb* to write a series of items one after the other ○ *to list products by category* ○ *to list representatives by area* ○ *to list products in a catalogue* ○ *The catalogue lists ten models of smartphone.*

list broker /ˈlɪst ˌbrəʊkə/ *noun* a person who arranges to sell mailing lists to users, but who does not own the lists

list building /ˈlɪst ˌbɪldɪŋ/ *noun* finding names and addresses and entering them into a database for direct marketing purposes

list cleaning /ˈlɪst ˌkliːnɪŋ/ *noun* checking the details of a mailing list to make sure they are correct

listen /ˈlɪs(ə)n/ *verb* to pay attention to someone who is talking or to something which you can hear

listening area /ˈlɪs(ə)nɪŋ ˌeəriə/ *noun* the area covered by a radio station's signal

listening share /ˈlɪs(ə)nɪŋ ˌʃeə/ *noun* the share of the total audience enjoyed by a radio station

list host /ˈlɪst həʊst/ *noun* a company that provides connections to the Internet and storage space on its computers which can store the files for a user's website (NOTE: also called a 'host service; *or* 'hosting service provider')

list maintenance /ˈlɪst ˌmeɪn-tənəns/ *noun* the process of keeping a mailing list up to date

list manager /ˈlɪst ˌmænɪdʒə/ *noun* a person who promotes a mailing list to potential users

list price /ˈlɪst praɪs/ *noun* the price for something as given in a catalogue

list rental /ˈlɪst ˌrent(ə)l/ *noun* the action of renting a mailing list

list renting /ˈlɪst ˌrentɪŋ/ *noun* an arrangement in which a company that owns a direct mail list lets another company use it for a fee

literature /ˈlɪt(ə)rətʃə/ *noun* written information about something ○ *Please send me literature about your new product range.*

lithography /lɪˈθɒɡrəfi/ *noun* a printing process by which a design is applied to a smooth flat surface with greasy ink or a crayon. The surface is wetted and ink will adhere to the greasy parts, but not to the wet parts.

livery /ˈlɪvəri/ *noun* a company's own special design and colours, used e.g. on uniforms, office decoration, and vehicles

living /ˈlɪvɪŋ/ *noun* □ **she does not earn a living wage** she does not earn enough to pay for essentials such as food, heat, and rent

load /ləʊd/ *noun* an amount of goods which are transported in a particular vehicle or aircraft □ **the load of a lorry** *or* **of a container** the goods carried by a lorry or in a container □ **maximum load** the largest weight of goods which a lorry or plane can carry ■ *verb* **1.** □ **to**

load a lorry *or* **a ship** to put goods into a lorry or a ship for transporting ○ *to load cargo onto a ship* ○ *a truck loaded with boxes* ○ *a ship loaded with iron* □ **a fully loaded ship** a ship which is full of cargo **2.** (*of a ship*) to take on cargo ○ *The ship is loading a cargo of wood.* **3.** to put a program into a computer ○ *Load the word-processing program before you start keyboarding.* **4.** to add extra charges to a price

load-carrying capacity /ˈləʊd ˌkæriɪŋ kəˌpæsɪti/ *noun* the amount of goods which a lorry is capable of carrying

loaded price /ˌləʊdɪd ˈpraɪs/ *noun* a price which includes an unusually large extra payment for some service ○ *That company is notorious for loading its prices.*

loading /ˈləʊdɪŋ/ *noun* the process of assigning work to workers or machines ○ *The production manager has to ensure that careful loading makes the best use of human resources.*

loading dock /ˈləʊdɪŋ dɒk/ *noun* the part of a harbour where ships can load or unload

load time /ˈləʊd taɪm/ *noun* in computing, the time it takes for a page of data to open completely in a window

lobby /ˈlɒbi/ *noun* a group that tries to persuade a government or law-makers to support a particular cause or interest

local /ˈləʊk(ə)l/ *adjective* located in or providing a service for a restricted area

'…each cheque can be made out for the local equivalent of £100 rounded up to a convenient figure' [*Sunday Times*]

'…the business agent for Local 414 of the Store Union said his committee will recommend that the membership ratify the agreement' [*Toronto Star*]

'EC regulations insist that customers can buy cars anywhere in the EC at the local pre-tax price' [*Financial Times*]

local advertising /ˌləʊk(ə)l ˈædvətaɪzɪŋ/ *noun* advertising in the area where a company is based

localisation /ˌgləʊkələaɪˈzeɪʃ(ə)n/ *noun* **1.** the process of restricting something to a particular area or adapting it for use in a particular area **2.** the translation of a website into a language or

idiom that can be easily understood by the target user

localised /ˈləʊkəlaɪzd/, **localized** *adjective* which occurs in one area only

localised advertising strategy /ˌləʊkəlaɪzd ˈædvətaɪzɪŋ ˌstrætədʒi/ *noun* planning an advertising campaign for a particular country or area of a market rather than a global campaign

local media /ˌləʊk(ə)l ˈmiːdiə/ *plural noun* newspapers and radio and TV stations in a small area of the country

local newspaper /ˌləʊk(ə)l ˈnjuːzpeɪpə/ *noun* a newspaper which is sold only in a restricted area, and mainly carries news about that area

local press /ˌləʊk(ə)l ˈpres/ *noun* newspapers which are sold in a small area of the country ○ *The product was only advertised in the local press as it was only being distributed in that area of the country.*

local radio station /ˌləʊk(ə)l ˈreɪdiəʊ ˌsteɪʃ(ə)n/ *noun* a radio station which broadcasts over a small area of the country

location /ləʊˈkeɪʃ(ə)n/ *noun* **1.** a place where something is **2.** a place, especially a site where still photographs or films are made ○ *We still have to decide on locations for the advertisements.*

logical models /ˌlɒdʒɪk(ə)l ˈmɒd(ə)lz/ *plural noun* models of buyer decision-making which assume that purchasing is the result of a set of rational decisions made by the purchaser ○ *Logical models do not allow for the unpredictable side of buying behaviour.*

logistics /ləˈdʒɪstɪks/ *noun* the task or science of managing the movement, storage, and processing of materials and information in a supply chain (NOTE: Logistics includes the acquisition of raw materials and components, manufacturing or processing, and the distribution of finished products to the end user.)

logistics management /ləˈdʒɪstɪks ˌmænɪdʒmənt/ *noun* the management of the distribution of products to the market

logo /ˈləʊgəʊ/ *noun* a symbol, design, or group of letters used by a company as a mark on its products and in advertising

London gold fixing /ˌlʌndən ˈɡəʊld ˌfɪksɪŋ/ *noun* a system whereby the world price for gold is set each day in London

long lease /ˌlɒŋ ˈliːs/ *noun* a lease which runs for fifty years or more ○ *to take an office building on a long lease*

long-range /ˌlɒŋ ˈreɪndʒ/ *adjective* for a long period of time in the future □ **long-range economic forecast** a forecast which covers a period of several years

long-standing /ˌlɒŋ ˈstændɪŋ/ *adjective* which has been arranged for a long time ○ *a long-standing agreement* □ **long-standing customer**, **customer of long standing** a person who has been a customer for many years

long-term /ˌlɒŋ ˈtɜːm/ *adjective* relating to a long time into the future ○ *The management projections are made on a long-term basis.* ○ *Sound long-term planning will give the company more direction.* ○ *It is in the company's long-term interests to have a contented staff.* □ **on a long-term basis** continuing for a long period of time □ **long-term debts** debts which will be repaid many years later □ **long-term forecast** a forecast for a period of over three years □ **long-term loan** a loan to be repaid many years later □ **long-term objectives** aims which will take years to achieve

look and feel /ˌlʊk ən ˈfiːl/ *noun* the appeal of the design, layout, and ease of use of a website to potential customers and the way the site fits the image the company is trying to put across

loose /luːs/ *adjective* not attached

loose insert /ˌluːs ˈɪnsɜːt/ *noun* a sheet of advertising material slipped between the pages of a publication

lorry-load /ˈlɒri ləʊd/ *noun* the amount of goods carried on a lorry ○ *They delivered six lorry-loads of coal.* Same as **truckload**

lose /luːz/ *verb* not to have something any more □ **to lose an order** not to get an order which you were hoping to get ○ *During the strike, the company lost six orders to American competitors.* □ **to lose customers** to have fewer customers

○ *Their service is so slow that they have been losing customers.* □ **the company is losing sales, is losing market share** the company has fewer sales or a smaller share of the market than before

lose out *phrasal verb* to suffer as a result of something ○ *The company has lost out in the rush to make cheap computers.* ○ *We lost out to a Japanese company who put in a lower tender for the job.*

loss /lɒs/ *noun* **1.** the state or process of not having something any more □ **loss of customers** not keeping customers because of bad service, high prices, etc. □ **loss of an order** not getting an order which was expected □ **the company suffered a loss of market penetration** the company found it had a smaller share of the market **2.** the state of having less money than before or of not making a profit □ **the company suffered a loss** the company did not make a profit □ **to report a loss** not to show a profit in the accounts at the end of the year ○ *The company reported a loss of £1m on the first year's trading.* □ **the car was written off as a dead loss or a total loss** the car was so badly damaged that the insurers said it had no value □ **at a loss** making a loss, not making any profit ○ *The company is trading at a loss.* ○ *We sold the shop at a loss.* □ **to cut your losses** to stop doing something which is losing money **3.** the state of being worth less or having a lower value ○ *Shares showed losses of up to 5% on the Stock Exchange.* **4.** the state of weighing less □ **loss in weight** goods which weigh less than when they were packed □ **loss in transport** the amount of weight which is lost while goods are being transported

'…against losses of FFr 7.7m two years ago, the company made a net profit of FFr 300,000 last year' [*Financial Times*]

loss-leader /ˈlɒs ˌliːdə/ *noun* an article which is sold at a loss to attract customers ○ *We use these cheap films as a loss-leader.*

low-grade /ˈləʊ ɡreɪd/ *adjective* **1.** not very important ○ *a low-grade official from the Ministry of Commerce* **2.** of not very good quality ○ *The car runs best on low-grade petrol.*

low-hanging fruit /ˌləʊ hæŋɪŋ ˈfruːt/ *noun* an easy short-term sales or market opportunity which provides a quick profit without too much effort (*informal*)

low-involvement hierarchy /ˌləʊ ɪnˈvɒlvmənt ˌhaɪərɑːki/ *noun* a hierarchy of response to advertising where the customer is relatively indifferent to the product or service and only responds to repeated marketing

low-involvement product /ˌləʊ ɪnˈvɒlvmənt ˌprɒdʌkt/ *noun* a low-priced product for everyday use that is bought by consumers without giving much thought to brands

low-pressure /ˌləʊ ˈpreʃə/ *adjective* □ **low-pressure sales** sales where the salesperson does not force someone to buy, but only encourages them to do so

low-quality /ˌləʊ ˈkwɒlɪti/ *adjective* not of good quality ○ *They tried to sell us some low-quality steel.*

low season /ˌləʊ ˈsiːz(ə)n/ *noun* a period when there are few travellers ○ *Air fares are cheaper in the low season.*

loyal /ˈlɔɪəl/ *adjective* always buying the same brand or using the same shop ○ *The aim of the advertising is to keep the customers loyal.*

loyalty /ˈlɔɪəlti/ *noun* the state of being faithful to someone or something

loyalty card /ˈlɔɪəlti kɑːd/ *noun* a special plastic card which gives discounts to customers over a period of time and so encourages them to remain as customers

loyalty scheme /ˈlɔɪəlti skiːm/ *noun* a scheme to keep the business of existing customers, e.g. by special discounts for loyalty card holders

Ltd *abbreviation* limited company

lull /lʌl/ *noun* a quiet period ○ *After last week's hectic trading this week's lull was welcome.*

lump sum /ˌlʌmp ˈsʌm/ *noun* money paid in one single amount, not in several small sums ○ *When he retired he was given a lump-sum bonus.* ○ *She sold her house and invested the money as a lump sum.*

luxury /ˈlʌkʃəri/ *noun, adjective* referring to an expensive thing which is not necessary but which is good to have ○ *a black market in luxury articles* ○ *Luxury items are taxed very heavily.*

luxury goods /ˈlʌkʃəri ɡʊdz/, **luxury items** /ˈlʌkʃəri ˌaɪtəmz/ *plural noun* expensive items which are not basic necessities

luxury product /ˈlʌkʃəri ˌprɒdʌkt/ *noun* a product which people buy more of as their incomes rise ○ *Luxury products such as designer handbags are selling poorly since the slump.* ○ *The company has gone upmarket and is now selling luxury products.*

M

macro- /ˈmækrəʊ/ *prefix* very large, covering a wide area

macroeconomics /ˌmækrəʊiːkəˈnɒmɪks/ *plural noun* a study of the economics of a whole area, a whole industry, a whole group of the population or a whole country, in order to help in economic planning. Compare **micro-economics** (NOTE: takes a singular verb) □ **macroeconomic conditions** factors that influence the state of the overall economy, e.g. changes in gross national product, interest rates, inflation, recession, and employment levels

macroenvironment /ˈmækrəʊɪnˌvaɪrənmənt/ *noun* **1.** the general environmental factors that affect an organisation, such as legislation or the country's economy ○ *We must develop a flexible planning system to allow for major changes in the macroenvironment.* **2.** factors outside the area of marketing which cannot be influenced by the marketing effort, including demographics, the natural environment, etc.

macromarketing /ˈmækrəʊˌmaːkɪtɪŋ/ *noun* the study of trading activity within a whole economic system such as a country, with its political, economic, and social implications

Macromedia Flash™ /ˌmækrəʊmiːdiə ˈflæʃ/ *noun* a trade name for a type of animation software used on the Web, which is characterised by small file sizes, easy scaleability and the use of streaming technology

made-to-measure /ˌmeɪd tə ˈmeʒə/ *adjective* made to fit the requirements of the customer ○ *made-to-measure kitchen cabinets* ○ *a made-to-measure suit*

magazine /ˌmægəˈziːn/ *noun* a special type of newspaper, usually pub-lished only weekly or monthly, often with a glossy cover and often devoted to a particular subject □ **magazine insert** an advertising sheet put into a magazine when it is mailed or sold □ **to insert a leaflet in a specialist magazine** to put an advertising leaflet into a magazine before it is mailed or sold

magazine mailing /mægəˈziːn ˌmeɪlɪŋ/ *noun* the sending of copies of a magazine by post to subscribers

magazine network /mægəˈziːn ˌnetwɜːk/ *noun* a group of magazines owned by one publisher and offering advertisers the possibility of buying space in several publications as a packaged deal

mail /meɪl/ *noun* **1.** a system of sending letters and parcels from one place to another ○ *The cheque was lost in the mail.* ○ *The invoice was put in the mail yesterday.* ○ *Mail to some of the islands in the Pacific can take six weeks.* □ **by mail** using the postal services, not sending something by hand or by messenger □ **to send a package by surface mail** to send a package by land or sea, not by air □ **by sea mail** sent by post abroad, using a ship □ **by air mail** sent by post abroad, using a plane □ **we sent the order by first-class mail** we sent the order by the most expensive mail service, designed to be faster **2.** letters sent or received ○ *Has the mail arrived yet?* ○ *The first thing I do is open the mail.* ○ *The receipt was in this morning's mail.* **3.** same as **email** ■ *verb* **1.** to send something by post ○ *to mail a letter* ○ *We mailed our order last Wednesday.* ○ *They mailed their catalogue to three thousand customers in Europe.* **2.** to send something by mail

mail box /ˈmeɪl bɒks/ *noun* a box where letters which are being sent are put to be collected

mail drop /'meɪl drɒp/ *noun* **1.** the mailing of promotional material to a large number of addresses **2.** the practice of sending unsolicited promotional material to potential customers as a way of advertising, or the material that is mailed

mailer /'meɪlə/ *noun* packaging made of folded cardboard, used to mail items which need protection ○ *a CD ROM mailer*

mailing /'meɪlɪŋ/ *noun* the sending of something by post ○ *the mailing of publicity material*

mailing house /'meɪlɪŋ haʊs/ *noun* a company which specialises in carrying out mailings for other companies

mailing list /'meɪlɪŋ lɪst/ *noun* a list of names and addresses of people who might be interested in a product, or a list of names and addresses of members of an organisation ○ *to build up a mailing list* ○ *Your name is on our mailing list.* □ **to buy a mailing list** to pay a society or other organisation money to buy the list of members so that you can use it to mail publicity material

mailing shot /'meɪlɪŋ ʃɒt/ *noun* same as **mail shot**

mailing tube /'meɪlɪŋ tjuːb/ *noun* a stiff cardboard or plastic tube, used for mailing large pieces of paper such as posters

mail interview /'meɪl ˌɪntəvjuː/, **mail survey** /'meɪl ˌsɜːveɪ/ *noun* US the sending of a questionnaire to respondents by post for a survey ○ *Not enough consumers responded to the mail interview.* ○ *To encourage people to co-operate in the mail survey we'll include a free sample with the questionnaire.*

mail merge /'meɪl mɜːdʒ/ *noun* a word-processing program that allows a standard form letter to be printed out to a series of different names and addresses

mail order /ˌmeɪl 'ɔːdə/ *noun* a system of buying and selling from a catalogue, placing orders, and sending goods by mail ○ *We bought our kitchen units by mail order.*

mail-order catalogue /'meɪl ɔːdə ˌkæt(ə)lɒg/ *noun* a catalogue from which a customer can order items to be sent by mail

mail-order selling /'meɪl ɔːdə ˌselɪŋ/ *noun* a method of selling in which orders are taken and products are delivered by mail

mail out /ˌmeɪl 'aʊt/ *verb* to send promotional material by mail

mailout /'meɪlaʊt/ *noun* a piece of promotional material sent by direct mail, usually accompanied by a letter which may be personalised

mail room /'meɪl ruːm/ *noun* US same as **post room**

mail shot /'meɪl ʃɒt/ *noun* **1.** leaflets sent by post to possible customers. Also called **mailing shot 2.** a single mailing of direct-mail advertising literature

> '…the building of media lists, the mailing out of releases tailored to the reader interests of newspapers and periodicals, and the follow-up phone calls all have their parallel in direct marketing' [*PR Week*]

mailsort /'meɪlsɔːt/ *noun* computer software used by mailing companies to sort mailings before they are sent to the post office, usually by using special labels with bar codes

Main Street /'meɪn striːt/ *noun* US the most important street in a town, where the shops and banks usually are

majority /mə'dʒɒrɪti/ *noun* more than half of a group

major selling idea /ˌmeɪdʒə 'selɪŋ aɪˌdiə/ *adjective* the central theme in an advertising campaign

make /meɪk/ *noun* a brand or type of product manufactured ○ *Japanese makes of cars* ○ *a standard make of equipment* ○ *What make is the new computer system What's the make of the new computer system?* ■ *verb* **1.** to produce or to manufacture ○ *The employees spent ten weeks making the table.* ○ *The factory makes three hundred cars a day.* (NOTE: **making – made**) **2.** □ **to make a profit** to have more money after a deal

make out *phrasal verb* to write something ○ *to make out an invoice* ○ *The bill is made out to Smith & Co.* □ **to make out a cheque to someone** to write someone's name on a cheque

makegood /'meɪkgʊd/ *noun* an advertisement placed again in a magazine or newspaper free of charge, because a mistake was made in it when it was previously published

maker /ˈmeɪkə/ *noun* in the VALS lifestyle classification, a practical, independent person who is interested in products that are good value but not necessarily fashionable

make-to-order /ˌmeɪk tʊ ˈɔːdə/ *noun* the making of goods or components to fulfil an existing order (NOTE: Make-to-order products are made to the customer's specification, and are often processed in small batches.)

manage /ˈmænɪdʒ/ *verb* **1.** to direct or to be in charge of something ○ *to manage a branch office* **2.** □ **to manage property** to look after rented property for the owner **3.** □ **to manage to** to be able to do something ○ *Did you manage to see the head buyer?* ○ *She managed to write six orders and take three phone calls all in two minutes.*

'…the research director will manage and direct a team of graduate business analysts reporting on consumer behaviour throughout the UK' [*Times*]

manageable /ˈmænɪdʒəb(ə)l/ *adjective* which can be dealt with ○ *The problems which the company faces are too large to be manageable by one person.*

managed economy /ˌmænɪdʒd ɪˈkɒnəmi/ *noun* an economy that is controlled by a government

managed hosting /ˌmænɪdʒd ˈhəʊstɪŋ/ *noun* a hosting option in which the hosting company is mainly responsible for a client's servers, often supplying and managing not only the hardware but the software as well

management /ˈmænɪdʒmənt/ *noun* **1.** the process of directing or running or a business ○ *a management graduate a graduate in management* ○ *She studied management at university.* ○ *Good management* or *efficient management is essential in a large organisation.* ○ *Bad management* or *inefficient management can ruin a business.* **2.** a group of managers or directors ○ *The management has decided to give everyone a pay increase.* (NOTE: Where **management** refers to a group of people it is sometimes followed by a plural verb.)

'…the management says that the rate of loss-making has come down and it expects further improvement in the next few years' [*Financial Times*]

management accountant /ˈmænɪdʒmənt əˌkaʊntənt/ *noun* an accountant who prepares financial information for managers so that they can take decisions

management accounting /ˈmænɪdʒmənt əˌkaʊntɪŋ/, **management accountancy** /ˌmænɪdʒmənt əˈkaʊntənsi/ *noun* the providing of information to managers, which helps them to plan, to control their businesses and to take decisions which will make them run their businesses more efficiently. Compare **financial accounting**

management accounts /ˈmænɪdʒmənt əˌkaʊnts/ *plural noun* financial information prepared for a manager so that decisions can be made, including monthly or quarterly financial statements, often in great detail, with analysis of actual performance against the budget

management buyout /ˌmænɪdʒmənt ˈbaɪaʊt/ *noun* the takeover of a company by a group of employees, usually senior managers and directors. Abbreviation **MBO**

management by exception /ˌmænɪdʒmənt baɪ ɪkˈsepʃən/ *noun* a management system whereby deviations from plans are located and corrected

management by objectives /ˌmænɪdʒmənt baɪ əbˈdʒektɪvz/ *noun* a way of managing a business by planning work for the managers to do and testing if it is completed correctly and on time

management consultant /ˈmænɪdʒmənt kənˌsʌltənt/ *noun* a person who gives advice on how to manage a business

management course /ˈmænɪdʒmənt kɔːs/ *noun* a training course for managers

management development /ˈmænɪdʒmənt dɪˌveləpmənt/ *noun* the selection and training of potential managers

management team /'mænɪdʒ-mənt tiːm/ *noun* all the managers who work in a particular company

management technique /'mæn-ɪdʒmənt tek,niːk/ *noun* a way of managing a business

manager /'mænɪdʒə/ *noun* **1.** the head of a department in a company ○ *She's a department manager in an engineering company.* ○ *Go and see the human resources manager if you have a problem.* ○ *The production manager has been with the company for only two weeks.* ○ *Our sales manager started as a rep in London.* **2.** the person in charge of a branch or shop ○ *Mr Smith is the manager of our local Lloyds Bank.* ○ *The manager of our Moscow branch is in London for a series of meetings.*

'…the No. 1 managerial productivity problem in America is managers who are out of touch with their people and out of touch with their customers' [*Fortune*]

managerial /,mænə'dʒɪəriəl/ *adjective* referring to managers ○ *All the managerial staff are sent for training every year.* □ **to be appointed to a managerial position** to be appointed a manager □ **decisions taken at managerial level** decisions taken by managers

managership /'mænɪdʒəʃɪp/ *noun* the job of being a manager ○ *After six years, she was offered the managership of a branch in Scotland.*

managing director /,mænədʒɪŋ daɪ'rektə/ *noun* the director who is in charge of a whole company. Abbreviation **MD**

mandatory /'mændət(ə)ri/ *adjective* required by law or stipulated in a contract

'…the wage talks are focusing on employment issues such as sharing of work among employees and extension of employment beyond the mandatory retirement age of 60 years' [*Nikkei Weekly*]

mandatory blurb /,mændət(ə)ri 'blɜːb/, **mandatory copy** /,mæn-dət(ə)ri 'kɒpi/ *noun* certain words which are required by law to be included in an advertisement, e.g. a health warning on cigarette advertisements

manifest /'mænɪfest/ *noun* a list of goods in a shipment

mannequin /'mænɪkɪn/ *noun* a model of a person, used to display clothes in a shop window or inside a store

manpower /'mænpaʊə/ *noun* the number of employees in an organisation, industry, or country (NOTE: **manpower** does not mean only men.)

manpower forecasting /'mæn-paʊə ,fɔːkɑːstɪŋ/ *noun* the process of calculating how many employees will be needed in the future, and how many will actually be available

manpower planning /'mænpaʊə ,plænɪŋ/ *noun* the process of planning to obtain the right number of employees in each job

manpower requirements /'mæn-paʊə rɪ,kwaɪəmənts/, **manpower needs** /'mænpaʊə niːdz/ *plural noun* the number of employees needed

manufacture /,mænjʊ'fæktʃə/ *verb* to make a product for sale, using machines ○ *The company manufactures spare parts for cars.* ■ *noun* the making of a product for sale, using machines □ **products of foreign manufacture** products made in foreign countries

manufactured goods /,mæn-jufæktʃəd 'gʊdz/ *plural noun* items which are made by machine

manufacturer /,mænjʊ'fæktʃərə/ *noun* a person or company that produces machine-made products ○ *a big Indian cotton manufacturer* ○ *Foreign manufacturers have set up factories here.*

manufacturer's agent /mæn-jʊ,fæktʃərəz 'eɪdʒənt/ *noun* a person who sells on behalf of a manufacturer and earns a commission

manufacturer's brand /mænjʊ,-fæktʃərəz 'brænd/ *noun* a brand which belongs to the manufacturer and has the same name

manufacturer's recommended price /,mænjufæktʃərəz ,rekə-mendɪd 'praɪs/ *noun* a price at which the manufacturer suggests the product should be sold on the retail market, which is often reduced by the retailer ○ *'All china – 20% off the manufacturer's recommended price'* Abbreviation **MRP**

manufacturing /ˌmænjʊˈfækt-ʃərɪŋ/ *noun* the production of machine-made products for sale ○ *We must try to reduce the manufacturing overheads.* ○ *Manufacturing processes are continually being updated.*

manufacturing capacity /ˌmæn-jʊˈfæktʃərɪŋ kəˌpæsɪti/ *noun* the amount of a product which a factory is capable of making

manufacturing industries /ˌmæ-njʊˈfæktʃərɪŋ ˌɪndəstriz/ *plural noun* industries which take raw materials and make them into finished products

map /mæp/ *noun* a chart which shows a geographical area

mapping /ˈmæpɪŋ/ *noun* the drawing up of a map of an area

margin /ˈmɑːdʒɪn/ *noun* **1.** the difference between the money received when selling a product and the money paid for it □ **we are cutting our margins very fine** we are reducing our margins to the smallest possible in order to be competitive □ **our margins have been squeezed** profits have been reduced because our margins have to be smaller to stay competitive **2.** extra space or time allowed

'…profit margins in the industries most exposed to foreign competition – machinery, transportation equipment and electrical goods – are significantly worse than usual' [*Australian Financial Review*]

marginal /ˈmɑːdʒɪn(ə)l/ *adjective* **1.** hardly worth the money paid **2.** not very profitable ○ *a marginal return on investment*

marginal cost /ˌmɑːdʒɪn(ə)l ˈkɒst/ *noun* the cost of making a single extra unit above the number already planned

marginal cost pricing /ˌmɑːdʒɪ-n(ə)l ˈkɒst ˌpraɪsɪŋ/ *noun* a pricing method that involves fixing a price per unit that covers marginal costs and makes an acceptable contribution to fixed costs

marginal land /ˌmɑːdʒɪn(ə)lˈlænd/ *noun* land which is almost not worth farming

marginal pricing /ˌmɑːdʒɪn(ə)l ˈpraɪsɪŋ/ *noun* the practice of basing the selling price of a product on its variable costs of production plus a margin, but excluding fixed costs

marginal productivity /ˌmɑːdʒɪ-n(ə)l prɒdʌkˈtɪvɪti/ *noun* extra productivity achieved by the use of one more factor of production

marginal purchase /ˌmɑːdʒɪn(ə)l ˈpɜːtʃɪs/ *noun* something which a buyer feels is only just worth buying

marginal rate of tax /ˌmɑːdʒɪn(ə)l reɪt əv ˈtæks/, **marginal rate of taxation** /ˌmɑːdʒɪn(ə)l reɪt əv tæks-ˈeɪʃ(ə)n/ *noun* the percentage of tax which a taxpayer pays at the top rate, which he or she therefore pays on every further pound or dollar he or she earns. Also called **marginal tax rate**

'…pensioner groups claim that pensioners have the highest marginal rates of tax. Income earned by pensioners above \$30 a week is taxed at 62.5%, more than the highest marginal rate' [*Australian Financial Review*]

marginal revenue /ˌmɑːdʒɪn(ə)l ˈrevɪnjuː/ *noun* the income from selling a single extra unit above the number already sold

marginal tax rate /ˌmɑːdʒɪn(ə)l ˈtæks reɪt/ *noun* same as **marginal rate of tax**

marginal utility /ˌmɑːdʒɪn(ə)l juː-ˈtɪlɪti/ *noun* satisfaction gained from using one more unit of a product

margin of error /ˌmɑːdʒɪn əv ˈerə/ *noun* the number of mistakes which can be accepted in a document or in a calculation

marine /məˈriːn/ *adjective* referring to the sea

marine insurance /məˌriːn ɪnˈʃʊ-ərəns/ *noun* the insurance of ships and their cargoes

marine underwriter /məˌriːn ˈʌn-dəraɪtə/ *noun* a person or company that insures ships and their cargoes

maritime /ˈmærɪtaɪm/ *adjective* referring to the sea

maritime lawyer /ˌmærɪtaɪm ˈlɔːjə/ *noun* a lawyer who specialises in legal matters concerning ships and cargoes

maritime trade /ˌmærɪtaɪm ˈtreɪd/ noun the transporting of commercial goods by sea

mark /mɑːk/ noun **1.** a sign put on an item to show something **2.** a former unit of currency in Germany. verb to put a sign on something ○ to mark a product 'for export only' ○ an article marked at £1.50 ○ She used a black pen to mark the price on the book.

mark down phrasal verb to make the price of something lower

mark up phrasal verb to make the price of something higher

mark-down /ˈmɑːk daʊn/ noun **1.** a reduction of the price of something to less than its usual price **2.** the percentage amount by which a price has been lowered ○ There has been a 30% mark-down on all goods in the sale.

marked price /mɑːkt ˈpraɪs/ noun the price which is marked on or attached to an article for sale

market /ˈmɑːkɪt/ noun **1.** a place, often in the open air where farm produce and household goods are sold ○ The fish market is held every Thursday. ○ The open-air market is held in the central square. ○ Here are this week's market prices for sheep. **2.** an area where a product might be sold or the group of people who might buy a product ○ There is no market for this product. ○ Our share of the Far East market has gone down. **3.** the possible sales of a specific product or demand for a specific product ○ There's no market for word processors ○ The market for home computers has fallen sharply. ○ We have 20% of the UK car market. **4.** □ **to pay black market prices** to pay high prices to get items which are not easily available **5.** □ **to go up market** or **to go down market** to make products which appeal to a wealthy section of the market or to a wider, less wealthy section of the market **6.** □ **to be in the market for secondhand cars** to look for secondhand cars to buy □ **to come on to the market** to start to be sold ○ This soap has just come on to the market. □ **to put something on the market** to start to offer something for sale ○ They put their house on the market. ○ I hear the company has been put on the market.

□ **the company has priced itself out of the market** the company has raised its prices so high that its products do not sell ■ verb to sell a product, or to present and promote a product in a way which will help to sell it ○ This product is being marketed in all European countries.

'…market analysts described the falls in the second half of last week as a technical correction to a market which had been pushed by demand to over the 900 index level' [Australian Financial Review]

marketable /ˈmɑːkɪtəb(ə)l/ adjective easily sold

market analysis /ˌmɑːkɪt əˈnæləsɪs/ noun the detailed examination and report of a market

market area /ˈmɑːkɪt ˌeəriə/ noun a geographical area which represents a particular market, e.g. a TV viewing area or a representative's territory

market build-up method /ˌmɑːkɪt ˈbɪld ʌp ˌmeθəd/ noun a method of assessing the sales potential of a product by adding up the number of potential buyers in each market segment

market challenger strategy /ˌmɑːkɪt ˈtʃælɪndʒə ˌstrætədʒi/ noun a strategy adopted by a company which is challenging the market leaders through pricing, promotion, or product design ○ It's a new aggressive company adopting a market challenger strategy.

market coverage /ˌmɑːkɪt ˈkʌv(ə)rɪdʒ/ noun a market share or measurement of what proportion of the sales of an article is accounted for by a particular brand ○ The marketing director's brief was to increase market coverage by at least 10%.

market day /ˈmɑːkɪt deɪ/ noun the day when a market is regularly held ○ Tuesday is market day, so the streets are closed to traffic.

market demand /ˌmɑːkɪt dɪˈmɑːnd/ noun the total demand for a product in the market ○ Market demand for this product is falling, as fashions have changed.

market development /ˌmɑːkɪt dɪˈveləpmənt/ noun a strategy involving the search for and exploitation of new markets for a product ○ Market *development for our tractors is part of the company's growth strategy.*

market-driven /'mɑːkɪt ˌdrɪv(ə)n/ *adjective* which is driven by market forces

market dues /ˌmɑːkɪt 'djuːz/ *plural noun* the rent to be paid for a stall in a market

market economist /ˌmɑːkɪt ɪ'kɒnəmɪst/ *noun* a person who specialises in the study of financial structures and the return on investments in the stock market

market economy /ˌmɑːkɪt ɪ'kɒnəmi/ *noun* same as **free market economy**

marketeer /ˌmɑːkɪ'tɪə/ *noun* same as **marketer**

marketer /'mɑːkɪtə/ *noun* a person or company that carries out marketing activities ○ *The company has been in manufacturing for ten years, and is now becoming a marketer of its own products as well.* ○ *Most direct marketers support the Post Office, which is almost the sole channel for their services.*

marketface /'mɑːkɪtfeɪs/ *noun* the point of contact between suppliers and their customers

market-facing enterprise /'mɑːkɪt feɪsɪŋ ˌentəpraɪz/ *noun* an organisation that is sensitive to the needs of its markets and customers and arranges its activities with them in mind

market factor analysis /ˌmɑːkɪt ˌfæktə ə'næləsɪs/ *noun* a forecasting method which concentrates on key market factors that are believed to affect demand

market follower strategy /ˌmɑːkɪt 'fɒləʊə ˌstrætədʒi/ *noun* a strategy of a company which does not directly challenge the market leaders, but attempts to benefit from their innovations and gain a profitable corner of the market ○ *Adopting a market follower strategy greatly reduces expenditure on research and development.*

market forces /ˌmɑːkɪt 'fɔːsɪz/ *plural noun* the influences on the sales of a product which bring about a change in prices

market forecast /ˌmɑːkɪt 'fɔːkɑːst/ *noun* a forecast of prices on the stock market

market fragmentation /ˌmɑːkɪt ˌfrægmən'teɪʃ(ə)n/ *noun* the splitting of a market into many small segments, which are more difficult to sell into

market gap /ˌmɑːkɪt 'gæp/ *noun* an opportunity to sell a product or service which is needed but which no one has sold before. ⇨ **gap**

market hall /'mɑːkɪt hɔːl/ *noun* the building in which a market is held regularly

marketing /'mɑːkɪtɪŋ/ *noun* **1.** the business of presenting and promoting goods or services in such a way as to make customers want to buy them **2.** the techniques used in selling a product, such as packaging and advertising

'…reporting to the marketing director, the successful applicant will be responsible for the development of a training programme for the new sales force' [*Times*]

marketing agreement /'mɑːkɪtɪŋ əˌgriːmənt/ *noun* a contract by which one company will market another company's products

marketing audit /'mɑːkɪtɪŋ ˌɔːdɪt/ *noun* an examination of the effectiveness of a company's marketing plans

marketing board /'mɑːkɪtɪŋbɔːd/ *noun* an organisation set up by the government or by a group of producers to help market a certain type of product

marketing budget /'mɑːkɪtɪŋ ˌbʌdʒɪt/ *noun* money set aside by an organisation for its marketing activities

marketing channels /'mɑːkɪtɪŋ ˌtʃæn(ə)lz/ *plural noun* the means of communicating a message involved in the process of marketing

marketing communications /ˌmɑːkɪtɪŋ kəˌmjuːnɪ'keɪʃ(ə)nz/ *plural noun* all methods of communicating used in marketing, e.g. television, radio, and sales literature

marketing concept /'mɑːkɪtɪŋ ˌkɒnsept/ *noun* a business idea or philosophy based on the importance of profit, consumer satisfaction, and the welfare of the general public

marketing consultancy /'mɑːkɪt-ɪŋ kən‚sʌltənsi/ *noun* a firm which gives specialist advice on marketing

marketing department /'mɑːkɪt-ɪŋ dɪ‚pɑːtmənt/ *noun* the section of a company dealing with marketing and sales

marketing director /'mɑːkɪtɪŋ daɪ‚rektə/ *noun* a director who is responsible for an organisation's marketing activities

marketing information system /‚mɑːkɪtɪŋ ‚ɪnfə'meɪʃ(ə)n ‚sɪstəm/ *noun* computer software which analyses marketing information and produces material on which marketers can make decisions

marketing intelligence /'mɑːkɪtɪŋ ɪn‚telɪdʒəns/ *noun* information about a market that can help a marketing effort

marketing management /'mɑː-kɪtɪŋ ‚mænɪdʒmənt/ *noun* the organising of a company's marketing

marketing manager /'mɑːkɪtɪŋ ‚mænɪdʒə/ *noun* a person in charge of a marketing department ○ *The marketing manager has decided to start a new advertising campaign.*

marketing mix /'mɑːkɪtɪŋ mɪks/ *noun* the combination of all the elements that make up marketing such as price, distribution, and advertising ○ *Personal selling is a vital part of the company's marketing mix.*

marketing model /'mɑːkɪtɪŋ ‚mɒd(ə)l/ *noun* an overview of the entire marketing process which can be shown graphically, often using a computer, and used to solve problems

marketing myopia /‚mɑːkɪtɪŋ maɪ'əʊpiə/ *noun* a problem which occurs when a business is 'short-sighted' and only views the world from its own perspective, and fails to see the point of view of the customer

marketing objectives /'mɑːkɪtɪŋ əb‚dʒektɪvz/ *plural noun* aims set for an organisation's marketing programme, including sales, market share, and profitability

marketing plan /'mɑːkɪtɪŋ plæn/ *noun* a plan, usually annual, for a company's marketing activities, specifying expenditure and expected revenue and profits ○ *Has this year's marketing plan been drawn up yet?* ○ *The marketing plan is flexible enough to allow for an increase in advertising costs.*

marketing planning /'mɑːkɪtɪŋ ‚plænɪŋ/ *noun* making a plan for a company's marketing activities, specifying expenditure and expected revenue and profits

marketing policy /'mɑːkɪtɪŋ ‚pɒlɪsi/ *noun* the basic attitudes underlying a company's marketing activities

marketing research /‚mɑːkɪtɪŋ rɪ'sɜːtʃ/ *noun* all research carried out in the interests of successful marketing, including market research, media research, and product research

marketing services /'mɑːkɪtɪŋ ‚sɜːvɪsɪz/ *plural noun* marketing functions other than selling, e.g. market research and advertising ○ *Our sales drive is supported by well-developed and effective marketing services.*

marketing strategy /'mɑːkɪtɪŋ ‚strætədʒi/ *noun* a strategy or plan for marketing activities ○ *What marketing strategy should be adopted to reach these long-term objectives?* ○ *The marketing strategy was one of expansion through diversification and market development.*

market intelligence /'mɑːkɪt ɪn‚telɪdʒəns/ *noun* information about a market that can help a marketing effort

market leader /‚mɑːkɪt 'liːdə/ *noun* the company with the largest market share ○ *We are the market leader in televisions.*

'…market leaders may benefit from scale economies or other cost advantages; they may enjoy a reputation for quality simply by being at the top, or they may actually produce a superior product that gives them both a large market share and high profits' [*Accountancy*]

market leader strategy /‚mɑːkɪt 'liːdə ‚strætədʒi/ *noun* a strategy of a company which is a market leader and wants to maintain a dominant market share or to keep its reputation as an innovator

marketmaker /'mɑːkɪtmeɪkə/ *noun* a person or firm that buys and sells shares on the stock market and offers to do so (NOTE: Marketmakers list the securities they are willing to buy or sell and their bid and offer prices. If the prices are met, they immediately buy or sell and make their money by charging a commission on each transaction. Marketmakers play an important part in maintaining an orderly market.)

market map /'mɑːkɪt mæp/ *noun* a graph showing the structure of a market in terms of the number and type of consumers and the activity of competitors ○ *One look at the market map shows we are aiming at the wrong target market.*

market niche /'mɑːkɪt niːʃ/ *noun* a particular segment or specialised area of a market ○ *In producing this unusual product, the company has found itself a market niche.*

market opening /'mɑːkɪt ˌəʊp(ə)nɪŋ/ *noun* the possibility of starting to do business in a new market

market opportunity /ˌmɑːkɪt ɒpəˈtjuːnɪti/ *noun* the possibility of going into a market for the first time

market penetration /ˌmɑːkɪt ˌpenɪˈtreɪʃ(ə)n/ *noun* the percentage of a total market which the sales of a company cover

market penetration pricing /ˌmɑːkɪt penɪˈtreɪʃ(ə)n ˌpraɪsɪŋ/ *noun* pricing a product low enough to achieve market penetration

marketplace /'mɑːkɪtpleɪs/ *noun* **1.** the open space in the middle of a town where a market is held ○ *You can park in the marketplace when there is no market.* **2.** the situation and environment in which goods are sold ○ *Our salespeople find life difficult in the marketplace.* ○ *What's the reaction to the new car in the marketplace?* ○ *What's the marketplace reaction to the new car?*

'…most discounted fares are sold by bucket shops but in today's competitive marketplace any agent can supply them' [*Business Traveller*]

market position /ˌmɑːkɪt pəˈzɪʃ(ə)n/ *noun* the place a company holds in a market

market potential /ˌmɑːkɪt pəˈtenʃəl/ *noun* the sales of a product that should be achieved with the right kind of marketing effort ○ *The product is promising but has not yet achieved its full market potential.*

market power /'mɑːkɪt ˌpaʊə/ *noun* the power of a business within a market, usually based on the firm's market position

market price /'mɑːkɪt praɪs/ *noun* the price at which a product can be sold

market profile /ˌmɑːkɪt ˈprəʊfaɪl/ *noun* the basic characteristics of a particular market

market rate /ˌmɑːkɪt ˈreɪt/ *noun* the usual price in the market ○ *We pay the market rate for temporary staff* or *We pay temporary staff the market rate.*

'…after the prime rate cut yesterday, there was a further fall in short-term market rates' [*Financial Times*]

market research /ˌmɑːkɪt rɪˈsɜːtʃ/ *noun* the process of examining the possible sales of a product and the possible customers for it before it is put on the market

market sector /ˌmɑːkɪt ˈsektə/ *noun* a particular section of a market, especially an area into which a firm sells

market segment /ˌmɑːkɪt ˈsegmənt/ *noun* a group of consumers in a market who are definable by their particular needs

market segmentation /ˌmɑːkɪt ˌsegmenˈteɪʃ(ə)n/ *noun* the division of the market or consumers into categories according to their buying habits ○ *Our strategy is based on satisfying the demands of many different types of buyer and therefore requires thorough market segmentation.*

market share /ˌmɑːkɪt ˈʃeə/ *noun* the percentage of a total market which the sales of a company's product cover ○ *We hope our new product range will increase our market share.*

market specialist /ˌmɑːkɪt ˈspeʃəlɪst/ *noun* a person who concentrates on a few markets, and has an expertise in the media industry in these markets

market stall /'mɑːkɪt stɔːl/ *noun* a light wooden stand where a trader sells goods in a market

market structure /ˌmɑːkɪt ˈstrʌktʃə/ *noun* the way in which a market is organised, including the concentration of suppliers or consumers, the ease of entry or barriers to entry, and the competitiveness of players in the market

market survey /ˌmɑːkɪt ˈsɜːveɪ/ noun a survey or general report on market conditions ○ *The market survey suggests that there is no longer much demand for this type of product.*

market targeting /ˌmɑːkɪt ˈtɑːgɪtɪŋ/ noun planning how to sell a product or service into a particular market

market test /ˌmɑːkɪt ˈtest/ noun an examination to see if a sample of a product will sell in a market

market trends /ˌmɑːkɪt ˈtrendz/ plural noun gradual changes taking place in a market

market value /ˌmɑːkɪt ˈvæljuː/ noun the value of an asset, a share, a product or a company if sold today

mark-up /ˈmɑːk ʌp/ noun **1.** an increase in price ○ *We put into effect a 10% mark-up of all prices in June.* ○ *Since I was last in the store they have put at least a 5% mark-up on the whole range of items.* **2.** the difference between the cost of a product or service and its selling price (NOTE: Mark-up is often calculated as a percentage of the production and overhead costs, and represents the profit made on the product or service.) □ **we work to a 3.5 times mark-up** *or* **to a 350% mark-up** we take the unit cost and multiply by 3.5 to give the selling price

mark-up percentage /ˈmɑːk ʌp pəˌsentɪdʒ/ noun the mark-up expressed as a percentage either of the cost price or of the selling price ○ *What's the mark-up percentage on these items?*

marque /mɑːk/ noun a famous brand name for a car, e.g. Jaguar, MG, or Ferrari

mart /mɑːt/ noun a place where things are sold

mass /mæs/ noun **1.** a large group of people **2.** a large number ○ *We have a mass of letters* or *masses of letters to write.* ○ *They received a mass of orders* or *masses of orders after the TV commercials.*

mass customisation /ˌmæs ˌkʌstəmaɪˈzeɪʃ(ə)n/ noun a process that allows a standard, mass-produced item, e.g., a bicycle, to be altered to fit the specific requirements of individual customers

mass market /ˌmæs ˈmɑːkɪt/ noun the whole market, consisting of a very large number of customers

mass marketing /ˌmæs ˈmɑːkɪtɪŋ/ noun marketing which aims at reaching large numbers of people

'…in the good old days of mass marketing, the things marketers did to attract new customers tended to be the same as the things they did to keep existing customers – competitive prices, high quality and good service' [*Marketing Week*]

mass media /ˌmæs ˈmiːdiə/ noun the means of communication by which large numbers of people are reached, e.g. radio, television, or newspapers

mass-produce /ˌmæs prəˈdjuːs/ verb to manufacture identical products in large quantities ○ *to mass-produce cars*

master /ˈmɑːstə/ adjective main or original □ **master budget** a budget prepared by amalgamating budgets from various profit and cost centres such as sales, production, marketing, or administration in order to provide a main budget for the whole company □ **the master copy of a file** the main copy of a computer file, kept for security purposes

master franchise /ˈmɑːstə ˌfræntʃaɪz/ noun a franchise given to a single entrepreneur who then sells subsidiary franchises to others

mastermind /ˈmɑːstəmaɪnd/ verb to be in charge of a project

Master of Business Administration /ˌmɑːstər əv ˈbɪznɪs ədˌmɪnɪstreɪʃ(ə)n/ noun full form of **MBA**

master sample /ˈmɑːstə ˌsɑːmpəl/ noun a collection of basic sampling units (such as parliamentary constituencies) compiled by research organisations to help a company's market research

masthead /ˈmɑːsthed/ noun the area at the top of a webpage, which usually contains the logo of the organisation that owns the page, and often a search box and a set of links to important areas of the website

matched sample /ˌmætʃd ˈsɑːm-pəl/ *noun* the use of two samples of people with the same characteristics to compare reactions to different products in tests

material /məˈtɪəriəl/ *noun* a substance which can be used to make a finished product □ **materials control** a system to check that a company has enough materials in stock to do its work □ **materials handling** the moving of materials from one part of a factory to another in an efficient way

matrix /ˈmeɪtrɪks/ *noun* an arrangement of data in horizontal and vertical columns (NOTE: plural is **matrices**)

matrix management /ˈmeɪtrɪks ˌmænɪdʒmənt/ *noun* management that operates both through the hierarchical chain of command within the organisation, and through relationships at the same level with other managers working in other locations or on different products or projects

mature /məˈtʃʊə/ *adjective* □ **mature economy** a fully developed economy ■ *verb* to become due □ **bills which mature in three weeks' time** bills which will be due for payment in three weeks

mature market /məˌtʃʊə ˈmɑːkɪt/ *noun* a well-established market, with little potential for increased sales

maturity /məˈtʃʊərɪti/ *noun* the third stage in a product life cycle when a product is well established in the market though no longer enjoying increasing sales, after which sooner or later it will start to decline

maximal awareness /ˌmæksɪməl əˈweənəs/ *noun* the point at which a consumer is convinced enough by a product's advertising to buy the product ○ *The marketing director considered the advertisement's message too weak to achieve maximal awareness.*

maximisation /ˌmæksɪmaɪˈzeɪ-ʃ(ə)n/, **maximization** *noun* the process of making something as large as possible ○ *profit maximisation* or *maximisation of profit*

maximise /ˈmæksɪmaɪz/, **maximize** *verb* to make something as large as possible ○ *Our aim is to maximise prof-*

its. ○ *The cooperation of the workforce will be needed if we are to maximise production.* ○ *She is paid on results, and so has to work flat out to maximise her earnings.*

maximum /ˈmæksɪməm/ *noun* the largest possible number, price or quantity ○ *It is the maximum the insurance company will pay.* (NOTE: The plural is **maxima** or **maximums**.) □ **up to a maximum of £10** no more than £10 □ **to increase exports to the maximum** to increase exports as much as possible ■ *adjective* largest possible ○ *40% is the maximum income tax rate* or *the maximum rate of tax.* ○ *The maximum load for the truck is one ton.* ○ *Maximum production levels were reached last week.* □ **to increase production to the maximum level** to increase it as much as possible

maximum price /ˌmæksɪməm ˈpraɪs/ *noun* the highest legal price for a product ○ *The government insists on such a low maximum price that we'll never break even.* ○ *Demand for the product is so low that no company is charging the maximum price.*

MBA /ˌem biː ˈeɪ/ *noun* a degree awarded to graduates who have completed a further course in business studies. Full form **Master of Business Administration**

MBO *abbreviation* management buyout

m-commerce /ˈem ˌkɒmɜːs/ *noun* marketing functions other than selling, e.g. market research and advertising

MD *abbreviation* managing director ○ *She was appointed MD of a property company.*

mean /miːn/ *adjective* average ○ *The mean annual increase in sales is 3.20%.* ■ *noun* the average or number calculated by adding several quantities together and dividing by the number of quantities added ○ *Unit sales are over the mean for the first quarter* or *above the first-quarter mean.*

means /miːnz/ *noun* a way of doing something ○ *Do we have any means of copying all these documents quickly?* ○ *Bank transfer is the easiest means of payment.* (NOTE: The plural is **means**.) ■ *plural noun* money or resources ○ *The* *company has the means to launch the new product.* ○ *Such a level of investment is beyond the means of a small private company.*

means test /'miːnz test/ *noun* an inquiry into how much money someone earns to see if they are eligible for state benefits

mechanical /mɪ'kænɪk(ə)l/ *adjective* worked by a machine ○ *a mechanical pump*

mechanical data /mɪˌkænɪk(ə)l 'deɪtə/ *noun* information regarding the printing of newspapers or magazines, e.g. format or column width

media /'miːdiə/ *noun* the means of communicating a message about a product or service to the public (NOTE: **media** is followed by a singular or plural verb.)

'…both advertisers and agencies agree that the media owners do their bit to keep advertisers well informed' [*Marketing Workshop*]

'…media costs represent a major expense for advertisers' [*Marketing*]

media broker /'miːdiə ˌbrəʊkə/ *noun* a business which offers organisations a media-buying service and possibly additional services such as media planning

media buyer /'miːdiə ˌbaɪə/ *noun* a person in an advertising agency who places advertisements in the media on behalf of clients

media buying /'miːdiə ˌbaɪɪŋ/ *noun* the placing of advertisements in the media on behalf of an organisation ○ *Efficient media buying is impossible without a good knowledge of comparative media costs.*

media class /'miːdiə klɑːs/ *noun* a basic type of medium, e.g. TV, radio, or the press

media coverage /'miːdiə ˌkʌv(ə)rɪdʒ/ *noun* reports about something in the media ○ *We got good media coverage for the launch of the new model.*

media data form /ˌmiːdiə 'deɪtə ˌfɔːm/ *noun* a document giving basic data or information about a publication such as circulation, readership, and geographical distribution

media event /ˌmiːdiə ɪ'vent/ *noun* a happening which is staged by or organ-

ised so as to attract the attention of the mass media

media independent /ˌmiːdiə ˌɪndɪ'pendənt/, **media shop** /'miːdiə ʃɒp/ *noun* a business which offers organisations a media-buying service, but without the creative services usually offered by advertising agencies

media mogul /'miːdiə ˌməʊg(ə)l/ *noun* a media proprietor who controls, either through personal ownership or a dominant position in any media enterprise ○ *Rupert Murdoch is one of the world's most influential media moguls.*

media-multiplier effect /ˌmiːdiə 'mʌltɪplaɪə ɪˌfekt/ *noun* the effect of combining several types of media in an integrated communications plan which is more successful than using one channel alone

median /'miːdiən/ *noun* the middle number in a list of numbers

media-neutral planning /ˌmiːdiə ˌnjuːtr(ə)l 'plænɪŋ/ *noun* an approach to planning advertising campaigns to maximise response across different media according to consumer usage of these media

media objectives /ˌmiːdiə əb'dʒektɪvz/ *plural noun* aims which an advertiser has in advertising through the media

media option /'miːdiə ˌɒpʃən/ *noun* a single unit of advertising space or time

media organisations /'miːdiə ɔːgənaɪˌzeɪʃ(ə)nz/ *plural noun* organisations whose aim is to provide information or entertainment to their subscribers, viewers, or readers while at the same offering marketers a way of reaching audiences with print and broadcast messages

media owner /'miːdiə ˌəʊnə/ *noun* a person or company that owns a magazine or newspaper or radio or TV station

media plan /'miːdiə plæn/ *noun* a plan showing what type of media will be used and how much advertising will be done and when

media planner /'miːdiə ˌplænə/ *noun* a person who deals with media planning

media planning /ˈmiːdiə ˌplænɪŋ/ *noun* a strategy concerned with what type of media should be used and how much advertising should be done and when ○ *The marketing manager and media buyer are having a media planning session.* ○ *Proper media planning avoids overexpenditure on promotion.*

media research /ˈmiːdiə rɪˌsɜːtʃ/ *noun* the study or evaluation of a target audience in order to improve an organisation's promotional activities

media schedule /ˈmiːdiə ˌʃedʒuːl/ *noun* all the details of advertising to be used in a promotional campaign, e.g. the timing and positioning of advertisements

media selection /ˈmiːdiə sɪˌlek-ʃən/ *noun* the process of choosing the right type of media for a promotional campaign ○ *The agency will give us guidance on media selection.*

media service /ˈmiːdiə ˌsɜːvɪs/ *noun* an organisation which provides the full range of media functions to its clients

media shop /ˈmiːdiə ʃɒp/ *noun* same as **media independent**

media strategy /ˈmiːdiə ˌstræ-tədʒi/ *noun* action plans for achieving media objectives

media vehicle /ˈmiːdiə ˌviːɪk(ə)l/ *noun* the specific programme or publication used to carry an advertising message

medium /ˈmiːdiəm/ *noun* one particular means of communicating information to the public (NOTE: plural is **media**)

medium-term /ˌmiːdiəm ˈtɜːm/ *adjective* referring to a point between short term and long term □ **medium-term forecast** a forecast for two or three years

megastore /ˈmegəstɔː/ *noun* a very large store

member-get-member *noun* a customer recruitment technique that often offers an incentive to current members for referring new members. Abbreviation **MGM**

mentee /menˈtiː/ *noun* a less experienced employee who is offered special guidance and support by a respected and trusted person with more experience (a mentor)

mercantile /ˈmɜːkəntaɪl/ *adjective* commercial □ **mercantile country** a country which earns income from trade □ **mercantile law** laws relating to business

mercantile agent /ˈmɜːkəntaɪl ˌeɪdʒənt/ *noun* a person who sells on behalf of a business or another person and earns a commission

mercantile paper /ˈmɜːkəntaɪl ˌpeɪpə/ *noun* a negotiable document used in commerce

merchandise /ˈmɜːtʃəndaɪz/ *noun* goods which are for sale or which have been sold ○ *The merchandise is shipped through two ports.* ■ *verb* to sell goods by a wide variety of means, such as display, advertising, or sending samples ○ *to merchandise a product*

merchandiser /ˈmɜːtʃəndaɪzə/ *noun* a person or company that organises the display and promotion of goods

merchandising /ˈmɜːtʃəndaɪzɪŋ/ *noun* the process of organising the display and promotion of goods in retail outlets ○ *the merchandising of a product* ○ *the merchandising department*

merchant /ˈmɜːtʃənt/ *noun* a businessperson who buys and sells, especially one who buys imported goods in bulk for retail sale ○ *a coal merchant* ○ *a wine merchant*

merchantable /ˈmɜːtʃəntəb(ə)l/ *adjective* of good enough quality for sale and use

merchant account /ˈmɜːtʃənt əˌkaʊnt/ *noun* an account opened by an e-merchant at a financial institution to receive the proceeds of credit-card transactions

merchant bank /ˈmɜːtʃənt bæŋk/ *noun* a bank which arranges loans to companies, deals in international finance, buys and sells shares and launches new companies on the stock exchange, but does not provide banking services to the general public

merchanting /ˈmɜːtʃəntɪŋ/ *noun* the action of buying and selling

merchant marine /ˌmɜːtʃənt mə-ˈriːn/, **merchant navy** /ˌmɜːtʃənt ˈneɪvi/ *noun* all the commercial ships of a country

merge /mɜːdʒ/ *verb* to join together ○ *The two companies have merged.* ○ *The firm merged with its main competitor.*

merge-purge /'mɜːdʒ pɜːdʒ/ *noun* combining two mailing lists and checking to remove duplicate addresses

merger /'mɜːdʒə/ *noun* the joining together of two or more companies ○ *As a result of the merger, the company is now the largest in the field.*

message /'mesɪdʒ/ *noun* **1.** a piece of news which is sent to someone ○ *He says he never received the message.* ○ *I'll leave a message with her secretary.* **2.** an idea that is communicated by promotion ○ *The agency was given clear instructions as to what message the advertisement should convey.* ○ *Few people interviewed in the survey knew what the advertisement's message was supposed to be.* ○ *The message on the poster was conveyed in only three words.*

message effect /'mesɪdʒ ɪ,fekt/ *noun* the effect of an advertisement's message on the target audience ○ *The message effect was lost because so many people didn't understand the joke used in the advertisement.* ○ *After the campaign we'll try to assess what the message effect has been.*

metadata /'metədeɪtə/ *noun* essential information contained in a document or web page, e.g. its publication date, author, keywords, title, and summary, which is used by search engines to find relevant websites in response to a search request from a user. ⇨ **meta-tag** (NOTE: takes a singular or plural verb)

metamarketing /'metəmɑːkɪtɪŋ/ *noun US* marketing applied to all kinds of organisations, such as hospitals, churches, and religions, as well as to profit-making concerns

meta-tag /'metə tæg/ *noun* a keyword or description command used on a webpage to enable it to be found by search engines

Metcalfe's Law /'metkɑːfs lɔː/ *noun* the value of a telecommunications network is proportional to the square of the number of connected users of that system. The law characterises many

network effects of communication technologies e.g. the Internet and social networking.

me-too product /,miː 'tuː ,prɒdʌkt/ *noun* a product which is a very similar to an existing market leader

metro area /'metrəʊ ,eəriə/ *noun* the central part of a large city

MGM *abbreviation* member-get-member

micro- /maɪkrəʊ/ *prefix* very small

microblogging /'maɪkrəʊ,blɒgɪŋ/ *noun* the exchange by users of small elements of content such as short sentences, individual images, or video links to promote websites, services or products

microeconomics /'maɪkrəʊ iːkə-,nɒmɪks/ *plural noun* the study of the economics of people or single companies. Compare **macroeconomics** (NOTE: takes a singular verb) □ **microeconomic trends** trends in a country's economy, e.g. consumer income and patterns of spending, wages, savings, or debt

microenvironment /'maɪkrəʊɪn-,vaɪrənmənt/ *noun* the elements or factors outside a business organisation which directly affect it, such as supply of raw materials, demand for its products, and rival companies ○ *Unreliability of suppliers is one the greatest problems in our microenvironment.*

micromarketing /'maɪkrəʊ ,mɑː-kɪtɪŋ/ *prefix* the study of the marketing strategy of an individual business

microsite /'maɪkrəʊsaɪt/ *noun* an individual webpage with a separate URL which functions as a supplement to a primary website and is used for editorial or commercial purposes to give more detailed information about a product or service that is not covered fully by the main website

middleman /'mɪd(ə)l,mæn/ *noun* a businessperson who buys from the manufacturer and sells to retailers or to the public ○ *We sell direct from the factory to the customer and cut out the middleman.* (NOTE: The plural is **middlemen.**)

milk /mɪlk/ *verb* to make as much profit for as long as possible from a particular product or service ○ *We intend to milk the product hard for the next two years, before it becomes obsolete.*

mindset /'maɪndset/ *noun* a way of thinking or general attitude to things

mindshare /'maɪndʃeə/ *noun* the density of the interconnects found by a search engine, that is the number of pages that have links to a website

minimum frequency /ˌmɪnɪməm 'friːkwənsi/ *noun* the minimum number of exposures for an advertisement to be effective

minority /maɪ'nɒrɪti/ *noun* a section of the population from a specific racial group, which does nor make up the majority of the population

miscellaneous /ˌmɪsə'leɪniəs/ *adjective* various, mixed, or not all of the same sort ○ *miscellaneous items on the agenda* ○ *a box of miscellaneous pieces of equipment* ○ *Miscellaneous expenditure is not itemised in the accounts.*

misrepresentation /ˌmɪsˌreprɪzen'teɪʃ(ə)n/ *noun* the act of making a wrong statement in order to persuade someone to enter into a contract such as one for buying a product or service

mission /'mɪʃ(ə)n/ *noun* a group of people going on a journey for a special purpose

missionary sales /'mɪʃ(ə)n(ə)ri seɪlz/ *plural noun* a sales pitch where a salesperson emphasises support services rather than taking orders

missionary salesperson /'mɪʃ(ə)n(ə)ri ˌseɪlzpɜːs(ə)n/ *noun* a salesperson who approaches a new market with a product

missionary selling /'mɪʃ(ə)n(ə)ri ˌselɪŋ/ *noun* the act of approaching new customers with a product ○ *We have never sold there before, so be prepared for missionary selling.* ○ *Some sales reps are not aggressive enough for missionary selling.*

mission statement /'mɪʃ(ə)n ˌsteɪtmənt/ *noun* a short statement of the reasons for the existence of an organisation

mix /mɪks/ *noun* an arrangement of different things together

mixed /mɪkst/ *adjective* made up of different sorts or of different types of things together

'...prices closed on a mixed note after a moderately active trading session' [*Financial Times*]

mixed economy /ˌmɪkstɪ'kɒnəmi/ *noun* a system which contains both nationalised industries and private enterprise

mixed media /ˌmɪkst 'miːdiə/ *plural noun* various types of media used together in a promotional campaign

mnemonic /nɪ'mɒnɪk/ *noun* a word, sentence, or little poem which helps you remember something

mobile /'məʊbaɪl/ *adjective* which can move about

mock-up /'mɒk ʌp/ *noun* the model of a new product for testing or to show to possible buyers ○ *The sales team were shown a mock-up of the new car.*

mode /məʊd/ *noun* a way of doing something □ **mode of payment** the way in which payment is made, e.g. cash or cheque

model /'mɒd(ə)l/ *noun* 1. a small copy of something made to show what it will look like when finished ○ *They showed us a model of the new office building.* 2. a style or type of product ○ *This is the latest model.* ○ *The model on display is last year's.* ○ *I drive a 2010 model Range Rover.* 3. a person whose job is to wear new clothes to show them to possible buyers 4. a description in the form of mathematical data ■ *adjective* which is a perfect example to be copied ○ *a model agreement* ■ *verb* to wear new clothes to show them to possible buyers ○ *She has decided on a career in modelling.* (NOTE: **modelling – modelled**. The US spelling is **modeling – modeled**.)

modem /'məʊdem/ *noun* a device which links a computer to a telephone line, allowing data to be sent from one computer to another

moderate /'mɒd(ə)rət/ *adjective* not holding very extreme views ○ *a moderate trade union leader*

modification /ˌmɒdɪfɪ'keɪʃ(ə)n/ *noun* a change ○ *The board wanted to make* or *to carry out modifications to the* *plan.* ○ *The new model has had several important modifications.* ○ *The client pressed for modifications to the contract.*

modified rebuy /ˌmɒdɪfaɪd ˈriː-baɪ/ *noun* a buying decision where either the product or the supplier has changed from the time of the previous purchase

modify /ˈmɒdɪfaɪ/ *verb* to change or to make something fit a different use ○ *The management modified its proposals.* ○ *This is the new modified agreement.* ○ *The car will have to be modified to pass the government tests.* ○ *The refrigerator was considerably modified before it went into production.* (NOTE: **modifies – modifying – modified**)

modular /ˈmɒdjʊlə/ *adjective* made of various sections

mom-and-pop operation /ˌmɒm ən ˈpɒp ɒpəˌreɪʃ(ə)n/ *noun US* a small business owned and run by a couple

monadic test /mɒˈnædɪk test/ *noun* a product test involving only one product

monetary /ˈmʌnɪt(ə)ri/ *adjective* referring to money or currency

'...the decision by the government to tighten monetary policy will push the annual inflation rate above the year's previous high' [*Financial Times*]

'...it is not surprising that the Fed started to ease monetary policy some months ago' [*Sunday Times*]

'...a draft report on changes in the international monetary system' [*Wall Street Journal*]

monetary policy /ˌmʌnɪt(ə)ri ˈpɒlɪsi/ *noun* the government's policy relating to finance, e.g. bank interest rates, taxes, government expenditure, and borrowing

monetary standard /ˌmʌnɪt(ə)ri ˈstændəd/ *noun* a fixed exchange rate for a currency

money /ˈmʌni/ *noun* coins and notes used for buying and selling □ **to earn money** to have a wage or salary □ **to earn good money** to have a large wage or salary □ **to lose money** to make a loss, not to make a profit □ **the company has been losing money for months** the company has been working at a loss for months □ **to get your money back** to

make enough profit to cover your original investment □ **to make money** to make a profit □ **to put money into the bank** to deposit money into a bank account □ **to put money into a business** to invest money in a business ○ *She put all her redundancy money into a shop.* □ **to put money down** to pay cash, especially as a deposit ○ *We put £25 down and paid the rest in instalments.* □ **money up front** payment in advance ○ *They are asking for £10,000 up front before they will consider the deal.* ○ *He had to put money up front before he could clinch the deal.*

money-back guarantee /ˌmʌni ˈbæk gærənˌtiː/, **money-back offer** /ˌmʌni ˈbæk ˌɒfə/ *noun* a guarantee that money will be paid back to customers who are not satisfied with their purchases

money-making /ˈmʌni ˌmeɪkɪŋ/ *adjective* able to turn over a profit ○ *a money-making plan*

money-off coupon /ˌmʌni ˈɒf ˌkuːpɒn/ *noun* a coupon in a newspaper or on a package which can be cut off and used to claim a discount on the next purchase

money order /ˈmʌni ˌɔːdə/ *noun* a document which can be bought as a way of sending money through the post

money rates /ˈmʌni reɪts/ *plural noun* rates of interest for borrowers or lenders

money-spinner /ˈmʌni ˌspɪnə/ *noun* an item which sells very well or which is very profitable ○ *The home-delivery service has proved to be a real money-spinner.*

money supply /ˈmʌni səˌplaɪ/ *noun* the amount of money in a country's economy, consisting mainly of the money in circulation and that held in savings and cheque accounts

monies /ˈmʌniz/ *plural noun* sums of money ○ *monies owing to the company* ○ *to collect monies due*

monopolisation /məˌnɒpəlaɪ-ˈzeɪʃ(ə)n/, **monopolization** *noun* the process of making a monopoly

monopolise /məˈnɒpəlaɪz/, **monopolize** *verb* to create a monopoly or to get control of all the supply of a product

monopolist /məˈnɒpəlɪst/ *noun* a business which is the sole seller in a market

monopolistic competition /mən-ɒpə,lɪstɪk ˌkɒmpəˈtɪʃ(ə)n/ *noun* a situation where there are only a few producers who therefore control the market between them ○ *With only three suppliers of cotton in the country it was a clear case of monopolistic competition.* Also called **imperfect competition**

monopoly /məˈnɒpəli/ *noun* a situation where one person or company is the only supplier of a particular product or service ○ *to be in a monopoly situation* ○ *The company has the monopoly of imports of Brazilian wine.* ○ *The factory has the absolute monopoly of jobs in the town.*

monopoly profit /məˈnɒpəli ˌprɒ-fɪt/ *noun* profit earned by a business through having a monopoly

monopsonist /məˈnɒpsənɪst/ *noun* a sole buyer of a particular product or service

monopsony /məˈnɒpsəni/ *noun* a situation where there is only one buyer for a particular product or service ○ *Monopsony gives the buyer leverage in demanding a low price.*

monthly /ˈmʌnθli/ *noun* a magazine which is published each month ○ *The holidays were advertised in all the monthlies.* (NOTE: The plural is **monthlies**.)

monthly sales report /ˌmʌnθli ˈseɪlz rɪˌpɔːt/ *noun* a report made every month showing the number of items sold or the amount of money a company has received for selling stock

morphological analysis /ˌmɔːfə-ˌlɒdʒik(ə)l əˈnæləsɪs/ *noun* a method of identifying the most profitable market segments by exploring various dimensions such as countries and market types

Mosaic /məʊˈzeɪɪk/ a targeting tool based on the analysis of trends in UK society. There are 115 person types, 67 household types, and 15 groups, creating a three-tier classification of consumers that can be used at the individual, household or postcode level.

motivate /ˈməʊtɪveɪt/ *verb* to encourage someone to do something, especially to work or to sell □ **highly motivated sales staff** sales staff who are very eager to sell

'…creative people aren't necessarily motivated by money or titles, they may not want a larger office or more work, they don't often want more responsibility. They want to see their ideas implemented' [*Nation's Business*]

motivation /ˌməʊtɪˈveɪʃ(ə)n/ *noun* **1.** an encouragement to staff **2.** eagerness to work well or sell large quantities of a product □ **the sales staff lack motivation** the sales staff are not eager enough to sell

motivation research /ˌməʊtɪˈveɪ-ʃən rɪˌsɜːtʃ/, **motivational research** /ˌməʊtɪveɪʃ(ə)nəl rɪˈsɜːtʃ/ *noun* research designed to find out the consumer's motives for purchasing a product or service

motive /ˈməʊtɪv/ *noun* something that forces someone to take a particular action

move /muːv/ *verb* to be sold, or to sell ○ *Over Christmas the stock hardly moved at all but with the January sales it is finally starting to sell.* ○ *The sales staff will have to work hard if they want to move all that stock by the end of the month.*

moving averages /ˌmuːvɪŋ ˈæv(ə)rɪdʒɪz/ *plural noun* a method for working out averages while allowing for seasonal variations, in which the period under consideration is moved forward at regular intervals

MRP *abbreviation* manufacturer's recommended price

multi- /mʌlti/ *prefix* referring to many things or many of one thing

multi-channel /ˌmʌlti ˈtʃæn(ə)l/ *adjective* using both online and offline methods of communication to do business

multi-channel system /ˈmʌlti ˌtʃæn(ə)l ˌsɪstəm/ *noun* a distribution system used by a producer which makes use of more than one distribution channel

multi-dimensional scaling /ˌmʌlti daɪˌmenʃ(ə)nəl ˈskeɪlɪŋ/ *noun* a method of carrying out market research, in which the respondents are given a scale (usually 1 to 5) on which they base their replies

multilateral /ˌmʌlti'læt(ə)rəl/ *adjective* between several organisations or countries ○ *a multilateral agreement* □ **multilateral trade** trade between several countries

multilevel marketing /mʌlti'lev(ə)l ˌmɑːkɪtɪŋ/ *noun* same as **network marketing**

multimagazine deal /ˌmʌltimægə'ziːn diːl/ *plural noun* a deal where different publishers offer advertisers the opportunity to buy space in their magazines at the same time

multimedia /ˌmʌlti'miːdiə/ *adjective* referring to several media used in a project ○ *We are going for an all-out multimedia advertising campaign.*

multimedia document /ˌmʌlti-'miːdiə ˌdɒkjʊmənt/ *noun* an electronic document that contains interactive material from a range of different media such as text, video, sound, graphics, and animation

multinational /ˌmʌlti'næʃ(ə)nəl/ *noun, adjective* (a company) which has branches or subsidiary companies in several countries ○ *The company has been bought by one of the big multinationals.* Also called **transnational**

'…the number of multinational firms has mushroomed in the past two decades. As their sweep across the global economy accelerates, multinational firms are posing pressing issues for nations rich and poor, and those in between' [*Australian Financial Review*]

multi-pack offer /ˌmʌltɪ pæk 'ɒfə/ *noun* a special promotional offer in which an extra pack is offered free, or at a reduced price, for each pack bought at full price

multiple /'mʌltɪp(ə)l/ *adjective* many ■ *noun* a company with stores in several different towns

'…many independents took advantage of the bank holiday period when the big multiples were closed' [*The Grocer*]

'…the multiple brought the price down to £2.49 in some stores. We had not agreed to this deal and they sold out very rapidly. When they reordered we would not give it to them. This kind of activity is bad for the brand and we cannot afford it' [*The Grocer*]

multiple choice question /ˌmʌltɪp(ə)l 'tʃɔɪs ˌkwetʃən/ *noun* a type of question used in a survey which allows the respondent to choose a single answer from several possible ones ○ *The questionnaire had eight multiple choice questions, two dichotomous questions, and one open question.*

multiple correlation /ˌmʌltɪp(ə)l kɒrə'leɪʃ(ə)n/ *noun* a method for measuring the effect of several independent variables on one dependent variable

multiple discriminant analysis /ˌmʌltɪp(ə)l dɪ'skrɪmɪnənt ə,næləsɪs/ *noun* a method for assessing products by separating out their various attributes, and estimating the relative values of these attributes to different market segments. The whole process produces an assessment of the general potential of a product.

multiple pricing /ˌmʌltɪp(ə)l 'praɪsɪŋ/ *noun* the practice of fixing the same price for several different products

multiple regression analysis /ˌmʌltɪp(ə)l rɪ'greʃ(ə)n ə,næləsɪs/ *noun* a method for discovering the relationship between several independent variables and one dependent variable

multiple store /'mʌltɪp(ə)l stɔː/ *noun* one store in a chain of stores

multiplexing /'mʌltɪpleksɪŋ/ *noun* an arrangement where several TV channels are transmitted by one cable network, or where several messages are combined in the same transmission medium

multi-stage sample /mʌltɪ ˌsteɪdʒ 'saːmpəl/ *noun* a sample selected by ensuring equal proportions of various categories existing in the population and then using random sampling to select respondents within these categories

multitasking /'mʌlti,taːskɪŋ/ *noun* the action of performing several different tasks at the same time

'New research suggests that multi-tasking may be counterproductive. Mounting evidence shows that a crowded calendar calling for a lot of jumping back and forth between activities can diminish rather than enhance productivity.' [*Harvard Business Review*]

multivariate testing /ˌmʌltiveəriət ˌtestɪŋ/ *a process in which two or more components of a website may be tested in a live environment. An example of multi-variate testing is regression analysis.

mystery shopper /ˈmɪst(ə)ri ˌʃɒpə/ *noun* a person employed by a market-research company to visit shops anonymously to test the quality of service

mystery shopping /ˈmɪst(ə)ri ˌʃɒpɪŋ/ *noun* shopping done by anonymous employees of a market-research company to test staff reactions, etc.

MySpace /ˈmaɪˌspeɪs/ a trade name for an online social community in which users upload a profile and can share information about themselves such as interests, photos, and musical tastes

N

name /neɪm/ *noun* the word used for referring to a person, animal, or thing ○ *I cannot remember the name of the managing director of Smith Ltd* ○ *His first name is John, but I am not sure of his other names.* □ **under the name of** using a particular name □ **trading under the name of 'Best Foods'** using the name 'Best Foods' as a commercial name, and not the name of the company

named /neɪmd/ *adjective* □ **the person named in the policy** the person whose name is given on an insurance policy as the person insured

narcotising dysfunction /ˌnɑː-kətaɪzɪŋ dɪsˈfʌŋkʃ(ə)n/ *noun* the social consequence of the mass media overloading audiences with so much information that they are reduced to apathy

narrowcasting /ˈnærəʊkɑːstɪŋ/ *noun* the act of reaching only a small special audience through an electronic medium such as cable television

nation /ˈneɪʃ(ə)n/ *noun* a country and the people living in it

national /ˈnæʃ(ə)nəl/ *adjective* referring to the whole of a particular country □ **national advertising** advertising in every part of a country, not just in the capital ○ *We took national advertising to promote our new 24-hour delivery service.* □ **national campaign** a sales or publicity campaign in every part of a country

national account /ˌnæʃ(ə)nəl əˈkaʊnt/ *noun* a customer with branches or offices all over the country

national advertiser /ˌnæʃ(ə)nəl ˈædvətaɪzə/ *noun* a company that advertises in every part of a country, not just in the capital city

national brand /ˈnæʃ(ə)nəl brænd/ *noun* a brand which is recognised throughout a whole country, not just in a local area

National Debt /ˌnæʃ(ə)nəl ˈdet/ *noun* money borrowed by a government

national income /ˌnæʃ(ə)nəl ˈɪnkʌm/ *noun* the value of income from the sales of goods and services in a country

nationalisation /ˌnæʃ(ə)nəlaɪˈzeɪʃ(ə)n/, **nationalization** *noun* the taking over of private industry by the state

national launch /ˌnæʃ(ə)nəl ˈlɔːntʃ/ *noun* a launch of a product over the whole country at the same time, as opposed to launching it in some areas only

national newspaper /ˌnæʃ(ə)nəl ˈnjuːzpeɪpə/ *noun* a newspaper which is sold throughout a whole country and carries national and international news

national press /ˌnæʃ(ə)nəl ˈpres/ *noun* newspapers which sell in all parts of the country ○ *The new car has been advertised in the national press.*

national retailer /ˌnæʃ(ə)nəl ˈriːteɪlə/ *noun* a retailing company which has branches throughout a country

nationwide /ˈneɪʃ(ə)nwaɪd/ *adjective* all over a country ○ *We offer a nationwide delivery service.* ○ *The new car is being launched with a nationwide sales campaign.*

natural /ˈnætʃ(ə)rəl/ *adjective* **1.** found in the earth ○ *The offices are heated by natural gas.* **2.** not made by people ○ *They use only natural fibres for their best cloth.* **3.** normal ○ *It was only natural that the shopkeeper should feel annoyed when the hypermarket was* *built close to his shop.* ○ *It was natural for the workers to feel aggrieved when production methods were changed without consultation.*

natural break /ˌnætʃ(ə)rəl 'breɪk/ *noun* a convenient or reasonable point in a TV programme for a commercial break

natural listings /'nætʃ(ə)rəl ˌlɪs-tɪŋz/ *plural noun* results listed from a search engine query that are displayed according to relevance of a match between the keyword typed into the search engine and a webpage. The match is made according to a ranking algorithm used by the search engine as opposed to pay-per-click advertising. Also called **organic listings**

natural resources /ˌnætʃ(ə)rəl rɪ'zɔːsɪz/ *plural noun* raw materials which are found in the earth, e.g. coal, gas, or iron

navigation /ˌnævɪ'geɪʃ(ə)n/ *noun* the action of guiding and steering, in particular the graphics which lead users to different websites

necessity /nə'sesɪti/ *noun* something which is vitally important, without which nothing can be done or no one can survive ○ *Being unemployed makes it difficult to afford even the basic necessities.* (NOTE: The plural is **necessities**.)

necessity product /nə'sesɪti ˌprɒdʌkt/ *noun* an ordinary everyday product which consumers tend not to buy much more of as their incomes rise ○ *Consumers find shopping for necessity products boring.* ○ *Fancy packaging will not increase sales of necessity products.*

negative /'negətɪv/ *adjective* meaning 'no' □ **the answer was in the negative** the answer was 'no'

negative cash flow /ˌnegətɪv 'kæʃ fləʊ/ *noun* a situation where more money is going out of a company than is coming in

negative demand /ˌnegətɪv dɪ-'mɑːnd/ *noun* firm decisions by consumers not to buy a particular product ○ *Negative demand was due to offensive advertising.*

negative variance /ˌnegətɪv 'veəriəns/ *noun* a difference between a financial plan and its outcome that means a less favourable profit than

expected ○ *The unexpected increase in raw material prices meant a negative variance of $5,000.* ○ *A sudden fall in revenue resulted in a negative variance for the year as a whole.*

negotiable /nɪ'gəʊʃiəb(ə)l/ *adjective* transferable from one person to another or exchanged for cash □ **not negotiable** which cannot be exchanged for cash □ **'not negotiable'** words written on a cheque to show that it can be paid only to a specific person □ **negotiable cheque** a cheque made payable to bearer, i.e. to anyone who holds it

negotiable instrument /nɪ,gəʊ-ʃiəb(ə)l 'ɪnstrʊmənt/ *noun* a document which can be exchanged for cash, e.g. a bill of exchange or a cheque

negotiable paper /nɪ,gəʊʃiəb(ə)l 'peɪpə/ *noun* a document which can be transferred from one owner to another for cash

negotiate /nɪ'gəʊʃieɪt/ *verb* □ **to negotiate with someone** to discuss a problem or issue formally with someone, so as to reach an agreement ○ *The management refused to negotiate with the union.* □ **to negotiate terms and conditions** *or* **a contract** to discuss and agree the terms of a contract □ **he negotiated a £250,000 loan with the bank** he came to an agreement with the bank for a loan of £250,000

negotiated commission /nɪ,gəʊ-ʃieɪtɪd kə'mɪʃ(ə)n/ *noun* a commission agreed with an advertising agency before work starts, and which may be different from standard commissions

negotiation /nɪ,gəʊʃi'eɪʃ(ə)n/ *noun* the discussion of terms and conditions in order to reach an agreement □ **contract under negotiation** a contract which is being discussed □ **a matter for negotiation** something which must be discussed before a decision is reached □ **to enter into** *or* **to start negotiations** to start discussing a problem □ **to resume negotiations** to start discussing a problem again, after talks have stopped for a time □ **to break off negotiations** to stop discussing a problem □ **to conduct negotiations** to negotiate □ **negotiations broke down after six hours** discussions stopped because no agreement was possible

'…after three days of tough negotiations, the company reached agreement with its 1,200 unionized workers' [*Toronto Star*]

negotiator /nɪˈgəʊʃieɪtə/ *noun* a person who discusses a problem with the aim of achieving agreement between different people or groups of people

nester /ˈnestə/ *noun* a person who has left the family home and is buying his or her own home

net /net/ *adjective* referring to a price, weight, pay, etc., after all deductions have been made (NOTE: The spelling **nett** is sometimes used on containers.) ■ *verb* to make a true profit ○ *to net a profit of £10,000* (NOTE: **netting – netted**)

'…out of its earnings a company will pay a dividend. When shareholders receive this it will be net, that is it will have had tax deducted at 30%' [*Investors Chronicle*]

net assets /ˌnet ˈæsets/ *plural noun* same as **net worth**

net cash flow /ˌnet ˈkæʃ ˌfləʊ/ *noun* the difference between the money coming in and the money going out of a firm

net circulation /ˌnet ˌsɜːkjʊˈleɪ-ʃ(ə)n/ *noun* the total sales figure of a publication after adjusting for error and discounting unsold copies

net cover /net ˈkʌvə/ *noun* the proportion of a target audience exposed to an advertisement at least once

Net imperative /ˌnet ɪmˈperətɪv/ *noun* the idea that an ability to use the Internet for business purposes is vital for organisations that wish to be successful in the future

netiquette /ˈnetɪket/ *noun* the rules for proper procedure and good manners that are usually observed when communicating on the Internet (NOTE: The term derives from the word 'etiquette'.)

net loss /ˌnet ˈlɒs/ *noun* an actual loss, after deducting overheads

net margin /ˌnet ˈmɑːdʒɪn/ *noun* the percentage difference between received price and all costs, including overheads

net names /net ˈneɪmz/ *plural noun* the names left in a mailing list after a merge-purge has removed the duplicate entries

net national product /net ˌnæʃ(ə)nəl ˈprɒdʌkt/ *noun* the gross national product less investment on capital goods and depreciation. Abbreviation **NNP**

net price /ˌnet ˈpraɪs/ *noun* the price of goods or services which cannot be reduced by a discount

net profit /ˌnet ˈprɒfɪt/ *noun* the amount by which income from sales is larger than all expenditure. Also called **profit after tax**

net reach /net ˈriːtʃ/ *noun* the total number of people who have seen an advertisement at least once

net receipts /ˌnet rɪˈsiːts/ *plural noun* receipts after deducting commission, tax, discounts, etc.

net sales /ˌnet ˈseɪlz/ *plural noun* the total amount of sales less damaged or returned items and discounts to retailers

net weight /ˌnet ˈweɪt/ *noun* the weight of goods after deducting the packing material and container

network /ˈnetwɜːk/ *noun* a system which links different points together ■ *verb* to link together in a network □ **to network a television programme** to send out the same television programme through several TV stations

network analysis /ˈnetwɜːk əˌnæləsɪs/ *noun* an analysis of a project that charts the individual activities involved, each with the time needed for its completion, so that the timing of the whole can be planned and controlled

networked system /ˌnetwɜːkt ˈsɪstəm/ *noun* a computer system where several PCs are linked together so that they all draw on the same database or use the same server

networking /ˈnetwɜːkɪŋ/ *noun* the practice of keeping in contact with former colleagues, school friends, etc., so that all the members of the group can help each other in their careers

network marketing /ˈnetwɜːk ˌmɑːkɪtɪŋ/ *noun* a marketing campaign carried out through a complete magazine network

network programming /ˌnetwɜːk ˈprəʊgræmɪŋ/ *noun* the practice of scheduling TV programmes over the whole network

network society /ˈnetwɜːk səˌsaɪəti/ *noun* a society that regularly uses global networks for the purposes of work, communication, and government

net worth /ˌnet 'wɜːθ/ *noun* the value of all the property of a person or company after taking away what the person or company owes ○ *The upmarket product is targeted at individuals of high net worth.*

net yield /ˌnet 'jiːld/ *noun* the profit from investments after deduction of tax

neural network /ˌnjʊərəl 'netwɜːk/ *noun* a computer system designed to imitate the nerve patterns of the human brain

neurolinguistic programming /ˌnjʊərəʊlɪŋgwɪstɪk 'prəʊgræmɪŋ/ *noun* a theory of behaviour and communication based on how people avoid change and how to help them to change. Abbreviation **NLP**

never-never /ˌnevə 'nevə/ *noun* buying on credit (*informal*) ○ *She bought her car on the never-never.*

new /njuː/ *adjective* recent or not old

new buy /njuː 'baɪ/ *noun* a type of organisational buying in which a completely new product is bought

new entrant /ˌnjuː 'entrənt/ *noun* a company which is going into a market for the first time

'The virtuous cycle that the new entrants appear to be building will add pressure on established members to reform' [*Business Week*]

new product committee /njuː 'prɒdʌkt kəˌmɪti/ *noun* a group of people from different departments in a company who work together on a new product development project ○ *The new product committee met regularly to monitor the progress in the product's development.*

new product development /ˌnjuː 'prɒdʌkt dɪˌveləpmənt/ *noun* the process of developing completely new products or improving existing ones ○ *The company fell behind because it failed to invest enough in new product development.* Abbreviation **NPD**

news /njuːz/ *noun* information about things which have happened ○ *She always reads the business news or financial news first in the paper.* ○ *Financial markets were shocked by the news of the devaluation.*

news agency /'njuːz ˌeɪdʒənsi/ *noun* an office which distributes news to newspapers and television stations

new season /ˌnjuː 'siːz(ə)n/ *noun* the start of the TV 'year', usually taken to be the autumn and winter programming season

newsletter /'njuːzletə/ *noun* □ **company newsletter** a printed sheet or small newspaper giving news about a company

newspaper /'njuːzpeɪpə/ *noun* a regular publication, usually daily or weekly, which gives items of general news, sold to the general public

news release /'njuːz rɪˌliːs/ *noun* a sheet giving information about a new event which is sent to newspapers and TV and radio stations so that they can use it ○ *The company sent out a news release about the new product launch.*

news stand /'njuːz stænd/ *noun* a small shop on a pavement, for selling newspapers and magazines

new technology /ˌnjuː tekˈnɒlədʒi/ *noun* electronic devices which have recently been invented

next matter /'nekst ˌmætə/, **next-to-reading matter** /ˌnekst tə 'riːdɪŋ ˌmætə/ *noun* advertising material placed next to editorial matter in a publication

niche /niːʃ/ *noun* a special place in a market, occupied by one company (a 'niche company') ○ *They seem to have discovered a niche in the market.*

niche audience /ˌniːʃ 'ɔːdiəns/ *noun* a small target audience that is highly specific

niche market /ˌniːʃ 'mɑːkɪt/ *noun* a small speciality market, where there is little competition

niche marketing /ˌniːʃ 'mɑːkɪtɪŋ/ *noun* the promotion of a product aimed at one particular area of the market. ➪ **concentrated marketing**

Nielsen Index /'niːlsən ˌɪndeks/ *noun* a US publication belonging to A.C. Nielsen, with a number of different retail and wholesale audit services referring to various types of outlet and different areas of the country

night rate /ˈnaɪt reɪt/ *noun* a cheap rate for telephone calls at night

nixies /ˈnɪksiz/ *plural noun US (informal)* **1.** records that do not match a file correctly **2.** mail returned as unable to be delivered

NLP *abbreviation* neurolinguistic programming

NNP *abbreviation* net national product

no-change discount /nəʊ ˈtʃeɪndʒ ˌdɪskaʊnt/ *noun* a reduction in the price of an advertisement which uses the same artwork as a previous one

noise /nɔɪz/ *noun* a random signal present in addition to any wanted signal, caused by static, temperature, power supply, magnetic or electric fields, and also from stars and the sun

noise level /ˈnɔɪz ˌlev(ə)l/ *noun* the amount of unwanted information found when searching the Internet

nominal ledger /ˌnɒmɪn(ə)l ˈledʒə/ *noun* a book which records a company's transactions in the various accounts

nominal value /ˌnɒmɪn(ə)lˈvæljuː/ *noun* same as **face value**

non- /nɒn/ *prefix* not

non-acceptance /ˌnɒnəkˈseptəns/ *noun* a situation in which the person who is to pay a bill of exchange does not accept it

non-business organisation /nɒn ˌbɪznɪs ˌɔːɡənaɪˈzeɪʃ(ə)n/ *noun US* an organisation (such as a club) which is not allowed by law to make a profit ○ *Though only a non-business organisation, the charity used highly sophisticated marketing techniques.* ○ *He became a fundraiser for a non-business organisation.*

non-delivery /ˌnɒndɪˈlɪv(ə)ri/ *noun* the failure to deliver goods that have been ordered

non-directive interview /nɒn daɪˈrektɪv ˌɪntəvjuː/, **non-directed interview** /nɒndaɪˈrektɪd ˌɪntəvjuː/ *noun* an interview in which the questions are not set in advance and no fixed pattern is followed ○ *Non-directed interviews give candidates a good chance to show their creative potential.*

non-durables /nɒnˈdjʊərəb(ə)lz/, **non-durable goods** /ˌnɒn ˈdjʊə-rəb(ə)l ɡʊdz/ *plural noun* goods which are used up soon after they have been bought, e.g. food or newspapers

non-franchise-building promotion /nɒn ˌfræntʃaɪz ˌbɪldɪŋ prə-ˈməʊʃ(ə)n/ *noun* sales promotion aimed at increasing sales in the short term, without increasing customer loyalty or repeat sales

non-negotiable instrument /ˌnɒn nɪˌɡəʊʃəb(ə)l ˈɪnstrʊmənt/ *noun* a document which cannot be exchanged for cash, e.g. a crossed cheque

non-payment /ˌnɒn ˈpeɪmənt/ *noun* □ **non-payment of a debt** the act of not paying a debt that is due

non-personal /nɒn ˈpɜːs(ə)n(ə)l/ *adjective* which does to apply to an individual person

non-personal channels /nɒn ˌpɜːs(ə)n(ə)l ˈtʃæn(ə)lz/ *plural noun* channels that carry a message without involving any contact between the advertiser and an individual customer

non-price competition /ˌnɒn ˈpraɪs kɒmpəˌtɪʃ(ə)n/ *noun* an attempt to compete in a market through other means than price such as quality of product and promotion

non-profit-making organisation /ˌnɒn ˌprɒfɪtmeɪkɪŋ ˌɔːɡənaɪˈzeɪ-ʃən/, **non-profit organisation** /nɒn ˈprɒfɪt ɔːɡənaɪˌzeɪʃ(ə)n/ *noun* an organisation which is not allowed by law to make a profit ○ *Non-profit-making organisations are exempted from tax.* (NOTE: Non-profit-making organisations include charities, professional associations, trade unions, and religious, arts, community, research, and campaigning bodies. The US term is **nonprofit organization**.)

non-refundable /ˌnɒn rɪˈfʌndəb-(ə)l/ *adjective* not refunded in normal circumstances ○ *You will be asked to make a non-refundable deposit.*

non-returnable /ˌnɒn rɪˈtɜːnəb-(ə)l/ *adjective* which cannot be returned

non-returnable packing /nɒn rɪˌtɜːnəb(ə)l ˈpækɪŋ/ *noun* packing which is to be thrown away when it has been used and not returned to the sender

non-statistical error /nɒn stə-ˌtɪstɪk(ə)l ˈerə/ *noun* a distortion of the results of a survey owing to bias and mistakes made in conducting the survey

non-store retailing /ˌnɒn stɔː ˈriː-teɪlɪŋ/ *noun* the selling of goods and services electronically without setting up a physical shop

non-tariff barriers /ˌnɒn ˈtærɪf ˌbæriəz/ *plural noun* barriers to international trade other than tariffs. They include over-complicated documentation, verification of goods for health and safety reasons and blocked deposits payable by importers to obtain foreign currency. Abbreviation **NTBs**

non-traditional media /ˌnɒn trə-ˌdɪʃ(ə)n(ə)l ˈmiːdiə/ *noun* ➡ **support media**

non-verbal communication /ˌnɒn ˌvɜːb(ə)l kəˌmjuːnɪˈkeɪʃ(ə)n/ *noun* any form of communication that is not expressed in words (NOTE: Non-verbal communication, which includes, for example, body language, silence, failure or slowness to respond to a message, and lateness in arriving for a meeting, is estimated to make up 65–90% of all communication.)

non-virtual hosting /ˌnɒn ˌvɜː-tjuəl ˈhəʊstɪŋ/ *noun* the most basic type of hosting option, often provided free, in which clients do not have their own domain names, but attach their names to the web address of the hosting company (NOTE: This hosting option is only suitable for small companies and has the disadvantage that clients cannot change their hosting company without changing their web address.)

no returns policy /nəʊ rɪˈtɜːnz ˌpɒlɪsi/ *noun* a trading policy where the supplier will not take back unsold merchandise in exchange for credit, and in return allows the retailer an extra discount

normal /ˈnɔːm(ə)l/ *adjective* usual or which happens regularly ○ *Normal deliveries are made on Tuesdays and Fridays.* ○ *Now that supply difficulties have been resolved we hope to resume normal service as soon as possible.* □ **under normal conditions** if things work in the usual way ○ *Under normal conditions a package takes two days to get to Copenhagen.*

normal distribution /ˌnɔːm(ə)l ˌdɪstrɪˈbjuːʃ(ə)n/ *noun* a term used in sampling theory, referring to the results of a sample and meaning a symmetrical distribution of values around a mean or average, so that you can be confident that the sample is properly representative of the people being surveyed in a study

normal price /ˌnɔːm(ə)l ˈpraɪs/ *noun* the price that can be expected for a product under normal market conditions

normal product /ˌnɔːm(ə)l ˈprɒ-dʌkt/ *noun* a product which people buy more of as their incomes rise and less of as their incomes fall

normal profit /ˌnɔːm(ə)l ˈprɒfɪt/ *noun* a minimum profit that can motivate a business to carry on a type of production or selling

note /nəʊt/ *noun* a short document or piece of writing, or a short piece of information ○ *to send someone a note* ○ *I left a note on her desk.* ■ *verb* to notice an advertisement in a publication but not necessarily read or understand it

notice /ˈnəʊtɪs/ *noun* **1.** an official warning that a contract is going to end or that terms are going to be changed □ **until further notice** until different instructions are given ○ *You must pay £200 on the 30th of each month until further notice.* **2.** the time allowed before something takes place ○ *We require three months' notice.* □ **at short notice** with very little warning ○ *The bank manager will not see anyone at short notice.* □ **you must give seven days' notice of withdrawal** you must ask to take money out of the account seven days before you want it

noticeboard /ˈnəʊtɪsbɔːd/ *noun* a board fixed to a wall where notices can be put up ○ *Did you see the new list of prices on the noticeboard?*

noting /ˈnəʊtɪŋ/ *noun* the act of noticing, though not necessarily reading and understanding, an advertisement in a publication

noting score /ˈnəʊtɪŋ skɔː/ *noun* the percentage of total readers who note an advertisement ○ *The* *amount of advertising we will need to do depends on the anticipated noting score.*

novelty /ˈnɒv(ə)lti/ *noun* an original, amusing article which is often bought as a gift ○ *A novelty shop provided paper hats for parties.*

NPD *abbreviation* new product development

NTBs *abbreviation* non-tariff barriers

Nth name a method of selecting sample names at random from a mailing list in regular increments, such as every 10th name. This process is used to test the validity of mailing lists.

null /nʌl/ *adjective* **1.** with no meaning **2.** which cannot legally be enforced □ **the contract was declared null and void** the contract was said to be not valid □ **to render a decision null** to make a decision useless or to cancel it

nullification /ˌnʌlɪfɪˈkeɪʃ(ə)n/ *noun* an act of making something invalid

nullify /ˈnʌlɪfaɪ/ *verb* to make something invalid or to cancel something (NOTE: **nullifying- nullified**)

numeric /njuːˈmerɪk/, **numerical** /njuːˈmerɪk(ə)l/ *adjective* referring to numbers

numeric data /njuːˌmerɪk ˈdeɪtə/ *noun* data in the form of figures

numeric keypad /njuːˌmerɪk ˈkiːpæd/ *noun* the part of a computer keyboard which is a programmable set of numbered keys

O

O & M *abbreviation* organisation and methods

objective /əb'dʒektɪv/ *noun* something which you hope to achieve ○ *The company has achieved its objectives.* ○ *We set the sales forces specific objectives.* ■ *adjective* considered from a general point of view rather than from that of the person involved ○ *You must be objective in assessing the performance of the staff.* ○ *They have been asked to carry out an objective survey of the market.*

objective and task method /əb,dʒektɪv ən 'tɑːsk ,meθəd/ *noun* a method of calculating an advertising appropriation by setting objectives, deciding what tasks are needed to achieve them and then calculating the actual costs involved

obligation /,ɒblɪ'geɪʃ(ə)n/ *noun* **1.** a duty to do something ○ *There is no obligation to help out in another department* ○ *There is no obligation to buy.* □ **two weeks' free trial without obligation** the customer can try the item at home for two weeks without having to buy it at the end of the trial □ **to be under an obligation to do something** to feel it is your duty to do something □ **he is under no contractual obligation to buy** he has signed no contract which forces him to buy **2.** a debt □ **to meet your obligations** to pay your debts

observation method /,ɒbzə'veɪʃən ,meθəd/, **observational research** /ɒbzə,veɪʃ(ə)n(ə)l rɪ'sɜːtʃ/ *noun* a market research method that obtains information through personal observation, rather than interviews ○ *The observation method does not tell you anything about the consumers' attitudes to the product.*

observe /əb'zɜːv/ *verb* to watch or to notice what is happening ○ *Officials have been instructed to observe the conduct of the ballot for union president.*

obsolescence /,ɒbsə'les(ə)ns/ *noun* the process of a product going out of date because of progress in design or technology, and therefore becoming less useful or valuable

obsolescent /,ɒbsə'les(ə)nt/ *adjective* becoming out of date

obsolete /'ɒbsəliːt/ *adjective* no longer used ○ *Computer technology changes so fast that hardware soon becomes obsolete.*

odd /ɒd/ *adjective* one of a group □ **we have a few odd boxes left** we have a few boxes left out of the total shipment □ **to do odd jobs** to do various pieces of work

odd-even pricing /ɒd 'iːv(ə)n ,praɪsɪŋ/ *noun* the practice of using odd numbers such as 0.95 or 0.99 or even numbers such as 1.00 or 2.50 when pricing, because this seems to be most effective psychologically in persuading customers to buy ○ *Students can study the psychological bases of odd-even pricing.*

odd lot /,ɒd 'lɒt/ *noun* a group of miscellaneous items for sale at an auction

oddments /'ɒdmənts/ *plural noun* **1.** items left over **2.** left-over pieces of large items, sold separately

odd size /,ɒd 'saɪz/ *noun* a size which is not usual

OFCOM /'ɒfkɒm/ *noun* the telecommunications regulator in the UK. Formed in 2003, it took over the licensing and regulatory duties formerly undertaken by the Radio Authority, the Broadcasting Standards Commission, the Independent Television Commission, the Office of Telecommunications and the Radiocommunications Agency. Full form **Office of Communications**

off /ɒf/ *adjective* not working or not in operation ○ *to take three days off* ○ *The agreement is off.* ○ *They called the strike off.* ○ *We give the staff four days off at Christmas.* ○ *It's my day off tomorrow.* ■ *adverb* lower than a previous price ○ *The shares closed 2% off.* ■ *preposition* subtracted from ○ *to take £25 off the price* ○ *We give 10% off our usual prices.*

'...its stock closed Monday at $21.875 a share in NYSE composite trading, off 56% from its high last July' [*Wall Street Journal*]

off-card rate /ˌɒf ˈkɑːd ˌreɪt/ *noun* a specially arranged price, lower than that on the rate card, for advertising space or time ○ *The newspaper offered us an off-card rate for space which was still empty the day before publication.*

offensive spending /əˌfensɪv ˈspendɪŋ/ *noun* spending on advertising which aims to attract users of a rival brand or to attack the competition

offer /ˈɒfə/ *noun* **1.** a statement that you are willing to give or do something, especially to pay a specific amount of money to buy something ○ *to make an offer for a company* ○ *We made an offer of £10 a share.* ○ *We made a written offer for the house.* ○ *£1,000 is the best offer I can make.* ○ *We accepted an offer of £1,000 for the car.* □ **the house is under offer** someone has made an offer to buy the house and the offer has been accepted provisionally □ **we are open to offers** we are ready to discuss the price which we are asking □ **or near offer** *US*, **or best offer** or an offer of a price which is slightly less than the price asked (often shortened to **o.n.o.** or **o.b.o.**) ○ *The car is for sale at £2,000 or near offer.* **2.** a statement that you are willing to sell something □ **offer for sale** a situation where a company advertises new shares for sale to the public as a way of launching the company on the Stock Exchange. The other ways of launching a company are a 'tender' or a 'placing'. **3.** a statement that you are willing to employ someone □ **she received six offers of jobs** *or* **six job offers** six companies told her she could have a job with them ■ *verb* **1.** to say that you are willing to pay a specific amount of money for something ○ *to offer someone £100,000 for their house* ○ *She offered £10 a share.* **2.** to say that you are willing to sell something ○ *They are offering special prices on winter holidays in the US* ○ *We offered the house for sale.*

Office of Communications /ˌɒfɪs əv kəˌmjuːnɪˈkeɪʃ(ə)nz/ *noun* full form of **OFCOM**

Office of Fair Trading /ˌɒfɪs əv feə ˈtreɪdɪŋ/ *noun* a department of the UK government that protects consumers against unfair or illegal business. Abbreviation **OFT**

office park /ˈbɪznɪs pɑːk/ *noun* same as **business park**

official receiver /əˌfɪʃ(ə)l rɪˈsiːvə/ *noun* a government official who is appointed to run a company which is in financial difficulties, to pay off its debts as far as possible and to close it down ○ *The company is in the hands of the official receiver.* Also called **receiver**

off-licence /ˈɒf ˌlaɪs(ə)ns/ *noun* **1.** a shop which sells alcohol for drinking at home **2.** a licence to sell alcohol for drinking away from the place where you buy it

offline /ˌɒf ˈlaɪn/ *adverb* not connected to a network or central computer

offload /ɒfˈləʊd/ *verb* to pass something which you do not want to someone else (NOTE: You offload something **from** a thing or person **on to** another thing or person.) □ **to offload excess stock** to try to sell excess stock □ **to offload costs on to a subsidiary company** to try to get a subsidiary company to pay some charges so as to reduce tax

off-peak /ˌɒf ˈpiːk/ *adjective* not during the most busy time

off-peak period /ɒf ˈpiːk ˌpɪəriəd/ *noun* the time when business is less busy

off-price label /ɒf ˈpraɪs ˌleɪb(ə)l/ *noun* a label on a product which shows a reduced price

off-season /ˈɒf ˌsiːz(ə)n/ *noun* the less busy season for travel, usually during the winter ○ *Air fares are cheaper in the off-season.*

offset /ˈɒfset/ *noun* a method of printing from a plate to a rubber surface and then to paper

offset lithography /ˌɒfset lɪˈθɒɡrəfi/ *noun* a printing process used for printing books, where the ink sticks to image areas on the plate and is transferred to an offset cylinder from which it is printed on to the paper

off-the-page /ˌɒf ðə ˈpeɪdʒ/ *adjective* referring to a sale made as a direct result of an print advertisement. Abbreviation **OTP**

off-the-page buying /ˌɒf ðə ˈpeɪdʒ ˌbaɪɪŋ/ *noun* the buying of items which have been advertised in magazines or newspapers

off-the-peg /ˌɒf ðə ˈpeɡ/ *adjective, adverb* made in standard sizes, and not fitted specially ○ *She buys all her clothes off-the-peg.*

off-the-peg research /ˌɒf ðə peɡ rɪˈsɜːtʃ/ *noun* the practice of taking research which has already been carried out in another context, and using it as the basis for taking particular decisions

off-the-screen /ˌɒf ðə ˈskriːn/ *adjective* referring to a sale made as a direct result of a television advertisement

OFT *abbreviation* Office of Fair Trading

oil-exporting country /ˈɔɪl ɪkˌspɔːtɪŋ ˌkʌntri/ *noun* a country which produces oil and sells it to others

OINK /ɔɪŋk/ *abbr* a demographic term which describes a professional person with no children. Full form **one income, no kids**

OIRO /ɔɪrəʊ/ *abbr* a term often seen in classified advertisements ○ *The advertisement said 'house for sale. OIRO £500k'.* Full form **offer(s) in the region of**

oligopoly /ˌɒlɪˈɡɒpəli/ *noun* a situation where only a few sellers control the market ○ *An oligopoly means that prices can be kept high.*

oligopsony /ˌɒlɪˈɡɒpsəni/ *noun* a situation where only a few buyers control the market

omnibus advertisement /ˈɒmnɪbəs ədˌvɜːtɪsmənt/ *noun* an advertisement which covers several different products

omnibus agreement /ˈɒmnɪbəs əˌɡriːmənt/ *noun* an agreement which covers many different items

omnibus research /ˈɒmnɪbəs rɪˌsɜːtʃ/, **omnibus survey** /ˈɒmnɪbəs ˌsɜːveɪ/ *noun* a survey to which several companies subscribe, each adding specific questions of its own

oncosts /ˈɒnkɒsts/ *plural noun* business costs that cannot be charged directly to a particular good or service and must be apportioned across the business

one-sided /ˌwʌn ˈsaɪdɪd/ *adjective* favouring one side and not the other in a negotiation

one-sided message /wʌn ˌsaɪdɪd ˈmesɪdʒ/ *noun* a message which only gives the benefits of a product or service

one-step approach /ˌwʌn ˈstep əˌprəʊtʃ/ *noun* a form of direct marketing where advertisements are used to obtain orders directly

one-stop /ˈwʌn stɒp/ *adjective* offering a wide range of services to a customer, not necessarily services which are related to the product or services which the company normally sells

one-stop shopping centre /ˌwʌn stɒp ˈʃɒpɪŋ ˌsentə/ *noun* a shopping centre with a comprehensive choice of shops and supermarkets, designed to cover all of a customer's shopping needs

one-time order /ˌwʌn taɪm ˈɔːdə/ *noun* an order for an advertising spot for a particular time which is not scheduled to be repeated

one-time rate /wʌn ˈtaɪm reɪt/ *noun* a special rate for an advertisement that is only placed once

one-to-one /ˌwʌn tə ˈwʌn/ *adjective* where one person has to deal with one other person only

one-to-one marketing /ˌwʌn tə wʌn ˈmɑːkɪtɪŋ/ *noun* marketing through a website which aims to establish a personal relationship with a customer, selling to each customer as an individual and trying to differentiate between customers

on-hold advertising /ˌɒn ˈhəʊld ˌædvətaɪzɪŋ/ *noun* advertising to telephone callers while they are waiting to be connected to the person they want to speak to, usually involving voice messages about the firm and its products

online /ɒnˈlaɪn//ˈɒnlaɪn/ *adjective, adverb* linked via a computer directly to another computer, a computer network or, especially, the Internet; on the Internet ○ *The sales office is online to the warehouse.* ○ *We get our data online from the stock control department.*

'…there may be a silver lining for 'clicks-and-mortar' stores that have both an online and a high street presence. Many of these are accepting returns of goods purchased online at their traditional stores. This is a service that may make them more popular as consumers become more experienced online shoppers' [*Financial Times*]

'…a survey found that even among experienced users – those who shop online at least once a month – about 10% abandoned a planned purchase because of annoying online delays and procedures' [*Financial Times*]

'…some online brokers failed to foresee the huge increase in private dealing and had problems coping with the rising volume. It has been the year when private investors were able to trade online quickly, cheaply, and on the whole, with little bother' [*Financial Times*]

online community /ˌɒnlaɪn kəˈmjuːnɪti/ *noun* a network of people who communicate with one another and with an organisation through interactive tools such as email, discussion boards and chat systems

online reputation management /ˌɒnlaɪn ˌrepjʊˈteɪʃə)n ˌmænɪdʒmənt/ *noun* the process of monitoring the Internet reputation of a person, brand, or business, by controlling messages placed about them and either suppressing negative mentions entirely or pushing them lower on search engine results pages

online shopping /ˌɒnlaɪn ˈʃɒpɪŋ/ *noun* same as **electronic shopping**

online shopping mall /ˌɒnlaɪn ˈʃɒpɪŋ mɔːl/ *noun* same as **cyber mall**

ONO *abbr* a term often seen in classified advertisements ○ *Our car is for sale for £10,000 ONO.* Full form **or nearest offer**

on-pack promotion /ˌɒn ˈpæk prəˌməʊʃ(ə)n/ *noun* advertising material on the outside of packaged goods ○ *We use on-pack promotion to stimulate buying at the point-of-sale.* ○ *Our on-pack promotion is designed to complement the TV advertising campaign.*

op-ed /ˌɒp ˈed/ *noun* in a newspaper, a page that has signed articles expressing personal opinions, usually found opposite the editorial page

open /ˈəʊpən/ *adjective* ready to accept something □ **the job is open to all applicants** anyone can apply for the job □ **open to offers** ready to accept a reasonable offer □ **the company is open to offers for the empty factory** the company is ready to discuss an offer which is lower than the suggested price ■ *verb* to start a new business ○ *She has opened a shop in the High Street.* ○ *We have opened a branch in London.*

'…after opening at 79.1 the index touched a peak of 79.2 and then drifted to a low of 78.8' [*Financial Times*]

open up *phrasal verb* □ **to open up new markets** to work to start business in markets where such business has not been done before

open account /ˌəʊpən əˈkaʊnt/ *noun* an account where the supplier offers the purchaser credit without security

open-air market /ˌəʊpən eə ˈmɑːkɪt/ *noun* a market which is held on stalls in the open air

open cheque /ˌəʊpən ˈtʃek/ *noun* same as **uncrossed cheque**

open communication /ˌəʊpən kəmjuːnɪˈkeɪʃ(ə)n/ *noun* a policy intended to ensure that employees are able to find out everything they want to know about their organisation

open credit /ˌəʊpən ˈkredɪt/ *noun* credit given to good customers without security

open dating /ˌəʊpən ˈdeɪtɪŋ/ *noun* the practice of putting the sell-by date on a packet in an uncoded form which can be understood by the consumers ○ *Open dating is considered by many to be an important feature of consumer protection in food products.*

open-door policy /ˌəʊpən ˈdɔː ˌpɒlɪsi/ *noun* a policy in which a country accepts imports from all other countries on equal terms

open-end /ˌəʊpən ˈend/ *adjective* US same as **open-ended**

open-ended /ˌəʊpən ˈendɪd/ *adjective* with no fixed limit or with some items not specified ○ *They signed* *an open-ended agreement.* ○ *The candidate was offered an open-ended contract with a good career plan.* (NOTE: The US term is **open-end**.)

open-ended credit /ˌəʊpən ˌendɪd ˈkredɪt/ *noun* same as **revolving credit**

open-ended question /ˌəʊpən endɪd ˈkwestʃən/ *noun* a question in a questionnaire which allows respondents to answer in some detail as they like without having simply to say 'yes' or 'no' ○ *Open-ended questions elicit answers that are original but hard to evaluate.* ○ *An open-ended question is needed here, since the question involves the respondent's personal feelings.*

open general licence /ˌəʊpən ˌdʒen(ə)rəl ˈlaɪs(ə)ns/ *noun* an import licence for all goods which are subject to special import restrictions

opening /ˈəʊp(ə)nɪŋ/ *noun* **1.** the act of starting a new business ○ *the opening of a new branch* ○ *the opening of a new market* or *of a new distribution network* **2.** an available job ○ *She's applied for the opening in the sales department.* **3.** an opportunity to do something ■ *adjective* being at the beginning, or the first of several

opening balance /ˈəʊp(ə)nɪŋ ˌbæləns/ *noun* a balance at the beginning of an accounting period

opening bid /ˌəʊp(ə)nɪŋ ˈbɪd/ *noun* the first bid at an auction

opening entry /ˈəʊp(ə)nɪŋ ˌentri/ *noun* the first entry in an account

opening hours /ˈəʊp(ə)nɪŋ ˌaʊəz/ *plural noun* the hours when a shop or business is open

opening sentence /ˌəʊp(ə)nɪŋ ˈsentəns/ *noun* the first sentence in an email

opening stock /ˌəʊp(ə)nɪŋ ˈstɒk/ *noun* on a balance sheet, the closing stock at the end of one accounting period that is transferred forward and becomes the opening stock in the one that follows (NOTE: The US term is **beginning inventory**.)

open market /ˌəʊpən ˈmɑːkɪt/ *noun* a market where anyone can buy or sell

open pricing /ˌəʊpən ˈpraɪsɪŋ/ *noun* the attempt by companies to achieve some cooperation and conformity in pricing ○ *Representatives from the major companies in the industry are meeting to establish an open-pricing policy.*

open rate /ˈəʊpən reɪt/ *noun* an advertising rate where discounts are available for frequent or bulk orders

open standard /ˌəʊpən ˈstændəd/ *noun* a standard that allows computers and similar pieces of equipment made by different manufacturers to operate with each other

operant conditioning /ˈɒpərənt kənˌdɪʃ(ə)nɪŋ/ *noun* a learning theory stating that behaviour can be modified by stimuli and also by the consequences which follow on from the behaviour itself. Also called **instrumental conditioning**

operate /ˈɒpəreɪt/ *verb* **1.** to be in force ○ *The new terms of service will operate from January 1st.* ○ *The rules operate on inland postal services only.* **2.** to make something work or function □ **to operate a machine** to make a machine work ○ *He is learning to operate the new telephone switchboard.*

'…the company gets valuable restaurant locations which will be converted to the family-style restaurant chain that it operates and franchises throughout most parts of the US' [*Fortune*]

operating /ˈɒpəreɪtɪŋ/ *noun* the general running of a business or of a machine

'…the company blamed over-capacity and competitive market conditions in Europe for a £14m operating loss last year' [*Financial Times*]

operating budget /ˈɒpəreɪtɪŋ ˌbʌdʒɪt/ *noun* a forecast of income and expenditure over a period of time

operating manual /ˈɒpəreɪtɪŋ ˌmænjuəl/ *noun* a book which shows how to work a machine

operating statement /ˈɒpəreɪtɪŋ ˌsteɪtmənt/ *noun* a financial statement which shows a company's expenditure and income, and consequently its final profit or loss ○ *The operating statement shows unexpected electricity costs.* ○ *Let's look at the operating statement to find last month's expenditure.*

operating supplies /ˈɒpəreɪtɪŋ səˌplaɪz/ *plural noun* low-priced industrial products that are normally bought by producers ○ *Production came to a standstill for lack of operating supplies.* ○ *We are now ordering operating supplies for next month's production.*

operating system /ˈɒpəreɪtɪŋ ˌsɪstəm/ *noun* the main program which operates a computer

operation /ˌɒpəˈreɪʃ(ə)n/ *noun* an activity or a piece of work, or the task of running something ○ *the company's operations in West Africa* ○ *He heads up the operations in Northern Europe.*

'…a leading manufacturer of business, industrial and commercial products requires a branch manager to head up its mid-western Canada operations based in Winnipeg' [*Globe and Mail (Toronto)*]

operational /ˌɒpəˈreɪʃ(ə)nəl/ *adjective* **1.** referring to the day-to-day activities of a business or to the way in which something is run **2.** working or in operation

operational budget /ˌɒpəreɪʃ(ə)nəl ˈbʌdʒɪt/ *noun* same as **operating budget**

operational costs /ˌɒpəreɪʃ(ə)nəl ˈkɒsts/ *plural noun* the costs of running a business

operational planning /ˌɒpəreɪʃ(ə)nəl ˈplænɪŋ/ *noun* the planning of how a business is to be run

operational research /ˌɒpəreɪʃ(ə)nəl rɪˈsɜːtʃ/ *noun* a study of a company's way of working to see if it can be made more efficient and profitable

operations review /ˌɒpəˈreɪʃ(ə)nz rɪˌvjuː/ *noun* an act of examining the way in which a company or department works to see how it can be made more efficient and profitable

opinion-former /əˈpɪnjən ˌfɔːmə/, **opinion-leader** /əˈpɪnjən ˌliːdə/ *noun* someone well known whose opinions influence others in society ○ *A pop-star is the ideal opinion-leader if we are aiming at the teenage market.* ○ *The celebrity used in the sales promotion campaign was not respected enough to be a true opinion-former.*

opinion-leader research /əˌpɪnjən liːdə rɪˈsɜːtʃ/ *noun* research into the attitudes of opinion-leaders

opinion poll /əˈpɪnjən pəʊl/ *noun* the activity of asking a sample group of people what their opinion is, so as to guess the opinion of the whole population ○ *Opinion polls showed that the public preferred butter to margarine.* ○ *Before starting the new service, the company carried out nationwide opinion polls.*

opinion shopping /əˈpɪnjən ˌʃɒpɪŋ/ *noun* the practice of trying to find an auditor who interprets the law in the same way that the company does, is likely to view the company's actions sympathetically, and will approve the company's financial statements, even if the company has been involved in dealings that other auditors might consider questionable

opportunities to see /ˌɒpəˌtjuːnɪtiz tə ˈsiː/ *plural noun* the number of opportunities an average member of the target audience will have to see an advertisement. Abbreviation **OTS**

opportunity /ˌɒpəˈtjuːnɪti/ *noun* a chance to do something successfully

'…the group is currently undergoing a period of rapid expansion and this has created an exciting opportunity for a qualified accountant' [*Financial Times*]

opportunity and threat analysis /ˌɒpəˌtjuːnɪti ən ˈθret əˌnæləsɪs/ *noun* a company's analysis of both the advantages and disadvantages in its situation, done in order to ensure sound strategic planning

opportunity cost /ˌɒpəˈtjuːnɪti kɒst/ *noun* the cost of a business initiative in terms of profits that could have been gained through an alternative plan ○ *It's a good investment plan and we will not be deterred by the opportunity cost.* Also called **alternative cost**

optimal /ˈɒptɪm(ə)l/ *adjective* best

optimal balance /ˌɒptɪm(ə)l ˈbæləns/ *noun* the best combination of elements or activities that can be achieved in a marketing mix ○ *If it achieves optimal balance the company will soon be a market leader.*

opt-in /ˈɒpt ɪn/ *noun* a method by which users can register with a website if they want to receive particular information or services from it. In opt-in, users must provide their email addresses, so that the website owner can send them emails.

opt-in mailing list /ˌɒpt ɪn ˈmeɪlɪŋ lɪst/ *noun* a list of email addresses in which each recipient has specifically asked to receive advertising email messages, normally so that they can keep up to date with a topic or industry

option /ˈɒpʃən/ *noun* the opportunity to buy or sell something, such as a security, within a fixed period of time at a fixed price □ **to have first option on something** to have the right to be the first to have the possibility of deciding something □ **to grant someone a six-month option on a product** to allow someone six months to decide if they want to manufacture the product □ **to take up an option** *or* **to exercise an option** to accept the option which has been offered and to put it into action ○ *They exercised their option* or *they took up their option to acquire sole marketing rights to the product.* □ **I want to leave my options open** I want to be able to decide what to do when the time is right

optional /ˈɒpʃ(ə)n(ə)l/ *adjective* able to be done or not done, taken or not taken, as a person chooses ○ *The insurance cover is optional.*

optional extra /ˌɒpʃən(ə)l ˈekstrə/ *noun* an item that is not essential but can be added if wanted

opt out /ˌɒpt ˈaʊt/ *noun* **1.** the action of asking not to receive advertising email messages and being removed from an email list **2.** a type of permission marketing where the customer can decide whether or not to reject further promotional messages from a marketer. Often this option appears as a tick box on a reply coupon or response email.

OR *abbreviation* operational research

oral contract /ˌɔːrəl ˈkɒntrækt/ *noun* a type of business agreement that is spoken, not written down and is legally binding even though the terms of the contract can be difficult to prove in the event of a breach

orange goods /ˈɒrɪndʒ ɡʊdz/ *plural noun* goods which are not bought as often as fast-moving items but are replaced from time to time, e.g. clothing. Compare **red goods, yellow goods**

orbit /ˈɔːbɪt/ *noun* the practice of rotating advertisements among different programmes on a TV station

order /ˈɔːdə/ *noun* **1.** an official request for goods to be supplied ○ *to give someone an order* or *to place an order with someone for twenty tablet computers* □ **to fill an order, to fulfil an order** to supply items which have been ordered ○ *We are so understaffed we cannot fulfil any more orders before Christmas.* □ **items available to order only** items which will be manufactured only if someone orders them □ **on order** ordered but not delivered ○ *This item is out of stock, but is on order.* **2.** an item which has been ordered ○ *The order is to be delivered to our warehouse.* **3.** an instruction **4.** a document which allows money to be paid to someone ○ *She sent us an order on the Chartered Bank.* **5.** □ **pay to Mr Smith or order** pay money to Mr Smith or as he orders □ **pay to the order of Mr Smith** pay money directly to Mr Smith or to his account ■ *verb* **1.** to ask for goods to be supplied ○ *They ordered a new Rolls Royce for the managing director.* **2.** to give an official request for something to be done or for something to be supplied ○ *to order twenty laptops to be delivered to the warehouse*

order book /ˈɔːdə bʊk/ *noun* a book which records orders received

order confirmation /ˈɔːdə kɒnfˌmeɪʃ(ə)n/ *noun* an email message informing a purchaser that an order has been received

order form /ˈɔːdə fɔːm/ *noun* a pad of blank forms for orders to be written on

order fulfilment /ˈɔːdə fʊlˌfɪlmənt/ *noun* the process of supplying items which have been ordered

order number /ˈɔːdə ˌnʌmbə/ *noun* the reference number printed on an order

order picking /ˈɔːdə ˌpɪkɪŋ/ *noun* the process of collecting various items in a warehouse in order to make up an order to be sent to a customer

order taking /ˈɔːdə ˌteɪkɪŋ/ *noun* the action of taking an order, the main responsibility of the salesperson

organic listings /ɔːˈɡænɪk ˌlɪstɪŋz/ *plural noun* same as **natural listings**

organisation /ˌɔːɡənaɪˈzeɪʃ(ə)n/, **organization** noun **1.** a way of arranging something so that it works efficiently ○ *the organisation of the head office into departments* ○ *The chairman handles the organisation of the AGM.* ○ *The organisation of the group is too centralised to be efficient.* **2.** a group or institution which is arranged for efficient work

'…working with a client base which includes many major commercial organizations and nationalized industries' [*Times*]

organisational buying /ˌɔːɡənaɪ-ˈzeɪʃ(ə)nəl ˌbaɪɪŋ/ noun buying by a large organisation, such as a company or government department, as opposed to purchases by individual consumers

organisational chart /ˌɔːɡənaɪ-ˈzeɪʃ(ə)n(ə)l tʃɑːt/ noun a chart that shows the relationships of people in an organisation in terms of their areas of authority and responsibility

organisation and methods /ˌɔːɡənaɪzeɪʃ(ə)n ən ˈmeθədz/ noun a process of examining how an office works, and suggesting how it can be made more efficient. Abbreviation **O & M**

organisation chart /ˌɔːɡən-aɪˈzeɪʃ(ə)n tʃɑːt/ noun same as **organisational chart**

organise /ˈɔːɡənaɪz/, **organize** verb to set up a system for doing something ○ *The company is organised into six profit centres.* ○ *The group is organised by sales areas.*

'…we organize a rate with importers who have large orders and guarantee them space at a fixed rate so that they can plan their costs' [*Lloyd's List*]

organised market /ˌɔːɡənaɪzd ˈmɑːkɪt/ noun a market controlled by regulations set down by government or an official organisation ○ *The government feels that an organised market is not conducive to business initiative.*

orientation /ˌɔːriənˈteɪʃ(ə)n/ noun the main interest or type of activity ○ *The company's orientation is towards production and it has little marketing experience.*

oriented /ˈɔːriəntɪd/, **orientated** /ˈɔːriənteɪtɪd/ adjective interested in or involved with ○ *Our strategy is ori-*

ented towards achieving further growth in the export market. ○ *The promotion is entirely product-oriented.*

origin /ˈɒrɪdʒɪn/ noun the place where something or someone originally comes from ○ *spare parts of European origin*

original /əˈrɪdʒən(ə)l/ adjective which was used or made first ○ *They sent a copy of the original invoice.* ○ *He kept the original receipt for reference.* ■ noun the first copy made ○ *Send the original and file two copies.*

originally /əˈrɪdʒən(ə)li/ adverb first or at the beginning

original purchase /əˌrɪdʒən(ə)l ˈpɜːtʃɪs/ noun a copy of a magazine or newspaper which is actually bought by the reader, rather than simply read by them

OS abbreviation outsize

O/S abbreviation out of stock

OTO abbreviation one time only

OTS abbreviation opportunities to see

outbid /aʊtˈbɪd/ verb to offer a better price than someone else ○ *We offered £100,000 for the warehouse, but another company outbid us.* (NOTE: **outbidding – outbid**)

outdoor /aʊtˈdɔː/ adjective in the open air

outdoor advertising /ˈaʊtdɔːr ˌædvətaɪzɪŋ/ noun **1.** advertising on the outside of a building or in the open air, using posters on hoardings or neon signs **2.** advertising in the open air, including advertising in public transport, on roadsides, at bus stops, skywriting, etc.

outer /ˈaʊtə/ noun a piece of packaging which covers items which already are in packages

outer pack /ˈaʊtə pæk/ noun a container which holds a number of smaller packaged items ○ *The goods are sold in outer packs, each containing twenty packets.*

outlet /ˈaʊtlət/ noun a place where something can be sold

out-of-date /ˌaʊt əv ˈdeɪt/ adjective, adverb old-fashioned or no longer modern ○ *Their computer system is years out of date.* ○ *They're still using out-of-date equipment.*

out-of-home advertising /ˌaʊt əv ˈhəʊm ˌædvətaɪzɪŋ/ *noun* outdoor advertising including transport, skywriting, etc.

out of stock /ˌaʊt əv ˈstɒk/ *adjective, adverb* with no stock left ○ *Those books are temporarily out of stock.* ○ *Several out-of-stock items have been on order for weeks.* Abbreviation **O/S**

output /ˈaʊtpʊt/ *noun* the amount which a company, person, or machine produces ○ *Output has increased by 10%.* ○ *25% of our output is exported.*

'…crude oil output plunged during the last month and is likely to remain near its present level for the near future' [*Wall Street Journal*]

output bonus /ˈaʊtpʊt ˌbəʊnəs/, **output-based bonus** /ˌaʊtpʊt beɪst ˈbəʊnəs/ *noun* an extra payment for increased production

output per hour /ˌaʊtpʊt pər ˈaʊə/ *noun* the amount of something produced in one hour

output tax /ˈaʊtpʊt tæks/ *noun* VAT charged by a company on goods or services sold, and which the company pays to the government

outsell /aʊtˈsel/ *verb* to sell more than someone ○ *The company is easily outselling its competitors.* (NOTE: **outselling – outsold**)

outside broadcast /ˌaʊtsaɪd ˈbrɔːdkɑːst/ *noun* a programme not transmitted from a studio

outside poster /ˌaʊtsaɪd ˈpəʊstə/ *noun* a poster on public transport such as buses, taxis, trains, and the underground

outsize /ˈaʊtsaɪz/ *noun* a size which is larger than usual. Abbreviation **OS** □ **outsize order** a very large order

outsource /ˈaʊtsɔːs/ *verb* to use a source outside a company or business to do the work that is needed

'The services unit won outsourcing contracts from the Environmental Protection Agency and NASA, which the company says played a significant part in the increase.' [*Information Week*]

outsourcing /ˈaʊtsɔːsɪŋ/ *noun* the transfer of work previously done by employees of an organisation to another organisation, usually one that specialises in that type of work (NOTE: Things that have usually been outsourced in the

past include legal services, transport, catering, and security, but nowadays IT services, training, and public relations are often added to the list.)

'…organizations in the public and private sectors are increasingly buying in specialist services – or outsourcing – allowing them to cut costs and concentrate on their core business activities' [*Financial Times*]

outstanding /aʊtˈstændɪŋ/ *adjective* not yet paid or completed □ **outstanding debts** debts which are waiting to be paid □ **outstanding orders** orders received but not yet supplied □ **what is the amount outstanding?** how much money is still owed? □ **matters outstanding from the previous meeting** questions which were not settled at the previous meeting

outward mission /ˌaʊtwəd ˈmɪʃ(ə)n/ *noun* a visit by a group of businesspeople to a foreign country

over- /əʊvə/ *prefix* more than □ **shop which caters for the over-60s** a shop which has goods which appeal to people who are more than sixty years old

overall /ˌəʊvərˈɔːl/ *adjective* covering or including everything □ **the company reported an overall fall in profits** the company reported a general fall in profits □ **overall plan** a plan which covers everything

overcharge ■ *noun*/ˈəʊvətʃɑːdʒ/ a charge which is higher than it should be ○ *to pay back an overcharge* ■ *verb*/ˌəʊvəˈtʃɑːdʒ/ to ask someone for too much money ○ *They overcharged us for our meals.* ○ *We asked for a refund because we'd been overcharged.*

overhead /ˈəʊvəhed/ *noun US* same as **overheads**

overhead budget /ˌəʊvəhed ˈbʌdʒɪt/ *noun* a plan of probable overhead costs

overhead costs /ˌəʊvəhed ˈkɒsts/, **overhead expenses** /ˌəʊvəhed ɪkˈspensɪz/ *plural noun* same as **overheads**

overheads /ˈəʊvəhedz/ *plural noun* the indirect costs of the day-to-day running of a business, i.e. not money spent of producing goods, but money spent on such things as renting or maintaining buildings and machinery ○ *The sales* *revenue covers the manufacturing costs but not the overheads.* (NOTE: The US term is **overhead**.)

overkill /ˈəʊvəkɪl/ *noun* a very intensive and expensive marketing campaign which has the effect of putting potential customers off

overlay /ˈəʊvəleɪ/ *noun* a transparent plastic sheet placed over artwork with instructions for changing it, or showing the artwork is to be printed

overmatter /ˈəʊvəmætə/, **over-setting** /ˈəʊvəsetɪŋ/ *noun* text which, when it is typeset, is too long for the space available

overpayment /ˌəʊvəˈpeɪmənt/ *noun* an act of paying too much

overprice /ˌəʊvəˈpraɪs/ *verb* to give a higher price to something than seems reasonable

overpricing /ˌəʊvəˈpraɪsɪŋ/ *noun* the charging of a higher price than is justified by demand ○ *Overpricing led to the producer being priced out of the market.*

overprint /ˌəʊvəˈprɪnt/ *verb* to print text on paper which already contains printed matter ○ *The retailer's name and address is overprinted on the catalogue.* ○ *We will overprint the catalogue with the retailer's name and address.*

overproduce /ˌəʊvəprəˈdjuːs/ *verb* to produce too much of a product

overproduction /ˌəʊvəprəˈdʌkʃən/ *noun* the manufacturing of too much of a product

overrider /ˈəʊvəraɪdə/, **overriding commission** /ˌəʊvəraɪdɪŋ kəˈmɪʃ(ə)n/ *noun* a special extra commission which is above all other commissions

overseas *adjective* /ˈəʊvəsiːz/ *adverb* /ˌəʊvəˈsiːz/ across the sea, or to or in foreign countries ○ *Management trainees knew that they would be sent overseas to learn about the export markets.* ○ *Some workers are going overseas to find new jobs.* ■ *noun* /ˈəʊvəsiːz//ˌəʊvəˈsiːz/ foreign countries ○ *The profits from overseas are far higher than those of the home division.*

overseas division /ˌəʊvəsiːz dɪˈvɪʒ(ə)n/ *noun* the section of a com-

pany dealing with trade with other countries

overseas markets /ˌəʊvəsiːz ˈmaːkɪts/ *plural noun* markets in foreign countries

oversell /ˌəʊvəˈsel/ *verb* to sell more than you can produce (NOTE: **overselling – oversold**) □ **he is oversold** he has agreed to sell more product than he can produce □ **the market is oversold** stock-market prices are too low, because there have been too many sellers

overspend /ˌəʊvəˈspend/ *verb* to spend too much (NOTE: **overspending – overspent**)

overstock /ˌəʊvəˈstɒk/ *verb* to have a bigger stock of something than is needed □ **to be overstocked with spare parts** to have too many spare parts in stock

'Cash paid for your stock: any quantity, any products, overstocked lines, factory seconds' [*Australian Financial Review*]

overstocks /ˈəʊvəstɒks/ *plural noun* US a surplus of stock ○ *We will have to sell off the overstocks to make room in the warehouse.*

over-the-counter sales /ˌəʊvə ðə ˈkaʊntə ˌseɪlz/ *plural noun* the legal selling of shares that are not listed in the official stock exchange list, usually carried out by telephone

overweight /ˌəʊvəˈweɪt/ *adjective* □ **the package is sixty grams overweight** the package weighs sixty grams too much

own brand /ˌəʊn ˈbrænd/ *noun* the name of a store which is used on products which are specially packed for that store

own-brand goods /ˌəʊn brænd ˈɡʊdz/ *plural noun* products specially packed for a store with the store's name on them

owner /ˈəʊnə/ *noun* a person who owns something ○ *The owners of a company are its shareholders.* □ **goods sent at owner's risk** a situation where the owner has to insure the goods while they are being transported

own label /ˌəʊn ˈleɪb(ə)l/ *noun* goods specially produced for a store with the store's name on them

own-label goods /ˌəʊn ˌleɪb(ə)l ˈɡʊdz/ *plural noun* goods specially produced for a store with the store's name on them

'...the company is hunting for a marketing director as part of an effort to expand its non-food division and introduce own-label. It will also review its entire own-label ranges and look at the possibility of rolling out the non-food division own-label brands' [*Marketing Week*]

'...its survey of brand development indicates that whereas branded goods appeal to over-45 year olds, supermarket own-label goods are favoured by consumers under the age of 34' [*Marketing Week*]

P

P2P /ˌpiː tə ˈpiː/ *adjective* used to describe a file-sharing connection between computer users, without a central server being involved. Full form **peer-to-peer**

pack /pæk/ *noun* items put together in a container or shrink-wrapped for selling □ **items sold in packs of 200** items sold in boxes containing 200 items □ **blister pack** *or* **bubble pack** a type of packing where the item for sale is covered with a stiff plastic cover sealed to a card backing ■ *verb* to put things into a container for selling or sending ○ *to pack goods into cartons* ○ *Your order has been packed and is ready for shipping.* ○ *The biscuits are packed in plastic wrappers.*

package /ˈpækɪdʒ/ *noun* **1.** goods packed and wrapped for sending by mail ○ *The Post Office does not accept bulky packages.* ○ *The goods are to be sent in airtight packages.* **2.** a group of different items joined together in one deal **3.** a group of TV or radio programmes or commercial spots offered with a discount by a station ■ *verb* **1.** □ **to package goods** to wrap and pack goods in an attractive way **2.** □ **to package holidays** to sell a holiday package including travel, hotels, and food

'…airlines offer special stopover rates and hotel packages to attract customers to certain routes' [*Business Traveller*]

'…the remuneration package will include an attractive salary, profit sharing and a company car' [*Times*]

'…airlines will book not only tickets but also hotels and car hire to provide a complete package' [*Business Traveller*]

packaged /ˈpækɪdʒd/ *adjective* put into a package ○ *packaged goods*

'…in today's fast-growing packaged goods area many companies are discovering that a well-

recognized brand name can be a priceless asset' [*Duns Business Month*]

package deal /ˈpækɪdʒ ˌdiːl/ *noun* an agreement which covers several different things at the same time ○ *They agreed a package deal which involves the construction of the factory, training of staff, and purchase of the product.*

package holiday /ˌpækɪdʒ ˈhɒlɪdeɪ/, **packaged holiday** *noun* a holiday whose price includes transport and accommodation, and sometimes also meals ○ *The travel company is arranging a package holiday to the international trade fair.*

packaging /ˈpækɪdʒɪŋ/ *noun* **1.** the act of putting things into packages **2.** material used to protect goods which are being packed ○ *bubble wrap and other packaging material* ○ *The fruit is sold in airtight packaging.* **3.** material used to wrap goods for display

'…the consumer wants to be challenged by more individual products and more innovative packaging' [*Marketing*]

'…promotional packaging can mean rethinking more than just the pack graphics' [*Marketing*]

packer /ˈpækə/ *noun* a person who packs goods

packet /ˈpækɪt/ *noun* a small box of goods for selling ○ *Can you get me a packet of cigarettes?* ○ *She bought a packet of biscuits.* ○ *We need two packets of filing cards.* □ **item sold in packets of 20** items are sold in boxes containing 20 items each

packing /ˈpækɪŋ/ *noun* **1.** the act of putting goods into boxes and wrapping them for shipping ○ *What is the cost of the packing?* ○ *Packing is included in the price.* **2.** material used to protect goods ○ *packed in airtight packing* ○ *The fruit is packed in airtight packing.*

packing case /'pækɪŋ keɪs/ *noun* a large wooden box for carrying items which can be easily broken

packing charges /'pækɪŋ ˌtʃɑːdʒɪz/ *plural noun* money charged for putting goods into boxes

packing station /'pækɪŋ ˌsteɪʃ(ə)n/ *noun* a place where goods are packed for transport ○ *From the production line the goods are taken directly to the packing station.* ○ *The company has three packing stations, each one dealing with goods for a particular part of the world.*

packshot /'pækʃɒt/ *noun* an image in an advertisement which shows the packaging of the product being sold ○ *The television advertisement for the new breakfast cereal featured a ten second packshot.*

page /peɪdʒ/ *noun* one side of a sheet of printed paper in a book, newspaper, or magazine

page impressions /'peɪdʒ ɪmˌpreʃ(ə)nz/ *plural noun* the number of customers who land on a webpage, e.g. in an ad view

page make-up /'peɪdʒ ˌmeɪk ʌp/ *noun* the arranging of material into pages in a publication

page proof /'peɪdʒ pruːf/ *noun* a proof after the text has been made up into pages, ready for checking before printing

page pushing /'peɪdʒ ˌpʊʃɪŋ/ *noun* same as **co-browsing**

page rate /'peɪdʒ reɪt/ *noun* the cost of a whole page of advertising space ○ *What's the page rate in that paper?* ○ *The page rate is lower in August when circulation is at its lowest.*

page traffic /'peɪdʒ ˌtræfɪk/ *noun* the proportion of readers of a publication who read a particular page ○ *Let's find out the page traffic before we decide to advertise on page two.*

page view /'peɪdʒ vjuː/ *noun* the number of times a page containing an advertisement is seen or how many times a page is displayed

paid circulation /ˌpeɪd ˌsɜːkjʊ'leɪʃ(ə)n/ *noun* the number of copies of a newspaper or magazine which have been bought. ⇨ **controlled circulation**, **subscribed circulation**

pallet /'pælət/ *noun* a flat wooden base on which goods can be stacked for easy handling by a fork-lift truck, and on which they remain for the whole of their transportation

palletise /'pælətaɪz/, **palletize** *verb* to put goods on pallets ○ *palletised cartons*

palmtop /'pɑːmtɒp/ *noun* a very small computer which can be held in your hand and which usually has a character recognition screen instead of a keyboard

pamphlet /'pæmflət/ *noun* a small booklet of advertising material or of information

panel /'pæn(ə)l/ *noun* **1.** a flat vertical surface **2.** a group of people who give advice on a problem ○ *a panel of experts*

panel study /'pæn(ə)l ˌstʌdi/ *noun* a study that collects and analyses the opinions of a selected group of people over a period of time

panic buying /'pænɪk ˌbaɪɪŋ/ *noun* a rush to buy something at any price because stocks may run out

pantry check /'pæntri tʃek/, **pantry audit** /'pæntri ˌɔːdɪt/ *noun* a survey method where a panel or sample of householders keep records of purchases so that these can be regularly checked for quantity and brand ○ *The pantry check suggests that there is little brand loyalty for that type of product.*

paper /'peɪpə/ *noun* **1.** a document which can represent money, e.g. a bill of exchange or a promissory note **2.** a newspaper

paper gain /ˌpeɪpə 'geɪn/ *noun* same as **paper profit**

'…the profits were tax-free and the interest on the loans they incurred qualified for income tax relief; the paper gains were rarely changed into spending money' [*Investors Chronicle*]

paper loss /ˌpeɪpə 'lɒs/ *noun* a loss made when an asset has fallen in value but has not been sold. Also called **unrealised loss**

paper profit /ˌpeɪpə 'prɒfɪt/ *noun* a profit on an asset which has increased in price but has not been sold ○ *He is showing a paper profit of £25,000 on his investment.* Also called **paper gain**, **unrealised profit**

parallel billboard /ˌpærəlel ˈbɪl-bɔːd/ *noun* a billboard which is parallel to a main road

parallel economy /ˌpærəlel ɪˈkɒnəmi/ *noun* same as **black economy**

parcel /ˈpɑːs(ə)l/ ■ *noun* goods wrapped up in paper or plastic to be sent by post ○ *to do up goods into parcels* □ **to tie up a parcel** to fasten a parcel with string □ **parcel rates** the charges for sending parcels by post ■ *verb* to wrap and tie up in a parcel ○ *to parcel up a consignment of books* (NOTE: **parcelling – parcelled**. The US spelling is **parceling – parceled**.)

parcel delivery service /ˌpɑːs(ə)l dɪˈlɪv(ə)ri ˌsɜːvɪs/ *noun* a private company which delivers parcels within a specific area

parcel post /ˈpɑːs(ə)l pəʊst/ *noun* a mail service for sending parcels ○ *Send the order by parcel post.*

parcels office /ˈpɑːs(ə)lz ˌɒfɪs/ *noun* an office where parcels can be handed in for sending by mail

Pareto's Law /pəˈriːtəʊz lɔː/, **Pareto Effect** /pəˈriːtəʊ ɪˌfekt/ *noun* the theory that incomes are distributed in the same way in all countries, whatever tax regime is in force, and that a small percentage of a total is responsible for a large proportion of value or resources. Also called **eighty/twenty law**

part exchange /ˌpɑːt ɪksˈtʃeɪndʒ/ *noun* the act of giving an old product as part of the payment for a new one ○ *to take a car in part exchange*

participation /pɑːˌtɪsɪˈpeɪʃ(ə)n/ *noun* taking part in something, e.g. when advertisers buy commercial time on TV

partnering /ˈpɑːtnərɪŋ/ *noun* same as **strategic partnering**

partnership /ˈpɑːtnəʃɪp/ *noun* a business set up by two or more people who make a contract with each other agreeing to share the profits and losses (NOTE: A partnership is not an incorporated company and the individual partners are responsible for decisions and debts.)

part payment /ˌpɑːt ˈpeɪmənt/ *noun* a partial payment that leaves a balance to pay at some future time ○ *I*

gave him £250 as part payment for the car.

party /ˈpɑːti/ *noun* **1.** a person or organisation involved in a legal dispute or legal agreement ○ *How many parties are there to the contract?* ○ *The company is not a party to the agreement.* **2.** a group of people who meet to celebrate something or to enjoy themselves

party-plan selling /ˈpɑːti plæn ˌselɪŋ/ *noun* selling by salespeople who present their products at parties organised in their homes ○ *Party-plan selling provides a relaxed atmosphere in which people are more inclined to buy the products being shown.*

par value /ˌpɑː ˈvæljuː/ *noun* same as **face value**

pass /pɑːs/ *verb*

pass off *phrasal verb* □ **to pass something off as something else** to pretend that something is another thing in order to cheat a customer ○ *She tried to pass off the wine as French, when in fact it came from outside the EU.*

passenger manifest /ˌpæsɪndʒə ˈmænɪfest/ *noun* a list of passengers on a ship or plane

passing trade /ˌpɑːsɪŋ ˈtreɪd/ *noun* selling to people who go past the shop without intending to buy

pass-on readership /ˈpɑːs ɒn ˌriːdəʃɪp/ *noun* the number of people who read a publication who have not bought it, but have borrowed it from a purchaser ○ *We know the magazine's circulation, but will have to estimate the level of pass-on readership.* (NOTE: The US term is **pass-along readership**.)

patent /ˈpeɪtənt ˈpætənt/ *noun* an official document showing that a person has the exclusive right to make and sell an invention ○ *to take out a patent for a new type of light bulb* ○ *to apply for a patent for a new invention* □ **'patent applied for'**, **'patent pending'** words on a product showing that the inventor has applied for a patent for it □ **to forfeit a patent** to lose a patent because payments have not been made □ **to infringe a patent** to make and sell a product which works in the same way as a patented product and not pay a royalty for it □ **to file a patent application** to apply for a patent ■ *verb* □ **to patent an**

invention to register an invention with the patent office to prevent other people from copying it

patent agent /ˈpeɪtənt ˌeɪdʒənt/ *noun* a person who advises on patents and applies for patents on behalf of clients

patented /ˈpeɪtəntɪd ˈpætəntɪd/ *adjective* which is protected by a patent

patentee /ˌpeɪtənˈtiː/ *noun* a person or business that has acquired a patent ○ *We shall have to obtain the patentee's permission to manufacture the product.*

patent medicine /ˌpeɪtənt ˈmed-(ə)sɪn/ *noun* a medicine which is registered as a patent

patent office /ˈpeɪtənt ˌɒfɪs/ *noun* a government office which grants patents and supervises them

patent rights /ˈpeɪtənt raɪts/ *plural noun* the rights which an inventor holds because of a patent

patron /ˈpeɪtrən/ *noun* **1.** a regular customer, e.g. of a hotel, restaurant, etc. ○ *The car park is for the use of hotel patrons only.* **2.** a person who gives an organisation or charity financial support ○ *She is a patron of several leading charities.*

patronage /ˈpætrənɪdʒ/ *noun US* same as **custom**

patronise /ˈpætrənaɪz/, **patronize** *verb* to be a regular customer ○ *I stopped patronising that restaurant when their prices went up.*

pattern /ˈpæt(ə)n/ *noun* the general way in which something usually happens ○ *The pattern of sales* or *The sales pattern is quite different this year.*

pattern advertising /ˈpæt(ə)n ˌædvətaɪzɪŋ/ *noun* an advertising campaign that follows a general global approach

pattern book /ˈpæt(ə)n bʊk/ *noun* a book showing examples of design

patterned interview /ˌpæt(ə)nd ˈɪntəvjuː/ *noun* an interview using questions set in advance and following a fixed pattern

pay /peɪ/ *verb* **1.** to give money to buy an item or a service ○ *to pay £1,000 for a car* ○ *How much did you pay to have the office cleaned?* (NOTE: **paying – paid**) □ **'pay cash'** words written on a crossed

cheque to show that it can be paid in cash if necessary □ **to pay in advance** to pay before you receive the item bought or before the service has been completed ○ *We had to pay in advance to have the new telephone system installed.* □ **to pay in instalments** to pay for an item by giving small amounts regularly ○ *We are buying the van by paying instalments of £500 a month.* □ **to pay cash** to pay the complete sum in cash □ **to pay by cheque** to pay by giving a cheque, not by using cash or credit card □ **to pay by credit card** to pay using a credit card, not a cheque or cash **2.** to give money which is owed or which has to be paid ○ *He was late paying the bill.* ○ *We phoned to ask when they were going to pay the invoice.* ○ *You will have to pay duty on these imports.* ○ *She pays tax at the highest rate.* □ **to pay on demand** to pay money when it is asked for, not after a period of credit □ **please pay the sum of £10** please give £10 in cash or by cheque

'…recession encourages communication not because it makes redundancies easier, but because it makes low or zero pay increases easier to accept' [*Economist*]

'…the yield figure means that if you buy the shares at their current price you will be getting 5% before tax on your money if the company pays the same dividend as in its last financial year' [*Investors Chronicle*]

pay down *phrasal verb* □ **to pay money down** to make a deposit ○ *They paid £50 down and the rest in monthly instalments.*

payable /ˈpeɪəb(ə)l/ *adjective* due to be paid □ **payable in advance** which has to be paid before the goods are delivered □ **payable on delivery** which has to be paid when the goods are delivered □ **payable on demand** which must be paid when payment is asked for □ **payable at sixty days** which has to be paid by sixty days after the date on the invoice □ **cheque made payable to bearer** a cheque which will be paid to the person who has it, not to any particular name written on it □ **shares payable on application** shares which must be paid for when you apply to buy them

payback period /ˈpeɪbæk ˌpɪəriəd/ *noun* the length of time it will take to earn back the money invested in a project

pay-cheque /'peɪ tʃek/ *noun* a monthly cheque by which an employee is paid (NOTE: The US spelling is **paycheck**.)

pay differentials /'peɪ dɪfə,renʃəlz/ *plural noun* the difference in salary between employees in similar types of jobs. Also called **salary differentials, wage differentials**

payee /peɪ'iː/ *noun* a person who receives money from someone, or the person whose name is on a cheque

payer /'peɪə/ *noun* a person who gives money to someone

payload /'peɪləʊd/ *noun* the cargo or passengers carried by a ship, train, or plane for which payment is made

payment /'peɪmənt/ *noun* **1.** the act of giving money in exchange for goods or a service ○ *We always ask for payment in cash* or *cash payment and not payment by cheque.* ○ *The payment of interest* or *the interest payment should be made on the 22nd of each month.* □ **payment after delivery** paying for goods at an agreed upon date after delivery ○ *There is a 10% discount for payment on delivery, but none for payment after delivery.* □ **payment on account** paying part of the money owed □ **payment on delivery** paying for goods when they are delivered ○ *Some customers won't agree to payment on delivery and want more time to settle up.* □ **payment on invoice** paying money as soon as an invoice is received □ **payment in kind** paying by giving goods or food, but not money □ **payment by results** money given which increases with the amount of work done or goods produced □ **payment supra protest** payment of a bill of exchange by a third party to protect the debtor's honour **2.** money paid □ **repayable in easy payments** repayable with small sums regularly

payment gateway /'peɪmənt ,geɪtweɪ/ *noun* software that processes online credit-card payments. It gets authorisation for the payment from the credit-card company and transfers money into the retailer's bank account.

payment terms /'peɪmənt tɜːmz/ *plural noun* the conditions laid down by a business regarding when it should be paid for goods or services that it sup-

plies, e.g. cash with order, payment on delivery, or payment within a particular number of days of the invoice date

pay package /'peɪ ,pækɪdʒ/ *noun* the salary and other benefits offered with a job ○ *The job carries an attractive pay package.*

PayPal /'peɪpæl/ an e-commerce business allowing payments and money transfers to be made through the Internet

pay parity /'peɪ ,pærɪti/ *noun* earning the same pay for the same job (NOTE: also called **wage parity**)

pay-per-click /,peɪ pe 'klɪk/ *noun* **1.** an Internet advertising model used on websites, in which advertisers pay an agreed price to their host only when their ad is clicked on. Abbreviation **PPC 2.** same as **pay-per-view**

pay-per-play /,peɪ pɜː 'pleɪ/ *noun* a website where the user has to pay to play an interactive game over the Internet

pay-per-view /,peɪ pə 'vjuː/ *noun* a website where the user has to pay to see digital information, e.g., an e-book or e-magazine. Also called **pay-per-click**

pay scale /'peɪ skeɪl/ *noun* a hierarchy of wage levels, typically varying according to job title, salary or length of service. Also called **salary scale, wage scale**

pay television /'peɪ telɪ,vɪʒ(ə)n/, **pay TV** /'peɪ tiː viː/ *noun* a television service that is paid for by regular subscriptions

PC /,piː 'siː/ *abbreviation* personal computer

PD *abbreviation* physical distribution

peak /piːk/ *noun* the highest point ○ *The shares reached their peak in January.* ○ *The share index has fallen 10% since the peak in January.* ○ *Withdrawals from bank accounts reached a peak in the week before Christmas.* ○ *He has reached the peak of his career.* ■ *verb* to reach the highest point ○ *Productivity peaked in January.* ○ *Shares have peaked and are beginning to slip back.* ○ *He peaked early and never achieved his ambition of becoming managing director.* ○ *Demand peaks in August, after which sales usually decline.*

peak output /ˌpiːk ˈautput/ *noun* the highest output

peak period /ˈpiːk ˌpɪəriəd/ *noun* the time of the day when something is at its highest point, e.g. when most commuters are travelling or when most electricity is being used

peak time /ˈpiːk taɪm/ *noun* the time during the day when the greatest number of people are watching television ○ *For the price of a 30-second spot at peak time we can get two minutes in mid-morning.*

peak year /ˌpiːk ˈjɪə/ *noun* the year when the largest quantity of products was produced or when sales were highest

pedestrian precinct /pəˌdestriən ˈpriːsɪŋkt/ *noun* the part of a town which is closed to traffic so that people can walk about and shop

peer group /ˈpɪə ˌgruːp/ *noun* the class of people that a person can respect or identify with, because they belong to the same age group, social class, or have the same opinions ○ *Consumers are found to be especially influenced by the tastes and opinions of those in their peer groups.*

peer-to-peer /ˌpɪə tə ˈpɪə/ *adjective* full form of **P2P**

peg /peg/ *verb* to maintain or fix something at a specific level (NOTE: **pegging – pegged**)

pen /pen/ *noun* an instrument for writing with, using ink

penalty clause /ˈpen(ə)lti klɔːz/ *noun* a clause which lists the penalties which will be imposed if the terms of the contract are not fulfilled ○ *The contract contains a penalty clause which fines the company 1% for every week the completion date is late.*

penetrate /ˈpenɪtreɪt/ *verb* □ **to penetrate a market** to get into a market and capture a share of it

penetrated market /ˌpenɪtreɪtɪd ˈmaːkɪt/ *noun* a market where more of a company's products are sold, shown as a percentage of the total market, using aggressive pricing and advertising

penetration /ˌpenɪˈtreɪʃ(ə)n/ *noun* **1.** the percentage of a target market that accepts a product **2.** the percentage of a target audience reached by an advertisement

penetration pricing /ˌpenɪˈtreɪʃ(ə)n ˌpraɪsɪŋ/ *noun* the practice of pricing a product low enough to achieve market penetration ○ *Penetration pricing is helping us acquire a bigger market share at the expense of short-term profits.*

penetration strategy /penɪˈtreɪʃ(ə)n ˌstrætədʒi/ *noun* selling more of a company's products into a market segment, shown as a percentage of the total market, by aggressive pricing and advertising. ⇨ **market penetration**

per annum /pər ˈænəm/ *adverb* in a year ○ *What is their turnover per annum?* ○ *What is his total income per annum?* ○ *She earns over £100,000 per annum.*

per capita /pə ˈkæpɪtə/ *adjective, adverb* for each person

per-capita expenditure /pə ˌkæpɪtə ɪkˈspendɪtʃə/ *noun* the total money spent divided by the number of people involved

per capita income /pə ˌkæpɪtə ˈɪnkʌm/ *noun* the average income of each member of a particular group of people, e.g., the citizens of a country

percentage bounced back /pəˌsentɪdʒ baʊnst ˈbæk/ *noun* the number of email messages returned as undeliverable, shown as a percentage of the total sent

percentile /pəˈsentaɪl/ *noun* one of a series of ninety-nine figures below which a percentage of the total falls

perception /pəˈsepʃən/ *noun* the way in which something is viewed and assessed by a person

perceptual map /pəˌseptʃuəl ˈmæp/ *noun* a map or diagram which represents how consumers view various comparative products on the basis of specific factors or attributes ○ *Thorough analysis of perceptual maps was followed by decisions on changes in product design and marketing strategy.*

perfect *adjective*/ˈpɜːfɪkt/ completely correct with no mistakes ○ *We check each batch to make sure it* *is perfect.* ○ *She did a perfect keyboarding test.* ■ *verb*/pə'fekt/ to develop or improve something until it is as good as it can be ○ *They perfected the process for making high-grade steel.*

perfect competition /ˌpɜːfɪkt ˌkɒmpə'tɪʃ(ə)n/ *noun* (*in economic theory*) the ideal market, where all products are equal in price and all customers are provided with all information about the products. Also called **atomistic competition**

perfect market /ˌpɜːfɪkt 'mɑːkɪt/ *noun* an imaginary market where there is perfect competition

performance review /pə'fɔːməns rɪˌvjuː/ *noun* a yearly interview between a manager and each employee to discuss how the employee has worked during the year

periodical /ˌpɪəri'ɒdɪk(ə)l/ *noun* a magazine which comes out regularly, usually once a month or once a week

perishable /'perɪʃəb(ə)l/ *adjective* which can go bad or become rotten easily ○ *perishable goods* ○ *perishable items* ○ *a perishable cargo*

perishables /'perɪʃəb(ə)lz/ *plural noun* goods which can go bad easily

'…the survey, which covered 7,376 supermarkets run by 119 companies, found that sales of food at the stores dropped by 2.9%. That decline, also the largest on record, was due to increasing price awareness among customers and the lower price of perishables' [*Nikkei Weekly*]

permanent /'pɜːmənənt/ *adjective* which will last for a long time or for ever ○ *the permanent staff and part-timers* ○ *She has found a permanent job.* ○ *She is in permanent employment.*

permanent-income hypothesis /ˌpɜːmənənt 'ɪnkʌm haɪˌpɒθəsɪs/ *noun* the theory that people spend according to the average income they expect to receive in their lifetime

permission marketing /pə'mɪʃ(ə)n ˌmɑːkɪtɪŋ/ *noun* any form of online direct marketing that requires the seller to get permission from each recipient, usually through an opt-in, before sending him or her any promotional material

permit *noun*/'pɜːmɪt/ an official document which allows someone to do something ■ *verb*/pə'mɪt/ to allow

someone to do something ○ *This document permits you to export twenty-five computer systems.* ○ *The ticket permits three people to go into the exhibition.* ○ *Will we be permitted to use her name in the advertising copy?* ○ *Smoking is not permitted in the design studio.* (NOTE: **permitting – permitted**)

persistent demand /pəˌsɪstənt dɪ'mɑːnd/ *noun* a continuous or stable demand for a product ○ *Persistent demand for the product means that there is very little pressure to adapt it.* ○ *The product is so useful that it is not surprising there is a persistent demand for it.*

personal /'pɜːs(ə)n(ə)l/ *adjective* referring to one person

personal call /'pɜːs(ə)n(ə)l kɔːl/ *noun* a telephone call not related to business ○ *Staff are not allowed to make personal calls during office hours.*

personal computer /ˌpɜːs(ə)n(ə)l kəm'pjuːtə/ *noun* a small computer which can be used by one person in the home or office. Abbreviation **PC**

Personal Identification Number /ˌpɜːs(ə)n(ə)l aɪˌdentɪfɪ'keɪʃ(ə)n ˌnʌmbə/ *noun* a unique number allocated to the holder of a cash card or credit card, by which he or she can enter an automatic banking system, as e.g., to withdraw cash from a cash machine or to pay in a store. Abbreviation **PIN**

personal interview /ˌpɜːs(ə)n(ə)l 'ɪntəvjuː/ *noun* an act of questioning respondents in a survey directly, by meeting them ○ *The advantage of a personal interview is that we have the chance to explain the questions.* ○ *It's possible that interviewers' bias may influence results in a personal interview.*

personalisation /ˌpɜːs(ə)nəlaɪ'zeɪʃ(ə)n/, **personalization** *noun* **1.** the process by which a website presents customers with information that is selected and adapted to meet their specific needs **2.** using personal information such as the addressee's first name in a mailing campaign

personalised /'pɜːs(ə)nəlaɪzd/, **personalized** *adjective* with the name or initials of a person printed on it ○ *She has a personalised briefcase.*

personalised mailing /ˌpɜːs(ə)nəlaızd ˈmeɪlɪŋ/ *noun* a mailing of letters addressed to particular people by name

personality /ˌpɜːsəˈnælɪti/ *noun* **1.** a famous person, usually connected with television or sport **2.** the character, especially the tone, of an advertising email, e.g. serious, cheerful, etc.

personality advertising /ˌpɜːsə-ˈnælɪti ˌædvətaɪzɪŋ/, **personality promotion** /ˌpɜːsəˈnælɪti prə-ˈməʊʃ(ə)n/ *noun* a promotion which makes use of a famous person to endorse a product ○ *Personality promotion is a tried and tested method of promoting beauty products.* ○ *A famous pop star was chosen for the personality promotion because of her widespread popularity among the target audience.*

personal selling /ˈpɜːs(ə)n(ə)l ˌselɪŋ/ *noun* selling to a customer by personal contact, either face to face or by telephone ○ *Personal selling allows any doubts the prospective customer may have to be cleared up by the salesman.*

PersonicX a trade name for a consumer segmentation solution that gives insight into customer behaviour based on recent demographic and lifestyle profiles from 25 million households. This analysis enables marketers to identify advertising opportunities and target media spend more effectively.

personnel /ˌpɜːsəˈnel/ *noun* all the people who work for an organisation or at a particular location ○ *The personnel of the warehouse* or *the warehouse personnel have changed their shift system.* ○ *The company is famous for the way it looks after its personnel.* (NOTE: now replaced in some cases by **human resources**)

persuade /pəˈsweɪd/ *verb* to talk to someone and get them to do what you want ○ *We could not persuade the French company to sign the contract.*

persuasibility /pəˌsweɪzɪˈbɪlɪti/ *noun* US the degree to which a target audience can be persuaded through advertising that a product has good qualities ○ *Persuasibility will depend on consumers' experience with products similar to the ones we are promoting.*

persuasion /pəˈsweɪʒ(ə)n/ *noun* the act of persuading

persuasion matrix /pəˈsweɪʒ(ə)n ˌmeɪtrɪks/ *noun* a planning model which shows how responses are affected by the communications they receive

pester power /ˈpestə ˌpaʊə/ *noun* the technique of selling to adults (who have the money) by appealing to children (who do not) and relying on them to pester their parents into buying the item for them

PESTLE /ˈpes(ə)l/ *noun* analysis of the various outside influences on a firm, shown as Political, Environmental, Social, Technological, Legislative, and Economic

phishing /ˈfɪʃɪŋ/ *noun* the act of tricking someone into providing bank or credit-card information by sending a fraudulent email claiming to be from a bank, Internet provider, etc. asking for account and password information

photoengraving /ˌfəʊtəʊɪnˈgreɪvɪŋ/ *noun* a process of producing a metal plate for printing, by photographing an image onto the plate which is then etched in such a way that prints can be taken from it

photogravure /ˌfəʊtəʊgrəˈvjʊə/ *noun* a type of photoengraving where the design is etched into the metal rather than in relief

photo opportunity /ˈfəʊtəʊ ˌɒpətjuːnɪti/ *noun* an arranged situation where a famous person can be filmed or photographed by journalists

phototypesetting /ˌfəʊtəʊˈtaɪpsetɪŋ/ *noun* typesetting by photographic means rather than by using metal type

physical distribution /ˌfɪzɪk(ə)l ˌdɪstrɪˈbjuːʃ(ə)n/ *noun* the process of moving goods from the producer to the wholesaler, then to the retailer and so to the end user ○ *Physical distribution is always a problem because of high transportation costs.* Abbreviation **PD**

physical inventory /ˌfɪzɪk(ə)l ˈɪnvənt(ə)ri/ *noun* US same as **physical stock**

physical retail shopping /ˌfɪzɪk(ə)l ˈriːteɪl ˌʃɒpɪŋ/ *noun* shopping that involves visiting actual shops rather than buying online

physical stock /ˌfɪzɪk(ə)l ˈstɒk/ *noun* the actual items of stock held in a warehouse

picking /ˈpɪkɪŋ/ *noun* the selecting of a product according to its packaging or place on the shelf, rather than by making a conscious decision to buy

picking list /ˈpɪkɪŋ lɪst/ *noun* a list of items in an order, listed according to where they can be found in the warehouse

pickup and delivery service /ˌpɪkʌp ən dɪˈlɪv(ə)ri ˌsɜːvɪs/ *noun* **1.** a service which takes goods from the warehouse and delivers them to the customer **2.** a service which takes something away for cleaning or servicing and returns it to the owner when finished

picture messaging /ˈpɪktʃə ˌmesɪdʒɪŋ/ *noun* the transmission of images and photographs from one mobile phone to another

pieceworker /ˈpiːswɜːkə/ *noun* a person who is employed at a piece rate

piggy-back advertising /ˈpɪgi bæk ˌædvətaɪzɪŋ/, **piggy-back promotion** /ˈpɪgi bæk prəˌməʊʃ(ə)n/ *noun* the sales promotion for one product which accompanies promotion for another product made by the same company

piggy-back freight /ˌpɪgi bæk ˈfreɪt/ *noun US* the transport of loaded trucks on freight trains. Compare **fishy-back freight**

pilferage /ˈpɪlfərɪdʒ/, **pilfering** /ˈpɪlfərɪŋ/ *noun* the stealing of small amounts of money or small items from an office or shop

pilot /ˈpaɪlət/ *adjective* used as a test, which if successful will then be expanded into a full operation ○ *The company set up a pilot project to see if the proposed manufacturing system was efficient.* ○ *The pilot factory has been built to test the new production processes.* ○ *She is directing a pilot scheme for training unemployed young people.* ■ *verb* to test a project on a small number of people, to see if it will work in practice ■ *noun* **1.** a trial episode of a proposed TV series **2.** a test project, undertaken to see

whether something is likely to be successful or profitable

pilot survey /ˈpaɪlət ˌsɜːveɪ/ *noun* a preliminary survey carried out to see if a full survey would be worth while

PIN /pɪn/ *abbreviation* Personal Identification Number

pink advertising /ˈpɪŋk ˌædvətaɪzɪŋ/ *noun* advertising aimed specifically at the gay and lesbian market

pink dollar /ˌpɪŋk ˈdɒlə/ *noun US* money spent by gay and lesbian customers

pink market /ˈpɪŋk ˌmɑːkɪt/ *noun* the market that consists of gay and lesbian people

pink pound /ˌpɪŋk ˈpaʊnd/ *noun* money spent by gay and lesbian customers

pioneer /ˌpaɪəˈnɪə/ *verb* to be the first to do something ○ *The company pioneered developments in the field of electronics.*

pioneer selling /paɪəˈnɪə ˌselɪŋ/ *noun* hard intensive selling in new markets ○ *A campaign of pioneer selling was organised to educate the public in the use of the new product.* ○ *There was a lot of consumer resistance to pioneer selling, since few customers had heard of the product or thought they needed it.*

pipeline /ˈpaɪplaɪn/ *noun* a distribution channel from the manufacturer through wholesalers and retailers to the customer ○ *How many different businesses are involved in the product's pipeline?*

piracy /ˈpaɪrəsi/ *noun* the copying of patented inventions or copyright works

pirate /ˈpaɪrət/ *noun* a person who copies a patented invention or a copyright work and sells it ■ *verb* to copy a copyright work ○ *a pirated book* ○ *The designs for the new dress collection were pirated in the Far East.* ■ *adjective* copied without permission ○ *a pirate copy of a book*

pitch /pɪtʃ/ *noun* a presentation by an advertising agency to a potential customer

'…the head of marketing says the company is reviewing its advertising agency arrangements, but does not have a pitch list at this stage' [*Marketing Week*]

pix /pɪks/ *plural noun* pictures used in advertising or design (*informal*)

pixel /'pɪksəl/ *noun* the smallest single unit or point on a display or on a printer whose colour or brightness can be controlled. A monitor normally has a resolution of 72 pixels per inch, whereas a laser printer has a resolution of 300–600 pixels (also called dots) per inch.

placard /'plækɑːd/ *noun* **1.** a poster of double crown size (i.e. 30 inches deep by 20 inches wide) **2.** a large advertisement on a stiff card

placement test /'pleɪsmənt test/ *noun* a test where different versions of a new product are tested in different places and with different types of consumer (as opposed to market tests, where the new product is actually sold through normal distribution channels in the test areas)

placement testing /'pleɪsmənt ˌtestɪŋ/ *noun* the practice of sending a product to different places for trial and then interviewing the users on its performance ○ *Placement testing revealed that the product was too easily breakable.*

place utility /'pleɪs juːˌtɪlɪti/ *noun* the usefulness to a customer of receiving a product at a particular place

plain cover /ˌpleɪn 'kʌvə/ *noun* □ **to send something under plain cover** to send something in an ordinary envelope with no company name printed on it

plan /plæn/ *noun* an idea of how something should be done, which has been decided on and organised in advance ■ *verb* to decide on and organise something in advance (NOTE: **planning – planned**)

'…the benefits package is attractive and the compensation plan includes base, incentive and car allowance totalling $50,000+' [*Globe and Mail (Toronto)*]

planned obsolescence /ˌplænd ˌɒbsəˈles(ə)ns/ *noun* same as **built-in obsolescence** ○ *Planned obsolescence was condemned by the consumer organisation as a cynical marketing ploy.*

planning /'plænɪŋ/ *noun* the process of organising how something should be done in the future ○ *Setting up a new incentive scheme with insufficient planning could be a disaster.* ○ *The long-term planning or short-term planning of the project has been completed.*

'…buildings are closely regulated by planning restrictions' [*Investors Chronicle*]

plans board /'plænz bɔːd/ *noun* a group of senior managers that meets to discuss campaign strategy ○ *The plans board will meet on Monday to discuss the latest sales figures.* ○ *The plans board has decided to concentrate the campaign in those areas where there are most sales representatives.*

plastic /'plæstɪk/ *noun* credit cards and charge cards (*informal*)

plateau /'plætəʊ/ *noun* a level point, e.g. when sales or costs stop increasing

plateau pricing /'plætəʊ ˌpraɪsɪŋ/ *noun* the setting of a medium price for a product where the raw materials used in making it are likely to change a lot in price

platform /'plætfɔːm/ *noun* a basic product that can be added to in order to develop more complex products

Plc, PLC, plc *abbreviation* public limited company

PLC *abbreviation* product life cycle

ploy /plɔɪ/ *noun* a trick or gimmick, used to attract customers

plug /plʌg/ *noun* □ **to give a plug to a new product** to publicise a new product ■ *verb* to publicise or advertise ○ *They ran six commercials plugging holidays in Spain.* (NOTE: **plugging – plugged**)

POA *abbreviation* point of action

podcast /'pɒdkɑːst/ *noun* a series of digital media files (either audio or video) that are downloaded by subscribers through web syndication

podcasting /'pɒdˌkɑːstɪŋ/ *noun* the act of offering audio or video files over the Internet to subscribing users

point /pɔɪnt/ *noun* a place or position

point of action /ˌpɔɪnt əv 'ækʃən/ *noun* a place in a presentation that encourages the prospective purchaser to take action. Abbreviation **POA**

point of purchase /ˌpɔɪnt əv 'pɜː-tʃɪs/ *noun* **1.** a place where a product is bought, which is usually the same as point of sale, though not always, as in the case of mail-order purchases. Abbreviation **POP 2.** same as **point of sale**

point-of-purchase advertising /ˌpɔɪnt əv ˌpɜːtʃɪs ˈædvətaɪzɪŋ/ *noun* advertising at the place where the products are bought, e.g. posters or dump bins. Abbreviation **POPA**

point-of-purchase display /ˌpɔɪnt əv ˌpɜːtʃɪs dɪsˈpleɪ/ *noun* an arrangement of products and marketing material at the place where an item is bought, which is designed to encourage sales

point of sale /ˌpɔɪnt əv ˈseɪl/ *noun* **1.** a place where a product is sold, e.g. a shop. Abbreviation **POS 2.** the place where a product is bought by the customer (NOTE: The point of sale can be a particular shop, or a display case or even a particular shelf inside a shop.)

point-of-sale material /ˌpɔɪnt əv ˈseɪl məˌtɪəriəl/ *noun* a display material to advertise a product where it is being sold, e.g. posters or dump bins. Abbreviation **POS material**

policy /ˈpɒlɪsi/ *noun* **1.** a course of action or set of principles determining the general way of doing something ○ *a company's trading policy* ○ *The country's economic policy seems to lack any direction.* ○ *Our policy is to submit all contracts to the legal department.* □ **company policy** the company's agreed plan of action or the company's way of doing things ○ *What is the company policy on credit?* ○ *It is against company policy to give more than thirty days' credit.* **2.** a course of action or set of principles **3.** a contract for insurance

poll /pəʊl/ *noun* same as **opinion poll** ■ *verb* □ **to poll a sample of the population** to ask a sample group of people what they feel about something

poly bag /ˌpɒli ˈbæg/ *noun US* a plastic bag used in packaging

polycentric stage /ˌpɒliˌsentrɪk ˈsteɪdʒ/ *noun US* the stage in a company's international marketing when there is a separate marketing planning unit for each country ○ *It's an expanding multinational in its polycentric stage.*

POP /pɒp/ *abbreviation* point of purchase

POPA *abbreviation* point-of-purchase advertising

popular /ˈpɒpjʊlə/ *adjective* liked by many people ○ *This is our most popular model.* ○ *The South Coast is the most popular area for holidays.*

popular price /ˌpɒpjʊlə ˈpraɪs/ *noun* a price which is low and therefore liked

popular pricing /ˌpɒpjʊlə ˈpraɪsɪŋ/ *noun* a pricing method which tries to attract prices that will be popular with customers ○ *Our competitor's popular pricing strategy is a serious threat to our sales.*

population /ˌpɒpjʊˈleɪʃ(ə)n/ *noun* **1.** all the people living in a particular country or area ○ *Paris has a population of over three million.* ○ *Population statistics show a rise in the 18–25 age group.* ○ *Population trends have to be taken into account when drawing up economic plans.* ○ *The working population of the country is getting older.* **2.** the group of items or people in a survey or study

population forecast /ˌpɒpjʊˈleɪʃ(ə)n ˌfɔːkɑːst/ *noun* a calculation of how many people will be living in a country or in a town at some point in the future

pop-under ad /ˈpɒp ʌndər ˌæd/ *noun* a web advertisement that appears in a separate browser window from the rest of a website

port /pɔːt/ *noun* a harbour where ships come to load or unload ○ *the port of Rotterdam* □ **to call at a port** to stop at a port to load or unload cargo

portal /ˈpɔːt(ə)l/ *noun* a website that provides access and links to other sites and pages on the web (NOTE: *Search engines* and directories are the most common portal sites.)

portfolio /pɔːtˈfəʊliəʊ/ *noun* a folder containing a selection of samples ○ *The student brought a portfolio of designs to show the design department manager.*

'...the Italian manufacturer has shaken up its drinks portfolio with a new launch and two relaunches' [*Marketing Week*]

portrait /ˈpɔːtrɪt/ *noun* an illustration, page, or book whose height is greater than its width. Compare **landscape**

POS /pɒz/, **p.o.s.** *abbreviation* point of sale

position /pə'zɪʃ(ə)n/ *noun* **1.** a situation or state of affairs □ **what is the cash position?** what is the state of the company's current account? **2.** a point of view

positioning /pə'zɪʃ(ə)nɪŋ/ *noun* **1.** the creation of an image for a product in the minds of consumers **2.** the placing of an advertisement in a specific place on a specific page of a magazine **3.** the promotion of a product in a particular area of a market

positive /'pɒzɪtɪv/ *adjective* meaning 'yes' ○ *The board gave a positive reply.*

positive appeal /ˌpɒzɪtɪv ə'piːl/ *noun* advertising which shows why a product is attractive

positive cash flow /ˌpɒzɪtɪv 'kæʃ fləʊ/ *noun* a situation in which more money is coming into a company than is going out

positive variance /ˌpɒzɪtɪv 'veəriəns/ *noun* a difference between a financial plan and its outcome, that means a more favourable profit than expected ○ *The managing director is pleased because costs this year show a £60,000 positive variance.*

possession utility /pə'zeʃ(ə)n juːˌtɪlɪti/ *noun* same as **marginal utility**

post /pəʊst/ *noun* **1.** a system of sending letters and parcels from one place to another ○ *to send an invoice by post* ○ *He put the letter in the post.* ○ *The cheque was lost in the post.* □ **to send a reply by return of post** to reply to a letter immediately □ **post free** without having to pay any postage ○ *The game is obtainable post free from the manufacturer.* **2.** letters sent or received ○ *Has the post arrived yet?* ○ *The first thing I do is open the post.* ○ *The receipt was in this morning's post.* ○ *The letter didn't arrive by the first post this morning.* (NOTE: UK English uses both *mail* and *post* but American English only uses *mail*) ■ *verb* to send something by post ○ *to post a letter* or *to post a parcel*

post- /pəʊst/ *prefix* after

postage /'pəʊstɪdʒ/ *noun* payment for sending a letter or parcel by post ○ *What is the postage for this airmail packet to China?* □ **'postage paid'** words printed on an envelope to show that the sender has paid the postage even though there is no stamp on it

postal /'pəʊst(ə)l/ *adjective* referring to the post

postal interview /ˌpəʊst(ə)l 'ɪntəvjuː/ *noun* same as **postal survey**

postal order /'pəʊst(ə)l ˌɔːdə/ *noun* a document bought at a post office, used as a method of paying small amounts of money by post

postal packet /'pəʊst(ə)l ˌpækɪt/ *noun* a small container of goods sent by post

postal sales /'pəʊst(ə)l seɪlz/ *plural noun* sales of products by post, through advertisements in the press ○ *The company carried out postal sales from a big warehouse in the north.*

postal survey /'pəʊst(ə)l ˌsɜːveɪ/ *noun* a survey in which questionnaires are sent by post for respondents to fill in and send back ○ *Not enough consumers responded to the postal survey.*

postcode /'pəʊstkəʊd/ *noun* a series of numbers and letters which forms part of an address, indicating the street and the town in a way which can be read by a scanner (NOTE: The US term is **ZIP code**.)

poster /'pəʊstə/ *noun* a large eye-catching notice or advertisement which is stuck up outdoors or placed prominently inside a store

poster site /'pəʊstə saɪt/ *noun* a hoarding, wall, or other surface, where posters are put up ○ *We want a poster site in a busy street.* ○ *I wish we could afford a prime poster site for our fund-raising campaign.* ⇨ **bill poste, fly poster**

postpaid /pəʊst'peɪd/ *adjective* with the postage already paid ○ *The price is £5.95 postpaid.*

post-purchase /ˌpəʊst 'pɜːtʃɪs/ *adjective* after a purchase has been made

post-purchase advertising /ˌpəʊst 'pɜːtʃɪs ˌædvətaɪzɪŋ/ *noun* advertising designed to minimise post-purchase anxiety

post-purchase anxiety /ˌpəʊst pɜːtʃɪs ænˈzaɪəti/ *noun* feelings of doubt about a purchase after it has been made

post-purchase assessment /ˌpəʊst pɜːtʃɪs əˈsesmənt/ *noun* the assessment of a product by the purchaser after it has been bought and used

post room /ˈpəʊst ruːm/ *noun* a room in a building where the mail is sorted and sent to each department or collected from each department for sending

post-test /ˈpəʊst test/ *noun* an evaluation of an advertising campaign after it has taken place, or of a product after it has been launched ○ *The post-test showed that an unnecessary amount of money had been spent.*

post-testing /ˈpəʊst ˌtestɪŋ/ *noun* the evaluation of an advertising campaign after it has been run, or of a product after it has been launched

potential /pəˈtenʃəl/ *adjective* possible □ **potential customers** people who could be customers □ **potential market** a market which could be exploited □ **the product has potential sales of 100,000 units** the product will possibly sell 100,000 units □ **she is a potential managing director** she is the sort of person who could become managing director ■ *noun* the possibility of becoming something □ **a product with considerable sales potential** a product which is likely to have very large sales □ **to analyse the market potential** to examine the market to see how large it possibly is

'...career prospects are excellent for someone with growth potential' [*Australian Financial Review*]

'...for sale: established general cleaning business; has potential to be increased to over 1 million dollar turnover' [*Australian Financial Review*]

potential demand /pəˌtenʃəl dɪˈmaːnd/ *noun* a situation where there is no demand as yet for a product but there is money to buy it ○ *Though there is no interest in our product in Saudi Arabia as yet, there is considerable potential demand.*

power /ˈpaʊə/ *noun* the ability to control people or events

power brand /ˈpaʊə brænd/ *noun* a very powerful brand which covers several best-selling products and is known worldwide

PPC *abbreviation* pay-per-click

PR *abbreviation* public relations ○ *A PR firm is handling all our publicity.* ○ *She works in PR.* ○ *The PR people gave away 100,000 balloons.*

preapproach /ˈpriːəˌprəʊtʃ/ *noun* the stage in a salesperson's preparation for a sale devoted to planning actual meetings with customers ○ *Preapproach sessions cover techniques in assessing customers and their needs.*

precinct /ˈpriːsɪŋkt/ *noun* a separate area

pre-coding /priː ˈkəʊdɪŋ/ *noun* the process of assigning codes to items on questionnaires in order to facilitate reference and evaluation ○ *Much time was lost in the survey through a confusing pre-coding system.* ○ *Freelance interviewers should be given a complete explanation of the pre-coding of questionnaires.*

predatory /ˈpredət(ə)ri/ *adjective* which tries to attack □ **a predatory pricing policy** a policy of reducing prices as low as possible to try to get market share from weaker competitors

pre-empt /ˌpriː ˈempt/ *verb* to stop something happening or stop someone doing something by taking action quickly before anyone else can ○ *They staged a management buyout to pre-empt a takeover bid.*

pre-emption /ˌpriː ˈempʃən/ *noun* getting an advantage by doing something quickly before anyone else

pre-emptselling /priːˈemptˌselɪŋ/ *noun* the practice of selling television advertising time at a lower rate with the proviso that another advertiser can take it over if the full rate is offered ○ *As we're on a tight advertising budget we'll have to go for pre-empt selling.*

preferred position /prɪˌfɜːd pəˈzɪʃ(ə)n/ *noun* the place in a publication where an advertiser asks for the advertisement to be put

preferred position rate /prɪˌfɜːd pəˈzɪʃ(ə)n reɪt/ *noun* a higher rate charged for placing an advertisement in the position requested

prejudice /ˈpredʒʊdɪs/ *noun* bias or unjust feelings against someone

prelaunch /ˈpriːlɔːntʃ/ *adjective* before a launch

prelaunch period /ˈpriːlɔːntʃ ˌpɪəriəd/ *noun* the period before the launch of a new product

premium /ˈpriːmiəm/ *noun* **1.** the amount added to a normal price or rate for a product or service **2.** free gift offered to a prospective purchaser as an inducement to make a purchase

premium offer /ˈpriːmiəm ˌɒfə/ *noun* a free gift offered to attract more customers

premium pricing /ˈpriːmiəm ˌpraɪsɪŋ/ *noun* the act of giving products or services high prices either to give the impression that the product is worth more than it really is, or as a means of offering customers an extra service

prepack /priːˈpæk/, **prepackage** /priːˈpækɪdʒ/ *verb* to pack something before putting it on sale ○ *The fruit are prepacked in plastic trays.* ○ *The watches are prepacked in attractive display boxes.*

prepaid /priːˈpeɪd/ *adjective* paid in advance

prepaid reply card /ˌpriːpeɪd rɪˈplaɪ kɑːd/ *noun* a stamped addressed card which is sent to someone so that they can reply without paying the postage

preparatory set /prɪˈpærət(ə)ri set/ *noun* the principle that people have preconceived ideas about brands which influence their buying decisions

prepay /priːˈpeɪ/ *verb* to pay something in advance (NOTE: **prepaying – prepaid**)

prepayment /priːˈpeɪmənt/ *noun* a payment in advance, or the act of paying in advance □ **to ask for prepayment of a fee** to ask for the fee to be paid before the work is done

pre-press /ˌpriː ˈpres/ *adjective* before going to press

pre-press work /priː ˈpres wɜːk/ *noun* the work needed to change original copy and artwork into the form required for printing

prequalification /ˌpriːkwɒlɪfɪˈkeɪʃ(ə)n/ *noun* researching the value of a potential customer, especially one who wants to take out a loan, or a contractor for a project

presence /ˈprez(ə)ns/ *noun* a measurement of an advertisement's real audience as opposed to its potential audience ○ *With an impressive presence our advertisement should have considerable effect.*

present /ˈprez(ə)nt/;/prɪˈzent/ *vti* to give a talk about or demonstration of something ○ *I've been asked to present at the sales conference.* ○ *The HR director will present the new staff structure to the Board.*

presentation /ˌprez(ə)nˈteɪʃ(ə)n/ *noun* **1.** the showing of a document □ **cheque payable on presentation** a cheque which will be paid when it is presented □ **free admission on presentation of this card** you do not pay to go in if you show this card **2.** a demonstration or exhibition of a proposed plan ○ *The distribution company gave a presentation of the services they could offer.* ○ *We have asked two PR firms to make presentations of proposed publicity campaigns.*

press /pres/ *noun* newspapers and magazines ○ *We plan to give the product a lot of press publicity.* ○ *There was no mention of the new product in the press.*

press advertising /ˈpres ˌædvətaɪzɪŋ/ *noun* advertising in newspapers and magazines

press clipping /ˈpres ˌklɪpɪŋ/ *noun/ US* same as **press cutting**

press communications /ˈpres kəˌmjuːnɪkeɪʃ(ə)nz/ *plural noun* communications which increase the awareness of journalists of a product or firm, e.g. press releases or news flashes

press conference /ˈpres ˌkɒnf(ə)rəns/ *noun* a meeting where newspaper and TV reporters are invited to hear news of something such as a new product or a takeover bid

press cutting /ˈpres ˌkʌtɪŋ/ *noun* a piece cut out of a newspaper or magazine which refers to an item which you find interesting ○ *We have kept a file of press cuttings about the new car.*

press cutting agency /ˈpres ˌkʌtɪŋ ˌeɪdʒənsi/ *noun* a company which cuts out references to clients from newspapers and magazines and sends them on to them

press date /'pres deɪt/ *noun* the date on which a publication is printed

press office /'pres ˌɒfɪs/ *noun* an office in a company which deals with relations with the press, sends out press releases, organizes press conferences, etc.

press officer /'pres ˌɒfɪsə/ *noun* a person who works in a press office

press relations /'pres rɪˌleɪʃ(ə)nz/ *plural noun* part of the public relations activity of an organisation, aimed at building up good relations with the press ○ *If the company image is to improve we must first improve our press relations.*

press release /'pres rɪˌliːs/ *noun* a sheet giving news about something which is sent to newspapers and TV and radio stations so that they can use the information ○ *The company sent out a press release about the launch of the new car.*

pressure /'preʃə/ *noun* something which forces you to do something

pressure group /'preʃə gruːp/ *noun* a group of people who try to influence the government, the local town council or some other organisation

prestige /pre'stiːʒ/ *noun* **1.** importance because of factors such as high quality or high value □ **prestige product** an expensive luxury product □ **prestige offices** expensive offices in a good area of the town **2.** status achieved because of being successful, wealthy, or powerful

prestige advertising /pre'stiːʒ ˌædvətaɪzɪŋ/ *noun* advertising in high-quality magazines to increase a company's reputation

prestige pricing /pre'stiːʒ ˌpraɪsɪŋ/ *noun* same as **premium pricing**

pretax profit /ˌpriːtæks 'prɒfɪt/ *noun* the amount of profit a company makes before taxes are deducted ○ *The dividend paid is equivalent to one quarter of the pretax profit.* Also called **profit before tax**

pretest /'priːtest/ *noun* evaluation of an advertising campaign before it is run

pre-testing /ˌpriː 'testɪŋ/ *noun* the testing or evaluation of a product or advertising campaign before it is launched or run ○ *Pre-testing has shown that the product would do well in the country as a whole. ○ The area chosen for pre-testing may not be representative enough of the whole country.*

preview /'priːvjuː/ *noun* a showing of a film, a television commercial, or an exhibition to a specially invited audience before the general public sees it

price /praɪs/ *noun* money which has to be paid to buy something □ **competitive price** a low price aimed to compete with a rival product □ **to sell goods off at half price** to sell goods at half the price at which they were being sold before □ **cars in the £18–19,000 price range** cars of different makes, selling for between £18,000 and £19,000 □ **price ex ship** the price that includes all costs up to the arrival of the ship at port □ **price ex warehouse** the price for a product which is to be collected from the manufacturer's or agent's warehouse and so does not include delivery □ **to increase in price** to become more expensive ○ *Petrol has increased in price* or *the price of petrol has increased.* □ **to increase prices, to raise prices** to make items more expensive □ **we will try to meet your price** we will try to offer a price which is acceptable to you □ **to cut prices** to reduce prices suddenly □ **to lower prices, to reduce prices** to make items cheaper ■ *verb* to give a price to a product ○ *We have two used cars for sale, both priced at £5,000.* □ **competitively priced** sold at a low price which competes with that of similar goods from other companies □ **the company has priced itself out of the market** the company has raised its prices so high that its products do not sell

price band /'praɪs bænd/ *noun* a method of grouping articles within a narrow range of prices

price ceiling /'praɪs ˌsiːlɪŋ/ *noun* a limit beyond which prices will not or cannot rise

price competition /'praɪs kɒmpəˌtɪʃ(ə)n/ *noun* the attempt to compete in a market through skilful pricing

price controls /'praɪs kənˌtrəʊlz/ *plural noun* legal measures to prevent prices rising too fast

price cutting /'praɪs ˌkʌtɪŋ/ *noun* a sudden lowering of prices

'…in today's circumstances, price-cutting is inevitable in an attempt to build up market share' [*Marketing Week*]

price-cutting war /ˈpraɪs ˌkʌtɪŋ wɔː/ *noun* same as **price war**

price differential /ˈpraɪs dɪfəˌrenʃəl/ *noun* the difference in price between products in a range

price differentiation /ˈpraɪs dɪfərenʃiˌeɪʃ(ə)n/ *noun* a pricing strategy in which a company sells the same product at different prices in different markets

price discrimination /ˈpraɪs dɪskrɪmɪˌneɪʃ(ə)n/ *noun* the practice of charging different prices in different markets or to different types of customer ○ *Price discrimination has caused some ill-feeling among customers.*

price effect /ˈpraɪs ɪˌfekt/ *noun* the result of a change in price on a person's buying habits ○ *Before fixing the price, we'll have to carry out a survey to determine the price effect.*

price elasticity /ˈpraɪs iːlæˌstɪsɪti/ *noun* a situation where a change in price has the effect of causing a big change in demand

price escalation clause /ˌpraɪs ˌeskəˈleɪʃ(ə)n ˌklɔːz/ *noun* a clause in a contract that permits the seller to raise prices if its costs increase

price fixing /ˈpraɪs ˌfɪksɪŋ/ *noun* an illegal agreement between companies to charge the same price for competing products

price-insensitive /ˌpraɪs ɪnˈsensətɪv/ *adjective* used to describe a good or service for which sales remain constant no matter what its price because it is essential to buyers

price leadership /ˈpraɪs ˌliːdəʃɪp/ *noun* a situation where the producers model their prices on those of one leading producer

price level /ˈpraɪs ˌlev(ə)l/ *noun* the average price of a particular product in a country at a particular time

price list /ˈpraɪs lɪst/ *noun* a sheet giving prices of goods for sale

price maintenance /ˈpraɪs ˌmeɪntənəns/ *noun* an agreement between producers or distributors on a minimum price for a product

price-off label /ˈpraɪs ˈɒf ˌleɪb(ə)l/ *noun* a label on a product showing a reduced price

price pegging /ˈpraɪs ˌpegɪŋ/ *noun* the practice of maintaining prices at a specific level

price point /ˈpraɪs pɔɪnt/ *noun* the exact price for a range of different products which is psychologically important for the customer, since if an article is given a higher price it will discourage sales ○ *We must have a meeting to determine price points for our products.*

price range /ˈpraɪs reɪndʒ/ *noun* a series of prices for similar products from different suppliers

price ring /ˈpraɪs rɪŋ/ *noun* a group of producers or distributors who agree to control prices and market conditions in their industry

price-sensitive /ˌpraɪs ˈsensətɪv/ *adjective* referring to a product for which demand will change significantly if its price is increased or decreased

price tag /ˈpraɪs tæg/ *noun* **1.** a label attached to an item being sold that shows its price **2.** the value of a person or thing ○ *The takeover bid put a $2m price tag on the company.*

price ticket /ˈpraɪs ˌtɪkɪt/ *noun* a piece of paper showing a price

price war /ˈpraɪs wɔː/ *noun* a competition between companies to get a larger market share by cutting prices. Also called **price-cutting war**

pricing /ˈpraɪsɪŋ/ *noun* the act of giving a price to a product

pricing policy /ˈpraɪsɪŋ ˌpɒlisi/ *noun* a company's policy in giving prices to its products ○ *Our pricing policy aims at producing a 35% gross margin.*

primacy /ˈpraɪməsi/ *noun* the fact of being in first place or being the most important

primacy effect theory /ˈpraɪməsi ɪˌfekt ˌθɪəri/ *noun* the theory that the first information in a message is most likely to be remembered

primary /ˈpraɪməri/ *adjective* basic

'…farmers are convinced that primary industry no longer has the capacity to meet new capital taxes or charges on farm inputs' [*Australian Financial Review*]

primary brand /ˈpraɪməri brænd/ *noun* a brand owned by a distributor rather than by a producer. Compare **private brand**

primary commodities /ˌpraɪməri kəˈmɒdɪtiz/ *plural noun* raw materials or food

primary data /ˌpraɪməri ˈdeɪtə/, **primary information** /ˌpraɪməri ˌɪnfəˈmeɪʃ(ə)n/ *noun* data or information which has not yet been published and must therefore be found by field research ○ *The company's market research proved very expensive since it needed so much primary data.*

primary demand /ˌpraɪməri dɪˈmɑːnd/ *noun* demand for a product in general, as opposed to demand for a particular brand ○ *The main producer companies are cooperating to create primary demand since this type of product is quite new to the public.*

primary industry /ˌpraɪməri ˈɪndəstri/ *noun* an industry dealing with basic raw materials such as coal, wood, or farm produce

primary products /ˌpraɪməri ˈprɒdʌkts/ *plural noun* products which are basic raw materials, e.g. wood, milk, or fish

prime /praɪm/ *adjective* most important ■ *noun* same as **prime rate**

prime cost /ˌpraɪm ˈkɒst/ *noun* the cost involved in producing a product, excluding overheads

prime rate /ˈpraɪm reɪt/ *noun US* the best rate of interest at which a bank lends to its customers. Also called **prime**

prime time /ˈpraɪm taɪm/ *noun* the most expensive advertising time for TV commercials ○ *We are putting out a series of prime-time commercials.*

principal /ˈprɪnsɪp(ə)l/ *noun* a person or company that is represented by an agent ○ *The agent has come to London to see his principals.* ■ *adjective* most important ○ *The principal shareholders asked for a meeting.* ○ *The country's principal products are paper and wood.* ○ *The company's principal asset is its design staff.*

'...the company was set up with funds totalling NorKr 145m with the principal aim of making capital gains on the secondhand market' [*Lloyd's List*]

print /prɪnt/ *noun* the action of marking letters or pictures on paper by a machine, and so producing a book, leaflet, newspaper, etc.

printed matter /ˈprɪntɪd ˌmætə/ *noun* printed items, e.g. books, newspapers, and publicity sheets

print farming /ˈprɪnt ˌfɑːmɪŋ/ *noun* organising the printing by outside printers of printed material required by an organisation, such as advertising leaflets, catalogues, letterheads, etc.

print media /ˈprɪnt ˌmiːdiə/ *plural noun* advertising media, e.g. magazines and newspapers

print run /ˈprɪnt rʌn/ *noun* the number of copies of a publication or piece of advertising material which are printed ○ *The company has ordered a print run of 100,000 for their new catalogue.*

privacy /ˈprɪvəsi/ *noun* a situation of not being disturbed by other people, especially the knowledge that communications are private and cannot be accessed by others

private /ˈpraɪvət/ *adjective* belonging to a single person or to individual people, not to a company or the state □ **a letter marked 'private and confidential'** a letter which must not be opened by anyone other than the person it is addressed to

private brand /ˈpraɪvət brænd/ *noun* a brand owned by a distributor rather than by a producer. Compare **primary brand**

private enterprise /ˌpraɪvət ˈentəpraɪz/ *noun* businesses that are owned privately, not nationalised ○ *The project is completely funded by private enterprise.*

private label /ˈpraɪvət ˌleɪb(ə)l/ *noun* a brand name which is owned by a store, rather than the producer

private label goods /ˈpraɪvət ˌleɪb(ə)l gʊdz/ *plural noun* goods with a brand name which is owned by the store, rather than the producer

private limited company /ˌpraɪvət ˌlɪmɪtɪd ˈkʌmp(ə)ni/ *noun* **1.** a company with a small number of shareholders, whose shares are not traded on the stock exchange **2.** a subsidiary company whose shares are not listed on the stock exchange, while those of its parent company are ▶ abbreviation **Pty Ltd**

privately /'praɪvətli/ *adverb* away from other people ○ *The deal was negotiated privately.*

private means /ˌpraɪvət 'miːnz/ *plural noun* income from dividends, interest, or rent which is not part of someone's salary

private property /ˌpraɪvət 'prɒpəti/ *noun* property which belongs to a private person, not to the public

private sector /'praɪvət ˌsektə/ *noun* one of the parts of the economy of a country, which itself is made up of the corporate sector (firms owned by private shareholders), the personal sector (individuals and their income and expenditure), and the financial sector (banks and other institutions dealing in money) ○ *The expansion is completely funded by the private sector.* ○ *Salaries in the private sector have increased faster than in the public sector.*

'…in the private sector the total number of new house starts was 3% higher than in the corresponding period last year, while public sector starts were 23% lower' [*Financial Times*]

privatisation /ˌpraɪvətaɪ'zeɪʃ(ə)n/, **privatization** *noun* the process of selling a nationalised industry to private owners

'…even without privatization, water charges would probably have to rise to pay for meeting EC water-quality rules' [*Economist*]

privatise /'praɪvətaɪz/, **privatize** *verb* to sell a nationalised industry to private owners

PRO *abbreviation* public relations officer

probability /ˌprɒbə'bɪlɪti/ *noun* the likelihood that something will happen, expressed mathematically

probability sampling /ˌprɒbə'bɪlɪti ˌsɑːmplɪŋ/ *noun* the choosing of samples for testing without any special selection method

probability tables /ˌprɒbə'bɪlɪti ˌteɪb(ə)lz/ *plural noun* statistical estimates that show the expectation rate that something will occur

probable /'prɒbəb(ə)l/ *adjective* likely to happen ○ *They are trying to prevent the probable collapse of the*

company. ○ *It is probable that the company will collapse if a rescue package is not organised before the end of the month.*

probing /'prəʊbɪŋ/ *noun* an attempt by an interviewer to get the interviewee to develop an answer ○ *No amount of probing would induce the housewife to say why she did not like the new washing powder.*

problem children /'prɒbləm ˌtʃɪldr(ə)n/ *plural noun* in the Boston matrix, products which are not very profitable, and have a low market share and a high growth rate ○ *The problem children in our range make very little contribution to the company profits.* Also called **question marks**, **wild cats** (NOTE: the singular is **problem child**)

procurement /prə'kjʊəmənt/ *noun* the act of buying equipment or raw materials for a company ○ *Procurement of raw materials is becoming very complicated with the entry of so many new suppliers into the market.*

produce *noun* /'prɒdjuːs/ products from farms and gardens, especially fruit and vegetables ○ *home produce* ○ *agricultural produce* ○ *farm produce* ■ *verb* /prə'djuːs/ to make or manufacture something ○ *The factory produces cars engines.*

producer /prə'djuːsə/ *noun* a person, company or country that manufactures ○ *a country which is a producer of high-quality watches* ○ *The company is a major car producer.* Also called **supplier**

producer market /prə'djuːsə ˌmɑːkɪt/ *noun* customers who buy goods to be used in production

producer's surplus /prəˌdjuːsəz 'sɜːpləs/ *noun* the amount by which the actual price of a product is more than the minimum which the producer would accept for it ○ *There is a considerable producer's surplus because the product is in short supply.* ○ *If our customer knew the producer's surplus she would have offered much less than the asking price.*

product /'prɒdʌkt/ *noun* **1.** something which is made or manufactured **2.** a manufactured item for sale

'...today new marketing is about new products based on consumer understanding and technology' [*Marketing Week*]

'...consistency of product is probably essential for successful branding' [*Marketing Workshop*]

'...any expansion or change in market share is most likely to come from the development and improvement of existing products' [*Marketing*]

product abandonment /ˌprɒdʌkt əˈbændənmənt/ *noun* the stopping of production and selling of a product

product acceptance /ˌprɒdʌkt əkˈseptəns/ *noun* the degree to which a product is accepted by the market and so sells well ○ *We do not know what product acceptance will be in such an unknown market.*

product advertising /ˈprɒdʌkt ˌædvətaɪzɪŋ/ *noun* the advertising of a particular named product, not the company which makes it

product analysis /ˈprɒdʌkt əˌnæləsɪs/ *noun* an examination of each separate product in a company's range to find out why it sells, who buys it, etc.

product assortment /ˌprɒdʌkt əˈsɔːtmənt/ *noun* a collection of different products for sale

product churning /ˈprɒdʌkt ˌtʃɜː-nɪŋ/ *noun* the practice of putting many new products onto the market in the hope that one of them will become successful (NOTE: Product churning is especially prevalent in Japan.)

product concept /ˈprɒdʌkt ˌkɒn-sept/ *noun* same as **product idea**

product deletion /ˌprɒdʌkt dɪ-ˈliːʃ(ə)n/ *noun* the removal of old products from the market as new ones are added to the company's range ○ *Product deletion was caused by poor sales.* ○ *If production costs continue to rise then product deletion will be the only answer.*

product design /ˈprɒdʌkt dɪˌzaɪn/ *noun* the design of consumer products

product development /ˈprɒdʌkt dɪˌveləpmənt/ *noun* the process of improving an existing product line to meet the needs of the market. ⇨ **new product development**

product development cycle /ˈprɒdʌkt dɪˌveləpmənt ˌsaɪk(ə)l/

noun the stages in the development of a new product

product differentiation /ˌprɒdʌkt dɪfəˌrenʃiˈeɪʃ(ə)n/ *noun* the process of ensuring that a product has some unique features that distinguish it from competing ones ○ *We are adding some extra features to our watches in the interest of product differentiation.*

product elimination /ˌprɒdʌkt ɪlɪmɪˈneɪʃ(ə)n/ *noun* same as **product deletion**

product endorsement /ˈprɒdʌkt ɪnˌdɔːsmənt/ *noun* advertising which makes use of famous or qualified people to endorse a product ○ *Which celebrities have agreed to contribute to our endorsement advertising?* ○ *Product endorsement will, we hope, help our fund-raising campaign.*

product family /ˈprɒdʌkt ˌfæm-(ə)li/ *noun* a group of interrelated products made by the same manufacturer

product idea /ˈprɒdʌkt aɪˌdɪə/ *noun* an idea for a totally new product or an adaptation of an existing one

product idea testing /ˌprɒdʌkt aɪˈdɪə ˌtestɪŋ/ *noun* the evaluation of a new product idea, usually by consulting representatives from all main departments in a company and interviewing a sample of consumers

product image /ˈprɒdʌkt ˌɪmɪdʒ/ *noun* the general idea which the public has of a product ○ *We need a huge promotional campaign to create the desired product image.*

production /prəˈdʌkʃən/ *noun* the work of making or manufacturing goods for sale ○ *We are hoping to speed up production by installing new machinery.*

production cost /prəˈdʌkʃən kɒst/ *noun* the cost of making a product

production department /prəˈdʌkʃən dɪˌpɑːtmənt/ *noun* the section of a company which deals with the making of the company's products

production line /prəˈdʌkʃən laɪn/ *noun* a system of making a product, where each item such as a car moves slowly through the factory with new sections added to it as it goes along ○ *He works on the production line.* ○ *She is a production-line employee.*

production manager /prə'dʌkʃən ˌmænɪdʒə/ *noun* the person in charge of the production department

production standards /prə'dʌkʃən ˌstændədz/ *plural noun* the quality levels relating to production

production target /prə'dʌkʃən ˌtɑːgɪt/ *noun* the number of units a business is expected to produce

production unit /prə'dʌkʃən ˌjuːnɪt/ *noun* a separate small group of employees producing a product

productive /prə'dʌktɪv/ *adjective* producing something, especially something useful □ **productive discussions** useful discussions which lead to an agreement or decision

productive capital /prə,dʌktɪv 'kæpɪt(ə)l/ *noun* capital which is invested to give interest

productivity /ˌprɒdʌk'tɪvɪti/ *noun* the rate of output per employee, or per item of equipment, in a business ○ *Bonus payments are linked to productivity.* ○ *The company is aiming to increase productivity.* ○ *Productivity has fallen or risen since the company was taken over.*

'...though there has been productivity growth, the absolute productivity gap between many British firms and their foreign rivals remains' [*Sunday Times*]

productivity agreement /ˌprɒdʌk'tɪvɪti əˌgriːmənt/ *noun* an agreement to pay a productivity bonus

productivity bonus /ˌprɒdʌk'tɪvɪti ˌbəʊnəs/ *noun* an extra payment made to employees because of increased production per employee

productivity drive /ˌprɒdʌk'tɪvɪti draɪv/ *noun* an extra effort to increase productivity

product launch /'prɒdʌkt lɔːntʃ/ *noun* the act of putting a new product on the market

product leader /ˌprɒdʌkt 'liːdə/ *noun* the person who is responsible for managing a product line

product liability /ˌprɒdʌkt laɪə'bɪlɪti/ *noun* the liability of the maker of a product for negligence in the design or production of the product

product life cycle /ˌprɒdʌkt 'laɪf ˌsaɪk(ə)l/ *noun* stages in the life of a product in terms of sales and profitability, from its launch to its decline ○ *Growth is the first stage in the product life cycle.* ○ *The machine has reached a point in its product life cycle where we should be thinking about a replacement for it.*

product line /'prɒdʌkt laɪn/ *noun* a series of different products which form a group, all made by the same company ○ *We do not stock that line.* ○ *Computers are not one of our best-selling lines.* ○ *They produce an interesting line in garden tools.*

product management /'prɒdʌkt ˌmænɪdʒmənt/ *noun* the process of overseeing the making and selling of a product as an independent item

product manager /'prɒdʌkt ˌmænɪdʒə/ *noun* the manager or executive responsible for the marketing of a particular product ○ *To co-ordinate the selling of our entire range we need more consultation between product managers.*

product market /ˌprɒdʌkt 'mɑːkɪt/ *noun* a group of consumers for a product which is different from other groups to which the product is also sold

product-market strategies /ˌprɒdʌkt ˌmɑːkɪt 'strætɪdʒiz/ *plural noun* basic marketing strategies consisting of either market penetration, market development, product development, or diversification

product mix /'prɒdʌkt mɪks/ *noun* the range of different products which a company has for sale

product placement /'prɒdʌkt ˌpleɪsmənt/ *noun* placing products as props on TV shows or in films as a form of advertising

product-plus /'prɒdʌkt plʌs/ *noun* features of a product which make it particularly attractive

product portfolio /ˌprɒdʌkt pɔːt'fəʊliəʊ/ *noun* a collection of products made by the same company

product portfolio analysis /ˌprɒdʌkt pɔːt'fəʊliəʊ əˌnæləsɪs/ *noun* a model for a marketing strategy with various categories of product based on present performance and growth rate, which can help a business to plan its product development and strategy ○ *Product portfolio analysis showed that some products were neither performing well nor showing any signs of increasing their market share.*

product positioning /ˈprɒdʌkt pəˌzɪʃ(ə)nɪŋ/ *noun* the placing of a product in the market so that it is recognisable to the public

product range /ˈprɒdʌkt reɪndʒ/ *noun* **1.** a series of products from which the customer can choose **2.** a series of different products made by the same company which form a group

product recall /ˌprɒdʌkt ˈriːkɔːl/ *noun* the removal from sale of products that may constitute a risk to consumers because of contamination, sabotage, or faults

product research /ˌprɒdʌkt rɪˈsɜːtʃ/ *noun* research carried out to examine various competing products in a market and the potential market for such products

product strategy /ˈprɒdʌkt ˌstrætədʒi/ *noun* the various elements which a company has to take into account when developing a product, e.g. price, design, and availability

product testing /ˈprɒdʌkt ˌtestɪŋ/ *noun* the testing of a product by allowing a sample of consumers to use it without knowing which brand it is ○ *Product testing showed that unfortunately consumers preferred two other brands to this one.*

profile /ˈprəʊfaɪl/ *noun* a brief description of the characteristics of something or someone ○ *They asked for a profile of the possible partners in the joint venture.* ○ *Her CV provided a profile of her education and career to date.*

'…the audience profile does vary greatly by period: 41.6% of the adult audience is aged 16 to 34 during the morning period, but this figure drops to 24% during peak viewing time' [*Marketing Week*]

profit /ˈprɒfɪt/ *noun* money gained from a sale which is more than the money spent on making the item sold or on providing the service offered □ **profit after tax** profit after tax has been paid □ **to take your profit** to sell shares at a higher price than was paid for them, and so realise the profit, rather than to keep

them as an investment □ **to show a profit** to make a profit and state it in the company accounts ○ *We are showing a small profit for the first quarter.* □ **to make a profit** to have more money as a result of a deal □ **to move into profit** to start to make a profit ○ *The company is breaking even now, and expects to move into profit within the next two months.* □ **to sell at a profit** to sell at a price which gives you a profit □ **healthy profit** quite a large profit

profitability /ˌprɒfɪtəˈbɪlɪti/ *noun* **1.** the ability to make a profit ○ *We doubt the profitability of the project.* **2.** the amount of profit made as a percentage of costs

profitable /ˈprɒfɪtəb(ə)l/ *adjective* making a profit ○ *She runs a very profitable employment agency.*

profit after tax /ˌprɒfɪt ɑːftə ˈtæks/ *noun* same as **net profit**

profit and loss account /ˌprɒfɪt ənd ˈlɒs ˌsteɪtmənt/ *noun* the accounts for a company showing expenditure and income over a period of time, usually one calendar year, balanced to show a final profit or loss. Also called **consolidated profit and loss account**, **P&L statement** (NOTE: The UK term is **consolidated profit and loss account**.)

profit before tax /ˌprɒfɪt bɪfɔː ˈtæks/ *noun* same as **pretax profit**

profit centre /ˈprɒfɪt ˌsentə/ *noun* a person, unit or department within an organisation which is considered separately for the purposes of calculating a profit ○ *We count the kitchen equipment division as a single profit centre.*

profiteer /ˌprɒfɪˈtɪə/ *noun* a person who makes too much profit, especially when goods are rationed or in short supply

profiteering /ˌprɒfɪˈtɪərɪŋ/ *noun* the practice of making too much profit

profit-making /ˈprɒfɪt ˌmeɪkɪŋ/ *adjective* making a profit, or operated with the primary objective of making a profit ○ *The whole project was expected to be profit-making by 2001 but it still hasn't broken even.* ○ *It is hoped to make it into a profit-making concern.*

profit margin /ˈprɒfɪt ˌmɑːdʒɪn/ *noun* the percentage difference between sales income and the cost of sales

profit maximisation /ˈprɒfɪt ˌmæksɪmaɪˌzeɪʃ(ə)n/ *noun* a business strategy or policy based on achieving as high a profit as possible ○ *The company considers profit maximisation a socially irresponsible policy.*

profit on ordinary activities before tax /ˌprɒfɪt ɒn ˌɔːd(ə)n(ə)ri ækˌtɪvɪtiz bɪˌfɔː ˈtæks/ *noun* same as **pretax profit**

pro forma /ˌprəʊ ˈfɔːmə/ *noun* a document issued before all relevant details are known, usually followed by a final version

pro forma invoice /ˌprəʊ ˌfɔːmə ˈɪnvɔɪs/, **pro forma** /ˌprəʊ ˈfɔːmə/ *noun* an invoice sent to a buyer before the goods are sent, so that payment can be made or so that goods can be sent to a consignee who is not the buyer ○ *They sent us a pro forma invoice.* ○ *We only supply that account on pro forma.*

progress report /ˈprəʊgres rɪˌpɔːt/ *noun* a document which describes what progress has been made

project /ˈprɒdʒekt/ *noun* **1.** a plan ○ *She has drawn up a project for developing new markets in Europe.* **2.** a particular job of work which follows a plan ○ *We are just completing an engineering project in North Africa.* ○ *The company will start work on the project next month.*

project analysis /ˈprɒdʒekt əˌnæləsɪs/ *noun* the examination of all the costs or problems of a project before work on it is started

projected /prəˈdʒektɪd/ *adjective* planned or expected □ **projected sales** a forecast of sales ○ *Projected sales in Europe next year should be over £1m.*

projection /prəˈdʒekʃən/ *noun* a forecast of something which will happen in the future ○ *Projection of profits for the next three years.* ○ *The sales manager was asked to draw up sales projections for the next three years.*

project management /ˈprɒdʒekt ˌmænɪdʒmənt/ *noun* the coordination of the financial, material, and human resources needed to complete a project and the organisation of the work that the project involves

project manager /ˌprɒdʒekt ˈmænɪdʒə/ *noun* the manager in charge of a project

promissory note /ˈprɒmɪsəri ˌnəʊt/ *noun* a document stating that someone promises to pay an amount of money on a specific date

promote /prəˈməʊt/ *verb* to advertise a product □ **to promote a new product** to increase the sales of a new product by a sales campaign, by TV commercials or free gifts, or by giving discounts

promotion /prəˈməʊʃ(ə)n/ *noun* all means of conveying the message about a product or service to potential customers, e.g. publicity, a sales campaign, TV commercials or free gifts ○ *Our promotion budget has been doubled.* ○ *The promotion team has put forward plans for the launch.* ○ *We are offering free holidays in France as part of our special in-store promotion.* ○ *We a running a special promotion offering two for the price of one.*

'…finding the right promotion to appeal to children is no easy task' [*Marketing*]

'…you have to study the profiles and people involved very carefully and tailor the promotion to fill those needs' [*Marketing Week*]

promotional /prəˈməʊʃ(ə)n(ə)l/ *adjective* used in an advertising campaign ○ *The admen are using balloons as promotional material.*

'…the simplest way to boost sales at the expense of regional newspapers is by a heavyweight promotional campaign' [*Marketing Week*]

promotional allowance /prəˌməʊʃ(ə)n(ə)l əˈlaʊəns/ *noun* a discount which is offered to a buyer in return for some promotional activity in connection with the product sold

promotional budget /prəˌməʊʃ(ə)n(ə)l ˈbʌdʒɪt/ *noun* a forecast of the cost of promoting a new product

promotional discount /prəˌməʊʃ(ə)n(ə)l ˈdɪskaʊnt/ *noun* a special discount offered as part of the promotion for a product

promotional mix /prəˌməʊʃ(ə)n(ə)l ˈmɪks/ *noun* the combination of all the elements that make up a company's promotion ○ *Our promotional mix consists of an extended TV and radio* *advertising campaign.* ○ *The exact promotional mix will depend on the costs of the various media available.*

promotional price /prə'məʊ-ʃ(ə)n(ə)l praɪs/ *noun* a reduced price offered in order to maximise sales (often when a product is launched)

promotional products /prə'məʊ-ʃ(ə)n(ə)l ˌprɒdʌkts/ *plural noun* premium offers, gifts, prizes, etc.

promotional tools /prə'məʊ-ʃ(ə)n(ə)l tuːlz/ *plural noun* material used in promotion, e.g. display material and sales literature ○ *A draw for a free holiday on the exhibition stand is one of the best promotional tools I know.* ○ *The sales reps are armed with a full range of promotional tools.*

promotools /'prəʊməʊtuːlz/ *plural noun* same as **promotional tools** (*informal*)

prompt /prɒmpt/ *adjective* rapid or done immediately ○ *We got very prompt service at the complaints desk.* ○ *Thank you for your prompt reply to my letter.* □ **prompt payment** payment made rapidly □ **prompt supplier** a supplier who delivers orders rapidly ■ *noun* information or an idea offered to people to help them answer a question in a survey ■ *verb* to give someone help in answering a question ○ *In order to avoid influencing the answers, the interviewer must prompt the respondent only when it is really necessary.*

prompted awareness test /ˌprɒmptɪd ə'weənəs test/ *noun* a test where the respondents are asked if they know the named product

prompted recall /ˌprɒmptɪd 'riː-kɔːl/ *noun* a test to see how well people can remember an advertisement in which the respondents are given some help such as a picture which they might associate with the advertisement ○ *After a prompted recall test, the company and its advertising agency decided to change the advertisement.*

proof /pruːf/ *noun* evidence which shows that something is true

proof of purchase /ˌpruːf əv 'pɜːtʃɪs/ *noun* evidence, e.g. a sales slip, to show that an article has been purchased, used in order to claim some benefit such as a free gift, or in order to claim reimbursement

propaganda /ˌprɒpə'gændə/ *noun* an attempt to spread an idea through clever use of the media and other forms of communication ○ *The charity has been criticised for spreading political propaganda.*

propensity /prə'pensɪti/ *noun* a tendency

propensity to consume /prə-ˌpensɪti tə kən'sjuːm/ *noun* the ratio between consumers' needs and their expenditure on goods

propensity to import /prə,pensɪti tə ɪm'pɔːt/ *noun* the ratio between changes in the national income and changes in expenditure on imports

propensity to invest /prə,pensɪti tə ɪn'vest/ *noun* the tendency of producers to invest in capital goods

propensity to save /prə,pensɪti tə 'seɪv/ *noun* the tendency of consumers to save instead of spending on consumer goods

property developer /'prɒpəti dɪ,veləpə/ *noun* a person who buys old buildings or empty land and plans and builds new houses or factories for sale or rent

property market /'prɒpəti ,mɑːkɪt/ *noun* same as **housing market**

proprietary goods /prə'praɪət(ə)ri gʊdz/ *plural noun* brands of a product such as medicines that are owned by the company which makes them

prospect /'prɒspekt/ *noun* **1.** a chance or possibility that something will happen in the future □ **prospects for the market** *or* **market prospects are worse than those of last year** sales in the market are likely to be lower than they were last year **2.** a person who may become a customer ○ *The sales force were looking out for prospects.*

prospecting /prə'spektɪŋ/ *noun* the act of looking for new customers

prospective /prə'spektɪv/ *adjective* possibly happening in the future □ **a prospective buyer** someone who may buy in the future ○ *There is no* *shortage of prospective buyers for the computer.*

prospects /'prɒspekts/ *plural noun* the possibilities for the future

prospectus /prə'spektəs/ *noun* a document which gives information to attract buyers or customers ○ *The restaurant has people handing out prospectuses in the street.*

'…when the prospectus emerges, existing shareholders and any prospective new investors can find out more by calling the free share information line; they will be sent a leaflet. Non-shareholders who register in this way will receive a prospectus when it is published; existing shareholders will be sent one automatically' [*Financial Times*]

protectionism /prə'tekʃənɪz(ə) m/ *noun* the practice of protecting producers in the home country against foreign competitors by banning or taxing imports or by imposing import quotas

protest *noun*/'prəʊtest/ an official document which proves that a bill of exchange has not been paid ■ *verb*/ prə'test/ □ **to protest a bill** to draw up a document to prove that a bill of exchange has not been paid

prototype /'prəʊtətaɪp/ *noun* the first model of a new product before it goes into production ○ *a prototype car* ○ *a prototype plane* ○ *The company is showing the prototype of the new model at the exhibition.*

provisional /prə'vɪʒ(ə)n(ə)l/ *adjective* temporary, not final or permanent ○ *The sales department has been asked to make a provisional forecast of sales.* ○ *The provisional budget has been drawn up for each department.* ○ *They faxed their provisional acceptance of the contract.*

prune /pruːn/ *verb* to reduce a product range by deleting old products ○ *The new marketing director insisted on pruning the product line to streamline the company's functions.*

psychogalvanometer /ˌsaɪkəʊ-gælvə'nɒmɪtə/ *noun* an instrument used to measure emotional reactions to advertising by checking the degree of sweating on the palms of the hands ○ *The results of the psychogalvanometer test suggested that the ad was*

so dull it had no effect whatever on the public.

psychographics /ˌsaɪkəʊ'græ-fɪks/ *noun* the study of the life style of different sectors of society for marketing purposes ○ *Psychographics can help define the market segment we should be aiming for with our product.* (NOTE: takes a singular verb)

psychographic segmentation /ˌsaɪkəʊˌgræfɪk ˌsegmən'teɪʃ(ə)n/ *noun* the division of a market into segments according to the lifestyles of the customers

public /'pʌblɪk/ *adjective* referring to all the people in general ■ *noun* □ **the public, the general public** the people

publication /ˌpʌblɪ'keɪʃ(ə)n/ *noun* **1.** the act of making something public by publishing it ○ *the publication of the latest trade figures* **2.** a printed document which is to be sold or given to the public ○ *We asked the library for a list of government publications.*

public image /ˌpʌblɪk 'ɪmɪdʒ/ *noun* an idea which the people have of a company or a person ○ *The minister is trying to improve her public image.*

publicise /'pʌblɪsaɪz/, **publicize** *verb* to attract people's attention to a product for sale, a service, or an entertainment ○ *The campaign is intended to publicise the services of the tourist board.* ○ *We are trying to publicise our products by advertisements on buses.*

publicity /pʌ'blɪsɪti/ *noun* the process of attracting the attention of the public to products or services by mentioning them in the media

publicity budget /pʌ'blɪsɪti ˌbʌd-ʒɪt/ *noun* money allowed for expenditure on publicity

publicity copy /pʌ'blɪsɪti ˌkɒpi/ *noun* the text of a proposed advertisement before it is printed ○ *She writes publicity copy for a travel firm.*

publicity department /pʌ'blɪsɪti dɪˌpɑːtmənt/ *noun* the section of a company which organizes the company's publicity

publicity expenditure /pʌ'blɪsɪti ɪkˌspendɪtʃə/ *noun* money spent on publicity

publicity handout /pʌˈblɪsɪti ˌhændaʊt/ *noun* an information sheet which is given to members of the public

publicity manager /pʌˈblɪsɪti ˌmænɪdʒə/ *noun* the person in charge of a publicity department

publicity matter /pʌˈblɪsɪti ˌmætə/ *noun* sheets, posters, or leaflets used for publicity

publicity slogan /pʌˈblɪsɪti ˌsləʊgən/ *noun* a group of words which can be easily remembered and which is used in publicity for a product ○ *We are using the slogan 'Smiths can make it' on all our publicity.*

public limited company /ˌpʌblɪk ˌlɪmɪtɪd ˈkʌmp(ə)ni/ *noun* a company whose shares can be bought on the stock exchange. Abbreviation **Plc, PLC, plc.** Also called **public company**

public opinion /ˌpʌblɪk əˈpɪnjən/ *noun* what people think about something

public relations /ˌpʌblɪk rɪˈleɪʃ(ə)nz/ *plural noun* the practice of building up and keeping good relations between an organisation and the public, or an organisation and its employees, so that people know and think well of what the organisation is doing ○ *She works in public relations.* ○ *A public relations firm handles all our publicity.* Abbreviation **PR** (NOTE: takes a singular verb)

public relations consultancy /ˌpʌblɪk rɪˈleɪʃ(ə)nz kənˌsʌltənsi/ *noun* a firm which advises on public relations

public relations department /ˌpʌblɪk rɪˈleɪʃ(ə)nz dɪˌpɑːtmənt/ *noun* the section of a company which deals with relations with the public. Abbreviation **PR department**

public relations exercise /ˌpʌblɪk rɪˈleɪʃ(ə)nz ˌeksəsaɪz/ *noun* a campaign to improve public relations

public relations officer /ˌpʌblɪk rɪˈleɪʃ(ə)nz ˌɒfɪsə/ *noun* a person in an organisation who is responsible for public relations activities. Abbreviation **PRO**

publics /ˈpʌblɪks/ *plural noun* groups of people that are identified for marketing purposes ○ *What publics is this product likely to appeal to?* ○ *Dif-*

ferent marketing messages need to be aimed at different publics.

public sector /ˈpʌblɪk ˌsektə/ *noun* nationalised industries and services ○ *a report on wage rises in the public sector* or *on public-sector wage settlements* Also called **government sector**

public service advertising /ˌpʌblɪk ˈsɜːvɪs ˌædvətaɪzɪŋ/ *noun* the advertising of a public service or cause such as famine relief

public transport /ˌpʌblɪk ˈtrænspɔːt/ *noun* transport which is used by any member of the public, e.g. buses and trains

public transport system /ˌpʌblɪk ˈtrænspɔːt ˌsɪstəm/ *noun* a system of trains, buses, etc., used by the general public

public warehouse /ˌpʌblɪk ˈweəhaʊs/ *noun* a warehouse which stores goods which are awaiting shipment or which have just been landed

puff /pʌf/ *noun* a claim made for a product or an organisation in order to promote it ○ *The magazine article was supposed to be about telecommunications, but was just a puff for a new modem.*

puffery /ˈpʌfəri/ *noun* advertising which praises the product or service being sold in an exaggerated way, without any specific factual data

puff piece /ˈpʌf piːs/ *noun* a supposedly objective newspaper or magazine article about a product or service, which reads as if it were written by an in-house publicity department and may in fact be written by advertising people on behalf of a client

pull-push strategy /ˌpʊl ˈpʊʃ ˌstrætədʒi/ *noun* a combination of both pull and push strategies

pull strategy /ˈpʊl ˌstrætədʒi/ *noun* an attempt by a producer to use heavy advertising to persuade final users to buy a product, so 'pulling' the product through the distribution channel to the point of sale ○ *We must develop a better pull strategy to allow retailers to sell off their excess stocks.*

pump priming /ˈpʌmp ˌpraɪmɪŋ/ *noun* government investment in new projects which it hopes will benefit the economy

purchase /'pɜːtʃɪs/ *noun* a product or service which has been bought □ **to make a purchase** to buy something ■ *verb* to buy something □ **to purchase something for cash** to pay cash for something

purchase book /'pɜːtʃɪs bʊk/ *noun* a book in which purchases are recorded

purchase history /'pɜːtʃɪs ˌhɪst(ə)ri/ *noun* a record of purchases which a customer has made in the past, or of sales made by a retail outlet, or of sales of a product over a specific period

purchase ledger /'pɜːtʃɪs ˌledʒə/ *noun* a book in which purchases are recorded

purchase order /'pɜːtʃɪs ˌɔːdə/ *noun* an official order made out by a purchasing department for goods which a company wants to buy ○ *We cannot supply you without a purchase order number.*

purchase price /'pɜːtʃɪs praɪs/ *noun* a price paid for something

purchaser /'pɜːtʃɪsə/ *noun* a person or company that purchases ○ *The company has found a purchaser for its warehouse.* □ **the company is looking for a purchaser** the company is trying to find someone who will buy it

purchase tax /'pɜːtʃɪs tæks/ *noun* a tax paid on things which are bought

purchasing /'pɜːtʃɪsɪŋ/ *noun, adjective* buying

purchasing department /'pɜːtʃɪsɪŋ dɪˌpɑːtmənt/ *noun* the section of a company which deals with the buying of stock, raw materials, equipment, etc.

purchasing manager /'pɜːtʃɪsɪŋ ˌmænɪdʒə/ *noun* the head of a purchasing department

purchasing officer /'pɜːtʃɪsɪŋ ˌɒfɪsə/ *noun* a person in a company or organisation who is responsible for buying stock, raw materials, equipment, etc.

purchasing opportunity /'pɜːtʃɪsɪŋ ˌɒpəˌtjuːnɪti/ *noun* a possibility for a customer to make a purchase

pure competition /ˌpjʊə ˌkɒmpɪˈtɪʃ(ə)n/ *noun* a hypothetical model of a market where all products of a particular type are identical, where there is complete information about market conditions available to buyers and sellers, and complete freedom for sellers to enter or leave the market

push /pʊʃ/ *noun* the action of making something move forward ◇ **push the envelope** /ˌpʊʃ ði ˈenvələʊp/ to go beyond normal limits and try to do something that is new and sometimes risky (*slang*)

push advertising /'pʊʃ ˌædvətaɪzɪŋ/ *noun* proactive and dynamic advertising to an entire group of potential customers in order to attract the few that many be interested in a product or service e.g. magazine, billboard, newspaper, and TV advertising and banner ads and email broadcasts

push money /'pʊʃ ˌmʌni/ *noun* cash given to a sales force to encourage them to promote a product

push-pull strategy /ˌpʊʃ 'pʊl ˌstrætɪdʒi/ *noun* same as **pull-push strategy**

push strategy /'pʊʃ ˌstrætədʒi/ *noun* **1.** an attempt by a manufacturer to push the product towards the customer **2.** an attempt by a producer to persuade distributors to take part in the marketing of a product, so 'pushing' it through the distribution channel

put /pʊt/ *verb*

put down *phrasal verb* to make a deposit ○ *to put down money on a house*

put in *phrasal verb* □ **to put an ad in a paper** to have an ad printed in a newspaper □ **to put in a bid for something** to offer to buy something, usually in writing □ **to put in an estimate for something** to give someone a written calculation of the probable costs of carrying out a job □ **to put in a claim for damage** to ask an insurance company to pay for damage

pyramid /'pɪrəmɪd/ *noun* a hierarchical staff structure in an organisation, with few employees at the top and many more at the bottom

pyramid selling /ˈpɪrəmɪd ˌselɪŋ/ *noun* an illegal way of selling goods or investments to the public, where each selling agent pays for the franchise to sell the product or service, and sells that right on to other agents together with stock, so that in the end the person who makes the most money is the original franchiser, and sub-agents or investors may lose all their investments

'…much of the population had committed their life savings to get-rich-quick pyramid investment schemes – where newcomers pay the original investors until the money runs out – which inevitably collapsed' [*Times*]

Q

quad crown /ˈkwɒd kraʊn/ *noun* a poster size corresponding to twice a double crown

qualified prospects /ˌkwɒlɪfaɪd ˈprɒspekts/ *plural noun* prospective customers who can make buying decisions

qualitative /ˈkwɒlɪtətɪv/ *adjective* referring to quality

qualitative audit /ˈkwɒlɪtətɪv ˌɔːdɪt/ *noun* examining an advertising agency's work in planning and developing a client's advertising programme

qualitative data /ˌkwɒlɪtətɪvˈdeɪtə/ *noun* data found in qualitative research

qualitative research /ˈkwɒlɪtətɪv rɪˌsɜːtʃ/ *noun* research based on finding the opinions and attitudes of respondents rather than any scientifically measurable data ○ *Qualitative research can be used to ascertain consumers' attitudes to a new advertising campaign.* ○ *Qualitative research will not give objective information.*

quality /ˈkwɒlɪti/ *noun* what something is like or how good or bad something is ○ *The poor quality of the service led to many complaints.* ○ *There is a market for good-quality secondhand computers.* □ **we sell only quality farm produce** we sell only farm produce of the best quality □ **high quality, top quality** of the very best quality ○ *The store specialises in high-quality imported items.*

quality control /ˈkwɒlɪti kənˌtrəʊl/ *noun* the process of making sure that the quality of a product is good

quality controller /ˈkwɒlɪti kənˌtrəʊlə/ *noun* a person who checks the quality of a product

quality label /ˈkwɒlɪti ˌleɪb(ə)l/ *noun* a label which states the quality of something

quality press /ˈkwɒlɪti pres/ *noun* newspapers aiming at the upper end of the market ○ *We advertise in the quality press.*

quantitative /ˈkwɒntɪtətɪv/ *adjective* referring to quantity

'…the collection of consumer behaviour data in the book covers both qualitative and quantitative techniques' [*Quarterly Review of Marketing*]

quantitative data /ˌkwɒntɪtətɪv ˈdeɪtə/ *noun* data gathered in quantitative research

quantitative research /ˈkwɒntɪtətɪv rɪˌsɜːtʃ/ *noun* research based on measurable data gathered by sampling ○ *Quantitative research will provide a firm basis for strategy decisions.*

quantity /ˈkwɒntɪti/ *noun* **1.** the amount or number of items ○ *a small quantity of illegal drugs* ○ *She bought a large quantity of spare parts.* **2.** an amount, especially a large amount

quantity discount /ˌkwɒntɪti ˈdɪskaʊnt/ *noun* a discount given to people who buy large quantities

quantity purchase /ˈkwɒntɪti ˌpɜːtʃɪs/ *noun* a large quantity of goods bought at one time ○ *The company offers a discount for quantity purchase.*

quarterly /ˈkwɔːtəli/ *noun* a newspaper or magazine which appears four times a year ○ *We're advertising in a medical quarterly.*

quasi- /ˈkweɪzaɪ/ *prefix* almost or which seems like ○ *a quasi-official body*

quasi-retailing /ˌkweɪzaɪ 'riːte-ɪlɪŋ/ *prefix* retailing relating to the provision of services, as in restaurants or hairdressers

question marks /'kwestʃ(ə)n maːks/ *plural noun* same as **problem children**

questionnaire /ˌkwestʃə'neə/ *noun* a printed list of questions aiming at collecting data in an unbiased way, especially used in market research ○ *We'll send out a questionnaire to test the opinions of users of the system.* ○ *We were asked to answer or to fill in a questionnaire about holidays abroad.*

quota /'kwəʊtə/ *noun* a limited amount of something which is allowed to be produced, imported, etc.

'Canada agreed to a new duty-free quota of 600,000 tonnes a year' [*Globe and Mail (Toronto)*]

quota sample /'kwəʊtə ˌsaːmpəl/ *noun* a sample which is preselected on the basis of specific criteria so as best to represent the group of people sampled ○ *The quota sample was used to represent the various ethnic groupings in their correct proportions.*

quota system /'kwəʊtə ˌsɪstəm/ *noun* a system where imports or supplies are regulated by fixed maximum amounts

quotation /kwəʊ'teɪʃ(ə)n/ *noun* an estimate of how much something will cost ○ *They sent in their quotation for the job.* ○ *Our quotation was much lower than all the others.* ○ *We accepted the lowest quotation.*

quote /kwəʊt/ *verb* **1.** to repeat words or a reference number used by someone else ○ *He quoted figures from the annual report.* ○ *In reply please quote this number.* ○ *When making a complaint please quote the batch number printed on the box.* ○ *She replied, quoting the number of the account.* **2.** to estimate what a cost or price is likely to be ○ *to quote a price for supplying stationery* ○ *Their prices are always quoted in dollars.* ○ *He quoted me a price of £1,026.* ○ *Can you quote for supplying 20,000 envelopes?* ■ *noun* an estimate of how much something will cost (*informal*) ○ *to give someone a quote for supplying computers* ○ *We have asked for quotes for refitting the shop.* ○ *Her quote was the lowest of three.* ○ *We accepted the lowest quote.*

R

rack /ræk/ *noun* a frame to hold items for display ○ *a magazine rack* ○ *Put the birthday-card display rack near the checkout.* ○ *We need a bigger display rack for these magazines.*

rack board /'ræk bɔːd/ *noun* a board on which items can be displayed, showing the names and prices of products

rack jobber /'ræk ˌdʒɒbə/ *noun* a wholesaler who sells goods by putting them on racks in retail shops

radio button /'reɪdiəʊ ˌbʌt(ə)n/ *noun* a device on a computer screen that can be used to select an option from a list

rail /reɪl/ *noun* a railway system ○ *Six million commuters travel to work by rail each day.* ○ *We ship all our goods by rail.* ○ *Rail travellers are complaining about rising fares.* ○ *Rail travel is cheaper than air travel.* □ **free on rail (FOR)** a price including all the seller's costs until the goods are delivered to the railway for shipment

railhead /'reɪlhed/ *noun* the end of a railway line ○ *The goods will be sent to the railhead by lorry.*

railroad /'reɪlrəʊd/ *noun US* same as **railway**

railway /'reɪlweɪ/ *noun* a system using trains to carry passengers and goods ○ *The local railway station has frequent trains to London.* ○ *They are planning to close the railway line as it isn't economic.* ○ *The country's railway network is being modernised.* (NOTE: The US term is **railroad**.)

rake-off /'reɪk ɒf/ *noun* a person's share of profits from a deal, especially if obtained illegally ○ *The group gets a rake-off on all the company's sales.* ○ *He got a £100,000 rake-off for intro-*ducing the new business. (NOTE: The plural is **rake-offs**.)

R&D *abbreviation* research and development

random /'rændəm/ *adjective* done without making any special selection □ **at random** without special selection ○ *The director picked out two sales reports at random.*

random check /ˌrændəm 'tʃek/ *noun* a check on items taken from a group without any special selection

random error /ˌrændəm 'erə/ *noun* a computer error for which there is no special reason

random fluctuation /ˌrændəm ˌflʌktʃu'eɪʃ(ə)n/ *noun* unforeseeable deviation from an expected trend

random observation method /ˌrændəm ˌɒbzə'veɪʃ(ə)n ˌmeθəd/ *noun* same as **activity sampling**

random sample /ˌrændəm 'sɑːmpəl/ *noun* a sample taken without any selection

random sampling /ˌrændəm 'sɑːmplɪŋ/ *noun* the action of choosing samples for testing without any special selection

random walk /ˌrændəm 'wɔːk/ *noun* a sampling technique which allows for random selection within specific limits set up by a non-random technique

range /reɪndʒ/ *noun* **1.** a series of items ○ *Their range of products or product range is too narrow.* ○ *We offer a wide range of sizes* or *range of styles.* **2.** a spread of sizes or amounts within fixed limits ○ *We make shoes in a wide range of prices.* **3.** a set of activities or products of the same general type or variety ○ *This falls within the company's range* *of activities.* ■ *verb* to be within a group of sizes or amounts falling within fixed limits ○ *The company sells products ranging from cheap pens to imported luxury items.* ○ *The company's salary scale ranges from £10,000 for a trainee to £150,000 for the managing director.* ○ *Our activities range from mining in the US to computer services in Scotland.*

'…the latest addition to the range features two hotplates, a storage cupboard, a refrigerator and a microwave oven' [*Sales & Marketing Management*]

'…the range has been extended to nine products' [*Marketing Week*]

rapport /ræˈpɔː/ *noun* good communication and understanding between two people ○ *The interviewer managed to establish a good rapport with the interviewees.* ○ *Co-ordination is difficult owing to lack of rapport between the marketing manager and the managing director.*

rate /reɪt/ *noun* **1.** the money charged for time worked or work completed **2.** the value of one currency against another ○ *What is today's rate* or *the current rate for the dollar?* □ **to calculate costs on a fixed exchange rate** to calculate costs on an exchange rate which does not change **3.** an amount, number or speed compared with something else ○ *the rate of increase in redundancies* ○ *The rate of absenteeism* or *The absenteeism rate always increases in fine weather.*

rate card /ˈreɪt kɑːd/ *noun* a list of charges for advertising issued by a newspaper or magazine

rate of exchange /ˌreɪt əv ɪksˈtʃeɪndʒ/ *noun* same as **exchange rate** ○ *The current rate of exchange is $1.60 to the pound.*

rate of interest /ˌreɪt əv ˈɪntrəst/ *noun* same as **interest rate**

rate of return /ˌreɪt əv rɪˈtɜːn/ *noun* the amount of interest or dividend which comes from an investment, shown as a percentage of the money invested

rate of sales /ˌreɪt əv ˈseɪlz/ *noun* the speed at which units are sold

rate of turnover /ˌreɪt əv ˈtɜːnəʊvə/ *noun* the length of time taken from the purchase of an item of stock to its replacement after being sold ○ *The rate of turnover is so low that*

some articles have been in the shop for more than a year.

rate of unemployment /ˌreɪt əv ˌʌnɪmˈplɔɪmənt/ *noun* same as **unemployment rate**

rating /ˈreɪtɪŋ/ *noun* the act of giving something a value, or the value given

ratings /ˈreɪtɪŋz/ *plural noun* the estimated number of people who watch TV programmes ○ *The show is high in the ratings, which means it will attract good publicity.*

ratings point /ˈreɪtɪŋz pɔɪnt/ *noun* one percentage point of a TV audience in a given area

ratio /ˈreɪʃiəʊ/ *noun* a proportion or quantity of something compared to something else ○ *the ratio of successes to failures* ○ *Our product outsells theirs by a ratio of two to one.*

rational /ˈræʃ(ə)n(ə)l/ *adjective* sensible, based on reason

rational appeal /ˈræʃ(ə)n(ə)l əˌpiːl/ *noun* advertising appeal to a prospective customer that uses logical arguments to show that the product satisfies the customer's practical needs (as opposed to an emotional appeal)

rationalise /ˈræʃ(ə)nəlaɪz/, **rationalize** *verb* to make something more efficient ○ *The rail company is trying to rationalise its freight services.*

raw /rɔː/ *adjective* in the original state or not processed

'…it makes sense for them to produce goods for sale back home in the US from plants in Britain where raw materials are relatively cheap' [*Duns Business Month*]

raw data /ˌrɔː ˈdeɪtə/ *noun* data as it is put into a computer, without being analysed

raw materials /ˌrɔː məˈtɪəriəlz/ *plural noun* basic materials which have to be treated or processed in some way before they can be used, e.g. wood, iron ore or crude petroleum

reach /riːtʃ/ *verb* to get to something ■ *noun* the actual number of people who will see an advertisement once (as opposed to the frequency, which is the number of times one person sees an advertisement over a given period of time) ○ *The success of an advertisement depends on its reach.*

readability /ˌriːdəˈbɪlɪti/ *noun* the fact of being easy to read (either copy for an advertisement or the advertisement itself)

reader /ˈriːdə/ *noun* a person who reads a newspaper or magazine

reader advertisement /ˈriːdər ədˌvɜːtɪsmənt/ *noun* an advertisement in the form of editorial matter

reader loyalty /ˌriːdə ˈlɔɪəlti/ *noun* the inclination of a person to keep reading and buying the same publication

readership /ˈriːdəʃɪp/ *noun* all the people who read a particular publication ○ *Our readership has increased since we included more feature articles in the magazine.*

reader's inquiry card /ˌriːdəz ɪnˈkwaɪəri kɑːd/, **reader's service card** /ˌriːdəz ˈsɜːvɪs kɑːd/ *noun* a card bound into a magazine which contains a matrix of numbers and letters on which readers can mark codes for products they wish to have further information about. The card is returned to the publisher, who gets the advertiser to send the relevant information to the reader.

reading and noting /ˌriːdɪŋ ən ˈnəʊtɪŋ/ *noun* a research statistic showing the proportion of the readership of a publication who actually read a given advertisement

readvertise /riːˈædvətaɪz/ *verb* to advertise again ○ *All the candidates failed the test so we will just have to readvertise the job.* □ **to readvertise a post** to put in a second advertisement for a vacant post

readvertisement /ˌriːədˈvɜːtɪsmənt/ *noun* a second advertisement for a vacant post ○ *The readvertisement attracted only two new applicants.*

ready /ˈredi/ *adjective* **1.** fit to be used or to be sold ○ *The order will be ready for delivery next week.* ○ *The driver had to wait because the shipment was not ready.* **2.** quick □ **these items find a ready sale in the Middle East** these items sell rapidly or easily in the Middle East

ready cash /ˌredi ˈkæʃ/ *noun* money which is immediately available for payment

ready-made /ˌredi ˈmeɪd/, **ready-to-wear** /ˌredi tə ˈweə/ *adjective* referring to clothes which are mass-produced and not made for each customer personally ○ *The ready-to-wear trade has suffered from foreign competition.*

ready market /ˌredi ˈmɑːkɪt/ *noun* a market with a high turnover of goods ○ *Distribution has to be good in such a ready market.*

ready money /ˌredi ˈmʌni/ *noun* cash or money which is immediately available

ready sale /ˌredi ˈseɪl/ *noun* a sale that is easily achieved ○ *Lengthy negotiations are a trial for salespeople used to ready sales.*

real /rɪəl/ *adjective* **1.** genuine and not an imitation ○ *His case is made of real leather* or *he has a real leather case.* ○ *That car is a real bargain at £300.* **2.** (*of prices or amounts*) shown in terms of money adjusted for inflation □ **in real terms** actually or really ○ *Salaries have gone up by 3% but with inflation running at 5% that is a fall in real terms.*

'…real wages have been held down dramatically: they have risen as an annual rate of only 1% in the last two years' [*Sunday Times*]

'…sterling M3 rose by 13.5% in the year to August – seven percentage points faster than the rate of inflation and the biggest increase in real terms for years' [*Economist*]

'Japan's gross national product for the April-June quarter dropped 0.4% in real terms from the previous quarter' [*Nikkei Weekly*]

'…the Federal Reserve Board has eased interest rates in the past year, but they are still at historically high levels in real terms' [*Sunday Times*]

realised profit /ˌrɪəlaɪzd ˈprɒfɪt/ *noun* an actual profit made when something is sold, as opposed to paper profit

Really Simple Syndication /ˌrɪəli ˌsɪmp(ə)l ˌsɪndɪˈkeɪʃ(ə)n/ *noun* a type of XML file format which allows news websites to update regularly using a tagged-up source feed. Abbreviation **RSS**

real time credit card processing /ˌrɪəl taɪm ˈkredɪt kɑːd ˌprəʊsesɪŋ/ *noun* online checking of a credit card that either approves or rejects it for use during a transaction

real time transaction /ˌrɪəl taɪm trænˈzækʃən/ *noun* an Internet payment transaction that is either approved or rejected immediately when the customer completes the online order form

rebate /ˈriːbeɪt/ *noun* **1.** a reduction in the amount of money to be paid ○ *We are offering a 10% rebate on selected goods.* **2.** money returned to someone because they have paid too much ○ *She got a tax rebate at the end of the year.*

rebating /riːˈbeɪtɪŋ/ *noun* the offering of a rebate

rebound /rɪˈbaʊnd/ *verb* to go back up again quickly ○ *The market rebounded on the news of the government's decision.*

rebuy /ˈriːbaɪ/ *noun* the act of buying a product again

recall /rɪˈkɔːl/ *verb* (*of a manufacturer*) to ask for products to be returned because of possible faults ○ *They recalled 10,000 washing machines because of a faulty electrical connection.* ■ *noun* the ability to remember an advertisement

recall test /ˈriːkɔːl test/ *noun* in advertising, a research test that checks how well someone can remember an advertisement ○ *A disappointing number of respondents in the recall test failed to remember the advertisement.*

receipt /rɪˈsiːt/ *noun* a piece of paper showing that money has been paid or that something has been received ○ *He kept the customs receipt to show that he had paid duty on the goods.* ○ *She lost her taxi receipt.* ○ *Keep the receipt for items purchased in case you need to change them later.*

receipts /rɪˈsiːts/ *plural noun* money taken in sales ○ *to itemise receipts and expenditure* ○ *Receipts are down against the same period of last year.*

'…the public sector borrowing requirement is kept low by treating the receipts from selling public assets as a reduction in borrowing' [*Economist*]

'…gross wool receipts for the selling season to end June appear likely to top $2 billion' [*Australian Financial Review*]

recession /rɪˈseʃ(ə)n/ *noun* a period where there is a decline in trade or in the economy ○ *The recession has reduced profits in many companies.* ○ *Several firms have closed factories because of the recession.*

recipient /rɪˈsɪpiənt/ *noun* a person who receives something ○ *She was the recipient of an allowance from the company.* ○ *He was the recipient of the award for salesperson of the year.* ○ *A registered letter must be signed for by the recipient.*

reciprocal /rɪˈsɪprək(ə)l/ *adjective* done by one person, company, or country to another one, which does the same thing in return ○ *We signed a reciprocal agreement* or *a reciprocal contract with a Russian company.*

reciprocal holdings /rɪˌsɪprək(ə)l ˈhəʊldɪŋz/ *plural noun* a situation in which two companies own shares in each other to prevent takeover bids

reciprocal trade /rɪˌsɪprək(ə)l ˈtreɪd/ *noun* trade between two countries

reciprocate /rɪˈsɪprəkeɪt/ *verb* to do the same thing for someone as that person has done for you ○ *They offered us an exclusive agency for their cars and we reciprocated with an offer of the agency for our buses.*

recognise /ˈrekəgnaɪz/ *verb* **1.** to know someone or something because you have seen or heard them before ○ *I recognised his voice before he said who he was.* ○ *Do you recognise the handwriting on the application form?* **2.** to record an item in an account or other financial statement □ **to recognise a union** to agree that a union can act on behalf of employees in a company ○ *Although more than half the staff had joined the union, the management refused to recognise it.*

recognised agent /ˌrekəgnaɪzd ˈeɪdʒənt/ *noun* an agent who is approved by the company for which they act

recognition /ˌrekəgˈnɪʃ(ə)n/ *noun* the act of recognising something or somebody

recognition test /ˌrekəgˈnɪʃ(ə)n test/ *noun* a research test in advertising that checks to see how well someone can remember an advertisement either with or without prompting or aided recall

recommended retail price /ˌrekəmendɪd ˈriːteɪl ˌpraɪs/ *noun* the price at which a manufacturer suggests a product should be sold on the retail market, though this may be reduced by the retailer. Abbreviation **RRP** Also called **administered price**

record /'rekɔːd/ *noun* **1.** a description of what has happened in the past ○ *the salesperson's record of service* or *service record* ○ *the company's record in industrial relations* **2.** a success which is better than anything before ○ *Last year was a record year for the company.* ○ *Our top sales rep has set a new record for sales per call.* □ **we broke our record for June** we sold more than we have ever sold before in June ○ *Sales last year equalled the record set in 1997.* ■ *verb* /rɪ'kɔːd/ to note or report something ○ *The company has recorded another year of increased sales.*

record-breaking /'rekɔːd ˌbreɪkɪŋ/ *adjective* better or worse than anything which has happened before ○ *We are proud of our record-breaking profits in 2000.*

recorded delivery /rɪˌkɔːdɪd dɪ-'lɪv(ə)ri/ *noun* a mail service where the letters are signed for by the person receiving them ○ *We sent the documents (by) recorded delivery.*

recording /rɪ'kɔːdɪŋ/ *noun* the act of making a note of something ○ *the recording of an order* or *of a complaint*

records /'rekɔːdz/ *plural noun* documents which give information ○ *The names of customers are kept in the company's records.* ○ *We find from our records that our invoice number 1234 has not been paid.*

recruit /rɪ'kruːt/ *verb* □ **to recruit new staff** to search for and appoint new staff to join a company ○ *We are recruiting staff for our new store.*

recruitment /rɪ'kruːtmənt/, **recruiting** /rɪ'kruːtɪŋ/ *noun* □ **the recruitment of new staff** the process of looking for new staff to join a company

recruitment advertising /rɪ'kruːtmənt ˌædvətaɪzɪŋ/ *noun* the advertising of jobs ○ *A sudden need for labour has led to a huge demand for recruitment advertising.*

recycle /riː'saɪk(ə)l/ *verb* to take waste material and process it so that it can be used again

recycled paper /riːˌsaɪk(ə)ld 'peɪpə/ *noun* paper made from waste paper

redeem /rɪ'diːm/ *verb* to exchange a voucher, coupon, or stamp for a gift or a reduction in price

redemption /rɪ'dempʃən/ *noun* the exchanging of vouchers, coupons, or stamps for a gift or a reduction in price

red goods /'red gʊdz/ *plural noun* fast-selling convenience goods, especially food items. Compare **orange goods, yellow goods**

reduced rate /rɪˌdjuːst 'reɪt/ *noun* a specially cheap charge

reduction /rɪ'dʌkʃən/ *noun* an act of making something smaller or less ○ *Reduction in demand has led to the cancellation of several new projects.* ○ *The company was forced to make reductions in its advertising budget.* ○ *Price reductions have had no effect on our sales.*

re-export *noun* /riː'ekspɔːt/ the exporting of goods which have been imported ○ *The port is a centre for the re-export trade.* ○ *We import wool for re-export.* ○ *The value of re-exports has increased.* ■ *verb* /ˌriːek'spɔːt/ to export something which has been imported

re-exportation /ˌriː ekspɔː'teɪʃ(ə)n/ *noun* the exporting of goods which have been imported

refer /rɪ'fɜː/ *verb* □ **the bank referred the cheque to drawer** the bank returned the cheque to person who wrote it because there was not enough money in the account to pay it (NOTE: **referring – referred**)

reference group /'ref(ə)rəns gruːp/ *noun* a group of people who share some interest or aim and are used by consumers as a model to be imitated

reference site /'ref(ə)rəns saɪt/ *noun* a customer site where a new technology is being used successfully

refund *noun* /'riːfʌnd/ money paid back ○ *The shoes don't fit – I'm going to ask for a refund.* ○ *She got a refund after complaining to the manager.* ■ *verb* /rɪ'fʌnd/ to pay back money ○ *to refund the cost of postage* ○ *All money will be refunded if the goods are not satisfactory.*

refundable /rɪˈfʌndəb(ə)l/ *adjective* possible to pay back ○ *We ask for a refundable deposit of £20.* ○ *The entrance fee is refundable if you purchase £5 worth of goods.*

refusal /rɪˈfjuːz(ə)l/ *noun* an act of saying no

regiocentre stage /ˈriːdʒiəʊsentə ˌsteɪdʒ/ *noun US* the stage in a company's international marketing when a region consisting of several countries is treated as one market

registered /ˈredʒɪstəd/ *adjective* having been noted on an official list ○ *a registered share transaction*

registered design /ˌredʒɪstəd dɪˈzaɪn/ *noun* a design which is legally registered to protect the owner against unauthorised use of it by others

registered letter /ˌredʒɪstəd ˈletə/, **registered parcel** /ˌredʒɪstəd ˈpaːs(ə)l/ *noun* a letter or parcel which is noted by the post office before it is sent, so that the sender can claim compensation if it is lost

registered trademark /ˌredʒɪstəd ˈtreɪdmaːk/ *noun* a name, design or symbol which has been registered by the manufacturer and which cannot be used by other manufacturers. It is an intangible asset. ○ *You can't call your beds 'Softn'kumfi' – it is a registered trademark.*

registration /ˌredʒɪˈstreɪʃ(ə)n/ *noun* the act of having something noted on an official list ○ *the registration of a trademark of a share transaction*

registration fee /ˌredʒɪˈstreɪʃ(ə)n fiː/ *noun* **1.** money paid to have something registered **2.** money paid to attend a conference

registration number /ˌredʒɪˈstreɪʃ(ə)n ˌnʌmbə/ *noun* an official number, e.g. the number of a car

regression analysis /rɪˈgreʃ(ə)n əˌnæləsɪs/, **regression model** /rɪˈgreʃ(ə)n ˌmɒd(ə)l/ *noun* a method of discovering the ratio of one dependent variable and one or more independent variables, so as to give a value to the dependent variable

regular /ˈregjʊlə/ *adjective* ordinary or standard ○ *The regular price is $1.25, but we are offering them at 99 cents.*

regular customer /ˌregjʊlə ˈkʌstəmə/ *noun* a customer who always buys from the same shop

regular model /ˌregjʊlə ˈmɒd(ə)l/ *noun* the main product in a company's product range ○ *We estimate that 65% of the customers interested in our product range will buy the regular model.*

regular size /ˈregjʊlə saɪz/ *noun* the standard size (smaller than economy size or family size)

regular staff /ˌregjʊlə ˈstaːf/ *noun* the full-time staff

regulate /ˈregjʊleɪt/ *verb* **1.** to adjust something so that it works well or is correct **2.** to change or maintain something by law □ **prices are regulated by supply and demand** prices are increased or lowered according to supply and demand □ **government-regulated price** a price which is imposed by the government

regulation /ˌregjʊˈleɪʃ(ə)n/ *noun* **1.** a law or rule ○ *the new government regulations on housing standards* ○ *Fire regulations or Safety regulations were not observed at the restaurant.* ○ *Regulations concerning imports and exports are set out in this leaflet.* **2.** the use of laws or rules stipulated by a government or regulatory body, such as the FSA, to provide orderly procedures and to protect consumers and investors ○ *government regulation of trading practices*

'EC regulations which came into effect in July insist that customers can buy cars anywhere in the EC at the local pre-tax price' [*Financial Times*]

'…a unit trust is established under the regulations of the Department of Trade, with a trustee, a management company and a stock of units' [*Investors Chronicle*]

'…fear of audit regulation, as much as financial pressures, is a major factor behind the increasing number of small accountancy firms deciding to sell their practices or merge with another firm' [*Accountancy*]

regulator /ˈregjʊleɪtə/ *noun* a person whose job it is to see that regulations are followed

'…the regulators have sought to protect investors and other market participants from the impact of a firm collapsing' [*Banking Technology*]

reimport *noun* /riːˈɪmpɔːt/ the importing of goods which have been exported from the same country ■ *verb* /ˌriːɪmˈpɔːt/ to import goods which have already been exported

reimportation /ˌriːɪmpɔːˈteɪʃ(ə)n/ *noun* the importing of goods which have already been exported

reinforcement advertising /ˌriːɪnˈfɔːsmənt ˈædvətaɪzɪŋ/ *noun* advertising aimed at making the positive features of a product stronger in order to reassure people who have already purchased it

reject /ˈriːdʒekt/ *noun, adjective* (something) which has been thrown out because it is not of the usual standard ○ *sale of rejects of reject items* ○ *to sell off reject stock*

reject shop /ˈriːdʒekt ʃɒp/ *noun* a shop which specialises in the sale of goods which have not passed all of their producers quality-control tests, but which are still suitable for sale at a reduced price

relational database /rɪˌleɪʃ(ə)n(ə)l ˈdeɪtəbeɪs/ *noun* a computer database in which different types of data are linked for analysis

relationship /rɪˈleɪʃ(ə)nʃɪp/ *noun* a link or connection

relationship building /rɪˈleɪʃ(ə)nʃɪp ˌbɪldɪŋ/ *noun* taking actions to develop a long-term relationship with the customer

relationship management /rɪˈleɪʃ(ə)nʃɪp ˌmænɪdʒmənt/ *noun* the management of customers so as to build long-term relationships with them

relationship marketing /rɪˈleɪʃ(ə)nʃɪp ˌmɑːkɪtɪŋ/ *noun* a long-term marketing strategy to build relationships with individual customers

relative /ˈrelətɪv/ *adjective* compared to something else

relative cost /ˌrelətɪv ˈkɒst/ *noun* the relationship between the cost of advertising space and the size of the audience

relaunch *noun*/ˈriːlɔːnʃ/ the act of putting a product back on the market again, after adapting it to changing market conditions ○ *The relaunch is scheduled for August.* ■ *verb* /riːˈlɔːntʃ/ to put a product on the market again ○ *The product will be relaunched with some minor modifications next autumn.*

release /rɪˈliːs/ *noun* **1.** the act of setting someone free or of making something or someone no longer subject to an obligation or restriction ○ *release from a contract* ○ *the release of goods from customs* **2.** the act of making something public, or a public announcement **3.** □ **new release** a new CD or a piece of software put on the market ■ *verb* to put something on the market ○ *They released several new CDs this month.* □ **to release dues** to send off orders which had been piling up while a product was out of stock

'…pressure to ease monetary policy mounted yesterday with the release of a set of pessimistic economic statistics' [*Financial Times*]

'…the national accounts for the March quarter released by the Australian Bureau of Statistics showed a real increase in GDP' [*Australian Financial Review*]

remainder /rɪˈmeɪndə/ *verb* □ **to remainder books** to sell new books off cheaply ○ *The shop was full of piles of remaindered books.*

remainder merchant /rɪˈmeɪndə ˌmɜːtʃənt/ *noun* a book dealer who buys unsold new books from publishers at a very low price

remainders /rɪˈmeɪndəz/ *plural noun* new books sold cheaply

reminder /rɪˈmaɪndə/ *noun* a letter to remind a customer that he or she has not paid an invoice ○ *to send someone a reminder*

reminder advertising /rɪˈmaɪndər ˌædvətaɪzɪŋ/ *noun* advertising designed to remind consumers of a product already advertised ○ *Reminder advertising is particularly important in a highly competitive market.*

reminder line /rɪˈmaɪndə laɪn/ *noun* a little advertising gimmick, e.g. a giveaway pen with the company's name on it

remnant /ˈremnənt/ *noun* an odd piece of a large item such as, a carpet or fabric sold separately ○ *a sale of remnants a remnant sale*

remnant space /ˈremnənt speɪs/ *noun* odd unsold advertising space, which is usually available at a discount

render /ˈrendə/ *verb* □ **to render an account** to send in an account ○ *Please find enclosed payment per account rendered.*

rental list /ˈrent(ə)l lɪst/ *noun* a mailing list of names and addresses which can be rented

reorder /riːˈɔːdə/ *noun* a further order for something which has been ordered before ○ *The product has only been on the market ten days and we are already getting reorders.* ■ *verb* to place a new order for something ○ *We must reorder these items because stock is getting low.*

reorder level /riːˈɔːdə ˌlev(ə)l/ *noun* a minimum amount of an item which a company holds in stock, such that, when stock falls to this amount, the item must be reordered

rep /rep/ *noun* same as **representative** (*informal*) ○ *to hold a reps' meeting* ○ *Our reps make on average six calls a day.*

repack /riːˈpæk/ *verb* to pack again

repacking /riːˈpækɪŋ/ *noun* the act of packing again

repeat /rɪˈpiːt/ *verb* □ **to repeat an order** to order something again

repeat business /rɪˌpiːt ˈbɪznɪs/ *noun* business which involves a new order for something which has been ordered before

repeat order /rɪˌpiːt ˈɔːdə/ *noun* a new order for something which has been ordered before ○ *The product has been on the market only ten days and we are already flooded with repeat orders.*

repeat purchasing /rɪˌpiːt ˈpɜː-tʃɪsɪŋ/ *noun* **1.** the purchasing of the same product a second time **2.** the frequent buying of a low-priced item that is for everyday use such as soap or bread

repertory grid technique /ˌre-pət(ə)rɪ ˈɡrɪd tekˌniːk/ *noun* a market-research technique in which a test is first run to discover what the respondents' main criteria are in judging product brands. This is followed by another test in which the respondents evaluate brands on the basis of these established criteria.

replacement cost accounting /rɪˈpleɪsmənt kɒst əˌkaʊntɪŋ/ *noun* same as **current cost accounting**

reply /rɪˈplaɪ/ *noun* an answer ○ *the company's reply to the takeover bid* ○ *There was no reply to my letter* or *to my phone call.* ○ *I am writing in reply to your letter of the 24th.* ■ *verb* to answer ○ *We forgot to reply to the solicitor's letter.* ○ *The company has replied to the takeover bid by offering the shareholders higher dividends.* (NOTE: **replies – replying – replied**)

reply coupon /rɪˈplaɪ ˌkuːpɒn/ *noun* a form attached to a coupon ad which has to be filled in and returned to the advertiser

report /rɪˈpɔːt/ *noun* **1.** a statement describing what has happened or describing a state of affairs ○ *to make a report* *to present a report* or *to send in a report on market opportunities in the Far East* ○ *The accountants are drafting a report on salary scales.* ○ *The sales manager reads all the reports from the sales team.* ○ *The chairman has received a report from the insurance company.* **2.** an official document from a government committee ○ *The government has issued a report on the credit problems of exporters.* ■ *verb* **1.** to make a statement describing something ○ *The sales force reported an increased demand for the product.* ○ *He reported the damage to the insurance company.* ○ *We asked the bank to report on his financial status.* **2.** □ **to report to someone** to be responsible to or to be under someone ○ *She reports direct to the managing director.* ○ *The sales force reports to the sales director.*

'…a draft report on changes in the international monetary system' [*Wall Street Journal*]

'…responsibilities include the production of premium quality business reports' [*Times*]

'…the research director will manage a team of business analysts monitoring and reporting on the latest development in retail distribution' [*Times*]

'…the successful candidate will report to the area director for profit responsibility for sales of leading brands' [*Times*]

reposition /ˌriːpəˈzɪʃ(ə)n/ *verb* to change the position of a product or company in the market

'…it is thought that the company will reposition the range in the mass market or relaunch it' [*Marketing Week*]

repositioning /ˌriːpəˈzɪʃ(ə)nɪŋ/ *noun* a change or adjustment to the position of a product in the market, or the consumers' idea of it, by changing its design or by different advertising ○ *If this spring's promotional campaign* *doesn't achieve a repositioning of the product, sales will continue to fall.*

repossess /ˌriːpəˈzes/ *verb* to take back an item which someone is buying under a hire-purchase agreement, or a property which someone is buying under a mortgage, because the purchaser cannot continue the payments

represent /ˌreprɪˈzent/ *verb* to work for a company, showing goods or services to possible buyers ○ *He represents an American car firm in Europe.* ○ *Our French distributor represents several other competing firms.*

representation /ˌreprɪzenˈteɪʃ(ə)n/ *noun* the right to sell goods for a company, or a person or organisation that sells goods on behalf of a company ○ *They have no representation in the US* ○ *We offered them exclusive representation in Europe.*

representative /ˌreprɪˈzentətɪv/ *adjective* which is an example of what all others are like ○ *We displayed a representative selection of our product range.* ○ *The sample chosen was not representative of the whole batch.* ■ *noun* **1.** a company which works for another company, selling their goods ○ *We have appointed Smith & Co our exclusive representatives in Europe.* **2.** same as **salesperson**

resale /ˈriːseɪl/ *noun* the selling of goods which have been bought ○ *to purchase something for resale* ○ *The contract forbids resale of the goods to the US*

resale price maintenance /ˌriː-seɪl ˈpraɪs ˌmeɪntənəns/ *noun* a system in which the price for an item is fixed by the manufacturer, and the retailer is not allowed to sell it at a lower price. Abbreviation **RPM**

research /rɪˈsɜːtʃ/ *noun* the process of trying to find out facts or information ■ *verb* to study or try to find out information about something ○ *They are researching the market for their new product.*

research and development /rɪ-ˌsɜːtʃ ən dɪˈveləpmənt/ *noun* **1.** a scientific investigation which leads to making new products or improving existing products ○ *The company spends*

millions on research and development. Abbreviation **R&D 2.** activities that are designed to produce new knowledge and ideas and to develop ways in which these can be commercially exploited by a business (NOTE: Research and development activities are often grouped together to form a separate division or department within an organisation.)

'...drug companies must make a massive investment in research and development if they are to ensure their future, according to a recently published report' [*Marketing*]

COMMENT: Research costs can be divided into (a) applied research, which is the cost of research leading to a specific aim, and (b) basic, or pure research, which is research carried out without a specific aim in mind: these costs are written off in the year in which they are incurred. Development costs are the costs of making the commercial products based on the research.

research brief /rɪˈsɜːtʃ briːf/ *noun* the basic objectives and instructions concerning a market-research project

research department /rɪˈsɜːtʃ dɪˌpaːtmənt/ *noun* the section of a company which carries out research

researcher /rɪˈsɜːtʃə/ *noun* a person who carries out research ○ *Government statistics are a useful source of information for the desk researcher.*

research unit /rɪˈsɜːtʃ ˌjuːnɪt/ *noun* a separate small group of research workers

research worker /rɪˈsɜːtʃ ˌwɜːkə/ *noun* a person who works in a research department

resell /riːˈsel/ *verb* to sell something which has just been bought ○ *The car was sold in June and the buyer resold it to an dealer two months later.* (NOTE: **reselling – resold**)

reseller /riːˈselə/ *noun* somebody in the marketing chain who buys to sell to somebody else, e.g. wholesalers, distributors, and retailers

reseller market /riːˈselə ˌmaːkɪt/ *noun* a market in which customers buy products in order to resell them as wholesalers or retailers ○ *Fewer and fewer consumers are buying the product, so prices are falling in the reseller market.*

reserved market /rɪˌzɜːvd ˈmaːkɪt/ *noun* a market in which producers agree not to sell more than a specific amount in order to control competition. Also called **restricted market**

reserve price /rɪˈzɜːv praɪs/ *noun* the lowest price which a seller will accept, e.g. at an auction or when selling securities through a broker ○ *The painting was withdrawn when it failed to reach its reserve price.*

resistance /rɪˈzɪstəns/ *noun* opposition felt or shown by people to something ○ *There was a lot of resistance from the team to the new plan.* ○ *The chairman's proposal met with strong resistance from the banks.* ○ *There was a lot of resistance from the shareholders to the new plan.*

resources /rɪˈzɔːsɪz/ *plural noun* **1.** a supply of something □ **we are looking for a site with good water resources** a site with plenty of water available **2.** the money available for doing something □ **the cost of the new project is easily within our resources** we have quite enough money to pay for the new project

respond /rɪˈspɒnd/ *verb* to reply to a question

respondent /rɪˈspɒndənt/ *noun* a person who answers questions in a survey ○ *Some of the respondents' answers were influenced by the way the questions were asked.*

response /rɪˈspɒns/ *noun* a reply or reaction ○ *There was no response to our mailing shot.* ○ *We got very little response to our complaints.*

'…forecasting consumer response is one problem which will never be finally solved' [*Marketing Week*]

response booster /rɪˈspɒns ˌbuːstə/ *noun* anything that will help increase the response rate

response function /rɪˈspɒns ˌfʌŋkʃən/ *noun* a figure which represents the value of a particular quantity of advertising impressions on a person

response level /rɪˈspɒns ˌlevəl/, **response rate** /rɪˈspɒns reɪt/ *noun* the proportion of people approached in a survey who agree to answer questions ○ *The response rate has been very disappointing.*

response marketing /rɪˈspɒns ˌmaːkɪtɪŋ/ *noun* in e-marketing, the

process of managing responses or leads from the time they are received through to conversion to sale

response mechanism /rɪˈspɒns ˌmekənɪz(ə)m/ *noun* a method of showing a response to an Internet advertisement, or the way in which a customer can reply to an advertisement or direct mailshot, such as sending back a coupon or a faxback sheet

response rate /rɪˈspɒns reɪt/ *noun* the proportion of people who respond to a questionnaire or survey

re-sticker /riː ˈstɪkə/ *verb* to put new stickers on stock, e.g. when increasing the price

restock /riːˈstɒk/ *verb* to order more stock or inventory ○ *to restock after the Christmas sales*

restocking /riːˈstɒkɪŋ/ *noun* the ordering of more stock or inventory

restraint /rɪˈstreɪnt/ *noun* control

restraint of trade /rɪˌstreɪnt əv ˈtreɪd/ *noun* **1.** a situation where employees are not allowed to use their knowledge in another company on changing jobs **2.** an attempt by companies to fix prices, create monopolies, or reduce competition, which could affect free trade

restrict /rɪˈstrɪkt/ *verb* to limit something or to impose controls on something ○ *to restrict credit* ○ *to restrict the flow of trade* ○ *We are restricted to twenty staff by the size of our offices.*

restricted market /rɪˌstrɪktɪd ˈmaːkɪt/ *noun* same as **reserved market**

restriction /rɪˈstrɪkʃ(ə)n/ *noun* a limit or control ○ *import restrictions* or *restrictions on imports* □ **to impose restrictions on imports *or* credit** to start limiting imports or credit □ **to lift credit restrictions *or* import restrictions** to allow credit to be given freely or imports to enter the country freely

restrictive /rɪˈstrɪktɪv/ *adjective* not allowing something to go beyond a point

restrictive trade practices /rɪˌstrɪktɪv ˈtreɪd ˌpræktɪsɪz/, **restrictive practices** /rɪˌstrɪktɪv 'præktɪsɪz/ *plural noun* an arrangement between companies to fix prices or to share the market in order to restrict trade

résumé /'rezjuː,meɪ/ *noun US* same as **curriculum vitae**

retail /'riːteɪl/ *noun* the sale of small quantities of goods to the general public □ **the goods in stock have a retail value of £1m** the value of the goods if sold to the public is £1m, before discounts and other factors are taken into account ■ *adverb* □ **he buys wholesale and sells retail** he buys goods in bulk at a wholesale discount and sells in small quantities to the public ■ *verb* **1.** □ **to retail goods** to sell goods direct to the public **2.** to sell for a price □ **these items retail at** *or* **for £2.50** the retail price of these items is £2.50

'…provisional figures show retail sales dropped 1.5% in January but wholesale prices released this week reveal a 1% increase last month' [*Marketing*]

retail audit /'riːteɪl ˌɔːdɪt/ *noun* a market research method by which a research company regularly checks a sample of retailers for unit sales and stock levels of different brands ○ *Since subscribing to the retail audit we've been able to compare our performance with that of our competitors.*

retail cooperative /'riːteɪl kəʊˌɒp(ə)rətɪv/ *noun* an organisation whose business is the buying and selling of goods that is run by a group of people who share the profits between them (NOTE: Retail cooperatives were the first offshoot of the cooperative movement.)

retail dealer /'riːteɪl ˌdiːlə/ *noun* a person who sells to the general public

retailer /'riːteɪlə/ *noun* a person who runs a retail business, selling goods direct to the public

'…voucher schemes are very attractive from the retailers' point of view' [*Marketing Week*]

retailer cooperative /'riːteɪlə kəʊˌɒp(ə)rətɪv/ *noun* a group of retailers who buy together from suppliers so as to be able to enjoy quantity discounts

retailing /'riːteɪlɪŋ/ *noun* the selling of full-price goods to the public ○ *From car retailing the company branched out into car leasing.*

retail management /ˌriːteɪl 'mænɪdʒmənt/ *noun* managing the retail side of a business such as points of sale, stock control, and just-in-time purchasing

retail media /'riːteɪl ˌmiːdiə/ *noun* advertising media in retail outlets, e.g. ads on supermarket trolleys

retail outlet /'riːteɪl ˌaʊtlet/ *noun* a shop which sells to the general public

retail price /'riːteɪl ˌpraɪs/ *noun* the price at which the retailer sells to the final customer

retail price index /ˌriːteɪl 'praɪs ˌɪndeks/, **retail prices index** /ˌriːteɪl 'praɪsɪz ˌɪndeks/ *noun* an index which shows how prices of consumer goods have increased or decreased over a period of time. Abbreviation **RPI** (NOTE: The US term is **Consumer Price Index.**)

COMMENT: In the UK, the RPI is calculated on a group of essential goods and services; it includes both VAT and mortgage interest; the US equivalent is the Consumer Price Index.

retail trade /'riːteɪl treɪd/ *noun* all people or businesses selling goods retail

retention /rɪ'tenʃ(ə)n/ *noun* the act of keeping the loyalty of existing customers, as opposed to acquisition, which is the act of acquiring new customers. Both can be aims of advertising campaigns.

'…a systematic approach to human resource planning can play a significant part in reducing recruitment and retention problems' [*Personnel Management*]

retrenchment /rɪ'trentʃmənt/ *noun* a reduction of expenditure or of new plans ○ *The company is in for a period of retrenchment.*

return /rɪ'tɜːn/ *noun* **1.** the act of sending something back □ **he replied by return of post** he replied by the next of post service back **2.** an official statement or form that has to be sent in to the authorities ■ *verb* to send back ○ *to return unsold stock to the wholesaler* ○ *to return a letter to sender*

'Section 363 of the Companies Act 1985 requires companies to deliver an annual return to the Companies Registration Office. Failure to do so before the end of the period of 28 days after the company's return date could lead to directors and other officers in default being fined up to £2000' [*Accountancy*]

returnable /rɪˈtɜːnəb(ə)l/ *adjective* which can be returned ○ *These bottles are not returnable.*

return address /rɪˈtɜːn əˌdres/ *noun* the address to which you send back something

returns /rɪˈtɜːnz/ *plural noun* unsold goods, especially books, newspapers, or magazines, sent back to the supplier

revenue /ˈrevənjuː/ *noun* money received ○ *revenue from advertising* or *advertising revenue* ○ *Oil revenues have risen with the rise in the dollar.*

revenue accounts /ˈrevənjuː əˌkaʊnts/ *plural noun* accounts of a business which record money received as sales, commission, etc.

reverse /rɪˈvɜːs/ *adjective* opposite or in the opposite direction

'…the trade balance sank $17 billion, reversing last fall's brief improvement' [*Fortune*]

reverse engineering /rɪˌvɜːs ˌendʒɪˈnɪərɪŋ/ *noun* the taking apart of a product in order to find out how it was put together (NOTE: Reverse engineering can help a company redesign a product, but it can also enable competitors to analyse how their rivals' products are made.)

reverse takeover /rɪˌvɜːs ˈteɪkə-ʊvə/ *noun* a takeover in which the company that has been taken over ends up owning the company which has taken it over. The acquiring company's shareholders give up their shares in exchange for shares in the target company.

revocable /ˈrevəkəb(ə)l/ *adjective* which can be revoked

revocable letter of credit /ˌrevəkəb(ə)l ˌletər əv ˈkredɪt/ *noun* a letter of credit that can be cancelled

revoke /rɪˈvəʊk/ *verb* to cancel something ○ *to revoke a decision a clause in an agreement* ○ *The quota on luxury items has been revoked.*

revolving credit /rɪˌvɒlvɪŋ ˈkredɪt/ *noun* a system where someone can borrow money at any time up to an agreed amount, and continue to borrow while still paying off the original loan. Also called **open-ended credit**

risk /rɪsk/ *noun* **1.** possible harm or a chance of danger □ **to run a risk** to be likely to suffer harm □ **to take a risk** to do something which may make you lose money or suffer harm **2.** □ **at the owner's risk** a situation where goods shipped or stored are insured by the owner, not by the transport company or the storage company ○ *Goods left here are at the owner's risk.* ○ *The shipment was sent at the owner's risk.* **3.** loss or damage against which you are insured **4.** □ **he is a good** *or* **bad risk** it is not likely or it is very likely that the insurance company will have to pay out against claims where he is concerned

'…remember, risk isn't volatility. Risk is the chance that a company's earnings power will erode – either because of a change in the industry or a change in the business that will make the company significantly less profitable in the long term' [*Fortune*]

risk analysis /ˈrɪsk əˌnæləsɪs/ *noun* analysis of how much can be lost and gained through various marketing strategies ○ *After protracted risk analysis a very ambitious strategy was adopted.* ○ *Our risk analysis must concentrate on competitor activity.*

risk-averse /ˌrɪsk əˈvɜːs/ *adjective* not wanting to take risks

risk capital /ˈrɪsk ˌkæpɪt(ə)l/ *noun* same as **venture capital**

risk-free /ˌrɪsk ˈfriː/, **riskless** /ˈrɪskləs/ *adjective* with no risk involved ○ *a risk-free investment*

'…there is no risk-free way of taking regular income from your money higher than the rate of inflation and still preserving its value' [*Guardian*]

'…many small investors have also preferred to put their spare cash with risk-free investments such as building societies rather than take chances on the stock market. The returns on a host of risk-free investments have been well into double figures' [*Money Observer*]

risky /ˈrɪski/ *adjective* dangerous or which may cause harm ○ *We lost all our money in some risky ventures in South America.*

'…while the bank has scaled back some of its more risky trading operations, it has retained its status as a top-rate advisory house' [*Times*]

rival /ˈraɪv(ə)l/ *noun* a person or company that competes in the same market ○ *a rival company* ○ *to undercut a rival*

rival brand /ˌraɪv(ə)l ˈbrænd/, **rival product** /ˌraɪv(ə)l ˈprɒdʌkt/ *noun* a brand or product that is competing for sales with another brand or product ○ *We are analysing the rival brands on the market.*

road /rəʊd/ *noun* a way used by cars, lorries, etc. to move from one place to another ○ *to send to ship goods by road* ○ *The main office is in London Road.* ○ *Use the Park Road entrance to get to the buying department.* (NOTE: in addresses, **Road** is usually shortened to **Rd**) □ **on the road** travelling ○ *The sales force is on the road thirty weeks a year.* ○ *We have twenty salesmen on the road.*

road haulage /ˈrəʊd ˌhɔːlɪdʒ/ *noun* the moving of goods by road

road haulage depot /rəʊd ˈhɔːlɪdʒ ˌdepəʊ/ *noun* a centre for goods which are being moved by road, and the lorries which carry them

road haulier /ˈrəʊd ˌhɔːliə/ *noun* a company which transports goods by road

ROB *abbreviation* run of book

rock bottom /ˌrɒk ˈbɒtəm/ *noun* □ **sales have reached rock bottom** sales have reached the lowest point possible

'…investment companies took the view that secondhand prices had reached rock bottom and that levels could only go up' [*Lloyd's List*]

rocket /ˈrɒkɪt/ *verb* to rise fast ○ *Investors are rushing to cash in on rocketing share prices.* ○ *Prices have rocketed on the commodity markets.*

roll /rəʊl/ *verb*

roll over *phrasal verb* □ **to roll over a credit** to make credit available over a continuing period □ **to roll over a debt** to allow a debt to stand after the repayment date

'…at the IMF in Washington, officials are worried that Japanese and US banks might decline to roll over the principal of loans made in the 1980s to Southeast Asian and other developing countries' [*Far Eastern Economic Review*]

rolling /ˈrəʊlɪŋ/ *adjective* continuing with no break

rolling launch /ˌrəʊlɪŋ ˈlɔːntʃ/ *noun* a gradual launch of a new product onto the market by launching it in different areas over a period

rolling plan /ˌrəʊlɪŋ ˈplæn/ *noun* a plan which runs for a period of time and is updated regularly for the same period

roll out /ˌrəʊl ˈaʊt/ *verb* to extend a company's marketing of a product from its original test marketing area to the whole country

'…the company is expected to make a decision in the new year on whether to roll out the name through its electrical division' [*Marketing Week*]

rollout /ˈrəʊlaʊt/ *noun* **1.** extending the marketing of a product from the original test marketing area to the whole country **2.** same as **rolling launch**

RON *abbreviation* run of network

ROP *abbreviation* run of paper

ROS *abbreviation* **1.** run of site **2.** run of station

rough /rʌf/ *noun* the outline plan of an illustration for an advertisement ○ *The agency sent the rough to the advertisers for approval.* ○ *The advertising department will consider the rough carefully before telling the agency to go ahead and run the advertisement.*

rough out *phrasal verb* to make a draft or a general design of something, which may be changed later ○ *The finance director roughed out a plan of investment.*

ROW *abbreviation* run of week

royalties /ˈrɔɪəltiz/ *plural noun* a proportion of the income from the sales of a product such as a new invention, a book, or a piece of music that is paid to its creator

royalty /ˈrɔɪəlti/ *noun* money paid to an inventor, writer, or the owner of land for the right to use their property, usually a specific percentage of sales, or a specific amount per sale ○ *The country will benefit from rising oil royalties.* ○ *He is still receiving substantial royalties from his invention.*

RPI *abbreviation* retail price index

RPM *abbreviation* resale price maintenance

RRP *abbreviation* recommended retail price

RSS /ˌɑː es ˈes/ *abbreviation* Really Simple Syndication

run /rʌn/ *noun* a period of time during which a machine is working □ **a cheque**

run a series of cheques processed through a computer

'…applications for mortgages are running at a high level' [*Times*]

'…with interest rates running well above inflation, investors want something that offers a return for their money' [*Business Week*]

run down *phrasal verb* **1.** to reduce a quantity gradually ○ *We decided to run down stocks* or *to let stocks run down at the end of the financial year.* **2.** to slow down the business activities of a company before it is going to be closed ○ *The company is being run down.*

running total /ˌrʌnɪŋ ˈtəʊt(ə)l/ *noun* the total carried from one column of figures to the next

run of book /ˌrʌn əv ˈbʊk/, **run of paper** /ˌrʌn əv ˈpeɪpə/ *noun* an advertiser's order to the advertising department of a publication that buys advertising space at the basic rate and does not specify the position of the advertisement in the publication. Abbreviation **ROB, ROP**

run of network /ˌrʌn əv ˈnetwɜːk/ *noun* banner advertising that runs across a network of websites. Abbreviation **RON**

run of site /ˌrʌn əv ˈsaɪt/ *noun* banner advertising that runs on one single website. Abbreviation **ROS**

run of station /ˌrʌn əv ˈsteɪʃ(ə)n/ *noun* TV advertising for which a particular time period has not been requested. Abbreviation **ROS**

run of week /ˌrʌn əv ˈwiːk/ *noun* an advertiser's order to the advertising department of a publication that buys advertising space at the basic rate and does not specify the issue it will appear in. Abbreviation **ROW**

run-on /ˌrʌn ˈɒn/ *noun* copies of a publication printed in addition to the original print order, as in the case of a leaflet whose setting-up costs have been covered. More copies of it can be printed at a relatively cheap unit cost.

S

salary cheque /ˈsæləri tʃek/ *noun* a monthly cheque by which an employee is paid

salary package /ˈsæləri ˌpækɪdʒ/ *noun* same as **pay package**

salary scale /ˈsæləri skeɪl/ *noun* same as **pay scale** ○ *He was appointed at the top end of the salary scale.*

salary structure /ˈsæləri ˌstrʌktʃə/ *noun* the organisation of salaries in a company with different rates of pay for different types of job

'...the union of hotel and personal service workers has demanded a new salary structure and uniform conditions of service for workers in the hotel and catering industry' [*Business Times (Lagos)*]

sale /seɪl/ *noun* **1.** an act of giving an item or doing a service in exchange for money, or for the promise that money will be paid □ **for sale** ready to be sold □ **to offer something for sale** *or* **to put something up for sale** to announce that something is ready to be sold ○ *They put the factory up for sale.* ○ *His shop is for sale.* ○ *These items are not for sale to the general public.* □ **sale as seen** a sale with no guarantee of quality ○ *If the equipment is for sale as seen, we shall have no comeback if it breaks down.* □ **sale by description** a sale on condition that the goods match the description of them given by the seller □ **sale or return** a system where the retailer sends goods back if they are not sold, and pays the supplier only for goods sold ○ *We have taken 4,000 items on sale or return.* **2.** an act of selling goods at specially low prices ○ *The shop is having a sale to clear old stock.* ○ *The sale price is 50% of the usual price.*

'...many on Wall Street are suspicious of the recent sales and production gains posted by American Industry' [*Management Today*]

'...the latest car sales for April show a 1.8% dip from last year's total' [*Investors Chronicle*]

saleability /ˌseɪləˈbɪlɪti/, **salability** *noun* a quality in an item which makes it easy to sell

saleable /ˈseɪləb(ə)l/, **salable** *adjective* which can easily be sold ○ *The company is not readily saleable in its present state.*

sale and lease-back /ˌseɪl ən ˈliːs bæk/ *noun* the sale of an asset, usually a building, to somebody else who then leases it back to the original owner

saleroom /ˈseɪlruːm/ *noun* a room where an auction takes place

sales /seɪlz/ *plural noun* □ **the sales** period when major stores sell many items at specially low prices ○ *I bought this in the sales* or *at the sales* or *in the January sales.*

sales agent /ˈseɪlz ˌeɪdʒənt/ *noun* a person who sells for a business or another person and earns a commission ○ *How many sales agents do we have in this area?* ○ *She's a competent sales agent representing several non-competing companies.*

sales aids /ˈseɪlz eɪdz/ *plural noun* various tools used for selling, e.g. samples, display cases, and sales literature ○ *The sales manager gave a talk on new sales aids which had just become available.* ○ *An exhibition of sales aids was held at the sales conference.*

sales analysis /ˈseɪlz əˌnæləsɪs/ *noun* an examination of the reports of sales to see why items have or have not sold well

sales appeal /ˈseɪlz əˌpiːl/ *noun* a quality in a product which makes customers want to buy it

sales assistant /'seɪlz əˌsɪstənt/ *noun* a person in a shop who sells goods to customers

sales audit /'seɪlz ˌɔːdɪt/ *noun* an analysis of a company's sales in terms of such factors as product, revenue, and area

sales book /'seɪlz bʊk/ *noun* a record of sales

sales budget /'seɪlz ˌbʌdʒɪt/ *noun* a plan of probable sales

sales call /'seɪlz kɔːl/ *noun* a visit by a salesperson to a prospective customer in order to make a sale ○ *How many sales calls does the manager expect us to make each day?* ○ *She kept reports on all her sales calls.*

sales campaign /'seɪlz kæmˌpeɪn/ *noun* a series of planned activities to achieve higher sales

sales channel /'seɪlz ˌtʃæn(ə)l/ *noun* any means by which products can be brought into the marketplace and offered for sale, either directly to the customer or indirectly through retailers or dealers

sales chart /'seɪlz tʃɑːt/ *noun* a diagram showing how sales vary from month to month

sales clerk /'seɪlz klɑːk/ *noun US* same as **shop assistant**

> '...the wage agreement includes sales clerks and commission sales people in stores in Toronto' [*Toronto Star*]

sales contest /'seɪlz ˌkɒntest/ *noun* an incentive scheme that rewards the salesperson who has the best results

sales contract /'seɪlz ˌkɒntrækt/ *noun* a contract between a buyer and a seller, whereby the buyer agrees to pay money to the seller in return for goods ○ *The sales contract was signed after lengthy negotiations over price and delivery.* ○ *The sales contract commits us to the purchase.*

sales department /'seɪlz dɪˌpɑːtmənt/ *noun* the section of a company which deals with selling the company's products or services

sales director /'seɪlz daɪˌrektə/ *noun* a director who is responsible for an organisation's sales

sales drive /'seɪlz draɪv/ *noun* a vigorous effort to increase sales

sales executive /'seɪlz ɪgˌzekjʊtɪv/ *noun* a person in a company or department in charge of sales

sales force /'seɪlz fɔːs/ *noun* a group of sales staff

sales forecast /'seɪlz ˌfɔːkɑːst/ *noun* an estimate of future sales

sales incentive /'seɪlz ɪnˌsentɪv/ *noun* something offered to encourage higher sales, e.g. paying the salespeople a higher commission or bonuses, or giving them prizes such as holidays for increased sales

sales interview /'seɪlz ˌɪntəvjuː/ *noun* a meeting between a salesperson and a prospective customer in which the customer obtains all information about a product necessary for them to be able to make a buying decision ○ *At the beginning of the sales interview, the salesperson established exactly what the prospective customer's needs were.*

sales lead /'seɪlz liːd/ *noun* a piece of information about a potential customer which may lead to a sale ○ *It has been difficult approaching this territory with no sales leads to follow up.* ○ *I was given some useful sales leads by the sales rep who used to operate here.*

sales ledger clerk /'seɪlz ˌledʒə ˌklɑːk/ *noun* an office employee who deals with the sales ledger

sales letter /'seɪlz ˌletə/ *noun* a letter sent to prospective customers, especially as part of a direct-mail operation

sales literature /'seɪlz ˌlɪt(ə)rətʃə/ *noun* printed information which helps sales, e.g. leaflets or prospectuses

salesman /'seɪlzmən/ *noun* a man who sells an organisation's products or services to customers, especially to retail shops ○ *He is the head salesman in the carpet department.* ○ *His only experience is as a used-car salesman.*

sales manager /'seɪlz ˌmænɪdʒə/ *noun* a person in charge of a sales department

salesmanship /'seɪlzmənʃɪp/ *noun* the art of selling or of persuading customers to buy

sales network /'seɪlz ˌnetwɜːk/ *noun* the network of retailers, distributors, and agents who all contribute to selling a product

sales office /'seɪlz ˌɒfɪs/ *noun* a local office of a large organisation, which deals only with sales

sales outlet /'seɪlz ˌaʊt(ə)let/ *noun* a shop which sells to the general public

'…that aims to offer a one-stop sales outlet for companies that need to sell a diverse mix of used equipment and surplus inventory' [*Information Week*]

salesperson /'seɪlzˌpɜːs(ə)n/ *noun* **1.** a person who sells goods or services to members of the public **2.** a person who sells products or services to retail shops on behalf of a company (NOTE: The plural is **salespeople**.)

sales pitch /'seɪlz pɪtʃ/ *noun* a talk by a salesperson to persuade someone to buy

sales plan /'seɪlz plæn/ *noun* a plan that sets out the future aims of a sales department and shows ways in which it can improve its performance and increase sales

sales potential /'seɪlz pəˌtenʃəl/ *noun* the maximum market share that can be achieved by a product

sales presentation /'seɪlz prez(ə)nˌteɪʃ(ə)n/ *noun* a demonstration by a salesperson of a product

sales promotion /'seɪlz prəˌməʊ‐ʃ(ə)n/ *noun* promotional and sales techniques aimed at short-term increases in sales, e.g. free gifts, competitions, and price discounts ○ *We need some good sales promotion to complement our advertising campaign.* ○ *Let's hope this sales promotion will help us sell off our stock.*

'…the novelty in the £1m sales promotion is that the consumer will know immediately if he or she has won a bottle of champagne' [*Marketing Week*]

sales promotion agency /'seɪlz prəˌməʊʃ(ə)n ˌeɪdʒənsi/ *noun* an agency that specialises in the planning of promotions such as games, premium offers, and other incentives

sales promotion trap /'seɪlz prə‐ˌməʊʃ(ə)n træp/ *noun* a problem that occurs when a number of competing firms use promotions, with the result that there is no advantage to any of them

sales quota /'seɪlz ˌkwəʊtə/ *noun* a sales target given to salespeople which

is based on either unit sales or revenue ○ *The sales manager intends to introduce sales quotas, in order to put extra pressure on the sales force.*

sales representative /'seɪlz re‐prɪˌzentətɪv/, **sales rep** /'seɪlz rep/ *noun* same as **salesperson** ○ *We have six sales representatives in Europe.* ○ *They have vacancies for sales representatives to call on accounts in the north of the country.*

sales resistance /'seɪlz rɪˌzɪs‐təns/ *noun* a lack of willingness by the public to buy a product

sales response /'seɪlz rɪˌspɒns/ *noun* the degree to which customers buy a product in response to the promotion of it ○ *There was a very poor sales response to the advertising campaign.* ○ *Although the product was not spectacular, the sales response was enormous.*

sales revenue /'seɪlz ˌrevənjuː/ *noun* US the income from sales of goods or services

sales statistics /'seɪlz stəˌtɪs‐tɪks/ *plural noun* figures relating a company's sales

sales target /'seɪlz ˌtɑːgɪt/ *noun* the amount of sales a sales representative is expected to achieve

sales tax /'seɪlz tæks/ *noun* US same as **VAT**

sales team /'seɪlz tiːm/ *noun* all representatives, sales staff, and sales managers working in a company

sales technique /'seɪlz tekˌniːk/ *noun* a method used by a salesperson to persuade customers to buy, e.g. presentation of goods, demonstrations, and closing of sales

sales territory /'seɪlz ˌterɪt(ə)ri/ *noun* an area visited by a salesman

saleswoman /'seɪlzwʊmən/ *noun* a woman who sells an organisation's products or services to customers

salutation /ˌsæljuˈteɪʃ(ə)n/ *noun* the way of addressing an email to a customer

sample /'sɑːmpəl/ *noun* **1.** a small part of an item which is used to show what the whole item is like ○ *Can you provide us with a sample of the cloth?* **2.** a small group which is studied in order to show what a larger group is like ○ *We interviewed a sample of potential customers.* ■ *verb* **1.** to test or to try something by taking a small amount of it ○ *to sample a product before buying it* **2.** to ask a representative group of people questions to find out what the reactions of a much larger group would be ○ *They sampled 2,000 people at random to test the new drink.*

'…all firms in the sample received the same questionnaire along with a covering letter explaining the objectives of the study' [*International Journal of Advertising*]

sample size /ˈsɑːmpəl saɪz/ *noun* the number of individuals included in a statistical survey

sample survey /ˈsɑːmpəl ˌsɜːveɪ/ *noun* a statistical study of a selected group of individuals designed to collect information on specific subjects such as their buying habits or voting behaviour

sampling /ˈsɑːmplɪŋ/ *noun* **1.** the testing of a product by taking a small amount ○ *a sampling of European Union produce* **2.** the testing of the reactions of a small group of people to find out the reactions of a larger group of consumers

sampling error /ˈsɑːmplɪŋ ˌerə/ *noun* the difference between the results achieved in a survey using a small sample and what the results would be if you used the entire population

sampling fraction /ˈsɑːmplɪŋ ˌfrækʃən/ *noun* a proportion of a group of people being surveyed that is chosen as a sample ○ *The sampling fraction will have to be small since we cannot afford many interviews with respondents.*

sampling frame /ˈsɑːmplɪŋ freɪm/ *noun* the definition of the group of people being surveyed out of which a sample is to be taken

sampling point /ˈsɑːmplɪŋ pɔɪnt/ *noun* a place where sampling is carried out ○ *The sampling point was just outside the main railway station.*

sandwich board /ˈsændwɪtʃ bɔːd/ *noun* a pair of boards with advertisements on them that is suspended from shoulder straps in front of and behind the person wearing them

sandwich man /ˈsændwɪdʒ mæn/ *noun* a man who carries a sandwich board

satellite television /ˌsæt(ə)laɪt ˈtelɪvɪʒ(ə)n/ *noun* a television service which is broadcast from a satellite, and which the viewer receives using a special aerial

satisfaction /ˌsætɪsˈfækʃən/ *noun* a good feeling of happiness and contentment ○ *He finds great satisfaction in the job even though the pay is bad.*

satisfy /ˈsætɪsfaɪ/ *verb* **1.** to give satisfaction or to please (NOTE: **satisfies – satisfying – satisfied**) □ **to satisfy a client** to make a client pleased with what they have purchased □ **a satisfied customer** a customer who has got what they wanted **2.** to fill the requirements for a job (NOTE: **satisfies – satisfying – satisfied**) □ **to satisfy a demand** to fill a demand ○ *We cannot produce enough to satisfy the demand for the product.*

satisfying /ˈsætɪsfaɪɪŋ/ *noun* the act of making satisfactory profits and maintaining an acceptable market share rather than making maximum profits at all costs

saturate /ˈsætʃəreɪt/ *verb* to fill something completely ○ *They are planning to saturate the market with cheap mobile phones.* ○ *The market for sportswear is saturated.*

saturation /ˌsætʃəˈreɪʃ(ə)n/ *noun* **1.** the process of filling completely □ **saturation of the market, market saturation** a situation where the market has taken as much of the product as it can buy □ **the market has reached saturation point** the market is at a point where it cannot buy any more of the product **2.** the fourth stage in a product's life cycle where sales level off

saturation advertising /ˌsætʃə-ˈreɪʃ(ə)n ˌædvətaɪzɪŋ/ *noun* a highly intensive advertising campaign ○ *Saturation advertising is needed when there are large numbers of rival products on the market.*

savings account /ˈseɪvɪŋz əˌkaʊnt/ *noun* an account where you put money in regularly and which pays interest, often at a higher rate than a deposit account

SBU *abbreviation* strategic business unit

scale /skeɪl/ *noun* a system which is graded into various levels □ **scale of**

charges or scale of prices a list showing various prices

scale down *phrasal verb* to lower something in proportion

COMMENT: If a share issue is oversubscribed, applications may be scaled down; by doing this, the small investor is protected. So, in a typical case, all applications for 1,000 shares may receive 300; all applications for 2,000 shares may receive 500; applications for 5,000 shares receive 1,000, and applications for more than 5,000 shares will go into a ballot.

scale up *phrasal verb* to increase something in proportion

scaling technique /ˈskeɪlɪŋ tekˌniːk/ *noun* the use of a scale in questionnaires to make interpretation of results easier ○ *The scaling technique was so complicated that the respondents did not understand the questions.*

scam /skæm/ *noun* a fraud, an illegal or dishonest scheme (*informal*) ○ *Many financial scams only come to light by accident.*

scarce /skeəs/ *adjective* not easily found or not common ○ *scarce raw materials* ○ *Reliable trained staff are scarce.*

scarceness /ˈskeəsnəs/, **scarcity** /ˈskeəsɪti/ *noun* the state of being scarce ○ *There is a scarcity of trained staff.*

scarcity value /ˈskeəsɪti ˌvæljuː/ *noun* the value something has because it is rare and there is a large demand for it

scatter /ˈskætə/ *noun* a strategy by which an advertising message is put out through several different vehicles at the same time

scattered market /ˌskætəd ˈmɑːkɪt/ *noun* a market which is spread around a wide area, and therefore can only be reached by a company with an efficient distribution system

scenario /sɪˈnɑːriəʊ/ *noun* the way in which a situation may develop, or a description or forecast of possible future developments

'…on the upside scenario, the outlook is reasonably optimistic, bankers say, the worst scenario being that a scheme of arrangement cannot be achieved, resulting in liquidation' [*Irish Times*]

scenario planning /sɪˈnɑːriəʊ ˌplænɪŋ/ *noun* a planning technique in which the planners write down several different descriptions of what they think might happen in the future and how future events, good or bad, might affect their organisation (NOTE: Scenario planning can help managers to prepare for changes in the business environment, to develop strategies for dealing with unexpected events, and to choose between alternative strategic options.)

schedule /ˈʃedjuːl/ *noun* **1.** a timetable, a plan of how time should be spent, drawn up in advance ○ *The managing director has a busy schedule of appointments.* ○ *Her assistant tried to fit us into her schedule.* □ **on schedule** at the time or stage set down in the schedule ○ *The launch took place on schedule.* **2.** a list, especially a list forming an additional document attached to a contract ○ *the schedule of territories to which a contract applies* ○ *Please find enclosed our schedule of charges.* ○ *See the attached schedule* or *as per the attached schedule.*

science /ˈsaɪəns/ *noun* study or knowledge based on observing and testing

scientific /ˌsaɪənˈtɪfɪk/ *adjective* referring to science

scientific management /ˌsaɪənˈtɪfɪk ˈmænɪdʒmənt/ *noun* a theory of management which believes in the rational use of resources in order to maximise output, thus motivating workers to earn more money

scope /skəʊp/ *noun* an opportunity or possibility ○ *There is considerable scope for expansion into the export market.* □ **there is scope for improvement in our sales performance** the sales performance could be improved

scrambled merchandising /ˌskræmbəld ˈmɜːtʃəndaɪzɪŋ/ *noun* the displaying and selling of products which are unrelated to most of the others in the store such as groceries in a newsagent's or sandwiches in a pharmacy

screen /skriːn/ *noun* **1.** a glass surface on which computer information or TV pictures can be shown ○ *She brought up the information on the screen.* ○ *I'll just call up details of your account on the screen.* **2.** a grid of dots or lines placed between the camera and the artwork, which has the effect of dividing the picture up into small dots, creating an image which can be used for printing ■ *verb* to examine something carefully to evaluate or assess it □ **to screen candidates** to examine candidates to see if they are completely suitable

screening /ˈskriːnɪŋ/ *noun* **1.** □ **the screening of candidates** the examining of candidates to see if they are suitable **2.** the act of evaluating or assessing new product ideas ○ *Representatives from each department concerned will take part in the screening process.* ○ *Screening showed the product idea to be unrealistic for our production capacity.*

screensaver /ˈskriːnˌseɪvə/ *noun* a program that shows moving images on the screen when a computer is not being used, because a static image can damage the monitor by burning itself into the phosphor coating on the inside of the screen

script /skrɪpt/ *noun* the written text of a commercial

SDRs *abbreviation* special drawing rights

seal /siːl/ *noun* **1.** a special symbol, often one stamped on a piece of wax, which is used to show that a document is officially approved by the organisation that uses the symbol □ **contract under seal** a contract which has been legally approved with the seal of the company **2.** a piece of paper, metal, or wax attached to close something, so that it can be opened only if the paper, metal, or wax is removed or broken ■ *verb* to close something tightly ○ *The computer disks were sent in a sealed container.*

sealed bid price /ˌsiːld ˈbɪd ˌpraɪs/ *noun* a price of goods or a service for which suppliers are invited to submit bids. The bids are considered together by the buyer who then chooses the lowest bidder.

sealed tender /ˌsiːld ˈtendə/ *noun* a tender sent in a sealed envelope that will be opened with others at a specific time (NOTE: The US term is **sealed bid**.)

seal of approval /ˌsiːl əv əˈpruːv(ə)l/ *noun* a certificate from an organisation to show that a product has been officially approved

seaport /ˈsiːpɔːt/ *noun* a port by the sea

search /sɜːtʃ/ *noun* the facility that enables visitors to go a website to look for the information they want

search engine /ˈsɜːtʃ ˌendʒɪn/ *noun* a computer program that searches through a number of documents, especially on the Internet, for particular keywords and provides the user with a list of the documents in which those keywords appear

search engine optimisation /ˌsɜːtʃ ˌendʒɪn ˌɒptɪmaɪˈzeɪʃ(ə)n/ *noun* the process of improving the visibility of a website or webpage in search engine results by using relevant keywords or phrases to ensure that the website appears higher in the natural or organic listings in the search engine's results page. Abbreviation **SEO**

search engine registration /ˈsɜːtʃ ˌendʒɪn ˌredʒɪˌstreɪʃ(ə)n/ *noun* the process of registering a website with a search engine, so that the site can be selected when a user requests a search

search query /ˈsɜːtʃ ˌkwɪəri/ *noun* a set of keywords or phrases that a user enters into web search engine in order to find documents or articles relating to their enquiry

season /ˈsiːz(ə)n/ *noun* **1.** one of four parts into which a year is divided, i.e. spring, summer, autumn, and winter **2.** a period of time when some activity usually takes place ○ *the selling season*

seasonal /ˈsiːz(ə)n(ə)l/ *adjective* which lasts for a season or which only happens during a particular season ○ *seasonal variations in sales patterns* ○ *The demand for this item is very seasonal.*

seasonal adjustment /ˌsiːz(ə)n(ə)l əˈdʒʌstmənt/ *noun* a change made to figures to take account of seasonal variations

seasonal business /ˌsiːz(ə)n(ə)l ˈbɪznɪs/ *noun* trade that varies depending on the time of the year, e.g. trade in goods such as suntan products or Christmas trees

seasonal demand /ˌsiːz(ə)n(ə)l dɪˈmaːnd/ *noun* a demand which exists only during the high season

seasonal discount /ˌsiːz(ə)n(ə)l ˈdɪskaʊnt/ *noun* a discount offered at specific times of the year during periods of slack sales, such as by media owners to advertisers

seasonally adjusted /ˌsiːz(ə)nəli əˈdʒʌstɪd/ *adjective* referring to statistics which are adjusted to take account of seasonal variations

seasonal product /ˈsiːz(ə)n(ə)l ˌprɒdʌkt/ *noun* a product such as skis or swimwear which is only bought for use at a specific time of year

seasonal variation /ˌsiːz(ə)n(ə)l ˌveəriˈeɪʃ(ə)n/ *noun* variation in data that happens at particular times of the year, e.g. during the winter months or a tourist season

second /ˈsekənd/ *noun, adjective* the thing which comes after the first

secondary /ˈsekənd(ə)ri/ *adjective* second in importance

secondary audience /ˌsekənd(ə)ri ˈɔːdiəns/, **secondary readership** /ˌsekənd(ə)ri ˈriːdəʃɪp/ *noun* people who do not buy a newspaper or magazine themselves, but read a copy after the original purchaser has finished with it

secondary bank /ˌsekənd(ə)ri ˈbæŋks/ *noun* a finance company which provides money for hire-purchase deals

secondary data /ˈsekənd(ə)ri ˌdeɪtə/ *noun* data or information which has already been compiled and is therefore found through desk research ○ *All this secondary data can be found in our files.* ○ *We found the secondary data in the embassy library.*

secondary industry /ˈsekənd(ə)ri ˌɪndəstri/ *noun* an industry which uses basic raw materials to produce manufactured goods

secondary meaning /ˌsekənd(ə)ri ˈmiːnɪŋ/ *noun* a nickname given to a brand deliberately by the producer or by the consumer

secondary products /ˈsekənd(ə)ri ˌprɒdʌkts/ *plural noun* products which have been processed from raw materials (as opposed to primary products)

second-class /ˌsekənd ˈklɑːs/ *adjective, adverb* referring to a less expensive or less comfortable way of travelling ○ *The group will travel second-class to Holland.* ○ *The price of a second-class ticket is half that of a first class.*

second-generation product /ˌsekənd ˌdʒenəreɪʃ(ə)n ˈprɒdʌkt/ *noun* a product which has been developed from another

second half-year /ˌsekənd ˈhɑːf jɪə/ *noun* the six-month period from July to the end of December

secondhand /ˌsekəndˈhænd/ *adjective, adverb* which has been owned by someone before ○ *a secondhand car* ○ *the market in secondhand computers* or *the secondhand computer market* ○ *to buy something secondhand*

secondhand dealer /ˌsekəndˈhænd ˈdiːlə/ *noun* a dealer who buys and sells secondhand items

seconds /ˈsekəndz/ *plural noun* items which have been turned down by the quality controller as not being top quality ○ *The shop has a sale of seconds.*

second season /ˌsekənd ˈsiːz(ə)n/ *noun* the period when a second series of a network television programme is shown

sector /ˈsektə/ *noun* a part of the economy or the business organisation of a country ○ *All sectors of the economy suffered from the fall in the exchange rate.* ○ *Technology is a booming sector of the economy.*

'…government services form a large part of the tertiary or service sector' [*Sydney Morning Herald*]

'…in the dry cargo sector, a total of 956 dry cargo vessels are laid up – 3% of world dry cargo tonnage' [*Lloyd's List*]

secured loan /sɪˌkjʊəd ˈləʊn/ *noun* a loan which is guaranteed by the borrower giving assets as security

secure server /sɪˌkjʊə ˈsɜːvə/ *noun* a combination of hardware and software that makes e-commerce credit card transactions safe by stopping unauthorised people from gaining access to credit card details online

secure sockets layer /sɪˌkjʊə ˈsɒkɪts ˌleɪə/ *noun* full form of **SSL**

secure website /sɪˌkjʊə ˈwebsaɪt/ *noun* a website on the Internet that encrypts the messages between the visitor and the site to ensure that no hacker or eavesdropper can intercept the information

security /sɪˈkjʊərɪti/ *noun* the fact of being protected against attack

seed /siːd/ *noun* details of the address of the person who owns a list, put into a rented mailing list to check if it is being used correctly ■ *verb* to put the names and addresses of the mailers into a rented mailing list to check that it is being used correctly

see-safe /ˈsiː seɪf/ *adverb* under an agreement where a supplier will give credit for unsold goods at the end of a period if the retailer cannot sell them ○ *We bought the stock see-safe.*

segment /ˈsegmənt/ *noun* a part of the sales of a large business defined by specific criteria ■ *verb*/segˈment/ to divide a potential market into different segments

'…like direct mail, telemarketing has assumed greater importance as consumer markets have become segmented' [*Financial Times*]

'…different market segments and, ultimately, individual consumers, must be addressed separately' [*Financial Times*]

segmentation /ˌsegmənˈteɪʃ(ə)n/ *noun* the division of the market or consumers into categories according to their buying habits

select /sɪˈlekt/ *adjective* of top quality or specially chosen ○ *The firm offers a select range of merchandise.* ○ *Our customers are a select group.* ■ *verb* to choose ○ *The board will meet to select three candidates for a second interview.* □ **selected items are reduced by 25%** some items have been reduced by 25%

selection /sɪˈlekʃən/ *noun* **1.** a choice **2.** a thing which has been chosen ○ *Here is a selection of our product line.*

selection procedure /sɪˈlekʃən prəˌsiːdʒə/ *noun* the general method of choosing a candidate for a job

selective /sɪˈlektɪv/ *adjective* choosing carefully

selective attention /sɪˌlektɪv əˈtenʃ(ə)n/, **selective perception** /sɪˌlektɪv pəˈsepʃən/ *noun* an individual's tendency to unconsciously select what they want from an advertisement ○ *We must take selective perception into account when deciding what to stress in the advertising.*

selective demand /sɪˌlektɪv dɪˈmaːnd/ *noun* demand for a particular brand

selective demand advertising /sɪˌlektɪv dɪˈmaːnd ˌædvətaɪzɪŋ/ *noun* advertising that stimulates demand for a specific product or brand

selective distribution /sɪˌlektɪv dɪstrɪˈbjuːʃ(ə)n/ *noun* use by a producer of a limited number of wholesalers and retailers in a particular area ○ *This specialised product will need selective distribution.* ○ *Selective distribution may not enable the goods to reach consumers in sufficient quantities.*

selective exposure /sɪˌlektɪv ɪkˈspəʊʒə/ *noun* the process by which consumers decide whether they will watch or listen to advertising information

selective mailing /sɪˌlektɪv ˈmeɪlɪŋ/ *noun* the mailing out of promotional material to a selected address list

selective retention /sɪˌlektɪv rɪˈtenʃən/ *noun* the process by which people remember some information but not everything they hear

self- /self/ *prefix* referring to yourself

self-completion /self kəmˈpliːʃ(ə)n/ *noun* a type of questionnaire that can be filled in without an interviewer being present ○ *These self-completion questionnaires can be sent out through the post.* ○ *Self-completion is not a good idea if the respondents don't understand the questions.*

self-image /ˌself ˈɪmɪdʒ/ *noun* an idea that a person has about their own character and abilities

self-liquidating offer /self lɪkwɪˌ-deɪtɪŋ ˈɒfə/ *noun* the offer of a free gift or the sale of another product at a discount, made when a product is bought, usually against proof of purchase. The intention is to encourage the customer to adopt the brand, and at the same time to cover the cost of the offer and reduce overall promotional costs for the product. ○ *Even with the self-liquidating offer our sales have not gone up very much.*

self-mailer /self ˈmeɪlə/ *noun* an item of promotional material sent through the post, which includes a post-age-paid reply section which can be sent back without an envelope and on which customers can make an order ○ *Only 10% of the self-mailers we sent out have elicited any response.*

self-reference criterion /self ˈrefrəns kraɪˌtɪəriən/ *noun* the assumption that a product can success-fully be sold abroad on the basis of its success in the home market (NOTE: plural is **criteria**)

self-regulation /ˌself ˌregjʊˈleɪʃ(ə)n/ *noun* the regulation of an industry by its own members, usually by means of a committee that issues guidance and sets standards that it then enforces (NOTE: For example, the stock exchange is regu-lated by the Stock Exchange Council.)

'…he blamed a tiny minority for breaking the codes and warned against agencies and clients trying to outwit the ASA. He called for honest dealings within the spirit of self-regulation and warned that the alternative to self-regulation was statutory restrictions' [*Marketing*]

self-regulatory /ˌself ˌregjʊˈleɪt-(ə)ri/ *adjective* referring to an organisa-tion which regulates itself

sell *noun* an act of selling □ **to give a product the hard sell** to make great efforts to persuade customers to buy it ■ *verb* **1.** to exchange something for money ○ *to sell something on credit* ○ *The shop sells washing machines and refrigerators.* ○ *They tried to sell their house for £450,000.* ○ *Their products are easy to sell.* **2.** to be bought ○ *These items sell well in the pre-Christmas period.* ○ *Those packs sell for £25 a dozen.* (NOTE: **selling – sold**)

sell forward *phrasal verb* to sell for-eign currency, commodities, etc. for delivery at a later date

sell off *phrasal verb* to sell goods quickly to get rid of them

sell out *phrasal verb* **1.** □ **to sell out of an item** to sell all the stock of an item ○ *to sell out of a product line* ○ *We have sold out of plastic bags.* ○ *This item has sold out.* **2.** to sell your business ○ *They sold out and retired to the seaside.*

sell-by date /ˈsel baɪ ˌdeɪt/ *noun* a date on a food packet which is the last

date on which the food is guaranteed to be good

seller /ˈselə/ *noun* **1.** a person who sells ○ *There were few sellers in the market, so prices remained high.* **2.** something which sells ○ *This book is a steady seller.*

seller's market /ˌseləz ˈmɑːkɪt/ *noun* a market where the seller can ask high prices because there is a large demand for the product. Opposite **buy-er's market**

sell-in /ˈsel ɪn/ *noun* the amount of stock of a product taken by retailers when it is launched

-selling /ˈselɪŋ/ *suffix* □ **best-selling car** a car which sells better than other models

selling agent /ˈselɪŋ ˌeɪdʒənt/ *noun* a person who sells for a business or another person and earns a commission

selling costs /ˈselɪŋ kɒsts/, **sell-ing overhead** /ˈselɪŋ ˌəʊvəhed/ *plural noun* the amount of money to be paid for the advertising, reps' commis-sions, and other expenses involved in selling something

selling price /ˈselɪŋ praɪs/ *noun* the price at which someone is willing to sell something

selling space /ˈselɪŋ speɪs/ *noun* the amount of space in a retail outlet which is used for displaying goods for sale

sellout /ˈselaʊt/ *noun* □ **this item has been a sellout** all the stock of the item has been sold

semantic differential /səˌmæntɪk ˌdɪfəˈrenʃ(ə)l/ *noun* a scaling tech-nique which provides a range of possible answers between two opposite descrip-tive words

semi- /semi/ *prefix* half or part

semi-display advertisement /ˌsemi dɪˈspleɪ ədˌvɜːtɪsmənt/ *noun* an advertisement that has some of the features of a display advertisement such as a border and its own typeface or illustrations, but which is printed on the classified advertisement page

semi-finished product /ˌsemi ˈfɪnɪʃt ˌprɒdʌkt/ *noun* a product which is partly finished

semi-fixed cost /ˌsemi fɪkst ˈkɒst/ *noun* same as **semi-variable cost**

semiotics /ˌsemiˈɒtɪks/ *noun* the use of such promotional tools as package design, logos, and slogans in marketing (NOTE: takes a singular verb)

semi-solus /ˌsemi ˈsəʊləs/ *noun* an advertisement that shares a page with other advertisements, but is not immediately next to any of them

semi-structured interview /ˌsemi ˌstrʌktʃəd ˈɪntəvjuː/ *noun* an interview using some pre-set questions but allowing some questions that have been chosen by the interviewer as well ○ *Part of a semi-structured interview consists in respondents describing their first reactions to the advertisement.*

semi-variable cost /ˌsemi ˌveəriəb(ə)l ˈkɒst/ *noun* the amount of money paid to produce a product, which increases, though less than proportionally, with the quantity of the product made ○ *Stepping up production will mean an increase in semi-variable costs.* Also called **semi-fixed cost**

send /send/ *verb*

send away for *phrasal verb* to write asking for something to be sent to you ○ *We sent away for the new catalogue.*

send off for *phrasal verb* to write asking for something to be sent to you ○ *We sent off for the new catalogue.*

sender /ˈsendə/ *noun* a person who sends □ **'return to sender'** words on an envelope or parcel to show that it is to be sent back to the person who sent it

sensitive /ˈsensɪtɪv/ *adjective* quick to respond to something ○ *The market is very sensitive to the result of the elections.* ⇨ **price-sensitive**

sequential sampling /sɪˌkwen-ʃ(ə)l ˈsɑːmplɪŋ/ *noun* the process of carrying on the process of sampling until enough respondents have been interviewed to provide the necessary information

serial number /ˈsɪəriəl ˌnʌmbə/ *noun* a number in a series ○ *This batch of shoes has the serial number 25–02.*

SERVQUAL /ˈsɜːvkwæl/ *noun* a model developed to measure service quality. SERVQUAL measures five dimensions of service quality: tangibles, reliability, responsiveness, assurance, and empathy.

service /ˈsɜːvɪs/ *noun* **1.** the fact of working for an employer, or the period of time during which an employee has worked for an employer ○ *retiring after twenty years service to the company* ○ *The amount of your pension depends partly on the number of your years of service.* **2.** the act of keeping a machine in good working order ○ *the routine service of equipment* ○ *The machine has been sent in for service.* ■ *verb* **1.** to keep a machine in good working order ○ *The car needs to be serviced every six months.* ○ *The computer has gone back to the manufacturer for servicing.* **2.** □ **to service a debt** to pay interest on a debt ○ *The company is having problems in servicing its debts.*

service bureau /ˈsɜːvɪs ˌbjʊərəʊ/ *noun* an office which specialises in helping other offices

service centre /ˈsɜːvɪs ˌsentə/ *noun* an office or workshop which specialises in keeping machines in good working order

service charge /ˈsɜːvɪs tʃɑːdʒ/ *noun* a charge which a bank or business makes for carrying out work for a customer (NOTE: The UK term is **bank charge**.)

service department /ˈsɜːvɪs dɪˌpɑːtmənt/ *noun* the section of a company which keeps customers' machines in good working order

service engineer /ˈsɜːvɪs endʒɪˌnɪə/ *noun* an engineer who specialises in keeping machines in good working order

service history /ˈsɜːvɪs ˌhɪst(ə)ri/ *noun* a record of the times a machine has been serviced

service level /ˈsɜːvɪs ˌlev(ə)l/ *noun* a measurement of how efficient a producer is in distributing goods, e.g. the minimum number of back orders at any one time or delivery frequency to an area ○ *Service levels must be improved to fight competition.* ○ *The product is competitive in itself, but sales are affected by a low service level.*

service level agreement /ˈsɜːvɪs ˌlev(ə)l əˌgriːmənt/ *noun* an agreement between a supplier and a customer which stipulates the level of services to be rendered. Abbreviation **SLA**

services /ˈsɜːvɪsɪz/ *plural noun* benefits which are sold to customers or clients, e.g. transport or education ○ *We give advice to companies on the marketing of services.* ○ *We must improve the exports of both goods and services.*

set /set/ *noun* a group of items which go together, which are used together, or which are sold together ○ *a set of tools* ■ *adjective* fixed, or which cannot be changed ○ *There is a set fee for all our consultants.* ■ *verb* to fix or to arrange something ○ *We have to set a price for the new computer.* ○ *The price of the calculator has been set low, so as to achieve maximum unit sales.* (NOTE: **setting – set**) □ **the auction set a record for high prices** the prices at the auction were the highest ever reached

set up *phrasal verb* to begin something, or to organise something new ○ *to set up an inquiry* or *a working party* □ **to set up a company** to start a company legally □ **to set up in business** to start a new business ○ *She set up in business as an insurance broker.* ○ *He set himself up as a freelance representative.*

'…the concern announced that it had acquired a third large tanker since being set up' [*Lloyd's List*]

setting up costs /ˌsetɪŋ ˈʌp kɒsts/, **setup costs** /ˈsetʌp kɒsts/ *plural noun* the costs of getting a machine or a factory ready to make a new product after finishing work on the previous one

settle /ˈset(ə)l/ *verb* **1.** □ **to settle an account** to pay what is owed **2.** to solve a problem or dispute

settlement /ˈset(ə)lmənt/ *noun* the payment of an account □ **we offer an extra 5% discount for rapid settlement** we take a further 5% off the price if the customer pays quickly □ **settlement in cash** *or* **cash settlement** payment of an invoice in cash, not by cheque

'…he emphasised that prompt settlement of all forms of industrial disputes would guarantee industrial peace in the country and ensure increased productivity' [*Business Times (Lagos)*]

shadow economy /ˌʃædəʊ ɪˈkɒnəmi/ *noun* same as **black economy**

share /ʃeə/ *noun* a part of something that has been divided up among several people or groups ■ *verb* to divide something up among several people or groups ○ *to share computer time* ○ *to share the profits among the senior executives* ○ *Three companies share the market.* □ **to share information or data** to give someone information which you have

'…falling profitability means falling share prices' [*Investors Chronicle*]

'…the share of blue-collar occupations declined from 48% to 43%' [*Sydney Morning Herald*]

share capital /ˈʃeə ˌkæpɪt(ə)l/ *noun* the value of the assets of a company held as shares

shared mailing /ʃeəd ˈmeɪlɪŋ/ *noun* a mailing where two or more producers insert mailing pieces in the same envelope

shelf /ʃelf/ *noun* a horizontal flat surface attached to a wall or in a cupboard on which items for sale are displayed ○ *The shelves in the supermarket were full of items before the Christmas rush.*

shelf barker /ˈʃelf ˌbɑːkə/, **shelf talker** /ˈʃelf ˌtɔːkə/, **shelf wobbler** /ˈʃelf ˌwɒblə/ *noun* a card placed on or hung from a shelf to promote an item for sale

shelf filler /ˈʃelf ˌfɪlə/ *noun* a person whose job is to make sure that the shelves in a shop are kept full of items for sale

shelf life /ˈʃelf laɪf/ *noun* the length of time during which a product can stay in the shop and still be good to use

shelf space /ˈʃelf speɪs/ *noun* the amount of space on shelves in a shop

shift /ʃɪft/ *noun* a movement or change ○ *a shift in the company's marketing strategy* ○ *The company is taking advantage of a shift in the market towards higher-priced goods.*

ship /ʃɪp/ *noun* a large boat for carrying passengers and cargo on the sea □ **to drop ship** to deliver a large order direct to a customer's shop or warehouse, without going through an agent ■ *verb* to send goods, but not always on a ship

○ *to ship goods to the US* ○ *We ship all our goods by rail.* ○ *The consignment of cars was shipped abroad last week.*

shipbroker /'ʃɪpˌbrəʊkə/ *noun* a person who arranges shipping or transport of goods for customers on behalf of ship owners

ship chandler /ʃɪp 'tʃɑːndlə/ *noun* a person who supplies goods such as food to ships

shipment /'ʃɪpmənt/ *noun* **1.** goods which have been sent or are going to be sent ○ *Two shipments were lost in the fire.* ○ *A shipment of toys was damaged.* **2.** an act of sending goods ○ *We make two shipments a week to France.*

shipper /'ʃɪpə/ *noun* a person who sends goods or who organises the sending of goods for other customers

shipping /'ʃɪpɪŋ/ *noun* the sending of goods ○ *shipping charges* ○ *shipping costs* (NOTE: **shipping** does not always mean using a ship.)

shipping agent /'ʃɪpɪŋ ˌeɪdʒənt/ *noun* a company which specialises in the sending of goods

shipping confirmation /'ʃɪpɪŋ kɒnfəˌmeɪʃ(ə)n/ *noun* an email message informing the purchaser that an order has been shipped

shipping instructions /'ʃɪpɪŋ ɪnˌstrʌkʃənz/ *plural noun* the details of how goods are to be shipped and delivered

shipping note /'ʃɪpɪŋ nəʊt/ *noun* a note which gives details of goods being shipped

shoddy /'ʃɒdi/ *adjective* of bad quality ○ *shoddy workmanship*

shop /ʃɒp/ *noun* **1.** a retail outlet where goods of a certain type are sold ○ *a computer shop* ○ *an electrical goods shop* ○ *All the shops in the centre of town close on Sundays.* ○ *She opened a women's clothes shop.* (NOTE: The usual US term is **store**.) **2.** an advertising agency

shop around *phrasal verb* to go to various shops or suppliers and compare prices before making a purchase or before placing an order ○ *You should shop around before getting your car serviced.* ○ *He's shopping around for a*

new suit. ○ *It pays to shop around when you are planning to get a mortgage.*

shop assistant /'ʃɒp əˌsɪstənt/ *noun* a person who serves the customers in a shop

shop audit /'ʃɒp ˌɔːdɪt/ *noun* a market-research method by which a research company regularly checks a sample of retailers for unit sales and stock levels of different brands ○ *Since subscribing to the shop audit we have seen how much better we're doing than our competitors.*

shopbot /'ʃɒpbɒt/ *noun* an Internet search device that searches for particular products or services and allows the user to compare prices and specifications

shop floor /ʃɒp 'flɔː/ *noun* **1.** the space in a shop given to the display of goods for sale **2.** □ **on the shop floor** in the factory, in the works or among the ordinary workers ○ *The feeling on the shop floor is that the manager does not know his job.*

shop front /'ʃɒp frʌnt/ *noun* a part of a shop which faces the street, including the entrance and windows

shopkeeper /'ʃɒpkiːpə/ *noun* a person who owns or runs a shop

shoplifter /'ʃɒplɪftə/ *noun* a person who steals goods from shops

shoplifting /'ʃɒplɪftɪŋ/ *noun* the practice of stealing goods from shops

shopper /'ʃɒpə/ *noun* a person who buys goods in a shop ○ *The store stays open to midnight to cater for late-night shoppers.*

shoppers' charter /ˌʃɒpəz 'tʃɑː-tə/ *noun* a law which protects the rights of shoppers against shopkeepers who are not honest or against manufacturers of defective goods

shopping /'ʃɒpɪŋ/ *noun* **1.** goods bought in a shop ○ *a basket of shopping* **2.** the act of going to shops to buy things ○ *to do your shopping in the local supermarket*

shopping arcade /'ʃɒpɪŋ ɑːˌkeɪd/ *noun* a covered passageway with small shops on either side

shopping cart /'ʃɒpɪŋ kɑːt/ *noun* **1.** a software package that records the items that an online buyer selects for purchase together with associated data, e.g. the price of the item and the number of items required **2.** *US* same as **shopping trolley**

shopping centre /'ʃɒpɪŋ ˌsentə/ *noun* a group of shops linked together with car parks and restaurants

shopping experience /'ʃɒpɪŋ ɪkˌspɪəriəns/ *noun* the virtual environment in which a customer visits an e-merchant's website, selects items, places them in an electronic shopping cart, and notifies the merchant of the order (NOTE: The shopping experience does not include a payment transaction, which is initiated by a message to a point-of-sale program when the customer signals that he or she has finished shopping and wishes to pay.)

shopping goods /'ʃɒpɪŋ ɡʊdz/ *plural noun* high-priced goods whose purchase has to be considered carefully by customers, who compare the good points of competing brands

shopping mall /'ʃɒpɪŋ mɒl/ *noun* *US* same as **shopping centre**

shopping precinct /'ʃɒpɪŋ ˌpriː-sɪŋkt/ *noun* a part of a town where the streets are closed to traffic so that people can walk about and shop

shopping trolley /'ʃɒpɪŋ ˌtrɒli/ *noun* **1.** a metal basket on wheels, used by shoppers to put their purchases in as they go round a supermarket **2.** same as **shopping cart** 1

shop-soiled /'ʃɒp sɔɪld/ *adjective* dirty because of having been on display in a shop ○ *These items are shop-soiled and cannot be sold at full price.*

shopwalker /'ʃɒpwɔːkə/ *noun* an employee of a department store who advises the customers and supervises the shop assistants in a department

shop window /ˌʃɒp 'wɪndəʊ/ *noun* a large window in a shop front, where customers can see goods displayed

shop window website /ˌʃɒp 'wɪndəʊ ˌwebsaɪt/ *noun* a website that provides information about an organisation and its products, but does not allow visitors to interact with it

shop-within-shop /ˌʃɒp ˌwɪðɪn 'ʃɒp/ *noun* an arrangement in large department stores, where space is given to smaller specialised retail outlets to trade

short /ʃɔːt/ *adjective, adverb* **1.** for a small period of time □ **in the short term** in the near future or quite soon **2.** less than what is expected or desired ○ *The shipment was three items short.* ○ *My change was £2 short.* □ **when we cashed up we were £10 short** we had £10 less than we should have had □ **to give short weight** to sell something which is lighter than it should be □ **short of** lacking ○ *We are short of staff* or *short of money.* ○ *The company is short of new ideas.*

shortage /'ʃɔːtɪdʒ/ *noun* a lack or low availability of something ○ *a shortage of skilled staff* ○ *We employ part-timers to make up for staff shortages.* ○ *The import controls have resulted in the shortage of spare parts.* □ **there is no shortage of investment advice** there are plenty of people who want to give advice on investments

short-change /ˌʃɔːt 'tʃeɪndʒ/ *verb* to give a customer less change than is right, either by mistake or in the hope that it will not be noticed

short credit /ˌʃɔːt 'kredɪt/ *noun* terms which allow the customer only a little time to pay

shorthanded /ʃɔːt'hændɪd/ *adjective* without enough staff ○ *We're rather shorthanded at the moment.*

short lease /ˌʃɔːt 'liːs/ *noun* a lease which runs for up to two or three years ○ *We have a short lease on our current premises.*

short-range forecast /ˌʃɔːt reɪndʒ 'fɔːkɑːst/ *noun* a forecast which covers a period of a few months

short-staffed /ˌʃɔːt 'stɑːft/ *adjective* with not enough staff ○ *We're rather short-staffed at the moment.*

short-term /ˌʃɔːt 'tɜːm/ *adjective* for a period of weeks or months ○ *to place money on short-term deposit* ○ *She is employed on a short-term contract.* □ **on a short-term basis** for a short period

short-term debt /ˌʃɔːt tɜːm 'det/ *noun* a debt which has to be repaid within a few weeks

short-term forecast /ˌʃɔːt tɜːm ˈfɔːkɑːst/ *noun* a forecast which covers a period of a few months

short-term gain /ˌʃɔːt tɜːm ˈɡeɪn/ *noun* an increase in price made over a short period

short-term planning /ˌʃɔːt tɜːm ˈplænɪŋ/ *noun* planning for the immediate future

shout /ʃaʊt/ *noun* a bold statement promoting a book, either printed on the cover or on posters and leaflets ○ *The author disliked the shout on the cover suggested by the publisher's promotional manager.*

show /ʃəʊ/ *noun* an exhibition or display of goods or services for sale ○ *a motor show* ○ *a computer show*

showcard /ˈʃəʊkɑːd/ *noun* a piece of cardboard with advertising material, put near an item for sale

showcase /ˈʃəʊkeɪs/ *noun* **1.** a cupboard with a glass front or top to display items **2.** the presentation of someone or something in a favourable setting ■ *verb* to present someone or something in a way that is designed to attract attention and admiration

showing /ˈʃəʊɪŋ/ *noun* a measurement of an audience's exposure to outdoor advertising

showroom /ˈʃəʊruːm/ *noun* a room where goods are displayed for sale ○ *a car showroom*

shrink /ʃrɪŋk/ *verb* to get smaller ○ *The market has shrunk by 20%.* ○ *The company is having difficulty selling into a shrinking market.* (NOTE: **shrinking – shrank – has shrunk**)

shrinkage /ˈʃrɪŋkɪdʒ/ *noun* **1.** the amount by which something gets smaller ○ *to allow for shrinkage* **2.** losses of stock through theft, especially by the shop's own staff (*informal*)

SIC *abbreviation* Standard Industrial Classification

sideline /ˈsaɪdlaɪn/ *noun* a business which is extra to your normal work ○ *He runs a profitable sideline selling postcards to tourists.*

sight /saɪt/ *noun* the act of seeing □ **bill payable at sight** a bill which

must be paid when it is presented □ **to buy something sight unseen** to buy something without having inspected it

'…if your company needed a piece of equipment priced at about $50,000, would you buy it sight unseen from a supplier you had never met?' [*Nation's Business*]

sight draft /ˈsaɪt drɑːft/ *noun* a bill of exchange which is payable when it is presented

sign /saɪn/ *noun* a board or notice which advertises something ○ *They have asked for planning permission to put up a large red shop sign.* ○ *Advertising signs cover most of the buildings in the centre of the town.*

signage /ˈsaɪnɪdʒ/ *noun* all the signs and logos which identify an organisation such as a retail group, chain of restaurants, or motorway service area

'…if planning permission is granted and the Department of Transport is happy to grant motorway signage and access permission, you can buy or lease the land and start building' [*Caterer & Hotelkeeper*]

signature /ˈsɪɡnɪtʃə/ *noun* a special authentication code, such as a password, which a user must enter to prove his or her identity

signature file /ˈsɪɡnətʃə faɪl/ *noun* text at the end of an email message that identifies the sender and company name, address, etc. Abbreviation **sig file**

silver market /ˈsɪlvə ˌmɑːkɪt/ *noun* a market consisting of retired people (NOTE: also called **grey market**)

silver surfer /ˌsɪlvə ˈsɜːfə/ *noun* an older or retired person who regularly uses the Internet ○ *Her grandad uses the Internet every day. He loves being a silver surfer!*

SINBAD *abbreviation* single income no boyfriend absolutely desperate

single /ˈsɪŋɡ(ə)l/ *adjective* not married ○ *marital status: single*

single column centimetre /ˌsɪŋɡ(ə)l ˌkɒləm ˈsentɪmiːtə/ *noun* a unit of measurement for newspaper and magazine advertisements, representing one column which is one centimetre in depth

single-currency /ˌsɪŋɡ(ə)l ˈkʌrənsi/ *adjective* using or shown as an amount in only one currency

single European market /ˌsɪŋg(ə)l ˌjʊərəpiːən ˈmɑːkɪt/, **single market** /ˌsɪŋg(ə)l ˈmɑːkɪt/ *noun* ➡ **European Union**

single sourcing /ˌsɪŋg(ə)l ˈsɔː-sɪŋ/ *noun* the practice of obtaining all of a company's supplies from one source or supplier ○ *The buying department believes that single sourcing will lead to higher raw-material costs.* ○ *Single sourcing has simplified our purchasing plans.*

site /saɪt/ *noun* the place where something is located ○ *We have chosen a site for the new factory.* ○ *The supermarket is to be built on a site near the station.*

situation /ˌsɪtʃuˈeɪʃ(ə)n/ *noun* a state of affairs ○ *the financial situation of a company* ○ *the general situation of the economy*

situation analysis /ˌsɪtʃuˈeɪʃ(ə)n əˌnæləsɪs/, **situation audit** /ˌsɪtʃuˈeɪʃ(ə)n ˌɔːdɪt/ *noun* the stage in marketing planning concerned with investigating an organisation's strengths and weaknesses ○ *In the situation analysis particular attention was paid to existing production capacity.* ○ *It is clear from the situation analysis that distribution is our biggest problem.*

Skills Funding Agency /ˌskɪlz ˈfʌndɪŋ ˌeɪdʒənsi/ *noun* an agency of the Department for Business, Innovation and Skills which funds and regulates adult further education in England

skim /skɪm/ *verb* to fix a high price on a new product in order to achieve high short-term profits. The high price reflects the customer's appreciation of the added value of the new product, and will be reduced in due course as the product becomes established on the market. ○ *We are skimming the market with a product that will soon be obsolete.*

skip scheduling /ˈskɪp ʃedʒuːlɪŋ/ *noun* the act of arranging for an advertisement to appear in every other issue of a publication

SKU /ˌes keɪ ˈjuː/ *noun* a unique code made up of numbers or letters and numbers which is assigned to a product by a retailer for identification and stock control. Full form **stockkeeping unit**

SLA *abbreviation* service level agreement

slack season /ˈslæk ˌsiːz(ə)n/ *noun* a period when a company is not very busy

slash /slæʃ/ *verb* to reduce something sharply ○ *We have been forced to slash credit terms.* ○ *Prices have been slashed in all departments.* ○ *The banks have slashed interest rates.*

sleeper /ˈsliːpə/ *noun* a product which does not sell well for some time, then suddenly becomes very popular

sleeper effect /ˈsliːpər ɪˌfekt/ *noun* an effect shown where a message becomes more persuasive over a period of time

slot /slɒt/ *noun* the period of time available for a TV or radio commercial ○ *They took six 30-second slots at peak viewing time.*

slowdown /ˈsləʊdaʊn/ *noun* a reduction in business activity ○ *a slowdown in the company's expansion*

slow payer /ˌsləʊ ˈpeɪə/ *noun* a person or company that does not pay debts on time ○ *The company is well known as a slow payer.*

slump /slʌmp/ *noun* **1.** a rapid fall ○ *the slump in the value of the pound* ○ *We experienced a slump in sales* or *a slump in profits.* **2.** a period of economic collapse with high unemployment and loss of trade ○ *We are experiencing slump conditions.* **3.** the world economic crisis of 1929–33 ■ *verb* to fall fast ○ *Profits have slumped.* ○ *The pound slumped on the foreign exchange markets.*

small and medium-sized enterprises /ˌsmɔːl ən ˌmiːdiəm ˌsaɪzd ˈentəpraɪzɪz/ *plural noun* organisations that have between 10 and 250 employees and are usually in the start-up or growth stage of development. Abbreviation **SMEs**

small business /ˌsmɔːl ˈbɪznɪs/ *noun* a company which has an annual turnover of less than £5.6 million and does not employ more than 50 staff

small businessman /ˌsmɔːl ˈbɪznɪsmæn/ *noun* a man who owns a small business

small print /ˈsmɔːl prɪnt/ *noun* items printed at the end of an official document such as a contract in smaller letters than the rest of the text. People sometimes do not pay attention to the small print, but it can contain important information, and unscrupulous operators may deliberately try to hide things such as additional charges, unfavourable terms, or loopholes in it.

'An emergency fiscal program is on the table providing for tax cuts next year. But there's some small print that provides for new taxes two years down the road' [*Business Week*]

small-scale enterprise /ˌsmɔːl skeɪl ˈentəpraɪz/ *noun* a small business

SMART /smɑːt/ *noun* a simple acronym used to set objectives. SMART stands for: specific, measurable, achievable, realistic, time.

smart market /ˌsmɑːt ˈmɑːkɪt/ *noun* a market where all business is conducted electronically using network communications

smartphone /ˈsmɑːtˌfəʊn/ *noun* a mobile telephone with built-in applications and Internet access. Smartphones provide digital voice services as well as text messaging, email, Web browsing, still and video cameras, MP3 players, video viewing and video calling. In addition to their built-in functions, smartphones can run a number of applications, turning the telephone into a mobile computer. ○ *There are over twenty smartphones listed in our catalogue.*

SMEs *abbreviation* small and medium-sized enterprises

smuggle /ˈsmʌɡ(ə)l/ *verb* to take goods illegally into a country or without declaring them to customs ○ *They had to smuggle the spare parts into the country.*

smuggler /ˈsmʌɡlə/ *noun* a person who smuggles

smuggling /ˈsmʌɡlɪŋ/ *noun* the practice of taking goods illegally into a country or without declaring them to customs ○ *They made their money in arms smuggling.*

snap /snæp/ *verb*

snap up *phrasal verb* to buy something quickly ○ *to snap up a bargain*

○ *She snapped up 15% of the company's shares.* (NOTE: **snapping – snapped**)

snip /snɪp/ *noun* a bargain (*informal*) ○ *These printers are a snip at £50.*

social /ˈsəʊʃ(ə)l/ *adjective* referring to society in general

social audit /ˌsəʊʃ(ə)l ˈɔːdɪt/ *noun* a systematic assessment of an organisation's effects on society or on all those who can be seen as its stakeholders. A social audit covers such issues as internal codes of conduct, business ethics, human resource development, environmental impact, and the organisation's sense of social responsibility. ○ *The social audit focused on the effects of pollution in the area.* ○ *The social audit showed that the factory could provide jobs for 5% of the unemployed in the small town nearby.*

social cost /ˈsəʊʃ(ə)l kɒsts/ *noun* a negative effect of a type of production on society ○ *The report examines the social costs of building the factory in the middle of the town.* ○ *The industry's representative denied that any social cost was involved in the new development.*

social costs /ˈsəʊʃ(ə)l kɒsts/ *plural noun* the ways in which something will affect people

social marketing /ˌsəʊʃ(ə)l ˈmɑːkɪtɪŋ/ *noun* marketing with the purpose of contributing to society rather than just making a profit

social media /ˌsəʊʃ(ə)l ˈmiːdiə/ *noun* the use of web-based and mobile technologies to turn communication into instantaneous, interactive dialogue on platforms such as Twitter, Facebook, and LinkedIn. It relies on the creation and exchange of user-generated content, is non-hierarchical, and is available to the public for little or no cost, compared with traditional print media.

social networking /ˌsəʊʃ(ə)l ˈnetwɜːkɪŋ/ *noun* the interaction between a group of people who share a common interest using online social sites such as Facebook, MySpace, LinkedIn, or Twitter ○ *The company found that social networking was the best way to attract new customers in the youth market.* ⇨ **Facebook, MySpace, LinkedIn, Twitter**

social security /ˌsəʊʃ(ə)l sɪˈkjʊə-rɪti/, **social insurance** /ˌsəʊʃ(ə)l ɪnˈʃʊərəns/ *noun* a government scheme where employers, employees, and the self-employed make regular contributions to a fund which provides unemployment pay, sickness pay, or retirement pensions ○ *He gets weekly social security payments.* ○ *She never worked but lived on social security for years.*

social system /ˈsəʊʃ(ə)l ˌsɪstəm/ *noun* the way society is organised

societal /səˈsaɪət(ə)l/ *adjective* referring to society

societally conscious /səˌsaɪətəli ˈkɒnʃəs/ *plural noun* people who are successful in life and want to work with groups of people

societal marketing /səˌsaɪət(ə)l ˈmɑːkɪtɪŋ/ *noun* same as **social marketing**

society /səˈsaɪəti/ *noun* **1.** the way in which the people in a country are organised **2.** a club for a group of people with the same interests ○ *She joined a social networking society.*

socio-cultural research /ˌsəʊʃiəʊ ˌkʌltʃərəl rɪˈsɜːtʃ/ *noun* research into problems of society and culture, which gives insights into consumers and their needs

socio-economic /ˌsəʊʃiəʊ iːkə-ˈnɒmɪk/ *adjective* referring to social and economic conditions, social classes and income groups ○ *We have commissioned a thorough socio-economic analysis of our potential market.*

socio-economic groups /ˌsəʊʃiəʊ iːkəˌnɒmɪk ˈgruːps/ *plural noun* groups in society divided according to income and position

COMMENT: The British socio-economic groups are: **A: upper middle class**: senior managers, administrators, civil servants and professional people; **B: middle class**: middle-ranking managers, administrators, civil servants and professional people; **C1: lower middle class**: junior managers and clerical staff; **C2: skilled workers**: workers with special skills and qualifications; **D: working class**: unskilled workers and manual workers; **E: subsistence level**: pensioners, the unemployed and casual manual workers.

socio-economic segmentation /ˌsəʊʃiəʊ iːkəˌnɒmɪk segmən-ˈteɪʃ(ə)n/ *noun* dividing the population into segments according to their incomes and social class

soft bounce /ˌsɒft ˈbaʊns/ *noun* an email message that reaches the recipient's mail server but is bounced back before it is delivered, sometimes because the recipient's inbox is full. It may be forwarded at a later date by the recipient's network administrator.

soft currency /ˌsɒft ˈkʌrənsi/ *noun* the currency of a country with a weak economy, which is cheap to buy and difficult to exchange for other currencies. Opposite **hard currency**

soft sell /ˌsɒft ˈsel/ *noun* the process of persuading people to buy, by encouraging and not forcing them to do so

software /ˈsɒftweə/ *noun* computer programs

sole /səʊl/ *adjective* only

sole agency /ˌsəʊl ˈeɪdʒənsi/ *noun* an agreement to be the only person to represent a company or to sell a product in a particular area ○ *He has the sole agency for Ford cars.*

sole agent /ˌsəʊl ˈeɪdʒənt/ *noun* a person who has the sole agency for a company in an area ○ *She is the sole agent for Ford cars in the locality.*

sole distributor /ˌsəʊl dɪˈstrɪbjutə/ *noun* a retailer who is the only one in an area who is allowed to sell a product

sole owner /ˌsəʊl ˈəʊnə/ *noun* a person who owns a business on their own, with no partners, and has not formed a company

sole proprietor /ˌsəʊl prə-ˈpraɪətə/, **sole trader** /ˌsəʊl ˈtreɪdə/ *noun* a person who runs a business, usually by him- or herself, but has not registered it as a company

solicit /səˈlɪsɪt/ *verb* □ **to solicit orders** to ask for orders, to try to get people to order goods

solus /ˈsəʊləs/ *adjective* alone

solus (advertisement) /ˈsəʊləs/ *noun* an advertisement which does not appear near other advertisements for similar products

solus position /ˈsəʊləs pəˌzɪ-ʃ(ə)n/ *noun* a position for an advertisement which is alone on a page, or not near advertisements for similar products

solus site /'səʊləs saɪt/ *noun* a shop which only carries products from one supplier

solution brand /sə'luːʃ(ə)n brænd/ *noun* a combination of a product and related services, e.g. a computer system plus installation and maintenance, that meets a customer's needs more effectively than the product on its own

sorting /'sɔːtɪŋ/ *noun* the process of organising a mailing list in a certain order (by name, by country, etc.)

source /sɔːs/ *noun* **1.** the place where something comes from ○ *What is the source of her income?* ○ *You must declare income from all sources to the tax office.* □ **income which is taxed at source** income where the tax is removed and paid to the government by the employer before the income is paid to the employee **2.** the person who sends a message ■ *verb* to get supplies from somewhere ○ *We source these spare parts in Germany.*

source credibility /'sɔːs kredə-ˌbɪlɪti/ *noun* the image people have of someone which will determine that person's credibility

source power /'sɔːs ˌpaʊə/ *noun* the power derived by a source from being able to reward a customer

sourcing /'sɔːsɪŋ/ *noun* the process of finding suppliers of goods or services ○ *The sourcing of spare parts can be diversified to suppliers outside Europe.* ⇨ **outsourcing**

space /speɪs/ *noun* an empty place or empty area □ **to take advertising space in a newspaper** to place a large advertisement in a newspaper

space buyer /'speɪs ˌbaɪə/ *noun* a person who buys advertising space in magazines and newspapers

spam /spæm/ *noun* **1.** articles that have been posted to more than one newsgroup, and so are likely to contain unsolicited commercial messages **2.** the use of electronic messaging systems to send unsolicited bulk messages indiscriminately, most commonly in the form of emails

spare parts /speə 'paːts/ *plural noun* a stock of components for a machine that are kept in case the machine breaks down and needs to be repaired

spatial segmentation /ˌspeɪʃ(ə)l ˌsegmən'teɪʃ(ə)n/ *noun* the segmentation or division of a market according to areas or regions

spec /spek/ *noun* same as **specification** □ **to buy something on spec** to buy something without being sure of its value

special /'speʃ(ə)l/ *noun* a product which a retailer buys for a special purpose, e.g. a premium offer

'…airlines offer special stopover rates and hotel packages to attract customers to certain routes' [*Business Traveller*]

special drawing rights /ˌspeʃ(ə)l 'drɔːɪŋ raɪts/ *plural noun* units of account used by the International Monetary Fund, allocated to each member country for use in loans and other international operations. Their value is calculated daily on the weighted values of a group of currencies shown in dollars. Abbreviation **SDRs**

specialisation /ˌspeʃəlaɪ'zeɪ-ʃ(ə)n/, **specialization** *noun* the act of dealing with one specific type of product ○ *The company's area of specialisation is accounts packages for small businesses.*

specialise /'speʃəlaɪz/, **specialize** *verb* to deal with one particular type of skill, product, or service ○ *The company specialises in electronic components.* ○ *They have a specialised product line.* ○ *He sells very specialised equipment for the electronics industry.*

'…the group specializes in the sale, lease and rental of new and second-user hardware' [*Financial Times*]

specialist /'speʃəlɪst/ *noun* a person or company that deals with one particular type of product or one subject ○ *You should go to a specialist in computers to a computer specialist for advice.*

speciality /ˌspeʃi'æləti/, **specialty** /'speʃ(ə)lti/ *noun* the specific business interest or specific type of product that a company has ○ *Their speciality is computer programs.*

special offer /ˌspeʃ(ə)l ˈɒfə/ *noun* a situation where goods are put on sale at a specially low price ○ *We have a range of men's shirts on special offer.*

special position /ˌspeʃ(ə)l pəˈzɪ-ʃ(ə)n/ *noun* an especially good place in a publication for advertising ○ *If we are prepared to invest the money we could choose a special position for the advertisement.*

specialty goods /ˈspeʃ(ə)lti gʊdz/ *plural noun* a special type of product which sells to a limited market ○ *We only deal in specialty goods.* ○ *These specialty goods require expert personal selling.* ○ *There's a high profit margin on specialty goods.*

specialty store /ˈspeʃ(ə)lti stɔː/ *noun* US a shop selling a limited range of items of good quality

specification /ˌspesɪfɪˈkeɪʃ(ə)n/ *noun* detailed information about what or who is needed or about a product to be supplied ○ *to detail the specifications of a computer system* □ **to work to standard specifications** to work to specifications which are acceptable anywhere in an industry □ **the work is not up to specification or does not meet our specifications** the product is not made in the way which was detailed

specify /ˈspesɪfaɪ/ *verb* to state clearly what is needed ○ *to specify full details of the goods ordered* ○ *Do not include VAT on the invoice unless specified.* ○ *Candidates are asked to specify which of the three posts they are applying for.* (NOTE: **specifies – specifying – specified**)

specimen /ˈspesɪmɪn/ *noun* something which is given as a sample □ **to give specimen signatures on a bank mandate** to write the signatures of all the people who can sign cheques for an account so that the bank can recognise them

spend /spend/ *verb* **1.** to pay money ○ *They spent all their savings on buying the shop.* ○ *The company spends thousands of pounds on research.* **2.** to use time ○ *The company spends hundreds of person-hours on meetings.* ○ *The chairman spent yesterday afternoon with the auditors.* (NOTE: **spending – spent**)

■ *noun* an amount of money spent ○ *What's the annual spend on marketing?*

spending /ˈspendɪŋ/ *noun* the act of paying money for goods and services ○ *Both cash spending and credit card spending increase at Christmas.*

spending money /ˈspendɪŋ ˌmʌni/ *noun* money for ordinary personal expenses

spending power /ˈspendɪŋ ˌpaʊə/ *noun* **1.** the fact of having money to spend on goods ○ *the spending power of the student market* **2.** the amount of goods which can be bought for a sum of money ○ *The spending power of the pound has fallen over the last ten years.*

sphere /sfɪə/ *noun* an area ○ *a sphere of activity* ○ *a sphere of influence*

spiff /spɪf/ *noun* special commission or special premium offers given to sales personnel or agents, based on sales over a specific period. Full form **special incentive for affiliates** ■ *verb* □ **to spiff up a product** to enhance the sales of a product by offering special incentives to sales personnel

spinner /ˈspɪnə/ *noun* a revolving stand on which goods are displayed in a shop ○ *There was a spinner with different types of confectionery at each checkout.*

spinoff /ˈspɪnɒf/ *noun* a useful product developed as a secondary product from a main item ○ *One of the spinoffs of the research programme has been the development of the electric car.*

splash page /ˈsplæʃ peɪdʒ/ *noun* a page, usually containing advertisements, that is displayed to visitors to a website before they reach the homepage

split run /ˈsplɪt rʌn/ *noun* the printing of the same issue of a publication in several production runs, so that different advertisements may be placed in different printings, allowing the effects of the advertising to be compared

sponsor /ˈspɒnsə/ *noun* **1.** a person who recommends another person for a job **2.** a company which pays part of the cost of making a TV programme by taking advertising time on the programme ■ *verb* to act as a sponsor for something

○ *a government-sponsored trade exhibition* ○ *The company has sponsored the football match.*

sponsorship /ˈspɒnsəʃɪp/ *noun* the act of sponsoring ○ *the sponsorship of a season of concerts* ○ *The training course could not be run without the sponsorship of several major companies.*

spot /spɒt/ *noun* **1.** a place for an advertisement on a TV or radio show **2.** the buying of something for immediate delivery ■ *adjective* done immediately

spot cash /ˌspɒt ˈkæʃ/ *noun* cash paid for something bought immediately

spot check /ˈspɒt tʃek/ *noun* a rapid and unannounced check to see if things are working properly

spot colour /ˈspɒt ˌkʌlə/ *noun* one colour, apart from black, used in an advertisement

spot market /ˈspɒt ˌmɑːkɪt/ *noun* a market that deals in commodities or foreign exchange for immediate rather than future delivery

'…with most of the world's oil now traded on spot markets, Opec's official prices are much less significant than they once were' [*Economist*]

spread /spred/ *noun* two facing pages in a magazine or newspaper used by an advertiser for a single advertisement running across the two pages

SRDS *abbreviation* Standard Rate & Data Service

SSL /ˌes es ˈel/ *abbreviation* a method of providing a safe channel over the Internet to allow a user's credit card or personal details to be safely transmitted ○ *I only purchase goods from a website that has SSL security installed.* ○ *The little key logo on my web browser appears when I am connected to a secure site with SSL.* Full form **secure sockets layer**

stabilisation /ˌsteɪbɪlaɪˈzeɪʃ(ə)n/, **stabilization** *noun* the process of making something stable, e.g. preventing sudden changes in prices □ **stabilisation of the economy** keeping the economy stable by preventing inflation from rising, cutting high interest rates and excess money supply

stabilise /ˈsteɪbəlaɪz/, **stabilize** *verb* to become steady, or to make something steady □ **prices have stabilised** prices have stopped moving up or down □ **to have a stabilising effect on the economy** to make the economy more stable

stability /stəˈbɪlɪti/ *noun* the state of being steady or not moving up or down ○ *price stability* ○ *a period of economic stability* ○ *the stability of the currency markets*

stable /ˈsteɪb(ə)l/ *adjective* steady or not moving up or down ○ *stable prices* ○ *a stable exchange rate* ○ *a stable currency* ○ *a stable economy*

stable market /ˌsteɪb(ə)l ˈmɑːkɪt/ *noun* a market where sales do not change much in response to changes in price and where demand is therefore steady

staff appraisal /stɑːf əˈpreɪz(ə)l/, **staff assessment** /stɑːf əˈsesmənt/ *noun* a report on how well a member of staff is working

stage-gate model /ˈsteɪdʒ ɡeɪt ˌmɒd(ə)l/ *noun* a business model for developing a new product from conception to its launch, where the development is divided into several stages at the end of which is a 'gate' where the management has to take a decision as to how to proceed to the next stage

stagflation /stægˈfleɪʃ(ə)n/ *noun* inflation and stagnation happening at the same time in an economy

stagnation /stægˈneɪʃ(ə)n/ *noun* the state of not making any progress, especially in economic matters ○ *The country entered a period of stagnation.*

stake /steɪk/ *noun* an amount of money invested □ **to have a stake in a business** to have money invested in a business □ **to acquire a stake in a business** to buy shares in a business ○ *He acquired a 25% stake in the company.* ■ *verb* □ **to stake money on something** to risk money on something

'…her stake, which she bought at $1.45 per share, is now worth nearly $10 million' [*Times*]

'…other investments include a large stake in a Chicago-based insurance company, as well as interests in tobacco products and hotels' [*Lloyd's List*]

stakeholder /ˈsteɪkhəʊldə/ *noun* **1.** a person such as a shareholder, employee, or supplier who has a stake in a business **2.** a person or body that is directly or indirectly involved with a company or organisation and has an interest in ensuring that it is successful (NOTE: A stakeholder may be an employee, customer, supplier, partner, or even the local community within which an organisation operates.)

'…the stakeholder concept is meant to be a new kind of low-cost, flexible personal pension aimed at those who are less well-off. Whether it will really encourage them to put aside money for retirement is a moot point. Ministers said companies would be able to charge no more than 1% a year to qualify for the stakeholder label' [*Financial Times*]

stakeholder theory /ˈsteɪkhəʊldə ˌθɪəri/ *noun* the theory that it is possible for an organisation to promote the interests of its shareholders without harming the interests of its other stakeholders such as its employees, suppliers and the wider community

stall /stɔːl/ *noun* a small moveable wooden booth, used for selling goods in a market

stallholder /ˈstɔːlhəʊldə/ *noun* a person who has a stall in a market and pays rent for the site it occupies

stamp duty /ˈstæmp ˌdjuːti/ *noun* a tax on legal documents such as those used, e.g., for the sale or purchase of shares or the conveyance of a property to a new owner

stamp trading /ˈstæmp ˌtreɪdɪŋ/ *noun* the giving out of stamps or vouchers to customers according to the value of their purchases, the stamps being exchangeable for more goods or for cash. Compare **trading stamp**

stand /stænd/ *noun* an arrangement of shelves or tables at an exhibition for showing a company's products

standard /ˈstændəd/ *noun* the usual quality or usual conditions which other things are judged against □ **up to standard** of acceptable quality ○ *This batch is not up to standard* or *does not meet our standards.* ■ *adjective* normal or usual ○ *a standard model car* ○ *We have a standard charge of £25 for a thirty-minute session.*

standard costing /ˌstændəd ˈkɒstɪŋ/ *noun* the process of planning costs for the period ahead and, at the end of the period, comparing these figures with actual costs in order to make necessary adjustments in planning

standard costs /ˌstændəd ˈkɒsts/ *plural noun* planned costs for the period ahead

standard deviation /ˌstændəd ˌdiːviˈeɪʃ(ə)n/ *noun* the way in which the results of a sample deviate from the mean or average

standard error /ˌstændəd ˈerə/ *noun* the extent to which chance affects the accuracy of a sample

Standard Industrial Classification /ˌstændəd ɪnˌdʌstriəl ˌklæsɪfɪˈkeɪʃ(ə)n/ *noun* the official listing and coding of industries and products. Abbreviation **SIC**

standardisation /ˌstændədaɪˈzeɪʃ(ə)n/, **standardization** *noun* the process of making sure that everything fits a standard or is produced in the same way ○ *standardisation of measurements throughout the EU* ○ *Standardisation of design is necessary if we want to have a uniform company style.* □ **standardisation of products** the process of reducing a large number of different products to a series which have the same measurements, design, packaging, etc.

standardise /ˈstændədaɪz/, **standardize** *verb* to make sure that everything fits a standard or is produced in the same way

standard letter /ˌstændəd ˈletə/ *noun* a letter which is sent without change to various correspondents

standard rate /ˈstændəd reɪt/ *noun* a basic rate of income tax which is paid by most taxpayers

Standard Rate & Data Service /ˌstændəd reɪt ənd ˈdeɪtə ˌsɜːvɪs/ *noun* an American publication listing advertising rates, circulation, and other details of major American magazines, newspapers, and other advertising media. Abbreviation **SRDS** (NOTE: The comparable UK publication is **British Rate and Data**.)

standing /ˈstændɪŋ/ *noun* a good reputation ○ *The financial standing of a company.* □ **company of good standing** very reputable company

standing order /ˌstændɪŋ ˈɔːdə/ noun an order written by a customer asking a bank to pay money regularly to an account ○ *I pay my subscription by standing order.*

standing room only /ˌstændɪŋ ruːm ˈəʊnli/ noun a sales technique which suggests to the customer that the current offer will be available only for a very short time or may be changed in the near future

stand-out test /ˈstænd aʊt ˌtest/ noun a test designed to assess how well a package stands out or catches the eye on a shelf ○ *Stand-out tests were carried out to evaluate how effective the colour of the new product packaging was.*

staple commodity /ˌsteɪp(ə)l kəˈmɒdɪti/ noun a basic food or raw material

staple industry /ˌsteɪp(ə)l ˈɪndəstri/ noun the main industry in a country

staple product /ˌsteɪp(ə)l ˈprɒdʌkt/ noun the main product

star /stɑː/ noun in the Boston matrix, a product which has a high market share and a high growth rate. It will need cash to finance its growth, but eventually should become a cash cow. ○ *We have only one star product but it's put our company on the map.* ○ *They're hoping that at least two of their new product range will turn out to be stars.*

starch ratings /ˈstɑːtʃ ˌreɪtɪŋz/ plural noun US a method of assessing the effectiveness of an organisation's advertising

start /stɑːt/ noun the beginning

starting point /ˈstɑːtɪŋ pɔɪnt/ noun the place where something starts

start-up /ˈstɑːt ʌp/ noun 1. the beginning of a new company or new product ○ *We went into the red for the first time because of the costs for the start-up of our new subsidiary.* 2. a new, usually small business that is just beginning its operations, especially a new business supported by venture capital and in a sector where new technologies are used

'It's unusual for a venture capitalist to be focused tightly on a set of companies with a common technology base, and even more unusual for the investment fund manager to be picking start-ups that will be built on a business he's currently running.' [*Information Week*]

state enterprise /ˌsteɪt ˈentəpraɪz/ noun a company run by the state

statement /ˈsteɪtmənt/ noun □ **statement (of account)** a list of invoices and credits and debits sent by a supplier to a customer at the end of each month

state-of-the-art /ˌsteɪt əv ði ˈɑːt/ adjective as technically advanced as possible

static market /ˌstætɪk ˈmɑːkɪt/ noun a market which does not increase or decrease significantly over a period of time

statistical /stəˈtɪstɪk(ə)l/ adjective based on statistics ○ *statistical information* ○ *They took two weeks to provide the statistical analysis of the opinion-poll data.*

statistical discrepancy /stəˌtɪstɪk(ə)l dɪˈskrepənsi/ noun the amount by which sets of figures differ

statistical error /stəˌtɪstɪk(ə)l ˈerə/ noun the difference between results achieved in a survey using a sample and what the results would be using the entire group of people surveyed.

statistics /stəˈtɪstɪks/ plural noun facts or information in the form of figures ○ *to examine the sales statistics for the previous six months* ○ *Government trade statistics show an increase in imports.* (NOTE: takes a plural verb)

steady demand /ˌstedi dɪˈmɑːnd/ noun demand for a product which continues in a regular way

sticker /ˈstɪkə/ noun a small piece of gummed paper or plastic to be stuck on something as an advertisement or to indicate a price ■ verb to put a price sticker on an article for sale ○ *We had to sticker all the stock.*

stickiness /ˈstɪkinəs/ noun a website's ability to retain the interest of visitors and to keep them coming back

sticky site /ˈstɪki saɪt/ noun a website that holds the interest of visitors for a substantial amount of time and is therefore effective as a marketing vehicle

stock /stɒk/ *noun* **1.** the available supply of raw materials ○ *large stocks of oil* or *coal* ○ *the country's stocks of butter* or *sugar* **2.** *especially UK* the quantity of goods for sale in a warehouse or retail outlet. Also called **inventory** □ **in stock** available in the warehouse or store ○ *to hold 2,000 lines in stock* □ **out of stock** not available in the warehouse or store ○ *The item went out of stock just before Christmas but came back into stock in the first week of January.* ○ *We are out of stock of this item.* □ **to take stock** to count the items in a warehouse **3.** shares in a company ■ *adjective* usually kept in stock ○ *Butter is a stock item for any good grocer.* ■ *verb* to hold goods for sale in a warehouse or store ○ *The average supermarket stocks more than 4500 lines.*

'US crude oil stocks fell last week by nearly 2.5m barrels' [*Financial Times*]

'…the stock rose to over $20 a share, higher than the $18 bid' [*Fortune*]

stock up *phrasal verb* to buy supplies of something which you will need in the future ○ *They stocked up with computer paper.*

stockbroker /'stɒkbrəʊkə/ *noun* a person who buys or sells shares for clients

stock control /'stɒk kən,trəʊl/ *noun* the process of making sure that the correct level of stock is maintained, to be able to meet demand while keeping the costs of holding stock to a minimum

stock controller /'stɒk kən–,trəʊlə/ *noun* a person who notes movements of stock

stock depreciation /'stɒk dɪpri:ʃi,eɪʃ(ə)n/ *noun* a reduction in value of stock which is held in a warehouse for some time

stock figures /'stɒk ,fɪgəz/ *plural noun* details of how many goods are in the warehouse or store

stocking agent /'stɒkɪŋ ,eɪdʒənt/ *noun* a wholesaler who stocks goods for a producer, sells them, and earns a commission

stocking filler /'stɒkɪŋ ,fɪlə/ *noun* a small item which can be used to put into a Christmas stocking

stock-in-hand /,stɒk ɪn 'hænd/ *noun* stock held in a shop or warehouse

stock-in-trade /,stɒk ɪn 'treɪd/ *noun* goods held by a business for sale

stockist /'stɒkɪst/ *noun* a person or shop that stocks an item

stockkeeping /'stɒk,ki:pɪŋ/ *noun* the process of making sure that the correct level of stock is maintained (to be able to meet demand while keeping the costs of holding stock to a minimum)

stockkeeping unit /'stɒkki:pɪŋ ,ju:nɪt/ *noun* full form of **SKU**

stock level /'stɒk ,lev(ə)l/ *noun* the quantity of goods kept in stock ○ *We try to keep stock levels low during the summer.*

stocklist /'stɒklɪst/ *noun* a list of items carried in stock

stockout /'stɒkaʊt/ *noun* a situation where an item is out of stock

stockpile /'stɒkpaɪl/ *noun* the supplies kept by a country or a company in case of need ○ *a stockpile of raw materials* ■ *verb* to buy items and keep them in case of need ○ *to stockpile tinned food*

stockroom /'stɒkru:m/ *noun* a room where stores are kept

stock size /'stɒk saɪz/ *noun* a normal size ○ *We only carry stock sizes of shoes.*

stocktaking /'stɒkteɪkɪŋ/, **stocktake** /'stɒkteɪk/ *noun* the counting of goods in stock at the end of an accounting period ○ *The warehouse is closed for the annual stocktaking.*

stocktaking sale /'stɒkteɪkɪŋ ,seɪl/ *noun* a sale of goods cheaply to clear a warehouse before stocktaking

stock transfer form /,stɒk 'trænsfɜ: fɔ:m/ *noun* a form to be signed by the person transferring shares

stock turn /'stɒk tɜ:n/, **stock turnround** /'stɒk ,tɜ:nraʊnd/**stock turnover** /'stɒk ,tɜ:nəʊvə/ *noun* the total value of stock sold in a year divided by the average value of goods in stock

stock valuation /,stɒk ,vælju'-eɪʃ(ə)n/ *noun* an estimation of the value of stock at the end of an accounting period

stop /stɒp/ *noun* a situation in which someone is not supplying or not paying something □ **account on stop** an account which is not supplied because it has not paid its latest invoices ○ *We put their account on stop and sued them for the money they owed.* □ **to put a stop on a cheque** to tell the bank not to pay a cheque which you have written ■ *verb* □ **to stop an account** not to supply an account any more on credit because bills have not been paid □ **to stop payments** not to make any further payments (NOTE: [all verb senses] **stopping – stopped**)

stoppage /'stɒpɪdʒ/ *noun* the act of stopping ○ *stoppage of payments* ○ *Bad weather was responsible for the stoppage of deliveries.* ○ *Deliveries will be late because of stoppages on the production line.*

'...the commission noted that in the early 1960s there was an average of 203 stoppages each year arising out of dismissals' [*Employment Gazette*]

stoppage in transit /ˌstɒpɪdʒ ɪn 'trænzɪt/ *noun* the legal right of sellers to stop delivery of goods that are in transit if they have reason to believe customers will not pay for them owing to insolvency

storage /'stɔːrɪdʒ/ *noun* **1.** the act of keeping something in store or in a warehouse ○ *We let our house and put the furniture into storage.* □ **to put a plan into cold storage** to postpone work on a plan, usually for a very long time **2.** the cost of keeping goods in store ○ *Storage rose to 10% of value, so we scrapped the stock.* **3.** the facility for storing data in a computer ○ *the hard drive has a storage capacity of 500Gb*

storage capacity /'stɔːrɪdʒ kə-ˌpæsɪti/ *noun* the space available for storage

storage company /'stɔːrɪdʒ ˌkʌmp(ə)ni/ *noun* a company which keeps items for customers

storage facilities /'stɔːrɪdʒ fə-ˌsɪltiz/ *plural noun* equipment and buildings suitable for storage

storage unit /'stɔːrɪdʒ juːnɪt/ *noun* a device attached to a computer for storing information on disk or tape

store /stɔː/ *noun* **1.** a place where goods are kept **2.** a quantity of items or materials kept because they will be needed ○ *I always keep a store of envelopes ready in my desk.* **3.** a large shop ○ *a furniture store* ○ *a big clothing store* ■ *verb* **1.** to keep in a warehouse ○ *to store goods for six months* **2.** to keep for future use ○ *We store our pay records on computer.*

store audit /'stɔːr ˌɔːdɪt/ *noun* a market-research method by which a research company regularly checks a sample of stores for unit sales and stock levels of different brands

store brand /'stɔː brænd/ *noun* a brand owned by the retailer and not by the manufacturer

store card /'stɔː kaːd/ *noun* a credit card issued by a large department store, which can only be used for purchases in that store

storekeeper /'stɔːkiːpə/, **store-man** /'stɔːmən/ *noun* a person in charge of a storeroom

storeroom /'stɔːruːm/ *noun* a room or small warehouse where stock can be kept

store traffic /'stɔː ˌtræfɪk/ *noun* the number of customers who enter a store

storyboard /'stɔːribɔːd/ *noun* a series of drawings which give the outline of a film or TV advertisement ○ *If the advertiser likes the storyboard, the agency will go ahead with the idea.*

straight line depreciation /ˌstreɪt laɪn dɪˌpriːʃi'eɪʃ(ə)n/ *noun* a form of depreciation that divides the cost of a fixed asset evenly over each year of its anticipated lifetime

COMMENT: Various methods of depreciating assets are used; under the 'straight line method', the asset is depreciated at a constant percentage of its cost each year, while with the 'reducing balance method' the asset is depreciated at the same percentage rate each year, but calculated on the value after the previous year's depreciation has been deducted.

straight rebuy /streɪt 'riːbaɪ/ *noun* a type of organisational buying decision where the same product is bought as before from the same supplier

strapline /'stræplaɪn/ *noun* a subheading in a piece of print, e.g. in a newspaper article or advertisement

○ *The strapline in our advertisement contains our full company name.*

strategic /strəˈtiːdʒɪk/ *adjective* based on a plan of action

strategic alliance /strəˌtiːdʒɪk əˈlaɪəns/ *noun* an agreement between two or more organisations to co-operate with each other and share their knowledge and expertise in a particular business activity, so that each benefits from the others' strengths and gains a competitive edge (NOTE: Strategic alliances can reduce the risk and costs involved in relationships with suppliers and the development of new products and technologies and have been seen as a response to *globalisation* and the increasing uncertainty in the business environment.)

strategic business unit /strəˌtiːdʒɪk ˈbɪznɪs ˌjuːnɪt/ *noun* a part or division of a large company which forms its own business strategy. Abbreviation **SBU**

strategic marketing /strəˌtiːdʒɪk ˈmɑːkɪtɪŋ/ *noun* marketing according to a set strategy, which is developed after analysing the market, designing the advertising messages and launching the product

strategic partnering /strəˌtiːdʒɪk ˈpɑːtnərɪŋ/ *noun* collaboration between organisations in order to enable them to take advantage of market opportunities together, or to respond to customers more effectively than they could if each operated separately. Strategic partnering allows the partners to pool information, skills, and resources and to share risks.

strategic planning /strəˌtiːdʒɪk ˈplænɪŋ/ *noun* the process of planning the future work of a company

strategy /ˈstrætədʒi/ *noun* a course of action, including the specification of resources required, to achieve a specific objective ○ *a marketing strategy* ○ *a financial strategy* ○ *a sales strategy* ○ *a pricing strategy* ○ *What is the strategy of the HR department to deal with long-term manpower requirements?* ○ *Part of the company's strategy to meet its marketing objectives is a major recruitment and retraining programme.* (NOTE: The plural is **strategies**.)

stratification /ˌstrætɪfɪˈkeɪʃ(ə)n/ *noun* **1.** the structure of a questionnaire which should help to ensure reliable answers and make it easy to evaluate results ○ *The results of the survey are hard to interpret owing to poor questionnaire stratification.* ○ *Good stratification will streamline the whole process.* **2.** a framework for the selection of a sample that ensures that it adequately represents the entire group of people surveyed

streaming /ˈstriːmɪŋ/ *noun* technology that allows material to be downloaded from the Web and viewed at the same time. For example, a user can download enough of a multimedia file to start viewing or listening to it, while the rest of the file is downloaded in the background.

streamline /ˈstriːmlaɪn/ *verb* to make something more efficient or more simple ○ *to streamline the accounting system* ○ *to streamline distribution services*

streamlined /ˈstriːmlaɪnd/ *adjective* efficient or rapid ○ *We need a more streamlined payroll system.* ○ *The company introduced a streamlined system of distribution.*

streamlining /ˈstriːmlaɪnɪŋ/ *noun* the process of making something efficient

street furniture /ˈstriːt ˌfɜːnɪtʃə/ *noun* lamps, litter bins, bus shelters, etc., on which advertising can be placed

striver /ˈstraɪvə/ *noun* in the VALS lifestyle classification, someone who likes spending money and wants to appear successful, rich, and fashionable

structure /ˈstrʌktʃə/ *noun* the way in which something is organised ○ *the price structure in the small car market* ○ *the career structure within a corporation* ○ *The paper gives a diagram of the company's organisational structure.* ○ *The company is reorganising its discount structure.* ■ *verb* to arrange in a specific way ○ *to structure a meeting*

structured interview /ˌstrʌktʃəd ˈɪntəvjuː/ *noun* an interview using pre-set questions and following a fixed pattern. Compare **unstructured interview**

stuff /stʌf/ *verb* to put papers into envelopes ○ *We pay casual workers by* *the hour for stuffing envelopes* or *for envelope stuffing.*

style /staɪl/ *noun* a way of doing or making something ○ *a new style of product* ○ *old-style management techniques*

style obsolescence /'staɪl ɒbsə-ˌles(ə)ns/ *noun* the redesign of a product in order to make previous models obsolete and therefore encourage buying of the latest one

suasionetics /sweɪʒə'netɪks/ *plural noun US* the techniques used to persuade people to adopt ideas or behaviour patterns (NOTE: takes a singular verb)

sub- /sʌb/ *prefix* under or less important

sub-agency /'sʌb ˌeɪdʒənsi/ *noun* a small agency which is part of a large agency

sub-agent /'sʌb ˌeɪdʒənt/ *noun* a person who is in charge of a sub-agency

subcontract *noun*/'sʌbˌkɒntrækt/ a contract between the main contractor for a whole project and another firm which will do part of the work ○ *They have been awarded the subcontract for all the electrical work in the new building.* ○ *We will put the electrical work out to subcontract.* ■ *verb*/ˌsʌbkən'trækt/ *(of a main contractor)* to agree with a company that they will do part of the work for a project ○ *The electrical work has been subcontracted to Smith Ltd*

subcontractor /'sʌbkənˌtræktə/ *noun* a company which has a contract to do work for a main contractor

subculture /'sʌbkʌltʃə/ *noun* a part or sector of society identifiable by factors such as lifestyle, religion, and race ○ *Studies were made of spending in the student subculture.* ○ *Different subcultures have different buying priorities.*

subhead /'sʌbhed/, **subheading** /'sʌbhedɪŋ/ *noun* a heading used to divide up text such as an email into separate sections

subject /'sʌbdʒɪkt/ *noun* the thing which you are talking about or writing about

subject line /'sʌbdʒɪkt laɪn/ *noun* the space at the top of an email template in which the sender types the title or subject of the email. It is the only part of the email, apart from the sender's name, that can be read immediately by the receiver.

sublease /'sʌbliːs/ *noun* a lease from a tenant to another tenant ○ *They signed a sublease for the property.*

subliminal advertising /sʌbˌlɪmɪn(ə)l 'ædvətaɪzɪŋ/ *noun* advertising that attempts to leave impressions on the subconscious mind of the person who sees it or hears it without that person realising that this is being done

subsample /'sʌbsɑːmpəl/ *noun* a subdivision of a sample

subscribe /səb'skraɪb/ *verb* □ **to subscribe to a magazine or website** to pay for a series of issues of a magazine or for information available on a website

'…the rights issue is to be a one-for-four, at FFr 1,000 a share; it will grant shareholders free warrants to subscribe to further new shares' [*Financial Times*]

subscribed circulation /səbˌskraɪbd sɜːkjʊ'leɪʃ(ə)n/ *noun* circulation of a publication that is paid for in advance

subscriber /səb'skraɪbə/ *noun* **1.** □ **subscriber to a magazine** *or* **magazine subscriber** a person who has paid in advance for a series of issues of a magazine or to have access to information on a website ○ *The extra issue is sent free to subscribers.* **2.** a user who chooses to receive information, content, or services regularly from a website

subscription /səb'skrɪpʃən/ *noun* money paid in advance for a series of issues of a magazine, for membership of a society, or for access to information on a website ○ *Did you remember to pay the subscription to the computer magazine?* ○ *She forgot to renew her club subscription.* □ **to take out a subscription to a magazine** to start paying for a series of issues of a magazine □ **to cancel a subscription to a magazine** to stop paying for a series of issues of a magazine

subscription-based publishing /səbˌskrɪpʃən beɪst 'pʌblɪʃɪŋ/ *noun* a form of publishing in which content from a website, magazine, book, or other publication is delivered regularly by email or other means to a group of subscribers

subscription process /səb'skrɪpʃən ˌprəʊses/ *noun* the process by which users register and pay to receive information, content, or services, from a website

subscription rate /səb'skrɪpʃən reɪt/ *noun* the amount of money to be paid for a series of issues of a magazine

subsidiary /səb'sɪdiəri/ *adjective* less important ○ *They agreed to most of the conditions in the contract but queried one or two subsidiary items.* ■ *noun* same as **subsidiary company** ○ *Most of the group profit was contributed by the subsidiaries in the Far East.*

subsidiary company /səb,sɪdiəri 'kʌmp(ə)ni/ *noun* a company which is more than 50% owned by a holding company, and where the holding company controls the board of directors

subsidise /'sʌbsɪdaɪz/, **subsidize** *verb* to help by giving money ○ *The government has refused to subsidise the car industry.*

subsidised accommodation /ˌsʌbsɪdaɪzd əˌkɒmə'deɪʃ(ə)n/ *noun* cheap accommodation which is partly paid for by an employer or a local authority

subsidy /'sʌbsɪdi/ *noun* **1.** money given to help something which is not profitable ○ *The industry exists on government subsidies.* ○ *The government has increased its subsidy to the car industry.* **2.** money given by a government to make something cheaper ○ *the subsidy on rail transport* (NOTE: The plural is **subsidies**.)

substitute /'sʌbstɪtjuːt/ *noun* a person or thing that takes the place of someone or something else ■ *adjective* taking the place of another person or thing ■ *verb* to take the place of someone or something else

substitute product /'sʌbstɪtjuːt ˌprɒdʌkt/, **substitute good** /'sʌbstɪtjuːt gʊd/ *noun* a product which may be bought instead of another when the price of the original product changes or if it becomes unavailable ○ *We must match our competitors*

since they produce substitute products to ours. ○ *As the price of substitute products falls, they will be much in demand.*

substitution effect /ˌsʌbstɪ'tjuːʃ(ə)n ɪˌfekt/ *noun* the extent to which consumers will change from one product to another when the price of the product rises

suggestion /sə'dʒestʃən/ *noun* an idea which is put forward

suggestion box /sə'dʒestʃən bɒks/, **suggestions box** /sə'dʒestʃənz bɒks/ *noun* a place in a company where employees can put forward their ideas for making the company more efficient and profitable

suggestion scheme /sə'dʒestʃən skiːm/ *noun* a scheme in which employees are asked to suggest ways in which the work they do or the way their organisation operates can be improved and receive a gift or cash reward for useful suggestions

suggestion selling /sə'dʒestʃən ˌselɪŋ/ *noun* selling in such a way that the customer believes they really want the product ○ *Trainee salespeople learn the application of psychology to suggestion selling.*

sums chargeable to the reserve /ˌsʌmz ˌtʃɑːdʒəb(ə)l tə ðə rɪ'zɜːv/ *plural noun* sums which can be debited to a company's reserves

Sunday closing /ˌsʌndeɪ 'kləʊzɪŋ/ *noun* the practice of not opening a shop on Sundays

Sunday supplement /ˌsʌndeɪ 'sʌplɪmənt/ *noun* a special extra section of a Sunday newspaper, usually on a special subject

supermarket /'suːpəmɑːkɪt/ *noun* a large store, usually selling food and household goods, where customers serve themselves and pay at a checkout ○ *Supermarket sales account for half the company's turnover.*

supermarket trolley /'suːpəmɑːkɪt ˌtrɒli/ *noun* a metal basket on wheels, used by shoppers to put their purchases in as they go round a supermarket

supernormal profit /ˌsuːpənɔːm(ə)l 'prɒfɪt/ *noun* profit earned by a business through having a monopoly ○ *This company has survived the recession owing to supernormal profits.*

supersite /ˈsuːpəsaɪt/ *noun* a particularly large poster site ○ *If we cannot afford a supersite we will have to settle for a site on an Underground station.* ○ *There are some key supersites at the side of the motorway.*

superstore /ˈsuːpəstɔː/ *noun* a very large self-service store (more than 2,500 square metres) which sells a wide range of goods ○ *We bought the laptop at a computer superstore.*

supplement /ˈsʌplɪmənt/ *noun* a special addition to a magazine or newspaper which is given free to customers ○ *The colour supplement is mostly full of advertising.* ○ *The supplement contains special articles on recent marketing strategies.* ○ *What are the advertising rates in that paper's supplement?*

supplier /səˈplaɪə/ *noun* a person or company that supplies or sells goods or services ○ *We use the same office equipment supplier for all our stationery purchases.* ○ *They are major suppliers of spare parts to the car industry.* Also called **producer**

supplier development /səˈplaɪə dɪˌveləpmənt/ *noun* the development of close and long-term relationships between customers and suppliers that are intended to benefit both

supplier evaluation /səˈplaɪə ɪvæljuˌeɪʃ(ə)n/ *noun* the process of assessing potential suppliers of materials, goods, or services before placing an order, to find out which one of them will best satisfy the customer's requirements (NOTE: When this process is undertaken after an order has been fulfilled, it is known as vendor rating.)

supplier rating /səˈplaɪə ˌreɪtɪŋ/ *noun* same as **vendor rating**

supply /səˈplaɪ/ *noun* **1.** the act of providing something which is needed **2.** □ **in short supply** not available in large enough quantities to meet the demand ○ *Spare parts are in short supply because of the strike.* **3.** stock of something which is needed ○ *Garages were running short of supplies of petrol.* ○ *Supplies of coal to the factory have*

been hit by the rail strike. ○ *Supplies of stationery have been reduced.* ■ *verb* to provide something which is needed ○ *to supply a factory with spare parts* ○ *The finance department supplied the committee with the figures.* ○ *Details of staff addresses and phone numbers can be supplied by the HR department.*

supply and demand /sə ˌplaɪ ən dɪˈmaːnd/ *noun* the amount of a product which is available and the amount which is wanted by customers

supply chain /səˈplaɪ tʃeɪn/ *noun* the manufacturers, wholesalers, distributors, and retailers who produce goods and services from raw materials and deliver them to consumers, considered as a group or network

'Only companies that build supply chains that are agile, adaptable, and aligned get ahead of their rivals.' [*Harvard Business Review*]

supply chain management /səˈplaɪ tʃeɪn ˌmænɪdʒmənt/ *noun* the work of co-ordinating all the activities connected with supplying of finished goods (NOTE: Supply chain management covers the processes of materials management, logistics, physical distribution management, purchasing, and information management.)

supply price /səˈplaɪ praɪs/ *noun* the price at which something is provided

supply-side economics /səˈplaɪ saɪd iːkəˌnɒmɪks/ *plural noun* an economic theory that governments should encourage producers and suppliers of goods by cutting taxes, rather than encourage demand by making more money available in the economy (NOTE: takes a singular verb)

support advertising /səˈpɔːt ˌædvətaɪzɪŋ/ *noun* advertising which is designed to support other advertising in other media

support media /səˈpɔːt ˌmiːdiə/ *plural noun* non-traditional media which are used to reinforce messages sent to target markets through other more traditional media

surcharge /ˈsɜːtʃɑːdʒ/ *noun* an extra charge

surplus /ˈsɜːpləs/ *noun* more of something than is needed □ **these items are surplus to our requirements** we do not need these items ■ *adjective* more than is needed ○ *Profit figures are lower than is needed because of surplus labour.* ○ *Some of the machines may have to be sold off as there is surplus production capacity.* ○ *We are proposing to put our surplus staff on short time.*

'Both imports and exports reached record levels in the latest year. This generated a $371 million trade surplus in June, the seventh consecutive monthly surplus and close to market expectations' [*Dominion (Wellington, New Zealand)*]

survivors /səˈvaɪvəz/ *plural noun* in the VALS lifestyle classification, elderly people who have no economic future

suspect /ˈsʌspekt/ *noun* any individual taken from a database of prospective customers

sustainers /sʌˈsteɪnəz/ *plural noun* in the VALS lifestyle classification, people who are living at subsistence level and resent the fact that they have no money

swatch /swɒtʃ/ *noun* a small sample of a fabric ○ *The interior designer showed us swatches of the curtain fabric.*

sweep periods /ˈswiːp ˌpɪəriədz/ *plural noun* times of the year when television audiences are measured

sweepstake /ˈswiːpsteɪk/ *noun* a form of gambling promotion where customers put in their names for a draw and the lucky number wins a prize

sweetener /ˈswiːt(ə)nə/ *noun* an incentive offered to help persuade somebody to take a particular course of action (*informal*)

switch /swɪtʃ/ *verb* to change from one thing to another ○ *to switch funds from one investment to another* ○ *The job was switched from our British factory to the States.*

switch selling /ˈswɪtʃ ˌselɪŋ/ *noun* a selling technique which involves trying to persuade customers to buy something very different from what they wanted to buy in the first place ○ *Trainee sales staff are coached in switch selling.* ■ *verb* the practice of offering an apparently good bargain as bait in order to gain the attention of prospective customers then approaching them with a different offer which is more profitable to the seller

SWOT analysis /ˈswɒt əˌnæləsɪs/ *noun* a method of assessing a person, company or product by considering their Strengths, Weaknesses, and external factors which may provide Opportunities or Threats to their development. Full form **Strengths, Weaknesses, Opportunities, Threats**

symbol /ˈsɪmbəl/ *noun* a sign, picture, or object which represents something ○ *They use a bear as their advertising symbol.*

symbol group /ˈsɪmbəl gruːp/ *noun* a group to which symbol retailers belong

symbol retailer /ˈsɪmbəl ˌriːteɪlə/ *noun* a retailer that is a member of an independent group which secures favourable prices from suppliers through buying in bulk and has its own symbol or logo

synchro marketing /ˈsɪŋkrəʊ ˌmaːkɪtɪŋ/ *noun* the practice of finding ways to use spare resources during periods of low demand ○ *Synchro marketing will stop wastage of our production and storage capacity in the off-season.*

syndicate /ˈsɪndɪkeɪt/ *verb* to produce an article, a cartoon, etc., which is then published in several newspapers or magazines

'…over the past few weeks, companies raising new loans from international banks have been forced to pay more, and an unusually high number of attempts to syndicate loans among banks has failed' [*Financial Times*]

syndicated programme /ˌsɪndɪkeɪtɪd ˈprəʊgræm/ *noun* a programme which is sold to a range of different stations across the country

syndicated research /ˌsɪndɪkeɪtɪd rɪˈsɜːtʃ/ *noun* market research carried out by agencies and sold to several different companies

syndication /ˌsɪndɪˈkeɪʃ(ə)n/ *noun* an article, drawing, etc., which is published in several newspapers or magazines at the same time

synectics /sɪˈnektɪks/ *plural noun* group discussions designed to elicit creative solutions to problems ○ *We are beginning to apply synectics to our strategy formulation.* ○ *Synectics is being* *encouraged as a method of approaching case-studies in business school.* (NOTE: takes a singular verb)

synergy /'sɪnədʒi/ *noun* the process of producing greater effects by joining forces than by acting separately ○ *There is considerable synergy between the two companies.*

synthetic materials /sɪnˌθetɪk məˈtɪəriəlz/ *plural noun* substances made as products of a chemical process

system /'sɪstəm/ *noun* an arrangement or organisation of things which work together ○ *Our accounting system has worked well in spite of the large increase in orders.* □ **to operate a quota system** to regulate supplies by fixing quantities which are allowed ○ *We arrange our distribution using a quota*

system – each agent is allowed only a specific number of units.

systems analysis /'sɪstəmz əˌnæləsɪs/ *noun* the process of using a computer to suggest how a company can work more efficiently by analysing the way in which it works at present

systems analyst /'sɪstəmz ˌænəlɪst/ *noun* a person who specialises in systems analysis

systems management /'sɪstəmz ˌmænɪdʒmənt/ *noun* the directing and controlling of all the elements in an organisation to achieve its basic objectives

systems selling /'sɪstəmz ˌselɪŋ/ *noun* the selling of an integrated system, not just separate products plus related services

T

table /ˈteɪb(ə)l/ *noun* **1.** a diagram or chart **2.** a list of figures or facts set out in columns □ **table of random numbers** a table of numbers in no particular order or pattern, which is used for selecting samples in market research

table of discounts /ˌteɪb(ə)l əv ˈdɪskaʊnts/ *noun* a table showing discounts for various prices and quantities ○ *According to the table of discounts, there was no discount for purchases involving less than 100 items of each product.* Also called **discount table**

tablet computer /ˈtæblət kəm,ˈpjuːtə/ *noun* a general-purpose computer contained in a single panel. Its distinguishing characteristic is the use of a touch screen as the input device. Modern tablet computers are operated by fingers, whereas earlier models required a stylus. ○ *Our tablet computers come with a free carry case.*

tabloid /ˈtæblɔɪd/ *noun* a small size of newspaper, as opposed to a broadsheet ○ *We're advertising in three tabloids concurrently.*

tachistoscope /təˈkɪstəskəʊp/, **T-scope** /ˈtiː skəʊp/ *noun* a device used to measure the recognition level when a customer is exposed to a brand package or advertising material

tactic /ˈtæktɪk/ *noun* a way of doing things so as to be at an advantage ○ *Securing a key position at an exhibition is an old tactic which always produces good results* ○ *Concentrating our sales force in that area could be a good tactic.* ○ *The directors planned their tactics before going into the meeting.*

tactical /ˈtæktɪk(ə)l/ *adjective* referring to tactics

tactical campaign /ˌtæktɪk(ə)l kæmˈpeɪn/ *noun* a promotion that is planned according to a series of targets, in particular when attacking a competitor

tag /tæg/ *noun* a label ○ *a price tag* ○ *a name tag*

tailor /ˈteɪlə/ *verb* to design something for a specific purpose ○ *We mail out press releases tailored to the reader interests of each particular newspaper or periodical.*

tailor-made /ˌteɪlə ˈmeɪd/ *adjective* made to fit specific needs

tailor-made promotion /ˌteɪlə meɪd prəˈməʊʃ(ə)n/ *noun* a promotion which is specifically made for an individual customer

take /teɪk/ *noun* the money received in a shop ○ *Our weekly take is over £5,000.* ■ *verb* to receive or to get (NOTE: **taking – took – has taken**) □ **the shop takes £2,000 a week** the shop receives £2,000 a week in cash sales □ **she takes home £450 a week** her salary, after deductions for tax, etc. is £450 a week

take-ones /ˈteɪk wʌnz/ *plural noun* advertising leaflets or promotional cards which are delivered to shops where they are displayed in racks

takeover /ˈteɪkəʊvə/ *noun* **1.** an act of buying a controlling interest in a business by buying more than 50% of its shares. Compare **acquisition 2.** the act of starting to do something in place of someone else

takeover bid /ˈteɪkəʊvə bɪd/ *noun* an offer to buy all or a majority of the shares in a company so as to control it ○ *They made a takeover bid for the company.* ○ *She had to withdraw her takeover bid when she failed to find any backers.* ○ *Share prices rose sharply on the disclosure of the takeover bid.*

taker /ˈteɪkə/ *noun* a person who wants to buy something ○ *There were very few takers for the special offer.*

takings /ˈteɪkɪŋz/ *plural noun* the money received in a shop or a business ○ *The week's takings were stolen from the cash desk.*

tannoy /ˈtænɔɪ/ *noun* a loudspeaker system for making public announcements

target /ˈtɑːɡɪt/ *noun* something to aim for ○ *performance targets* □ **to set targets** to fix amounts or quantities which employees have to produce or reach □ **to meet a target** to produce the quantity of goods or sales which are expected □ **to miss a target** not to produce the amount of goods or sales which are expected ○ *They missed the target figure of £2m turnover.* ■ *verb* to aim to sell to somebody ○ *I'll follow up your idea of targeting our address list with a special mailing.* □ **to target a market** to plan to sell goods in a specific market

'…he believes that increased competition could keep inflation below the 2.5% target' [*Investors Chronicle*]

'…the minister is persuading the oil, gas, electricity and coal industries to target their advertising towards energy efficiency' [*Times*]

target audience /ˈtɑːɡɪt ˌɔːdiəns/ *noun* consumers at whom an advertisement is aimed ○ *TV advertising will fail unless we have a clear idea of who the target audience is for our product.* ○ *What is the best media to reach our target audience?*

target cost /ˈtɑːɡɪt kɒst/ *noun* a product cost estimate derived by subtracting a desired profit margin from a competitive market price. This may be less than the planned initial product cost, but will be expected to be achieved by the time the product reaches the mature production stage.

target market /ˈtɑːɡɪt ˌmɑːkɪt/ *noun* the market in which a company is planning to sell its goods

target marketing /ˈtɑːɡɪt ˌmɑːkɪtɪŋ/ *noun* the aiming of advertising or selling at a specific group of consumers who all have similar characteristics

target population /ˈtɑːɡɪt pɒpjuˌleɪʃ(ə)n/ *noun* a group of individuals or regions that are to be investigated in a statistical study

target price /ˈtɑːɡɪt praɪs/ *noun* a wholesale price within the EU for certain products, such as wheat, which market management is intended to achieve; it is linked to the intervention price

target pricing /ˈtɑːɡɪt ˌpraɪsɪŋ/ *noun* the setting of a selling price with the aim of producing a particular rate of return on investment for a specific volume of production

tariff /ˈtærɪf/ *noun* **1.** a tax to be paid on imported goods. Also called **customs tariff**. Compare **import levy 2.** a rate of charging for something such as electricity, hotel rooms, or train tickets

tariff barrier /ˈtærɪf ˌbæriə/ *noun* the customs duty intended to make imports more difficult ○ *to impose tariff barriers on* or *to lift tariff barriers from a product*

task /tɑːsk/ *noun* work which has to be done ○ *The job involves some tasks which are unpleasant and others which are more rewarding.* ○ *The candidates are given a series of tasks to complete within a time limit.* □ **to list task processes** to make a list of various parts of a job which have to be done ■ *verb* to give someone a task to do

task method /ˈtɑːsk ˌmeθəd/ *noun* the way of calculating an advertising appropriation by basing it on the actual amount needed to achieve the objectives

taste /teɪst/ *noun* a very small quantity of something taken to try it out

taste space /ˈteɪst speɪs/ *noun* different individuals or groups brought together into a database based on common interests

TAT *abbreviation* thematic apperception test

tax credit /ˈtæks ˌkredɪt/ *noun* **1.** a sum of money which can be offset against tax **2.** the part of a dividend on which the company has already paid tax, so that the shareholder is not taxed on it

tax-exempt /ˌtæks ɪɡˈzempt/ *adjective* **1.** referring to a person or organisation not required to pay tax **2.** not subject to tax

tax-free /ˌtæks ˈfriː/ *adjective* with no tax having to be paid ○ *tax-free goods*

TC *abbreviation* till countermanded

team /tiːm/ *noun* a group of people who work together and co-operate to share work and responsibility

team approach /ˈtiːm əˌprəʊtʃ/ *noun* a method of measuring the effectiveness of an advertising campaign when the evaluators are actually involved in the campaign

team-building /ˈtiːm ˌbɪldɪŋ/ *noun* a set of training sessions designed to instil co-operation and solidarity in a group of employees who work together as a team

tear sheet /ˈteə ʃiːt/ *noun* a page taken from a published magazine or newspaper, sent to an advertiser as proof that their advertisement has been run

teaser /ˈtiːzə/, **teaser ad** /ˈtiːzər æd/ *noun* an advertisement that gives a little information about a product in order to attract customers by making them curious to know more

technical /ˈteknɪk(ə)l/ *adjective* referring to a particular machine or process ○ *The document gives all the technical details on the new computer.*

'…market analysts described the falls in the second half of last week as a technical correction' [*Australian Financial Review*]

'…at the end of the day, it was clear the Fed had not loosened the monetary reins, and Fed Funds forged ahead on the back of technical demand' [*Financial Times*]

technical press /ˈteknɪk(ə)l pres/ *noun* newspapers and magazines on scientific or technical subjects ○ *We need to advertise this product in the technical press.*

technique /tekˈniːk/ *noun* a skilled way of doing a job ○ *The company has developed a new technique for processing steel.* ○ *We have a special technique for answering complaints from customers.*

technology adoption life cycle /tekˌnɒlədʒi əˌdɒpʃən ˈlaɪf ˌsaɪk(ə)l/ *noun* a model that describes the stages in which various types of individuals and organisations start to use new technologies. The individual and organisations are usually classified as innova-

tors, early adopters, early majority, late majority, or technology laggards.

technology laggard /tekˈnɒlədʒi ˌlægəd/ *noun* an individual or organisation that is very slow or reluctant to adopt new technology

telcos /ˈtelkəʊz/ *plural noun* telecommunications companies (*informal*)

telecommunications /ˌtelikəˌmjuːnɪˈkeɪʃ(ə)nz/ *plural noun* systems of passing messages over long distances (by cable, radio, etc.)

telecoms /ˈtelikɒmz/ *noun* same as **telecommunications**(*informal*)

teleconferencing /ˈteliˌkɒnf(ə)rənsɪŋ/ *noun* the use of telephone or television channels to connect people in different locations in order to conduct group discussions, meetings, conferences, or courses

telemarketer /ˈtelɪˌmaːkɪtə/ *noun* a person who markets a product by telephone

telemarketing /ˈtelɪˌmaːkɪtɪŋ/ *noun* the selling of a product or service by telephone

telephone /ˈtelɪfəʊn/ *noun* a machine used for speaking to someone over a long distance ○ *We had a new telephone system installed last week.*

telephone interview /ˈtelɪfəʊn ˌɪntəvjuː/ *noun* same as **telephone survey**

telephone interview survey /ˌtelɪfəʊn ɪntəvjuː ˈsɜːveɪ/ *noun* a survey conducted by telephoning a selected group of people and asking them for their views on a particular subject

telephone order /ˈtelɪfəʊn ˌɔːdə/ *noun* an order received by telephone ○ *Since we mailed the catalogue we have received a large number of telephone orders.*

telephone research /ˈtelɪfəʊn rɪˌsɜːtʃ/ *noun* same as **telephone survey**

telephone sales representative /ˌtelɪfəʊn ˈseɪlz reprɪˌzentətɪv/ *noun* someone who sells to customers over the phone. Abbreviation **TSR**

telephone selling /ˈtelɪfəʊn ˌselɪŋ/ *noun* the practice of making sales by phoning prospective customers and trying to persuade them to buy

telephone survey /ˈtelɪfəʊn rɪˌsɜːtʃ/ *noun* an act of interviewing respondents by telephone for a survey ○ *How many people in the sample hung up before replying to the telephone survey?*

telesales /ˈteliseɪlz/ *plural noun* sales made by telephone

teleshopping /ˈteliˌʃɒpɪŋ/ *noun* shopping from home by means of a television screen and a home computer

television /ˌtelɪˈvɪʒ(ə)n/ *noun* the broadcasting of moving images. Abbreviation **TV**

television consumer audit /ˌtelɪˈvɪʒ(ə)n kənˈsjuːmə ˌɔːdɪt/ *noun* an act of questioning a sample of television viewers on their viewing and impressions

television network /ˌtelɪvɪʒ(ə)n ˈnetwɜːk/ *noun* a system of linked television stations covering the whole country

television ratings /telɪˈvɪʒ(ə)n ˌreɪtɪŋz/ *plural noun* statistics showing the size and type of television audiences at different times of day for various channels and programmes ○ *We will have to consult the television ratings before buying a spot.* Abbreviation **TVR**

tender /ˈtendə/ *noun* an offer to do something for a specific price ○ *a successful tender* ○ *an unsuccessful tender* (NOTE: The US term is **bid**.) □ **to put a project out to tender, to ask for or invite tenders for a project** to ask contractors to give written estimates for a job □ **to put in or submit a tender** to make an estimate for a job □ **to sell shares by tender** to ask people to offer in writing a price for shares ■ *verb US* to sell shares, usually at a price above the current price, in response to a tender offer

tenderer /ˈtendərə/ *noun* a person or company that puts forward an estimate of cost ○ *The company was the successful tenderer for the project.* (NOTE: The US term is **bidder**.)

tendering /ˈtendərɪŋ/ *noun* the act of putting forward an estimate of cost ○ *To be successful, you must follow the*

tendering procedure as laid out in the documents. (NOTE: The US term is **bidding**.)

terminal /ˈtɜːmɪn(ə)l/ *noun* the building where you end a journey

terminal poster /ˈtɜːmɪn(ə)l ˌpəʊstə/ *noun* an advertising display in stations or airline terminals, etc.

terminate /ˈtɜːmɪneɪt/ *verb* to end something or to bring something to an end ○ *His employment was terminated.*

termination clause /ˌtɜːmɪˈneɪʃ(ə)n klɔːz/ *noun* a clause which explains how and when a contract can be terminated

terms /tɜːmz/ *plural noun* the conditions or duties which have to be carried out as part of a contract, or the arrangements which have to be agreed before a contract is valid ○ *to negotiate for better terms* ○ *She refused to agree to some of the terms of the contract.* ○ *By* or *Under the terms of the contract, the company is responsible for all damage to the property.* □ **'terms: cash with order'** the terms of sale showing that payment has to be made in cash when the order is placed

'…companies have been improving communications, often as part of deals to cut down demarcation and to give everybody the same terms of employment' [*Economist*]

'…the Federal Reserve Board has eased interest rates in the past year, but they are still at historically high levels in real terms' [*Sunday Times*]

terms of payment /ˌtɜːmz əv ˈpeɪmənt/ *plural noun* the conditions for paying something

terms of sale /ˌtɜːmz əv ˈseɪl/ *plural noun* the conditions attached to a sale

terms of trade /ˌtɜːmz əv ˈtreɪd/ *plural noun* the ratio of a country's import prices to export prices

territorial planning /ˌterɪtɔːriəl ˈplænɪŋ/ *noun* the planning of a salesperson's calls, taking into account the best use of time in travelling and the priority of important customers ○ *The sales manager is giving the sales team some guidelines on territorial planning.* ○ *Bad territorial planning means time wasted in travelling.*

territorial rights /ˌterɪtɔːriəl ˈraɪts/ *plural noun* the rights of a distributor, granted by the producer or supplier, to sell a product in a particular geographical area, often on condition that specific methods are used in the selling

territory /'terɪt(ə)ri/ *noun* an area visited by a salesperson ○ *We are adding two new reps and reducing all the reps' territories.* ○ *Her territory covers all the north of the country.*

tertiary industry /ˌtɜːʃəri 'ɪndəstri/ *noun* an industry which does not produce raw materials or manufacture products but offers a service such as banking, retailing, or accountancy

tertiary readership /ˌtɜːʃəri 'riːdəʃɪp/ *noun* the people who do not buy a newspaper or magazine but come across it as a result of another activity such as waiting for an appointment with the dentist ○ *Many glossy magazines have a relatively small circulation but a high tertiary readership.*

tertiary sector /'tɜːʃəri ˌsektə/ *noun* the section of the economy containing the service industries

test /test/ *noun* an examination to see if something works well or is possible ■ *verb* to examine something to see if it is working well ○ *We are still testing the new computer system.* □ **to test the market for a product** to show samples of a product in a market to see if it will sell well ○ *We are testing the market for the toothpaste in Scotland.*

test certificate /'test səˌtɪfɪkət/ *noun* a certificate to show that something has passed a test

test close /'test kləʊz/ *noun* an act of trying to obtain at least one immediate order from a buyer to see how promising a customer they are

test-drive /'test draɪv/ *verb* □ **to test-drive a car** to drive a car before buying it to see if it works well

testimonial /ˌtestɪ'məʊniəl/ *noun* a written report about someone's character or ability ○ *She has asked me to write her a testimonial.*

testimonial advertising /ˌtestɪ'məʊniəl ˌædvətaɪzɪŋ/ *noun* advertising which makes use of testimonials from famous or qualified people, or from satisfied customers, to endorse a product

testing /'testɪŋ/ *noun* the act of examining something to see if it works well ○ *During the testing of the system several defects were corrected.*

testing bias /'testɪŋ baɪəs/ *noun* bias that occurs when respondents to questionnaires know they are being tested and change their responses accordingly

test market /'test ˌmɑːkɪt/ *noun* a geographic region or demographic group, representative of the entire market, used to test the viability of a product or service prior to a large scale roll-out

test-market /'test ˌmɑːkɪt/ *verb* □ **to test-market a product** to show samples of a product in a market to see if it will sell well ○ *We are test-marketing a new computer game.*

test marketing /'test ˌmɑːkɪtɪŋ/ *noun* marketing a product in a specific area or to a specific audience to test the validity of the approach before launching a nationwide marketing campaign

test panel /'test ˌpæn(ə)l/ *noun* a group of people used to test a product or service

test run /'test rʌn/ *noun* a trial made on a machine

text /tekst/ *verb* to send a text message on a mobile phone

text message /'tekst ˌmesɪdʒ/ *noun* a message sent in text form, especially from one mobile phone to another

T-group /'tiː gruːp/ *noun* a group of trainees following a training method, often used in training sales staff, which uses group discussions and activities to develop social skills and general self-awareness

thematic apperception test /θɪˌmætɪk ˌæpə'seps(ə)n test/ *noun* a test used to find out attitudes or reactions to a brand, which consists of showing pictures to the subject who then constructs a story round them. Abbreviation **TAT**

thinker /'θɪŋkə/ *noun* in the VALS lifestyle classification system, a well-educated person with strong ideals who buys products that last a long time and are good value

threshold /ˈθreʃhəʊld/ *noun* the point at which something changes

tie /taɪ/ *verb* to attach or to fasten with string, wire, or other material ○ *He tied the parcel with thick string.* ○ *She tied two labels on to the parcel.* (NOTE: **tying – tied**)

tied shop /taɪd ˈʃɒp/ *noun* a business which has agreed to sell only a particular supplier's products ○ *The store felt constrained by the tied shop agreement and wanted to offer a wider range of brands.*

tie-in /ˈtaɪ ɪn/ *noun* an advertisement linked to advertising in another media, e.g. a magazine ad linked to a TV commercial (NOTE: The plural is **tie-ins**.)

tie-up /ˈtaɪ ʌp/ *noun* a link or connection ○ *The company has a tie-up with a German distributor.* (NOTE: The plural is **tie-ups**.)

tight money /ˌtaɪt ˈmʌni/ *noun* same as **dear money**

till /tɪl/ *noun* a drawer for keeping cash in a shop

till countermanded /ˌtɪl ˈkaʊntəmɑːndɪd/ *noun* a clause in a contract which states that an advertisement will run until stopped by the advertiser. Abbreviation **TC**

time /taɪm/ *noun* **1.** a period during which something takes place, e.g. one hour, two days, or fifty minutes **2.** a period before something happens □ **to keep within the time limits** *or* **within the time schedule** to complete work by the time stated

time and duty study /ˌtaɪm ən ˈdjuːti ˌstʌdi/ *noun* a study to see how effectively salespeople are using their time ○ *The time and duty study showed that 30% of time is wasted.* ○ *The aim of the time and duty study was to streamline our sales activities.*

time and motion expert /ˌtaɪm ən ˈməʊʃ(ə)n ˌekspɜːt/ *noun* a person who analyses time and motion studies and suggests changes in the way work is done

time buyer /ˈtaɪm ˌbaɪə/ *noun* a person who buys advertising time on radio or TV

timelength /ˈtaɪmleŋkθ/ *noun* the length of a cinema, television, or radio

advertisement ○ *Find out the rates for the various timelengths before placing the commercial.*

time limit /ˈtaɪm ˌlɪmɪt/ *noun* the maximum time which can be taken to do something ○ *to set a time limit for acceptance of the offer* ○ *The work was finished within the time limit allowed.* ○ *The time limit on applications to the industrial tribunal is three months.*

time limitation /ˈtaɪm lɪmɪˌteɪʃ(ə)n/ *noun* the restriction of the amount of time available

time of peak demand /ˌtaɪm əv ˌpiːk dɪˈmɑːnd/ *noun* the time when something is being used most

time segment /ˈtaɪm ˌsegmənt/ *noun* a period set aside for advertisements on television

time series analysis /ˈtaɪm ˌsɪəriːz əˌnæləsɪs/ *noun* a method of assessing variations in data over regular periods of time such as sales per month or per quarter in order to try to identify the causes for the variations

time utility /ˈtaɪm juːˌtɪlɪti/ *noun* the usefulness to a customer of receiving a product at a particular time ○ *Time utility has meant avoiding unreliable suppliers.* ○ *Some customers put time utility before place utility.*

tip *noun* **1.** money given to someone who has helped you ○ *The staff are not allowed to accept tips.* **2.** a piece of advice on buying or doing something which could be profitable ○ *The newspaper gave several stock market tips.* ○ *She gave me a tip about a share which was likely to rise because of a takeover bid.* ■ *verb* to say that something is likely to happen or that something might be profitable ○ *He is tipped to become the next chairman.* ○ *Two shares were tipped in the business section of the paper.* (NOTE: **tipping – tipped**)

tip sheet /ˈtɪp ʃiːt/ *noun* a newspaper which gives information about shares which should be bought or sold

TIR *abbreviation* Transports Internationaux Routiers

token /ˈtəʊkən/ *noun* **1.** something which acts as a sign or symbol **2.** a device which involves the customer in an offer, e.g. a piece cut out of a newspaper which can be redeemed for a special premium offer **3.** a plastic or metal disk, similar to a coin, used in some slot machines

token charge /ˌtəʊkən ˈtʃɑːdʒ/ *noun* a small charge which does not cover the real costs ○ *A token charge is made for heating.*

token payment /ˈtəʊkən ˌpeɪmənt/ *noun* a small payment to show that a payment is being made

tone /təʊn/ *noun* the impression given by a text or media product of its creator's attitude, e.g. serious, humorous etc.

top-down information /ˌtɒp ˈdaʊn ɪnfəˌmeɪʃ(ə)n/ *noun* a system of passing information down from management to the workforce

top-grade /ˈtɒp greɪd/ *adjective* of the best quality ○ *top-grade petrol*

top management /ˌtɒp ˈmænɪdʒmənt/ *noun* the main directors of a company

top-selling /ˌtɒp ˈselɪŋ/ *adjective* which sells better than all other products ○ *top-selling brands of toothpaste*

tort /tɔːt/ *noun* harm done to a person or property which can be the basis of a civil lawsuit

torture testing /ˈtɔːtʃə ˌtestɪŋ/ *noun* the act of pushing products to their limits during product testing ○ *Torture testing will show up any product deficiencies while changes can still be made.*

total /ˈtəʊt(ə)l/ *adjective* complete, or with everything added together ○ *The company has total assets of over £1bn* ○ *The total amount owed is now £1000.* ○ *The total cost was much more than expected.* ○ *Total expenditure on publicity is twice that of last year.* ○ *Our total income from exports rose last year.*

total audience package /ˌtəʊt(ə)l ˈɔːdiəns ˌpækɪdʒ/ *noun* a media owner's arrangement or scheduling of advertisements across time segments on television and radio

total cost of ownership /ˌtəʊt(ə)l kɒst əv ˈəʊnəʃɪp/ *noun* a systematic method of calculating the total cost of buying and using a product or service. It takes into account not only the purchase price of an item but also related costs

such as ordering, delivery, subsequent use and maintenance, supplier costs, and after-delivery costs.

total distribution system /ˌtəʊt(ə)l dɪstrɪˈbjuːʃ(ə)n ˌsɪstəm/ *noun* a system where all distribution decisions, including the purchasing of raw materials and parts, as well as the movement of finished products, are taken globally

total invoice value /ˌtəʊt(ə)l ˈɪnvɔɪs ˌvæljuː/ *noun* the total amount on an invoice, including transport, VAT, etc.

total offer /ˌtəʊt(ə)l ˈɒfə/ *noun* a complete package offered to the customer including the product or service itself, its price, availability, and promotion

total quality management /ˌtəʊt(ə)l ˌkwɒlɪti ˈmænɪdʒmənt/ *noun* a philosophy and style of management that gives everyone in an organisation responsibility for delivering quality to the customer (NOTE: Total quality management views each production process as being in a customer/supplier relationship with the next, so that the aim at each stage is to define and meet the customer's requirements as precisely as possible.)

tracking /ˈtrækɪŋ/ *noun* monitoring changes in the way the public sees a product or a firm, done over a period of years

trade /treɪd/ *noun* **1.** the business of buying and selling □ **to do a good trade in a range of products** to sell a large number of a range of products **2.** □ **to impose trade barriers on** to restrict the import of some goods by charging high duty **3.** a particular type of business, or people or companies dealing in the same type of product ○ *He's in the second-hand car trade.* ○ *She's very well known in the clothing trade.*

'…a sharp setback in foreign trade accounted for most of the winter slowdown. The trade balance sank $17 billion' [*Fortune*]

'…trade between Britain and other countries which comprise the Economic Community has risen steadily from 33% of exports to 50% last year' [*Sales & Marketing Management*]

trade in *phrasal verb* **1.** to buy and sell specific items ○ *The company trades in* imported goods. ○ *They trade in French wine.* **2.** to give in an old item as part of the payment for a new one ○ *The chairman traded in his old Rolls Royce for a new model.*

trade advertising /ˈtreɪd ˌædvə-taɪzɪŋ/ *noun* advertising to trade customers and not to the general public

trade agreement /ˈtreɪd əˌgriː-mənt/ *noun* an international agreement between countries over general terms of trade

trade association /ˈtreɪd əˌsəʊ-sieɪʃ(ə)n/ *noun* a group which links together companies in the same trade

trade barrier /ˈtreɪd ˌbæriə/ *noun* a limitation imposed by a government on the free exchange of goods between countries. ➪ **import restrictions** (NOTE: NTBs, safety standards, and tariffs are typical trade barriers.)

trade counter /ˈtreɪd ˌkaʊntə/ *noun* a shop in a factory or warehouse where goods are sold to retailers

trade cycle /ˈtreɪd ˌsaɪk(ə)l/ *noun* a period during which trade expands, then slows down, then expands again

trade debtor /ˈtreɪd ˌdetə/ *noun* a debtor who owes money to a company in the normal course of that company's trading

trade deficit /ˈtreɪd ˌdefɪsɪt/ *noun* the difference in value between a country's low exports and higher imports. Also called **balance of payments deficit, trade gap**

trade delegation /ˈtreɪd deləˌ-geɪʃ(ə)n/ *noun* a group of official delegates on a commercial visit

trade description /ˌtreɪd dɪ'skrɪpʃən/ *noun* a description of a product to attract customers

Trade Descriptions Act /ˌtreɪd dɪ'skrɪpʃənz ækt/ *noun* an act which limits the way in which products can be described so as to protect customers from wrong descriptions made by manufacturers

trade directory /ˈtreɪd daɪˌrekt(ə)ri/ *noun* a book which lists all the businesses and business people in a town

trade down /ˌtreɪd ˈdaʊn/ *verb* to move to selling at lower prices to

increase sales volume ○ *We're trading down now because too many customers were put off by our high prices.*

trade fair /ˈtreɪd feə/ *noun* a large exhibition and meeting for advertising and selling a specific type of product ○ *There are two trade fairs running in London at the same time – the carpet manufacturers' and the mobile telephone companies'.*

trade gap /ˈtreɪd gæp/ *noun* same as **trade deficit**

trade-in /ˈtreɪd ɪn/ *noun US* same as **part exchange**

trade-in price /ˈtreɪd ɪn ˌpraɪs/, **trade-in allowance** /ˈtreɪd ɪn əˌlaʊəns/ *noun* an amount allowed by the seller for an old item being traded in for a new one

trade magazine /ˈtreɪd mægə-ˌziːn/ *noun* a magazine aimed at working people in a specific industry

trademark /ˈtreɪdmɑːk/, **trade name** /ˈtreɪd neɪm/ *noun* same as **registered trademark**

trade mission /ˈtreɪd ˌmɪʃ(ə)n/ *noun* a visit by a group of businesspeople to discuss trade ○ *He led a trade mission to China.*

trade-off /ˈtreɪd ɒf/ *noun* an act of exchanging one thing for another as part of a business deal (NOTE: The plural is **trade-offs**.)

trade-off analysis /ˈtreɪd ɒf əˌnæləsɪs/ *noun* same as **conjoint analysis**

trade paper /ˌtreɪd ˈpeɪpə/ *noun* a newspaper aimed at people working in a specific industry

trade practices /ˈtreɪd ˌpræktɪsɪz/ *plural noun* same as **industrial practices**

trade press /ˈtreɪd pres/ *noun* all magazines produced for people working in a certain trade

trade price /ˈtreɪd praɪs/ *noun* a special wholesale price paid by a retailer to the manufacturer or wholesaler

trade promotion /ˈtreɪd prəˌməʊʃ(ə)n/ *noun* the promotion of products to distributors ○ *The new trade promotion campaign is designed* *to attract wholesalers in all our areas of distribution.*

trader /ˈtreɪdə/ *noun* a person who does business

trade route /ˈtreɪd ruːt/ *noun* a route along which goods are transported for trade ○ *The main trade routes were studied to see which areas of the country were most accessible.* ○ *When the Suez Canal was closed some vital trade routes were affected.*

trade show /ˈtreɪd ʃəʊ/ *noun* same as **trade fair**

tradesman /ˈtreɪdzmən/ *noun* a shopkeeper or someone who does business (NOTE: The plural is **tradesmen**.)

tradespeople /ˈtreɪdzˌpiːp(ə)l/ *plural noun* shopkeepers or people who do business

trade terms /ˈtreɪd tɜːmz/ *plural noun* a special discount for people in the same trade

trade up /ˌtreɪd ˈʌp/ *verb* to move to selling more expensive goods or to offering a more up-market service

trading /ˈtreɪdɪŋ/ *noun* the business of buying and selling

trading account /ˈtreɪdɪŋ əˌkaʊnt/ *noun* a company bank account administered by an investment dealer and used for managing trading activity, rather than for investment purposes

trading area /ˈtreɪdɪŋ ˌeəriə/ *noun* a group of countries which trade with each other

trading channel /ˈtreɪdɪŋ ˌtʃæn(ə)l/ *noun* a series of purchases and sales from company to company which are made until the finished product is purchased by the customer

trading company /ˈtreɪdɪŋ ˌkʌmp(ə)ni/ *noun* a company which specialises in buying and selling goods

trading estate /ˈtreɪdɪŋ ɪˌsteɪt/ *noun* an area of land near a town specially for building factories and warehouses

trading loss /ˌtreɪdɪŋ ˈlɒs/ *noun* a situation where a company's receipts are less than its expenditure

trading partner /ˈtreɪdɪŋ ˌpɑːtnə/ *noun* a company or country which trades with another

trading profit /ˈtreɪdɪŋ ˌprɒfɪt/ *noun* a result where the company' receipts are higher than its expenditure

trading stamp /ˈtreɪdɪŋ stæmp/ *noun* a special stamp given away by a shop, which the customer can collect and exchange later for free goods

Trading Standards Office /ˌtreɪdɪŋ ˈstændədz ˌɒfɪs/ *noun* a UK government department responsible for such matters as making sure that advertisements are true or that weighing machines are correct

traffic /ˈtræfɪk/ *noun* **1.** the flow of data on the Internet ○ *Analysts rated the website's success by monitoring traffic over a week.* **2.** an illegal trade ○ *drugs traffic or traffic in drugs*

traffic builder /ˈtræfɪk ˌbɪldə/ *noun* a software programme which increases traffic to a website, by linking with search engines, etc.

train /ˈtreɪn ɒn/ *verb* to learn how to do something

training levy /ˈtreɪnɪŋ ˌlevi/ *noun* a tax to be paid by companies to fund the government's training schemes

tramp ship /ˈtræmp ʃɪp/ *noun* a ship with no fixed schedule or itinerary that can be chartered by a company to transport goods

transaction /trænˈzækʃən/ *noun* an instance of doing business, e.g. a purchase in a shop or a withdrawal of money from savings □ **fraudulent transaction** a transaction which aims to cheat someone

'...the Japan Financial Intelligence Office will receive reports on suspected criminal transactions from financial institutions, determine where a probe should be launched and provide information to investigators' [*Nikkei Weekly*]

transaction e-commerce /trænˌzækʃən ˈiː kɒmɜːs/ *noun* the electronic sale of goods and services, either business-to-business or business-to-customer

transfer *noun*/ˈtrænsfɜː/ an act of moving an employee to another job in the same organisation ○ *She applied for a transfer to our branch in Scotland.* ■ *verb*/trænsˈfɜː/ to move someone or something to a different place, or to move someone to another job in the same organisation ○ *The accountant was transferred to our Scottish branch.* ○ *He transferred his shares to a family trust.* ○ *She transferred her money to a deposit account.*

transferable skill /trænsˌfɜːr-əb(ə)l ˈskɪl/ *noun* a skill that is not related to the performance of a particular job or task (NOTE: The skills that make people good at leadership, communication, critical thinking, analysis, or organisation are among those thought of as transferable skills.)

transfer pricing /ˈtrænsfɜː ˌpraɪ-sɪŋ/ *noun* prices used in a large organisation for selling goods or services between departments in the same organisation; also used in multinational corporations to transfer transactions from one country to another to avoid paying tax

transformational advertising /ˌtrænsfəˈmeɪʃ(ə)nəl ˌædvətaɪzɪŋ/ *noun* a form of emotional advertising that aims to relate emotional experiences to the product or service being advertised, and then tries to change these emotions into an active interest in purchasing

tranship /trænˈʃɪp/, **transship** *verb* to move cargo from one ship to another (NOTE: **transhipping – transhipped**)

transient advertisement /ˌtræn-ziənt ədˈvɜːtɪsmənt/ *noun* an advertisement which the target audience cannot keep to look at again, e.g. a cinema advertisement, as opposed to an intransient one in a newspaper or magazine

transit /ˈtrænzɪt/ *noun* the movement of passengers or goods on the way to a destination ○ *Some of the goods were damaged in transit.* □ **goods in transit** goods being transported from warehouse to customer

transit advertising /ˈtrænzɪt ˌædvətaɪzɪŋ/ *noun* advertisements on or inside buses, taxis, trains, etc.

transnational /trænzˈnæʃ(ə)nəl/ *noun* same as **multinational**

transnational corporation /ˌtrænz ˌnæʃ(ə)nəl ˌkɔːpəˈreɪ-ʃ(ə)n/ *noun* a large company which operates in various countries

transport /ˈtrænspɔːt/ *noun* **1.** the moving of goods or people from one place to another ○ *air transport* or *trans-*

port by air ○ *rail transport* or *transport by rail* ○ *road transport* or *transport by road* ○ *the passenger transport services into London* ○ *What means of transport will you use to get to the factory?* **2.** vehicles used to move goods or people from one place to another ○ *The company will provide transport to the airport.*

■ *verb* /trænsˈpɔːt/ to move goods or people from one place to another in a vehicle ○ *The company transports millions of tons of goods by rail each year.* ○ *The visitors will be transported to the factory by air* or *by helicopter* or *by taxi.*

transport advertising /ˈtrænspɔːt ˌædvətaɪzɪŋ/ *noun* advertising appearing on or in forms of transportation such as buses or trains ○ *Transport advertising will reach too broad a public for our product.* ○ *Is your transport advertising on the sides of buses or in Underground trains?*

transportation /ˌtrænspɔːˈteɪ-ʃ(ə)n/ *noun US* same as **transport**

transporter /trænsˈpɔːtə/ *noun* a company which transports goods

Transports Internationaux Routiers /ˌtrɔːnspɔːz ˌæntenæsjə-ˈnəʊ ruːtieɪ/ *noun* a system of international documents which allows dutiable goods to cross several European countries by road without paying duty until they reach their final destination. Abbreviation **TIR**

travel /ˈtræv(ə)l/ *verb* to go from one place to another, showing a company's goods to buyers and taking orders from them ○ *She travels in the north of the country for an insurance company.* (NOTE: **travelling – travelled**. The US spelling is **traveling – traveled**.)

traveller /ˈtræv(ə)lə/ *noun* a person who travels (NOTE: The US spelling is **traveler**.)

traveller's cheques /ˈtræv(ə)ləz tʃeks/ *plural noun* cheques bought by a traveller which can be cashed in a foreign country

travelling expenses /ˈtræv(ə)lɪŋ ekˌspensɪz/ *plural noun* money spent on travelling and hotels for business purposes

travelling salesman /ˌtræv(ə)-lɪŋ ˈseɪlzmən/ *noun* a salesman who travels around an area visiting customers on behalf of his company ○ *Travelling salesmen must make regular contact with company headquarters by phone.*

travel magazine /ˈtræv(ə)l ˌmægəˌziːn/ *noun* a magazine with articles on holidays and travel

travel organisation /ˈtræv(ə)l ˌɔːɡənaɪzeɪʃ(ə)n/ *noun* a body representing companies in the travel business

treaty /ˈtriːti/ *noun* **1.** an agreement between countries ○ *The two countries signed a commercial treaty.* **2.** an agreement between individual persons □ **to sell a house by private treaty** to sell a home to another person not by auction

trend /trend/ *noun* a general way in which things are developing ○ *a downward trend in investment* ○ *There is a trend away from old-established food stores.* ○ *The report points to inflationary trends in the economy.* ○ *We notice a general trend towards selling to the student market.* ○ *We have noticed an upward trend in sales.*

'…the quality of building design and ease of accessibility will become increasingly important, adding to the trend towards out-of-town office development' [*Lloyd's List*]

trend analysis /ˈtrend əˌnæləsɪs/ *noun* analysis of particular statistics over a period of time in order to identify trends ○ *Trend analysis has shown how soon major competitors begin to copy innovations.*

trial /ˈtraɪəl/ *noun* a test to see if something is good □ **on trial** in the process of being tested ○ *The product is on trial in our laboratories.* ■ *verb* to test a product to see how good it is (NOTE: **trialling – trialled**)

trial balance /ˈtraɪəl ˌbæləns/ *noun* the draft calculation of debits and credits to see if they balance

trial offer /ˈtraɪəl ˌɒfə/ *noun* a promotion where free samples are given away

trial period /ˌtraɪəl ˈpɪəriəd/ *noun* the time when a customer can test a product before buying it

trial sample /ˈtraɪəl ˌsɑːmpəl/ *noun* a small piece of a product used for testing

triplicate /ˈtrɪplɪkət/ *noun* □ **invoicing in triplicate** the preparing of three copies of invoices

troll /trəʊl, trɒl/ *verb* to search websites for Internet addresses which are then added to an email address list for promotional purposes

trolley /ˈtrɒli/ *noun* a small metal cart which is used by customers in supermarkets to carry their shopping (NOTE: The US term is **shopping cart**)

truck /trʌk/ *noun* **1.** a large motor vehicle for carrying goods **2.** an open railway wagon for carrying goods

truckage /ˈtrʌkɪdʒ/ *noun* the carriage of goods in trucks ○ *What will the truckage costs be for these goods?*

truck distributor /ˈtrʌk dɪˌstrɪbjutə/, **truck jobber** /ˈtrʌk ˌdʒɒbə/ *noun US* a wholesaler who usually only delivers goods directly by truck to retailers

trucking /ˈtrʌkɪŋ/ *noun* the carrying of goods in trucks ○ *a trucking firm*

truckload /ˈtrʌkləʊd/ *noun* a quantity of goods that fills a truck

trust /trʌst/ *noun US* a small group of companies which control the supply of a product

trustbusting /ˈtrʌstbʌstɪŋ/ *noun US* the breaking up of monopolies to encourage competition

T-scope /ˈtiː skəʊp/ *noun* same as **tachistoscope**

TSR *abbreviation* telephone sales representative

tube card /ˈtjuːb kɑːd/ *noun* a card with an advertisement on which is either put on the walls of Underground stations or inside Underground trains ○ *Half the tube cards in one carriage were advertising the same product.* ○ *The Underground railway system uses tube cards to advertise its own services.*

turn /tɜːn/ *verb*

turn over *phrasal verb* to have a specific amount of sales ○ *We turn over £2,000 a week.*

turn round *phrasal verb* to make a company change from making a loss to becoming profitable □ **they turned the company round in less than a year** they made the company profitable in less than a year

turnaround /'tɜːnəˌraʊnd/ *noun*
especially US same as **turnround**

turnkey contract /'tɜːnkiː ˌkɒn-trækt/ *noun* an agreement by which a contractor undertakes to design, construct, and manage something and only hand it over to the client when it is in a state where it is ready for immediate use

turnover /'tɜːnəʊvə/ *noun* **1.** the amount of sales of goods or services by a company ○ *The company's turnover has increased by 235%.* ○ *We based our calculations on the forecast turnover.* **2.** the number of times something is used or sold in a period, usually one year, expressed as a percentage of a total

turnround /'tɜːnraʊnd/ *noun* **1.** the value of goods sold during a year divided by the average value of goods held in stock **2.** the action of emptying a ship, plane, etc., and getting it ready for another commercial journey **3.** the act of making a company profitable again (NOTE: [all senses] The US term is **turnaround**.)

TV /ˌtiː 'viː/ *abbreviation* television

TVR *abbreviation* television ratings

TV spot /ˌtiː 'viː ˌspɒt/ *noun* a short period on TV which is used for commercials ○ *We are running a series of TV spots over the next three weeks.*

tweet /twiːt/ *noun* a text-based post of up to 140 characters displayed on the author's profile page on Twitter and read by subscribers to the author's page, known as followers ■ *verb* to post a comment on your or someone else's Twitter page ○ *She tweeted about her company's latest product launch.*

24/7 /ˌtwenti fɔː 'sev(ə)n/ *adverb* twenty-four hours a day, every day of the week (NOTE: Businesses often advertise themselves as being 'open 24/7'.)

24-hour service /ˌtwenti fɔːr aʊə 'sɜːvɪs/ *noun* help which is available for the whole day

twenty-four-hour trading /ˌtwenti fɔː aʊə 'treɪdɪŋ/ *noun* trading in bonds, currencies, or securities that can take place at any time of day or night (NOTE: Twenty-four-hour trading does not involve one trading floor being open all the time, but instead refers to the possibility of conducting operations at different locations in different time zones.)

twin-pack /'twɪn pæk/ *noun* a banded pack of two items sold together

Twitter /'twɪtə/ a trade name for a social networking and microblogging service where users send and read messages of no longer than 140 characters. ⇨ **social networking**

two-sided message /ˌtuː saɪdɪd 'mesɪdʒ/ *noun* a message which presents two arguments for purchasing a product or service

tying contract /'taɪɪŋ ˌkɒntrækt/ *noun* a contract under which a producer sells a product to a distributor on condition that the distributor also buys another product ○ *Tying contracts are used to get wholesalers acquainted with lesser-known products.*

typological analysis /taɪpəˌlɒd-ʒɪk(ə)l əˈnæləsɪs/ *noun* a categorisation of households based on socio-economic factors and buying habits ○ *Typological analysis helped the company clarify what market segments the new product should be aimed at.*

tyrekicker /'taɪəˌkɪkə/ *noun* a prospective customer who wants to examine every option before making up his or her mind about a purchase (as opposed to a 'first choice' who chooses the first option available) (NOTE: The usual US spelling is **tirekicker**.)

U

ultimate /ˈʌltɪmət/ *adjective* last or final

ultimate consumer /ˌʌltɪmət kən-ˈsjuːmə/ *noun* the person who actually uses the product

umbrella advertising /ʌmˈbrelə ˌædvətaɪzɪŋ/ *noun* the advertising of an organisation or an association of companies rather than a single product

umbrella organisation /ʌmˈbrelə ˌɔːɡənaɪzeɪʃ(ə)n/ *noun* a large organisation which includes several smaller ones

unaided recall /ʌnˌeɪdɪd ˈriːkɔːl/ *noun* same as **unprompted recall**

unavailability /ˌʌnəveɪləˈbɪlɪti/ *noun* the fact of not being available ○ *The unavailability of any reliable sales data makes forecasting difficult.*

unavailable /ˌʌnəˈveɪləb(ə)l/ *adjective* not available ○ *The following items on your order are temporarily unavailable.*

uncontrollable /ˌʌnkənˈtrəʊləb(ə)l/ *adjective* not possible to control ○ *uncontrollable inflation*

uncontrollable variable /ʌnkən-ˌtrəʊləb(ə)l ˈveəriəb(ə)l/ *noun* a variable or factor in marketing that cannot be controlled, e.g. legislation or the state of the country's economy ○ *There are too many uncontrollable variables for any real planning.* ○ *Changes in fashion constitute a dangerous uncontrollable variable for a clothes shop.*

uncrossed cheque /ˌʌnkrɒst ˈtʃek/ *noun* a cheque which does not have two lines across it, and can be cashed anywhere (NOTE: They are no longer used in the UK, but are still found in other countries.)

under- /ˈʌndə/ *prefix* less important than or lower than

underbid /ˌʌndəˈbɪd/ *verb* to bid less than someone (NOTE: **underbidding – underbid**)

underbidder /ˈʌndəbɪdə/ *noun* a person who bids less than the person who buys at an auction

undercharge /ˌʌndəˈtʃɑːdʒ/ *verb* to ask someone for too little money ○ *She undercharged us by £25.*

underclass /ˈʌndəklɑːs/ *noun* a group of people who are underprivileged in a way that appears to exclude them from mainstream society

undercut /ˌʌndəˈkʌt/ *verb* to offer something at a lower price than someone else ○ *They increased their market share by undercutting their competitors.* (NOTE: **undercutting – undercut**)

underdeveloped /ˌʌndədɪˈveləpt/ *adjective* which has not been developed ○ *Japan is an underdeveloped market for our products.*

underdeveloped countries /ˌʌndədɪveləpt ˈkʌntriz/ *plural noun* countries which are not fully industrialised

underdeveloped market /ˌʌndədɪveləpt ˈmɑːkɪt/ *noun* a market which has not been fully exploited ○ *Japan is an underdeveloped market for our products.*

underlease /ˈʌndəliːs/ *noun* a lease from a tenant to another tenant

underline /ˈʌndəlaɪn/ *noun* a short description printed underneath an illustration

underpayment /ˌʌndəˈpeɪmənt/ *noun* a payment of less than the correct invoiced amount

underpricing /ˌʌndə'praɪsɪŋ/ *noun* the charging of a lower price than is justified by demand ○ *The company's underpricing is due to ignorance of the growing market.* ○ *Underpricing can be used as a strategy to increase market share.*

undersell /ˌʌndə'sel/ *verb* to sell more cheaply than someone ○ *to undersell a competitor* (NOTE: **underselling – undersold**) □ **the company is never undersold** no other company sells goods as cheaply as this one

undertake /ˌʌndə'teɪk/ *verb* to carry out ○ *They are undertaking a study on employee reactions to pay restraint.* ○ *We asked the research unit to undertake an investigation of the market.*

under-the-counter sales /ˌʌndə ðə ˌkaʊntə 'seɪlz/ *plural noun* black-market sales

undervaluation /ˌʌndəvæljʊ'eɪ-ʃ(ə)n/ *noun* the state of being valued, or the act of valuing something, at less than the true worth

undervalued /ˌʌndə'vælju:d/ *adjective* not valued highly enough ○ *The dollar is undervalued on the foreign exchanges.* ○ *The properties are undervalued on the company's balance sheet.*

'…in terms of purchasing power, the dollar is considerably undervalued, while the US trade deficit is declining month by month' [*Financial Weekly*]

underweight /ˌʌndə'weɪt/ *adjective* not heavy enough □ **the pack is twenty grams underweight** the pack weighs twenty grams less than it should

undifferentiated /ˌʌndɪfə'rən-ʃieɪtɪd/ *adjective* which has no unique feature

undifferentiated marketing strategy /ˌʌndɪfəˌrənʃieɪtɪd 'mɑːkɪtɪŋ ˌstrætədʒi/ *noun* a marketing strategy which seeks to present a product to the public without stressing any unique feature of the product, thus appealing to all segments of the market. ⇨ **concentrated marketing**, **differentiated marketing strategy**

undifferentiated product /ˌʌndɪfə-ˌrenʃieɪtɪd 'prɒdʌkt/ *noun* a product which has no unique feature to set it apart from others on the market ○ *Only an extra-low price will sell an undifferenti-*

ated product in a market where there is already a wide choice of brands.

undue influence /ˌʌndjuː 'ɪnfluəns/ *noun* unfair pressure put on someone to sign a contract ○ *The sales force were discouraged from exerting undue influence on prospective buyers.*

unemployment rate /ˌʌnɪm-'plɔɪmənt reɪt/ *noun* the number of people out of work, shown as a percentage of the total number of people available for work. Also called **rate of unemployment**

uneven /ʌn'iːv(ə)n/ *adjective* not smooth or flat

uneven playing field /ʌnˌiːv(ə)n 'pleɪɪŋ fiːld/ *noun* a situation where the competing groups do not compete on the same terms and conditions. Opposite **level playing field**

unfair /ʌn'feə/ *adjective* not just or reasonable

unfair competition /ˌʌnfeə ˌkɒm-pə'tɪʃ(ə)n/ *noun* the practice of trying to do better than another company by using techniques such as importing foreign goods at very low prices or by wrongly criticising a competitor's products

unfavourable /ʌn'feɪv(ə)rəb(ə)l/ *adjective* not favourable (NOTE: The US spelling is **unfavorable**.) □ **unfavourable balance of trade** a situation where a country imports more than it exports □ **unfavourable exchange rate** an exchange rate which gives an amount of foreign currency for the home currency which is not good for trade ○ *The unfavourable exchange rate hit the country's exports.*

unfulfilled /ˌʌnfʊl'fɪld/ *adjective* (*of an order*) which has not yet been supplied

unilateral /ˌjuːnɪ'læt(ə)rəl/ *adjective* on one side only or done by one party only ○ *They took a unilateral decision to cancel the contract.*

unilaterally /ˌjuːnɪ'læt(ə)rəli/ *adverb* by one party only ○ *The decision was taken to cancel the contract unilaterally.*

unionism /'juːnjənɪz(ə)m/ *noun* the fact of being a member of a trade union

unique /juːˈniːk/ *adjective* unlike anything else

unique selling point /juːˌniːk ˈselɪŋ pɔɪnt/, **unique selling proposition** /juːˌniːk ˈselɪŋ ˌprəpəzɪʃ(ə)n/ *noun* a special quality of a product which makes it different from other goods and is used as a key theme in advertising ○ *A five-year guarantee is a USP for this product.* ○ *What's this product's unique selling proposition?* Abbreviation **USP**

unit /ˈjuːnɪt/ *noun* **1.** a single product for sale **2.** a separate piece of equipment or furniture **3.** a group of people set up for a special purpose

unit cost /ˈjuːnɪt kɒst/ *noun* the cost of one item, i.e. the total product costs divided by the number of units produced

United Nations /juːˌnaɪtɪd ˈneɪʃ(ə)nz/ *noun* an organisation which links almost all the countries of the world to promote good relations between them

unit pack /ˈjuːnɪt pæk/ *noun* a pack containing only one unit of a product ○ *Will the product be sold in unit packs, or in packs of ten or twenty units?*

unit price /ˈjuːnɪt praɪs/ *noun* the price of one item

unit pricing /ˈjuːnɪt ˌpraɪsɪŋ/ *noun* the pricing of items by showing how much each costs per unit of measurement, e.g. per metre or per kilo

Universal Product Code /juːnɪˌvɜːs(ə)l ˈprɒdʌkt kəʊd/ *noun* the code which identifies an article for sale, usually printed as a bar code on the packet or item itself. Abbreviation **UPC**

universe /ˈjuːnɪvɜːs/ *noun* the total population which is being studied in a survey and out of which a sample is selected ○ *Is this sample really representative of the universe?* ○ *In the survey, the universe is all British men between the ages of forty and fifty.* ○ *From a universe of two million, a sample of two thousand was chosen by random selection.*

unladen /ʌnˈleɪd(ə)n/ *adjective* without a cargo ○ *The ship was unladen when she arrived in port.*

unlimited /ʌnˈlɪmɪtɪd/ *adjective* with no limits ○ *The bank offered him unlimited credit.*

unlimited liability /ʌnˌlɪmɪtɪd ˌlaɪəˈbɪlɪti/ *noun* a situation where a sole trader or each partner is responsible for all a firm's debts with no limit on the amount each may have to pay

unload /ʌnˈləʊd/ *verb* **1.** to take goods off a ship, lorry etc. ○ *The ship is unloading at Hamburg.* ○ *We need a fork-lift truck to unload the lorry.* ○ *We unloaded the spare parts at Barcelona.* ○ *There are no unloading facilities for container ships.* **2.** to sell stock which is no longer needed at a lower price than usual ○ *They tried to unload some unsellable items onto the Far Eastern market.*

unloading /ʌnˈləʊdɪŋ/ *noun* the act of selling off goods at a lower price than usual, often when they are no longer being produced and the producers merely want to get rid of remaining stock ○ *Many customers are taking advantage of our unloading and are buying in bulk.*

unmentionables /ʌnˈmenʃənəb(ə)lz/ *plural noun* groups of products that are considered too delicate to mention or to advertise. These may include sanitary towels, condoms or incontinence pads. ○ *The company manufactures a number of unmentionable products that are difficult to market effectively.*

unprofitable /ʌnˈprɒfɪtəb(ə)l/ *adjective* not profitable

unprompted awareness test /ʌnˌprɒmptɪd əˈweənəs test/, **unprompted recall** /ʌnˌprɒmptɪd ˈriːkɔːl/ *noun* an advertising research test to see how well a respondent can remember an advertisement when he or she is given no help in remembering it ○ *A disappointing number of respondents did not remember the advertisement at all in an unprompted recall.* Compare **prompted recall**

unrealised loss /ˌʌnrɪəlaɪzd ˈlɒs/ *noun* same as **paper loss**

unrealised profit /ʌnˌrɪəlaɪzd ˈprɒfɪt/ *noun* same as **paper profit**

unseen /ʌnˈsiːn/ *adverb* not seen

unsold /ʌnˈsəʊld/ *adjective* not sold ○ *Unsold items will be scrapped.*

unsolicited /ʌnsəˈlɪsɪtɪd/ *adjective* which has not been asked for ○ *an unsolicited gift*

unsolicited testimonial /ʌnsə-ˌlɪsɪtɪd ˌtestɪˈməʊniəl/ *noun* a letter praising someone or a product, without the writer having been asked to write it

unstructured interview /ʌnˌstrʌk-tʃəd ˈɪntəvjuː/ *noun* an interview which is not based on a series of fixed questions and which encourages open discussion ○ *Unstructured interviews are effective in eliciting original suggestions for product improvement.* ○ *Shy respondents often perform well in unstructured interviews where they have more freedom of expression.* Compare **structured interview**

unsubsidised /ʌnˈsʌbsɪdaɪzd/, **unsubsidized** *adjective* with no subsidy

unused /ʌnˈjuːzd/ *adjective* which has not been used ○ *We are trying to sell off six unused computers.*

UPC *abbreviation* Universal Product Code

update *noun*/ˈʌpdeɪt/ information added to something to make it up to date ○ *Here is the latest update on sales.* ■ *verb*/ʌpˈdeɪt/ to revise something so that it is always up to date ○ *The figures are updated annually.*

up front /ˌʌp ˈfrʌnt/ *adverb* in advance

uplift /ˈʌplɪft/ *noun* an increase ○ *The contract provides for an annual uplift of charges.*

upmarket /ˌʌpˈmɑːkɪt/ *adverb, adjective* more expensive or appealing to a wealthy section of the population (NOTE: The opposite is **down market**.) □ **the company has decided to move upmarket** the company has decided to start to produce more luxury items

'…upmarket companies which are doing well need a conference venue to reflect this' [*Marketing Week*]

'…prices of upmarket homes (costing $350,000 or more) are falling in many areas' [*Economist*]

upscale /ˈʌpskeɪl/ *adjective* aimed at customers at the top end of the socio-economic ladder, who are well-educated and have higher incomes

upselling /ˈʌpselɪŋ/ *noun* selling extra products to go with the one the customer is planning to buy

upset price /ˈʌpset praɪs/ *noun* the lowest price which the seller will accept at an auction

up-to-date /ˌʌp tə ˈdeɪt/ *adjective, adverb* current, recent, or modern ○ *an up-to-date computer system* □ **to bring something up to date** to add the latest information or equipment to something □ **to keep something up to date** to keep adding information to something so that it always has the latest information in it ○ *We spend a lot of time keeping our mailing list up to date.*

upturn /ˈʌptɜːn/ *noun* a movement towards higher sales or profits ○ *an upturn in the economy* ○ *an upturn in the market*

usage /ˈjuːsɪdʒ/ *noun* the way in which something is used

usage pull /ˈjuːsɪdʒ pʊl/ *noun US* the degree to which those who see or hear advertisements for a product buy more of it than those who do not ○ *We're only able to assess usage pull some time after the advertising campaign.*

usage segmentation /ˈjuːsɪdʒ segmenˌteɪʃ(ə)n/ *noun* the dividing of a market into segments according to the type of use which customers will make of the product

use-by date /ˈjuːz baɪ ˌdeɪt/ *noun* a date printed on a packet of food showing the last date on which the contents should be used. Compare **best-before date**, **sell-by date**

user /ˈjuːzə/ *noun* a person who uses something

user experience questionnaire /ˈjuːzə ɪkˈspɪəriəns ˌkwestʃəneə/ *noun* a set of questions designed to establish how a person feels about using a product, system or service which is used by companies to improve existing products or create new ones ○ *The marketing department devised a user experience questionnaire to find out whether customers liked the new soft drinks range.*

user-friendly /ˌjuːzə ˈfrendli/ *adjective* which a user finds easy to work ○ *These programs are really user-friendly.*

user group /ˈjuːzə gruːp/ *noun* an organisation of users of a specific hardware or software product. Members share experiences and ideas to improve their understanding and use of a particular product. User groups are often responsible for influencing vendors to modify or enhance their products. ○ *The technology department has set up a user group to review the company's latest model of tablet computer.*

user's guide /ˈjuːzəz ɡaɪd/, **user's handbook** /ˈjuːzəz ˌhændbʊk/ **user's manual** /ˈjuːzəz ˌmænjʊəl/ *noun* a book showing someone how to use something

USP *abbreviation* **1.** unique selling point **2.** unique selling proposition

utility /juːˈtɪlɪti/ *noun* the usefulness or satisfaction that a consumer gets from a product ○ *The price charged depends on the product's utility.*

utility goods /juːˈtɪlɪti ɡʊdz/ *plural noun* basic goods that are necessary for everyday life ○ *Even some utility goods can be considered luxuries during a depression.* ○ *Consumers say that shopping for utility goods is routine and boring.*

V

valorem /vəˈlɔːrəm/ *noun* ➡ **ad valorem duty**

VALS *noun* a system of dividing people into segments according to their way of living. Full form **Values and Lifestyles**

valuation /ˌvæljuˈeɪʃ(ə)n/ *noun* an estimate of how much something is worth ○ *to ask for a valuation of a property before making an offer for it* □ **to buy a shop with stock at valuation** when buying a shop, to pay a price for the stock which is equal to the value as estimated by the valuer □ **to purchase stock at valuation** to pay the price for stock which it is valued at

value /ˈvæljuː/ *noun* the amount of money which something is worth ○ *the fall in the value of sterling* ○ *She imported goods to the value of £2,500.* ○ *The valuer put the value of the stock at £25,000.* □ **good value (for money)** a bargain, something which is worth the price paid for it ○ *That restaurant gives value for money.* ○ *Buy that computer now – it is very good value.* ○ *Holidays in Italy are good value because of the exchange rate.* □ **to rise or fall in value** to be worth more or less ■ *verb* to estimate how much money something is worth ○ *He valued the stock at £25,000.* ○ *We are having the jewellery valued for insurance.*

value added /ˌvæljuː ˈædɪd/ *noun* **1.** the difference between the cost of the materials purchased to produce a product and the final selling price of the finished product **2.** the amount added to the value of a product or service, being the difference between its cost and the amount received when it is sold. Also called **net output 3.** the features that make one product or service different from or better than another and so create value for the customer (NOTE: Value added in this sense is based on the customer's view of what makes a product or service more desirable than others and worth a higher price.)

value-added reseller /ˌvæljuː ædɪd ˈriːselə/ *noun* a merchant who buys products at retail prices and packages them with additional items for resale to customers

value-added services /ˌvæljuː ædɪd ˈsɜːvɪsɪz/ *plural noun* services which add value to a service or product being sold

Value Added Tax /ˌvæljuː ædɪd ˈtæks/ *noun* full form of **VAT**

value-adding intermediary /ˌvæljuː ædɪŋ ɪntəˈmiːdiəri/ *noun* a distributor who increases the value of a product before selling it to a customer, e.g. by installing software in a computer

value analysis /ˈvæljuː əˌnæləsɪs/ *noun* analysis by a producer of all aspects of a finished product to determine how it could be made at minimum cost ○ *Value analysis showed an excessive amount of rubber was used in manufacturing the product.*

value chain /ˈvæljuː tʃeɪn/ *noun* **1.** the sequence of activities a company carries out as it designs, produces, markets, delivers, and supports its product or service, each of which is thought of as adding value **2.** the pattern that people traditionally have in mind when considering their career prospects, which involves them identifying at each stage in their careers what the next, most obvious, upward move should be

'Competition is no longer limited to the realm of the enterprise. Entire value chains are now starting to act as formidable entities, competing against each other for similar markets' [*Harvard Business Review*]

valued impression per pound /ˌvæljuːd ɪmˌpreʃ(ə)n pə 'paʊnd/ *noun* a method of showing how many readers are reached by advertising for a given sum of money. Abbreviation **VIP**

value engineering /'væljuː endʒɪˌnɪərɪŋ/ *noun* analysis by a producer of all aspects of a product at the design stage to determine how it could be made at minimum cost ○ *Value engineering allows very economical production and competitive prices at every stage in the distribution channel.*

value map /'væljuː mæp/ *noun* an indication of the amount of value that the market considers a product or service to have, which helps to differentiate it from its competitors

value proposition /'væljuː prɒpəˌzɪʃ(ə)n/ *noun* a statement by an organisation of the way in which it can provide value for a customer

valuer /'væljʊə/ *noun* a person who estimates how much money something is worth

Values and Lifestyles /ˌvæljuː ən 'laɪfˌstaɪlz/ *noun* full form of **VALS**

van /væn/ *noun* a small goods vehicle

van ship /'væn ʃɪp/ *noun* a ship designed to carry goods in containers

VAR *abbreviation* value-added reseller

variable /'veəriəb(ə)l/ *adjective* changeable

variable costs /ˌveəriəb(ə)l 'kɒsts/ *plural noun* production costs which increase with the quantity of the product made, e.g. wages or raw materials

variable pricing /ˌveəriəb(ə)l 'praɪsɪŋ/ *noun* the practice of giving a product or service different prices in different places or at different times

variance /'veəriəns/ *noun* the discrepancy between the actual cost of an asset or business activity and the standard or expected cost □ **at variance with** not in agreement with ○ *The actual sales are at variance with the sales reported by the reps.*

variation /ˌveəri'eɪʃ(ə)n/ *noun* the amount by which something changes

□ **seasonal variations** variations which take place at different times of the year ○ *seasonal variations in buying patterns*

variety /və'raɪəti/ *noun* different types of things ○ *The shop stocks a variety of goods.* ○ *We had a variety of visitors at the office today.*

variety chain store /vəˌraɪəti 'tʃeɪn stɔː/ *noun* a chain store which sells a large range of goods ○ *The variety chain stores sell everything from jewellery to electrical products.*

variety store /və'raɪəti stɔː/ *noun* *US* a shop selling a wide range of usually cheap items

VAT /ˌviː eɪ 'tiːvæt/ *noun* a tax on goods and services, added as a percentage to the invoiced sales price ○ *The invoice includes VAT at 20%.* ○ *The government is proposing to increase VAT to 22%.* ○ *Some items (such as books) are zero-rated for VAT.* ○ *He does not charge VAT because he asks for payment in cash.* Full form **Value Added Tax**

'…the directive means that the services of stockbrokers and managers of authorized unit trusts are now exempt from VAT; previously they were liable to VAT at the standard rate. Zero-rating for stockbrokers' services is still available as before, but only where the recipient of the service belongs outside the EC' [*Accountancy*]

VAT declaration /'væt dekləˌreɪʃ(ə)n/ *noun* a statement declaring VAT income to the VAT office

VAT inspector /'væt ɪnˌspektə/ *noun* a government official who examines VAT returns and checks that VAT is being paid

VAT invoice /'væt ˌɪnvɔɪs/ *noun* an invoice which includes VAT

VAT invoicing /'væt ˌɪnvɔɪsɪŋ/ *noun* the sending of an invoice including VAT

VATman /'vætmæn/, **vatman** *noun* a VAT inspector(*informal*)

VAT office /'væt ˌɒfɪs/ *noun* the government office dealing with the collection of VAT in an area

VDU *abbreviation* visual display unit

Veblenian model /ve'bleɪniən ˌmɒd(ə)l/ *noun* a theory of buying behaviour proposed by Veblen, which explains consumption mainly in terms of social influences or pressures rather than economic ones ○ *A Veblenian model helps to illustrate the non-rational side of consumer behaviour.*

vending /ˈvendɪŋ/ *noun* selling

vending machine /ˈvendɪŋ məˈʃiːn/ *noun* same as **automatic vending machine**

vendor /ˈvendə/ *noun* **1.** a person who sells something, especially a property ○ *the solicitor acting on behalf of the vendor* **2.** a person who sells goods

vendor rating /ˈvendə ˌreɪtɪŋ/ *noun* an assessment of a vendor by a buyer on the basis of the vendor's reliability and the quality and price of the goods on offer ○ *Vendor rating has already disqualified three suppliers on the grounds of price.* ○ *A good reputation for quick delivery is a key factor in the buying department's vendor ratings.*

venture /ˈventʃə/ *noun* a commercial deal which involves a risk ○ *They lost money on several import ventures.* ○ *She's started a new venture – a clothing shop.* ■ *verb* to risk money

venture capital /ˌventʃə ˈkæpɪt(ə)l/ *noun* capital for investment which may easily be lost in risky projects, but can also provide high returns. Also called **risk capital**

venture team /ˈventʃə tiːm/ *noun* a group of people from different departments in a company who work together on a new product-development project ○ *The venture team met regularly to monitor progress in the product's development.*

version /ˈvɜːʃ(ə)n/ *verb* to adapt a website for different categories of customer by maintaining different versions of it

vertical /ˈvɜːtɪk(ə)l/ *adjective* upright, straight up or down

vertical communication /ˌvɜːtɪk(ə)l kəˌmjuːnɪˈkeɪʃ(ə)n/ *noun* communication between senior managers via the middle management to the workforce

vertical industrial market /ˌvɜːtɪk(ə)l ɪnˈdʌstriəl ˌmɑːkɪt/ *noun* a market in which a product is used by only one industry

vertical integration /ˌvɜːtɪk(ə)l ˌɪntɪˈgreɪʃ(ə)n/ *noun* the extent to which supply-chain activities are controlled within an organisation

vertical marketing system /ˌvɜːtɪk(ə)l ˈmɑːkɪtɪŋ ˌsɪstəm/ *noun* a distribution system that is a co-ordinated integrated unit involving the manufacturer, the wholesaler, and the retailer, where marketing decisions are taken globally

vertical publication /ˌvɜːtɪk(ə)l ˌpʌblɪˈkeɪʃ(ə)n/ *noun* a publication for people working at different levels in the same industry. Compare **horizontal publication**

viable /ˈvaɪəb(ə)l/ *adjective* which can work in practice □ **not commercially viable** not likely to make a profit

videoconferencing /ˈvɪdiəʊˌkɒnf(ə)rənsɪŋ/ *noun* the use of live video links that enable people in different locations to see and hear one another and so to discuss matters and hold meetings without being physically present together in one place

videotape /ˈvɪdiəʊteɪp/ *noun* a magnetic tape for recording sound and vision, used for making original recordings or taping existing television material ○ *The advertiser studied the videotape of the advertisement and sent comments to the agency.* ■ *verb* to record something on videotape ○ *The reactions of respondents trying the product for the first time were videotaped.*

view /vjuː/ *verb* to watch a TV programme

viewer /ˈvjuːə/ *noun* a person who watches television

viewing figures /ˈvjuːɪŋ ˌfɪgəz/ *plural noun* figures showing the numbers of people watching a TV programme

VIP *abbreviation* valued impression per pound

viral /ˈvaɪrəl/ *adjective* acting in the same way as a virus ■ *noun* a message spread by viral marketing

viral design /ˈvaɪrəl dɪˌzaɪn/ *noun* the design of a message that encourages recipients to forward the message on to others

viral effect /ˈvaɪrəl ɪˌfekt/ *noun* the number of recipients of a message who forward the message on to others

viral forwards /ˌvaɪrəl ˈfɔːwədz/ *plural noun* the number of messages forwarded

viral marketing /ˈvaɪrəl ˌmaːkɪtɪŋ/ *noun* marketing by word of mouth or by spreading advertising messages on the Internet

'...investment in new technology enabled marketing programs, such as viral marketing and E-care systems, to remain relevant to the changing needs of online buyers' [*Information Week*]

virtual hosting /ˌvɜːtʃuəl ˈhəʊstɪŋ/ *noun* a hosting option, suitable for small and medium-sized businesses, in which the customer shares space on the hosting company's server that with other organisations (NOTE: In virtual hosting, the hosting company carries out basic maintenance on hardware, but the customer is responsible for managing the content and software.)

virtual office /ˌvɜːtʃuəl ˈɒfɪs/ *noun* a workplace that has no physical location but is created when a number of employees use information and communications technologies to do their work and collaborate with one another (NOTE: A virtual office is characterised by the use of teleworkers, telecentres, mobile workers, hot-desking and hotelling.)

virtual team /ˌvɜːtʃuəl ˈtiːm/ *noun* a group of employees working in different locations who use communications technologies such as groupware, email, an intranet, or videoconferencing to collaborate with each other and work as a team

VISA /ˈviːzə/ a trademark for an international credit card system

visible /ˈvɪzɪb(ə)l/ *adjective* referring to real products which are imported or exported

visible exports /ˌvɪzɪb(ə)l ˈekspɔːts/ *plural noun* real products which are exported, as opposed to services

visible imports /ˌvɪzɪb(ə)l ˈɪmpɔːts/ *plural noun* real products which are imported, as opposed to services

vision statement /ˈvɪʒ(ə)n ˌsteɪtmənt/ *noun* a statement that sets out in general terms what an organisation is aiming or hoping to achieve in the future (NOTE: Vision statements express corporate vision, and are related to mission statements.)

visual /ˈvɪʒuəl/ *adjective* which can be seen ■ *noun* a photograph, picture, chart, or graph used to display information or promotional material

visual display terminal /ˌvɪzjuəl dɪˈspleɪ ˌtɜːmɪnəl/, **visual display unit** /ˌvɪzjuəl dɪˈspleɪ juːnɪt/ *noun* a screen attached to a computer which shows the information stored in the computer. Abbreviation **VDT, VDU**

visualizer /ˈvɪʒuəlaɪzə/ *noun* a person who produces visual ideas for advertisements or advertising campaigns

voicemail /ˈvɔɪsmeɪl/ *noun* an electronic communications system which stores digitised recordings of telephone messages for later playback

voiceover /ˈvɔɪs ˌəʊvə/ *noun* the commentary for a TV or cinema advertisement, spoken by an actor who does not appear in the advertisement

volume /ˈvɒljuːm/ *noun* a quantity of items

volume discount /ˈvɒljuːm ˌdɪskaʊnt/ *noun* the discount given to a customer who buys a large quantity of goods

volume of output /ˌvɒljuːm əv ˈaʊtpʊt/ *noun* the number of items produced

volume of sales /ˌvɒljuːm əv ˈseɪlz/ *noun* the number of items sold □ **low or high volume of sales** a small or large number of items sold

volume segmentation /ˈvɒljuːm segmenˌteɪʃ(ə)n/ *noun* the segmentation or division of a market on the basis of the quantity of the product bought

volumetrics /ˌvɒljuːˈmetrɪks/ *noun* analysis of the relative influence of various media by considering the number of people who are exposed to them, and their importance as buyers ○ *Volumetrics has been our most useful tool in media buying.* ○ *The marketing department consulted an expert in volumetrics to help plan the advertising campaign.* (NOTE: takes a singular verb)

voluntarily /ˈvɒlənt(ə)rəli/ *adverb* without being forced or paid

voluntary /ˈvɒlənt(ə)ri/ *adjective* **1.** done freely without anyone forcing you to act **2.** done without being paid

voluntary chain /ˈvɒlənt(ə)ri tʃeɪn/, **voluntary group** /ˈvɒlənt(ə)ri gruːp/ *noun* a group of distributors who join together to buy from suppliers so as to enjoy quantity discounts ○ *After joining the voluntary chain the shop saved up to 20% in buying.*

voluntary control /ˌvɒlənt(ə)ri kənˈtrəʊl/ *noun* a system adopted by the advertising industry for controlling possible abuses which involves following guidelines laid down for the industry as a whole ○ *If voluntary controls are not effective, the government will have to bring in legislation.*

voluntary organisation /ˈvɒlənt(ə)ri ˌɔːgənaɪzeɪʃ(ə)n/ *noun* an organisation which does not receive funding from the government, but relies on contributions from the public

voucher /ˈvaʊtʃə/ *noun* **1.** a piece of paper which is given instead of money **2.** a written document from an auditor to show that the accounts are correct or that money has really been paid

W

wage differentials /ˈweɪdʒ ˌdɪfə-ˌrenʃəlz/ *plural noun* same as **pay differentials**

wage parity /ˈweɪdʒ ˌpærɪti/ *noun* same as **pay parity**

waggon jobber /ˈwægən ˌdʒɒbə/ *noun US* a limited function wholesaler, usually one who delivers goods by truck to retailers

walk-in /ˈwɔːk ɪn/ *noun* a person who approaches an organisation for a job, without knowing if any jobs are available (NOTE: The plural is **walk-ins**.)

wall /wɔːl/ *noun* a webpage on Facebook that displays the status updates and conversations the user has with other users, or that can be used to advertise or promote an organisation's products or services. It is visible to everyone the user chooses to allow access. ○ *He posted a link to networking event on the company's wall.*

want /wɒnt/ *noun* a need felt by a person, which is formed by that person's education, culture, and character

WAP /wæp/ *noun* a technical language and set of processing rules that enables users of mobile phones to access websites (NOTE: WAP stands for Wireless Application Protocol and is the equivalent of HTML for mobile phones.)

warehouse /ˈweəhaʊs/ *noun* a large building where goods are stored □ **price ex warehouse** the price for a product which is to be collected from the manufacturer's or agent's warehouse and so does not include delivery ■ *verb* to store goods in a warehouse ○ *Our offices are in London but our stock is warehoused in Scotland.*

warehouse capacity /ˈweəhaʊs kəˌpæsɪti/ *noun* the space available in a warehouse

warehouseman /ˈweəhaʊsmən/ *noun* a person who works in a warehouse (NOTE: The plural is **warehousemen**.)

warehousing /ˈweəhaʊzɪŋ/ *noun* the act of storing goods in a warehouse ○ *Warehousing costs are rising rapidly.*

warm lead /ˌwɔːm ˈliːd/ *noun* a customer who already knows something about your company's products or services and is, therefore, easier to sell to than someone you are cold calling

warranty /ˈwɒrənti/ *noun* a legal document which promises that a machine will work properly or that an item is of good quality ○ *The car is sold with a twelve-month warranty.* ○ *The warranty covers spare parts but not labour costs.*

waste /weɪst/ *noun* an unnecessary use of time or money

waste coverage /ˈweɪst ˌkʌv(ə)rɪdʒ/ *noun* media coverage which goes beyond the target audience

waybill /ˈweɪbɪl/ *noun* a list of goods being transported, made out by the carrier

wealth management /ˈwelθ ˌmænɪdʒmənt/ *noun* investment services offered by banks to people with more than a specific amount of money in liquid assets

web /web/ *noun* same as **World Wide Web**

Web 2.0 /ˌweb tuː pɔɪnt ˈzɪərəʊ/ *noun* a range of Web applications that enable information sharing on the Web through user-driven technologies. Users interact with each other in a social media dialogue in a virtual community through blogs, wikis, social networks, and podcasting.

web analytics /ˈweb ænəˌlɪtɪks/ *noun* the measurement, collection, analysis, and reporting of Internet data such as user traffic, server performance and email response rates, for the purposes of optimising web usage and improving advertising campaigns

webcast /'webkɑːst/ *noun* a broadcast made over the web that enables an event to be viewed by a large number of people who are all connected to the same website at the same time (NOTE: Webcasts often use *rich media* technology.)

web commerce /'web ˌkɒmɜːs/ *noun* same as **e-commerce**

web content management /'web ˌkɒntent ˌmænɪdʒmənt/ *noun* formal organisation of the content on a company's website, including updating, branding, editorial access, formatting and supporting software considerations

web form /'web fɔːm/ *noun* an electronic document similar to a printed form, which can be used to collect information from a visitor to a website. When the form has been filled in the form, it is usually returned to the owner of the website by email.

web log /'web lɒg/ *noun* **1.** a record of activity taking place on a website, which can provide important marketing information, e.g. on how many users are visiting the site and what they are interested in, as well as highlighting any technical problems. Also called **server log 2.** a personal journal published on the Internet, which often encourages other users to make comments. Also called **blog**

web marketing /'web ˌmɑːkɪtɪŋ/ *noun* marketing that uses websites to advertise products and services and to reach potential customers

web marketplace /'web ˌmɑːkɪpleɪs/ *noun* a network of connections that enables business buyers and sellers to contact one another and do business on the web (NOTE: There are three types of web marketplace: online catalogues, auctions, and exchanges.)

webmaster /'webmɑːstə/ *noun* the person who looks after a website, changing and updating the information it contains and noting how many people visit it (NOTE: Several different people within an organisation may share the job of webmaster.)

webpage /'webpeɪdʒ/ *noun* a single file of text and graphics, forming part of a website

website /'websaɪt/ *noun* a position on the web, which is created by a company, organisation or individual, and which anyone can visit ○ *How many hits did we have on our website last week?*

weekly /'wiːkli/ *noun* a newspaper or magazine which is published each week ○ *The clothes were advertised in the fashion weeklies.* (NOTE: The plural is **weeklies.**)

weight /weɪt/ *noun* a measurement of how heavy something is □ **to sell fruit by weight** the price is per pound or per kilo of the fruit □ **to give short weight** to give less than you should

weighted average /ˌweɪtɪd 'æv(ə)rɪdʒ/ *noun* an average which is calculated taking several factors into account, giving some more value than others

weighted index /ˌweɪtɪd 'ɪndeks/ *noun* an index where some important items are given more value than less important ones

weighting /'weɪtɪŋ/ *noun* a statistical process which gives more importance to some figures or results than others in the process of reaching a final figure or result

weight limit /'weɪt ˌlɪmɪt/ *noun* the maximum weight ○ *The packet is over the weight limit for letter post, so it will have to go by parcel post.*

wet goods /'wet gʊdz/ *plural noun* goods that are sold in liquid form ○ *Special plastic containers have to be used for wet goods.* ○ *Inflammable wet goods are the most dangerous type of product to transport.*

wheel of retailing /ˌwiːl əv 'riːteɪlɪŋ/ *noun* a model which explains changes in the evolution of the retailing trade

COMMENT: This model explains that retailers start as low-price downmarket stores and gradually trade up, and sometimes eventually go out of business, being replaced by new downmarket stores.

white coat rule /ˌwaɪt 'kəʊt ˌruːl/ *noun* a rule for advertising on TV stating that doctors or actors in white coats cannot promote medical products

white goods /'waɪt gʊdz/ *plural noun* **1.** machines which are used in the kitchen, e.g. refrigerators, washing machines **2.** household linen, e.g. sheets and towels

white space /'waɪt speɪs/ *noun* the areas of any company where strategy and authority are vague, and where useful entrepreneurial activity can flourish. ⇨ **black space**

wholesale /'həʊlseɪl/ *adjective, adverb* referring to the business of buying goods from manufacturers and selling them in large quantities to traders (retailers) who then sell in smaller quantities to the general public ○ *I persuaded him to give us a wholesale discount.* □ **he buys wholesale and sells retail** he buys goods in bulk at a wholesale discount and then sells in small quantities to the public

wholesale dealer /'həʊlseɪl ˌdiːlə/ *noun* a person who buys in bulk from manufacturers and sells to retailers

wholesale price /'həʊlseɪl praɪs/ *noun* the price charged to customers who buy goods in large quantities in order to resell them in smaller quantities to others

wholesale price index /ˌhəʊlseɪl 'praɪs ˌɪndeks/ *noun* an index showing the rises and falls of prices of manufactured goods as they leave the factory

wholesaler /'həʊlseɪlə/ *noun* a person who buys goods in bulk from manufacturers and sells them to retailers

wholesale trade /'həʊlseɪl treɪd/ *noun* trade that involves buying goods in large quantities at lower prices in order to resell them in smaller quantities and at higher prices to others

WIIFM *noun* the basic thoughts that affect the decision taken by a prospective customer. Full form **what's in it for me?**

wild cats /'waɪld kæts/ *plural noun* same as **problem children**

win /wɪn/ *verb* to be successful □ **to win a contract** to be successful in tendering for a contract ○ *The company announced that it had won a contract worth $25m to supply buses and trucks.*

window /'wɪndəʊ/ *noun* an opening in a wall, with glass in it

window display /'wɪndəʊ dɪˌspleɪ/ *noun* the display of goods in a shop window

window dressing /'wɪndəʊ ˌdresɪŋ/ *noun* the practice of putting goods on display in a shop window, so that they attract customers

window shopping /'wɪndəʊ ʃɒpɪŋ/ *noun* the practice of looking at goods in shop windows, without buying anything

windscreen sticker /'wɪndskriːn ˌstɪkə/ *noun* an advertising sticker put onto the windscreen of a car

win-win situation /ˌwɪn ˌwɪn ˌsɪtjuˈeɪʃ(ə)n/ *noun* a situation in which, whatever happens or whatever choice is made, the people involved will benefit

WIP *abbreviation* work in progress

wireless /'waɪələs/ *adjective* referring to communications systems and devices that use mobile phone technology

women's magazine /'wɪmɪnz mæɡəˌziːn/ *noun* a magazine aimed at the women's market

word /wɜːd/ *noun* something spoken

word-of-mouth communications /ˌwɜːd əv maʊθ kəmjuːnɪˈkeɪʃ(ə)nz/ *plural noun* informal channels of communication such as friends and neighbours, colleagues, and members of the family

working capital /'wɜːkɪŋ ˌkæpɪt(ə)l/ *noun* capital in the form of cash, stocks, and debtors but not creditors, used by a company in its day-to-day operations. Also called **circulating capital, floating capital, net current assets**

work in progress /ˌwɜːk ɪn 'prəʊɡres/ *noun* the value of goods being manufactured which are not complete at the end of an accounting period ○ *Our current assets are made up of stock, goodwill and work in progress.* Abbreviation **WIP** (NOTE: The US term is **work in process**.)

work-life balance /ˌwɜːk 'laɪf ˌbæləns/ *noun* the balance between the amount of time and effort someone devotes to work and the amount they devote to other aspects of life (NOTE: Work-life balance is the subject of widespread debate on how to allow employees more control over their working arrangements so that they have more time for their outside activities and responsibilities, but in a way that will still benefit their employers.)

works /wɜːks/ *noun* a factory ○ *There is a small engineering works in the same street as our office.* ○ *The steel works is expanding.* (NOTE: takes a singular or plural verb)

workshop /ˈwɜːkʃɒp/ *noun* a small factory

world /wɜːld/ *noun* **1.** the Earth □ **the world market for steel** the possible sales of steel throughout the world **2.** the people in a specific business or people with a special interest ○ *the world of big business* ○ *the world of lawyers* or *the legal world*

world enterprise /wɜːld ˈentəpraɪz/ *noun* an advanced form of international marketing

world rights /ˌwɜːld ˈraɪts/ *plural noun* the right to sell the product anywhere in the world

worldwide /ˈwɜːldwaɪd/;/ˌwɜːld-ˈwaɪd/ *adjective, adverb* everywhere in the world ○ *The company has a worldwide network of distributors.* ○ *Worldwide sales* or *Sales worldwide have topped two million units.* ○ *This make of computer is available worldwide.*

World Wide Web /ˌwɜːld ˌwaɪd ˈweb/ *noun* an information system on the Internet that allows documents to be linked to one another by hypertext links and accommodates websites and makes them accessible. Also called **web**

wrap /ˌræp ˈʌp/, **wrap up** *verb* to cover something all over in paper ○ *He wrapped (up) the parcel in green paper.*

wrapper /ˈræpə/ *noun* a piece of material which wraps something ○ *The biscuits are packed in plastic wrappers.*

XYZ

xd *abbreviation* ex dividend

yappy /ˈjæpi/ *noun* a young affluent parent (*slang*)

yearbook /ˈjɪəbʊk/ *noun* a reference book which is published each year with updated or new information

yellow goods /ˈjeləʊ ɡʊdz/ *plural noun* high-priced goods which are kept in use for a relatively long time and so are not replaced very frequently. Compare **orange goods**, **red goods**

Yellow Pages /ˌjeləʊ ˈpeɪdʒɪz/ *trademark* a section of a telephone directory printed on yellow paper which lists businesses under various headings such as computer shops or newsagents

young old /jʌŋ ˈəʊld/ *noun* the market sector consisting of people aged between 60 and 75, that is with a median age of around 66

yuppies /ˈjʌpiz/ *plural noun* young professional people with relatively high incomes (NOTE: short for **young upwardly-mobile professionals**)

zero-rated /ˌzɪərəʊ ˈreɪtɪd/ *adjective* referring to an item which has a VAT rate of 0%

zero-rating /ˈzɪərəʊ ˌreɪtɪŋ/ *noun* the rating of a product or service at 0% VAT

ZIP code /ˈzɪp kəʊd/ *noun US* same as **postcode**

zone /zəʊn/ *noun* an area of a town or country for administrative purposes ■ *verb* to divide a town into different areas for planning and development purposes □ **land zoned for light industrial use** land where planning permission has been given to build small factories for light industry

SUPPLEMENT

VALS Lifestyle Segmentation

Social group	*Description of members*
Innovators	Successful, sophisticated people, often leaders in their profession, who are interested in new ideas and products and who buy a lot of expensive things
Thinkers	Well-educated and well-informed people, often idealistic, who buy things that last a long time and are good value for money
Achievers	Successful people with traditional tastes and values who buy expensive products that have a good reputation or that save them time
Experiencers	Young people who like new and unusual things and spend a lot of money on fashion and on their social life and hobbies
Believers	Conventional people with strong morals and ideals who like traditional, well-known products and are loyal customers
Strivers	People who want to appear successful, rich and fashionable, who enjoy shopping and would like to have more money to spend
Makers	Practical people who like to be independent and control their own lives and who buy goods that are good value for money but are not expensive or fashionable
Survivors	People without much money who cannot afford expensive things and buy only what they need, often at reduced prices

SWOT Analysis

Organisation

Strengths
The services or products or
skills which the organisation
is good at doing or making

Weaknesses
The services or products or skills
which the organisations can't do or
does not do well

Market

Opportunities
Segments of the market which are
attractive, and where changes in
the market might work

Threats
Segments of the market or changes
taking place in the market which are
in favour of the organisation

Make it difficult for the organisation to work there

Social Classes in the UK

This classification of social classes is based on the one used by the Office for National Statistics (ONS), the UK government service that provides statistical information on many areas of British life.

Code	*Description of members of group*
I	Senior managers, administrators, senior civil servants, leading professional people (doctors, lawyers, architects, etc.)
II	Middle managers and administrators, middle-level civil servants and professional people
III N (= non-manual)	Junior managers and administrators, clerical staff
III M (= manual)	Workers with skills and qualifications
IV	Unskilled workers, such as manual workers, in permanent jobs
V	Pensioners, unemployed people, casual manual workers

Technical Information for a Periodical

MECHANICAL DATA

Circulation:	25,000
Frequency:	Monthly
Publication day:	First Thursday in month
Printing process:	Offset litho
Binding:	Wire-stitched
Trim size:	285 × 210mm
Screen:	Black & White 120/48 line per cm
	Colour 150/60 lines per cm
Bleeds:	Bleed trim on all trimmed edges is 3mm
Colour:	Screened positives, emulsion-side down, right-reading, with progressives
Black & White:	Screened positives, emulsion-side down, right-reading
Copy for setting:	Double space typed
Artwork:	Digital artwork only, following file formats accepted: Quark Express, EPS with embedded fonts, TIFF, JPEG